Praise for Previous Editions

This well-written, comprehensive, and clear guide offers practical wisdom for both new and seasoned writers who want to communicate effectively with today's readers. Robert Hudson and Zondervan have performed an enormous service to the publishing community and to the reading public with this well-organized, easy-to-use version, making this the definitive style manual for religious writers and publishing professionals. I am grateful for this essential addition to my library.

> ***Ann Spangler,*** author of *Wicked Women of the Bible*, *Praying the Names of Jesus*, and *Praying the Names of God*

One-stop shopping. That's what makes *The Christian Writer's Manual of Style* so useful. Anyone serious about writing needs a copy.

> ***Jerry B. Jenkins,*** bestselling author

Style is how you do it. Class is where you arrive when you do it right. I've never known a classy writer who was indifferent to style. Robert Hudson is committed to excellence ... yours! So turn off your word processor. It doesn't matter what you are writing; you'll write it better when you spend some time with Robert Hudson. Strunk and White may be the final authority for style in general, but Robert Hudson is the last, most important word on style for the Christian writer. So give your Christian editor a break. Play by the rules. Write well. Pay attention to style. It's your ticket to class.

> ***The late Calvin Miller,*** pastor, professor, and bestselling author

Those of us in publishing who have long admired Robert Hudson's qualities as an editor will not be surprised at the dedication to editorial excellence on display in this volume. Kudos to the entire team that contributed to this splendid and helpful resource. It will certainly be at the editorial right hand of those of us at Eerdmans.

> ***Jon Pott,*** former vice president, editor-in-chief, Wm. B. Eerdmans Publishing Company

With comprehensive and easy-to-find information, *The Christian Writer's Manual of Style* is a must-have resource for all Christian authors.

> ***Brandilyn Collins,*** novelist, author of *Dark Justice* and *Getting Into Character: Seven Secrets a Novelist Can Learn From Actors*

In all my years in Christian publishing, I've never seen a manual of style so relevant, so accessible, so clear, and so complete. This one stays on my desk.

> ***Gregg Lewis,*** author

A wonderful compendium of information and advice. All religion writers would benefit from keeping this volume close at hand and referring to it often.

Andrew T. Le Peau, Associate Publisher, InterVarsity Press

The Christian Writer's Manual of Style is a clear, targeted, and insightful stylebook that answers the rubber-meets-the-road questions unique to Christian writers, editors, and publishers. The A-to-Z format is easy to access, and writers and editors will find the breezy tone helpful with even the most challenging editorial decisions.

Carolyn McCready, editor and former vice president of editorial, Harvest House Publishers

A practical, helpful resource for beginning and advanced writers and editors and others involved in religious writing and publishing. Walks readers through style-related complexities as well as basic how-tos. Wish I'd had a copy sooner.

Stephen W. Sorenson, author, editor, speaker

I think you could change the title. You could call it *The Only Christian Writer's Reference Book You'll Ever Need*. Putting that incredible amount of detailed information in one place makes the book an invaluable resource for anybody who is writing for the Christian market.

Dick Malone, VP Product Purchasing, Riverside Distributors

This manual is an invaluable tool—the most significant and thorough go-to guide for Christian writers and editors.

Rick Christian, founder and president, Alive Communications Literary Agency

the Christian Writer's Manual *of* Style

Also by Robert Hudson

Kiss the Earth When You Pray: The Father Zosima Poems

Companions for the Soul (with Shelley Townsend-Hudson)

Beyond Belief: What the Martyrs Said to God (with Duane W. H. Arnold)

ROBERT HUDSON

4th Edition

the Christian Writer's Manual of Style

ZONDERVAN®

ZONDERVAN

The Christian Writer's Manual of Style

This title is also available as a Zondervan ebook.

Requests for information should be addressed to:
Zondervan, *3900 Sparks Dr. SE, Grand Rapids, Michigan 49546*

Library of Congress Cataloging-in-Publication Data

Names: Hudson, Robert, 1953- editor.
Title: The Christian writer's manual of style / [edited by] Robert Hudson.
Description: 4th Edition. | Grand Rapids : Zondervan, 2016. | Includes bibliographical references and index.
Identifiers: LCCN 2016012022 | ISBN 9780310527909 (softcover)
Subjects: LCSH: Christian literature—Authorship. | Authorship—Style manuals.
Classification: LCC BR44 .C48 2016 | DDC 808.02/7—dc23 LC record available at http://lccn.loc.gov/2016012022

Cover design: Tammy Johnson
Interior design: Kait Lamphere and Beth Shagene

Printed in the United States of America

HB 09.12.2019

Since misunderstanding even a single word can hinder one's reading, . . . we have carefully annotated the meanings of foreign words; studied the spelling, style, etymology, and syntax of the ancients with untiring care; and taken pains to explain those terms time has obscured—so that the pathway before the reader might be smoothed.

Richard de Bury, *The Philobiblon* (1345)

Contents

Introduction 11

How to Use This Manual 13

Part One: The Style Guide. 17

Part Two: The Word List. 399

Notes. 598

Acknowledgments. 599

References Consulted 601

Index. 604

Personal Style Sheet 623

Introduction

The volume you hold in your hands is a manual of style, not a book of rules.

Why is that important? Because rules don't necessarily make for better writing; good style does. For the writer, style means clarity above all—the most effective and vitally charged transmission of thoughts from the writer's mind to the reader's. Style is putting words together so they will be clearly understood by the greatest number of readers, or, to echo Richard de Bury's phrase, so that "the pathway before the reader might be smoothed." It's that simple and that complex. While this manual takes a largely technical approach to that smoothing, focusing on such details as word choice, punctuation, capitalization, and more, it also tries to touch upon such intangibles as voice, tone, syntax, rhythm, and even individuality.

Why a *Christian* manual? Because American publishing comprises many readerships, one of the largest of which identifies itself as Christian. Much of the information in this manual relating to Christian writing and publishing is simply not found in other references. Who else will define *Teavangelical* or *emergent church* for you? Where else can you find *ichthus*, *megachurch*, or *parachurch* (none of which appear in *Webster*)? Who else will happily parse the nuances of *trespasses*, *debts*, and *sins* in the Lord's Prayer or the shades of difference between *abiblical* and *unbiblical*?

Even within the Christian market many readerships exist, each with its own style. Some are almost mutually exclusive. The reader of an Amish novel would throw the book down in disgust if it were written like a scholarly history of the Anabaptists. A pastor would be frustrated by a Bible commentary that read like a biblical novel. Even within genres one finds different audiences. The vocabulary, dialogue, and syntax of a biblical novel are completely different from those of an eschatological thriller.

What's new in this edition? This revised and expanded fourth edition of *The Christian Writer's Manual of Style* is eclectic, even bizarre at times. Everything we could think of is included: ordinary topics, like abbreviation, annotation, and punctuation—as well as the out-of-the-ordinary, like minced oaths, notorious versions of the Bible, and the correct names for the colleges at Oxford and Cambridge. From *abbot* to

Zealot, the words singled out for discussion in the Word List may seem hopelessly random, but each is included because it has, at one time or another, presented itself as a question in the course of editing an actual book. Hardly a day passes when a writer or editor doesn't ask: What *is* the best way to say that?

Do some of these entries seem frivolous? Yes. We include them anyway. The truth is, you don't need *anything* in this book—until you do.

Also new is the format. Rather than listing everything in one master list, this manual has now been divided into two: a Style Guide, which discusses general topics, and a Word List, which contains discussions of specific words. Also added is much new information about content development, whether for print, digital, or audio, and hundreds of new entries about style and usage.

This edition has been thoroughly updated to keep pace with the changing language. While holding tenaciously to the best of classic English style, we have also, without hesitation, scrapped the irrelevant to make way for the new, which may stir controversy. In the more than twenty years since the first edition of this manual appeared, the editors have been accused of heresy (for endorsing the lowercase deity pronoun), prudery (for recommending that profanity be avoided), liberalism (for advocating gender-accurate language), conservatism (for resisting trendy neologisms), and disrespect for proper English (for suggesting that certain time-honored rules be discarded).

Some correspondents have called the curses at the end of Revelation down upon our heads; some journals have accused us of conspiring with those who plot to destroy Christianity; and some readers have pegged us as conservative religious extremists while others accuse us of being liberal religious extremists. All of which means we are doing our job. It would be impossible to outline the main features of a relevant, contemporary Christian style without discussing such contentious issues, as upsetting as they may be, from prudery to license, from disrespect to orthodoxy.

May this volume be of help to you in your writing and editing and proofreading. We pray that you will find it descriptive of the best practices of the best Christian writers now putting pixels to screen so that the pathway before the reader might indeed be smoothed.

How to Use This Manual

The best way to use this manual is to apply its recommendations judiciously rather than mechanically. A surprising number of so-called rules may be ignored when they get in the way of clear communication. Readers have an uncanny ability to survive infractions against proper usage or the discarding of some time-honored dictum of standard English—as long as the bond between the writer and reader is strengthened. To paraphrase Søren Kierkegaard, this manual is like a sharp ceremonial sword: one must be careful which end of it one hands to others.

As mentioned before, *The Christian Writer's Manual of Style* is divided into two parts, a Style Guide and a Word List.

THE STYLE GUIDE

The Style Guide contains broad topic areas with guidelines and recommendations. The entries discuss such common topics as abbreviations and capitalization—and such arcane ones as grawlixes and scribal Latin. Style Guide topics are listed alphabetically and SET IN CAPITAL LETTERS IN THE HEADINGS. Throughout the book, all cross-references to Style Guide topics are set in all capital letters and also "CONTAINED WITHIN QUOTATION MARKS." (For example: See "DEITY PRONOUN, THE.") In some cases, a subsection within a Style Guide topic is cross-referenced, just as they are in the Word List. (For example: See "BIBLE, THE—WHAT IS IT?" section on *"The Hebrew Bible."*)

The Word List

The alphabetical Word List discusses specific words and phrases used in Christian writing and makes recommendations about their usage. Word List entries *are italicized in the headings*, and throughout the book, cross-references to entries in the Word List are also *"contained within quotation marks."* (For example: See *"trespasses, debts, sins."*)

Standard References

We encourage readers to consult the following standard references, which provided the basis for much of what is contained in this manual. But note that these references do not always agree with each other in matters of style and usage, so it would be impossible to conform to all of them. In *The Christian Writer's Manual of Style*, we have forged our own style for Christian writers, editors, and proofreaders. As mentioned before, any of the guidelines in this manual may be adapted as appropriate for specific purposes.

Merriam-Webster's Collegiate Dictionary

This manual generally accords with the print edition of *Merriam-Webster's Collegiate Dictionary, 11th Edition* (2004), as well as its online counterpart found at http://www.merriam-webster.com/, which we feel are the most concise and accessible dictionaries available. When this manual deviates from *Webster* (as that dictionary will be referred to in these pages), an explanation is given.

To help writers, editors, and proofreaders agree on matters of consistent spelling, meaning, and capitalization, this manual recommends a few guidelines in the use of *Webster*:

Use the First Alternative. When alternate spellings are given, use the first one listed unless the author has a strong preference otherwise. (The editor should note any exceptions or variations on the style sheet; see "STYLE SHEET.")

Use Main Entries. Use spellings given in main entries only. Avoid those from alternative entries that are followed by such phrases as *var of* (variant of).

Generally Avoid Entries Marked "Archaic," "Nonstand," and so on. Avoid words qualified by such terms as *archaic*, *nonstand* (nonstandard), *obs* (obsolete), *slang*, or *substand* (substandard), although certainly use or allow them if they are intentional and the reasons for their use will be clear to the reader. Such other-than-standard words can be effective in humor, fiction, dialect, dialogue, and other kinds of writing that require special vocabulary or spelling. As with all the recommendations, be flexible.

Capitalization. Capitalize words marked *cap* (capitalized) or *usu cap* (usually capitalized), but lowercase those marked *sometimes cap* (sometimes capitalized). Words marked *often cap* (often capitalized) may be capitalized or lowercased according to context, common sense, or author or editor preference.

The Chicago Manual of Style

The Chicago Manual of Style, 16th Edition, abbreviated as *CMoS* in these pages, is the definitive style guide for publishing in the US. *The Christian Writer's Manual of Style, 4th Edition,* is a supplement to that guide, listing variations and exceptions unique to religious publishing and adding information not covered there or elsewhere. You may buy a subscription to the online version of *CMoS* at http://www.chicagomanualofstyle.org/home.html.

The SBL Handbook of Style

Newly revised in 2014, *The SBL Handbook of Style, 2nd Edition*, is an essential reference for scholars working in the areas of biblical studies and related disciplines. Though *The Christian Writer's Manual of Style* differs in some points from *The SBL Handbook*, the two are generally compatible. Whenever it seemed redundant to duplicate material from that reference, we have simply stated, "See *SBL*." A student supplement to *The SBL Handbook of Style, 2nd Edition*, can be found at https://www.sbl-site.org/assets/pdfs/pubs/SBLHSsupp2015-02.pdf.

Abbreviations Used in This Manual

BCE = Before the Common Era
Britannica = *The Encyclopaedia Britannica* (online)
CE = Common Era
CMoS = *The Chicago Manual of Style, 16th Edition* (2010 and online)
CWMS = *The Christian Writer's Manual of Style, 4th Edition* (2016)
Fowler = H. W. Fowler, *A Dictionary of Modern English Usage* (1926)
Garner = *Garner's Modern American Usage, 3rd Edition* (2009)
KJV = Holy Bible: King James Version
MLA = *MLA Handbook for Writers of Research Papers, 6th Edition* (2008)
NIV = Holy Bible: New International Version (2011 revision)
NT = New Testament
OED = *The Oxford English Dictionary, 2nd Edition* (1989)
OP = out of print
OT = Old Testament
Oxford = *The Oxford Style Manual* (2003)
rev. = revised or revision
Rev. = Reverend
SBL = *The SBL Handbook of Style, 2nd Edition* (2014)
Strunk and White = William Strunk Jr. and E. B. White, *The Elements of Style* (1999)
Tyndale = Tyndale's New Testament
Webster = *Merriam-Webster's Collegiate Dictionary, 11th Edition* (print, 2004) or at http://www.merriam-webster.com/; full resources available by paid subscription.
Webster's Unabridged = *Webster's Third New International*

Dictionary, Unabridged (print 1993) or at http://unabridged.merriam-webster.com/, by paid subscription.
Wikipedia = *Wikipedia* online: https://en.wikipedia.org/wiki/Wiki.
Wycliffe = Wycliffe Bible

PART 1

The Style Guide

Always try to use the language so as to make quite clear what you mean and make sure your sentence couldn't mean anything else.

C. S. Lewis, *Letters to Children*

A

ABBREVIATIONS

As a shortened form of a name, word, or phrase, an abbreviation is used by convention or for convenience when the repetition of a spelled-out form would be monotonous or distracting. Some words and phrases, such as *Dr.*, *Mr.*, *Mrs.*, and *etc.*, as well as those used by scholars, such as *i.e.* and *e.g.* (see "ABBREVIATIONS: SCHOLARLY"), are nearly always abbreviated. Also, some people prefer the abbreviated form of their given names; for instance, *J. R. R. Tolkien* or *D. A. Carson.*

With or Without Periods. In most cases, don't use periods with abbreviations containing all capital letters (like *FM*, *GNP*, *MD*, *UNC*), but use periods with abbreviations containing lowercase letters or a combination of capital and lowercase letters (such as *a.m.*, *Dec.*, *Gov.*). Personal initials should always use periods (for example, *G. K. Chesterton*). Some writers and editors prefer periods in the abbreviations of academic degrees, since many of those abbreviations combine capital and lowercase letters. That style is acceptable, though this manual recommends setting the abbreviations for all academic degrees without periods (for instance, *PhD*, *ThD*, as well as *BA*, *MA*). If you opt to use periods with those abbreviations, such as *Ph.D.* and *Th.D.*, then use periods with all other academic abbreviations in the book: *B.A.*, *M.S.* Be sure to include such a preference on the book's style sheet. (See also "ACADEMIC DEGREES: TERMS AND ABBREVIATIONS.")

The following list summarizes instances when periods need not be used in abbreviations and shows common exceptions as well.

Academic degrees: BA, MA, MD, ThD, PhD; though *Th.D.* and *Ph.D.* are acceptable

Acronyms and initialisms: AFL-CIO, AIDS, jeep, NATO, Texaco; see "ACRONYMS AND INITIALISMS"

Agencies and organizations: CRC, GE, IBM, NSA, YMCA

Computer- and internet-related words: CPU, FTP, HCML

Famous people referred to by initials only: JFK, MLK

French forms of address: Mme (Madame), Mlle (Mademoiselle), though note that M. (Monsieur) uses a period; see "FRENCH STYLE"

Historical eras: AD, BC, BCE, CE, AH; see "*BC, AD*" and "*BCE/CE*")

Scholarly style for abbreviating books of the Bible: Exod, Rom, Col; though note the general style retains the periods: Ex., Rom., Col.; see "ABBREVIATIONS: BIBLE BOOKS AND RELATED MATERIAL"

Terms of biblical scholarship: NT, Q

Titles of books and periodicals commonly abbreviated: *CMoS, NYT, OED, TLS* (these are also italicized as titles)

UK style: UK publishers generally don't use periods with *Dr, Ltd, Mr, Mrs,* and other abbreviations when the eliminated letters fall in the middle rather than at the end of the word. See "UK STYLE"

Units of measurement: ft, mm, mpg, yd; though note that *in.* (inches) retains a period to avoid confusion with the preposition

With Other Punctuation. When an abbreviation that uses a period falls at the end of a sentence, do not double the period. Otherwise, any other punctuation mark may be placed next to a period in an abbreviation at any place in the sentence with no intervening word space.

Defining Abbreviations in Text. Familiar abbreviations, such as *FBI*, *CIA*, and *ASAP*, need not be defined when used in text, but whenever an abbreviation is likely to be unfamiliar, the author should define it at first use. As far as which abbreviations might be unfamiliar to readers, common sense should prevail. When in doubt, spell it out.

George Carey was one of the founders of the BMS (Baptist Missionary Society). [First use; thereafter BMS need not be spelled out.]

If an unfamiliar abbreviation appears first in a heading or a title, explain it at the next occurrence in the text.

Web Style. Because of the web's global reach, many abbreviations familiar to US readers will not be familiar to international web users, so spell out abbreviations on the web whenever possible, especially at first use.

Plurals of Abbreviations. Use an *'s* to form the plurals of most abbreviations that use periods: as in *Ph.D.'s* or *He scattered op. cit.'s throughout his thesis.* Add an *s* alone to create plurals from most abbreviations that don't use periods: *twenty ThDs* or *a conference of MDs.* Use an apostrophe in some common phrases (as in *Mind your p's and q's*) or when the absence of an apostrophe might look odd or cause misreading: such as *S's, A's, I's.*

Inflecting Abbreviations as Verbs. Abbreviations are sometimes inelegantly used as verbs. It is usually safe to form the past tense with *'d* (*RSVP'd*). Gerunds may be formed either with a hyphen (*RSVP-ing*) or without (*RSVPing*), though this manual recommends the hyphenated form.

Personal Initials. Abbreviate personal names according to the person's own preference or in the form given in a standard reference such as *Merriam-Webster's Biographical Dictionary* (rev. 2003) or *Wikipedia.* In its back matter, *Merriam-Webster's Collegiate Dictionary, 11th Edition* includes a condensed biographical dictionary that can resolve many questions; the online edition (http://www.merriam-webster.com) also allows biographical searches. Always use the form by which those people are most commonly known; for instance, *T. S. Eliot* rather than *Thomas S. Eliot*, or *G. K. Chesterton* rather than *Gilbert K. Chesterton*.

Normal word spacing (or a nonbreaking three-to-em or a three-point space) should separate two or more initials preceding a surname (*C. S. Lewis* and not *C.S. Lewis*), though two or more initials should not be allowed to break over line endings, nor should any initials be separated from the surname over a line or page. If a person's initials are commonly used as a nickname, set those initials without spaces or periods (such as *PJ* for *P. J. Zondervan*).

A few well-known figures are identified by their initials alone, such as *FDR* (Franklin Delano Roosevelt), *GBS* (George Bernard Shaw), *JFK* (John F. Kennedy), *LBJ* (Lyndon Baines Johnson), and *MLK* (Martin Luther King Jr.). Periods are not used and the letters are not spaced.

Using Rev. Spell out *Reverend* when the person is first referred to by name (*Reverend Billy Graham*, *the Reverend Billy Graham*, or *Reverend Graham*), but thereafter the abbreviation or the last name alone may be used (*Rev. Billy Graham*, *Rev. Graham*, or just *Graham*). (See "*reverend, Reverend.*")

Civil and Military Titles. Spell out a civil or military title when used with a surname alone or when used for the first time: *Governor Wallace*, *General Pershing*. It may be abbreviated with the full name; either *Gov. Lew Wallace* or *Governor Lew Wallace*; either *Gen. John J. Pershing* or *General John J. Pershing*. (See "TITLES, MILITARY.")

Corporations and Organizations. Do not use periods in the abbreviations of corporations and organizations (such as *AT&T*, *IBM*, or *LG*). The article *the* is used before a company abbreviation only if the article is used when the name is given in full; for example, *the SPCA* (*the Society for the Prevention of Cruelty to Animals*), but *PETA* (*People for the Ethical Treatment of Animals*). (See also "ACRONYMS AND INITIALISMS.") Whenever the name of a corporation or organization might be unfamiliar, give the full name on first reference, though the abbreviations *Inc.*, *LLC*, and *Ltd.* may usually be dropped. Thereafter, the acronym or abbreviated form may be used without further explanation.

Abbreviations Discussed Elsewhere in This Manual. For lists of abbreviations, see:

"ABBREVIATIONS: BIBLE BOOKS AND RELATED MATERIAL"
"ABBREVIATIONS: RELIGIOUS TERMS"
"ABBREVIATIONS: SCHOLARLY"
"ACADEMIC DEGREES: TERMS AND ABBREVIATIONS"

"ACRONYMS AND INITIALISMS"
"BIBLE VERSIONS IN ENGLISH"
"BIBLE VERSIONS NOT IN ENGLISH"
"HYMN METERS"
"ROMAN CATHOLIC ORDERS, ABBREVIATIONS OF"
"STATE AND PROVINCE ABBREVIATIONS"

For entries discussing specific abbreviations, see:

"a.m., p.m., noon, midnight"
"AS, AC"
"BC, AD"
"BCE/CE"
"DJ, dee-jay"
"e.g., i.e."
"HIV/AIDS"
"ID"
"okay, OK"
"pj's"
"v., versus"

ABBREVIATIONS: BIBLE BOOKS AND RELATED MATERIAL

Spell out the names of the books of the Old and New Testaments and the Apocrypha in works for a popular audience, though they may be abbreviated in citations, whether in parenthetical references, footnotes, or endnotes, and especially when such citations are numerous. In reference and scholarly works, the names of books of the Bible may be abbreviated in the text as well as the annotations at the discretion of the author and editor.

Three Styles. Three styles of abbreviation are common: the general style, the SBL (Society of Biblical Literature) style, and the NIV style, which is used primarily for ancillary content in NIV Bibles. In deciding which to use, keep the readership in mind. The general style is less formal, making it the choice for trade books in which a less academic appearance is desired. That style is also useful in academic and reference works intended to appeal to lay readers. The SBL style is more condensed and technical in appearance, making it appropriate for a scholarly readership. The NIV style is ideal when space is a consideration, as in cross-references, marginal or center-column notes, and reference works closely based on the NIV.

The titles and order of the books of the Bible in the following list are based on the NIV. The titles and order of books of the Apocrypha are based on *SBL*, and alternate titles are shown in parentheses. All abbreviations may be adapted according to the version used. Previous editions of this manual included abbreviations for the Old and New Testament Pseudepigrapha, but since they are so seldom used, they are no longer included here. For those abbreviations (and for all matters of style in biblical scholarship), refer to *The SBL Handbook of Style, 2nd Edition*, sections 8.3.13 and 8.3.4.

OLD TESTAMENT

Book of the Bible	General	SBL	NIV
Genesis	Gen.	Gen	Ge
Exodus	Ex.	Exod	Ex
Leviticus	Lev.	Lev	Lev
Numbers	Num.	Num	Nu
Deuteronomy	Deut.	Deut	Dt
Joshua	Josh.	Josh	Jos
Judges	Judg.	Judg	Jdg
Ruth	Ruth	Ruth	Ru
1 Samuel (1 Kingdoms [LXX])	1 Sam. 1 Kgdms.	1 Sam 1 Kgdms	1Sa
2 Samuel (2 Kingdoms [LXX])	2 Sam. 2 Kgdms.	2 Sam 2 Kgdms	2Sa
1 Kings (3 Kingdoms [LXX])	1 Kings 3 Kgdms.	1 Kgs 3 Kgdms	1Ki
2 Kings (4 Kingdoms [LXX])	2 Kings 4 Kgdms.	2 Kgs 4 Kgdms	2Ki
1 Chronicles	1 Chron.	1 Chr	1Ch
2 Chronicles	2 Chron.	2 Chr	2Ch
Ezra	Ezra	Ezra	Ezr
Nehemiah	Neh.	Neh	Ne
Esther	Est.	Esth	Est
Job	Job	Job	Job
Psalm/Psalms	Ps./Pss.	Ps/Pss	Ps/Ps
Proverbs	Prov.	Prov	Pr
Ecclesiastes	Eccl.	Eccl	Ecc
Song of Songs (Canticles)	Song Cant.	Song Cant	SS
Isaiah	Isa.	Isa	Isa
Jeremiah	Jer.	Jer	Jer
Lamentations	Lam.	Lam	La
Ezekiel	Ezek.	Ezek	Eze
Daniel	Dan.	Dan	Da
Hosea	Hos.	Hos	Hos
Joel	Joel	Joel	Joel
Amos	Amos	Amos	Am

OLD TESTAMENT

Book of the Bible	General	SBL	NIV
Obadiah	Obad.	Obad	Ob
Jonah	Jonah	Jonah	Jnh
Micah	Mic.	Mic	Mic
Nahum	Nah.	Nah	Na
Habakkuk	Hab.	Hab	Hab
Zephaniah	Zeph.	Zeph	Zep
Haggai	Hag.	Hag	Hag
Zechariah	Zech.	Zech	Zec
Malachi	Mal.	Mal	Mal

NEW TESTAMENT

Book of the Bible	General	SBL	NIV
Matthew	Matt.	Matt	Mt
Mark	Mark	Mark	Mk
Luke	Luke	Luke	Lk
John	John	John	Jn
Acts	Acts	Acts	Ac
Romans	Rom.	Rom	Ro
1 Corinthians	1 Cor.	1 Cor	1Co
2 Corinthians	2 Cor.	2 Cor	2Co
Galatians	Gal.	Gal	Gal
Ephesians	Eph.	Eph	Eph
Philippians	Phil.	Phil	Php
Colossians	Col.	Col	Col
1 Thessalonians	1 Thess.	1 Thess	1Th
2 Thessalonians	2 Thess.	2 Thess	2Th
1 Timothy	1 Tim.	1 Tim	1Ti
2 Timothy	2 Tim.	2 Tim	2Ti
Titus	Titus	Titus	Tit
Philemon	Philem.	Phlm	Phm
Hebrews	Heb.	Heb	Heb
James	James	Jas	Jas
1 Peter	1 Peter	1 Pet	1Pe

NEW TESTAMENT

Book of the Bible	General	SBL	NIV
2 Peter	2 Peter	2 Pet	2Pe
1 John	1 John	1 John	1Jn
2 John	2 John	2 John	2Jn
3 John	3 John	3 John	3Jn
Jude	Jude	Jude	Jude
Revelation	Rev.	Rev	Rev

APOCRYPHA AND SEPTUAGINT

Book of the Bible	General	SBL
Baruch	Bar.	Bar
Additions to Daniel	Add. Dan.	Add Dan
Prayer of Azariah	Pr. Azar.	Pr Azar
Song of the Three Young Men (Song of the Three Jews, NRSV)	Song Three	Sg Three
Susanna	Sus.	Sus
Bel and the Dragon	Bel.	Bel
1 Esdras	1 Esd.	1 Esd
2 Esdras	2 Esd.	2 Esd
Additions to Esther	Add. Esth.	Add Esth
Epistle of Jeremiah (Letter of Jeremiah, NRSV)	Ep. Jer.	Ep Jer
Judith	Judith	Jdt
1 Maccabees	1 Macc.	1 Macc
2 Maccabees	2 Macc.	2 Macc
3 Maccabees	3 Macc.	3 Macc
4 Maccabees	4 Macc.	4 Macc
Prayer of Manasseh	Pr. Man.	Pr Man
Psalm 151	Ps. 151	Ps 151
Sirach (Ecclesiasticus, NRSV)	Sir.	Sir
Tobit	Tobit	Tob
Wisdom of Solomon	Wisd. Sol.	Wis

ABBREVIATIONS: BIBLE VERSIONS AND TRANSLATIONS

See "BIBLE VERSIONS IN ENGLISH."

ABBREVIATIONS: RELIGIOUS TERMS

The following list contains abbreviations for general religious terms and names. An asterisk (*) indicates that a more complete discussion of that abbreviation, definition, or word may be found under its own entry in the Word List (Part Two of this manual).

ab.. . . . . abbot* *or* abbess*
ABMC. . . . . . . Ancient Biblical Manuscript Center
Abp. . . . . Archbishop*
AC. . . . . *Auditor Camerae* (auditor of the papal treasury)
AC. . . . . Anglican* Church *or* Anglican* calendar
AC. . . . . *ante Christum* ("before Christ"); do not use, since it can also mean "after Christ"
ACN . . . . *ante Christum natum* ("before the birth of Christ"); seldom used
AD*. . . . . *anno Domini* ("in the year of [our] Lord"; usually precedes date)
a.d. . . . . *ante diem* ("the day before")
Adm. Rev.. . . . *admodum reverendus* ("very reverend")
Adv. . . . . Advent*
AH. . . . . *anno Hebraico* ("in the Hebrew year")
AH. . . . . *anno Hegirae* ("in the year of the Hegira")
Akkad. . . . . . . Akkadian
AM . . . . *anno mundi* ("in the year of the world"; precedes date)
AM . . . . *artium magister* ("master of arts")
AM . . . . *ave Maria* ("Hail Mary"*)
AMDG . . . . . . *ad maiorem Dei gloriam* ("to the greater glory of God"), motto of the Jesuits
AME . . . . African Methodist Episcopal
an.. . . . . *annus* ("year")
ana., ant. . . . . antiphon
anc.. . . . . ancient
Angl.. . . . . Anglican*
ani. . . . . *anni* ("years")
ap.. . . . . apocryphon
ap.. . . . . apostle*
Apoc. . . . . Apocalypse
Apocr.. . . . . . . Apocrypha*
Ap. Sed.. . . . . *Apostolica Sedes* ("Apostolic See")
Aq. . . . . Aquila's Greek translation of OT
Arab.. . . . . Arabic
Aram. . . . . Aramaic

ARS . . . . *anno reparatae salutis* ("in the year of our redemption")
AS . . . . *anno salutis* ("in the year of salvation")
Assyr. . . . . Assyrian
AUC . . . . *ab urbe condita* ("after Rome's founding"; precedes date)
B, BB. . . . . *Beatus, Beati* (pl.) ("Blessed")
b. . . . . bar/ben (Aram./Heb. for "son of")
b. . . . . born
BA . . . . Babatha Archive
Bab. . . . . Babylonian
Bapt. . . . . Baptist
BC* . . . . before Christ
BCE* . . . . before the Common Era
BCP . . . . The Book of Common Prayer*
ben. . . . . *benedictio* ("blessing")
benevol. . . . . . *benevolentia* ("benevolence")
b.f. . . . . *bona fide* ("in good faith")
bib. . . . . biblical*
BK . . . . Bar Kochba
BL . . . . British Library
bl. . . . . blessed*
BM . . . . British Museum
bon. mem. . . . *bonae memoriae* ("of happy memory")
Bp. . . . . Bishop*
Bro., Br.. . . . . . Brother* (monk)
BV . . . . *beatitudo vestra* ("your holiness")
BVM . . . . Blessed Virgin Mary (*beata virgo Maria*)
Byz. . . . . Byzantine
c . . . . cross*
Can. . . . . Canaanite
Can(n). . . . . . . Canon(s), in Code of Canon Law
Card.. . . . . Cardinal*
CB . . . . Christian Brethren
CE, CofE. . . . . Church of England
CE . . . . Common Era (see "*BCE/CE*")
COC . . . . Church of Christ
CM . . . . Common Meter—86.86 (hymnody)
CMD. . . . . Common Meter Doubled—86.86.86.86 (hymnody)
CME . . . . Christian Methodist Episcopal Church
cod., codd.. . . codex, codices
comm(s). . . . . commentary (commentaries)
Con. . . . . Congregational
con.. . . . . *contra* ("against")

Copt. . . . . Coptic
cr. . . . . *credo* ("creed" in the Breviary)
CRC . . . . Christian Reformed Church
CS. . . . . Christian Science
D . . . . one of the supposed Deuteronomist sources of Pentateuch
D . . . . *Dominus* ("Lord")
d.. . . . . *dies* ("day")
D&C . . . . Doctrine and Covenants (Mormon)
Dec. . . . . Deacon*
def. . . . . *defunctus* ("deceased")
DG . . . . *Dei gratia** ("by the grace of God") (see "*Deo gratias, Dei gratia*")
DN . . . . *Dominus noster* ("our Lord")
DNJC . . . . *Dominus noster Jesus Christus* ("our Lord Jesus Christ")
doct. . . . . doctrine
DOM. . . . . *Deo optimo maximo* ("to God the best and greatest")
DP . . . . domestic prelate
DRC . . . . Dutch Reformed Church
DSS. . . . . Dead Sea Scrolls
Dtr. . . . . Deuteronomist
DV. . . . . *Deo volente* ("God willing")
E . . . . one of the supposed Elohist sources of Pentateuch
EC. . . . . Eastern calendar
eccl. . . . . ecclesiastic *or* ecclesiastical
Egyp. . . . . Egyptian
EO. . . . . Eastern Orthodox
ep(p). . . . . epistle(s)*
Episc. . . . . Episcopal *or* Episcopalian*
ET . . . . English translation
Eth. . . . . Ethiopic
extrabibl. . . . . extrabiblical* (see "*nonbiblical, abiblical, extrabiblical, unbiblical*")
fel. mem. . . . . *felicis memoriae* ("of happy memory")
Fr., F. (FF) . . . . Father (Fathers); priests
frag. . . . . fragment
GARBC . . . . . General Association of Regular Baptist Churches
Gk. . . . . Greek
H . . . . Law of Holiness
HB. . . . . Hebrew Bible
HC. . . . . Holy Communion*
HE. . . . . His Eminence
Heb. . . . . Hebrew*

Hel. . . . . Hellenistic
Hev./Se. . . . . . Used for documents earlier attributed to Seiyal
Hex. . . . . Hexateuch
HH. . . . . His Holiness (pope)
Hitt.. . . . . Hittite
IC, IX. . . . . *Iesus Christus* (Jesus Christ)
IHS (or IHC) . . monogram for Greek name for Jesus (ΙΗΣΟΥΣ)
IX. . . . . *in Christo* (in Christ)
INRI. . . . . *Iesus Nazarenus Rex Iudaeorum* ("Jesus of Nazareth, King of the Jews")
J . . . . one of the supposed Yahwist sources of Pentateuch
J" . . . . Jehovah
Jeh. . . . . Jehovah (Yahweh*)
Jerus. . . . . Jerusalem
JT . . . . Jerusalem Talmud
Jud.. . . . . Judaism
JW. . . . . Jehovah's Witnesses
K . . . . Kethib
Lat. . . . . Latin
LB . . . . Late Bronze Age
LDS. . . . . Latter-day Saints
lex. . . . . lexicon
LL . . . . Late Latin
LM. . . . . Long Meter—88.88 (hymnody)
LMD . . . . Long Meter Doubled—88.88.88.88 (hymnody)
Luth. . . . . Lutheran
LXX. . . . . Septuagint
M. . . . . Methodist
m., mg. . . . . . . marginal notes to Bible version
m., mm. . . . . . martyr, martyrs
MB . . . . Middle Bronze Age
MEC . . . . Methodist Episcopal Church
Meth. . . . . Methodist
Mird. . . . . Khirbet Mird
mk. . . . . monk
ML. . . . . Medieval* Latin
Mor. . . . . Mormon
MPΘY. . . . . . . "Mother of God" (Greek) on icons
MS(S) . . . . manuscript(s)
MT . . . . Majority Text
MT . . . . Masoretic Text of OT
Mur. . . . . Murabba'at

Naz. . . . . Nazarene
ND . . . . *nostra Domina* (Latin), *notre Dame* (French) ("our Lady")
NHC . . . . Nag Hammadi Codex
NIKA. . . . . "victor" (Greek) on icons
NS. . . . . New Series
NS. . . . . *nostro Signore* (Latin), *notre Seigneur* (French) ("our Lord")
NT. . . . . New Testament
Nub. . . . . Nubian
nup. . . . . nuptials
ob. . . . . *obiit* ("died")
OL. . . . . Our Lady
OS. . . . . Old Syriac
OT. . . . . Old Testament
OωN . . . . "the One who is" or "I Am" (Jesus) (Greek)
P . . . . Priestly Narrative, source of Pentateuch
P. . . . . *pater* ("father")
Pal. . . . . Palestine* *or* Palestinian
pap. . . . . papyrus
par. . . . . parallel
Patr.. . . . . Patriarch*
PB . . . . Plymouth Brethren
PC . . . . Priestly Code
PCA . . . . Presbyterian Church in America
PCUSA . . . . . . Presbyterian Church (USA)
Pent. . . . . Pentateuch
Pen.. . . . . Pentecostal*
Pesh. . . . . Peshitta
PG. . . . . Preacher General
Phoen. . . . . . . Phoenician
PM. . . . . Primitive Methodist
postbibl.. . . . . postbiblical
pr. . . . . priest
pr. bk. . . . . prayer book
Presb. (*or* Pre.) Presbyterian
Prot. . . . . Protestant*
Pseudep. . . . . Pseudepigrapha* *or* pseudepigraphal
Q. . . . . Quelle (one of the supposed sources of Synoptic Gospels)
Q. . . . . Qumran
Qua. . . . . Quaker
R . . . . with refrain (hymnody)
r. . . . . rabbi*
rab. . . . . rabbinic

RC.......... Roman calendar
RC.......... Roman Catholic
RCC .... Roman Catholic Church
relig......... religion
Rev.......... Reverend*
RIP.......... *requiescat in pace* ("[may he or she] rest in peace")
Rom......... Roman
Rev. P., RP.... *reverendus pater* ("reverend father")
Rt. Rev., RR... Right Reverend
SA.......... Salvation Army
Sab.......... *Sabbatum* ("Sabbath," or "Sunday")
SAG .... Saint Anthony Guide (prayer)
Sam......... Samaritan
Script........ Scripture*
SCS......... *Sanctus* ("Saint")
SD........... *servus Dei* ("servant of God")
s.d. .... *sine data* (a book without a date)
SDA......... Seventh-day Adventist
Sem......... Semitic*
SM.......... *santae memoriae* ("of holy memory")
SM.......... Short Meter—66.86 (hymnody)
SMD .... Short Meter Doubled—66.86.66.86 (hymnody)
Sr. .... Sister* (of a religious order)
SSL .... licentiate in sacred Scripture
St. .... Saint*
Sta.......... Saint* (female; Italian)
Ste.......... Saint* (female; French)
STL .... licentiate of sacred theology
Sum......... Sumerian
Symm........ Symmachus's Greek translation of OT
Syr. .... Syriac
Talm......... Talmud
Tan.......... Tanak (Hebrew Scriptures)
Targ......... Targum
Theod....... Theodotion's Greek translation of OT
theol. .... theology, theological
TLM .... Traditional Latin Mass
TR .... Textus Receptus
tr............ translation or translated
UIODG...... *ut in omnibus Deus glorificetur* ("that God may be glorified in all things"), motto of the Benedictine order
UM .... United Methodist

Uni. . . . . Unitarian
UR. . . . . United Reformed Church (formerly Congregational)
UU. . . . . Unitarian Universalist
V . . . . Vatican Library
v(v). . . . . verse(s)
VBS . . . . vacation Bible school
ven. (*or* V). . . . venerable
vers. . . . . vespers*
Vulg. . . . . Vulgate (Jerome's Latin Bible)
WM. . . . . Wesleyan Methodist
WWJD . . . . . . What would Jesus do?
XC (*or* XCS) . . *Christus* (Greek initials for "Christ")
Xmas* . . . . Christmas

ABBREVIATIONS: SCHOLARLY

Scholars use a number of conventional Latin terms and abbreviations to explain, insert expansions to, or cross-reference their writing. These abbreviations are usually set with periods and in roman type, except for *sic* (Latin for "thus"), which is usually set in italic to distinguish it from any quoted text into which that term has been inserted. When used in quoted text, *sic* is enclosed in square brackets—[*sic*]. Note that the brackets are in roman while the word *sic* is in italic. (See "*sic.*")

The use of scholarly abbreviations is discouraged in books for a popular readership. Avoid *e.g.*, *etc.*, and *i.e.* when *for example*, *and so on*, and *that is* will suffice. Still, the use of academic abbreviations can benefit technical and scholarly writing. The following are the most common.

Abbreviation	Meaning
ad loc..	*ad locum*; to indicate "the place referred to"; rarely used
aet.	*aetatis*; "of the same time or era"
c. or ca..	*circa*; "around," "approximately"; with dates
cf.	*confer*; "compare with" or "compare to"; in parentheses in text
e.g.	*exempli gratia*; "for example"; in text; see also "*e.g., i.e.*"
et al.	*et alia, et alii*; "and others"; in bibliographic references
etc. *or* &c. . . .	*et cetera*; "and other things," or "and so on"; in text; see also "etc."
et seq.	*et sequentes*; "and the following"
ff..	*folio*; "and the following [pages]"; in parentheses in text or in notes; avoid if possible
fl..	*floruit*; "flourished" (a person's prime); in parentheses
ibid.	*ibidem*; "identical to previous reference" in notes; generally avoid it, opting instead for shortened references

id. . . . . *idem*; "same author or work as previous reference," though other information has changed; in notes
i.e. . . . . *id est*; "that is"; in text; see also "*e.g., i.e.*"
inf. *or* infra . . . *infra*; "see below"; in parentheses or notes
loc. cit. . . . . . . *loco citato*; "in the place cited"; in parentheses or notes; rarely used; avoid it
NB *or* n.b.. . . . *nota bene*; "pay attention" or "note well"; commonly capitalized; in text or notes
non seq. . . . . . *non sequitur*; "does not follow"; used in parentheses
ob. . . . . *obit*; "died"; used in parentheses
op. cit. . . . . . . *opera citato*; "in the work cited"; in parentheses or notes, rarely used; avoid it
p., pp. . . . . "page," "pages"; in notes
passim . . . . . . *passim* (not abbreviated); "here and there," "throughout"; in notes
q.v. . . . . *quod vide*: "see which" ("see another reference elsewhere"); in notes
sic. . . . . *sic* (not abbreviated); "thus" or "as in original"; in text or notes; word in italic, always in roman brackets or parentheses; for more detail, see "*sic*"
supra. . . . . *supra* (not abbreviated); "see above"; in text or notes
s.v. . . . . *sub verbo*; "under the word," "listed under another heading"; in parentheses or notes
ut sup. . . . . . . *ut supra*; "as above"; in notes
v. inf. . . . . *vide infra*; "see below"; used in parentheses or text
viz. . . . . *videlicet*; "that is," "namely," or "more precisely"; in text, parentheses, or notes
v. *or* vs. . . . . . . *versus*; "versus" or "against"; in text or notes; see also "*v., vs., versus*"

These abbreviations sometimes cause problems when a book is recorded in an audio edition. To help resolve such problems, refer to "PRONUNCIATION GUIDE FOR AUDIO BOOKS," section on "*Pronouncing Latin Abbreviations.*"

ACADEMIC DEGREES: TERMS AND ABBREVIATIONS

Lowercase academic degrees when spelled out in text, even when they immediately follow a person's name (*Adam Cutliff, doctor of divinity*) and even though their abbreviations are capitalized (*She became a doctor of religious education after earning her BA and MRE*).

Blurb style. An exception is made in marketing copy (such as catalog copy, promotional material, and author biographies on book covers), when it is important to highlight the author's credentials (*Adam Cutliff, Doctor of Divinity, teaches at ...*).

Possessives. Use the possessive forms for such terms as *associate's*, *bachelor's*, and *master's*. For example, *a bachelor's degree in physics* or *a master's in comparative religions*. While saying *doctor's degree* is grammatically correct, most people say *doctorate* or *doctoral degree*.

Abbreviations. Set the abbreviations of academic degrees in capital letters without periods: *BA*, *MA*, *MD*, and so on. Even though a common rule states that periods should be used with abbreviations that incorporate lowercase letters (see "ABBREVIATIONS," section on "*With or Without Periods*"), we recommend that such abbreviations as *PhD* and *MDiv* be set without periods. Using periods (*Ph.D.* or *M.Div.*) may be warranted in certain situations as long as consistency is maintained (*B.A.*, *M.D.*, and so on). When used after a name, set the degree abbreviation apart with commas: *Wilfred Grenfell, MD, was a medical missionary* ... Also, use degree abbreviations with a full name, not a last name alone.

In Bylines. Abbreviations for academic degrees are not used with an author's name in a byline (on a cover or title page, for instance) unless the degree is highly relevant to the subject of the book or crucial to its marketing. For example, it may be essential for a reader to know that a nutrition book is written by an MD, in which case the abbreviation may appear after the author's name (*Preventing Disease through Diet, by Carolyn Kirchner, MD*). But a reader does not need to know that the author of a novel about the Civil War is a dentist. That information may be included in the author's biographical blurb, but the abbreviation *DDS* should not appear in the byline on the cover or title page.

For a list of general abbreviations for academic degrees, see *CMoS* 10.20. The following list shows the abbreviations common to religious studies, some of which are not included in the *CMoS* list.

Abbreviation	Meaning
ABT	bachelor of arts in theology, also *BTh*, *ThB*, or *BA in theology*
BCL	bachelor of canon law
BD	bachelor of divinity, or *BDiv*
BHL	bachelor of Hebrew letters
BMin	bachelor of ministry
BRE	bachelor of religious education
BSL	bachelor of sacred literature
BT	bachelor of theology, or *BTh* (*baccalaureus theologiae*)
CSB	bachelor of Christian science
CSD	doctor of Christian science

DB. . . . . bachelor of divinity (*divinitatis baccalaureus*)
DCL. . . . . doctor of canon law (*doctor canonicae legis*)
DD . . . . doctor of divinity (*divinitatis doctor*)
DHL. . . . . doctor of Hebrew letters
DMin. . . . . doctor of ministry
DRE. . . . . doctor of religious education
DST. . . . . doctor of sacred theology
DT . . . . doctor of theology, or *DTh* (*doctor theologiae*)
JCB. . . . . bachelor of canon law (*juris canonici baccalaureus*)
JCD. . . . . doctor of canon law (*juris canonici doctor*)
MDiv. . . . . master of divinity
MMin . . . . master of ministry
MRE . . . . master of religious education
MTS . . . . master of theological studies
STB. . . . . bachelor of sacred theology (*sacrae theologiae baccalaureus*)
STD. . . . . doctor of sacred theology
STM . . . . master of sacred theology
ThB . . . . bachelor of theology
ThD. . . . . doctor of theology (*theologiae doctor*)
ThM . . . . master of theology

ACCENT MARKS

See "DIACRITICAL MARKS (ACCENTS)."

ACKNOWLEDGMENTS PAGE

On an acknowledgments page an author expresses gratitude or gives credit to those who have helped conceive, create, or produce the work, and a brief description of the contribution of each person is often included. Some authors incorporate their appreciations, especially when brief, into a preface, an introduction, an author's note, or an afterword instead. (See also "PREFACE," "INTRODUCTION," "AUTHOR'S NOTE," and "AFTERWORD.")

Placement. While the acknowledgments page has conventionally been placed among the front matter in the past, placing it among the back matter is becoming more common. The reason is that many readers simply skip a book's front matter, which means they may be more likely to read an acknowledgments page placed at the end. If they enjoyed the content, they will want to know who contributed to it.

Still, some writers prefer to place their acknowledgments at the beginning so the spell of the narrative won't be broken by extraneous material at the end. The author should communicate any preference to the editor. If placed at the beginning, the acknowledgments should come after the foreword and preface, both of which have a looser connection to the content, but before the introduction, which has a closer relation to the content.

Tone. When writing an acknowledgments page, the author should avoid making the reader feel excluded by directing inside jokes and references at those being acknowledged (*... thanks to my Tweetsie girl*). Authors should also avoid making those acknowledged feel patronized, for example, by overpraising small matters (*... to my wife for making such excellent coffee*), or crediting those whose contributions were marginal (*... and to the tattooed Best Buy clerk who sold me my MacBook*). Make the tone warm and straightforward, not cheeky or off-putting.

Spelling. In the UK the word *acknowledgments* is often spelled with an internal *e*: *acknowledgements*. The *e* has been absent in the US since Noah Webster's 1828 dictionary.

ACRONYMS AND INITIALISMS

An acronym is a form of abbreviation in which the first letter or letters of a series of words are combined to create a new word that itself becomes a noun or proper name. Acronyms are usually pronounced as words themselves, such as *AIDS* (acquired immune deficiency syndrome), *Amway* (American Way), and *UNICEF* (United Nations International Children's Emergency Fund). An initialism is an abbreviation pronounced not as a word, but as a series of letters, such as *BBC* (British Broadcasting Company), *FAQ* (frequently asked questions), *IWW* (Industrial Workers of the World), and *SUV* (sport utility vehicle). A few abbreviations, like *CD-ROM*, combine an initialism and an acronym. Periods are not used with either acronyms or initialisms. Note that acronyms and initialisms are both popularly referred to as *acronyms* (and even more popularly as just plain *abbreviations*); the distinction is technical and only of interest to linguists and editors.

Common Nouns from Acronyms. The etymologies of many common English words are rooted in acronyms: for example, *awol* (absent without leave), *fubar* (fouled up beyond all recognition), *jeep* (probably from GP—general purpose), *laser* (light amplification by stimulated emission of radiation), *radar* (radio detecting and ranging), *scuba* (self-contained underwater breathing apparatus), *snafu* (situation normal, all fouled up), and *sonar* (sound navigation ranging). Computer technology has added a large number of acronyms to the language: for instance, *ROM* (read-only memory), *DAT* (digital audio tape), and *RAM* (random access memory).

Initialisms in Social Media. In the past two decades, initialisms for common phrases have come into vogue in digital communication, largely in emails, text messages, and social media sites: *imho* ("in my humble opinion"), *lol* ("laughing out loud"), *swak* ("sealed with a kiss"), *tmi* ("too much information"), and hundreds more. On the whole, such initialisms, called *chat abbreviations* or *net lingo*, may be set either capitalized or lowercase in text, the main point being that they should be at least minimally comprehensible. Such initialisms do not usually work well in books. (For more discussion, see "BLOG STYLE AND TURNING BLOGS INTO BOOKS.")

Styling Acronyms and Initialisms. An acronym that is pronounced as a word and contains four or fewer letters is usually spelled with all capitals, such as *SALT* (Strategic Arms Limitation Treaty), *SWAT team* (special weapons and tactics team), and *WAC* (Women's Army Corps). Organizational acronyms that have five or more letters and are pronounced as words are usually cap-lowercase, such as *Nasdaq* (National Association of Securities Dealers Automated Quotations) and *Amoco* (American Oil Company), though exceptions exist, which are established by the organizations themselves, such as *UNICEF*.

Those acronyms that have passed into ordinary parlance as common nouns, like *radar* or *sonar*, are lowercase, regardless of how many letters they contain, while others retain their capitals, often as a way of distinguishing them from already existing nouns, like *WASP* (white Anglo-Saxon Protestant). When in doubt, check a standard reference. Some computer-related acronyms are all caps by convention, such as *DAT* (digital audio tape) and *RAM* (random access memory), sometimes to distinguish them from already existing common nouns (*RAM*, for instance).

Initialisms are usually all caps when referring to organizations, regardless of the number of letters they contain: for instance, the *NAACP* (National Association for the Advancement of Colored People) and the *SPCA* (Society for the Prevention of Cruelty to Animals). When initialisms have passed into common parlance as common nouns, they are usually lowercase, like *jeep* and *laser*.

Initialisms in casual digital communications (blogs, emails, texts, and so on) may be set in either lowercase or uppercase letters, according to the writer's preferences (*lol* or *LOL*).

With an Indefinite Article. When in doubt as to which indefinite article, *a* or *an*, should precede an acronym, choose the one that would ordinarily be used when the acronym is spoken aloud: for instance, *an HIV test*; *a UNICEF worker*; *an ANSI character*. (See "*a, an*.")

Introducing Acronyms and Initialisms. Whenever an acronym or initialism is apt to be unfamiliar, define it or spell it out when first used in text unless it is used in a heading, in which case explain the acronym at the next opportunity in the text itself.

> While in graduate school, he was an active member of the Fellowship of Christians in Universities and Schools (FOCUS). [First use]

Lest we think of acronyms as a recent phenomenon, a common acronym among Jewish scholars through the centuries has been *Tanak*, which is short for *Torah* (Law), *Nevi'im* (the Prophets), and *Kethuvim* (the Writings), which are the three major sections of the Jewish Bible. (See "BIBLE, THE—WHAT IS IT?")

AD CARD

See "AUTHOR CARD, OR AD CARD."

ADDRESSES, STREET

With Numbers. Use numerals for street addresses (*520 Walker Road*) except for the number *one*, which is usually spelled out (*One United Nations Plaza*).

When streets with numeric names are referenced in text, one of two systems should be used. If many such streets are referenced, then the wisest course is to use newspaper style, which spells out the ordinals *First* through *Ninth* (*Fourth Street*, *Ninth Avenue*) and uses numerals for *10th* and higher (*10th Avenue, 52nd Street*). If only a few streets with numeric names are referenced, use the *CMoS* style of spelling out the ordinals for 100 and under (*Tenth Avenue, Fifty-Second Street*) and using numerals for 101 and higher (*101st Street, 120th Street*). No clear boundary can be drawn between "many" references and "a few," but common sense should prevail.

Abbreviations. The abbreviations *Ave.*, *Blvd.*, and *St.* are used only when a number also appears in the street address: *1600 Pennsylvania Ave.* Otherwise, spell them out when the number is spelled out or when no number is used at all: *Fifth Avenue* or *Red Dog Road*. In all cases, spell out less common designations such as *Alley, Center, Court, Drive, Highway, Route, Terrace*, and *Way*. Always spell out *Road*, because its all-cap postal style abbreviation, RD, can be mistaken for *Rural Delivery*.

Postal, List, and Text Styles. Mailing addresses are commonly set in one of three ways: (1) postal style, (2) list style, or (3) text style.

1. Postal Style. The US Postal Service prefers that addresses on envelopes be rendered in all capital letters with no punctuation and that words like *Street, Road*, and *Highway* be spelled out. Note the extra space (about three word spaces) that separates the city from the state and the state from the zip code in the following example.

LOUISE TAYLOR
SENIOR EDITOR
EXTREMELY ROMANTIC BOOKS
2200 EAST OF EDEN BOULEVARD SW
LA JOLLA DUNE CA 12345

2. List Style. Addresses often need to be shown in column format; for instance, publishers commonly put their addresses on the copyright page, authors often provide reference or resource lists, or authors may want to give the address of their own organization. In these cases, addresses should be set in caps and lowercase, with postal state code and regular punctuation as shown (a person's name and job title may be set on the same line to save space):

Louise Taylor, Senior Editor
Extremely Romantic Books
2200 East of Eden Blvd. SW
La Jolla Dune, CA 12345

3. Text Style. When an address is given in text or in dialogue, most elements should be spelled out. For instance, spell out such words as *Avenue*, *Street*, and so on. States names may be spelled out, abbreviated, or set as postal codes (see "STATE AND PROVINCE ABBREVIATIONS"). Do not spell out directional compass points that follow street addresses, such as NW or SE. Also, place commas after each element, though no comma should be placed between the state name and zip code.

All requests for information should be addressed to Louise Taylor, Senior Editor, Extremely Romantic Books, 2200 East of Eden Boulevard SW, La Jolla Dune, California 12345.

He told the court, "My last legal residence was 8405 Bailey Boulevard, San Jacinto, California 92582."

ADDRESSES, WEB

Web addresses, or *URLs*, are commonly cited in text and in source notes.

Format. The guidelines for formatting web addresses in print differ slightly from those for formatting them online. For instance, a final period or other punctuation mark may be added at the end of a web address in print, when the address is part of a sentence or a source reference. Avoid such punctuation online to prevent a user from highlighting and pasting an entire web address into a browser with faulty added punctuation.

In print, set web addresses in roman type and in the same font as the surrounding type. Formerly, italic was recommended for web addresses, but that proved hard to read.

For in-text references and source notes alike, always provide the complete URL, including the protocol *http://* and any other preliminary indicator, like *www*. Web browsers can usually find web addresses without those prefixes, but not always.

Hyphens with Web Addresses. When breaking an unusually long web address over one or more lines of type, do not add a hyphen or hyphens. Also, do not allow a period or a hyphen already within the web address itself to fall at the end of a line; rather, force the period or hyphen to drop down to the beginning of the next line. Other punctuation and symbols (/, ?, =, +, and so on) can usually safely be set at the end of a line.

Accuracy. The author is responsible for the accuracy of all URLs cited both in the text and in references. A copyeditor should also check them for accuracy.

In Source Notes. A web address should never stand alone as a source note. It should always be preceded by the name of the author (when known) and the title of the article, page, or website. Ideally, a citation to a printed book should be provided for any pre-internet-era book references. Such print sources, including page numbers, can often be easily traced through Google Books (http://books.google.com), Amazon's "Look Inside" feature, and other online tools. A pre-internet-era journal or newspaper article may be accompanied by a web reference, since such articles are commonly archived online. (See "NOTES," section on "*Referencing Websites*.")

Access Dates. Only provide an access date with a web address if it is crucial to the reference, for instance, when it is necessary for the reader to know the exact date of a piece of polling data or other time-sensitive information. Otherwise, access dates need not be included.

ADDRESSES OF PUBLISHER, MAILING AND WEB

Including the publisher's mailing and web addresses on the copyright page is customary, though not mandatory, among US publishers. If those addresses do not appear on the copyright page, they should appear elsewhere, most commonly on the title page or a "reader response card." (See "COPYRIGHT PAGE" and "READER RESPONSE CARD.") These addresses benefit readers and distributors who may want to contact the publisher. In practical terms these addresses can result in added income through additional orders and through individuals seeking permission to quote from the book.

ADJECTIVES, COMPOUND

When two or more adjectives or an adverb-adjective combination modify, as a unit, a noun or another adjective, they are called *compound adjectives.*

Standard Compounds. The most common way of showing that a multiple adjective or an adverb-adjective combination modifies a noun is to use a hyphen: *slow-moving currency*, *lime-green drapes*, *a once-respected institution*. Care should be taken to prevent misreading. For instance, a *broken-toy basket* is a basket for broken toys, while a *broken toy basket* is a toy basket that is broken. A *small-computer company* makes small computers, while a *small computer company* is a small company that makes computers. Hyphenate the modifying elements that go together, but don't use a hyphen when a compound is so common that being misunderstood is impossible: *a high school graduation*, *a life insurance policy*, *a Sunday school lesson*.

Adverbs with -ly. In such compounds, don't use a hyphen after an adverb ending in *-ly*: *a formerly respected institution*, *a deeply philosophical problem*. The *-ly*, in a sense, automatically links the adverb to the adjective that follows it.

When One Element Is Already a Compound. When creating a compound adjective from a noun phrase or another compound, use an en dash instead of a hyphen, and do not insert hyphens into the existing compound. For example: *a Civil War–reenactment weekend*, *an ECPA Christian Book Award–winning author*, *a United Methodist–sponsored mission trip*.

Adjectival Phrases. Extended phrases can be transformed into adjectives in two ways. When the compound is not quoted from another source, insert hyphens between all the elements: *a no-holds-barred-and-take-no-prisoners mentality*. When the compound is drawn from a proverb or a quotation, enclose it in quotation marks and don't use hyphens: *my "early bird catches the worm" philosophy* or *the ministry's "my grace is sufficient for you" emphasis*.

ADJECTIVES, MULTIPLE

The "And Test." When two elements modify a noun equally and independently, separate them with a comma, as in *a new, unflattering waistcoat*. In such cases the word *and* can be inserted between the modifiers with no awkwardness. When an element modifies everything that follows it, do not add a comma: *an elegant red waistcoat*. The "and test" is not foolproof, but it helps in most situations.

ADVERBIAL DOUBLES

An *adverbial double* is any adverbial phrase in which a single word is repeated, such as *day-to-day* or *side by side*. The challenge in using them is that they are inconsistently hyphenated, and dictionaries often contradict each other. To save you repeated trips to *Webster*, here is a convenient list. All the following phrases, unless otherwise noted, are hyphenated when used as compound adjectives preceding a noun (as in *day-to-day activities* or *hand-to-hand combat*), though they may be used without hyphens when used as adjectives elsewhere (as in *the combat was hand to hand*). Note that any similarly doubled adverbial phrases not specifically shown in *Webster* as being hyphenated should be set without hyphens: *they walked together year after year* or *he pulled in the rope hand over hand*.

arm in arm (adv. and adj. after noun without hyphens)
back-to-back
bit by bit
by and by (adv., but for *by-and-by* as a noun, see "*by-and-by, by and by*")
cheek-to-cheek (but *cheek by jowl*)
day after day
day by day
day-to-day
door-to-door
eye-to-eye (not in *Webster* but parallels *face-to-face*)
face-to-face (but note the NIV uses *face to face*)
half-and-half
hand in hand
hand to hand
head-to-head (but *head over heels*)
inch by inch
little by little
man-to-man
mano a mano (italicized as foreign phrase)
minute by minute
neck and neck (adv. and adj. after noun without hyphens)
one-on-one
over and over
piece by piece
side by side
step-by-step
time to time
toe-to-toe
vis-à-vis
word for word

AFTERWORD

An afterword is considered the first element of a book's back matter. An afterword (1) tends to be short, (2) is usually written by the author, and (3) usually comments on the writing of the work itself or on events in the author's life since completion of the project. Although one might expect an afterword to be a complement to the foreword, the afterword is more complementary to the preface, since prefaces, unlike most forewords, are usually written by the author. (See "FOREWORD" and "PREFACE.")

An afterword can also serve as an extended acknowledgments page, or as an epilogue in a nonfiction narrative, bringing the narrative up-to-date. In fiction, an *epilogue* would be more commonly used to tie together the loose ends of a story. If an afterword is also used, it should be written in the author's own voice, while an epilogue usually remains in the voice of the book's narrator. (See also "CONCLUSION" and "EPILOGUE.")

ALL-RIGHTS-RESERVED NOTICE

The use of the phrase *all rights reserved* on the copyright page of every book is recommended because it is the accepted formula for protection under the Buenos Aires Convention (1910), recognized by the US and most Latin American countries, some of which do not recognize the copyright symbol ©, the word *copyright*, or the abbreviation *copr.* as providing legal copyright protection. *All rights reserved* is considered one of the three essential elements of a copyright page. (See "COPYRIGHT PAGE.") Most publishers place the phrase *all rights reserved* at the beginning of the warning notice, though some place it on the same line as the copyright notice. (See "WARNING NOTICE.")

ALPHABET, SPELLING OUT LETTERS OF THE

See "LETTERS AS WORDS."

ALPHABETIZATION

The two styles of alphabetization are *letter-for-letter* and *word-for-word*. Letter-for-letter style alphabetizes words as though word spaces do not exist, while word-for-word style considers whole words first, stopping at the first word space unless further distinction is needed. Both styles alphabetize as though words with hyphens or apostrophes were set solid, and both alphabetize only those word units that precede any commas. If two words are identical up to the point of the comma, the information after the comma should be used for the basis of arranging the identical words alphabetically. The two styles may be contrasted by examining the following:

Letter-for-Letter

Old Believers	Oldham, Joseph	Old Latin Versions
Oldcastle, Sir John	Oldham, Martin	Olds, Benjamin
Old Catholics	Oldham Library	Olds, Ditmar
old covenant	Old-Home Week	

Word-for-Word

Old Believers	Oldcastle, Sir John	Old-Home Week
Old Catholics	Oldham, Joseph	Olds, Benjamin
old covenant	Oldham, Martin	Olds, Ditmar
Old Latin Versions	Oldham Library	

For most purposes, such as indexes, the letter-for-letter style is recommended. Although neither style is likely to confuse readers, the letter-for-letter style is slightly more common in popular and trade references, while word-for-word is somewhat more common in academic references. (See also "INDEXES.")

Articles and Pronouns. In alphabetizing entries and subentries in an index, initial articles (such as *the* and *a*) and initial pronouns (such as *him*, *her*, and *their*) are ignored, and the entry is alphabetized according to the key word.

Mac, Mc, and St. In both styles of alphabetization, names beginning with the prefixes *Mac* and *Mc* should be alphabetized letter-for-letter. *Mc* should not be listed as though it were spelled *Mac*, as was once commonly done. Likewise, place names that begin with the abbreviation *St.* should be alphabetized letter-for-letter and not as though they were spelled *Saint*.

ALPHA BRAVO COMMUNICATIONS CODE, THE

See "NATO PHONETIC ALPHABET."

AMERICANIZING UK PUBLICATIONS

Most readers in the US and UK are accustomed to reading books that have not been "translated" into their own version of English, but in some cases, publishers wish to make UK publications more accessible to a US readership. The most common reason is that the British character of some books is so extensive that it would baffle a US audience. Young readers in the US may be confused by British spelling, punctuation, and slang, which is why Scholastic, J. K. Rowling's US publisher, restyled its editions of the Harry Potter books for the US market.

Three levels of Americanization can be implemented.

Level One: Converting Spelling and Punctuation. The simplest level of Americanization replaces UK typographic and spelling conventions with US conventions. This involves converting UK single quotation marks to US double quotation marks, and vice versa (all of which are called *inverted commas* in the UK). Some UK punctuation placed outside the quotation marks are moved inside (mostly periods and commas), and some UK publications use spaced en dashes where US convention uses unspaced em dashes. Finally, and perhaps most importantly, British spellings are changed to American spellings for those words that have the same meaning in both cultures: *plough* is changed to *plow*; *Saviour* to *Savior*; *splendour* to *splendor*; *theatre* to *theater*; and so on. This level of Americanization creates the least distraction for the American reader while retaining the maximum amount of British character—an important factor in works of fiction, for instance, when other uniquely British words and cultural references need to be present.

Level Two: Converting Vocabulary. Added to the first level, the second level converts words for common objects that are completely different in the two cultures. For instance, *lorry* changes to *truck*; *vest* to *undershirt*; and so on. This can be done to a greater or lesser extent, depending on how much of the British flavor needs to be retained. For novels set in England, for example, it may be important to keep the British character of the original, so the editor would translate only those words that might seriously confuse the American reader. For nonfiction, this would also include converting weights and measures from metric.

Level Three: Converting Cultural Equivalents. The most thorough level, added to the others, is a complete conversion of all cultural and topical references. The editor, in a sense, disguises the fact that the writer is British, and scenes and characters may even be shifted to the US. This would only be done for books in which the British character is inessential to the book's appeal—for instance, in some self-help books or technical manuals that for clarity or safety need to be rendered in language as close to that of the target reader's as possible. The issue is not so much translating the individual words as it is finding recognizable cultural equivalents. *Prime minister* would become *president*, for example; *Houses of Parliament* would become *Congress*; and *BBC Radio* might be changed to *National Public Radio*. (See also "UK STYLE" and "MID-ATLANTIC STYLE.")

AMPERSAND

An *ampersand* (short for "and per se and"; sometimes called the *tironian sign*) is the typographic symbol *&*. It means simply "and," and its form is a stylistic ligature for the Latin *et* ("and") developed by medieval calligraphers. (See also "SCRIBAL LATIN CHARACTERS AND ABBREVIATIONS.") It can take on different forms, depending upon the typeface being used: for instance, & (Eras), & (Garamond), & (Goudy Old Style), & (Times New Roman).

Though seldom used in text type, it is often seen in advertising copy, on book covers and in other display typography, and in headings of charts, lists, and tables where space is limited. The editor should note its use on a style sheet so proofreaders won't convert it back to *and*.

An ampersand may be used at the discretion of the cover designer to replace *and* in a book's title as displayed on the cover, even if the *and* is retained elsewhere in the book or copyright registration.

Company Names. The ampersand should be retained in text in the initialisms of such company names as *A&P* and *AT&T* and in the names of those companies that prefer the ampersand in their official moniker (when such a preference is known), such as *Barnes & Noble*; *Farrar, Straus & Giroux*; *Grosset & Dunlap*; *Procter & Gamble*; and *Smith & Wesson.*

Drop the Serial Comma. Never use a serial comma before an ampersand; for instance, *Smith, Gundersen & Klein*, not *Smith, Gundersen, & Klein.* In the case of book titles, the serial comma may be dropped before an ampersand at the designer's discretion: for instance, *Gods, Graves & Scholars* may appear on the cover while *Gods, Graves, and Scholars* may appear on the copyright page and in the official registration.

ANACHRONISM

An *anachronism* is an error of chronology. In writing, it is usually the insertion of an object, word, concept, or fact from one time period into another, such as the famous clock that strikes the hour in Shakespeare's *Julius Caesar.* Anachronisms have been considered contrary to artistic and literary realism since about the eighteenth century; before then, it was common to see portraits showing the Virgin Mary garbed in the clothes of a Renaissance Dutch lady, for instance, or Joseph in the dress of a medieval peasant. The KJV translators intentionally used anachronisms from time to time, especially when the meanings of the Hebrew and Greek words were fuzzy. For instance, in Gen. 4:21, Jubal is said to be "the father of all such as handle the harp and organ." Most later translations render *organ* as *flute* or *pipe.*

While inadvertent anachronisms can be an embarrassment, creative writers know that intentional anachronism can be a useful tool of communication. They are a common source of humor and satire, as in Mark Twain's *Connecticut Yankee in King Arthur's Court*; they are part of the intrigue of most tales of time travel; and they are implicit in any modern translation of an older work. To give readers a sense of obsolete concepts and objects, a certain amount of deliberate anachronism is necessary. That is part of the process of finding "dynamic equivalents" in translation, as when the NIV renders the "ninth hour" as "three in the afternoon" (Matt. 27:45; see "HOURS, BIBLICAL") as though there were clocks in Jesus's time—which, when you think about it, is not too far removed from Shakespeare's clock in *Julius Caesar.* (See also "ARCHAISM.")

APOSTROPHE

The *apostrophe* (') dates back to Latin and medieval calligraphy and is used today with a word or number to show contraction (omission), possession, or pluralization.

Contraction. An apostrophe is most commonly used in contractions to show the absence of a letter or letters: *ma'am, M'Cheyne, shouldn't.* (For details, see "CONTRACTIONS.")

Possession. An apostrophe is used to denote possession: *the apostles' ministry, George MacDonald's novels, Jesus's disciples, the prophet's writings.* (For details, see "POSSESSIVES.")

Pluralization. For the use of the apostrophe with plurals, see "PLURALS," sections on "*Plurals of Single Letters*" and "*Plurals of Abbreviations.*"

APPENDIX

Information that is useful but intrusive in the main text may be contained in an *appendix*, though the author should avoid lumping unprocessed research or data in an appendix if it has only marginal value. An appendix should contain only information that will benefit the reader and enhance the text.

Design. Since appendixes are meant to be functional, they should be set in the same type size as the text of the book, or possibly one point size smaller if space is a problem. They should be readable and inviting. Also, the titles and headings in an appendix should match those in the main part of the book.

Reference in Text. Within the main text of the book, the author should be sure to make at least one detailed reference to every appendix, including the number and title of the appendix and a brief explanation of why it will be of value to the reader.

Enumerating. Although it was once common to use roman numerals to number appendixes, arabic numerals or capital letters are now predominantly used.

Plural. The plural of *appendix* is either *appendixes* or *appendices*, though this manual opts for *appendixes* for most books, since *appendices* can appear slightly pretentious.

ARCHAISM

If an anachronism is a modern thing in an old setting, then you might say an archaism is an old thing in a modern setting. Although this manual discourages the use of any word marked "archaic" in *Webster*, archaisms, like anachronisms, are useful tools for the skilled writer. (See "ANACHRONISM.") They lend authenticity to historical fiction, provide useful etymological illustrations, and create comic effects, among other things.

Some Christians, especially preachers, use archaisms to echo the authority of the KJV, with words like *begat*, *hither*, *howbeit*, *peradventure*, *saith*, *shalt*, *spake*, *verily*, and so on. But unless such words are used for humor, they are best avoided. The archaic second-person singular pronouns *thou*, *thee*, *thy*, and *thine* are still commonly used in hymns and some prayers (see "*thou, thee, thy, thine*"). An entire class of archaisms is remembered only because they survive in popular hymns and customs: *laud* ("praise") is limited to the Christmas song "What Child Is This?"; *ebenezer*, from 1 Sam. 7:12 (meaning "monument"), survives in Robert Robinson's hymn "Come Thou Fount of Every Blessing"; *langsyne* ("long ago") survives in Robert Burns's "Auld Lang Syne"; *troll* ("to sing") is found solely in "Troll the ancient yuletide carol" from "Deck the Halls"—and *yuletide* itself is an archaism. Other interesting examples: *rood* ("cross"), *sooth* ("truth," which survives in *soothsayer*), *mare* ("demon"; survives in *nightmare*), *shrove* ("to confess," as in *Shrove Tuesday*), *wedbreaker* (the Wycliffe Bible's colorful word for "adulterer"). Nearly all these are Anglo-Saxon words that were superseded by Latinate interlopers.

All words contain fossils of the past. An archaism is simply a fossil that has been left undisturbed for many years. When a good reason exists to unearth archaisms, do so. Otherwise, let them lie.

ASTERISK

An *asterisk* is a typographic symbol that looks like a star with six points in most serif fonts (*) and five points in most sans-serif fonts (*). It is used primarily for bottom-of-page footnote references in those instances when the asterisk-dagger system of footnoting is used rather than numerals, that is, when few footnotes are used on each page. (See "NOTES," section on "*Asterisk-Dagger System*," and also "FOOTNOTE SYMBOLS, BOTTOM-OF-PAGE.")

A sequence of three spaced asterisks is occasionally used to signal a break in the text, such as a shift in scene or a transition to a new section. (See "ASTERISM" and "TEXT BREAKS.")

Also, at the discretion of the designer, an asterisk is occasionally used in place of a bullet in bulleted lists. (See "BULLETS.")

ASTERISM

An *asterism* (⁂ or * * *) is used almost exclusively to signal a text break. (For a more complete discussion, see "TEXT BREAKS.")

AUDIO BOOKS

The recording of audio books for downloading presents few problems for authors and editors, though some issues arise. Correct pronunciation is perhaps the biggest challenge. (See "PRONUNCIATION GUIDE FOR AUDIO BOOKS" for a list of commonly mispronounced words and names.) Also, authors who depend on certain typographic devices to communicate—such as capitalizing special uses of words or arranging words in an unusual way on the page—should be aware that such devices are lost in an audio format.

AUTHOR BIOGRAPHY

A short biography of a book's author or authors, called the "author bio," is commonly placed on the back of softcover books and on the back cover or back flap of hardcover books. The same biographical blurb may be duplicated in the interior, usually as the last element of the back matter. While such duplication may seem redundant, it is common in hardcover books since the dust jacket may be lost or discarded. It is not advisable to duplicate the biography on the interior of softcover books.

At times, space may prohibit a lengthy biography from appearing on the cover, in which case a condensed version may be displayed while the longer version is placed in the back matter.

For ebooks, always include the author biography in the interior since it may not be included in whatever electronic cover or promotional material accompanies the ebook.

AUTHOR CARD, OR AD CARD

The *author card*, sometimes called the *ad card* or *card page*, is reserved for a list of the author's other publications. (It is called a *card* because it was once printed on a piece of card stock and distributed as a marketing piece or inserted into the book.) Articles, monographs, other short publications, derivative works, and audio versions of printed books are usually not included on a card page. Most publishers supply an author card as a way of promoting their own publications by that author, though the author or publisher may find it advantageous to provide a more comprehensive list that includes the author's works from other publishers.

Placement and Size. In print books, the author card is usually placed on the verso of the half-title page, across from the title page, and is commonly set in the same type size as the text or one point smaller. In ebook format, it is usually the page immediately before the title page.

Style. The list is headed by a phrase like "Also by [name of author]" or "Resources by [name of author]." The phrase "Other books by ..." is avoided because content is often available in other formats. When the author has coauthored works on the list, the name(s) of the coauthor(s) should be given in parentheses after the title so that it doesn't appear that the author is claiming sole authorship. Titles are usually set in italic and any accompanying information in roman. Subtitles should not be included unless they explain the title in a significant way.

Out of Print. Most often, only currently available titles are placed on the author card page, but OP titles may be included at the author's and publisher's discretion. With so many online book resources, many out-of-print books are readily available, and readers may want to search them out.

AUTHOR SIGNATURE

Nearly every author is asked to sign a copy of his or her book. A signature is written in black ink and usually takes one of two forms: (1) *A signature*: If the reader is a book collector or fan, it is customary for the author to sign only his or her name on the title page, directly beneath the author's printed name, unless asked to write it elsewhere. A signature with no personalization increases the book's value when it is resold on the collectors' market. (2) *An inscription*: If the author wishes to write a personal message, or if the author is requested to write such a message, it can be done on the title page (if the message is short) or on the half-title page (if it is longer). Long messages are best written on the blank flyleaf. A courteous author will ask the reader which form they prefer.

AUTHOR'S NOTE

An *author's note*, or *note from the author*, is sometimes included in a book's back matter. It is usually short and informal, sometimes taking the form of a personal letter from the author to the reader. Such notes are especially common in fiction when the author wishes to address the reader in his or her own voice rather than in the voice of the novel's narrator. Nonfiction authors often opt to call such an author-reader communication an *afterword*. (See "AFTERWORD.")

B

BACK MATTER, ELEMENTS OF A BOOK'S

A book's *back matter* comprises those elements that follow the main text. Ideally, all parts of the back matter should begin on recto pages, but they may begin verso if the design or space limitations dictate. The back matter is usually placed in the following order, as available:

Afterword, conclusion, or epilogue (though in some books, a conclusion or an epilogue may be considered the final element of the body matter); see "AFTERWORD," "CONCLUSION," and "EPILOGUE"
Note from the author; see "AUTHOR'S NOTE"
Acknowledgments (if not in the front matter); see "ACKNOWLEDGMENTS"
Appendix(es); see "APPENDIX"
Study questions (if not incorporated into the text)
Notes (if not set as footnotes or as chapter endnotes); see "NOTES"
Glossary
Chronological table(s)
Bibliography, Sources, "For Further Reading," or "References Consulted"; see "BIBLIOGRAPHIES AND SOURCE LISTS"
Index to maps; see "INDEXES"
Proper-name index; see "INDEXES"
Subject index; see "INDEXES"
Scripture index; see "INDEXES"
List of contributors
Author biographical note; see "AUTHOR BIOGRAPHY"
Colophon, publisher's note, or reader response page; see "COLOPHON" and "READER RESPONSE CARD"

BIBLE CITATIONS

See "QUOTING THE BIBLE."

BIBLE, NAMES FOR THE

Capitalize words and phrases that are used as alternate titles for the Bible and set them in roman type, though be careful not to confuse such words and phrases with those that may be descriptors.

the Book
the Good Book
Holy Scriptures
Holy Writ
the Scriptures
the Word
the Word of God
the Writings
but
the divine writings
God's personal word for us
the living words of God

BIBLE, NAMES FOR SPECIFIC PORTIONS OF THE

Many well-known portions of the Bible have titles of their own, given to them by scholars or by tradition. Capitalize them as titles and set them in roman. (See also "PSALMS, TRADITIONAL GROUPINGS OF.") Some common examples:

the Beatitudes
the Catholic Epistles
the Christ Hymn
the Commandments
the Decalogue
the General Epistles
the Gloria Patri
the Golden Rule
the Gospels
the Great Commandment
the Great Commission
the Great Hallel
the Hebrew Scriptures
the Historical Books
the Lord's Prayer
the Love Chapter
the Magnificat
the Minor Prophets
the New Testament
the Old Testament
the Pastoral Letters
the Penitential Psalms
the Pentateuch
the Poetic Books
the Prayer of Moses
the Prophetic Books
the Psalms of David
the Sermon on the Mount
the Songs of Ascent
the Synoptic Gospels
the Ten Commandments
the Testaments
the Twenty-Third Psalm

Such words as *book*, *epistle*, *gospel*, and *letter* are often lowercase as descriptors (unless they are capitalized in the specific version of the Bible being used): *the book of Genesis*, *the epistle to the Romans*, *the gospel of John*, *Paul's letter to the Corinthians*, and so on.

BIBLE PAPER

Bible paper is a thin, durable, opaque printing paper, often used for Bibles, though not exclusively. Printers refer to it as *India paper.*

BIBLE QUOTATION

See "QUOTING THE BIBLE."

BIBLE, RED-LETTER EDITIONS OF THE

See "RED-LETTER EDITIONS OF THE BIBLE."

BIBLE REFERENCING

See "QUOTING THE BIBLE."

BIBLES, ONLINE

The internet is an invaluable source for accessing complete Bible texts in many versions and languages, many of which are downloadable. One of the most comprehensive sites is Bible Gateway (a subsidiary of HarperCollins Christian; go to http://www.biblegateway.com/), which, as of February 2014, offers complete texts of the following Bibles in English:

American Standard Bible
Amplified Bible
Amplified Bible, Classic Edition
Common English Bible
Complete Jewish Bible
Contemporary English Version
Darby Translation
Disciples' Literary New Translation
Douay-Rheims 1899 American Edition
Easy-to-Read Version
English Standard Version (audio also available)
English Standard Version Anglicised
Expanded Bible
Geneva Bible (1599)
GOD'S WORD Translation
Good News Translation
Holman Christian Standard Bible (audio also available)
International Standard Version
J. B. Phillips New Testament
Jubilee Bible 2000
King James Version (audio also available)
Lexham English Bible (audio also available)
The Message
Modern English Version
Mounce Reverse-Interlinear New Testament
Names of God Bible
New American Bible
New American Standard Bible (audio also available)
New Century Version
New English Translation
New International Reader's Version
New International Version (audio also available)
New International Version (UK)
New King James Version
New Life Version
New Living Translation
New Revised Standard Version
New Revised Standard Version (Anglicized)
New Revised Standard Version (Catholic)
Orthodox Jewish Bible
Revised Standard Version
Revised Standard Version (Catholic)
Twenty-First Century King James Version

The Voice	Wycliffe Bible
World English Bible	Young's Literal Translation
Worldwide English (New Testament)	

Bible Gateway also includes Bibles in many foreign languages: ten in Chinese, four in French, five in German, five in Italian, fourteen in Spanish, as well as more than fifty other languages (including the original Greek and Hebrew).

Among the Bible versions and translations not found at Bible Gateway, the following can be found at these sites:

Analytical-Literal Translation	http://dtl.org/alt/index.html
Bible in Basic English	http://www.biblestudytools.com/bbe/
Hebrew Names Version	http://www.biblestudytools.com/hnv/
Jefferson Bible	http://www.angelfire.com/co/JeffersonBible/
Modern Young's Literal Version	http://ao-soft.com/mylt/index.htm
Third Millennium Bible	http://www.biblestudytools.com/tmb/
Webster's Bible	http://www.biblestudytools.com/wbt/
Weymouth New Testament	http://www.biblestudytools.com/wnt/

BIBLE STYLE: THE NEW INTERNATIONAL VERSION

See "NIV STYLE (NEW INTERNATIONAL VERSION)."

BIBLE VERSIONS AND TRANSLATIONS, TYPES OF

Bible translations are either literal, paraphrastic, or dynamic, though these are a gradation rather than three distinct categories.

Literal translations (such as NASB, ESV, and AB) provide an exact word-for-word English equivalent for each word in the original. While such translations are accurate, many readers find them a challenge because such translations often require extensive annotations to explain outmoded idioms, vocabulary, and references.

At the other extreme is the *paraphrase* (MSG, Phillips, and TLB, for example), which renders the original in easily understood modern equivalents so that little explanation is required. The extensive use of contemporary idiom results in Bible versions that are extremely readable, though some readers find that such paraphrases obscure certain shades of meaning or lend themselves too easily to the paraphraser's interpretation. Historical accuracy is often sacrificed.

A *dynamic* translation (for example, NIV and NRSV) splits the difference between the literal and the paraphrastic, adhering as closely as possible to the original language but trying to render obscure idioms, vocabulary, and references in modern "dynamic" equivalents. A dynamic translation tries to minimize the challenges of both the literal translation (obscurity and overexplanation) and the paraphrastic (inaccuracy).

In addition to those three general types, other specific kinds of Bible translations and versions exist, such as the following:

abridgment—from which certain passages, chapters, or entire books have been eliminated to facilitate reading

children's Bible—rewritten or heavily revised for children

chronological Bible—in which narrative elements are chronologically arranged

condensed Bible—shortened for ease of reading; more extensively abridged than an abridgment

devotional Bible—annotated with commentary and study helps, usually centering on a specific theme or readership (such as archaeological, men, women, youth, and so on)

easy-reader Bible—a Bible revised to use only the most common words in the language or geared to a specific reading level (usually about eighth grade)

family Bible—usually provides the text only, often with decorative illustrations; often oversized

inclusive Bible—in which gender-specific language has been made non-gender-specific in those cases when the gender-specific construction of the original is meant to be generic

interlinear Bible—in which the translation is given between the lines of the original language

lectern Bible—an oversize, often ornamental Bible designed to be displayed on a lectern or special stand in a church; the font size is usually large so that a reader standing at the lectern can read it easily

modernized version—usually refers to an older version of a Bible that has been rendered into more contemporary language

parallel Bible—in which two or more versions are presented side by side

paraphrase—a version in modern colloquial English, largely adapted from existing English versions or the author's own familiarity with the original texts

paraphrastic translation—a modernized version, usually in contemporary English, though it differs from a paraphrase in that it is translated exclusively from the original texts

pew Bible—specially printed and bound, to be used by worshipers in a church setting; often the type size is larger than normal, and most annotations are eliminated

presentation Bible—specially designed, usually small, and given on special occasions such as confirmations or weddings. See "PRESENTATION PAGE."

reading Bible, or reader's Bible—printed without verse numbers or intruding annotations; also with standard paragraphing

red-letter Bible—in which the words of Jesus are printed in red. See "RED-LETTER EDITIONS OF THE BIBLE."

study Bible—annotated with study helps, often with maps, charts, and illustrations

synchronized Bible—in which the Gospels or certain OT historical books have been melded into a single continuous narrative; also called a *harmony*

updated version—an older version of the Bible that has been revised or altered in some form to keep pace with changing times and tastes; usually more extensive than a *modernized version*, which implies just updating of vocabulary

wide-margin edition—a Bible printed with columns of white space on which the reader may write his or her own notes

BIBLE VERSIONS IN ENGLISH

The names of Bible versions and translations are usually set in roman type (for instance, the King James Version, the New International Version, the Douay Version), especially when those versions appear in many editions and formats. When a specific edition of a particular version is referred to, it should be italicized as an ordinary book title (for instance, *The Good News Bible, The NIV Study Bible, The King James 2000 Bible*).

Abbreviations of Bible translations, paraphrases, and significant editions are also usually set in roman type. If the abbreviation is an initialism incorporating the beginning letters of the version (see "ACRONYMS AND INITIALISMS"), the letters are set in full capitals; for instance, NIV for the New International Version. Likewise, if the abbreviation is the last name of the translator or paraphraser, it is set in roman type with an initial capital letter, followed by lowercase letters; for instance, Phillips is the abbreviation for that author's paraphrase, *The New Testament in Modern English*. If the abbreviation is a complete word taken from the title of a specific edition, then it is set in italic; for instance, *Anchor* is the correct abbreviation for *The Anchor Bible*.

This list presents a standard that can easily accommodate variations in typographic style as needed.

Abbreviation	Title (and Information)
ABUV	*American Bible Union Version* (1912)
Ælfric	Old English Hexateuch (c. 1000; Ælfric of Eynsham; Old English Pentateuch plus Joshua and Judges)
AENT	*Aramaic English New Testament* (2008; uses Hebrew terms)

Aitken. . . . . . . Aitken Bible (NT 1777, complete 1782; first English-language Bible printed in America; essentially adapted from KJV)

AIV . . . . *The New Testament and Psalms: An Inclusive Version* (1995; NT and Psalms only; gender-inclusive revision of NRSV)

AKJV. . . . . . . *American King James Version of the Holy Bible* (1999; M. P. Engelbrite modernization of KJV; public domain)

ALB . . . . *A Literary Bible* (2010; D. Rosenberg; OT Hebrew Bible)

ALT . . . . *Analytic-Literal Translation of the New Testament of the Holy Bible* (1999; Darkness to Light Ministries; online literal NT trans.: http://www.dtl.org/alt/index.html; print edition 2001)

AMP . . . . *Amplified Bible* (1958–65, rev. 2015)

AMPC. . . . . . . *Amplified Bible, Classic Edition* (1958–65, rev. 1987)

Anchor . . . . . . *Anchor Bible* (1964; each book is translated by a different scholar; published by Doubleday)

ARTB . . . . *Ancient Roots Translinear Bible* (OT 2006, complete Bible 2013; A. F. Werner; "restoration" partially incorporating revisions of other translations)

ARV. . . . . American Revised Version (1901; US edition of ERV; public domain)

ARV, MG . . . . American Revised Version (margin)

ASV. . . . . American Standard Version (1901; US edition of ERV; public domain)

AV7 . . . . *New Authorized Version in Present-Day English* (2006; NT and selected OT; not the same as NAV or TMB)

AV . . . . Authorized Version (1611; same as KJV; used in UK references; public domain in US; under British crown control in UK)

AVU. . . . . Authorized Version Update (2006; updated language; NT only)

Barclay . . . . . . Barclay's *New Testament* (1968–69; W. Barclay)

Barnstone . . . *The Restored New Testament* (2009; W. Barnstone; NT with some Pseudepigrapha)

Bassendyne. . Bassendyne Bible (first Bible printed in English in Scotland; NT 1576, complete 1579; used the text of the Geneva Bible)

BB . . . . *Basic Bible* (1950; C. K. Ogden; uses basic vocabulary of 850 words)

BBE. . . . . *Bible in Basic English* (NT 1941, OT 1949, updated 1962; public domain in US only)

Beck . . . . *Holy Bible: An American Translation* (1976; W. F. Beck, completed by E. Smick and E. Kiehl; Lutheran; reprinted in 1990 as *God's Word to the Nations*)

Berean . . . . . . *Berean Bible* (online, open source; trans. by Bible Hub and Discovery Bible teams; available online at http://biblehub.com; comprises *Berean Interlinear Bible* [BIB], *Berean Literal Bible* [BLB], and *Berean Study Bible* [BSB])

Bishop . . . . . . Bishop's Bible (1568; Archbishop Parker and others; revision of the Great Bible; sometimes called Matthew Parker's Bible; public domain)

BIB . . . . *Berean Interlinear Bible* (see Berean)

BLB . . . . *Berean Literal Bible* (see Berean)

BLE . . . . *Bible in Living English* (1972; used by Jehovah's Witnesses)

BSB . . . . *Berean Study Bible* (see Berean)

BV . . . . *Holy Bible: Berkeley Version in Modern English* (NT 1945, OT 1959)

CAB . . . . *Complete Apostles' Bible* (2004; P. W. Esposito; from Septuagint)

Cassirer . . . . . *Cassirer New Testament* (1989; H. W. Cassirer)

CB . . . . *Conservative Bible* (NT 2010, OT in progress; Conservative Bible Project; electronic only)

CCD . . . . *Confraternity Bible* (1941–69; series of translations and updates by the Confraternity of Christian Doctrine; Roman Catholic)

CENT . . . . *Common English New Testament* (1865; American Bible Union; public domain)

CEB . . . . *Common English Bible* (2011; Christian Resources Development Corporation; includes deuterocanonical books and Apocrypha)

CEV . . . . *Holy Bible: Contemporary English Version* (1995; American Bible Society; fifth-grade reading level)

CJB . . . . *Complete Jewish Bible* (1998; David H. Stern)

CLNT . . . . *Concordant Literal New Testament* (1926; A. E. Knoch; NT companion to CVOT)

CNT . . . . *Centenary New Testament* (1924)

Coverdale . . . Coverdale Bible (1535; Miles Coverdale; first full English translation printed, and its 1537 edition the first full version printed in England; incorporates Tyndale's Pentateuch and NT; public domain)

CPB . . . . *Cambridge Paragraph Bible* (1873 edition of the KJV)

CPV . . . . *Cotton Patch Version* (1973; loose paraphrase by Clarence Jordan; same as *Jordan*)

CPDV . . . . *Holy Bible: Catholic Public Domain Version* (2011; based on Vulgate and Challoner Douay-Rheims; public domain)

Cranmer . . . . . Cranmer's Bible (1540 edition of the Great Bible; prologue by Archbishop Thomas Cranmer)

Cressman . . . . See WE

CSB . . . . *Christian Standard Bible* (2017, same as HCSB)

CVOT . . . . *Concordant Version of the Old Testament* (1926; A. E. Knoch; OT companion to CLNT)

DB.......... *Dartmouth Bible* (1961; abridgment of KJV)

DBT.......... *Holy Bible: Darby Translation* (1871; dispensationalist; public domain)

DLNT .... *Disciples' Literal New Testament* (2011; companion to *New Testament TransLine*)

DNT .... *Documents of the New Testament* (1934; paraphrase by G. W. Wade)

DRB.......... Douay-Rheims Bible (NT 1582, OT 1609–10; based on Vulgate; also called the Douay Version)

DRC .... Douay-Rheims Bible (1750, 1752; Catholic Bishop Richard Challoner's updating of the Douay-Rheims Bible; also called Challoner's Bible)

Easy .... *Holy Bible: Easy-to-Read Version* (1987, rev. 2004, 2010; World Bible Translation Center; for deaf and ESL readers; fourth-grade reading level)

EB .... *Emphasized Bible* (NT 1897, OT 1902; J. B. Rotherham; public domain)

EEB.......... *Easy English Bible* (2001 and ongoing; restricted-vocabulary translation from Wycliffe Associates, UK, for English-as-a-second-language readers)

ERV.......... English Revised Version, Revised Version, or Revised English Bible (NT 1881, OT 1885, Apoc. 1895; first major revision of KJV; same as RV; public domain)

ERV, MG..... English Revised Version (margin)

ESV......... *Holy Bible: English Standard Version* (2001; Crossway; updating of RSV)

ESVUK ...... *Holy Bible: English Standard Version, Anglicized* (2001; updating of RSV for UK)

Everyday..... *The Everyday Bible* (1986; same as NCV)

EXB.......... *The Expanded Bible* (2011; based on the New Century Version)

Fenton ...... *Holy Bible in Modern English* (1903; F. Fenton)

Geneva...... Geneva Bible (1560; first English Bible with verse divisions; trans. by William Whittingham, Anthony Gilby, and Thomas Sampson; popularly referred to as the "Breeches Bible" for its translation of Gen. 3:7)

GNB .... *Good News Bible* (NT 1966, OT 1976; same as TEV; also called *Good News Translation* and *Good News for Modern Man*)

Goodspeed.. *The New Testament: An American Translation* (NT 1923; see Smith-Goodspeed for complete Bible)

Great .... Great Bible (1539; Coverdale's revision of Matthew Bible; 1539 edition is called Cromwell's Bible because of his portrait on title page; 1540 edition is called Cranmer's Bible for his portrait)

GWT........ *God's Word Translation* (1995; Luther Bible Society; update of Beck)
GWTN ...... *God's Word to the Nations* (1995; same as GWT)
Hammond ... Hammond's Paraphrase (1653; Henry Hammond; NT only, based on KJV)
HCSB .... *Holman Christian Standard Bible* (NT 1999, complete 2006; Southern Baptist Convention)
HNB .... *Holy Name Bible* (1963; A. B. Traina; first English Bible to use Hebrew names for God)
HNV .... *Hebrew Names Version of the World English Bible*, also called *World English Bible: Messianic Edition* (revision of WEB that uses Hebrew names; public domain; electronic only)
HSE......... *Holy Scriptures in English* (2001)
ICB .... *International Children's Bible* (1986; same as ICV)
ISR.......... *The Scriptures* (1998, rev. 2009; Institute for Scripture Research)
ICV .... *International Children's Version* (1986; original name for NCV; same as ICB)
ISV.......... *Holy Bible: International Standard Version* (NT 1998, complete 2011; ISV Foundation)
IV........... *The Holy Scriptures: Inspired Version* (1867; revision of the KJV by Joseph Smith, Mormon founder; also called the *Joseph Smith Translation* [JST]; public domain)
JB .... *Jerusalem Bible* (French 1956, English 1966; first Catholic Bible translated from original languages rather than from Vulgate; French version referred to as BJ: *La Bible de Jérusalem*)
Jefferson .... *Jefferson Bible* (c. 1820; Thomas Jefferson's redaction of KJV NT Gospels; public domain)
JNT......... *Jewish New Testament* (NT 1989; David H. Stern; became part of CJB 1998)
Jordan ...... *Cotton Patch Version* (1973; Clarence Jordan's dialect paraphrase; same as CPV)
JPS .... *Holy Scriptures: Jewish Publication Society Version of the Old Testament* (1917)
JST.......... *The Joseph Smith Translation* (1867; Joseph Smith, Mormon founder; see also "IV")
KJ2000...... *The King James 2000e* (2000; Robert A. Couric's modernization of KJV, electronic version)
KJ21 .... *Holy Bible: Twenty-First Century King James Version* (1994; modernized KJV)
KJII .... *Holy Bible: King James II Version* (1971; J. P. Green's modernization of KJV)
KJC.......... *King James, Clarified New Testament* (2010; Bill McGinnis; modernized KJV)

KJV . . . . Holy Bible: King James Version (1611; same as AV; public domain in US)
KJVER. . . . . . . *Holy Bible: King James Version, Easy Reading* (2001)
Knox . . . . *Holy Bible: A Translation from the Latin Vulgate in the Light of the Hebrew and Greek Original* (NT 1945, OT 1949; Knox)
KNT . . . . *The Kingdom New Testament: A Contemporary Translation* (2011; N. T. Wright)
Lamsa . . . . *Holy Bible from Ancient Eastern Manuscripts* (1933, 1939, 1940, 1957; Lamsa)
Lattimore . . . . *The Four Gospels and the Revelation* (1979; Lattimore); *Acts and Letters of the Apostles* (1982; Lattimore)
LB . . . . See TLB
Leeser. . . . . . . *The Twenty-Four Books of the Holy Scriptures* (1853; Jewish version of Hebrew Scriptures by Isaac Leeser; public domain)
LITV . . . . *Literal Translation of the Holy Bible* (1976; J. P. Green; electronic version only)
LO . . . . *Living Oracles* (NT 1835; Alexander Campbell; public domain)
Lorimer. . . . . . *The New Testament in Scots* (1983; Scots dialect NT by William L. Lorimer)
Matthew. . . . . Matthew Bible (1537; Thomas Matthew; first English Bible printed in England)
MEV . . . . *Holy Bible: Modern English Version* (2014; updating of KJV)
MGB . . . . *The Manga Bible* (2007; manga-style illustrations; uses TNIV text)
MKJV . . . . *Modern King James Version of the Holy Bible* (1999; J. P. Green; modernized KJV; updating of KJII)
MLB . . . . *Modern Language Bible* (NT 1945, OT 1959; same as NBV)
MLV. . . . . *Holy Bible: Modern Literal Version* (NT 1987; first computerized NT; OT 2000; updating of ASV; public domain)
Moffatt. . . . . . *A New Translation of the Bible* (NT 1913, OT 1924; rev. 1935; Moffatt)
Montgomery . *Centenary Translation of the New Testament in Modern English* (1924; Helen Montgomery and American Baptist Publication Society)
Moulton . . . . . *Modern Reader's Bible* (1907; Moulton; public domain)
MSG . . . . *The Message: The Bible in Contemporary Language* (NT 1993, complete 2000; paraphrastic translation by Eugene Peterson)
NAB . . . . *New American Bible* (NT 1941, OT 1969; Roman Catholic)
NABR . . . . *New American Bible, Revised Edition* (NT 1986, OT 2010; Roman Catholic)
NASB . . . . *New American Standard Bible* (NT 1963, OT 1971; rev. 1995; Lockman Foundation)

NASB95 . . . . . *New American Standard Bible* (1995 update of NASB; Lockman Foundation)
NAV . . . . *Third Millennium Bible: The New Authorized Version* (1998; updated KJV with Apocrypha; same as TMB)
NBV . . . . *Holy Bible: The New Berkeley Version in Modern English* (NT 1945, OT 1959; same as MLB)
NCPB . . . . *The New Cambridge Paragraph Bible with the Apocrypha* (2006 edition of complete KJV)
NCV . . . . *The New Century Version Bible* (NT 1978, complete 1986; third-grade reading level; same as ICB and ICV)
NE. . . . . *The New Evangelical New Testament* (1990; NT of GWT)
NEB . . . . *New English Bible* (NT 1961, OT and Apoc. 1970)
NET. . . . . *New English Translation* (1997; Biblical Studies Foundation; electronic version only)
NETS . . . . *New English Translation of the Septuagint* (2007; OT and Apocrypha)
NEV . . . . *New Testament: New European Version* (NT 2011; revised conflation of KJV and ASV)
NIrV . . . . *Holy Bible: New International Reader's Version* (1996; Biblica; third-grade-reading-level version of NIV; gender-inclusive language of British edition removed in US version. Note the lowercase "r" amid the full capitals)
NIV . . . . *Holy Bible: New International Version* (NT 1973, OT 1978; rev. 1984 and 2011; Biblica)
NIVI. . . . . *Holy Bible: New International Version, Inclusive Language Edition* (1996; published in UK; now out of print; superseded by NIV 2011)
NIVSB . . . . *NIV Study Bible* (1985)
NJB. . . . . *New Jerusalem Bible* (1985; update of JB)
NJPS. . . . . *Tanak: The Holy Scriptures: The New Jewish Publication Society Translation According to the Traditional Hebrew Text* (1988; update of JPS)
NJV. . . . . *New Jewish Version* (1962–82; Torah rev. 1985; rev. of JPS)
NJVSS. . . . . . . *The Beloved and I: New Jubilee's Version of Sacred Scripture* (OT 2007; T. McElwain; verse commentaries)
NKJV . . . . *Holy Bible: New King James Version* (1979; loosely based on KJV, though largely new translation)
NLT. . . . . *Holy Bible: New Living Translation* (1996; Tyndale House; based on TLB, but less paraphrastic, being largely a new translation; sixth-grade reading level)
NLV. . . . . *Bible: New Life Version* (1969; G. H. and K. Ledyard; third-grade reading level, using basic vocabulary of 850 words)

NNT . . . . *Noli New Testament* (1961; Albanian Orthodox Church in America)
Norlie . . . . *New Testament in Modern English* (1951; Norlie)
Noyes . . . . . . *The New Testament* (1868; Noyes; public domain)
NRSV . . . . *Holy Bible: The New Revised Standard Version* (1990; National Council of Churches; rev. of RSV; gender-inclusive)
NSRB . . . . *New Scofield Reference Bible* (1967; KJV)
NTUV . . . . *New Testament: An Understandable Version* (2006; W. E. Paul)
NWT . . . . *New World Translation of the Holy Scriptures* (1961; Watch Tower Bible and Tract Society [Jehovah's Witnesses]; loosely based on ASV)
OAB . . . . *Oxford Annotated Bible* (1962; RSV)
OJB . . . . *Orthodox Jewish Bible* (2002; P. Goble; Yiddish and Hasidic names and references)
OSB . . . . *Orthodox Study Bible* (2007; OT newly translated; NT from NKJV)
Parker . . . . *Holy Bible* (1876; Julia E. Smith Parker translation, first complete translation by a woman)
Phillips . . . . . . *New Testament in Modern English* (1958; paraphrase by J. B. Phillips; later editions less paraphrastic)
PNC . . . . *People's New Covenant* (1925; Christian Scientist)
Quaker . . . . . . "Quaker Bible"; *Purver's Translation of the Bible* (1764; Anthony Purver translation)
RDB . . . . *Reader's Digest Bible* (1982; heavily condensed RSV)
REB . . . . *Revised English Bible* (1989; 2nd edition and revision of NEB)
Rheims . . . . . . Rheims New Testament (1582; NT of DRB; public domain)
Rieu . . . . *Penguin Bible* (1952; the four gospels translated by E. V. Rieu)
RNT . . . . *Restored New Testament* (2009; W. Barnstone; NT translation with three Gnostic gospels included)
RSV . . . . Holy Bible: Revised Standard Version (NT 1946, OT 1952, Apoc. 1957; National Council of Churches; rev. of ASV)
RSVC . . . . *Revised Standard Version Catholic Bible* (2002; Catholic version of RSV)
RV . . . . Revised Version (NT 1881, OT 1885, Apoc. 1895; same as ERV; public domain)
RV, MG . . . . . . Revised Version (1899; marginal notes show differences between RV and AV)
Schocken . . . . *The Schocken Bible* (OT in process; trans. by Everett Fox; Pentateuch, 2000; Joshua, Judges, Samuel, and Kings, 2014)
SCM . . . . *New Testament*, often called *Spencer New Testament* (NT 1941; Spencer, Callan, McHugh; Roman Catholic)
SEB . . . . *Simple English Bible* (NT 1980; International Bible Translators, Inc.)
Smith . . . . *Joseph Smith Translation* (1867; Joseph Smith, Mormon

founder; public domain; also referred to as *Inspired Version*, IV, or JST)

Smith-Goodspeed . . . *Complete Bible: An American Translation* (NT 1923; OT 1927; Apoc. 1938; E. Goodspeed, J. M. P. Smith, and others)

SRB . . . . *Scofield Reference Bible* (1909; KJV)

SV . . . . *The Complete Gospels, Annotated Scholars Version*, 4th ed. (2010; R. J. Miller; includes extracanonical gospels)

Taverner . . . . . Taverner's Bible (1537; trans. by Richard Taverner; public domain; revision of Matthew)

TB . . . . *Today's Bible* (1995; retitling of GWTN)

TCNT . . . . *Twentieth Century New Testament* (1898–1901; based on Weymouth; public domain; note: "Twentieth Century" not hyphenated)

TEB . . . . *Transparent English Bible* (literal version was due 2012 from the Original Bible Project; portions available online; still in progress)

TEV . . . . *Today's English Version* (NT 1966, OT 1976; American Bible Society; also called *Good News Bible* and *Good News for Modern Man*; easy reading level)

Thomson . . . . *Holy Bible* (1808; Charles Thomson's translation of Septuagint and NT)

TIB . . . . *The Inclusive Bible: The First Egalitarian Translation* (2009; by Priests for Equality)

TLB . . . . *The Living Bible* (NT 1967, OT 1971; Kenneth Taylor; paraphrase of ASV; also called *The Book* and later reprinted as *The Way*)

TLS . . . . *The Living Scripture* (1982; Messianic Jewish revision of TLB)

TMB . . . . *Third Millennium Bible* (1998; modernized KJV with some Apocrypha; same as NAV)

TNIV . . . . *Holy Bible: Today's New International Version* (NT 2002, OT 2005; updating of NIV; now out of print, superseded by Biblica's NIV 2011 edition)

TS98 . . . . *The Scriptures* (1998; Messianic Jewish translation)

Tyndale. . . . . . Tyndale's New Testament (1526; based largely on both Erasmus's Greek Testament and Latin version, as well as the Vulgate and Luther's German version; the Pentateuch followed c. 1530; public domain)

VW . . . . *Voice in the Wilderness Bible* (2005; conflation of NKJV, LITV, and KJV)

Voice. . . . . *The Voice Bible* (2012; dynamic equivalent translation; Ecclesia Bible Society)

WE . . . . *Bible in Worldwide English* (1959; A. Cressman; also referred to as "Cressman"; some references use BWE as abbreviation)

WEB .... *World English Bible* (NT 2000, complete with Apocrypha 2012; based on ASV; public domain; electronic only; ebible.org/)
Webster..... Webster's Bible (1833; Noah Webster's rev. of KJV, with updated spelling; public domain)
Wesley ...... Wesley's New Testament (1790; John Wesley's rev. of KJV; public domain)
Wessex....... Wessex Gospels (c. 990; first trans. of gospels into West Saxon dialect of Old English; also called West-Saxon Gospels)
Weymouth... *Weymouth's New Testament in Modern Speech* (1903; rev. 1924 and 1929; Richard Weymouth)
WGCIB...... *Work of God's Children Illustrated Bible* (2010; Catholic, based on DRC, with illustrations)
Williams, C.B. *New Testament: A Translation in Language of the People* (1937; Charles B. Williams)
Williams, C.K. *New Testament in Plain English* (1963; Charles K. Williams)
WOTM ...... *Way of the Master Evidence Bible* (2003; R. Comfort's updating of KJV, also called *A Comfort-able KJV*)
WOY......... *Word of Yahweh* (2003; KJV, using *Yahweh* for *the Lord* and *Yahshua* for *Jesus*)
Wuest....... *Wuest Expanded Translation* (NT 1961; K. S. Wuest; follows Greek word order)
WVSS .... *Westminster Version of the Sacred Scriptures* (NT 1936, OT incomplete; English Roman Catholic)
Wycliffe ...... Wycliffe Bible (c. 1380; Middle English trans. from Vulgate by Nicholas of Hereford and an anonymous translator. Two early versions exist: Bodley [before 1382, catalogued in Bodley Library as MS Bodley 959] and Purvey [c. 1400]. Not actually printed in its complete form until 1810; public domain)
YLT .... *Young's Literal Translation of the Bible* (1862; rev. 1887, 1898; Young; based on KJV; public domain; the modernized version is ALT)

BIBLE VERSIONS NOT IN ENGLISH

Of the more than three thousand languages into which at least portions of the Bible have been translated (including invented languages like Klingon, Pig Latin, and emoji symbols), here is a select list of some of the better-known translations. This list also includes some seminal original-language documents.

Abbreviation	Title and Information
Aquila........	Version of Aquila (c. 130 CE; Greek OT)
BDS...........	*La Bible de Semeur* (2000; French)

Bedell . . . . . . Bedell's Irish Old Testament (1685; Bishop William Bedell's trans. of KJV OT into Irish Gaelic)

BFC . . . . *La Bible en français courant* (1987; French)

BHK . . . . *Biblia Hebraica* (1925; Rudolf Kittel and others; Hebrew OT text)

BHS . . . . *Biblia Hebraica Stuttgartensia* (1983; Hebrew OT text)

BJ . . . . *La Bible de Jérusalem* (1956, rev. 1973; French)

Clementine . . *Bibliorum Sacrorum Iuxta Vulgatam Clementinam* (1592; the Latin Vulgate as revised by Pope Clement VIII; official Bible of Roman Catholic Church until replaced by the Nova Vulgata in 1979)

CP . . . . Complutensian Polyglot (1513–17; first Bible printed in Greek and Hebrew; in six volumes)

Eliot . . . . Algonquin Bible (1663; John Eliot's Native American trans.; first Bible printed in America)

Erasmus . . . . . Erasmus's New Testament (1516; Latin trans. of Greek NT by Erasmus)

Ferrara . . . . . . Ferrara Bible (1553; first Spanish OT, trans. from Hebrew)

Gullah . . . . *De Nyew Testament* (2005; first translation of NT into Gullah, a distinct language with African and English influences)

Gutenberg . . . Gutenberg Bible (c. 1454; Johannes Gutenberg; first Bible printed on a printing press with movable type; the Latin Vulgate; sometimes called the Forty-Two Line Bible; followed c. 1458–59 by the Thirty-Six Line Bible)

HB . . . . Hebrew Bible (OT; general name for many editions)

Leopolita . . . . Biblia Leopolity (1561; first Polish trans. of Vulgate, by John Leopolita)

LSG . . . . *La Bible Sainte* (1880, rev. 1978; French trans. by Louis Segond)

Luther . . . . Luther Bible (1534; German trans. by Martin Luther)

LXX . . . . Septuagint (3rd and 2nd centuries BCE; Greek version of Hebrew Bible; the four notable editions are the Complutensian, the Aldine, the Grabian, and the Vatican Codex)

Mazarin . . . . . A specific copy of the Gutenberg Bible discovered in the Mazarin Library, Paris, in 1760

MT . . . . Masoretic Text (c. 1100; basis for Christian OT)

NA27 . . . . *Novum Testamentum Graece*, 27th ed. (1993; Erwin Nestle, Barbara Aland, and Kurt Aland)

NV, Neo-Vulgate . . . . *Bibliorum Sacrorum nova vulgata editio* (Psalter 1969; OT 1971; NT 1979; thorough updating of Latin Bible; official Bible of Roman Catholic Church since 1979)

O'Donnell . . . O'Donnell's Irish New Testament (1602; William O'Donnell's trans. of NT into Irish Gaelic)

Ostrog . . . . . . Ostrog Bible (1581; first complete Slavonic Bible, printed in Russia)

Pagninus . . . . *Veteris et Novi Testamenti nova translation* (1527; first complete Latin translation from original languages by a modern scholar, Santes Pagnino)
Sacy . . . . Bible de Sacy, or Bible de Port-Royal (c. 1670; early French translation by Louis de Sacy)
Sauer . . . . Sauer Bible (1743; German Luther Bible; first Bible printed in America in a European language)
Segond21 . . . *La Bible Sainte* (2007; French; updated LSG)
Stephanus . . . Greek New Testament (1551; printed in Paris by Robert Stephanus; first NT to have verse numbers; one of the sources for KJV and other translations)
Symmachus . . Version of Symmachus (late 2nd cent.; idiomatic Greek OT)
Theodotion . . Version of Theodotion (early 2nd cent.; Greek OT; partly a revision of LXX)
UBS4. . . . . *The Greek New Testament*, 4th ed. (1993, last rev. 2000; United Bible Societies)
Vulg. . . . . Vulgate, or Latin Vulgate (405; Jerome; also called the Jerome Bible)
WH . . . . *The New Testament in the Original Greek* (1881; B. F. Westcott and F. J. A. Hort)
Wuyck. . . . . . . Wuyck's Bible (1599; first authorized Polish translation)
Zurich . . . . The Zurich Bible (1530; incorporates Luther's NT and portions of his OT; predates Luther's complete translation by four years)

BIBLE VERSIONS, NOTORIOUS

The following list is for the reader's delectation, though it serves a serious purpose as well. While most books don't achieve fame based solely on their misprints, the Bible is an exception. Note some of the fine points of styling in these titles. For instance, when the misprint itself becomes part of the popular title, it is placed in quotation marks. If it is a generic term describing the mistake, the word is not set in quotes. (In the following list, the correct word is sometimes provided in brackets.) Otherwise, these titles are set in roman because they are actually descriptive epithets rather than formal titles.[1]

Name	Description
"Adultery" Bible	A 1631 KJV, printed for Charles I by Robert Barker and Martin Lucas, renders the seventh commandment "Thou shalt commit adultery." Also called the Wicked Bible.
Affinity Bible	A 1923 KJV contains a table of family affinities that includes the line "A man may not marry his grandmother's wife."

Name	Description
"Breeches" Bible	The first Geneva Bible (1560) renders Gen. 3:7 "They sowed figge tree leaves together, and made themselves breeches."
"Bug" Bible	The first Coverdale Bible (1535) translates *terrors* as *bugs* in Ps. 91:5: "Thou shalt not nede to be afrayed for eny bugges by night." In its defense, however, the word *bugges* at that time meant *bogies*, or *ghosts*.
"Camels" Bible	An 1823 KJV translates *camels* for *damsels* in Gen. 24:61: "And Rebekah arose, and her camels."
Denial Bible	A 1792 KJV has Philip denying Christ rather than Peter in Luke 22:34.
"Discharge" Bible	An 1806 KJV reads *discharge* for *charge* in 1 Tim. 5:21: "I discharge thee before God . . ."
"Ears to Ear" Bible	An 1810 KJV renders Matt. 13:43 "Who hath ears to ear, let him hear."
"Fool" Bible	A KJV printed for Charles I renders Ps. 14:1 "A fool hath said in his heart there is a God."
"Forgotten Sins" Bible	A 1638 KJV renders Luke 7:47 "Her sins which are many are forgotten [forgiven]."
Harwood's Bible	English minister Edward Harwood (eighteenth century) paraphrased the NT in the genteel language of the day. For example, in Rev. 3:15–16, Christ tells the Laodicean church: "Since, therefore, you are now in a state of lukewarmness, a disagreeable medium between the two extremes, I will, in no long time, eject you from my heart with fastidious contempt."
"He" Bible; "She" Bible	The first KJV of 1611 renders Ruth 3:15 "he went into the city," which is, according to the Hebrew, correct. The second printing incorrectly rendered it "she went into the city." Nearly all subsequent English versions reproduced the error until it was corrected in the Revised Version, 1885.
Incunabula Bible	Transposed numbers on the title page of this Elizabethan Bible dated its printing as 1495 rather than 1594.
"Judas" Bible	One printing of the 1611 KJV has Judas rather than Jesus initiating the Last Supper in Matt. 26:26.
Leda Bible	A 1572 Bishop's Bible scandalously borrows decorative woodcuts from an edition of Ovid's *Metamorphoses*, including one of Leda and the swan.

Name	Description
"Lions" Bible	A notoriously error-riddled printing of KJV that, among other errors, renders 1 Kings 8:19 "Thy son … shall come forth out of thy lions [loins]."
"More Sea" Bible	A 1641 KJV renders Rev. 21:1 as "there was more sea" rather than "there was no more sea."
"Murderers" Bible	An 1801 KJV puts *murderers* in place of *murmurers* in Jude 16: "These are murderers, complainers, walking after their own lusts."
"Placemakers" Bible	A 1562 Geneva Bible renders Matt. 5:9 "Blessed are the placemakers [peacemakers]."
"Printers" Bible	A 1702 KJV renders Ps. 119:161 "Printers [princes] have persecuted me without a cause."
"Rosin" Bible	The 1609 Douay Bible translates *balm* as *rosin* in Jer. 8:22: "Is there noe rosin in Galaad?" See also "Treacle" Bible.
"Sin On" Bible	The first English Bible printed in Ireland (1716) renders John 5:14 as "Sin on more" rather than "Sin no more."
"Standing Fishes" Bible	An 1806 KJV renders Ezek. 47:10 "The fishes [fishermen] shall stand upon it."
"To Remain" Bible	In 1805 a proofreader marked on some galleys that a comma was "to remain." His instructions were mistakenly transferred to the text of Gal. 4:29: "Persecuted him that was born after the spirit to remain, even so it is now."
"Treacle" Bible	The first Bishop's Bible (1568) translated *balm* as *treacle* in Jer. 8:22: "Is there no tryacle in Gilead?" See also "Rosin" Bible.
"Unrighteous" Bible	A 1653 KJV leaves out the word *not* in 1 Cor. 6:9: "The unrighteous shall inherit the Kingdom of God."
"Vinegar" Bible	A 1717 KJV titles Luke 20 "The Parable of the Vinegar [Vineyard]."
Wicked Bible	See "Adultery" Bible.
"Wife-Hater" Bible	An 1810 KJV renders Luke 14:26 "If any man come to me, and hate not his father and mother … yea, and his own wife [life] also …"

BIBLE VERSIONS PREFERRED BY CLASSIC WRITERS

Do not assume that most Christians writing in English quote from either the KJV (the most widely read Bible) or the NIV (the best-selling Bible). Many important writers prefer those Bibles, but others do not. Here's a brief list of well-known Christians and their preferences.

John Bunyan—like most Puritan writers, was familiar with the Geneva Bible, but unlike many, predominantly quoted the KJV in his writings
Geoffrey Chaucer—Vulgate; with some evidence he may have been familiar with Wycliffe
Oliver Cromwell—Geneva Bible
Emily Dickinson—KJV
John Donne—Geneva Bible
Jonathan Edwards—KJV
George Fox—KJV
John Foxe—Bishop's Bible
Billy Graham—KJV early in his career; later used NIV
Samuel Johnson—KJV
Martin Luther King Jr.—KJV
John Knox—Geneva Bible
C. S. Lewis—Greek NT, otherwise KJV, of which he was often critical; often quoted Moffatt for English translation
Abraham Lincoln—KJV
Max Lucado—NCV
Herman Melville—KJV
Thomas Merton—Latin Vulgate; Douay-Rheims
John Milton—Geneva Bible
Dwight L. Moody—KJV
Pilgrims and Puritans in general—Geneva Bible rather than KJV
William Shakespeare—Geneva Bible; often referenced Book of Common Prayer
Charles Spurgeon—KJV
Chuck Swindoll—NASB
J. R. R. Tolkien—translated the book of Jonah for the English version of the Jerusalem Bible
John Wesley—preferred Greek and Hebrew; read KJV, which he occasionally corrected, and other English versions

BIBLE, THE—WHAT IS IT?

We assume we know what is meant by the words *the Bible*, and yet no other book exists in more languages, paraphrases, versions, and translations. Even its basic canon is a matter of dispute among various traditions.

For instance, many people who staunchly defend the KJV as the authoritative English translation are surprised to find that the Apocrypha was included in the original 1611 edition (between the Old and New Testaments but seldom reproduced today). The following list defines what various denominations, faiths, and traditions mean by *the Bible.*

The Hebrew Bible (The Jewish Bible)

The Hebrew Bible, also referred to as the Hebrew Scriptures or the Jewish Bible, contains twenty-four books written in Hebrew. While roughly similar in content to the Christian OT, the two Samuels are one book in the Hebrew Bible, as are the two Kings and the two Chronicles, and the twelve shorter prophetic books are combined into one book called the Minor Prophets. Some differences in order also exist. The Hebrew Bible is divided into four groupings:

The Pentateuch (the Torah): Genesis, Exodus, Leviticus, Numbers, and Deuteronomy

The Former Prophets: Joshua, Judges, Samuel, and Kings

The Latter Prophets (the Former and Latter Prophets together are called the Nevi'im): Isaiah, Jeremiah, Ezekiel, and the Minor Prophets (incorporating Hosea, Joel, Amos, Obadiah, Jonah, Micah, Nahum, Habakkuk, Zephaniah, Haggai, Zechariah, and Malachi)

The Writings (the Kethuvim): Psalms, Proverbs, Job, Song of Songs, Ruth, Lamentations, Ecclesiastes, Esther, Daniel, Ezra, Nehemiah, and Chronicles

The acronym used for the major sections of the Hebrew Bible is Tanak (Torah, Nevi'im, Kethuvim).

Some writers feel that the Christian use of the terms *Old Testament* and *New Testament* is disrespectful toward Jews and prefer to use, respectively, *The Hebrew Bible* (or *Hebrew Scriptures*) and *The Christian Scriptures* as the two major divisions of the Christian Bible.

The Greek Old Testament (Septuagint)

Written in Greek, the Septuagint contains fifty books, including all those of the Hebrew Bible, though the Minor Prophets are separated, and many books are slightly altered in content. Job is shorter in the Greek, for instance; portions of 1 Samuel and Jeremiah are not found in the Greek; and some verses are in a different order in Ezekiel and Jeremiah.

The Septuagint adds the following books not found in the Hebrew Bible: 1 Esdras, Tobit, Judith, Wisdom of Solomon, Wisdom of the Son of Sirach (Ecclesiasticus), Baruch, Epistle of Jeremiah, Song of the Three Holy Children, Susanna, Bel and the Dragon, 1–4 Maccabees, and Prayer of Manasseh, all collectively known as the Apocrypha.

Some psalms are numbered differently in the Septuagint than in the Protestant Bible. Many Bibles based on the Septuagint, such as the Vulgate and many Catholic Bibles, retain the alternate numbering. (For a discussion and comparison, see "PSALMS, ALTERNATE NUMBERING OF.")

Theologians sometimes abbreviate the Septuagint with the roman numerals LXX, a reference to the seventy Jewish scholars who are said to have translated the Pentateuch portion.

The Vulgate

This is the earliest Latin version of the Old and New Testaments, based on the work of Jerome and extensively revised and edited throughout the Middle Ages. It contains seventy-three books, with basically the same order and format as the Catholic Bible, which is based on the Vulgate.

The Catholic Bible

The Catholic Bible is available in many languages, and most of those translations are based on the Vulgate. It contains seventy-three books (forty-six OT; twenty-seven NT), which are essentially the same as the Protestant Bible, though the writings of the Apocrypha are added, some of which are separate OT books and some of which are additions to existing OT books:

The Apocrypha: Tobit, Judith, Additions to the Book of Esther, Wisdom of Solomon, Sirach, Baruch, Additions to the Book of Daniel (Susanna, The Song of the Three Holy Children, and Bel and the Dragon), 1 Maccabees, and 2 Maccabees

In the Catholic Bible and the Vulgate, the books of the Apocrypha are interspersed throughout, whereas in the Protestant Bibles that include the Apocrypha (primarily the Anglican Bible), they are in a separate section between the OT and NT.

The Protestant Bible

The Bible as used by most Protestants contains sixty-six books and exists in many languages. The thirty-nine books of the OT are traditionally divided as follows:

The Historical Books: Genesis, Exodus, Leviticus, Numbers, Deuteronomy, Joshua, Judges, Ruth, 1 Samuel, 2 Samuel, 1 Kings, 2 Kings, 1 Chronicles, 2 Chronicles, Ezra, Nehemiah, and Esther

The Poetical Books: Job, Psalms, Proverbs, Ecclesiastes, and Song of Songs

The Prophetic Books: Isaiah, Jeremiah, Lamentations, Ezekiel, Daniel, Hosea, Joel, Amos, Obadiah, Jonah, Micah, Nahum, Habakkuk, Zephaniah, Haggai, Zechariah, and Malachi

The twenty-seven books of the NT are divided as follows:

The Gospels: Matthew, Mark, Luke, and John

The Acts of the Apostles

The Epistles, or the Letters: Romans, 1 Corinthians, 2 Corinthians, Galatians, Ephesians, Philippians, Colossians, 1 Thessalonians, 2 Thessalonians, 1 Timothy, 2 Timothy, Titus, Philemon, Hebrews, James, 1 Peter, 2 Peter, 1 John, 2 John, 3 John, and Jude

Revelation

The Anglican Bible

This is the same as the Protestant Bible except it often includes the writings from the Catholic Apocrypha as edifying though noncanonical. The books of the Apocrypha usually appear as a separate section between the OT and NT, as in the 1611 KJV.

The Eastern Orthodox Bible

This is available in many languages. Its content is the same as the Catholic Bible, with the addition of two more deuterocanonical books (1 Esdras and the Prayer of Manasseh) and two OT pseudepigraphal writings (Psalm 151 and 3 Maccabees).

The Muslim Bible

Although no book is referred to as the Muslim Bible (the Qur'an being the holy book of Islam), Muslims believe that the Hebrew and Christian Scriptures are divinely inspired and should be respected. They admire the Torah, the Psalms (called Zaboor), and the Gospels (called Injeel) in particular but believe both the OT and NT texts are corrupted, with original portions having been lost or tampered with by partisan faiths. They accept specific tenets of the Bible insofar as they are confirmed by the Qur'an, while any tenet contradictory to the Qur'an is rejected as a human corruption.

The Book of Mormon

The Church of Jesus Christ of the Latter-day Saints (Mormons) accepts the Protestant Bible in Joseph Smith's translation to be authoritative but considers the Book of Mormon, called Another Testament of Jesus Christ, equally canonical. The Book of Mormon contains the following fifteen books in this order:

1 Nephi, 2 Nephi, Jacob, Enos, Jarom, Omni, Words of Mormon, Mosiah, Alma, Helaman, 3 Nephi, 4 Nephi, Mormon, Ether, and Moroni

The Jehovah's Witness Bible

The same as the Protestant Bible except the Jehovah's Witnesses prefer their own translation, the *New World Translation of the Holy Scriptures* (completed in 1961, published by the Watch Tower Bible and Tract Society), which many Protestant theologians, not surprisingly, feel is slanted toward specific doctrines of the Jehovah's Witnesses.

BIBLICAL HOURS

See "HOURS, BIBLICAL."

BIBLIOGRAPHIES AND SOURCE LISTS

Some editors prefer the word *Sources* to the word *Bibliography* for that book element that lists works of interest to the reader or those cited in the text. The word *bibliography*, whose Latin root means "the writing of books," seems outdated in an era of online resources. Still, an insistence on the word *sources* seems uselessly purist—first, because *bibliography* can easily absorb other kinds of material (language grows by accommodating new ideas, after all); and second, the word *sources* finds its origin in an etymological root meaning a "spring of water," which is no better as a metaphor for digital or audio media than "books."

This manual recommends that both terms be used—with this distinction: a section headed *Bibliography* should list the significant works, whether in print, digital, or nonbook, related to the topic, to points discussed in the book, or to works on associated topics. Its purpose is to inform the reader of other works of interest. A section headed *Sources* or *Source List*, by contrast, is more limited, listing only those works actually quoted or referenced in the text or otherwise essential to the author's research.

Proper Names. Bibliographies and source lists are compiled alphabetically. Authors, editors, translators, or compilers are listed last name first. No titles or academic degrees are used with names. If the bibliography is broken down under subheads, each section is alphabetized separately.

Multiauthor Works. When two or more names are given for a single entry, the first is listed last name first, followed by a comma, and the other names are listed normally. List as many as three names for a multiauthor work, but when four or more names are given, show only the first (whichever is first on the title page or cover), and replace the remaining names with the abbreviation *et al.*, which is Latin for "and others" (*et alia*).

Citing Books. The following information should be included, as appropriate, in a bibliographic or source entry:

Full name of author(s) or editor(s), last name, then first name (subsequent names are given first name first)
Complete title (and subtitle, if any)
Full name of editor(s) or translator(s), if any
Name of series, and volume and number in the series
Edition, if other than the first
Number of volumes
City where book was published (and state if city is not well known)
Name of publisher
Year of publication

De Gasztold, Carmen Bernos. *Prayers from the Ark*. Trans. by Rumer Godden. New York: Viking, 1947.

Fickett, Harold, et al. *Stories for the Christian Year*. New York: Macmillan, 1992.

Johnson, James Weldon. *God's Trombones*. New York: Viking, 1927.

Tennyson, G. B., and Edward E. Ericson Jr., eds. *Religion and Modern Literature: Essays in Theory and Criticism*. Grand Rapids: Eerdmans, 1975.

Publisher's Name. **A shortened form for listing the publisher's name may be used, though the full name may also be given; keep the style consistent throughout.**

Citing Print Periodicals. **The following information should normally be included in a bibliographical entry for an article from a print periodical:**

Full name of author(s) or editor(s), last name first (subsequent names are given first name first)
Complete title (and subtitle, if any)
Name of periodical
Volume number (and issue number, if any)
Date (in parentheses)
Page number(s) of article

Not all this information is available for every periodical. In such cases, as much of the information as possible should be provided. Note also that a colon precedes the page number(s) if volume and/or issue numbers are given; otherwise a comma is used.

Aeschliman, M. D. "Flickering Candles in the Winds of Woe." *Books & Religion* 15, no. 6 (Winter 1988): 3, 29.

"Fighting Isms and Schisms." *Christian History* 4, no. 3 (1987): 29.

Ubell, Earl. "Surgeon General C. Everett Koop Has an Idea: A Battle Plan to Save Your Life." *Parade* (April 10, 1988), 16–17.

Citing Webpages. **The following information should normally be included in a bibliographical entry for material from a webpage:**

Full name of author(s), last name, then first name (subsequent names are given first name first)
Title of page, entry, or article
Title of the larger work of which the entry or article may be a part (if applicable)
Version or file number (if available)
Publication, posting, or last revision date (if available)
The website's name (in italic if a journal or online magazine)
The webpage's URL

Loconte, Joseph. "How to Really Keep the Commandments in Alabama—and Elsewhere." Posted September 3, 2003. *Christianity Today Online.* http://www.christianitytoday.com/ct/2003/septemberweb-only/9-1-31.0.html.

Diana M. Amadeo, "The Heart-Shaped Leaf: A Sign of Hope and God's Love." *Guideposts.* https://www.guideposts.org/the-heart-shaped-leaf-a-sign-of-hope-and-gods-love.

Access Dates. **Noting the date that the website was accessed is no longer necessary, though it may be provided in the notes when the author believes that information is important.**

Citing Software. **The following information should normally be included in a bibliographical entry for material from a software package, whether a download or physical CD, CD-ROM, or DVD.**

Full name of author(s), last name, then first name (if known) (subsequent names are given first name first)
Complete title of work, page, or article within the software package
Title of the software package of which the entry or article may be a part (if applicable)
Full name of editor(s) or translator(s), if any
Name of series, and volume and number in the series
Edition, if other than the first
City where the software was published (and state if city is not well known)
Name of publisher
Year of publication

Carson, D. A., Douglas J. Moo, and Leon Morris. *Introduction to the New Testament.* In *Zondervan Bible Study Library 5.0: Scholar's Edition* CD-ROM. Grand Rapids: Zondervan, 2003.

"For Further Reading" Lists. A less formal type of bibliography—a "For Further Reading" list—may be more appropriate in some books than a full bibliography. Such lists should follow the format of the formal bibliography but could conceivably contain only author and title. Most any book in print can be found in a library, ordered online, or referenced on the internet with only an author name and title as references. Of course, more information would help the reader in a "For Further Reading" list, but it is not necessary if an author wishes to avoid an overly academic appearance. (As examples, the editors of this manual recommend the following books for writers and editors.)

Hale, Constance. *Sin and Syntax: How to Craft Wickedly Effective Prose.*
Klinkenborg, Verlyn. *Several Short Sentences about Writing.*
Lerner, Betsy. *The Forest for the Trees: An Editor's Advice to Writers.*
Rabiner, Susan, and Alfred Fortunato. *Thinking Like Your Editor: How to Write Great Serious Nonfiction—and Get It Published.*

Design. Bibliographies and source lists may be set in a type size 1 or 2 points smaller than text size, to conserve space, though if they are quite short, they are best set in the same size as the text.

BLOCK QUOTATIONS

See "QUOTATIONS, GENERAL," section on "*Run-in versus Block Quotations.*"

BLOG STYLE AND TURNING BLOGS INTO BOOKS

Many of today's best writers learned their craft by blogging online, and publishers often adapt their blogs into books. How well does a series of blog entries translate into a book, and to what extent is the writing style of a blog appropriate for an ebook or print book? It all depends on the blog and the book, but the following comments might be helpful.

Editing. Since blogging is largely unjuried (that is, no one is paid to critique the writer's work), bloggers are sometimes surprised that editors trim, rewrite, revise, ask for expansions and transitions, and otherwise manipulate copy as aggressively as they do. Bloggers should expect a book editor to be frank about what works well in a print or ebook format and what doesn't, and bloggers should not be surprised by the micro-editing that occurs. Numerals and abbreviations may be spelled out, punctuation may be changed, capitalized words may be made lowercase, and vice versa—such micro-editing issues are what this manual is all about. The blog and book forms are distinct, and this often defeats the advantages of the book form to try to make it read like a blog.

Tone. The writing's tone often changes between formats. Writing that is chatty or charmingly intimate in a blog can come off as wordy or cloyingly overfamiliar in a book. Similarly, the profanity that sounds cheeky or amusingly provocative online can come across as overly aggressive or blatantly offensive in a book. Same words, different tone.

Structure. Editors use the word *arc* to mean the structure of a piece of writing, the way it builds from its opening exposition through an interesting development and finally to a rich climax and satisfying conclusion. A blog entry has its own unique arc, which is not necessarily the same as a book's section or chapter, nor does a series of blogs have the structure that a book needs to communicate well. The bane of many blogs is their episodic nature. While many bloggers are capable of envisioning the larger arc that their book should have, the advice of an experienced editor will be helpful more often than not.

Transitions. One of the strengths of the blog form is its accumulation of many short pieces. Books too are constructed one thought at a time, but the addition of smooth transitions is usually necessary to prevent the book from appearing directionless and episodic. Good editors can recommend ways to make those transitions.

Repetition. Because blogs often focus on a single theme, bloggers remind their readers of that theme with each new entry. In book form, the theme is usually stated early in the book, allowing the rest of the book to develop various related elements. Repetition, which is an aid to the blog reader, can be an irritant to the book reader.

Emphasis. Bloggers often emphasize entire phrases, sentences, or paragraphs with italic, all caps, alternate fonts, underscoring, or even different colors. These devices seldom transfer smoothly into books. All caps look like shouting, and large chunks of italic are hard to read. Alternate fonts can look like mistakes, and color printing is not an option in most books. Underscoring was once used to show emphasis in typewritten manuscripts, but now it is primarily used online to show that a word or phrase is a hyperlink.

As someone once said of the overuse of emphasis, "That's not writing; that's gesticulating." The craft of writing involves arranging words and phrases in such a way as to emphasize the important points without depending on typographic peculiarities. Such peculiarities are usually distracting, causing the reader to focus less on the content and more on the form. In the worst cases, such typography can cause confusion. Stick with italic as the most immediately recognized method of showing emphasis.

Periods. For. Emphasis. Another popular blogging device is the use of fragments and periods as a way of emphasizing each word in a short phrase. Again, this device distracts from the flow of thought, and if there was ever a cliché whose time has long passed, this is it. (See also "PERIOD.")

Overuse of Question Marks and Exclamation Marks. A single question mark or exclamation mark suffices. Adding a series of such marks after a word (as in, *He shouted, "No!!!!!!!!!"*) does not increase the intensity, nor does mixing them benefit the reader in any way (as in, *What was I thinking?!?!?*). Such devices are usually used for their humor, but the device (as well as the humor) wears thin quickly. It causes the reader to focus on the form rather than the content.

Web Shorthand. Such common web abbreviations as *OMG* and *LOL* often catch readers up short in print, and anyway, those abbreviations no longer look as intriguing, even online, as they used to. And emoticons and emojis usually look bewildering in print as well. (See "EMOTICON" and "EMOJI.")

Strikethroughs. One source of humor in blogs is the device of striking through a word or words. This gives the impression that the blogger is second-guessing or perhaps replacing an overly honest, harsh, or candid thought with a more considered alternative (*What this ~~repellent Neanderthal~~ elderly gentleman lacked was empathy.*) This device does not translate well into books because the word beneath the strikethrough can be hard to read. Many readers may also perceive it as a printer's error or miss the humor. It also breaks the flow of thought by forcing the reader to stop and consider what exactly is going on, increasing the risk of the reader missing the point. Still, it can occasionally be used in titles or headings as a novelty.

Lack of References. Bloggers often find it annoying that editors ask them to provide references for the direct quotations gathered from other, often online, sources. Just because something is quoted hundreds of times on the internet doesn't mean that it can go uncredited. While writing their original blog entries, bloggers should make it a habit to keep track of the exact source for every quotation, whether print or digital. Ideally, references to print sources should be provided for all pre-internet quotations, and those sources are now surprisingly easy to track down with help from Amazon.com (its searchable "Look Inside" feature) and Google Books. If a print source simply cannot be found, then a web reference will suffice. A web URL is sufficient for quoting from post-internet digital sources (though see "ADDRESSES, WEB," section on "*In Source Notes*"). Articles that are simultaneously published in print and on the web may reference the web address if that is the blogger's preference. (See also "NOTES.")

Copyright. Quotations found on the internet are subject to the same copyright laws as quotations in print. In a blog, it is easy to link to copyrighted material, but permission is often needed to reproduce the same quotation in an ebook or print book. Unless a "fair use defense" pertains (see "FAIR USE"), permission from the original publisher or author needs to be obtained for any of the following: extended quotes from an online article or ebook, comments from readers of the writer's own blog, reader comments on Amazon.com or any other website that collects user comments, other blogs, and quotes from any pre-internet, copyrighted material that may be reproduced online. (See guidelines in "QUOTATIONS.")

BLURBS

See "ENDORSEMENTS."

BODY MATTER, ELEMENTS OF A BOOK'S

A book's *body matter* is its essential content, its primary reason for being a book. (See also "BACK MATTER, ELEMENTS OF A BOOK'S" and "FRONT MATTER, ELEMENTS OF A BOOK'S.") The elements of any book's body matter are conventionally arranged in the following order, as appropriate:

Inside half-title page (recto, followed by a blank verso); see "HALF-TITLE PAGE"
Prologue; see "PROLOGUE"
Part-title page (recto, usually followed by a blank verso)
Part epigraph (if it applies to entire part; recto, verso, or on part-title page); see "EPIGRAPH"
Chapter title page (recto); see "CHAPTER OPENER"
Chapter epigraph (if it applies to chapter only; recto, verso, or on chapter-title page); see "EPIGRAPH"
Chapter number and title (usually recto; chapters may start on next blank page, either recto or verso if there are many chapters or if space is limited)
Text of chapter (usually recto, but may start verso if there is a separate chapter title page)
Chapter discussion questions (recto, verso, or on last page of chapter text)
Chapter endnotes (recto, verso, or on last page of chapter text); see "NOTES"
Chapter bibliography or "For Further Reading" list (recto, verso, or on last page of chapter text); see "BIBLIOGRAPHIES AND SOURCE LISTS"
Chapter epilogue or conclusion; see "EPILOGUE" and "CONCLUSION"

BOLDFACE

Avoid boldface type in text. It is not effective in content meant for sustained reading, whether in print or ebook form. The kind of emphasis gained from boldface in text can usually be achieved with less unevenness of appearance and distraction by using italic or caps-and-small-caps.

In Headings and Cross-References. Boldface is commonly used in headings and display type, and it is sometimes used in reference materials to indicate cross-references—though, again, italic is also used. Some editors and authors of academic books avoid both boldface and italic type for cross-references because both are too easily mistaken for emphasis. In those cases, either the word *see* or the abbreviation *cf.* is used (Latin *confer,* "compare"; see "ABBREVIATIONS: SCHOLARLY"). When boldface is used to note a cross-reference, that fact should be made clear in a note at the beginning of the book.

In Web Design. Web designers may effectively use boldface for emphasis in short blocks of text, especially when the italic font of the typeface being used looks weak. Boldface, though, is not recommended for links on webpages because the darker type can be mistaken for emphasis. An alternate color on webpages usually suffices to indicate a link.

BRACES

Braces { } are seldom used in ordinary typesetting. Sometimes referred to as *curly brackets,* they are primarily used as a means of grouping items together, such as several lines of type or items in a vertical list. Unlike brackets and parentheses, braces are not necessarily used in pairs, and because of their special function of bracketing many items, they may be extended over many lines of type as needed.

BRACKETS

Four typographic devices are commonly referred to as *brackets*:

Round brackets ( ), usually called *parentheses*
Square brackets [ ], usually called simply *brackets*
Curly brackets { }, usually called *braces*
Angle brackets < >, also called *the less than* and *greater than signs*

All these are used to enclose parenthetical or appended material in various contexts, but since, after parentheses, the square brackets are the most often used in text preparation, the term *brackets*, unmodified, refers to them. (For more detail about round brackets, see "PARENTHESES"; for more about curly brackets, see "BRACES.")

Appropriateness. By and large, all brackets, except for parentheses, should be used as seldom as possible since most readers are unfamiliar with their functions. Wherever possible, commas, em dashes, or ordinary parentheses should be used for parenthetical elements. (See "PARENTHESES.") In ordinary text, curly brackets and angle brackets are almost never used. Square brackets are unavoidable in certain situations, such as for interpolations in quoted material or within parentheses.

Square Brackets within Quoted Material. Square brackets are most commonly used to contain an editorial comment, substitution, or explanation within already quoted material. The bracketed word(s) may either replace a word in the original or be placed next to a word as an amplification or a correction to an error.

"On September 2, 1666, [Richard Baxter] witnessed the Great Fire of London." [Inserted in place of *he*, to clarify to whom *he* refers in the original quote]

"The creed was first proposed by Eusebius [of Caesarea] in 325 CE." [Amplifies the meaning of a word]

"Gutenberg [actually Fust and Shoeffer using Gutenberg's types] completed the Psalter in 1457." [Corrects an error]

Square Brackets for Parenthetical Thought. Brackets are also commonly used to mark a parenthetical statement made within an already parenthetical context (sometimes called *parentheses within parentheses*).

Daniel interpreted the mysterious inscription (*"Mene, mene, tekel, parsin"* [Dan. 5:25]) immediately before Belshazzar's death.

Square Brackets Adjacent to Parentheses. When an opening or closing square bracket is placed immediately adjacent to an opening or closing parenthesis, a thin space should be inserted between them.

Brackets with Font Changes. All types of brackets should be set in the same font as the surrounding sentence or text, not necessarily in the same font as the material contained within the brackets. (For examples, see "PARENTHESES," section on "*With Font Changes.*" Also see "*sic.*")

BRAND NAMES, TRADEMARKED

The distinction between trademarked brand names, which are capitalized, and their generic equivalents is often a useful one. The use of a well-known brand name in writing is acceptable as long as the writer has a reason for specifying the product by name, though the writer should avoid any negative or defamatory statements about the brand. If a product is singled out for criticism by name, the author or editor should always ask an attorney to review the manuscript before publication. A brand name should never be used in a way (in a title, on the cover, or in ad copy) that implies the brand's owner endorses the book or product.

In Fiction. Brand names add realism to fiction. Such use is acceptable as long as the context is not one that might give offense to the product's manufacturer (such as a character getting sick or dying after using a given product). Even that guideline is no guarantee that an especially aggressive trademark owner won't sue for perceived damages or to have the publisher cease using the name, but the guideline offers the best protection for the publisher. Caution is recommended, and when in doubt, seek legal advice.

Trademark Symbol. The trademark-registration symbol ® does not need to be shown after the brand or trade name when the name is used in text. Such a symbol is distracting and unnecessary in most contexts. A trademark symbol, ® or ™, should be used whenever the manufacturer requires it or whenever a registered trademark is used on the cover of a book or in advertising copy or anywhere else where its use might be taken as an endorsement by the product's manufacturers. Permission for its use in such locations must always be obtained in writing from the trademark owner. In most cases, obtaining such permission must be done by contract, and an attorney should be consulted.

Brands as Verbs. Though relatively rare, some brand names have become so common as verbs that those verb forms are commonly lowercase, even though the brand itself is capitalized. This is especially common with modern technologies. For instance: *to google*, *to tweet* (from *Twitter*), *to xerox*. Google has worked hard to keep its name from becoming the generic verb for any kind of internet search (*to google*), but Google is discovering it can't dictate English usage. The word *generic* here is key. The verb *to Skype* is still commonly capitalized, largely because the Skype software is the specific one used on most computers. *To Taser* is usually capitalized because the Taser company is still the primary maker of that product. When in doubt, capitalize brand names used as verbs, such as *to Facebook*, *to Simonize*, *to Windex*.

Brands as Plural Nouns. Retain the capital when writing brand names in the plural, even when the intention is to make them seem more generic: *Kleenexes*, *Porta-Potties*, and so on.

Generic Equivalents. Of the two lists that follow, the first itemizes common brand names often mistaken for generic ones. The generic name is given as an alternative. The second list shows brand names that, because of their age, common usage, or many imitators, have passed into general use and are lowercase—in a process whimsically referred to as *genericide*. The generic terms, as well as all the words in the second list, may be used in pejorative or negative contexts when needed, since no specific manufacturer is implied.

Common Brand Names and Their Generic Equivalents

Alka-Seltzer—effervescent antacid tablets
Anacin—analgesic tablets, aspirin
Aqua-Lung—underwater breathing apparatus
Astroturf—artificial grass
Autoharp—button-chord zither
Baggies—plastic bags
Band-Aid—adhesive bandage
Books on Tape—audio books
Botox—anti-wrinkle injection; capitalize it as a verb, *to Botox*
Bufferin—buffered aspirin
Bundt (pan)—decorative cake pan
ChapStick—lip balm
Coca-Cola, or Coke—cola, pop, soda, soft drink
Crock-Pot—slow cooker
Dacron—polyester fiber
Day-Glo paint—fluorescent paint
Dictaphone—dictating machine
Dobro—metal-bodied guitar
Dramamine—anti-nauseant
Drano—drain opener
Dumpster—trash bin
Fig Newton—fig cookie
Formica—laminated plastic
Freon—refrigerant
Frigidaire—refrigerator
Frisbee—toy flying disk
Fudgsicle—fudge-flavored Popsicle
Grand Marnier—liqueur
Jacuzzi—whirlpool bath
Jell-O—flavored gelatin dessert
Kitty Litter—cat-box filler
Kleenex—facial tissue or paper tissue
Kodak—film, camera, etc.
Kool-Aid—powdered soft-drink mix
Kotex—sanitary napkin (pl., *Kotex*)
Laundromat—coin-operated laundry
Levi's—denim jeans (note *'s*)
Librium—tranquilizer
Liquid Paper—correction fluid
Lycra—spandex, a synthetic fiber
Maalox—antacid liquid
Mace—tear gas
Magic Marker—felt-tipped or marking pen
Masonite—hardboard product
Muzak—background music (company now defunct)
Naugahyde—vinyl-coated fabric
Novocain—local anesthetic
NutraSweet—aspartame, nutritive sweetener
Olean—olestra, nonfat cooking oil
Pablum—pabulum; capitalized as a baby-food trade name. Lowercase, it means anything bland or "dumbed-down"
Pampers—disposable diapers
Paxil—antidepressant
Pepsi—cola soft drink
Perrier—carbonated mineral water
Pilates—a trademarked physical fitness program
Play-Doh—modeling clay
Plexiglas—acrylic plastic; a

trademarked name for a type of plexiglass (the term with two s's is not trademarked)
Popsicle—frozen dessert bars
Post-it notes—sticky notes, self-adhesive tags (note lowercase *i* and that *notes* is not part of the trade name)
PowerPoint—computer presentation program
Prozac—antidepressant
Pull-Ups—disposable underpants
Pyrex—heat-resistant glass
Q-Tip—cotton swab
Rollerblade—in-line skate
Rolodex—desktop address file
Saltines—soda crackers
Samsonite—luggage
Sanka—decaffeinated coffee
Saran Wrap—plastic wrapping film
Scotch tape—adhesive or cellophane tape
Sharpie—permanent marker
Sheetrock—plasterboard
Simoniz, Simonize—paste wax
Stetson—cowboy hat
Stryker frame—spinal-injury bed
Styrofoam—plastic foam
Sudoku—number-grid game
Super Ball—high-density plastic ball
Super Glue—super glue (this is both a trade and generic name; note the verb is *to super-glue*, with hyphen)
Sweet'N Low—sugar substitute
Tabasco—pepper sauce
Tampax—tampon
Tang—instant orange drink
Tarmac—blacktop
Technicolor—color movie processing
Teflon—nonstick surface
TelePrompTer—electronic cuing device
Tommy Gun—submachine gun
Transcendental Meditation—meditation technique
Tums—antacid
Tupperware—plastic storage container
U-Haul—rented moving truck or trailer
Valium—tranquilizer
Vaseline—petroleum jelly
Velcro—fabric fastener
Weed Eater—grass trimmer
Wi-Fi—wireless network
Windbreaker—light jacket
Wite-Out—correction fluid
X-Acto—modeler's knife, layout knife
Xerox—copier, duplicating machine, photocopier
Ziploc—resealable plastic bags or freezer bags

Former Brand Names Now Considered Generic

aspirin
cellophane
celluloid
elevator
escalator
hula hoop
kerosene
lanolin
linoleum
linotype
mah-jongg
mason jar
milk of magnesia
mimeograph
nylon
petri dish
ping-pong
raisin bran
shredded wheat
spandex
thermos
touch-tone phone
trampoline
yo-yo
zipper

BRAND, PRODUCT, AND COMPANY NAMES: COMMONLY MISSPELLED

Many brand, product, and company names are commonly misspelled. Sometimes this is because the author, editor, or proofreader has picked the spelling off the logotype of the company's website (see "LOGO STYLE"). Logotypes are not trustworthy sources of information. To get the correct spelling and style, always dig deeper into the website to see how the company spells its name, brand, or product in standard copy. The company's "About Us" page is a good place to start.

The following list highlights a few of those names that are most commonly misspelled.

7-Eleven—convenience store chain

7Up—soft drink; set solid

700 Club, The—italicize as the name of specific program

Adrenalin—pharmaceutical trade name, no final *e*; the commercial form of *adrenaline*, a chemical found in the body

Barnes & Noble—note ampersand

Bed Bath & Beyond—no comma; uses ampersand

BlackBerry—handheld computer; note internal cap

CliffsNotes—this is the current spelling; formerly *Cliff's Notes* and *Cliffs Notes*

Chock full 'oNuts—this unusual rendering is consistently used by the company

Coke, or Coca-Cola—always capitalize *Coke* when referring to the soda; lowercase, *coke*, is slang for "cocaine"; note that *Coca-Cola* is hyphenated

Crock-Pot—note the hyphen and capital *P*

Dr Pepper—soft drink; no period after *Dr*

eBay Inc., or just eBay—online auction house; lowercase *e*, midcap *B*; see also "MIDCAP"

Encyclopaedia Britannica—note the older *ae* form (but don't use the ligature æ)

Fox News, Fox, Fox News Network—not *FOXNews* or *FOX*

Goodyear Blimp, the—the *B* is capitalized

Harper & Row—former publisher preferred ampersand; now HarperCollins (with no space)

Harper's—magazine; note possessive

iPad—compact digital reading and internet-accessing device; midcap *P*; see also "MIDCAP"

iPod—tablet device; midcap *P*; see also "MIDCAP"

J. C. Penney—note: *Penney*, not *Penny*. May also be referred to casually as *Penney's*. The J. C. Penney, Inc., website refers to the stores as *jcpenney*, but since that might cause confusion, we opt to overrule the company and refer to the stores as *J. C. Penney* or *Penney's*.

Jell-O—note capital *O*

Kmart—their website shows the logo style as *kmart*, but capitalize it as normal

Lloyds—bank (no apostrophe); as distinguished from Lloyd's of London (with apostrophe), the insurance company

M & M—candy brand name; note ampersand, spaces, and no periods; plural is *M & M's*

Macy's—store chain; with apostrophe

McDonald's—restaurant chain; midcap *D* and apostrophe; the plural, by the way, is *McDonald's restaurants*, not *McDonald'ses*

Novocain—commercial trade name for the anesthetic *novocaine*, which is the generic name for the chemical

Pez—though the candy is trademarked in caps, *PEZ*, it is commonly spelled cap-lowercase; either is acceptable

Popeyes—restaurant chain; no apostrophe

Post-it notes—lowercase *it* and *notes*

Procter & Gamble—note the *e* in *Procter*, and the ampersand

Rolls-Royce—with hyphen

Sears, Roebuck & Company—note comma (also *Sears, Roebuck* or just *Sears*)

Starbucks—no apostrophe (*a Starbucks latte*)

***Time* magazine**—cap-lowercase in references; may be spelled *TIME* magazine in casual uses; see *"Time magazine, TIME magazine."*

V-8—brand name of vegetable juice, as distinguished from *V-eight*, which is an eight-cylinder engine

Volkswagen—note the final *-en*

Walmart—as of 2009, this company has stated that the individual stores are spelled *Walmart*; the corporation that owns them is *Wal-Mart, Inc.* Although some stores sport a star in the middle (*WAL*MART*), the company prefers *Walmart* for the stores.

Warner Bros.—second word is always abbreviated

Webster* or *Webster's—italic when referring to any edition of a dictionary that displays *Webster's* in the title, though *CWMS* uses *Webster* to refer only to *Merriam-Webster's Collegiate Dictionary, 11th Edition*.

BULLETS

Bullets are dotlike typographic devices used to call attention to items in a list. Here are some guidelines for their use:

- They should be modest in appearance, neither too bold nor too light, and they are usually separated from their accompanying text by a word space or small tab (usually not more than an em space).
- Bullets are not used for lists that contain only single words or short lines, none of which carry over to a second line; the reason is that a single row of single-line-spaced dots running down the left side of text is unsightly.
- Bullets are set to the left of the listed items, and the runover lines are set flush with the first word (as in this list). Some designers find an irregular column of left-hanging dots unsightly and recommend the runover text be aligned under the bullet or that the bullets be indented. It's a matter of taste.
- If the list contains only two or three items, indent the bullet from the left margin. If it has more, the bullets may be set flush with the left margin at the designer's discretion.
- On webpages, it is not always possible to control the spaces or margins for bullets. In these cases, a space need not follow the bullet; allow the bullet and runover lines to set wherever the software sets them.

BUTTONS (OR KEYS) ON ELECTRONIC DEVICES

Electronic devices, whether old-fashioned telephones or touchscreen tablets, are covered with buttons or touch-sensitive keys. When referring to these, capitalize the functional word and set it in regular type: as in *She hit Send on her smartphone* or *He couldn't find Pause on the player.*

C

CANONICAL HOURS

See “HOURS, CANONICAL.”

CAPITALIZATION: GUIDELINES

No surer sign of insanity exists than the attempt to formulate absolute rules of capitalization. The following guidelines provide a broad rationale, but as in other areas of life, consistency tempered by flexibility is the best one can hope for.

Reasons for Capitalizing. Aside from certain typographic conventions, such as capitalizing the first word of a sentence, the purpose of capitalization is to show that a given word has a specialized or specific meaning rather than a general one. This would include such words as place names and proper names, the titles of books and works of art, specialized vocabulary, and so on. Capitalization is not used to confer status or respect. We capitalize *Baker*, for instance, to single out the carpenter who lives down the street so that we may distinguish him from the baker next door, whose name happens to be *Carpenter*.

Recent editing practice has been to avoid capitalization whenever it is not needed for specification, and many words formerly capitalized are now lowercase without any loss of clarity. The first rule: Check *Webster*.

Specialized Vocabulary. Authors occasionally capitalize terms as part of a specialized or technical vocabulary. They should inform the editor of these special uses. For example, an author may wish to capitalize *the Silence* when referring to God or *the Canon* when referring to a specialized body of work.

Titles and Headings. Capitalize the first and last words of titles of books, software, or other major publications or works of art, and do the same for headings. Also capitalize the first word following a colon or a dash in a title. Capitalize all other words in titles and headings except for articles (*a*, *an*, and *the*); prepositions of any length; and coordinating conjunctions (*and*, *but*, *or*, *for*, and *nor*), unless they are the first or last word. An exception is made for any preposition used adverbially or otherwise emphasized. For example, *Lifting Up Our Hearts* or *One Flew Over the Cuckoo's Nest*.

Ordinary rules of capitalization in a title are ignored when a work is purposely titled contrary to common style (for example, E. E. Cummings's *is 5*). Caution should be exercised because, for design reasons, some book titles are rendered differently on the cover, sometimes irregularly lowercasing, bolding, or italicizing words. The title as listed in the copyright notice on the copyright page is the correct version for all references to that book. Do not use the title as shown in the Library of Congress Cataloging-in-Publication Data, since that uses a different capitalization style (only the first word and proper or place names are capitalized). If no title is shown accompanying the copyright notice, then consider the title as given on the title page to be definitive.

Hyphenated Compounds in Titles and Headings. Capitalize the first word of a hyphenated compound in a title or heading. Capitalize any subsequent word or words in the compound unless they are articles, prepositions, or coordinating conjunctions: *Orange-Red Leaves, Old-Fashioned Gospel Hymns, The Two-for-One-Sale Mystery, The Peanuts Page-a-Day Calendar.* Also, when a hyphenated number is used in a title, capitalize the second element: *The Ninety-Five Theses, The Twenty-Third Psalm, Tales of the Forty-Niners, "When I'm Sixty-Four."*

Adverbs in Titles and Headings. Capitalize an adverb in a title or heading even though the same word might not be capitalized when used as a preposition: *Looking Up to Jesus, Steady As She Goes, The Spy Who Came In from the Cold,* but *A Walk in the Woods.*

When Southernisms Beginning with "A-" Appear in Titles and Headings. The prefix *a-* is an old-fashioned way of expressing that the action of the verb to which it is attached is ongoing, as in *a-hunting* or *a-sailing.* Such formulations are common in folk songs and Southern colloquial speech. When such words appear in titles, they are commonly rendered in one of three ways. Penguin Press, in its seminal *Penguin Book of English Folk Songs*, opts to lowercase the *a* and capitalize the letter following it: "Ships Are a-Sailing." Other presses capitalize the *a* and lowercase the following letter: "Ships Are A-sailing." Oxford University Press in its extensive publishing on music and folklore has elected to capitalize both elements: "Ships Are A-Sailing." Any of these methods are workable as long as consistency is maintained throughout a publication, although we recommend the Oxford system: *"A-Hunting We Will Go," "Here We Come A-Wassailing," "The Times They Are A-Changing," Twenty Years A-Growing.*

After a Colon. Do not capitalize the first word after a colon in text unless the colon introduces two or more sentences in close sequence or in parallel, announces a definition, presents a proverb or quotation, or introduces a question or formal statement. (See "COLON.")

Merton's conflict was this: he didn't know whether the Trappists would accept him or whether the army would draft him first. [Lowercase: ordinary construction]

Here are the directions: Turn right at the first stoplight. Drive three miles and make a left. [Capitalized: two or more sentences after the colon]

William Carey will be remembered for this phrase: Expect great things from God; attempt great things for God. [Capitalized: announces a quotation or formal statement]

Racial Designations. As racial designations, lowercase *black* and *white* both as adjectives (as in, *a professor of black literature, a black gospel choir*) and as nouns (as in, *Many blacks and whites marched together in the sixties*) unless they form part of a phrase that would otherwise require capitalization (such as *Black Muslims*). Some contexts require capitalization for consistency, for instance, when those terms are included in a list of other racial designations that are commonly capitalized (as in, *The survey included Blacks, Whites, Native Americans, and Latinos*). Also, racial designations may be capitalized in the context of an academic study or a social movement (as in, *the Black Studies Department, the Black Power movement*). (See also "*African American, black*," "*black*," and "*ethnic, national, and racial designations*.")

Particles with Proper Names. Consult the internet or a biographical reference when in doubt about foreign proper names that use particles (such as *de, van, von*, etc.). The following guidelines should help in many cases:

1. Particles in well-known English and North American names adapted from other cultures are usually capitalized (*Mark Van Doren, Bernard De Voto*), although exceptions are made for individual preference (such as *Walter de la Mare, Aubrey de Vere*).
2. French, Italian, Portuguese, Spanish, Dutch, and German particles are usually lowercase if a name or title precedes them (*Baron Manfred von Richtofen*).
3. In French names, *La* and *Le* are usually capitalized (*La Bruyère*), but *d'*, *de*, *de la*, *des*, and *du* are usually not (*Charles d'Orléans, Honoré de Balzac*).
4. For some names, the particle is commonly dropped when the last name is used alone (*Vondel*, rather than *van den Vondel*), but when a particle is used but not preceded by a first name or a title (except for French names using *de* or *d'*), capitalize it (*Le Corbusier*).
5. Always capitalize a particle at the beginning of a sentence (*De la Mare was born in Charlton, Kent, in 1873*) or when used with an author name at the beginning of a bibliography or source list.

Here are more common examples:

Charles de Gaulle	Ludwig van Beethoven, *but* Beethoven
Catherine de Médici	Corrie ten Boom, *but* the Ten Boom family
Werner von Braun	Leonardo da Vinci, *but* Da Vinci
Thomas De Quincey	Henry Van Dyke

Personal Titles. When a title directly precedes a person's name, capitalize it: *President Barack Obama*, *Gen. Colin Powell*, *Queen Elizabeth.* When it follows or when it is used in place of the person's name, lowercase it: *Barack Obama, the president of the United States*, *the president*; *the general*; *the queen of England*, *the queen.*

Traditional titles of the nobility are often capitalized even when they follow the person's name or when the personal name is not given at all. When the full title is given, it may be capitalized according to custom: for instance, *the Duchess of York's latest children's book* or *an exhibition of watercolors by the Prince of Wales.*

Be aware of the "marketer's exception": that is, a person's title may be capitalized in a biographical blurb, in book back-ad or flap copy, or in promotional copy. Whenever it is important to tout an author or contributor's credentials, the person's title may be capitalized after the name: *Charles Colson, Founder of Prison Fellowship and Founder and Chairman of the Colson Center ...*

Organizations. The names of businesses, educational institutions, and other organizations are capitalized and otherwise styled according to the organization's preference. (See "BRAND, PRODUCT, AND COMPANY NAMES: COMMONLY MISSPELLED.") This is sometimes tricky because some businesses style their names differently in their logos than in their promotional copy. (See "LOGO STYLE.") When in doubt, style the name according to the company's usage in its website's text rather than in their logo (for example, although the logos for these companies show *amazon*, *BibleGateway*, *ebay*, and *WAL*MART*, the actual company names are spelled *Amazon*, *Bible Gateway*, *eBay*, and *Walmart*). To further complicate this situation, some online companies incorporate the extension into their company name while others do not (*FactCheck.org* but *Politifact*). If absolute accuracy is needed, query the online company directly.

While authors should adhere to an organization's own styling of its name, one exception is common: the article *the* need not be capitalized even if that organization insists that it should be. Such "in-house" styles are used only in official publications emanating from those organizations. The University of Michigan, for example, capitalizes the article when referring to the entire statewide network of universities under its umbrella (*The University of Michigan*) and lowercases it when referring to a particular campus (*the University of Michigan at Flint*). The problem is that this distinction is lost on most readers, rendering adherence to the rule meaningless. Lowercase the article in all cases. (See "*the, The* [BEFORE NAMES OF ORGANIZATIONS])."

Governmental Bodies. Capitalize the formal names of government organizations and bodies, though generally lowercase them as adjectives. Also lowercase generic and informal terms for governmental bodies.

United States Congress; Congress; congressional
House of Representatives; the House; the lower house of Congress
Committee on Foreign Affairs; Foreign Affairs Committee; the committee
Houses of Parliament; Parliament; parliamentary; early parliament
General Assembly of Illinois; Illinois legislature; assembly

administration
cabinet
the crown
district
electoral college
federal government
government ministry office
precinct
state
state's attorney

Political Organizations. Capitalize the names of official political organizations. Only capitalize the word *party* when it is part of an official name.

Common Market
Communist Party
Communists, the (party members); *but* the communist threat
Congressional Progressive Caucus
Democratic Party
Fascist Party (in Italy; otherwise *fascist*)
Grand Old Party (GOP)
Holy Alliance
Republican convention
Republican National Committee
Republican Party

Eras. Lowercase the names of most historical eras (except those derived from proper nouns and a few that have come to be capitalized by tradition).

Age of Reason
age of steam
ancient Greece
Christian Era
colonial period
Eighteenth Dynasty
Era of Good Feeling
fin de siècle
first century
information age
Middle Ages, *but* medieval era
Paleolithic times
post-war era
space age
Stone Age
the twenties, *but* the Roaring Twenties
Victorian era

Historical Events and Epithets. Capitalize the names of most specific historic events, as opposed to broad historical eras. Also capitalize popular epithets and nicknames for most cultural or historic moments or events.

Bamboo Curtain	Inquisition
California Gold Rush	Iron Curtain
Cold War	Kentucky Derby
Fall of Rome	Pickett's Charge
Great Depression; the Depression, *but* a depression; a recession	Prohibition
	Reconstruction
Holocaust	Vatican Council
Industrial Revolution	World War I

Systems of Thought. Lowercase most nouns and adjectives referring to broad systems of economic, philosophic, or political thought, though capitalize them when they are derived from proper names. Likewise, lowercase most nouns and adjectives referring to artistic, academic, religious, or philosophic schools of thought, though again, capitalize them when they are derived from proper nouns. Discretion is required, and in any given work a particular term must be treated consistently.

Aristotelian	expressionism	neoconservatism
baroque	Gregorian chant	neo-Nazi
bolshevism	impressionism	Neoplatonism
Cartesian	liberalism	Platonism
classical	Machiavellian	postmodernism
communism	Malthusianism	religious right
conservatism	Marxist-Leninism	romanticism
cubism	modernism	socialism
democracy	Nazism	transcendentalism
environmentalism	neoclassicism	

Personification. When abstract concepts are personified or made into allegorical characters, capitalize them as though they were proper names, as in *"A thousand men thronged together, crying aloft to Christ . . . that Grace might go with them in their search for Truth"* (William Langland, *Piers the Plowman*).

Place Names. The rules for capitalizing geographical nouns and adjectives are many and varied. Most specific questions can be answered by referring to *Webster* or other standard references. (See the "Geographical Names" section at the back of *Webster*.) The following brief summary and the list that follows it should help with most names.

Capitalize **Western, Eastern,** *etc.* when part of a formal place name or used in the sense of political division. *Continent* and *Continental* are capitalized to designate Europe. Capitalize such terms as *mountain* and *lake* when they are part of a formal place name.

the Arctic Circle *but* the equator
the Continent (Europe) *but* the Australian continent
the East; Far East(ern); the Near East
the East Coast or the West Coast
Lake Michigan; Lakes Huron and Michigan
the Midwest
the North
the North Atlantic *but* northern Atlantic
the Northwest
Ohio River; the Ohio and Wabash Rivers *but* the river Nile
the South, the Old South, the Deep South
Southerner (Civil War) *but* southerner (common usage)
the Tropics *but* the tropic of Cancer
the West, the Western world *but* the western plains
a westerner (from either the Western Hemisphere or the western United States)

When the article *the* is a traditional part of a place name, lowercase it: *the Hebrides, the Lesser Antilles, the Netherlands, the People's Republic of China, the Seychelles.* An exception is *The Hague*, the capital of the Netherlands, from the Dutch *Den Haag.*

Family Relationship. Lowercase any term indicating a family relationship when it is used generically or preceded by a modifier. Capitalize it when it is used as a family member's common appellation, that is, as though it were a proper name. For instance, *"Did Cousin Ed lead the singing, Dad?" his son asked hopefully. "No, Son, but Mother's brothers and her sister Carol all sang solos."*

Terms of Endearment. Lowercase such common terms of affection as *dear*, *honey*, and *sweetheart* unless they are used so often as to have the force of a nickname.

Brand Names. Be sure to observe the distinction between brand names, which are trademarked and capitalized, and their generic equivalents, which are lowercase. (For an outline of how to use trademarked names in writing and a list of examples, see "BRAND NAMES, TRADEMARKED.")

Adjectives Derived from Proper Names. No rule satisfactorily resolves all doubt about when to capitalize adjectives derived from proper and place names. Usually, capitalize adjectives with direct biographical and geographical references (*Socratic*, *Hawaiian*), though some common exceptions exist; for instance, *platonic* and *romanesque* are lowercase because their primary meanings are somewhat removed from the proper names they are derived from. When an adjective's connotation is no longer immediate, a decision must be made. It is usually a question of evocation. On the one hand, the quintessentially American term *french fries* does not evoke France, so the adjective is usually lowercase. On the other hand, *French cuisine* does evoke French food, so it is capitalized. By the same token, *brussels sprouts* does not evoke Brussels any more than *lima beans* evokes Lima, Peru, the city for which they are named. Such lowercasing is more common with geographical adjectives, though it occasionally happens with biographical adjectives as well; for example, most style manuals lowercase *cesarean section*, which may have been named for an ancestor of Julius Caesar. When in doubt, check the dictionary.

Byzantine (referring to Constantinople) *but* byzantine (meaning devious or labyrinthine)
cesarean section—*but note*: C-section
Ferris wheel
Molotov cocktail
moroccan leather
russian dressing

Parts of a Book. Only capitalize a part of a book when that part appears in a title, heading, or caption. Otherwise, lowercase parts of a book in text: for instance, *Appendix A [title]*; *Refer to chapter 3 for more information*; *See figure 12*; *Turn to page 48*.

CAPITALIZATION OF BIBLICAL AND RELIGIOUS TERMS

The capitalization of biblical and religious terms has evolved over the centuries. Victorian devotional literature tended to overcapitalize, a style that looks antiquated to most readers today. In an effort to offer a consistent contemporary style, the following guidelines are offered.

Capitalize the Names of Persons of the Trinity and Deities of Other Religions. Capitalize commonly accepted names for the persons of the Trinity, such as *Adonai*, *Christ*, *El*, *God*, *the Holy Spirit*, *Jehovah*, *Jesus*, *the Messiah* (Jesus), *the Paraclete*, *Yahweh*, and so on. (See "TRINITY, NAMES FOR PERSONS OF THE.") Also capitalize the names of deities of other faiths and from mythology, such as *Allah*, *Isis*, *Jupiter*, *Ra*, and *Shiva*. Lowercase pronouns referring to persons of the Trinity and deities of other religions. (For a discussion, see "DEITY PRONOUN, THE.")

Capitalize Epithets Used Like Names. Capitalize common epithets for persons of the Trinity, biblical characters, or figures in church history, such as *the Alpha and Omega, the Ancient of Days, the Blessed Virgin, the Comforter, the Divine Doctor, the King of Kings, the Man of Sorrows, Saint John the Divine, the Venerable Bede.* Use judgment in determining which words and phrases are epithets that have the force of a proper name and are capitalized, and which are merely descriptive and lowercase. For instance, you would capitalize *the Twelve* when referring to the disciples while lowercasing it in phrases like *the twelve disciples.* Other examples: *the Evangelists,* but *the four evangelists*; *the Almighty,* but *almighty God.* Some names are descriptive and not meant to be used like proper names, such as *the second person of the Trinity, the angel Gabriel,* or *the gospel writer.* When in doubt, lowercase. In all cases, once a style is decided upon, maintain consistency throughout the book.

Religious Titles. Capitalize official religious titles of modern or historical personages according to the same guidelines as secular titles. When a title precedes a person's name, capitalize it. When it follows or is used in place of a person's name, lowercase it. Lowercase all names for religious offices when they are simply descriptive.

Archbishop Justin Welby, *but* the archbishop of Canterbury; the archbishop
Father Patrick O'Neil, Father O'Neil, *but* the father
Bishop John Shelby Spong, *but* John Shelby Spong, bishop of Newark
Pope Francis I, *but* the pope
evangelist Billy Graham (descriptive)
the ministry, the papacy, the bishopric, the pastorate

Names for Satan. Capitalize names and common epithets for Satan: *the Beast, Beelzebub, the Dragon, the Enemy* (but *the enemy,* meaning the forces of evil in general), *the Evil One, the Father of Lies, Lucifer, Satan.* (See also "*devil, Devil.*")

Adjectives Derived from Proper Names. Capitalize most adjectives derived from proper names, as in *Aaronic priesthood, Augustinian rhetoric, Christlike, Isaian passages, Matthean version, Pauline writings.* Lowercase most adjectives and adverbs derived from the words *God* and *Satan,* such as *godlike power, a godly woman, satanic rites.* (For more detail, see "'GOD' COMPOUNDS" and "PERSONAL NAMES, ADJECTIVES DERIVED FROM.")

Epithets for the Bible. Capitalize all names and common epithets for the Bible and for the sacred writings of other traditions, and set them in roman type: *the Bible, the Good Book, the Qur'an, Scripture* (but *scriptural*), *the Talmud, the Vedas, the Word,* and so on. Note that the word *bible* is lowercase when used figuratively: as in, *The* OED *is the bible of lexicographers.* (For more detail, see "TITLES OF COMMON TEXTS OF THE WORLD'S RELIGIONS.")

Adjectives Indicating the Bible. Lowercase adjectives and adverbs derived from names for the Bible or other sacred writings: ***biblical***, ***mishnaic***, ***pentateuchal***, ***qur'anic***, ***scriptural***, ***talmudic***, ***vedic***.

Names for Versions of the Bible. Capitalize names and nicknames of well-known or important versions and editions of the Bible, especially when they exist in many editions and formats, and set them in roman type. When a specific edition of a particular version is referred to, it should be set in italic like any ordinary book title. (See "bible versions in english.")

the King James Version, but *The King James Version, Easy Reading*
the New International Version, but *The NIV Study Bible*
the New King James Version, but *The King James 2000e*
the Syriac Version
the Vinegar Bible
the Vulgate

Books of the Bible. Capitalize the names of all books of the Bible, the Apocrypha, and pseudobiblical writings. The words *book*, *gospel*, *letter*, *psalm*, and *epistle* are generic terms that specify different forms of written documents and are lowercase unless they form part of the actual title of a book as given in the specific translation of the Bible being used. (For a discussion of the capitalization of the word *gospel*, see "*gospel, Gospel.*")

1 Corinthians, First Corinthians, Paul's first epistle to the Corinthians, the first book of Corinthians, *but* the First Letter of Paul to the Corinthians [RSV]
the Gospel of Thomas [actual title]
Job, the book of Job [NIV], *but* the Book of Job [MLB]
John, John's gospel, the gospel of John [NIV], *but* the Gospel According to John [KJV], the Gospel of John [Phillips]
the Protevangelion
Psalm 139
the Twenty-Third Psalm *but* a psalm of David

Parts of the Bible. Capitalize names for specific parts, groupings, or passages of the Bible when those names are used as the equivalents of titles in theological and devotional writing. (Note that in this instance *CWMS* departs from *CMoS*, which lowercases most parts, groupings, and passages of the Bible. The *CMoS* lowercase style is appropriate for books intended for a general readership.) Exercise judgment in determining whether a name is generic or used as the equivalent of a title. For instance: *David's psalms*, but *the Davidic Psalms*. When in doubt, lowercase. (See also "BIBLE, NAMES FOR SPECIFIC PORTIONS OF THE" and "PSALMS, TRADITIONAL GROUPINGS OF.")

the Accession Psalms
the Book of Jeremiah [RSV], *but* Jeremiah's book of prophecies
the Epistle of Paul to the Romans [MLB], *but* Paul's Roman epistle
the General Epistles
the Gospel According to Matthew [RSV], *but* Matthew's gospel
the Gospels, *but* the four gospels
the Historical Books
the Lord's Prayer
the Love Chapter
the Minor Prophets
the New Testament
the Olivet Discourse
the Pentateuch
the Poetical Books
the Synoptic Gospels
the Ten Commandments, *but* the first commandment
the Upper Room Discourse
Wisdom Literature

"Law" as a Word. Capitalize the word *Law* in references to the Pentateuch as a whole. Otherwise, lowercase it: *the Law* (Pentateuch), but *the law* (as opposed to grace); *Mosaic law*; *law of Moses*; *Davidic law*.

Biblical Events. Lowercase all accepted names for major biblical events, such as events in the life of Christ: *the advent of Christ* (but *Advent*, meaning the season), *the ascension, the captivity, the creation* (both the act and the things created), *the crucifixion, the exodus, the flood, the nativity, the resurrection*, and so on. (See also "EVENTS IN THE LIFE OF JESUS, LOWERCASING.")

Biblical and Sacred Objects. Lowercase words describing important biblical and sacred objects of veneration: for example, *the blood of Christ, the brazen altar, the cross* (both the object and the event), *the golden calf, the holy name of Jesus, the light of Christ in the world* (but *the Light of the World*), *Noah's ark, the seven seals, the star of Bethlehem, the tent*. Note the names of a few legendary objects and terms have become so common in literature and culture that they are still capitalized by tradition: *the Holy Grail, the Sacred Heart of Jesus, the Shroud of Turin, the Star of David, the True Cross.*

Biblical Eras. Lowercase names for biblical eras; for instance, *the age of the prophets, the end times, the exile, the exilic period, the last days, the millennial kingdom, the millennium.*

Religious Historical Eras. Capitalize common names for major periods and events in church history unless they are purely descriptive: *the Counter-*

Reformation, the Great Awakening (but *the age of revivalism*), *the Middle Ages* (but *the medieval era*), *the Reformation*, and so on.

Historic Documents. Capitalize the titles of creeds, confessions, and other important documents in church history, and set them in roman type, such as *the Apostles' Creed, the Baltimore Catechism, the Edict of Milan, the Nicene Creed, the Rule of St. Benedict, the Statutes of Mortmain, the Thirty-Nine Articles, Vatican II: Decree on Ecumenism, the Westminster Confession.*

Religious Observances. Capitalize common names for religious seasons, holy days, feast days, saints' days, and religious festivals and observances; for instance, *Advent, Ash Wednesday, Christian Unity Week, Conversion of Saint Paul, Epiphany, Holy Week, Lent, Michaelmas, National Day of Prayer, Passover, St. Valentine's Day.* (See "CHRISTIAN HOLIDAYS, FEASTS, AND THE LITURGICAL YEAR.")

Sacraments and Rites. Lowercase case most names of specific sacraments and rites (such as *last rites* and *sacred rites*), except those referring to Communion, or the Eucharist, which are traditionally capitalized (such as *Holy Eucharist, the Lord's Table*, and *the Sacred Host*). (See "*Communion.*") The seven sacraments recognized by the Roman Catholic Church are baptism, confirmation, the Eucharist, penance, anointing of the sick (which is now preferred to the term *extreme unction*), holy orders, and matrimony. (See "*Sacraments.*") Capitalize names for systems of rites (such as Latin Rite, Roman Rite, Eastern Rites, Masonic Rites, and Western Rites). (See "*Eastern Rites, Western Rites*" and "*Rite, rite.*")

Names of Denominations. Capitalize the names of official denominations and the common adjectives derived from them according to denominational usage; for instance, *Baptist, Brethren, the Church of God, the Christian Reformed Church, Episcopal, Methodism, Roman Catholic, Seventh-day Adventism.* The definitive resource for accurate denominational names is Frank S. Mead, Samuel S. Hill, and Craig D. Atwood, *The Handbook of Denominations in the United States* (Nashville: Abingdon Press, 2010), periodically updated.

Names for Places of Worship. Words like *assembly, cathedral, chapel, church, congregation, fellowship, hall, meeting, ministry, mission, synagogue, tabernacle*, and *temple* are capitalized as part of an official name of a religious meeting place. Otherwise, lowercase them as common nouns. Do not capitalize the article *the* in front of a church or denomination's name, though if the denomination or church itself uses the article, honor such "in-house" styles in all publications emanating from those denominations or churches.

Brick Bible Chapel, *but* the chapel
the Brooklyn Tabernacle (even though the church prefers The Brooklyn Tabernacle, with the article capitalized)
Church of the Servant, *but* the church
Holy Spirit Catholic Church, *but* a Catholic church
St. Paul's Cathedral, *but* the cathedral
Temple Emmanuel, *but* the temple
Westminster Presbyterian Church, *but* the local Presbyterian church

Religious Groups and Movements. Capitalize the names for major historical religious groups and movements, including historical heresies and schisms, and the adjectives derived from them; for instance, *Adoptionism, Antinomianism, Donatism, the Great Schism, Pentecostal(ism), the Pharisees, Protestant(ism), Puritan(ism).* (See also "*heresy, schism.*") Lowercase the names of broad modern religious movements that are not official denominations, the names of broad religious philosophies, and the adjectives derived from all such words; for example, *agnostic(ism), charismatic renewal, charismatics, conservative church, ecumenical, ecumenism, evangelical(ism), liberal theologians, secular humanism, theistic.*

"Movement" as a Word. Capitalize the word *movement* only when the adjective preceding it is capitalized. Tradition is a factor here; recognized historical movements are more likely to be capitalized, while contemporary movements are less likely to be: *the Holiness Movement* (but *the ecumenical movement*), *the Pentecostal Movement* (but *the charismatic movement*), *the Temperance Movement.*

"Heaven," "Hell," etc. Although place names in the Bible and other religious texts are capitalized, terms like *the abode of the saints, the garden of Eden, hades, heaven, hell, the new Jerusalem,* and *seventh heaven* are lowercase. This is done to match the style used by most of the popular versions of the Bible (though note the NIV capitalizes *Hades* [Matt. 16:18] as well as *the Abyss* [Luke 8:31]). The seven heavens of Islamic tradition are also lowercase: *the first heaven, the second heaven,* and so on. Only capitalize the word *Paradise* when it refers specifically to the garden of Eden. Note that the NRSV and the NASB capitalize the word *Sheol* (as in Job 11:8). The word *kingdom* is usually lowercase (as in *Christ's kingdom* and *the kingdom of God*). (See "*heaven, Heaven,*" "*hell,*" and "*paradise, Paradise.*")

In classical and Western literary tradition, names for heaven and hell are often capitalized, as in the Greek mythological *Hades*; Dante's *Inferno, Purgatorio,* and *Paradiso*; and Milton's *Heaven, Hell,* and *Paradise* (as in *Paradise Lost*). Other literary place names and geographical locations referring to heaven, hell, and the other various abodes of the dead are capitalized as though they were ordinary geographical references: *Acheron*, *Cocytus*, *Elysium*, *First Circle of Hell*, *Lethe*, *Olympus*, *Pandemonium*, *Phlegethon*, *Styx*, and others.

Epithets for Place Names. Capitalize epithets for geographical places when they are commonly used like place names. Be careful to distinguish between those words and phrases that are capitalized as epithets and those that are lowercase as descriptive terms; for instance, *the City of David* (but *the city where David reigned*), *the Eternal City*, *the Holy Land* (but *the land of Jesus*), *the Land of Promise* (but *the land of Canaan*).

CAPITALIZATION OF RELIGIOUS TERMS

The following list shows the capitalization of some common Christian terms. An asterisk (*) indicates that the term may be found under its own heading elsewhere in the book.

Aaronic priesthood
Aaronide (genealogy of Aaron)
Abba (name for God)
abomination of desolation
Abrahamic* covenant
Abraham's bosom
Abraham's side
Abyss, the
Achaemenid
Adonai
advent,* the
Advent season
Advocate, the
agape
age of grace
age to come, the
agnosticism, agnostic*
Agora (Athens; otherwise *agora*)
agrapha (pl.), agraphon (sing.)
Ahiram inscription
alleluia*
Almighty,* the
almighty* God
Alpha and Omega (Christ)
amen*
Amidah
amillenarian
amillennial(ism)(ist)
Amoraic era, Amoraim
Amun-Re
Anabaptist*
ancient Near East(ern)
Ancient of Days, the (God)
angel* (capitalized if theophany)
angel* Gabriel, the
angel* of the Lord (capitalized if theophany)
Anglican church, an
Anglican Church, the
anno mundi
annunciation,* the (the event)
Annunciation,* the (the holy day)
Anointed, the (Christ)
Anointed One, the (Christ)
anointed Savior
anointing of the sick
ante-Christian
antediluvian
ante-Nicene fathers (people)
Ante-Nicene Fathers, the (collected writings)
anti-Catholic

antichrist* (the general spirit)
Antichrist* (the person)
anti-Christian*
antichurch
anti-God
antilegomena
anti-Semite,* anti-Semitic, anti-Semitism
anti-Trinitarian
Apocalypse, the (Revelation of John)
apocalyptic
Apocrypha,* the
apocryphal*
apostle* Paul, Peter, et al.
apostles, the
Apostles' Creed,* the
Apostle to the Gentiles (Paul)
apostolic
apostolic age
apostolic benediction (2 Cor. 13)
apostolic council (Acts 15)
apostolic faith
apostolic fathers* (the people)
Apostolic Fathers,* the (the writings)
Aramaean
archangel
archbishop* of Canterbury (*but* Archbishop Welby)
Arche, L'*
ark,* the (Noah's)
ark* of the covenant
ark* of the testimony
Armageddon
Arminian(ism)
ascension,* the
Ascension* Day (holy day)
Assyrian Empire
Athanasian Creed
atheism, atheist*
atonement, the
Atonement, the Day of (Yom Kippur)
Augsburg Confession
Baal*
Baalism
babe in the manger, the
baby Jesus,* the
Babylonian captivity (Jews)
Babylonian Empire
baptism
baptism, the (of Jesus)
Baptist, the (John the Baptist)
battle of Armageddon (final battle)
Beast,* the (Antichrist)
beatification
beatific vision (theology)
beatitude,* a
Beatitudes,* the
bedouin (sing. and pl.)
Beelzebub*
Beelzebul*
Being (God)
Beloved Disciple, the
Benedictus (Luke 1:68–79)
betrayal, the
Bible,* the
Bible Belt,* the
Bible school
biblical*
Biblicism (-ist)
bidding prayer
bishop of Rome (the pope)
blessed* name (Christ)
Blessed* Virgin
blood of Christ
body, the (of Christ)
Body and Blood, the (Eucharistic elements)
body of Christ (the church)
Book,* the (Bible)
book of* Genesis, et al.
Book of* Life (book of judgment)
Book of Noah
book of the covenant
book of the law

Book of the Twelve, the
Book of Truth
boy Jesus, the
brazen altar
Bread of Life (Bible or Christ)
Bridegroom, the (Christ)
bride of Christ (the church)
Bronze Age
brotherhood of man
bulla (pl. bullae)
burning bush, the (Ex. 3)
burnt offering
Calvary
Calvinist(ic), (-ism)
Canon,* the (Scripture)
canonical*
canonical hours*
canonization
canon law
canon of Scripture, the
captivity, the (of the Jews)
catechumen
catholic* (universal)
Catholic* church, a (the building)
Catholic* Church, the (the Roman Catholic Church*)
Catholic Epistles (James, et al.)
Catholicism
Celestial City* (abode of the redeemed)
cereal offering
charismatic*
charismatic church
charismatic movement
cherub(im)*
chief priest
Chief Shepherd (Christ)
child Jesus, the
children of Israel
chosen people (Jews)
Christ*
Christ child
Christendom*
christen(ing)
Christian (n. and adj.)
Christian era
Christianize* (-ization)
Christian socialism
Christlike, Christlikeness
Christmas (Day, Eve)
Christmastide (-time)
Christocentric(ism)
Christogram
christological
Christology
christophany
Chronicler, the
church,* the (body of Christ)
church* (building)
church* (service)
Church* (as part of name)
church age
church and state
church father(s)*
church in America
church invisible
church militant
Church of England
Church of Rome
church triumphant
church universal
church visible
city of David
classical age
Code of Hammurabi
College of Cardinals
Comforter, the (Holy Spirit)
commandment* (first, et al.)
Commandments,* the Ten
Common Meter
Communion* (sacrament)
compline
confirmation
co-regency

Council of Trent
Counselor, the (Holy Spirit)
Counter-Reformation*
covenant,* the (old, new)
Covenant Code (Ex. 21–23)
covenant of grace
covenant of the Lord, the
covenant of works
creation,* the (both the act and the result)
Creator,* the
creator God, the
creed, the (Apostles' Creed)
cross,* the (both the wooden object and the event)
crown
Crucified One, the (as name; lowercase as descriptor)
crucifixion,* the
crucifixion* of Christ, the
Crusades, the
cupbearer
curse, the
Daniel's Seventieth Week
Davidic
day hours (first seven canonical hours)
Day of Atonement (Yom Kippur)
day of grace
day of judgment
day of Pentecost
day of the Lord
Dead Sea Scrolls*
Decalogue* (Ten Commandments)
Defender (God)
deism (-ist)*
Deity, the
deity of Christ
deluge, the (the flood)
demiurge
demon(ic)
Desert Fathers, the
deuterocanonical
Deuteronomic
devil,* a
devil,* the (Satan)
Diaspora* (the event and the people)
diglot
disciple(s)*
dispensation(alism), (alist)
dispensation of the Law
dispersion, the
divided kingdom (period of history)
divine*
Divine Doctor (Christ)
Divine Father (God)
divine guidance
Divine King
Divine Liturgy (Eucharist, Eastern Orthodox)
Divine Office(s) (canonical)
Divine Providence (God)
divine providence (God's providence)
Divinity, the (God)
divinity of Christ, the
doctor(s) of the church*
Door, the (Christ)
Dordrecht Confession
doxology*
Dragon, the (Satan)
E (Elohist)
early church
early church fathers (the people)
Early Church Fathers (title of body of writings)
Easter
Eastern church(es)
Eastern Orthodox* church, an (a building)
Eastern Orthodox* Church, the
Eastern religions
Eastern Rites*

Easter season
Easter Sunday
ecumenism, -ical*
Eden
El
elect, the; God's elect
Eleven,* the
Elohim
Elohist source
El Shaddai
emergent church*
emerging church*
Emmanuel*
Emmaus road
emperor, the; but Emperor Nero
empire, the
Empire (Roman, Macedonian)
end-time* (adj.)
end time(s),* the
Enemy, the (Satan)
enemy, the (satanic forces)
Enlightenment
Epiphany (holy day)
Episcopal* (Church)
episcopal* (relating to bishops)
epistle* (John's epistle, etc.)
epistle to the Romans
Epistles, the (NT letters)
Eros (Greek god)
eros (n.)
eschatology, -ical
eschaton
Eternal, the (God)
Eternal City, the (Rome)
eternal God, the
eternal life
eternity
Eucharist* (n.)
eucharistic* (adj.)
Evangel (any of the four gospels)
evangelical* (adj.)
evangelical(s), (ism)
evangelist* (someone who evangelizes or a gospel writer)
Evangelists,* the (the gospel writers)
evensong
Evil One, the (Satan)
exile, the
exodus, the (from Egypt)
extrabiblical*
extreme unction (*prefer* anointing of the sick)
faith,* the (Christianity)
faith healing
fall,* the
fall of humanity
fall of Jerusalem
false christs
False Prophet, the (of Revelation)
false prophet(s)
Farewell Discourses (John)
Father (God)
fatherhood of God
Father of Lies (Satan)
Fathers, the (*see* fathers of the church)
fathers of the church,* the
Fathers of the Church* (the writings)
Feast (meaning Passover)
feast day
Feast of Booths (Sukkoth)
Feast of Esther (Purim)
Feast of Firstfruits
Feast of Tabernacles
Feast of the Dedication (Hanukkah)
Feast of the Lights (Hanukkah)
Feast of the Nativity
Feast of the Passover (Pesach)
Feast of Unleavened Bread
Fertile Crescent
fertility god(dess)
first Adam, the
first advent
Firstborn, the (Christ)
firstborn Son of God

First Cause, the
First Estate (Second Estate, etc.)
firstfruits
first person of the Trinity
First Temple,* the
First Vatican Council (1869–70)
flood,* the
footwashing
four evangelists, the
four gospels, the
fourth gospel, the
free will
Friend (Quaker)
fundamentalist(s), (-ism)*
fundamentals of the faith
Galilean, the (Christ)
garden,* the (Eden or Gethsemane)
garden of Eden
garden of Gethsemane
gehenna*
Gemara
General Epistles
General Letters
gentile,* a (distinguished from a Jew)
gentile laws
Gloria Patri
gnostic* (generic)
Gnostic(ism)* (specific sect)
god (pagan)
God* (Yahweh)
God Almighty
God-given
Godhead* (essential being of God)
godhead* (godhood or godship)
godless
godlike
godliness
godly
God-man
God Most High
godsend
God's house
Godspeed
God's Son
God's Spirit
God's word* (his statement or promise)
God's Word* (the Bible)
godward
golden calf, the
golden candlesticks, the
Golden Rule,* the
Good Book,* the
Good Friday
good news, the
Good Samaritan,* the (*but* the parable of the good Samaritan)
Good Shepherd (Jesus)
good shepherd, the parable of the
gospel* (the good news; the message; genre)
Gospel* (title of book; John's Gospel, et al.)
Gospel of Matthew (Mark, Luke, John)
Gospels, the (section of NT)
gospel truth
grain offering
Great Awakening, the
Great Commandment,* the
Great Commission, the
Great High Priest, the
great judgment, the
Great Physician, the
Great Schism (of 1054)
Great Shepherd, the
great tribulation, the
great white throne, the
Ground of Being
Guide, the (Holy Spirit)
guilt offering
Hades* (Greek mythology)
hades* (hell)
Haggadah

Hagiographa*
hagiography (-er, -ic)
Hail Mary*
halacha, or halakha
Hallel
hallelujah*
Hanukkah (Feast of the Dedication)
Hasidic
Hasidim
Head, the (Christ, head of the church)
heaven* (abode of the redeemed)
heavenly Father
Hebraism
Hebrew Bible
Heidelberg Catechism
Heilsgeschichte
hell*
Hellenism (-istic)
hellenize
Heptateuch
Herodian
Herod's Temple*
Hexapla
high church*
high priest, a
High Priest, the (Christ)
High Priestly Prayer, the (John 17)
Historical Books, the (of Bible)
Hittite Law Code
holiness
Holiness Movement, the
Holy Bible*
Holy Book* (Bible)
Holy City* (present or new Jerusalem)
Holy Communion*
holy day of obligation* (Roman Catholic)
Holy Eucharist
holy family*
Holy Father* (pope)
Holy Ghost* (*prefer* Holy Spirit)
Holy God (*but* a holy God)
Holy Grail*
Holy Island (Lindisfarne)
Holy Joe (slang for parson)
Holy Land* (Palestine)
Holy League (1510–11)
holy of holies*
holy oil
Holy One, the (God, Christ)
holy order(s)
Holy Place
Holy Roller*
Holy Roman Empire
Holy Saturday*
Holy Scriptures
Holy See
Holy Spirit*
Holy Thursday*
Holy Trinity*
holy war
holy water
Holy Week* (before Easter)
Holy Word
Holy Writ* (Bible)
Holy Year (Roman Catholic)
homologoumena
Host (Eucharist)
hours (canonical)
house church
house of David
house of the Lord
imago Dei
immaculate conception,* the
Immanuel*
incarnation, the
incarnation of Christ
Indo-European
infancy gospels, the
infant Jesus,* the
Inklings,* the (Lewis, Tolkien, et al.)
inner veil

Inquisition, the (historical)
Intercessor, the (Christ)
intertestamental
Iron Age
Isaian or Isaianic
Jacob's trouble
Jehovah
Jehovah's Witness(es)
jeremiad
Jeremian or Jeremianic
Jesus Prayer, the
Jewish Feast (Passover)
Jewish New Year (Rosh Hashanah)
Jewish War
Johannine
John's Gospel
John the Baptist
John the Beloved
John the Divine
John the Evangelist
John the Presbyter
Jordan River (*but* the river Jordan)
Jubilee (year of emancipation)
Judaic
Judaica
Judaism,* (-ist, -istic)
Judaize, Judaizer
Judean
Judeo-Christian*
judges, the
judgment day
judgment seat of Christ
Kabbalah* (the body of writings)
Kaddish
kerygma
Kethuvim (portion of OT)
King (God or Jesus)
King David (etc.)
kingdom,* the
kingdom age
kingdom of God
kingdom of heaven
kingdom of Israel
kingdom of Satan
King James Version*
King of Glory (Christ)
King of Kings* (title for Christ)
kingship of Christ
kinsman-redeemer
koine (noun)
Koine Greek
koinonia
Koran (Qur'an* *is preferred*)
koranic (qur'anic* *is preferred*)
Lady, our (Mary)
lake of fire
Lamb, the (Christ)
Lamb of God
Lamb's Book of Life
land of Canaan
Land of Promise
last day(s),* the
last judgment,* the
last rites*
Last Supper,* the
last times, the
Latin Rite
Latter Prophets, the
lauds
laver
law* (as opposed to grace)
Law,* the (Pentateuch)
Lawgiver (God)
law of Moses
Lent(en)*
Levant,* the
Leviathan
Levite
Levitical
Levitical decrees
Levitical priesthood
liberal(ism)
liberation theology
Light (Truth or Christ)

Light of the World (Christ)
Lion of Judah
Litany,* the (Anglican)
liturgy of the hours
living God
living Word, the (Bible)
loanword
Logos
Long Meter
Lord,* the
Lord Almighty, the
Lord of Hosts
Lord of Lords* (title for Christ)
Lord's Anointed, the (Christ)
Lord's anointed Savior, the (Christ)
Lord's Day,* the
lordship of Christ*
Lord's Prayer,* the
Lord's Supper,* the
Lord's Table,* the
Lost Tribes, the
lost tribes of Israel
Love Chapter, the (1 Cor. 13)
low church
Lucifer (Satan)
Lukan
Maccabean
Maccabees
magi*
Magnificat, the ("Song of Mary")
Major Hours (canonical)
Majority Text
Major Offices (canonical)
Major Prophets,* the (div. of OT)
major prophets* (people)
mammon* (capitalize when
    personified)
Manichaean
Man, the (Jesus)
Man of Sin (Satan)
Man of Sorrows
Mariology, Mariolatry
Markan
Martyrs Mirror
Masoretes
Masoretic text
Mass,* the (liturgy of the Eucharist)
masses (musical compositions)
Master, the (God)
matins
matrimony (sacrament)
Matthean
Mediator, the (Christ)
medieval*
megachurch*
Melchizedek priesthood
menorah
mercy seat
Messiah,* the (Christ)
messiahship
messianic*
metachurch*
mezuzah
Middle Ages*
midrash(ic)
midtribulation(al)
millenarian(ism)(ist)
millennial kingdom
millennium,* the
Minor Hours (canonical)
Minor Offices (canonical)
minor prophets* (people)
Minor Prophets,* the (div. of OT)
Miserere, the
Mishnah
mishnaic
modernist(s), (-ism)
moon-god
Mosaic
Mosaic law (Pentateuch or Ten
    Commandments)
Most High, the
Mount of Olives
Mount of Transfiguration

Mount Olivet
Mount Olivet Discourse
Mount Sinai
Muhammad*
Muslim
Nag Hammadi codices
name of Christ, the
name of God, the
nativity,* the
nativity of Christ, the
Near East
Neo-Babylonian Empire
neoorthodox(y)
neo-Pentecostalism
Neoplatonism, Neoplatonic
Nevi'im (portion of OT)
new age
New Atheism,* New Atheists
new birth
New City (part of modern Jerusalem)
new covenant (NT)
new heaven and new earth
new Jerusalem
New Testament
New Testament church
New World
Nicene Creed
Nicene fathers
night office (canonical hour)
Ninety-Five Theses*
noncanonical
non-Christian* (n. and adj.; *but* unchristian*)
Nonconformism (-ist)
none (canonical hour)
non-Pauline
Northern Kingdom (Israel)
Nunc Dimittis
office, offices (canonical hours)
Old City* (part of modern Jerusalem)
old covenant (OT)
Old World
Olivet Discourse
Omega, the
omnipotence of God
Omnipotent, the
One,* the (*but* the one true God and God is the one who . . .)
Only Begotten,* the
only begotten* of the Father
only begotten* Son of God
orders (sacrament)
original sin*
Orthodox (Eastern Orthodoxy)
Orthodox (Jewish)
orthodox(y) (general)
Our Father,* the (Lord's Prayer)
our Lady* (Mary)
outer court (of the temple*)
Palestinian covenant
Palm Sunday
papacy
parable* of the prodigal son, etc.
Paraclete, the
Paradise* (garden of Eden)
paradise* (heaven)
parochet
parousia
partial rapture
Paschal Lamb (Jesus)
paschal moon
Paschal Tridium (*but* the tridium)
passion*
Passion Sunday (fifth Sunday in Lent)
Passion Week
Passover
Passover Feast
Passover Lamb (Jesus)
Passover Seder
Pastoral Epistles
Pastoral Letters
Pater Noster, the

patriarch,* a
Patriarch,* the (Abraham)
patriarchs,* the (church fathers)
patristic(s)
Pauline Epistles
Paul's epistles
Paul's letters
Paul the Apostle
peace church(es)
peace offering
pearly gates
penance
Pentateuch
pentateuchal
Pentecost
Pentecostal(ism)*
people of God
person of Christ
persons of the Trinity
Pesach (Passover)
Petrine
Pharaoh* (when used as name or title without article)
pharaoh,* the
pharisaic* (attitude)
Pharisaic* (in reference to Pharisees)
Pharisee*
Pilgrim Fathers*
Pilgrims,* the
pillar of cloud
pillar of fire
Poetical Books, the
pontiff (pope)
pope,* the
Pope Francis I
postapostolic
postbiblical
post-Christian*
postdiluvian
postexilic
postmillennial(ism)(ist)
postmodern
post–Nicene fathers
postresurrection
pre-Christian*
predestination
prediluvian
preexilic
premillenarian
premillennial(ism)(ist)
pretribulation(al)
priesthood of believers
priesthood of Christ
Priestly (meaning P as source)
prime (canonical hour)
Prime Mover
Prince of Darkness
Prince of Peace (Christ)
Prison Epistles (Paul's)
Prison Letters (Paul's)
Prodigal Son, the (*but* the parable of the prodigal son)
promised land* (Canaan or heaven)
Promised One, the (Christ)
Proper Meter
Prophetic Books, the
prophet* Isaiah, the, et al.
Prophets,* the (books of OT)
prophets,* the (people)
Protestant(ism)*
Providence* (God)
providence* of God
providential
psalm,* a
Psalm* 119 (etc.)
psalmic
psalmist,* the
Psalms, the (OT book)
Psalter,* the (the Psalms)
Pseudepigrapha* (body of writings)
pseudepigraphal*
purgatory*
Purim (Feast of Esther)
Puritan*

Qumran
Qur'an*
qur'anic*
rabbi*
Rabbi* (as a title)
rabbinic(al)
rapture,* the
real presence
Received Text, the
Redeemer, the
Reformation, the
Reformed church
Reformed theology
Reformers (16th century)
Reform Judaism
religious right, the*
Renaissance*
resurrection,* the (of Christ)
return, the (of Christ)
risen Lord, the
rite(s)*
River of Life, the (Christ)
Rock, the (Christ)
Roman Catholic Church
Roman Empire
Roman Rite
Roman Senate
rosary* (beads)
Rosary* (prayer)
Rosh Hashanah (Jewish New Year)
Sabbath* (day; n. and adj.)
sabbath* rest (for the land)
Sabbath* rest (for the people of God)
sabbatical* (n. and adj.)
sacrament(s)*
sacramentalism, -ist
Sacramentarian(ism)
sacrament of baptism, confirmation, etc.
Sacred Host
sacred rite(s)
Sadducee*
Samaritan (in all meanings)
Sanctus
Sanhedrin
Satan*
satanic
satanism
Savior* (Jesus)
scribe*
scriptural*
Scripture(s)* (Bible; n. and adj.)
scripture(s)* (other religions)
Sea of Galilee
seat of judgment (in UK: seat of judgement)
second Adam, the (Christ)
second advent, the
second coming, the (of Christ)
second person of the Trinity
Second Temple*, the
Second Vatican Council (1962–65)
Seder, Seder meal
Semite,* -ic, -ism
Septuagesima
Septuagint
seraph(im)*
Sermon on the Mount
Sermon on the Plain
Serpent,* the (Satan)
Servant Songs (Isaiah 2)
seven deadly sins,* the
seven sacraments,* the
Seventh-day Adventist*
seventh heaven
Seventieth Week
sext (canonical hour)
Shabuoth (Pentecost)
shalom
shalom aleichem
shariah law*
shekinah
Sheol (italicized when referred to as a Hebrew word)

Shepherd Psalm, the
Shoah (Holocaust)
shofar
Short Meter
Shulammite (NIV), Shulamite (KJV)
Simon the Zealot
Sinai Desert
Sinai peninsula
Sin-Bearer, the
sin offering
Solomon's Temple*
Son, the (Christ)
son of David
Son of God
Son of Man
Song of Mary, the
sonship of Christ
Southern Kingdom (Judah)
Sovereign Lord
Spirit,* the (Holy Spirit)
spirit of God
star of Bethlehem*
Star of David*
stations of the cross*
Suffering Servant (name for Christ)
Sukkoth (Feast of Booths)
Sunday school*
Sunday school teacher
sun-god
Sun of Righteousness
Supreme Being, the
Sustainer (God)
synagogue*
synoptic (adj.)
Synoptic* Gospels
Synoptics, the
synoptic writers, the
tabernacle, the (OT)
table of showbread
Talmud
talmudic
Tanak
targum(ic)
Te Deum
temple,* the (Jerusalem) (*but* First Temple, etc.)
temptation,* the
temptation in the desert, the
temptation of Christ, the
Ten Commandments* (*but* the second commandment, etc.)
tent
Tent of Meeting
Tent of the Testimony
Ten Tribes, the
ten tribes of Israel, the
terce (canonical hour)
Testaments, the
tetragrammaton,* tetragram
Textus Receptus
third person of the Trinity
Thirty-Nine Articles (Anglican)
throne of grace
Thummim
time of Jacob's trouble, the
time of the gentiles, the
time of the judges, the
tomb, the
Torah (part of the canon)
Tower of Babel
transfiguration,* the
Transjordan
Tree of Knowledge of Good and Evil
Tree of Life
tribe of Judah
tribulation, the (historical event)
tridium (*but* Paschal Tridium)
Trinitarian
Trinity,* the (God)
triumphal entry
triune God, the
True Cross, the
Twelve,* the
twelve* apostles, the

twelve* disciples, the
twelve tribes, the
Twenty-Third Psalm, etc.
unchristian*
ungodly*
Unitarian
united kingdom (of Israel)
universal church
universalism, -ist
unscriptural
Upanishads
upper room, the
Upper Room Discourse
Urim
vacation Bible school*
Veda(s)
vedic
vespers*
viaticum
Victor, the (Christ)
Vine, the (Christ)
Virgin, the
Virgin and child
virgin birth,* the
Virgin Mary, the
visible church
voice of God
Vulgate*
Wailing Wall*
Wandering Jew, the (legend)
Water of Life (Christ)
Way, the (Christ)
way, the truth, and the life
Weeping Prophet, the (Jeremiah)
West Bank
Western church*
Western Rites
Western Wall*
Westminster Catechism
Wicked One, the (Satan)
Wisdom Literature,* the
wise men,* the
Word,* the (Bible or Christ)
Word made flesh (Christ)
word of God* (his statement or promise)
Word of God* (the Bible)
Word of Life
Word of Truth, the
Writings, the (part of the canon)
Yahweh (italicized only when referred to as a Hebrew word)
Year of Jubilee
YHWH
Yom Kippur (Day of Atonement)
Yuletide*
Zealot (religious sect)

CAPTIONS

Captions to photos, illustrations, charts, or other graphic matter, which should be as brief as possible, are provided by the author.

Type Size. A caption is usually set one or two point sizes smaller than the text type when the graphic matter is inserted in the text, though the caption may be set the same size when the graphic is set on its own page (as in a separate photo section). Still, if a caption runs more than two lines, it may be further reduced in size to save space.

With Periods. Periods should be used only when the caption forms a complete sentence.

When an Illustration Is Turned on Its Side. If the graphic material needs to be placed on its side to fit, then the caption should run along the right side of the page, that is, from the bottom of the page to the top.

From Left, From Right, Clockwise. When a caption identifies people in a photograph, say *from left* or *from right* rather than *left to right* or *right to left.* Avoid saying *clockwise* unless the reader is also informed as to where on the "clock" they are supposed to start; such as *Clockwise from lower left.*

CATALOGING-IN-PUBLICATION DATA (CIP)

Cataloging-in-publication (CIP) data is the accurate cataloging information for a print book or ebook as it will appear in the catalog of the Library of Congress. Providing this information helps libraries catalog and access the book. Although placing CIP information in a book is not legally mandated, its use is encouraged since many libraries find it impractical to purchase books in which this information does not appear.

Placement. Ordinarily, the CIP data appears on the copyright page. If the copyright page is too crowded, or if other reasons exist for displacing the CIP data, it may appear elsewhere, though a note stating where to find the CIP data customarily appears on the copyright page.

Accuracy. The CIP data should be printed line-for-line, space-for-space, and indent-for-indent as it appears on the form sent from the Library of Congress. The typeface may conform to that of the rest of the copyright page or book. The Library of Congress makes no typographic specifications other than legibility.

Occasionally mistakes creep into the CIP data because of errors on the publisher's submitted form, an error at the Library of Congress itself, or an error in keying the data at the time of typesetting. Mistakes in an author's birth date or in the spelling of the author's name, for instance, are common, and all CIP data should be proofread carefully. The publisher may correct any such error as long as the Library of Congress is informed of the change.

Changes. Other changes in the CIP data may be made by the publisher. For instance, if the author prefers not to reveal his or her birthdate, the publisher may substitute the word *date* for the birth year (though the actual birth year should be provided on the CIP application form). Also, if a pseudonymous author prefers that no one know his or her actual name, then a long dash may be substituted for the author's real name in the CIP data. Again, all such changes should be reported to the CIP Division of the Library of Congress. In this last case, CIP is best registered using the author's pseudonym to begin with.

For Coauthored Books. Only the first author's name is listed as the main catalog reference (that is, on the first line of the CIP data) in books by more than one author. Each coauthor is then listed as a secondary catalog reference.

For Reprints. In reprints, if no bibliographic information (title, author, publisher, ISBN, page count, and so on) other than the year of publication has changed, then a new CIP need not be applied for. This means, for instance, a reprint that has received a new cover does not need a new CIP. If a book has gone from hardcover to paper, then a new CIP should be applied for because the new format requires a new ISBN. If a publisher is reprinting another publisher's book, then a new CIP is needed even if no changes were made in the content.

Publications That Do Not Need CIP. Printed matter of a perceived ephemeral nature (tracts, chapbooks, pamphlets, catalogs, and so on) and books unlikely to be purchased by libraries (such as workbooks, some Bible studies, cartoon books, comic books, and some series books) do not need CIP data. In many cases, the Library of Congress will refuse to provide data for such books in the first place.

Contact. Questions about aspects of CIP data will be answered via email or phone by the Copyright Office at this address:

Library of Congress
Copyright Office
101 Independence Avenue SE
Washington, DC 20559-6000
Telephone: (202) 287-8700
website: www.copyright.gov
(various email addresses are available at the website for different kinds of questions)

CHAPTER OPENER

A chapter's first page, the *chapter opener*, is usually designed with more flair than a standard text page and should serve as an invitation to the content. It is an exception to the rule that typography should strive for invisibility. Ideally, chapter openers are set recto with the chapter number, title, and text starting lower on the page than a normal text page. If an overabundance of chapters is present, they may start random simply to conserve space. (See "RECTO VERSUS RANDOM SETTING OF PAGES.") In some mass-market books, chapters begin flush to the top of the page to save space.

Chapter *as a Word.* As in the table of contents (see "TABLE OF CONTENTS,") the word *chapter* is often omitted on a chapter opener since the numeral alone usually suffices. The exception is mode when the word is actually designed in such a way as to be a part of the page's aesthetics.

Chapter Number. Arabic numerals are standard for chapter numbers, though roman numerals may be used when there are few chapters (no more than ten). Chapter numbers may be spelled out for design reasons, but in books with many chapters, large numbers are cumbersome when spelled out. If the number is spelled out, it should be set in a contrasting type or located well apart from the title so that it won't appear the number is actually the first word of the chapter title.

Chapter Titles. If the chapter titles in a book tend to be long, the designer should set them in caps-and-lowercase rather than all caps. Also, a period should never follow a chapter title.

Initial Capitals. The first letter of the first word of a chapter is sometimes given a special treatment. A large capital letter sitting on the baseline of the first line is called a *standing cap*. If it is cut into the text so that it stands on the baseline of the second, third, or other succeeding line, it is called a *drop cap*. These may be indented for design reasons, but they can be set flush left or even hung out in the left margin. The first word or words can also be given this sort of display treatment at the discretion of the designer.

Chapters Beginning with Quotations. If the chapter actually begins with a quotation, the opening quotation mark is dropped whenever an enlarged initial capital is used. This causes consternation among authors, proofreaders, and readers with OCD, but it is a long-standing convention in printing to avoid oversized and ugly open quotation marks.

First Line of Text. When no oversized initial capital is used, and occasionally when it is used, the first line of text may be given a special treatment. The first word, phrase, or line may be set in small caps, italic, or a special font. Alternatively, the first word, phrase, or line may be set cap-lowercase like the rest of the text.

Running Heads and Folios. Running heads usually do not appear on a chapter opener. If the design calls for the folio to appear in the running heads, then an alternate location for the folio needs to be found for the chapter openers, customarily centered below the text in the lower margin (called a *drop folio*), though that placement can be altered to suit the needs of a particular design.

CHILDREN'S BOOKS: STYLE AND FORMAT

Christianity has had a special relationship with children's books. Most scholars credit European Christian educators with having developed the idea of a separate literature for children to provide moral education as a form of entertainment. The *Orbis Sensualum Pictus* (1657) by Jan Amos Comenius, a Moravian bishop, is thought to be the first children's picture book. Although children's books in our time vary widely in length, format, age of readership, and content, a few guidelines are offered here.

Type Size. Although children are able to read tiny type (as small as 8 point), larger types (12 point and above) are usually used for children through the age of ten. For the youngest readers, ages four through seven, type as large as 18 point is common. At a fifth-grade level or higher, children are capable of reading faces in adult type sizes: 9 through 12 point. By and large, the younger the audience, the larger the type, even when a publisher expects the parent to read the book to the child.

Type Face. Familiar medium- to heavy-weight typefaces are preferred by children themselves, especially in easy readers and some picture books that children are expected to read by themselves. Serif faces are the most often used: Times New Roman, Bookman Antique, Century Schoolbook, and similar typefaces common in adult books.

Picture books for preschool-age children are often set in attractive sans-serif fonts such as Arial, Eras, Lucida Sans, and others because they look more like a child's own block letters. Design-intensive books often sport handwritten text, elaborate fonts, or exotic calligraphy to achieve special effects. Typographic design of children's books is an opportunity for the author, editor, and designer to work together.

Word Breaks and Justification. Words should not be hyphenated or broken over lines in books for younger readers. Hyphens tend to confuse early readers, and ragged-right setting is the most reader friendly. In some cases—as in picture books—lines can even be set so that each line ends with a complete phrase or sentence.

Word and Letter Spacing. For books intended for beginning readers, a larger than normal word spacing may be used—up to a full em. The compositor should also be sure that no kerning is used, since letters that are artificially squeezed together may cause problems for young readers. By the same token, no extra letter space should be added. Always allow type to letter-space itself as it was designed to.

Paragraphing. In picture books and simple chapter books for beginning readers, it is common to avoid using paragraph indents, since it is felt they confuse young readers unnecessarily. This places a special burden on the writer, who has to be careful that the speakers in dialogue are kept distinct and that "said references" are placed earlier in dialogue rather than later. Names of speakers, if placed in the middle of a character's speech, should not come at a full stop. They should come midsentence so that it will be clear that the character is continuing to speak and that the sentence that follows is not spoken by a new character. If dialogue issues are too complex or cause confusion in an unparagraphed setting, then traditional paragraph indents should be used.

Margins. The margins in books for young readers should be wider than normal. Research has shown narrow margins actually lead the child's eyes off the page.

Lengths. The length of a children's book should be age-appropriate. Although firm rules cannot be established (who would have thought eight-year-olds would be reading a seven-hundred-page *Harry Potter* novel?), the publishing industry has developed some standards for length and age. Keep in mind that, especially for picture books and easy readers, part of the page count is taken up with title pages, copyright information, dedications, and sometimes author and artist information. So, in the following chart, subtract two to four pages from the total to estimate the number of pages available for the actual text.

Type of Book	Age	Approximate Number of Pages	Approximate Number of Words
Board books	0–3	8, 12, 16	0–20 per two-page spread
Picture books (to be read to children)	3–8	24–32	0–1,000 (with 0–40 per two-page spread); 100–500 average for youngest readers (with 4–20 per two-page spread)
Easy (early) readers			
Level 1 (can read and write with help)	4–5	32	300–500
Level 2 (can almost read and write)	5–8	32, 48	500–1,000
Level 3 (can read and write alone)	7–8	48, 56, 64	1,000–1,500
Chapter books	8–12	80, 96, 112, 128	18,000–25,000 total, unless there is a lot of design or art

Type of Book	Age	Approximate Number of Pages	Approximate Number of Words
Young adult books (teen-age readers; teens who read at their level should be able to read adult books by age 16 or 17)	13+	varies, usually 144+	30,000–40,000

Other kinds of children's books have parameters that are not as easily quantifiable. For example, "hi-lo readers" are for children of various ages whose interest in reading is exceptionally high even though their skills are below average for their age. Also available are "family readers," which are picture books with higher-than-average word or page counts meant to be read to children in several sittings. "Novelty," or "special format," books for children can take whatever shape the imaginations of the author and designer can conceive, and they follow no set pattern. In this group are foldout books, pop-up books, scratch-and-sniff books, and books enhanced with computer chips to play music or make sounds.

Copyright Page. Because of the design-intensive nature of picture books and some other kinds of children's books, the copyright page is often shifted to the end. There is no legal requirement for the location of the copyright page, so this practice is acceptable and common. Publishers often put only the bare minimum of information required on the copyright pages of their children's books—the copyright notice, the country of printing notice, and the all-rights-reserved notice. (See "COPYRIGHT PAGE.")

Dedication Page. Because space is limited in books for young children, the dedication is commonly incorporated on either the copyright or title page.

Cadet Edition. Whenever a book written for adults is simplified or otherwise adapted for younger readers, it is called a *cadet edition*. For example, Dr. Ben Carson's book (with Gregg Lewis) *Think Big* (Zondervan, 1996) was adapted in 2015 as a cadet edition called *You Have a Brain: A Teen's Guide to T.H.I.N.K. B.I.G.*

CHINESE TRANSLITERATION

Two systems of rendering Chinese words in English are common: the older *Wade-Giles* and the more modern *pinyin*. A short list contrasting the two systems can be found in *CMoS*, 11.105, and a more comprehensive conversion chart can be found at http://library.ust.hk/guides/opac/conversion-tables.html, courtesy of the Hong Kong University of Science and Technology Library.

Use pinyin for most purposes. Not only is it preferred by the greater number of Chinese-English speakers and readers, but it is also easier in many ways. It is the system endorsed by the People's Republic of China as well as the government of the Republic of China (Taiwan), who used to use the Wade-Giles system but officially converted to pinyin in 2008. British and American libraries have largely converted to pinyin so that most book, subject, and author references are cataloged according to that system.

Exceptions. In books intended for a general trade market, exceptions to the pinyin system are usually made when a familiar Chinese word or name already has a long-established romanized form, such as the names of classic literary works and some historical personages. For instance, few English readers recognize the pinyin *Kong Fuzi*, but most readers will immediately know who *Confucius* is. (See also "TITLES OF COMMON TEXTS OF THE WORLD'S RELIGIONS.") It is not always easy to judge which forms are "long-established" and which aren't. When in doubt, use the pinyin. Also, render the names of even well-known modern Chinese personages in pinyin: *Mao Zedong* rather than *Mao Tse-tung*. Most academic writers use the pinyin system, even for those names and words long established in their Wade-Giles versions.

Here is a short sampling of some of the differences between pinyin and Wade-Giles. An asterisk follows the forms most often preferred for general readership, although author preference should always be taken into account.

Pinyin	Wade-Giles
Beijing*	Peking
Chan	Zen*
Dao, Daosim	Tao, Taoism*
Daodejing	Tao Te Ching*
do fu	tofu*
Du Fu	Tu Fu*
Gongfu	Kung Fu*
Laozi	Lao Tzu*
Li Bai	Li Po*
Mao Zedong*	Mao Tse-tung
Nanjing*	Nanking
qi*	ch'i
Qin dynasty*	Chin dynasty
Quanyin*	Kuan Yin
Sichuan Province*	Szechwan Province
Taichiquan	T'ai Chi Ch'uan*
Tang dynasty*	T'ang dynasty
Yangzi River*	Yang-tse River
Yi Ching	I Ching*
Zhou dynasty*	Chou dynasty
Zhou Enlai*	Chou En-Lai

Pronunciation. One disadvantage of pinyin is its occasionally un-Englishlike pronunciations, though if a few rules are observed, those problems are easily resolved.

Pinyin Character	Pronounced
c	*ts* (as in *its*)
q	*ch* (as in *chin* but a little softer)
u	(similar to the French *u* or the German *ü* when it follows *j*, *q*, *x*, or *y*)
x	*sh* (as in *she* but a little softer)
z	*dz* (as in *adz*)

CHRISTIAN BOOKS, TYPES OF

While Christian books are written in most of the same genres as books in the general market—fiction, memoir, poetry, history, personal essay, and so on—Christian writers have invented genres and forms that are largely unique to the faith. In the following list, those marked with asterisks are discussed in more detail under their own entries. (See also "GENRE FICTION.")

***Bible study**—a book, usually for lay readers, that interprets the meaning of Bible passages verse by verse, most often in an attempt to apply that meaning to daily life. Bible studies often include a basic interpretive essay for each passage, study or discussion questions, and blanks or rule lines for readers to record their thoughts (called a *fill-in-the-blanks Bible study*). (See "*Bible study*" and "*biblical studies, Bible study.*")

book of hours—a book, often elaborately decorated, containing prayers for each of the Divine Offices, short meditations, records of saints' days and holy days along with short lives of the saints, selected Bible passages, and liturgical readings. These were popular in the late Middle Ages and the Renaissance. (Example: *Les Très Riches Heures de Duc de Berry*, early fifteenth century)

clerical novel—a novel describing the daily life of a priest or minister. (Examples: Georges Bernanos's *Diary of a Country Priest* and Jan Karon's Mitford Series)

commentary—like the Bible study, a work that seeks to interpret Bible passages verse by verse, but with a focus not so much on application as on the precise meanings of words, phrases, and sections.

***concordance**—an alphabetical listing of words used in the Bible, along with their specific verse references and a short quote to show how the word is used in context. Concordances are helpful in tracking down references or doing word or thematic studies in the Bible. (Example: *Cruden's Concordance*, 1737)

***devotional**—a collection containing a short reading or meditation for each day, used as part of the reader's devotional practice. Each reading commonly includes a Bible verse, a meditation, and a prayer. (Example: Mrs. Charles E. Cowman's *Streams in the Desert*, 1926)

end-times novel—a subgenre of science fiction and fantasy dealing with the end times, the tribulation, and the return of Christ. End-times novels, also called apocalyptic fiction, are inspired by Revelation, Daniel, and some noncanonical writings that discuss apocalyptic events. (Examples: C. S. Lewis's *That Hideous Strength* and Tim LaHaye and Jerry Jenkins's Left Behind Series)

illuminated manuscript—a book so-called because of its form rather than its content; often a unique copy of a Bible or a book of hours that has been rendered in calligraphy with marginal drawings and elaborate initial letters. These books are considered works of art in themselves. (Example: *The Book of Kells*, ninth century)

lectionary—a list of recommended readings, usually Bible readings, for personal devotional use.

martyrology—a collection of stories of noted martyrs. (Example: *Acts and Monuments*, familiarly known as *Foxe's Book of Martyrs*, 1563)

prayer book—a collection of prayers and rites for either private devotions or public liturgy. (Example: *The Book of Common Prayer*, 1549)

***red-letter Bible**—an edition of the Bible in which the words of Jesus are printed in red. Most modern Bibles are available in this form.

saints' lives—also called a *hagiography*, a genre that collects inspirational biographies of noted saints; most common in the Roman Catholic Church. (Example: Butler's *Lives of the Saints*, 1756–59)

spiritual thriller—a subgenre of fiction that describes supernatural forces being unleashed in everyday life. It is the Christian counterpart to the *supernatural thriller*. (Examples: Charles Williams's *War in Heaven* [1930] and Bill Myers's *Blood of Heaven* [2002])

CHRISTIAN HOLIDAYS, FEASTS, AND THE LITURGICAL YEAR

Movable and Immovable Feasts. Western Christian tradition recognizes eight primary *movable feasts* (that is, their date changes from year to year), all of which are determined in relation to the date of Easter, and together they are called the *paschal cycle*. They are Sexagesima Sunday (sixty days before Easter), Palm Sunday, Ash Wednesday, Good Friday, Easter, Ascension Day (or Holy Thursday; forty days after Easter), Pentecost, and Trinity Sunday. Note that the Eastern Orthodox Church dates its feasts according to the older Julian calendar, which adds thirteen days to the modern Gregorian calendar.

All the other feast days and holidays are considered *fixed*, or *immovable, feasts* (that is, they occur on the same day each year). The four primary ones are the Annunciation (March 25), the Nativity of John the Baptist (June 24), Michaelmas (September 29), and Christmas (December 25). These are also called the *quarter days*, because they roughly correspond to the changing of the seasons.

The following paragraphs describe those holidays and holy seasons, and their calendar placement, spelling, and styling, that have had historical importance to the worldwide church.

Advent. Advent spans the period between Advent Sunday and Christmas. Advent (from Latin *adventus*, meaning "coming") is the season commemorating Christ's nativity.

1. *Advent Sunday.* In Western churches, Advent begins on the fourth Sunday before Christmas (which is also the Sunday closest to November 30). That Sunday is considered the beginning of the church year, or church calendar.
2. *Christmas (December 25).* Christmas (short for *Christ Mass*) is the day on which the birth of Jesus is commemorated. It is referred to as the *Feast of the Nativity of Jesus Christ* in some traditions, and although it actually ranks after Easter, Pentecost, and Epiphany in liturgical importance, it is the most popular holiday of the church year.
3. *Boxing Day (December 26 or 27).* Though not part of the official celebration of Advent, *Boxing Day* is observed in the UK and much of its Commonwealth on the day after Christmas (unless Christmas falls on a Saturday, in which case Boxing Day is observed on Monday). It was formerly the day on which families distributed gift boxes to the household servants. Today the tradition survives by remembering those who perform other public services, such as the mail carrier and the trash collector.

Epiphany (January 6). Epiphany (from Greek *epiphainein*, "to manifest") is the celebration of Christ's manifestation to the magi and to the gentile world. This is a particularly important holiday in the Eastern churches, as the commemoration of Christ's baptism. In England, the evening before Epiphany is referred to as *Twelfth Night*. The span of days from December 25 to January 5 (inclusive) are the traditional *twelve days of Christmas*. In the old-style Julian calendar, Epiphany is Christmas Day, and it is still a day of gift giving among many Christians.

Lent. The primary church season, Lent (from Anglo-Saxon *lencten*, meaning "spring" or "March") is traditionally a period of penitence and fasting commemorated between Ash Wednesday and Easter in preparation for Easter. The modern Western dating of Ash Wednesday and Easter were determined at the time of the Gregorian calendar reforms in 1582, so the dates often differ in the Eastern churches, which follow the Julian calendar. The following are the major dates of the Lenten season.

1. *Shrove Tuesday.* The day before Ash Wednesday is a time of preparation for Lent. Outside—and even inside—the church, the day is better known as *Mardi Gras*, the traditional day of feasting before the Lenten fast.
2. *Ash Wednesday.* A day of penance and the official beginning of Lent, Ash Wednesday falls forty-six days before Easter. Commonly, Ash Wednesday is considered to be forty days before Easter, though that traditional way of determining the date of Ash Wednesday does not count Sundays.
3. *Laetare Sunday*, also called *Mothering Sunday* or sometimes *Refreshment Sunday.* This is the fourth Sunday of Lent, on which some small respites from the Lenten penances are allowed.
4. *Passion Sunday.* The fifth Sunday of the Lenten season. In some traditions, the last two weeks of the Lenten season, from Passion Sunday to Holy Saturday, are referred to as *Passiontide.*
5. *Palm Sunday.* The sixth Sunday of the Lenten Season, that is, the Sunday before Easter, on which Christ's triumphant entry into Jerusalem is remembered. The seven-day period beginning on Palm Sunday is called *Holy Week.*
6. *Maundy Thursday.* This is the Thursday before Easter, traditionally the day on which Christ's institution of the sacrament of Communion, or the Eucharist, is commemorated. This day is sometimes referred to as *Holy Thursday*, though in some traditions *Holy Thursday* refers to Ascension Day (forty days after Easter). (See "*Holy Thursday.*") The word *maundy* is taken from the Bible verse read for that day: *"Mandatum novum do vobis"* ("A new command I give you"—John 13:34).
7. *Good Friday.* The Friday before Easter. On this day Christ's crucifixion and death are remembered.
8. *Holy Saturday.* This day commemorates the resting of Christ's body in the tomb and is honored in some churches with a Paschal Vigil Service, which begins late on this day and ends in the early hours of Easter Sunday morning.

Easter, Easter Sunday. Sometimes called the *Feast of the Resurrection of Christ*, Easter is the celebration of Christ's resurrection. Technically not part of Lent, which ends at midnight on Holy Saturday, Easter Sunday is meant to be a day of joy and celebration.

All dates preceding Easter in the Lenten season are established in relation to Easter Sunday. Several factors determine the date of Easter in the Western church from year to year. Easter is always on a Sunday, and that Sunday is the first to fall after the fourteenth day of the "paschal moon" (which is a new moon). The paschal moon is determined by considering which spring new moon will have a full moon (fourteen days after the new moon) that falls either on or closest after the vernal equinox (always March 21 for this calculation). These somewhat confusing conditions being met, Easter can never occur earlier than March 22 or later than April 25.

The following chart shows the dates for Ash Wednesday and Easter.

Year	Ash Wednesday	Easter	Year	Ash Wednesday	Easter
2017	March 1	April 16	2033	March 2	April 17
2018	February 14	April 1	2034	February 22	April 9
2019	March 6	April 21	2035	February 7	March 25
2020	February 26	April 12	2036	February 27	April 13
2021	February 17	April 4	2037	February 18	April 5
2022	March 2	April 17	2038	March 10	April 25
2023	February 22	April 9	2039	February 23	April 4
2024	February 14	March 31	2040	February 15	April 1
2025	March 5	April 20	2041	March 6	April 21
2026	February 18	April 5	2042	February 19	April 6
2027	February 10	March 28	2043	February 11	March 29
2028	March 1	April 16	2044	March 2	April 17
2029	February 15	April 1	2045	February 22	April 9
2030	March 6	April 21	2046	February 7	March 25
2031	February 26	April 13	2047	February 27	April 14
2032	February 11	March 28			

Pentecost. Celebrated on the seventh Sunday after Easter, this holy day commemorates the descent of the Holy Spirit upon the apostles (Acts 2) and officially marks the end of the fifty days of the Easter season. Pentecost Sunday is also called *Whitsun*, or *Whitsunday*, in England. In the Roman Catholic Church and the Church of England, *Paschaltide* is the period between Easter Sunday and Pentecost.

Trinity Sunday. This day is set aside to honor the Trinity and is celebrated the Sunday after Pentecost Sunday.

Other Christian Holidays, Feast Days, and Observances.

Week of Prayer for Christian Unity (January 18 to 25)

Conversion of Saint Paul (January 25)

Presentation of Christ, or Candlemas (February 2)

Annunciation, or Lady Day (March 25)
National Day of Prayer (first Thursday of May; interfaith observance in US; mandated by act of Congress)
Ascension Day (fifth Thursday after Easter)
Nativity of John the Baptist (June 24)
Feast of Saint Peter and Saint Paul (June 29)
Visitation (July 2)
Transfiguration of Our Lord (August 6)
Assumption of the Blessed Virgin Mary (August 15)
Michaelmas (September 29)
Worldwide Communion Sunday (first Sunday in October)
Reformation Sunday (Sunday nearest October 31)
Reformation Day (October 31)
All Saints' Day (November 1)
All Souls' Day (November 2)
Feast of the Immaculate Conception (December 8)
Feast of the Conception of Saint Anne (December 9)
Saint Lucy's Day, or Santa Lucia (December 13)
Saint Stephen's Day (December 26)
Holy Innocents' Day (December 28)

CHURCH LATIN PRONUNCIATION

See "PRONUNCIATION GUIDE FOR AUDIO BOOKS," section on "*Ecclesial Latin.*"

CITATIONS

See "NOTES."

CITING BIBLE VERSES

See "QUOTING THE BIBLE."

CITY NAMES

Some copyeditors insist a phrase like *they honeymooned in Paris* should be changed to *they honeymooned in Paris, France*, so the reader won't mistakenly assume the couple honeymooned in Paris, Idaho. But well-known, major cities of the world do not need to be qualified by country or state. Reserve the qualifier for those cases when the city either is not well known (*She was born in Lenoir, North Carolina*) or may be confused with a major city of the same name (*He dreamed of visiting Cairo, Illinois*).

CLERICAL TITLES AND CLERICAL POSITIONS

A *clerical title* is a formal title given to a religious official; it differs from a *clerical position*, which is a word used to describe a religious official but usually does not have the status of a formal title. Capitalize clerical titles only when they come immediately before the person's name: *Archbishop David Leon Cooper*. Note that clerical titles may be capitalized after a name in promotional or blurb copy. (See "CAPITALIZATION: GUIDELINES," section on "*Personal Titles*.") Confusion sometimes occurs when clerical titles shared by different denominations have slightly different meanings; the same word can be a formal title to some believers and a clerical position to others.

Specific titles and positions may be found in the Word List section. The most common clerical titles are *archbishop*, *archdeacon*, *auxiliary bishop*, *bishop*, *canon*, *cardinal*, *deacon*, *dean*, *father*, *general secretary*, *metropolitan*, *pastor*, *patriarch*, *presiding bishop*, *rabbi*, and *suffragan bishop*. The most common clerical positions are *canoness*, *deacon*, *elder*, *minister*, *pastor*, *priest*, *primate*, and *rector*.

CODE LANGUAGE

See "JARGON, RELIGIOUS."

COLON

A colon (:) is a pointer. It introduces an amplification, an example, a question, or a quotation. In a salutation to a letter, it points to the entire text itself. It acts as a substitute for such expressions as *for example*, *for instance*, *namely*, and *that is*. Though a colon was often used in the past to separate two closely related but independent clauses, a semicolon is now more commonly used.

> That is what faith is: God perceived intuitively by the heart, not by reason.—Pascal
>
> Remember the words of Augustine: "Hasten more slowly."
>
> Many Christian writers have been instrumental in shaping the genre of prison literature: Paul, Boethius, and Bunyan.
>
> It was the golden age of revivalism: Moody, Torrey, and Sunday were the familiar names of the time.
>
> It was the golden age of revivalism; Moody, Torrey, and Sunday were the familiar names of the time. [Either a colon or a semicolon is correct here.]

With Direct Quotations. A colon may introduce a direct quotation when no verb-of-saying is used: *Luther's answer was unapologetic: "Here I stand; I cannot do otherwise."*

Capitalization. Do not capitalize the first word after a colon unless that colon announces a definition, presents a proverb or quotation, introduces two or more parallel sentences in close sequence, or introduces a question or formal statement. *This old saying contains much truth: The hurrier I go, the behinder I get.*

To Introduce a Quotation or a List. Use a colon when quoted material or a list is placed in a separate paragraph after an introductory statement. An introductory statement should not be followed by a colon if the series completes the sentence.

> Consider this passage from Arthur Dent's *Plain Man's Pathway to Heaven*: [. . .]
>
> The five areas of Tolkien studies are
> the works of fantasy
> the literary criticism
> the personal writings
> the translations of older works
> the grammars and linguistic works

Between Titles and Subtitles. In bibliographies, source lists, and other references, a colon is used between a title and subtitle—even when no punctuation appears on the cover or title page (publishers commonly drop the colons before subtitles on such pages). When a dash is used in the title, the dash should be retained in any reference to that work.

Between Volume and Page Numbers. In bibliographies, source lists, and notes, a colon is used to separate a volume number (and an issue number, if present) from a page number or URL.

> Soho Machida, "Jesus, Man of Sin: Toward a New Christology in the Global Era," *Buddhist-Christian Studies* 19 (1990): 81–91.
>
> Malcolm Gladwell, "How I Rediscovered Faith," *Relevant Magazine* 67 (January/February 2014): http://www.relevantmagazine.com/culture/books/how-i-rediscovered-faith.

In Scripture References and Times. Place an unspaced colon between chapter and verse designations in Scripture references (*John 3:16*) and between hours and minutes in time references (*7:21 a.m.*).

COLOPHON

A colophon is a notice, usually on the last page of a book, in which the publisher provides details of a book's production, such as the typeface or the names of those who contributed. It was first used in the Mainz Psalter of 1457. Though now rare, a colophon is appropriate whenever the book's production values are unusually high—and this could include ebooks. Customarily, a colophon appears as a single page, verso or recto, though for space reasons it may appear on the copyright page. It can be as short or as long as can conveniently fit in the space allotted, though shorter is better. Colophons are often set one or two point sizes smaller than the text type and may contain any or all of the following information:

Notes on the typeface(s) used, including:

- style, size, and leading
- reasons for using that typeface
- the type's provenance (designer, year, first use)
- the design system in which it was set

A credit line for the compositor or designer

Notes on the paper (weight and maker) used for the print edition

A credit line for the printer or ebook producer (including location)

A credit line for graphic artists or illustrators who contributed to the book

A general note on the series or imprint of which the book is a part

COMMA

A comma serves many functions. It can separate clauses of a sentence, introduce a direct quotation, signal a parenthetical statement, separate items in a list, and much more. The word *comma* comes from Latin and Greek roots, meaning "a piece cut off," which suggests, metaphorically, the sort of uses to which the comma is put.

With Coordinating Conjunctions. A comma is placed before a coordinating conjunction (*and*, *but*, *for*, *nor*, *or*, *so*, *yet*) in a compound sentence. No comma is needed when both clauses of the compound sentence are fairly short. When one or both of the clauses are quite long or contain many other internal punctuation marks, a semicolon is often used before the conjunction in place of the comma. Bear in mind that a compound sentence differs from a sentence with a compound predicate (that is, two or more verbs with the same subject), in which case a comma should not be used.

True Christian love can sometimes get angry, but it is also constantly wary of anger's pitfalls. [Compound sentence]

We seek a human Christ but we also seek a transcendent Christ. [Short compound sentence; no comma needed]

Thus, therefore, they walked on together; and as they walked, ever and anon these trumpeters, even, with joyful sound, would, by mixing their music with looks and gestures, still signify to Christian and his brother how welcome they were into their company, and with what gladness they came to meet them.—John Bunyan, *The Pilgrim's Progress* [Complex compound sentence with internal punctuation; a semicolon used in place of a comma]

God teaches us patience and produces in us whatever other virtues we may exhibit. [Compound predicate, no comma]

With Restrictive Clauses. **Don't use a comma to set off an adjectival clause or phrase that restricts the meaning of the noun it modifies (a restrictive clause). Use a comma, though, whenever the phrase or clause does not strictly identify the noun (a nonrestrictive clause). The most helpful guiding principle is this: when the modifying phrase could be eliminated without essentially changing the reader's basic understanding of the sentence, commas should be used.**

The translation proposed to King James I in 1604 eventually became known as the Authorized Version. [The phrase *proposed to King James I in 1604* restricts, or defines in an essential way, the subject, telling precisely which translation is meant.]

The Authorized Version, largely translated from the original languages, was not printed until 1611. [The phrase *largely translated from the original languages* does not restrict or define, in an essential way, the subject.]

With Appositives. **When a word or phrase is placed in apposition to a noun, it is set off by commas. If the word or phrase is restrictive, no commas should be used. When the word or phrase can be eliminated without changing the basic meaning of the sentence, commas should be used. *CMoS* suggests the commas may be dropped in those cases where no likelihood of confusion exists, such as with spouses.**

John Wycliffe, the great fourteenth-century Bible translator, has been called "the Morning Star of the Reformation." [appositive; not restrictive]

the poet Milton [restrictive; tells which poet]

the short story "Revelation" [restrictive]

his brother, Charles, is ... [appositive; implies Charles is the only brother]

his brother Charles is ... [restrictive; implies more than one brother]

but his wife, Susannah, *or* his wife Susannah [since no confusion is likely to result]

With a Series of Elements. A comma is placed before *and*, *or*, and *nor* connecting the last two elements in a series of three or more. This is known as the *serial*, or *Oxford, comma.*

Though John is known for his sermons and Charles for his hymns, both Wesleys were prolific writers of letters, journals, sermons, and hymns.

Many manuals, especially those intended for journalists and for writers in the UK, discourage the use of the serial comma. They can usually be dropped without noticeable effect, though this manual recommends retaining them for two reasons. First, it is the more common style in American book publishing, so its use is familiar to readers, if not widely expected as well. Second, experience suggests misreading occurs more often when the serial comma is absent than when it is present. (See also "AMPERSAND," section on "*Drop the Serial Comma.*")

With "Namely," "That Is," and Similar Expressions. A comma follows such expressions as *namely*, *that is*, and *for example* (including the academic abbreviations *i.e.* and *e.g.*, though those abbreviations are discouraged in nonacademic books; see "*e.g., i.e.*"). For example, ***She wrote her thesis on three English mystics, namely, Richard Rolle, Walter Hilton, and Julian of Norwich.***

With Dependent Clauses. A comma usually follows a dependent clause (restrictive or nonrestrictive) when that clause comes before the main clause of the sentence. A comma is also used before nonrestrictive dependent clauses that follow the main clause. A comma should not be used when a restrictive dependent clause follows the main clause.

Although Merton entered the monastery in 1941, he continued to write poetry throughout his life. [Dependent clause preceding main clause]

Galileo finally agreed to recant, though he was later rumored to have recanted his recantation. [Dependent clause following main clause]

Dorothy Sayers was not allowed to graduate after earning her "first" at Oxford. [Restrictive, dependent clause that follows main clause]

With Adverbial Phrases. When an adverbial phrase comes before the main clause of the sentence, the comma should be omitted whenever the phrase is short and the omission will not result in confusion. The comma should also be omitted when the introductory adverbial phrase is immediately followed by the verb it modifies. Otherwise, if the adverbial phrase is long, complex, or would result in misreading, a comma should be used.

After the final decree Latimer was free to preach anywhere in England. [Short adverbial phrase, no comma]

Not many years after surviving a storm at sea, John Newton committed his life to Christ.

On the altar stood the completed carving of the nativity. [Adverbial phrase is followed by the verb it modifies.]

Two years before, his ministry had ended. [Were the comma omitted, misreading would result.]

With Two or More Adjectives. Two or more adjectives in sequence and without a coordinating conjunction should be separated by a comma (or commas) when each, by itself, modifies the noun alone—that is, if the word *and* could be inserted between them without changing the basic meaning of the phrase. If an adjective modifies both a subsequent adjective (or adjectives) and the noun, a comma should not be used. (See "ADJECTIVES, MULTIPLE.")

Margaret Fell proved a faithful, sincere friend. [Could be rewritten as "... a faithful *and* sincere friend"]

Caedmon was the first great devotional poet to write in English. [No comma needed; each adjective defines the group of words that follows it.]

With Numerals, Names, and Repeated Words. A comma should be placed between unrelated numerals, though rewriting is often a better way to deal with such situations. A comma should also be used when confusion would result from the juxtaposition of two unrelated proper names or when a word is juxtaposed to itself.

In August 1670, 450 people heard William Penn preach in front of his padlocked church. [Original]

In August 1670, William Penn preached to 450 people in front of his padlocked church. [Rewritten]

For Izaak Walton, Donne was the premier poet of his day.

His theology echoed Pope's opinion that whatever is, is right.

To Show Ellipsis. In some cases a comma may signal that a word or phrase has been dropped. If the meaning is clear without it, the comma is not needed.

Newman contributed twenty-four tracts to the series; Keble, nine; and Pusey, four.

We know the Corinthians received at least two letters from Paul, and the Ephesians one.

With Quotations and Sayings. Commas may be used to set off quotations or sayings, whether or not quotation marks are used. If the quotation is long or formal, a colon should be used instead of a comma. When the entire quotation is used as though it were a noun (for instance, as a subject of a sentence or as a predicate nominative), it should not be set off by commas.

> Meister Eckhart said, "The eye with which I see God is the very same eye with which God sees me." [Direct quotation, from *Sermons and Treatises*]
>
> The minister was fond of the old saw, Too heavenly minded to be any earthly good. [Indirect quotation]
>
> "I forgive you" is a primary assertion of the Christian life. [Quotation is subject of sentence]

With "Oh." Use a comma after *oh* when other words follow it, but not after the vocative O, which is usually only used in direct address (see "*oh, O*"). Phrases such as *oh yes* and *oh no* are so common, particularly in dialogue, that no comma is needed after *oh*.

> Oh, Jerusalem!
> O mighty king!
> "Oh no, I hadn't counted on being asked to give my testimony."

With "Too." Use commas around *too* only when the word is used in an odd or unexpected place in a sentence for rhetorical effect or emphasis. Otherwise, do not use commas around *too* in the middle of a sentence or before *too* at the end of a sentence. (For more detail, see "*too*.")

> Saint Colm too was noted for his love of animals.
> Saint Colm was noted for his love of animals too.
> Saint Colm was noted, too, for his love of animals. [Rhetorical effect]

To Show Disruption in the Flow of Thought. Adverbs, interjections, and other similar words should be set off by commas when they interrupt the flow of thought. Commas are not needed when these words do not disrupt the continuity.

> Margery Kempe, unsurprisingly, was too impulsive to attract disciples. [Disruptive adverb]
>
> The sincerity of Constantine's faith, alas, has often been questioned. [Disruptive interjection]
>
> Cowper eventually contributed to the *Olney Collection*. [The word *eventually* is not disruptive]
>
> "Sinners in the Hands of an Angry God" was indeed Jonathan Edwards's most famous sermon. [The word *indeed* is not disruptive]

With "Jr.," "Sr.," and Numerals after Names. Do not use a comma to separate *Jr., Sr., I, II, III*, and so on from a proper name: ***Martin Luther King Jr., Pope John Paul II, Henry V.***

After the Last Element in a Series. A comma is not needed after the last element of a series with no conjunction: *Pretentiousness, boasting, arrogance are symptoms of pride.* Likewise, a comma is unnecessary after expressions such as *etc.*, *and so on*, or *and so forth* if they are the last element of a series: *Pretentiousness, boasting, arrogance, and so forth are symptoms of pride.*

With Two or More Verbs. Two verbs with the same object should not be separated by commas, though a series of verbs with the same object should be separated by commas, as would a series of nouns. In a sense, this is the "serial comma" applied to verbs: *Jesus touched and healed the man with leprosy*, but *Jesus comforted, healed, and taught many people.*

The Drama Comma. The *drama comma* is used to show a slight dramatic pause, as in: *He saw the gun, and froze.* Many good writers use the device, though it is best used sparingly. This manual discourages its use for two reasons: (1) writers who use this comma tend to overuse it, and it loses its effectiveness when used too often; and (2) most readers will miss the pause completely, and among those who do notice it, many will think it is a mistake. English provides better ways of communicating dramatic pauses, such as an ellipsis (*He saw the gun ... and froze*) or, for more emphatic pauses, an em dash (*He saw the gun—and froze*).

CONCLUSION

A conclusion is usually the first element of a book's back matter (see "BACK MATTER, ELEMENTS OF A BOOK'S") and is the place for the author to summarize the main themes, fill in additional details, and tie up loose ends. It is usually longer than an afterword and more integral to understanding the book's content. It differs from an epilogue in that an epilogue is often more narrative based while a conclusion is more information based. (See also "AFTERWORD" and "EPILOGUE.")

CONCORDANCE

A concordance, which can be either an entire book in itself or a section of a book, alphabetically lists the words used in a given work, along with verse, page, or other references and often a short quotation to show how each word is used in context. The term is commonly applied to Bible concordances, the most famous of which is *A Complete Concordance to the Holy Scriptures* (1737), better known as Cruden's Concordance, though there are many scholarly concordances of literary works (for instance, Mary Cowden Clarke's *Complete Concordance to Shakespeare*, 1844–45) and sacred writings of other traditions (such as Gustave Flugel's *Concordance to the Quran*, 1842). Several types of Bible concordances exist:

analytical concordance—analyzes according to Greek and Hebrew words
compact concordance—abridged, usually in a pocket-size binding
complete concordance—contains many words, but not such common words as articles, prepositions, etc.
concise concordance—abridged for ease of use
condensed concordance—abridged, synonym for *concise concordance*
critical concordance—synonym for *analytical concordance*
exhaustive concordance—unabridged, contains every occurrence of every word and often analyzes them according to related Greek and Hebrew words
handy concordance—abridged, synonym for *compact concordance*
keyword concordance—abridged, using only words of special significance
red-letter concordance—prints in red the words spoken by Jesus
thematic concordance—organizes entries by theme
topical concordance—organizes entries by chief topics, synonymous with *thematic concordance*
unabridged concordance—a complete concordance that contains all words but does not analyze according to Greek and Hebrew words

An entry in a Bible concordance is typically formatted as follows:

Book (Books)

Ecc . . . 12:12 Of making many *b* there is no end.
Da . . . 7:10 and the *b* were opened.
Jn . . . . 21:25 for the *b* that would be written.
Rev . . . 20:12 the throne, and *b* were opened.
20:12 they had done as recorded in the *b*.

CONTENTS PAGE

See "TABLE OF CONTENTS."

CONTRACTIONS

Contractions are acceptable in most writing, especially to preserve an author's voice or intimate tone. Although the admonition to avoid contractions in formal writing is heard less now than it once was, contractions are still used sparingly in formal and academic writing, where they are considered inelegant. The book's tone, style, and genre will dictate the extent to which contractions are appropriate. Memoirs, for instance, in which an author's spoken cadence and voice are particularly colorful, may allow for a heavy use of contractions. Books of theology, by contrast, usually avoid contractions in an effort to elevate the tone and increase the perceived authority of the author's voice, since some readers may perceive contractions as being slangy.

In Quotations. Contractions are always preserved in direct quotation.

In Fiction. The judicious use of contractions is one way of making fictional dialogue more natural. Contractions are also effective in fiction when used as part of a character's thoughts or when a scene is from a particular character's point of view. It is part of "voicing." Using contractions can also be effective for the narrator's voice in fiction writing, depending on the tone the author wants to establish. Authors of Western romances, for instance, often have their stories' narrators use contractions to establish a rustic or rugged tone.

A good fiction writer also knows the trick of when *not* to use contractions. A novelist will sometimes avoid contractions in the speech of characters for whom English is a second language. Even though actual nonnative speakers learn the use of contractions, just that extra trick of avoiding contractions in fictional dialogue can subtly communicate that the character has learned formal English as a foreign language. Avoiding contractions can sometimes make a fictional villain's speech just a little more sinister. A lack of contractions can also quietly suggest that a character is stiff, highly educated, part of the gentry, or even a snob.

Emphasis. Using a full form rather than a contraction can subtly change the emphasis of a sentence. Many readers, for example, would sense a more emphatic negative in the statement *You are not going to the dance* as compared to *You aren't going to the dance.*

Be Careful with "Is." Be careful when contracting *is* with a noun since it can be construed as a possessive. For instance, it's unclear whether *the preacher's calling* means *the preacher is calling* or *the calling of the preacher.*

COPYRIGHT HOLDER AND COPYRIGHT OWNER

Usually, the *copyright holder* is the author or creator of a given work. Such a person (or persons) is sometimes called the *owner of copyright.* Under current law, that person owns the copyright from the instant the work is written or created. This person may then transfer some or all of those rights (to a publisher, for instance, by way of a contract). The person or organization to whom the author or creator has given legal responsibility to reproduce the book and usually to sell other rights (film, serial, subsidiary, and so on) is called the *copyright owner.*

COPYRIGHT NOTICE

A copyright notice is the publisher's and author's legal declaration that they alone have the right to reproduce and sell the book, ebook, or other material in which that notice is given.

The Essentials. A legal copyright notice for books consists of three essential elements, which are usually set immediately after the title of the work:

1. The copyright symbol (©) (often with the word *copyright* or the abbreviation *copyr.*; the symbol or the word may appear alone.)
2. The year of publication
3. The name of the owner of copyright (see "COPYRIGHT HOLDER AND COPYRIGHT OWNER")

For works published after March 1, 1989, a notice of copyright is not required to protect the copyright of the book, though most sources urge its use nonetheless—to make the legal status of the copyright unambiguous. Use of the correct copyright notice will defeat the defense of "innocent infringement," should anyone infringe on the copyright; and without the notice, the publisher may not be able to collect damages from the infringer.

The order of the three elements is not prescribed, though they should be juxtaposed in some fashion. The most common order is *copyright / year / by copyright owner*:

Through the Year with Jimmy Carter
Copyright © 2011 by Jimmy Carter

Although using both the word *Copyright* and the © symbol together is not required (either one alone is sufficient), it is often done as a convention.

Name of Copyright Holder. A book's contract should specify the name of the copyright holder to be used in the copyright notice. Usually, the author's full legal name is used. Abbreviations of names (*Wm.* for William, for example) are acceptable as long as their meaning is unambiguous. In one case, an author named Frederick abbreviated his name as *Fr.* to mislead people into thinking he was a Catholic monk. Pen names are acceptable. If the owner of the copyright is commonly known by a pseudonym, single name, or single initial, then that is acceptable as well.

Incorrect Copyright Notice. If one of the three essential elements is missing from the copyright notice, the notice could be considered legally invalid and a company lawyer should be contacted. Under the current copyright laws, this usually does not mean the copyright is forfeited, but it can result in some limitations to certain privileges or protections. If a single element is merely inaccurate, then the copyright is still valid, and most privileges and protections are not affected. A copyright attorney should be consulted nonetheless, and the correction made in later editions. If the name of the copyright holder is misspelled or wrongly given, then it should be corrected in the next printing. This is not usually a serious problem, though again, an attorney should be consulted. If the wrong year of publication is given, it is usually not a serious problem if the date is off by only one year before or after the actual date of publication. The publisher should be sure to correct the error when applying for copyright registration after publication. If the date in the notice is two or more years before or after the actual publication date, then the law treats the entire notice as omitted, and the publisher's lawyers should be contacted.

Placement. While the Copyright Act of 1976 does not insist that the copyright notice be placed on the copyright page, most publishers still do it since it is the most convenient and expected place. The law states that the copyright notice should be placed in such a way so as to be "perceived visually" on all copies of the work reproduced. This may seem obvious, but it is stated to cover certain ambiguities, such as unreadable material on ebook, download, or other electronic media. A mechanical aid to visual perception may be assumed, such as a projector, device or computer screen, or disc player. In the case of DVD, Blu-ray Disc, and CD-ROM, the copyright notice must be printed on the object itself or on its accompanying case as long as the case is not meant to be thrown away. A performance copyright should be obtained for any sound recordings contained therein.

Copyright Dates for New Editions. Whenever a new edition of a book contains any amount of fresh material not covered under the copyright for the previous edition, the entire copyright should be renewed and a new date provided in the copyright line. In that case, both the original copyright date and the new one should appear in the copyright notice. Technically, the first date need not be shown, but for a number of reasons it is advisable to provide it. When more than one year is given in the copyright notice, the lowest number is given first.

If the owner of the copyright has changed, then both the old and new dates—along with the names of the old and new owners—should be shown. This is needful especially when an author dies and the copyright is transferred to a surviving spouse, family member, or estate.

Compilations. Copyright experts recommend that in cases in which contributors to a compilation or an anthology retain the copyrights to their own works, the safest procedure is for each individual copyright holder to be listed in addition to the compiler's collective copyright for the whole work. This can be done on the copyright page, though it may mean providing additional pages at the front or back of the book to list all the copyrights for the individual pieces.

Library of Congress. The Library of Congress provides complete information about the legal registering of copyrights at http://www.copyright.gov/. Every publisher should have at least one person on their staff who is thoroughly familiar with the information at that website and has registered the company with the Electronic Copyright Office (eCO). For copyright information call the Copyright Public Information Office at 202-707-3000 or toll free at 1-877-476-0778. The address is: Library of Congress, Copyright Office, 101 Independence Avenue SE, Washington, DC 20559. For a list of frequently asked questions, check online at http://copyright.gov/help/faq/.

COPYRIGHT PAGE

The copyright page is prepared by the publisher, and its primary purpose is to display the legal copyright notice for the book. (See "COPYRIGHT NOTICE" for the essential elements of that notice.) An all-rights-reserved notice and a declaration of the country in which the book was printed should also appear on the page. (See "ALL-RIGHTS-RESERVED NOTICE" and "COUNTRY-OF-PRINTING NOTICE.") At the publisher's discretion, the copyright page may include any of the following elements:

- the International Standard Book Number (ISBN) (see "INTERNATIONAL STANDARD BOOK NUMBER [ISBN]"), which references a coding system used worldwide
- a brief printing and publishing history of the volume
- the publisher's address (see "ADDRESSES OF PUBLISHER, MAILING AND WEB")
- the Library of Congress Cataloging-in-Publication Data (see "CATALOGING-IN-PUBLICATION DATA [CIP]"), which is used for library classification
- any credits and permissions
- disclaimers (see "DISCLAIMER") and other brief notes from the editor or author
- a warning notice (see "WARNING NOTICE")
- a permission-to-copy notice (see "PERMISSION-TO-COPY NOTICE")
- a "printer's line," including edition, printer information, and printing reference numbers
- and any other information deemed important by the publisher

A copyright page is partially a legal notice and partially a notification to specialized users of the book regarding the book's edition and print run, certain exceptions to copyright, disclaimers, permissions and credits, and so on. It should not be used as a consumer page, and the publisher should assume the average reader will not look at the copyright page at all. Advertising and marketing copy and any information the reader needs to fully appreciate the book should be placed elsewhere.

One option for a copyright page is a listing (with publishing info) of the Bible versions quoted in the book. (See "QUOTING THE BIBLE.") If the book quotes many versions—more than there would be room for on the page—the main (default) version could be cited on the copyright page and the other versions listed on a separate page (in either the front matter or the rear matter) with a line on the copyright page indicating where to find that list.

Placement. Customarily, the copyright page is placed on the verso of the title page. Occasionally, in some art books, gift books, children's picture books, or other books in which graphic elements are dominant, the copyright page may be placed at the back of the book. The functional purpose is to make the page easy to find. The law states it must provide the reader with "reasonable notice" of copyright.

Page-a-day calendars usually place the copyright page at the very end of the calendar, so the page won't be thrown away at the beginning of the year. This provides the reader with "reasonable notice" and ensures the copyright notice may be "visually perceived" for the maximum amount of time.

Design. Most often the copyright page is set in the same font as the book's text and one font size smaller. Some designers prefer to set the entire copyright page in italic to give the page a lighter appearance.

COUNTING PAGES

See "PAGES, COUNTING."

COUNTRY-OF-PRINTING NOTICE

For all books printed in the US, the copyright page should carry the notice: "Printed in the United States of America." Anytime a book is printed in a foreign country (whether by a foreign printer or by a foreign division of a US printer), the name of that country should be specified in the country-of-printing notice. Even if only the dust jacket of a domestically printed book were to be printed in a foreign country, a notice of the country of printing should appear on the dust jacket. This notice is provided on printed material for customs reasons, and failure to do so can cause shipments of books or other materials to be impounded by the US Customs Service.

COVER COPY

A book's cover serves as a billboard for the contents. It is designed to draw attention, and any words on the cover should serve as a virtual sales pitch for the book. The copywriter is allowed a great deal of freedom in the way that pitch is expressed. The writer should be free to break rules of grammar and punctuation—call it "copywriter's license"—when necessary. For example, serial commas may be dropped, numerals may be used in text to facilitate rapid communication, and sentence fragments are common.

Titling. Book designers have the freedom to play with the style of the book's title on the cover. For instance, a subtitle does not need to be preceded by a colon even though a colon appears on the copyright or title page. The title may be set in all caps or all lowercase letters, some words may be emphasized in unusual ways, punctuation may be tampered with, an ampersand may replace the word *and*, and so on.

(See also "ENDORSEMENTS.")

DASH

Five marks are referred to as *dashes*: the hyphen (-), the en dash (–), the em dash (—), the two-em dash (——), and the three-em dash (———). After the hyphen, the em dash is the most frequently used and the one most commonly referred to as a *dash.* (For more detail, see "EM DASH," which also covers two- and three-em dashes, "EN DASH," "HYPHEN," and "HYPHENATION.") Most word-processing programs have an autoformatting feature that converts two hyphens to an em dash and a hyphen between two numbers to an en dash, but some authors prefer to use hyphens only. The following shortcuts can be used:

Kind of Dash	Manuscript	Typeset
hyphen	-	-
en dash	-	–
one-em dash	--	—
two-em dash	----	——
three-em dash	------	———

DATES

See "TIMES AND DATES."

DEAD COPY, LIVE COPY

In publishing, *dead copy*, sometimes called *fouls*, is any set of galleys marked up by an author, editor, or proofreader. *Live copy* is the unmarked, corrected version. Editors and proofreaders check the dead copy to verify that all the corrections have been made on the live copy.

DEATH DAGGER

An elegant old printing custom is to place a dagger symbol (†), representing Christ's cross, immediately before or after a recently deceased person's name. Though rarely seen now, the *death dagger* still occasionally shows up in some book dedications or acknowledgments, indicating that the person has died during the production of the book itself or relatively recently. (See also "*late, the [for deceased person]*.")

DEDICATION

An author may dedicate a work to one or more people and include a short sentiment by way of appreciation. The dedication has roots in the era when authors wrote effusive acknowledgments to the patrons who financed their work, though such effusiveness should be avoided today. A dedication is only likely to be read if it is short, simple, and heartfelt.

Placement. A dedication most often appears on the recto page immediately after the copyright page and before the table of contents and any other introductory material. It is customarily centered line-for-line and set a little above the center of the page, unless the page designer opts for an alternate setting. When space is scarce, a dedication may be placed on a convenient verso elsewhere in the front matter or at the top of the copyright page as long as sufficient space is available to distinguish it from the rest of the copy on that page.

Elements and Style. The words *dedication* or *dedicated to* should not be used, nor should the word *Dedication* be used as a heading. The page itself should not bear a folio number or a running head, and it should not be listed in the table of contents. Usually, no period is used at the end of a dedication, even if the dedication makes up a complete sentence. If the dedication is made up of two or more sentences, then periods should be used at the end of each sentence.

Coauthored Book. In coauthored books, the lead author's dedication comes first, followed by each coauthor's dedication. Each of those dedications should be followed by a credit line showing that author's name or initials.

DEFINING TERMS

In general, when a short definition of a term or phrase is provided in text, put the word or phrase in italic and the definition in quotation marks. (See also "WORDS AS WORDS.")

By *heterodox* we mean "unorthodox" or "opposed to the norm."

In many parts of the South, *to mash* simply means "to push," as in *to mash the buttons on the phone.*

DEITY PRONOUN, THE

The capitalization of pronouns referring to persons of the Trinity has long been a matter of debate. Should *he* be capitalized when referring to God or Jesus or the Holy Spirit? Impassioned arguments are offered on both sides. Although both the lowercase and capitalized styles have long histories in written English, this manual and others (including *CMoS*,

SBL, and the Catholic News Service's *Stylebook on Religion*) recommend using lowercase pronouns in most trade books and all academic books and references.

Most publishers, religious and general, use the lowercase style in large part to conform to the two most popular versions of the Bible (the best-selling NIV and the historically dominant KJV). It is the style recognized as contemporary by the greatest number of readers and writers both inside and outside the church. Because capitalizing the deity pronoun and some religious terms was common in late nineteenth- and early twentieth-century religious publishing, that style gives a book, at best, a dated, Victorian feel, and at worst, an aura of irrelevance to modern readers.

As an example of how written conventions change, one of the earliest English Bibles, Tyndale's (a major source for the KJV), not only didn't capitalize the deity pronoun but only inconsistently capitalized the word *God* ("… and geve vnto god that which is goddess," Matt. 22:21). Also, neither of the original Bible languages, Hebrew and Greek, distinguishes between capital and lowercase letters the way English does, so there is no appealing to them for typographic authority.

Contrary to popular perception, capitalization is not used in English as a way to confer respect or honor (we capitalize both *God* and *Satan*, *Churchill* and *Hitler* equally), nor does lowercasing convey disrespect (we commonly write *the president* and *the pope* with no disrespect intended). In general our language uses capitalization to distinguish specific things (a man named *Baker*, for instance) from general things (a man who happens to be a *baker* by trade). Jesus is no more specific, in that sense, than Peter, and both can be referred to as *he*.

The capitalized deity pronoun is particularly distracting in fiction because the reader may be confused as to whether the author, the story's narrator, or a fictional character is capitalizing the word. In biblical novels, it seems as odd to have Jesus refer to himself as *Me* and *Myself* as it does to have his enemies refer to him, seemingly reverentially, as *You*. Nearly all the classic biblical novels, such as Thomas B. Costain's *The Silver Chalice* (1952) and Lloyd C. Douglas's *The Robe* (1942), use lowercase pronouns.

Some writers argue that the capitalized style is helpful in avoiding confusion among antecedents in closely written text—for instance, whether Jesus or one of the disciples is being referred to as *he* in a given passage. Even in this case, a careful writer should be able to make the meaning clear without capitalization. After all, the writer should be able to distinguish between the twelve disciples without resorting to typographic tricks. Remember too that many books are available as audio downloads, which cannot distinguish between a capitalized and a lowercase pronoun. Using a capital letter to distinguish among antecedents is irrelevant in an audio format.

Many readers, especially younger ones, do not recognize the reasons for such typographic conventions, and a capitalized deity pronoun may actually cause confusion or be read as emphasis when none is implied.

Finally, an insistence on the capitalized style can introduce unintended political overtones into the writing. When *he* is capitalized for God or Jesus, it can appear to some readers as though the author is emphasizing the exclusive maleness of the deity, in direct response to feminist theologians who argue for the inclusiveness of God. Apart from the merits of either side of that debate, the capitalized deity pronoun may introduce a polemical tone that could detract from the topic.

Is Capitalization Ever Justified? Certainly. For instance, the deity pronoun is justifiably capitalized in books with a deliberately old-fashioned tone or when the author quotes predominantly from a Bible version that uses the capitalized style (such as the NKJV or the NASB). Some daily devotional writers prefer to capitalize the deity pronoun as a way of focusing on the persons of the Trinity. It is not a strategy this manual necessarily endorses, but the author's preference should be considered.

Amish writers and many of those in the Amish communities traditionally use the capitalized deity pronoun. This is partly because of the German origins of much of their literature, which, until the German spelling reforms of 1996, consistently stressed the use of the capitalized forms.

Also, *The U.S. Government Printing Office Style Manual* (2000) recommends capitalizing the deity pronoun (except for *who*, *whom*, and *whose*) in all government documents and publications—largely to avoid offense.

Mixed Style. It is possible to mix styles within one book as long as it is done with enough care so as not to confuse the reader. For instance, in his classic novel *Ben-Hur* (1880), Lew Wallace seems to use the lowercase style when referring to Jesus as a person in the narrative passages and reserves the capitalized style for formal references to the promised biblical Messiah (such as when the angels speak to the shepherds before the nativity). Some writers use the capitalized style only in formal prayers or when addressing God directly. In *Paradise Lost*, for instance, Milton lowercased the deity pronoun, though he occasionally capitalized the second-person pronoun *You* as part of a formal invocation when addressing God. In all cases, the mixing of styles should be a device for enhancing the reader's experience of the content.

Author Preference. An author should discuss any strong preference for capitalization with the editor, and that preference should be specified on a style sheet so others involved in the project will be informed.

Who, Whom, and Whose. Even when the deity pronouns are capitalized in a work, the words *who*, *whom*, and *whose* should not be.

You. The second person is most often lowercase when addressing persons of the Trinity. It may be capitalized when appropriate in prayers, especially in devotional contexts.

In Quotations. While the deity pronoun may be lowercase in any given publication, the capitalized pronoun should be retained in any quotations from other sources that capitalize it. Likewise, if the deity pronoun is capitalized in a publication, the lowercase should be retained in all quotes where the lowercase style is found in the original source. In other words, quotations should always retain the style of the original as a matter of accuracy. (See "QUOTING THE BIBLE.")

Bibles That Capitalize the Deity Pronoun. Most publishers of copyrighted Bibles do not grant permission to quote from their Bibles if the deity-pronoun style in those quotations is going to be changed. If it is essential to quote from a Bible that capitalizes the deity pronouns, the most familiar options are the Holman Christian Standard Bible (HCSB), the New American Standard Bible (NASB), and the New King James Version (NKJV), though be aware that each of those Bibles have the Pharisees and other enemies of Jesus referring to him, with seeming reverence, as *Him* and *You*, which may seem peculiar to many readers.

Another alternative is to capitalize the deity pronouns in any public-domain version of the Bible, such as the KJV, providing a note on the copyright page that explains this has been done. The practice is usually frowned upon for common use, but it can be done on those rare occasions when it is essential to maintain a consistent style of capitalization.

DEMONYMS

See "STATE AND PROVINCIAL RESIDENT NAMES."

DEVOTIONAL BOOKS

At one time, most books of religious reflection were termed *devotional books* because they were meant to be read in conjunction with a believer's devotions, or times of prayer. But since the Victorian era, the term *devotional book*, or just *devotional*, has come to mean a specific subgenre of religious literature that contains daily readings or reflections. The modern devotional of daily readings harks back to the medieval book of hours, which gathered prayers to be recited at specific hours of the day (see "HOURS, CANONICAL"). The earliest known daily devotional book is the

Feliré, written in Gaelic verse in the early ninth century by an Irish monk known as Saint Óengus the Culdee.

Daily devotional readers (books in which one entry is meant to be read each day over the course of a week, month, or year) are sometimes referred to in the general trade as *metered readers*. Many examples of nonreligious devotional, or metered, readers can be cited, such as *The Intellectual Devotional* (New York: Rodale, 2006).

Elements. The conventional, though by no means mandatory, elements of a Christian daily devotional reading are (1) a Bible verse; (2) a meditation, which may or may not relate to the Bible verse; and (3) a closing prayer, which incorporates some theme of the verse or meditation. Other elements can include (1) a title; (2) an epigraph or quote from another author; (3) an assigned reading, in which the reader is directed to read a portion from some other book or from the Bible; (4) a directed activity, in which the author suggests to the reader an activity that would put the message into practice; and (5) a blank or rule-lined workbook section, in which the reader is encouraged to write his or her responses and reflections in the book itself.

Types of Devotionals. The following are the most common types of devotionals, though they may be creatively adapted into any number of forms:

Type of Devotional	Description
daily devotional	This term most often refers to a complete year's worth of daily readings—usually 366 (accounting for February 29 in leap years). This is the most common and successful type of devotional book.
classics devotional	A book of daily readings from classic Christian authors.
devotional journal	A devotional in which rule lines are provided for readers to write out their own thoughts.
devotional reader	An anthology of selected and edited readings from one or more authors and formatted to be read devotionally each day.
seasonal devotional	Contains readings for each day of a holy season, usually Lent or Advent.
three-month devotional	Usually rounded off to 90 daily readings.
two-month devotional	Usually rounded off to 60 daily readings.
one-month devotional	Usually rounded off to 30 daily readings.
devotional Bible	The text of the Bible divided into daily readings or expanded with daily reflections on the Bible text; most often 366 readings.

Format and Design. Printed devotional books are often trimmed smaller than the average book to convey a feeling of intimacy or worshipfulness. The challenge is that daily devotionals can contain as many as 366 readings, which can result in extremely thick books. Smaller, more condensed fonts and thinner papers like those used for Bibles are sometimes used, and the margins around the text area are often reduced.

Since devotional books are sipped rather than drunk in long draughts, their page design allows for considerable graphic flourish—which would prove too distracting in other kinds of books. Such flourishes can include decorative borders, screened backdrops, dingbats, florets, or illustrations.

Year-long devotionals may dispense with conventional page numbers (folios) in favor of simply numbering the readings themselves from 1 through 366. All index references would be to the number of the particular reading rather than to the page number. To save space, running heads are often dispensed with.

Indexes. Many devotional books include a Scripture index, an author index (in a compilation), a topical index, or a subject index, depending on the uses to which the book might be put. (See "INDEXES.")

365 or 366. If a specific day of the year is listed with each reading (most commonly, January 1 through December 31), then 366 readings should be provided to account for February 29 of leap years. Otherwise, if the year's worth of readings are not tied to specific month-and-day dates, either 365 or 366 readings can be given.

DEVOTIONAL CAPS

The trend in eighteenth- and nineteenth-century Christian writing was to use capitalization for reverential purposes, so that many attributes and objects associated with the persons of the Trinity were capitalized; for example, *the Body and Blood of Jesus*, *the Indwelling of the Holy Spirit*, *the Omnipotence and Omniscience of God*. This practice lent a certain piety to the prose but is discouraged in contemporary writing because readers (1) are likely to find it odd or antiquated, (2) may mistake such capitalization for emphasis, (3) may not understand why the words are capitalized, and (4) may think such words are meant to be proper names or epithets for specialized concepts. (See more at "CAPITALIZATION: GUIDELINES" and "CAPITALIZATION OF BIBLICAL AND RELIGIOUS TERMS.")

DEVOTIONAL CONTEXTS

The term *devotional contexts* means a style of religious writing, often florid and poetic, meant to inspire the reader with the beauty and profundity of its insights about the nature of God and Christ. In this kind of literature, some standard style guidelines may be modified to achieve the devotional purpose. For instance, the deity pronoun can be capitalized; other words, conventionally lowercase, may be capitalized (such as *the Holy Name of Jesus* or *His Power and His Glory*); and a certain poetic license can be granted. (See "DEVOTIONAL CAPS.") Be sensitive to the intended readership and the effect such alternate styling might have; for instance, will such styles confuse younger readers or appear too breathlessly sentimental?

DIACRITICAL MARKS (ACCENTS)

Commonly referred to as *accents*, these typographic aids are more accurately called *diacritical marks*, or *diacritics*. Strictly speaking, an accent is used to indicate a stressed (accented) syllable within a multisyllabic word, and English uses only two: the acute accent (´) and the grave accent (`).

Some foreign languages use acute and grave accent marks, as well as a host of others, to show a change in the pronunciation of a letter or letters, rather than a stressed syllable. In those cases, the mark is called a *diacritical mark* (though some languages also use true accent marks as well). English commonly uses only two diacritical marks to aid in pronunciation—the breve (˘) for short vowels and the macron (¯) for long vowels—though they are only added as an aid to pronunciation in phonetic spellings and not as an integral part of the word. In English, those are referred to as *pronunciation marks*.

Many accents and diacritical marks made their way into English by being attached to words borrowed from other languages. Some of the more common diacritics are:

Mark	Name	Examples and Notes
´	acute	canapé, Cézanne, cliché, entrée, fiancée, résumé, José, auto-da-fé
˘	breve	(to show short vowels)
¸	cedilla	façade, garçon, François, Niçoise, français
^	circumflex	château, coup de grâce, fête, pâté, Rhône, papier-mâché
`	grave	Thomas à Kempis, à la carte, voilà, crèche, pietà
ˇ	haèek	(a Czech word pronounced HA-check; sometimes called an *inverted circumflex*)
¯	macron	(to show long vowels)

ʿ	okina, hamzah . . .	(to show glottal stop in Hawaiian, and sometimes used in Arabic)
~	tilde	mañana, señor, señora, São Paulo
¨	umlaut . . . . [diaeresis, trema, . zweipunct].	Brontë, Köln, Danaë, Möbius strip (the Scandinavians use a ° symbol instead of an umlaut)

Vanishing Accents. Over time, as foreign words become more familiar to English speakers, any accompanying diacritical marks tend to vanish. We no longer see *denouement* and *decoupage* spelled *dénouement* and *découpage*, though they were commonly spelled that way fifty years ago. No strict rule exists for when to retain or drop the diacritics in any given word. *Webster*, for instance, lists as its first options *facade*, *naive*, *senor* (as well as *senora* and *senorita*), though they still keep the accents in such words as *café*, *cliché*, *fiancé*, and *sauté* (although *cafe* and *cliche* are showing up more frequently in both print and electronic formats). The umlaut, once common in such words as *coöperation*, *reëlect*, and *naïve*, is seldom used.

Vanishing accents pose a problem for editors and proofreaders. Many electronic spell-checkers and autoformat programs automatically convert *facade* to *façade* and *naive* to *naïve*, after which a conscientious proofreader, to keep pace with *Webster*, will change them back, and a battle of correction and countercorrection ensues.

This manual recommends that whenever *Webster* lists both forms (for instance, "*cliché* or *cliche*" and "*naive* or *naïve*"), either form may be considered equally correct as long as each word is spelled consistently throughout the work. In most cases the author's preference should dictate—and the editor should note that preference on the style sheet. This would be an exception to the "first usage rule" for *Webster*.

When the author has no preference, the older forms with diacritical marks may be marginally more appropriate in printed works of a classic or literary nature. By contrast, any work planned for a digital format—which is most works—would probably best be served by minimizing diacritics whenever possible. Some electronic formats do not convert diacritics well.

When to Retain Diacritics. Retain the diacritics and accents in words likely to be perceived by readers as foreign, such as *crème brûlée*, *déjà vu*, *olé*, and *piñata*; in place names like *Córdoba*, *Göttingen*, *Périgord*, and *São Paulo*; and in personal names like *Beyoncé*, *Brontë*, *Karel Èapek*, *Salvador Dalí*, and *Molière*. Be sure to retain the marks whenever the unaccented form might be confused with another word, such as *exposé*, *maté*, *pâté*, or *résumé* (or *resumé*). Also retain all diacritics, when present, in foreign words not listed in *Webster* or so uncommon as to necessitate being set in italic. (See "ITALIC," section on "*Foreign Words and Phrases.*")

Alternate Forms. In many cases, alternate Anglicized forms exist that eliminate the diacritics, such as *Cologne* in place of *Köln*, or *George Mueller* in place of *George Müller* (though see "PERSONAL NAMES, COMMONLY MISSPELLED"). In each case the author and editor should decide which form would be more readily understood by the book's readers. The Anglicized forms, for instance, may be preferred by readers of web copy, while the diacritic forms may be more appropriate for a literary readership.

In Hymns, Plays, and Poetry. Occasionally in hymnody, theater scripts, and poetry, a grave accent is used to highlight unexpected syllabification or an unusually stressed syllable: as in the word *blessèd*. Some actors' editions of early English plays, such as Shakespeare's, use this device (not found in the original editions) to alert the actor to the correct pronunciation. Historically, some poets too have used accents to mark syllables for proper scansion or rhyme. These accents should always be retained in direct quotation; for instance, the grave accent in this quote from Francis Thompson's "Hound of Heaven":

> For, though I knew His love Who followèd,
> Yet was I sore adread
> Lest, having Him, I must have naught beside.

Poet-priest Gerard Manly Hopkins often used the acute accent to show a stressed beat within a line of his "sprung rhythm." Either one or more syllables within a word might be stressed or the entire word itself.

> Márgarét, áre you gríeving
> Over Goldengrove unleaving?
> Leáves, líke the things of man, you
> With your fresh thoughts care for, can you?
> ("*Spring and Fall: To a Young Child*")

For Accented Syllables. An acute accent is sometimes added in an explanatory reference or a pronunciation guide to show which syllable of a word should be emphasized when spoken. Often the syllables are separated by hyphens or even spelled phonetically as an aid to pronunciation: *An-ax-á-go-ras*, *Cynewulf (kí-nuh-wolf)*, *Eurípedes*. They are used as aids only and not part of the word itself.

DIALOGUE, FICTIONAL

For miscellaneous advice on techniques and styles for fictional dialogue, see:

"DIALOGUE, INTERRUPTED"
"DIALOGUE, SAYING WORDS SLOWLY IN"

"DIALOGUE SLANG"
"DISEMBODIED VOICES, CONVEYING IN DIALOGUE"
"INTERJECTIONS OF EXPRESSION"
"*try to, try and*"

DIALOGUE, INTERRUPTED

The interruption of dialogue in fiction (and in some nonfiction) is customarily conveyed in one of two ways. First, if the speaker is interrupted by an action or by another character's speaking, and the speaker does not continue, a single em dash is used inside the closing quotation mark:

> "What I think is—"
> "No one asked you what you think!"

Second, if an action intervenes within or is simultaneous with a character's speaking, a pair of em dashes set around the intervening or simultaneous action is used. Note that both em dashes are set outside the quotation marks. (See also "EM DASH," section on "*To Show When an Action Interrupts Dialogue*.")

> "I suspect someone in this very room"—suddenly the sound of nervous shuffling could be heard—"committed the crime."

Do not use suspension points (sometimes called *ellipses*) to convey interrupted speech. Reserve suspension points to convey hesitant speech or the trailing off of thought. (See "SUSPENSION POINTS.")

DIALOGUE, SAYING WORDS SLOWLY IN

When a writer needs to convey the idea that a speaker is saying something slowly, the best option is to use an appropriate adverb with the said reference: *"Keep your calm," he mouthed slowly over the traffic noise.* Another less attractive option, though popular with some writers, is to use hyphens between the letters: *"Hey," he yelled over the roar of the engine, "You've got to k-e-e-p c-a-l-m!"* (Contrast this with "SPELLING OUT WORDS IN TEXT," in which case all caps are used with hyphens.) Like so many typographic solutions to problems, the hyphens between the letters may cause the reader to think, "What's going on here?" Although the adverb solution seems less likely to break the spell of the fiction, it is a question that can only be answered by an author and an editor.

DIALOGUE SLANG

A common form of slang in fictional dialogue is to drop the final *g* in words ending with *-ing* (such as *goin'*, *waitin'*, *changin'*), a device that should be used sparingly and restricted to characters for whom colloquial or slangy speech is appropriate. The words in the following list, all of which are examples of what linguists call "relaxed pronunciation," are also surprisingly common in fictional dialogue, but since most are considered substandard, they sometimes do not appear in dictionaries. This list shows their recommended spellings. Use these terms carefully. When overused, they draw attention to themselves. They are unavoidable in many common catchphrases, such as *I'm outta here*, *you betcha*, and the triumphal *gotcha*, a word that has become a noun and an adjective (*a gotcha moment*).

awright = all right
betcha = bet you
can'tcha = can't you
c'mon = come on
coulda = could have
don'tcha = don't you
dunno = don't know
'em = them
getcha = get you
gimme = give me
gonna = going to
gotcha = got you
gotta = got to
howja = how do you
howya = how are you
-in' = -ing (livin', runnin', talkin', etc.)
kinda = kind of
ol' = old
oughta = ought to
outta = out of
shoulda = should have
sorta = sort of
wanna = want to
whaddya = what do you
whatcha = what are you
won'tcha = won't you
woulda = would have
ya = you

DIMENSIONS

See "MEASUREMENTS," section on "*Dimensions*."

DINGBAT

A *dingbat*, also called a *printer's ornament*, is a small character-size image used for some typographic purposes, such as replacing asterisms (see "ASTERISM") in text breaks or adding a simple graphic to a chapter opener or running head. Some common dingbats are: ⇧ ⅄ ▯ ☛. The dingbat is the forerunner of the modern emoji (see "EMOJI"), but because of the dingbat's typographic history, it is more appropriate than the emoji in book design. Unicode provides many traditional dingbats under the font names (also called *pi fonts*) of Webdings, Wingdings, and Zapf Dingbats.

DISABILITY DESIGNATIONS

A *disability* is not the same as a *handicap*. A *disability* is an individual's particular condition while a *handicap* is an obstacle in a particular instance. For instance, a person with a hearing impairment may be disabled, but a television program that is not closed-captioned creates a handicap for that person. A person in a wheelchair is presented with a handicap only if his or her workplace is not wheelchair accessible. We are all handicapped when our environment imposes limitations on our abilities. *Handicap*, in this sense, is synonymous with *barrier*.

The "People First" Principle. When writing about people with disabilities, always define them first as people. It is demeaning to use the disability as the primary descriptor for the person. For instance:

Use This	Not This
people with disabilities	the disabled
a child with epilepsy	an epileptic child
a man with a visual impairment	a blind man
a woman with quadriplegia	a quadriplegic
adults with mental challenges	the mentally retarded
a man with schizophrenia	a schizophrenic
a child with a learning disability	a slow learner

Avoid Emotionally Charged Terms and Be Positive Whenever Possible. Avoid the tendency, common to those who do not share a given disability, to assume the person is necessarily suffering because of it. Unless referring to a particular instance of struggle or hardship, avoid falling into locutions such as *a victim of epilepsy*, *suffering from hearing impairment*, *the burden of deafness*, or *afflicted with a learning disability*. Someone who has survived cancer, for instance, is a *cancer survivor*, not a *cancer victim*. Someone with AIDS is *living with AIDS* rather than *suffering with AIDS*.

Avoid using disabilities as metaphors in most cases. To say that *the candidate is a cancer on the party* is not only offensive to those with cancer, but especially offensive if the candidate in question has actually had cancer.

Avoid Antiquated and Insensitive Terms. A whole host of disability terms that were once common are now unacceptable. Such epithets express insensitivity to people with disabilities, such as *backward*, *crazy*, *crippled*, *deaf-mute*, *deformed*, *dwarf*, *hare-lip*, *lame*, *lunatic*, *midget*, *mongoloid*, *paranoid*, *retarded*, and so on. When in doubt, always check a dictionary or an online source for the appropriateness of a given term. Find alternatives.

Research Contexts. At times the writer needs to use a brief descriptor to define a group in terms of their specific challenge, as in a medical or sociological study. Some terms are acceptable in medical contexts, such as *dwarfism* or *mental retardation*, but not outside of those contexts. Whenever possible, use the "people first" principle.

Don't Assume Normality. Avoid using terms like *able-bodied*, *healthy*, *normal*, and *whole* to describe those who do not have a given disability. These terms assume the person with the disability is somehow abnormal or unhealthy. Use such terms as *those without this disability* or *a nondisabled person* instead.

DISCLAIMER

A disclaimer is the publisher or author's declaration, usually placed on a book's copyright page, that while every effort has been made to make the content of the book safe, accurate, and nondefamatory, the publisher and author cannot be held personally liable. It can also be used to assert that characters in a novel are not based on real people or that the publisher does not endorse products, companies, or websites referenced in the book. It can also notify readers when names have been changed in a memoir or other nonfiction narrative. Though a disclaimer is not usually legally protective, it puts readers on notice that they are expected to take responsibility for the way the content of the book is understood and applied.

Placement and Legibility. Unlike most information on the copyright page, which only needs to achieve a basic level of legibility, an important disclaimer should be prominently placed so as to be clearly noticeable. It is often positioned either at the very top or immediately after the copyright notice.

When to Use Disclaimers. Any book that an editor feels requires a special disclaimer involving reader safety or liability should be carefully reviewed by an attorney. While some publishers do not use disclaimers, most experts advise publishers to err on the side of overuse rather than underuse. Some common types of books that benefit from disclaimers are:

Advice books, in which a reader's financial status, reputation, or health could be negatively affected

Cookbooks, in which ingredients might be easily confused or create hazards

Health and fitness books, in which certain exercises, diets, or medications might cause injury

How-to books, in which some procedures might lead to injury

Nonfiction books, in which personal names and details have been changed to protect the privacy of individuals mentioned and to avoid libeling or otherwise identifying those whose stories are told

Novels, in which a person might feel he or she is being personally and identifiably libeled in the guise of a fictional character

Sample Disclaimers

For a Book of Health Advice:

This book contains advice and information relating to health and medicine. It is not intended to replace medical advice and should be used to supplement rather than replace regular care by your physician. Readers are encouraged to consult their physicians with specific questions and concerns.

For a Work of Fiction:

Names, characters, and events in this work of fiction are the products of the author's imagination and used for fictional purposes only. Any resemblance to actual persons, living or dead, or actual events is strictly coincidental.

For a Nonfiction Narrative, Such as a Memoir or Any Book Containing Case Studies:

Some names and identifying details have been changed to protect the privacy of individuals mentioned in this work.

For Nonendorsement of a Product, Company, or Website:

The [products, companies, websites] recommended in this book are offered as a resource to the reader. They are not intended in any way to be or imply an endorsement on the part of the publisher.

The web addresses (URLs) cited in this book are offered solely as a resource to the reader. The citation of these websites does not in any way imply an endorsement on the part of the author(s) or the publisher, nor does the author(s) or publisher vouch for their content for the life of this book.

DISEMBODIED VOICES, CONVEYING IN DIALOGUE

Sometimes in fiction, and occasionally in nonfiction, a character hears God, the conscience, or disembodied spirits, such as angels or demons, speaking, most often as an interior voice, but occasionally as an implied external voice. In such situations, the author and editor should decide on a typographic strategy, and the simpler, the better. Since such a voice is often intuited silently, authors and editors commonly opt to represent the voice as if it were an unspoken thought, that is, in italic without quotation marks. When the author wants to communicate that the voice is heard audibly and perhaps by people other than the primary listener, the words might best be set in quotation marks and, in some cases, italicized as well. This will communicate to the reader that the voice is an actual spoken voice but is also unique, that is to say, supernatural or uncommon. Avoid typographic tricks, such as setting disembodied words in color, in a larger size, or in a different font. Such devices distract from the text and cause confusion. (See also "THOUGHTS.")

DITTO MARK

A *ditto mark* (") shows the repetition of an element from one line of type to the next. In form, its mark is straight, which differs from a quotation mark, which is curved or slanted.

DIVINE OFFICE

See "HOURS, CANONICAL."

DOT

A *dot* is simply a period used in a web address. Technically, it is not a punctuation mark but a character that separates elements in a URL.

At the End of Sentences. Some writers and editors worry that when a web address appears at the end of a sentence in text, the final period might be mistaken as a final dot in the address. Still, most readers will understand the period in its correct context, and most search engines know to ignore a period mistakenly typed at the end of a URL. (See "WEB ADDRESSES [URLS].")

Spelling Out. Spell out *dot* in the term *dot-com* to mean "an online company."

DRAMA COMMA, THE

See "COMMA," section on "*The Drama Comma.*"

DUMMY COPY

When a book is being designed, *dummy copy* is often used in place of the text. This helps those evaluating the design to focus on the visual impact of the page rather than the words themselves. Since books are often designed before the edited and proofread text is available, an earlier, unedited version is sometimes appropriated as dummy copy. Authors shouldn't worry if they see errors in the design samples (sometimes called *castoffs*). The most famous bit of dummy copy is the Latin "Lorem ipsum" quote from Cicero, which begins, "Lorem ipsum dolor sit amet, consectetur adipiscing elit . . ." and has been in use for that purpose since the time of the early printers.

E

ECCLESIAL LATIN PRONUNCIATION

See "PRONUNCIATION GUIDE FOR AUDIO BOOKS," section on "*Ecclesial Latin.*"

E- COMPOUNDS

Insert a hyphen after the *e* (short for "electronic") in most *e-* compounds, such as *e-banking*, *e-card*, *e-church*, *e-commerce*, or *e-trading*. Still, this manual recommends that no hyphen be inserted in at least three of the most common terms: *ebook*, *email*, and *ezine*. (See "*ebook*," "*e-church*," "*email*," and "*ezine*.") The *e-* prefix will most likely vanish as books and ebooks, for instance, are increasingly undifferentiated or as commerce and e-commerce become synonymous.

EDITORS, TEN COMMANDMENTS FOR

Ambrose Bierce defined an editor as "a severely virtuous censor, but so charitable withal that he tolerates the virtues of others and the vices of himself" (*Devil's Dictionary*). With that in mind, here are ten things to keep in mind while editing.

1. *First, Do No Harm.*
2. *Look for Cuts, Additions, and Pathways.* Ask first, "What's extraneous or distracting?" Then ask, "What's missing that would help the reader if it were included?" Then ask, "Is everything presented step-by-step, each point leading to the next?"
3. *Check Your Gut.* If something doesn't feel right, don't move on. It probably won't feel right to the reader either. This covers a wide array of potential problems—from subliminal ethnic stereotyping to blatant misstatements of fact, from faulty arguments to insincerity. Keep in mind that challenging the author on these points helps the author win readers over. Read as if you were the most attentive reader the book will ever have, because you are.
4. *Don't Make Authors Sound Like You.* The goal of editing is to make authors sound more like themselves—and that usually means *not* sounding like you, the editor. The fact that a writer's word choices, syntax, and grammar are different from yours doesn't make them wrong. Forget about how you, as editor, would phrase something; focus on how the writer could phrase it better. It is a fine line sometimes, but know which side you're on.

5. *Don't Give in to Legalism.* English is a riotously flexible language, big enough to accommodate inconsistencies, optional spellings, and alternate usages while still communicating clearly. While consistent rules of grammar, spelling, and style make life easier for writers and editors as well as readers, they are *not* engraved in stone. Avoid the temptation to apply the same measure to all books and all authors. Readership, tone, formality/informality, author preference, cadence, and voice allow for wide variation. Many rules of grammar, spelling, and usage may be broken when there's a compelling reason to do so. (Ask E. E. Cummings and James Joyce.)
6. *Don't Make Fictional Characters Talk Like English Professors (Unless They Are).* Proofreaders and editors alike have a tendency to correct the grammar in fictional dialogue. Resist the temptation. Most people speak ungrammatically. They split infinitives, end sentences with prepositions, use *who* instead of *whom*, mix up *like* and *as*, use lots of contractions, say things like "between you and I," and so on. Even allow for creative misspelling (in slang and dialect, for instance), as long as it will be clear that the misspelling is intentional. Allow colloquial speech to characterize each character in a subtle way, though avoid anything so self-conscious it might "break the spell" of the narrative.
7. *Remember, It's the Author's Book.* Authors and editors don't always agree. On issues that are not likely to cause serious problems for the reader, the editor should tactfully present the reason for the publisher's viewpoint but be willing to let the author have the last word. On matters that *are* likely to cause serious problems, the editor should tactfully present the publisher's viewpoint, listen seriously to the author's counterarguments, then present counterarguments in return. If the author is still not convinced, the publisher can either decide not to publish the book (if the issue is serious enough) or let the author have his or her way. In the end, it is the author's book, which the publisher was willing to contract in the first place.
8. *Double-Check Names and Facts.* A copyeditor should always pause whenever there's a reference to a date, fact, source, or name that can be easily checked online or with a handy reference. Is it *Gutenburg* or *Gutenberg*? When did the Spanish-American War end? Was Franklin Delano Roosevelt the cousin or nephew of Theodore Roosevelt? (The answers are *Gutenberg*; the Spanish-American War began *and* ended in 1898; and the two Roosevelts were actually fifth cousins.)

9. *Always Speak Truth.* The editor, as middle-person between the author and the publisher, is often tempted to fudge the truth when speaking to the author ("Yes, I'm sure your book will be out on time") or to the publisher ("I'm sure the author will be able to get an endorsement from the pope"). White lies, as in all areas of life, catch up to you sooner than later, and it is best to confront problems early and honestly, even if the truth upsets you, the author, the publisher, or all three.
10. *Relationships Come First.* Authors are vulnerable beings and should be treated like people, not projects. Always couch your criticisms and suggestions in positive, honest, encouraging language. Make at least one unreservedly positive comment for every two points of criticism. Authors are also lonely people, so communicate with them at every opportunity. To see how two of the most brilliant editors of the twentieth century cultivated their author relationships, read Leonard S. Marcus's *Dear Genius: The Letters of Ursula Nordstrom* and John Hall Wheelock's *Editor to Author: The Letters of Maxwell Perkins.* They should be on every editor's shelf.

ELLIPSIS

An ellipsis (. . .) is used to indicate that words within a sentence—usually within a quotation—have been deliberately omitted. (The same three-dot character, though called a *suspension point*, is used to indicate a trailing off of or hesitancy in thought; see "SUSPENSION POINT.")

Punctuation with. If the statement preceding the ellipsis forms a complete sentence, insert a period before the ellipsis (with no intervening space), even if such a period is absent in the original quotation. If the preceding statement is fragmentary, allow the ellipsis to stand alone with a word space on either side. Include all other punctuation from the original quotation as appropriate. Adjacent punctuation marks are set solid with the ellipsis.

"The more often he feels without acting . . . the less he will be able to feel," wrote Screwtape to Wormwood. [Words omitted within the quotation, which is from C. S. Lewis, *Screwtape Letters*]

Job focuses on God, not on God's questions. He shows this by beginning his answer by saying, "I know that you . . ." (Job 42:2). [Incomplete sentence with no period]

"I am cold and weary, ink is bad. . . . The day is dark." [Omission between complete sentences]

"I have no drinking cup or goblet other than my shoe! . . ." [Exclamation point with ellipsis]

"But now, Lord, what do I look for?... Do not make me the scorn of fools" (Ps. 39:7–8). [Question mark with ellipsis]

"For he spoke,... he commanded, and it stood firm" (Ps. 33:9). [Comma with ellipsis]

Split over Line. Most typographers prefer to set an ellipsis at the end of a typeset line rather than the beginning of the next, but it is acceptable at the beginning if there is no alternative. Never allow an ellipsis to stand on a line by itself at the end of a paragraph.

Before or After Bible Quotations. Unless the context demands it (usually with a sentence fragment), do not place an ellipsis before or after a verse or a portion of a Bible verse. Introductory words like *and*, *for*, *but*, *verily*, or *therefore* may be omitted from the beginning of a Bible verse without inserting ellipsis points.

"God so loved the world that he gave his one and only Son" (John 3:16). [The word *For* has been omitted without using an ellipsis.]

EM DASH

An em dash (—) is often the same width as a font's uppercase letter *M*, though this varies. It is the mark usually meant by the word *dash*. Use it sparingly in the course of a manuscript, and do not allow more than two in a single sentence. The em dash serves several useful functions:

To Signal a Sharp Break in Continuity. An em dash can signal an abrupt shift in the continuity of a sentence or a thought, a strongly rhetorical turn of phrase, or an ironic or humorous contrast.

Nothing in this world is to be taken seriously—nothing except the salvation of a soul. (Bishop Fulton Sheen)

Feel for others—in your pocket. (C. H. Spurgeon)

I feel a very unusual sensation—if it is not indigestion, I think it must be gratitude. (Benjamin Disraeli)

To Add Immediacy to Dialogue. Broken, hesitating, or interrupted dialogue can be shown with an em dash, though an en dash is used to show stuttering.

"I can't—don't even ask—swear such an oath!" [Em dash]

"What was—" Just then, a peal of thunder shook the walls. [Em dash]

"I s–see. B–but why?" asked Brother Juniper. [En dash for stuttering]

To Show When an Action Interrupts Dialogue. Use an em dash to show that an action has interrupted a spoken sentence. In accord with *CMoS*, place the dashes around the narrated action, not inside the quotation marks themselves.

"And now it's time to remember"—he paused to choke back his emotion—"the kindhearted child who sacrificed so much."

To Serve as a Pointer. Like a colon, an em dash may be used as a kind of pointer to direct the reader to something that follows an introductory phrase, but use it only when a special emphasis is being placed on the words that follow the dash. In most cases a colon will suffice.

That is what we are here for—to do God's will. (Henry Drummond)

To Show Parenthetical Thought. Em dashes may be used to insert parenthetical matter that carries special emphasis or importance. Commas usually set off parenthetical matter that has a close affinity to the rest of the sentence but does not carry any special emphasis. Use parentheses for less essential matter.

We must become so pure in heart—and it needs much practice—that we shall see God. [From Henry Drummond, *The Ideal Life and Other Unpublished Addresses*, 83; em dashes used for special emphasis]

Mistress Anne Bradstreet—a woman and a Puritan no less—may be regarded as the first major American poet. [Em dashes for important matter]

Helen Waddell, who also wrote *Beasts and Saints* and the novel *Peter Abelard*, is probably best remembered for her translation of *The Desert Fathers*. [Commas for close affinity but no special emphasis]

Erasmus Darwin (the grandfather of Charles) and Lamarck postulated the inheritance of acquired characteristics. [Parentheses for peripherally related matter]

To Show Sources. An em dash can be used before the source or credit line of a quote when that quote is set off from the text, as in an epigraph or block quotation. Note that in these cases the period is used in conjunction with the em dash to avoid misreading.

Alms are but the vehicles of prayer.—John Dryden

To Signal the Summation of a List. When several items are listed and then summarized as a group by a single word in a concluding sentence or clause, an em dash separates the list from the concluding sentence or clause.

Wycliffe, Tyndale, Coverdale—all had a dream of seeing the Bible generally available in English. [*All* is the summarizing word in this case.]

Using with Other Punctuation. The em dash is often used in combination with other punctuation. When a dash concludes a quotation and is immediately followed by a said reference, a comma follows the dash. Often dashes are used in place of commas to introduce a parenthetical idea into a sentence; in these cases a question mark or exclamation point can be used in combination with the dash when appropriate.

> "Mine is comic art—," Flannery O'Connor quipped.
>
> Southwell knew the dangers—who more than he?—of returning to England.

Using at the Ends of Lines. When an em dash falls at the end of a line of type, set it on the right margin rather than allowing it to drop down to the next line (at the left margin) if at all possible. Because an em dash can appear faint in some fonts, it may be mistaken for an indent when set on the left.

Avoid Overusing Em Dashes. Some writers lean heavily on em dashes to give their writing immediacy and excitement, but if used too often, it can prove counterproductive by numbing the reader's attention. Even when not overused, em dashes have a tendency to cause the reader to pause a fraction of a second while reading. Too much of that leads to what one editor calls "stop-and-start" reading, something every author should avoid.

Web Use. Some web-management systems do not have actual em dashes in their fonts. In those cases two unspaced hyphens are used instead.

Two-Em Dash. A two-em dash with word spaces around it suggests that an entire word or name has been omitted from a sentence.

> A certain pastor in the village of⸺was known to have cooperated with the Nazis.

A two-em dash with no spaces around it can signal that a series of letters has been omitted from within a word: *The book was signed* C. W⸺*s [Williams?].*

Three-Em Dash. A three-em dash is usually only used to show that a name is repeated in a bibliography or source list.

> Jansson, Tove. *Comet in Moominland.* London: Ernest Benn, 1951.
>
> ⸻. *The Exploits of Moominpappa.* London: Ernest Benn, 1952.
>
> ⸻. *Finn Family Moomintrool.* London: Ernest Benn, 1950.

EMERGENCY PHONE NUMBERS

See "PHONE NUMBERS IN TEXT (TELEPHONE AND CELL PHONE)," section on "*Emergency 9-1-1.*"

EMOJI

An emoji (from a Japanese word combining *character* and *picture*) is a small, character-size pictographic symbol. Unlike emoticons (see "EMOTICON"), which are constructed from existing keyboard characters, emojis are individually designed illustrations with an extremely wide range of graphic representations. Entire books have been translated using nothing but emojis. The Library of Congress listed its first emoji translation in 2013, Fred Benenson's translation of *Moby Dick*, called *Emoji Dick*. Some traditional dingbats (see "DINGBATS"), like Zapf Dingbats and some Wingdings, are considered the prototypes for emojis but are more appropriate for book-design purposes. The newer, more representational emojis from Japan are largely not useful in print books and are best reserved for social media, blogs, and novelty publishing. (An emoji Bible is in the works.) 😎

EMOTICON

Such popular symbols (constructed out of punctuation marks and other typographic symbols) as :-) and ;-o are common (that is, overused) in online communications but are inappropriate in print books or ebooks, where they simply seem out-of-context at best and baffling at worst. (See also "EMOJI.")

EN DASH

An en dash is used to indicate successive, inclusive numbers, as in dates, page numbers, or Scripture references. An en dash is a visual stand-in for the words *to* or *through*. For example, *1852–53, May–June 1967, pages 29–41, John 4:3–6:2*. (See also "NUMBERS, INCLUSIVE (ELISION)" for guidelines governing elision of numbers.)

With Compound Adjectives. An en dash is also used to replace a hyphen in a compound adjective when one of the adjectives is already hyphenated or made up of two words: *the Norman–Anglo-Saxon church, pre–Civil War era, an Old Testament–New Testament contrast.*

Web Use. On webpages, use a hyphen when an en dash is not available.

The British Dash. In those places where American typography would insert an unspaced em dash in text, UK typography often uses an en dash with word spaces on either side:

> Night is drawing nigh – For all that has been – Thanks! For all that shall be – Yes! (Dag Hammarskjöld)

The advantage of the UK style is that the dashes appear less emphatic and flow more smoothly with the type. In some fonts the em dash is actually lighter in weight than the en, so many typographers complain that the em dash, if used too frequently, can make a page look like Swiss cheese—full of holes! Also, in some fonts, unless the em dash is hair spaced, it can appear to touch the letters on either side of it. Even in American publishing, the British en dash style can be used effectively in books that require a refined appearance, are of a high literary quality, or contain an inordinate number of dashes.

ENDNOTES

See "NOTES."

ENDORSEMENTS

Most books benefit from endorsements, or blurbs, which usually appear on a book's cover. The author and publisher draw up a list of potential endorsers, with the actual letter of solicitation coming from the one who has the best chance of securing a particular endorser. The list should be ambitious but realistic. Some well-known people are asked for endorsements so often that they routinely refuse to provide them unless the author or publisher has a close personal connection. Current members of the federal legislative, judicial, and executive branches of government are usually either barred from or unwilling to provide endorsements. Endorsers don't necessarily have to be well known, but ideally they are people whose opinion is respected in their field and relevant to the subject of the book. (See also "ENDORSERS, TEN COMMANDMENTS FOR.")

Placement. Endorsements are commonly found on the front cover, the back cover or jacket flaps, the first page or pages of the book itself, or in all three places. A front-cover endorsement (usually only one) needs to be catchy and short, and ideally by an endorser who is likely to be recognized by name alone. Just a few words or a single phrase is usually best so as not to clutter the front cover. Endorsements on the back cover or jacket flaps can afford to be longer and more numerous. The endorsers may be somewhat less well known, and their names may be qualified with their professional titles and publications.

Sometimes a publisher will use the first page or two of a book to list endorsements, especially those that did not fit on the cover or flaps. In some cases, these collected endorsements can run to more than two pages, but keep in mind that the prospective reader is unlikely to read so many endorsements. Having eight pages of endorsements at the beginning of a book might be not only counterproductive but immodest as well.

With or Without Quotations Marks. It is never wrong to insert quotation marks around endorsements on the front cover, back cover, or jacket flaps, although such quotation marks are often unnecessary. Some marketing people prefer quotation marks because they give a blurb a sense of urgency, as though the words have just been spoken. Always provide the endorser's byline. Quotation marks are not necessary for endorsements listed on the initial interior pages.

ENDORSERS, TEN COMMANDMENTS FOR

If you are asked to write an endorsement, keep the following things in mind:

1. *Keep It Short.* No more than two or three sentences (fewer than seventy words)—seriously. Anything more than a hundred words feels like a foreword!
2. *Know the Deadline.* If you weren't given one, ask.
3. *Be Pithy.* Be creative, clever, but honest. Think soundbite. Avoid clichés like "if you only read one book this year," "a must-read," and "a clarion call."
4. *Don't Overhype.* There's only one "best book you've ever read," and it's unlikely to be the book you're endorsing. Readers sense when an endorser is promising more than a book can deliver. Fulsome praise is no praise at all.
5. *Sentence Fragments? Okay!* Sentence fragments are integral to the genre. Things like "A novel of grace and beauty!" or "A book for your permanent collection" are fine.
6. *Find a Personal Connection.* It's okay to refer to yourself and how you personally connect with the book. It humanizes the endorsement. But again, keep it short.
7. *Be Specific.* Focus on specifics. "The case studies were enormously helpful" is better than "Good from beginning to end."
8. *Address the Reader.* Think about what is most likely to draw readers to the book, and focus on that. Avoid simply flattering the author.
9. *Allow for Editing and Review.* Let the author and publisher know they are free to shorten or alter the endorsement as needed, though it is fair to ask to be shown any major revisions. Expect small changes in style, such as capitalization or punctuation. If the endorsement is longer than seventy words, expect the publisher to edit it. If the publisher would like to use your endorsement on the front or back cover, expect them to shorten it to just the most memorable words or phrases. Consider it an honor.

10. *Keep Your Byline Short and Modest.* After your name, state your position or job title—but keep it brief. Don't provide a byline that is nearly as long as the endorsement itself! If you are an author, mention either a bestselling book or a recent one, but only one. Focus on the book you're endorsing and not on marketing your own.

ENDSHEET, ENDPAPER

The endsheets, or endpapers, of a hardcover book are part of the binding and hold the interior pages to the cover boards. The loose portion of the endsheet, in both the front and back, is called the *flyleaf* (see "FLYLEAF"), and they are not counted as part of the book's pagination. The endsheets are commonly the same color as the paper stock used in the book, though sometimes heavier in weight, or they may be colored or printed. For instance, fantasy novels frequently display a map of the fantasy world on their endsheets.

EPIGRAPH

An epigraph is a short quotation either at the beginning of a book (*book epigraph*), in which case it is usually set on a page by itself, or at the beginning of a chapter (*chapter epigraph*), where it is usually placed after the chapter title. A book epigraph can have several functions: to make a wry comment on the book's content; to summarize the book's thesis; to identify a recognized authority; to whet the reader's appetite; or, at times, to identify the source quotation from which the title of the book itself is taken. A chapter epigraph is more limited, usually simply glossing the content of the chapter in some way, though by the time the reader has finished the chapter, no doubt should exist in the reader's mind as to the relevance of the epigraph. A good epigraph can intrigue and even mystify, but it should never confuse.

Pitfalls. While the judicious use of epigraphs can enhance a book, some authors use them as a means of appearing more erudite than they are. Readers can usually distinguish between a writer who has actually read Pliny the Younger, for instance, and one who has simply done a Google search of famous quotations. The best epigraphs come from the author's own personal reading.

Style. An epigraph is customarily set in the same type size as the text or one size smaller and often indented from one or both margins. In most instances, do not place quotation marks around an epigraph, though retain any internal quotation marks from the original. When placed on the recto page ahead of the table of contents, which is its customary position, an *epigraph page* should not contain a running head or a folio number. Allow the epigraph to stand alone with only the author or source credited. Unless positioned otherwise by the book's designer, the epigraph itself is usually weighted toward the upper half of the page. Only when space is limited should it be relegated to the copyright page.

Credit Line. For most epigraphs, only the source author's name needs to be given. The title of the source work only needs to be provided if it helps the reader understand the context of the quotation more fully or is essential to the quotation.

Bible Quotes. When quoting a Bible verse as an epigraph, use a title or chapter-and-verse reference as the source. Don't just say "The Bible." Do not use *a*, *b*, *c*, and so on to indicate that only a portion of a verse was used.

Unknown Author. Avoid using the word *anonymous* as an attribution for a quotation whose source is unknown. Rather, credit the quotation honestly by using an applicable line like "source unknown" or "a proverb." With online search engines, there's little excuse for not being able to track down the source of most quotations.

Citations. Always provide a credit line right after the epigraph, but do not provide a source note, either as a footnote or an endnote. Such attributions appear pedantic. A source note is needed only if the quotation is copyrighted (a song or poem, for instance) and the original publisher has required a credit line. A source note may also be provided whenever the author expects the veracity or source of the epigraph to be questioned.

EPILOGUE

An *epilogue* is sometimes synonymous with an *afterword* or a *conclusion*, though it has a slightly more literary tone. In works of fiction, drama, or narrative nonfiction, an epilogue usually summarizes the events that take place after the main action, just as a prologue fills in the narrative before the story begins, and is, in that sense, distinct from both an afterword and a conclusion. Despite its name, an epilogue (from Greek, meaning "speaking after") is not part of a book's back matter but is usually considered the final element of the body. In fiction, an epilogue is usually, though not always, written in the same voice as the main part of the story, that is, in the narrator's or a character's voice rather than the author's. If an epilogue is written in the author's voice, distinct from the narrative voice of the body, it is more likely to be called an *afterword* or, if lengthy, a *conclusion*. (See also "AFTERWORD" and "CONCLUSION"; also contrast with "PROLOGUE.")

ERAS, HISTORICAL

See "MOVEMENTS AND ERAS, HISTORICAL."

ERRATA

Though now uncommon, an *errata slip* or an *errata page* is provided when the publisher feels that certain printing errors warrant being brought to the reader's attention even before those mistakes are corrected in the next printing or if no subsequent printing will take place. This is accomplished by inserting a small slip of paper, bookmark-like, into the front matter of the book, usually immediately following the contents page. In especially large print runs or for especially important books, the slip, or even a full-size errata page, is "tipped in" (glued in). Even though the word *errata* is the Latin plural of the word *erratum* (mistake), it is construed as a singular noun in publishing convention: *An errata is called for*. The notice should be as simple as possible, with the errors given first, followed by the corrections. The italicized words *for* and *read*, along with the page number, are used to indicate the incorrect and corrected versions respectively.

> Page 55, *for* Chuck Berry *read* Wendell Berry

Note that no punctuation is used unless the punctuation is actually part of the corrected copy. In his book *Language on a Leash*, editor and writer Bruce O. Boston defined errata as "flecks of spinach on the flashing editorial smile" (114).

ETHNIC, NATIONAL, AND RACIAL DESIGNATIONS

Only use terms describing ethnic, national, or racial groups when they are relevant. Choose such terms with care, and limit them to those that the groups use to describe themselves. Needless to say, avoid derogatory, vulgar, and slang terms. Also avoid the words *minority* and *minorities* in such phrases as *minority applications*, *minority populations*, or *ethnic minorities* because the terms are dismissive and condescending.

Self-identification. Allowing ethnic, racial, and other communities to define their own terms of reference is a common and accepted practice. Allowing groups to identify themselves is not a matter of political correctness, but a matter of civility. While determining such terms of reference may be difficult when subgroups disagree about the designation, nevertheless, to honor people is to honor their preferred forms of self-reference. For instance, the term *black* is now making a resurgence as a term preferred over *African American*, and such outdated terms as *colored person* or *negro* should be avoided. The same is true for *Latino*, which is preferred over *Hispanic*. Use *Asian* (or name a specific nationality) rather than

Oriental, and recently *American Indian* has come to be slightly preferred over *Native American*. Note that in Canada, the indigenous population is still referred to as *First Nations* or *First Peoples*. But be sensitive to these communities because all such preferences change over time.

Some self-referential terms are only for the use of the groups involved. Canadians may humorously refer to themselves as *Canucks* (which is even the name of one of their hockey teams), but that does not mean that outsiders may use the term unreservedly. Similarly, a rapper using the n-word does not justify its use by nonblacks. Be sensitive. When in doubt, don't use a problematic word at all.

Stereotyping. Avoid designations that involve stereotyping. Some media personalities have lost their jobs because they were too quick to generalize about Jews, blacks, or other groups. There is a gray area of terms that seem considerably less offensive. *Dutch door* is inoffensive (since that style of door originated in the Netherlands), but what about *Dutch-treat*, which implies that Dutch people are particularly stingy? The safest policy is to avoid all such terms, even when common in English, whenever a stereotype is at their heart. Such stereotypes often say more about those using the term than about the group described. For instance, the term *Indian giver* was coined in the 1840s at a time when it was actually the British (in Canada) and US governments rather than the First Nations who were reneging on their treaties.

Specificity. Ethnic, national, and racial designations should be as specific as possible. Even generic terms can have negative connotations in the wrong context. For instance, referring to someone simply as an *Arab* can be read as dismissive in some contexts when it would be more helpful to specify whether that person is *Jordanian*, *Saudi*, *Palestinian*, or so on. To say that American Indians practiced the sun dance is misleading, because relatively few of them did. It is more accurate to say that some Lakota practiced the sun dance.

Hyphenated Forms. Style guides differ on the question of whether to hyphenate compound forms of ethnic, national, and racial designations. Is it *Asian American* or *Asian-American*? *Webster* recommends hyphenating them as compound nouns (*Asian-Americans*) as well as adjectives (*an Asian-American scholar*). This manual follows the recommendation of *CMoS*, which drops the hyphens in both cases. The primary reason is that many people have reacted negatively to what is called the "hyphenated-American syndrome," feeling that the hyphen subtly suggests that these groups are only partially American. Such compounds are so familiar that they are unlikely to result in misreading when the hyphen is dropped.

Black and White. As mentioned elsewhere, the term *black* is now used more often for people of African descent in the US than the formerly predominant *African American*. Lowercase the term *black* unless it is used in phrases like *Black English* and *Black Studies*. Although *white* is also lowercase, both *Black* and *White* are occasionally capitalized in scientific or sociological studies.

People of Color. Use the term *people of color* cautiously. It has recently come to be a way of saying "nonwhite," but that doesn't define who the "whites" or the "nonwhites" are. For instance, many people consider Latinos and Asians to be people of color; others do not. Be precise, and always define terms.

EVENTS IN THE LIFE OF JESUS, LOWERCASING

After the lowercasing of the deity pronoun (see "DEITY PRONOUN, THE"), the lowercasing of words describing major events in Jesus's life is the next most hotly disputed topic in discussions of Christian writing style. For decades, editors have lowercased such words as *the crucifixion, the transfiguration, the ascension, the nativity, the resurrection*, and so on. This is the style used in most Bible translations (NIV, KJV, NRSV, and many others) and is also the style recommended by *SBL* and other style manuals.

Some writers argue that the capitalized forms are needed to distinguish between Christ's resurrection, for instance, and the general resurrection of believers, or between Christ's crucifixion and the crucifixion of common criminals in Jesus's time. But as the previous sentence shows, such distinctions are easily made without the use of capital letters. The article *the* is helpful in identifying those events that specify Jesus: *the crucifixion, the resurrection.*

An insistence on the capitalized forms is often a holdover from older devotional literature, when an overuse of capitals was in vogue for words relating to events and objects in the life of Jesus. When a capitalized style is used, it becomes hard to know where to draw the line. Every event tends to be viewed as special in some way and worthy of capitalization, at times to the point of absurdity: *the Birth of Jesus, the Entry into Jerusalem, the Feeding of the Five Thousand, the Raising of Lazarus*, or even *the Life of Jesus.* Such capitalizing usually does not suggest a more respectful or pious attitude toward the event, but rather a sort of Christian code language that will seem peculiar to those outside the faith. In a time when books are increasingly available as audio downloads, detailed schemes of capitalization for devotional reasons are largely irrelevant anyway.

Although this manual recommends lowercasing the names for the events in the life of Jesus, an exception is made for certain academic books or books of theology in which the author is implying specific, technical theological concepts.

EXCLAMATION POINT

The exclamation point (*!*), or exclamation mark, was developed by early printers as an abbreviation of the Latin *io*, meaning "joy." The character was originally rendered "oI," which was later stylized into the mark we know today. An exclamation point is used after a sentence or a word to express surprise, enthusiasm, astonishment, or special emphasis. Along with the period and the question mark, it is usually considered an "end stop" (a mark that ends a sentence). The use of exclamation points is traditionally minimized in formal writing, since overuse tends to limit the effectiveness of the device. Still, they are useful in fictional dialogue and in colloquial and informal writing.

With the Question Mark. Often an exclamation point is needed in the same place in the sentence that a question mark is needed. Since the stronger of two punctuation marks should be retained, that is usually the exclamation mark.

> Was it Quasimodo who shouted *Sanctuary!* [Question mark not placed at end of sentence]

Spanish Exclamation Points. In Spanish, an inverted exclamation point (*¡*) precedes an emphatic statement while a regular exclamation point (*!*) follows it. Do not reproduce this device when translating Spanish quotations into English, though it may be retained at the author's and editor's discretion when reproducing the quotation in Spanish.

EXPLICIT

Sometimes, at the end of a book, an author provides his or her name and the date of the completion of the writing to give the work a formal sense of closure. Sometimes the author's geographic location at the time of the book's completion is also provided. This is called an *explicit*. The name, date, and location can be set on separate lines or run together at the author and editor's discretion. An explicit is still occasionally used with a work to which the author wishes to lend an air of special dignity or literary significance. It is different from a byline, which appears on a book cover or following a foreword.

EXTRACTS, SETTING OF

See "QUOTATIONS, GENERAL," section on "*Run-in versus Block Quotations.*"

F

FAIR USE

In some limited circumstances, copyright law permits authors to use small amounts of copyrighted material without permission from the copyright owner. The fair use privilege is intended primarily for purposes of criticism, commentary, news reporting, teaching, scholarship, and research. What is commonly called "fair use" is not a legal guideline, but rather a defense used in court when a publisher or author is accused of plagiarism (see "PLAGIARISM"), so few rules govern its application, since each instance has its own peculiar set of facts that must be weighed. Such a determination takes into account the following factors:

1. The length of the quoted passage in relation to the length of the copyrighted work from which it is taken (not in relation to the work in which it is used by the borrowing author).
2. The qualitative significance of the passage in relation to the copyrighted work as a whole; that is, is the passage the "heart" of the copyrighted work or merely an incidental or minor segment?
3. The manner in which the borrowed passage is used: Is the passage used in an illustrative, critical, or instructive context? Or is the passage used to spare the author the burden of creating his or her own original expression? Is the passage quoted within the text of the book for purposes of comment or criticism, or is it used as a window dressing to enliven the new piece of writing?
4. The nature of the copyrighted work from which the passage is taken: Is it a published or unpublished source? (The scope of the fair use privilege is significantly reduced for unpublished works.) Is the passage factual and mostly informative, or is it more expressive and fanciful, more "literary"?
5. The effect of the use of the material on the potential market for the copyrighted work, including the market for granting rights and permissions to use the copyrighted work.

Although no easy formulas exist for analyzing those factors and applying them to a given set of facts, an author will usually have to obtain permission for the following material, assuming that material is already protected by copyright (no permissions are needed for material in the public domain):

1. Prose quotations or close paraphrasing of 300 words or more from any full-length book (either a single citation or the total of several shorter quotations from a single work)
2. Prose quotations or close paraphrasing of 100 words or more from a short article or periodical piece
3. More than 300 words from a full-length play or 100 words from a one-act play
4. One or more lines of a poem, unless it is of epic proportion, in which case more lines may be used depending on their qualitative and quantitative relationship to the entire copyrighted work
5. One or more lines from a song
6. All photographs and illustrations (including cartoons)
7. Any table, diagram, or map that is copied or closely adapted
8. More than a single line or two from any unpublished letter, memo, diary, manuscript, or other personal document. (Always bear in mind that the guidelines for unpublished material are more restrictive than those for published material.)

If the author has any doubts about whether borrowed material would be protected by a fair-use defense, he or she should advise the project's editor so the publisher's legal counsel can be consulted. It is also important to remember that although one need not obtain permission for fair use material, a source reference for any quoted or closely paraphrased passage should be provided in the notes.

(See also "PERMISSION GUIDELINES: GENERAL" and "PERMISSION GUIDELINES: QUOTING READER REVIEWS ON A WEBSITE.")

FAMILY RELATIONSHIPS, TERMS FOR

Terms for family relationship are capitalized when used like proper names (*he knew Mom would understand*) and lowercase when used generically (*he knew his mom would understand*). They are usually capitalized in direct address (*"So, Dad, how've you been?"*). Be sensitive to the distinction; a father may address his own offspring as *Son* if he uses that like a name (*"Listen, Son"*—capitalized), while an older person may address a younger person as *son* in a metaphorical sense (*"Listen, son"*—lowercase). Be aware that less common terms like *Pops*, *Mum*, *Sis*, *Bro*, and so on follow this same pattern.

"Grand." When the word *grand* precedes a term of family relation, it is set closed: *grandaunt, grandbaby, grandchild, granddaughter, grandfather, grandkid, grandma, grandmother, grandnephew, grandniece, grandpa, grandparent, grandson*, and so on.

"Great." In family relationships, the word *great* is followed by a hyphen: *great-grandmother, great-nephew.* The word *great* and the word that follows the hyphen are both capitalized when such terms are used in direct address (*Thank you, Great-Aunt Edna*), as an affectionate name (*I want to thank Great-Aunt Edna*), or in a title of a work (*In the article "The Great-Grandfather Syndrome" ...*). When the word is used simply as a descriptor (for instance, with an article or possessive pronoun) or is in apposition to the name, then the words are lowercase: *my only great-aunt, Edna, lives in ...* or *William, my mother's great-uncle, arrived....* Finally, a hyphen follows each use of the word *great* when it is repeated: *great-great-great-grandfather.*

"Half." In contrast to the word *great,* which uses a hyphen, the word *half* in family relationships is set apart with a space: *half brother, half siblings, half sister.*

"Step." Both *great* and *half* are in contrast to the term *step* in family relationship designations, which, like *grand,* is set solid: *stepbrother, stepfather, stepsister,* and so on. One could even have a *stepgrandmother.*

"Apposition." Formerly, commas were used when only one person could be identified with a specific family descriptor (for instance, *my wife, Michelle*), and no commas were used if several people could be identified by a family descriptor (*my brother Mike,* for instance, which presumes that other brothers exist; *my brother, Mike,* implies that Mike is the only brother). In other words, if the name is in apposition to the family title, commas are used; if the name is restrictive, no commas are used. *CMoS* recommends relaxing those rules as appropriate. In our culture, for instance, it can usually be assumed that *my wife Michelle* (without the comma) no longer suggests the existence of other wives besides Michelle (despite the way literalist grammarians might interpret it). If siblings are inessential in a narrative and never even mentioned, then saying *his brother Richard* is acceptable. Each author and publisher determines how relaxed they wish to be about this. It is still not wrong to insert the commas. Readers of fiction and memoir, for instance, are not likely to be confused by the presence or absence of such commas. Academic writers, by contrast, may wish to preserve a restrictive-versus-nonrestrictive distinction for precision's sake.

FIRST PERSON

An old precept of high school English is that first-person pronouns should not be used in expository writing, especially academic writing, though an exception is made for prefaces and introductions. Though the rule is now outmoded, some academic disciplines and departments still urge it on their students. While referring to oneself in formal writing is commonly accepted, establishing this voice early in the text by using *I* or *we* is recommended.

FLYLEAF

Technically, a flyleaf is part of a hardcover book's binding and not counted in the pagination. It is the loose half of the endsheet, or endpaper, and every hardcover book has one at the front and another at the back. The flyleaf is often the same color as the book's paper, though sometimes heavier in weight, but, it may be colored or printed attractively to complement the content. (See also "ENDSHEET, ENDPAPER.")

FOLIO

The *folio* is the page number as printed on the page. This may differ from the actual *page number*, which counts the first page after the flyleaf as page 1. A distinction is made between folios and page numbers because in some books, usually academic and reference books, the folio numbers in the front matter are in roman numerals, while the actual text begins with arabic numeral 1 in the first chapter. In such cases, the first page of text might actually be the eleventh page in the book (page number 11), but it bears folio number 1. A book that has no numbers printed on the pages, like some children's books, is called *unfoliated*.

Customarily, numbers are not printed on nontext pages, such as title pages, copyright pages, epigraphs, dedications, tables of content, blanks, and so on. Those pages are said to have *blind folios*. Usually, the first page to carry a printed folio number is the first page of text, whether that is the foreword, introduction, first chapter, or other section. The folio on that first page of text is often the same as the actual page number, but in some cases (at the designer's and editor's discretion) it may start with the numeral 1. In the latter case, the folio and the actual page number will differ by the number of pages before the first page of text. For most purposes, it is advisable to have the actual page numbers and the folios as printed on the pages align, except, as stated before, when the front matter is numbered with roman numerals. When a folio is printed at the bottom of a page or as part of a running footer, it is called a *drop folio* or *foot folio*.

FOOTNOTES

See "NOTES," section on "*Footnotes*"; see also "FOOTNOTE SYMBOLS, BOTTOM-OF-PAGE."

FOOTNOTE SYMBOLS, BOTTOM-OF-PAGE

The sequence of symbols conventionally used for callouts and references for bottom-of-page footnotes is *, †, ‡, §, ||, ¶, **, and so on, doubling each character. This is called the *asterisk-dagger system*. Most book designers find this system unwieldy whenever more than two or three footnotes appear on more than a few pages, in which case numbering the footnotes sequentially throughout the chapter is more practical. In some older books, an expanding sequence of asterisks alone was used to indicate the footnotes on each page: *, **, ***, and so on, though that practice is now obsolete. The asterisk-dagger system is more common in the US. In the UK, designers tend to use superior numbers for callouts and references for bottom-of-page footnoting. (See also "NOTES," section on "*Footnotes*.")

FOREIGN WORDS AND PHRASES COMMON TO CHRISTIAN LIFE AND WORSHIP

The pervasive influence of Christianity through the centuries and across cultures can be seen in the number of foreign phrases relating to Christian life and worship that have become more or less common in English. Many Latin phrases appear in the following list because that was the official language of the church for so long.

Abba—(Aramaic) "Father." Capitalized in reference to God.

Adeste Fideles—(Latin) "O Come, All Ye Faithful," a popular Christmas hymn.

ad majorem Dei gloriam—(Latin) "To the greater glory of God." Motto of the Jesuits; sometimes abbreviated *AMDG*.

agape—(Greek) "Love." Spiritual love; charity.

Agnus Dei—(Latin) Short for *Agnus Dei, qui tolles peccata mundi* ("Lamb of God, who takes away the sins of the world"). Also, the portion of the Catholic Mass or Episcopal Communion when these words are spoken or sung.

agrapha—(Greek) "Unwritten sayings." Usually refers to statements of Jesus that are not found in the four gospels.

Anima Christi—(Latin) "Soul of Christ." A well-known Eucharistic prayer: "Soul of Christ, sanctify me."

anno Domini—(Latin) "In the year of our Lord" (AD). Used for year designations after the time of Christ.

anno mundi—(Latin) "Year of the world." Dating system starting at biblical creation.

apologia pro vita sua—(Latin) "A defense of one's life." A confession, or self-justification. Capitalized, the title of Cardinal Newman's spiritual autobiography.

Ars Moriendi—(Latin) "The art of death." The shortened title of a fifteenth-century religious text, which eventually grew into an entire genre of books of meditations about death. Lowercase, the term refers to the spiritual practice of meditating upon one's own death.

Athanasius contra mundum—(Latin) "Athanasius against the world." A reference to Athanasius's stand, unpopular in the church at the time, against the fourth-century Arian heresy.

auto-da-fé—(Spanish) "Act of faith." The formulaic religious rites of the Spanish Inquisition, which preceded the judgment portion of a heresy trial. It has come to be synonymous with the burning at the stake of a person accused of heresy. The plural is *autos-da-fé*.

Ave, Maria—(Latin) "Hail, Mary." Traditionally, the first words of the angel's greeting to Mary at the annunciation (Luke 1:28). Also, the small beads of the Roman Catholic rosary. (The large beads are the *Paternosters*.)

benedicamus Domino—(Latin) "Let us bless the Lord." A closing salutation used in some Roman Catholic offices. The response is *Deo Gratias* ("Thanks be to God").

benedicite—(Latin) "Bless [the Lord]." A common blessing or grace. Also, capitalized, a song of praise based on Dan. 3:28–29.

Benedictus—(Latin) "Blessed." The first word of Zechariah's song of thanksgiving in Luke 1:68–79.

Benedictus qui venit—(Latin) The first words of *Benedictus qui venit in nomine Domini* ("Blessed is he who comes in the name of the Lord," Matt. 21:9). Capitalized, a portion of the Sanctus of the Roman Catholic Mass.

biblia pauperum—(Latin) "Bible of the poor." A reference to medieval picture books and sometimes stained-glass windows, illustrating Bible stories for the illiterate.

Capitalavium—(Latin) "Washing the head." An early medieval name for Palm Sunday.

Christus resurrexit—(Latin) "Christ is risen." Easter greeting, to which the response is *resurrexit vere* ("He is risen indeed").

confessio fidei—(Latin) "Confession of faith."

confiteor—(Latin) "I confess." The opening words of the Roman Catholic confession.

contemptus mundi—(Latin) "Contempt for the world," suggesting a focus on heavenly things as opposed to earthly.

contra mundum—See *Athanasius contra mundum* in this list.

credo—(Latin) "I believe." A creed, sometimes specifically referring to Augustine's paradox: "I believe because it is impossible."

Dei gratias—(Latin) "By the grace of God." Abbreviated *DG*.

Dei judicium—(Latin) "The judgment of God."

Deo favente—(Latin) "With God's favor."

Deo gratia—(Latin) "Thanks to God."

Deo optimo maximo—(Latin) "To God the best and greatest." Its abbreviation, *DOM*, is inscribed on bottles of wine made by the Benedictines.

Deo volente—(Latin) "God willing." Sometimes abbreviated *DV*.

de profundis—(Latin) "Out of the depths." The first words of Ps. 130, which is sometimes quoted at burial services. The phrase is used to express spiritual despair.

Deus absconditus—(Latin) "Hidden God." The idea that it is not possible to grasp God with human understanding.

Deus vult—(Latin) "God wills it." The (misguided) motto of the First Crusade.

Dies Irae—(Latin) "Day of Wrath." The name of a medieval hymn about the last judgment, based on Joel 2:31.

Dieu avec nous—(French) "God with us."

Dieu et mon droit—(French) "God and my right." Motto of the British monarchy.

Dieu vous garde—(French) "May God protect you."

dixit Dominus—(Latin) The first words of *Dixit Dominus Domino meo* ("The Lord says to my Lord," Ps. 110:1, or Ps. 109:1 in Vulgate). Capitalized, the first of five psalms sung on certain feast days in Roman Catholic vespers.

Dominus vobiscum—(Latin) "The Lord be with you." A salutation. The traditional Latin response is *Et cum spiritu tuo* ("And with your spirit").

dona nobis pacem—(Latin) "[Lord,] grant us peace." Used liturgically as a prayer response and, when capitalized, as the title of many musical compositions.

ecce agnus Dei—(Latin) "Behold the Lamb of God" (John 1:29). John the Baptist's words at Jesus's baptism.

ecce homo—(Latin) "Behold the man" (John 19:5). Pilate's words presenting Jesus to the crowd.

Ein Feste Burg Ist Unser Gott—(German) "A Mighty Fortress Is Our God." A hymn of Martin Luther.

ex cathedra—(Latin) "From the throne." A term often applied to any pronouncement of great authority; originally referring to papal announcements and decrees.

ex nihilo—(Latin) "From nothing." A phrase referring to God's creating the universe from nothing.

felix culpa—(Latin) "Happy fault." The idea that original sin was providential in that it provided a means for Christ's coming into the world.

fiat lux—(Latin) "Let there be light" (Gen. 1:3).

fides quaerens intellectum—(Latin) "Faith in search of understanding" (Thomas Aquinas). A term encouraging the pursuit of intellectual and scientific knowledge while remaining rooted in faith.

Formgeschichte—(German) "Form criticism." The study of determining the date and origins of Bible passages by their structure and form.

Fratres Minores—(Latin) "Little [or Inferior] Brothers." A term of intentional self-abasement with which Franciscan monks describe themselves.

gloria in excelsis—(Latin) "Glory to God in the Highest." Sung by the angels announcing Christ's birth (Luke 2:14); the basis for "The Greater Doxology." The *Gloria* is a portion of the Ordinary of the Roman Catholic Mass.

Gott ist über all—(German) "God is over all."

Gott mit uns—(German) "God with us."

hic jacet—(Latin) "Here lies . . ." A term used before a name on a tombstone inscription.

imago Dei—(Latin) "The image of God."

imitatio Christi—(Latin) "The imitation of Christ." The Latin title of Thomas à Kempis's fifteenth-century book is *De Imitatione Christi.*

imitatio Dei—(Latin) "The imitation of God."

imprimatur—(Latin) "Let it be printed." See "IMPRIMATUR."

in hoc signo vinces—(Latin) "In this sign you will conquer." The words of Constantine the Great, referring to the cross on his military banners.

ite missa est—(Latin) "Go, it's the dismissal." Words spoken by a priest after the completion of Holy Communion. These words are the origin of the term *the Mass.*

jus divinum—(Latin) "Holy law."

kirk—(Scottish) "Church."

kyrie eleison (Greek) "Lord, have mercy." A prayer used in Western and Eastern churches as a response during Mass. Also, capitalized, the title of any musical setting of this prayer.

laborare est orare—(Latin) "To work is to pray."

Lasciate ogni speranza, voi ch'entrate—(Italian) "Abandon all hope, you who enter." The words over the entrance to hell in Dante's *Inferno.*

laus Deo—(Latin) "Praise God."

Legenda Aurea—(Latin) "The Golden Legend." A thirteenth-century collection of Bible stories and saints' tales, categorized by feast days and compiled by Jacopo da Voragine.

magnificat—(Latin) First word of "My soul glorifies the Lord," the words of Mary to Elizabeth (Luke 1:46–55). Capitalized, a reading or song long used in church services.

maranatha—(Aramaic) From 1 Cor. 16:22, meaning "come, Lord" or "our Lord comes." It embodies the Christian desire for the speedy return of Christ.

mea culpa—(Latin) "Through my own fault." Used to acknowledge one's own guilt for sin, often accompanied by the gesture of striking one's fist to one's chest. Often used as a noun phrase to mean "I'm the one at fault."

me genoito—(Greek) "Not at all," emphatic. Rom. 3:4 and elsewhere.

memento mori—(Latin) "Remember that you will die." Used as a noun phrase, referring to any object, such as a skull or tombstone, that aids in the contemplation of mortality.

mene, mene, tekel, parsin—(Aramaic) From Dan. 5:25, the cryptic words that Daniel interprets to mean "numbered, weighed, divided," prophesying the end of Belshazzar's kingdom.

mirabile dictu—(Latin) "Wonderful to say." Often used sarcastically.

miserere—(Latin) The first word of Ps. 51, "Have mercy on me, O God." Capitalized, the name for a service during Lent when these words are sung. Also, a place in the church choir for kneeling.

Missa solemnis—(Latin) "High Mass" in the Roman Catholic Church.

missio Dei—(Latin) "Mission, or sending, of God." Theological term.

nomina sacra—(Latin) "Sacred names." Early scribal abbreviations for names of persons of the Trinity. Singular: *nomen sacrum*.

nunc dimittis—(Latin) The beginning of *Nunc dimittis servum tuum, Domine* ("Sovereign Lord, . . . you now dismiss your servant in peace"), the words of Simeon at the presentation of Jesus in the temple (Luke 2:29–32). Capitalized, it has become a common canticle sung at the conclusion of services in both the Anglican and Roman Catholic churches. Also, a term for dismissal.

obiit—(Latin) "He [or she] died."

ora et labora—(Latin) "Prayer and work." One of the mottos of the Benedictines.

ora pro nobis—(Latin) "Pray for us."

oremus—(Latin) "Let us pray."

pace—(Latin) "With all due respect."

pacem in terris—(Latin) "Peace on earth." Capitalized, the title of the influential 1963 encyclical of Pope John XXIII.

Pater noster—(Latin) First words of the Lord's Prayer, "Our Father" (Matt. 6:9–13). Also, closed up (*Paternoster*), the large beads of the Roman Catholic rosary.

pax Christi—(Latin) "Peace of Christ."

pax vobiscum—(Latin) "Peace be with you."

pietà—(Italian) "Pity." An artistic representation of Mary holding Jesus's dead body across her lap. Always retain the grave accent.

prie-dieu—(French) "Pray God." A small prayer desk with a sloping top and a kneeling board. The plural is *prie-dieux*.

quo vadis?—(Latin) "Where are you going?" From the pseudepigraphal Acts of Peter, in which Peter, fleeing Rome, encounters Christ. Peter asks, "Where are you going, Lord?" Christ answers, "To be crucified again." Peter is convicted and returns to face his own martyrdom. Capitalized, the title of a popular novel by Henry K. Sienkiewicz.

requiem—(Latin) First word of the prayer *Requiem aeternam dona eis, Domine* ("Give the eternal rest, O Lord"). Sung at the beginning of the Roman Catholic Mass for the Dead.

requiescat in pace—(Latin) "Rest in peace" (abbreviated *RIP*). Used on gravestone inscriptions.

salve, Regina—(Latin) First words of "Hail, holy Queen, mother of mercy," a hymn sung in the Roman Catholic Church from Trinity Sunday to Advent.

Sanctum Sanctorum—(Latin) "The holy of holies" in the Jewish temple, into which only the high priest may enter. By extension—the presence of God.

sanctus—(Latin) "Holy." The first word of *Sanctus, sanctus, sanctus, Dominus Deus Sabaoth* ("Holy, holy, holy, Lord, God of Sabaoth"). Capitalized, a portion of the Ordinary of the Roman Catholic Mass.

scriptio continua—(Latin) "Continuous writing." Manuscripts without words spaces or punctuation, as in some early biblical documents.

sic transit gloria mundi—(Latin) "Thus passes the glory of the world." Said to new popes upon their election.

similitudo Dei—(Latin) "The likeness of God."

sola fides, sola gratia, sola scriptura—(Latin) "Faith alone, grace alone, Scripture alone." A motto of the Protestant Reformation.

sola scriptura—(Latin) "Scripture only." The Bible as sole authority in matters of faith.

soli Deo gloria—(Latin) "To God alone be the glory" (abbreviated *SDG*). A motto used when one wishes to credit God as the source of one's successes or achievements. Bach and Handel often signed their works with the initials *SDG*.

stabat Mater—(Latin) "The Mother was standing." The opening words of a Latin hymn in the Roman Catholic Church recounting the seven sorrows of Mary at the cross. Capitalized, the title of the hymn sung the week before Easter.

Te Deum—(Latin) Opening words of a Latin hymn: *Te Deum laudamus* ("You, Father, we praise").

urbi et orbi—(Latin) "For the city [Rome] and the world." Used with papal blessings.

ut in omnibus Deus glorificetur—(Latin) "That God may be glorified in all things." The motto of the Benedictine order.

veritas—(Latin) "Truth." One of the mottos of the Dominican Order.

Via Dolorosa—(Latin) "Way of Sorrow." The name of the path through the streets of Jerusalem taken by Christ on the way to the cross.

via negativa—(Latin) "Way of denial." Reference to an approach to the Christian faith that denies worldly pleasures as distractions from God.

via positiva—(Latin) "Way of affirmation." Reference to an approach to the Christian faith that affirms the physical world as a gift from God to be enjoyed.

vita nuova—(Italian) "New life."

¡Viva Christo Rei!—(Spanish) "Long live Christ the King!"

vox populi vox Dei—(Latin) "The voice of the people is the voice of God."

FOREWORD

A *foreword* is usually written by someone other than the author. That person may be a well-known figure, someone who has a special relationship with the author, or someone who has expertise on the book's subject matter. A foreword illuminates some interesting aspect of the book's content or its author, and when the reader is finished, no doubt should exist as to why that writer was chosen to write the foreword. In some cases, it can read like an extended endorsement of the book. The name of the person writing the foreword appears as a byline either after the title, especially if that person is well known, or at the end of the foreword itself. If two or more forewords are reprinted from various editions of the book, the original foreword appears closest to the text itself. (See also "INTRODUCTION" and "PREFACE.")

FRAGMENTS

See "SENTENCE FRAGMENTS."

FRENCH STYLE

A few important conventions are worth noting when quoting French sources.

Diacritics. French contains a great number of diacritical marks (see "DIACRITICAL MARKS [ACCENTS]"), and these should be carefully reproduced when extracting a quotation in French or one that uses French words. While diacritical marks are often dropped with capital letters in English contexts, the marks are retained with capital letters in French titles and names: as in *L'École des ménages, the commune of Éloise, Étienne Brûlé.*

Abbreviations. Such abbreviations as *Mme* ("*madam*") and *Mlle* ("*mademoiselle*") are not followed by periods. French rules of abbreviation are similar to those of British English; if letters are excised from the middle of a word to form an abbreviation, that word is not followed by a period. The French abbreviation *M.* ("*monsieur*") is followed by a period because the end of that word was clipped off to form the abbreviation. The plural abbreviation *MM.* ("*messieurs*") also includes a final period. Honor those forms when referencing French names or quotations.

Titles of Works. When referencing the titles of French books, articles, artworks, and so on, convention dictates that only the first word of a title or subtitle and proper names are capitalized: *Rêverie de l'enfance de Pantagruel* and *L'Halitose: Une approach pluridisciplinaire.*

Quotation Marks. French typography uses what are called *guillemets* (« / ») to indicate open and closing quotation marks respectively. When quoting from a French source, use standard English quotation marks (" / ") instead of guillemets.

Particles before Names. When *L'*, *La*, *Le*, or *Les* comes before a French proper name, it is usually capitalized (*La Fontaine, Le Franc*), but *d'*, *de*, *des*, and *du* are not (*Théophile de Viau, Joachim du Bellay*), though many exceptions exist.

FRONTISPIECE

A *frontispiece* is an illustrative element placed across from the book's title page. In biographies, for instance, a portrait of the book's subject often appears as the frontispiece, or in reprints of works by classic authors, a portrait of that author might be used. When in color, a frontispiece is usually printed on high-quality paper and glued ("tipped") in. Most commonly—and more economically—it is set as a halftone or piece of line art on the verso of the half-title page, either replacing the author ad card or subsequent to it. If the book contains a list of illustrations, the frontispiece is listed first and labeled with the word *frontispiece* rather than a page number.

FRONT MATTER, ELEMENTS OF A BOOK'S

A book's front matter encompasses all the preliminary pages preceding the main content, or body, of the book. The elements of the front matter are traditionally arranged, as appropriate, in the order shown in the following list and usually only deviate from this order when there is a compelling reason to do so, such as a limitation of space or idiosyncratic design. (For more information, see the entries for each different kind of front matter.)

Half-title (on recto page immediately after the flyleaf)
Author card (sometimes called the *ad card*; lists the author's other books) or frontispiece or series title page (all appear on the verso of the half-title page)
Title page (on recto page)
Copyright page (on verso page, usually on back of title page; can be moved to the end of the book if space or design warrants it)
Dedication (usually on recto page, but may be verso for space reasons)
Epigraph (if it applies to the entire book; usually on recto page, but may be verso for space reasons)
Contents page, or table of contents (usually begins on recto page, but may be set on two-page spread)
Errata (if any, slipped in or set on verso of contents page)
List(s) of maps, illustrations, or charts (usually on recto page)
List of abbreviations (usually on recto page)
Foreword (usually by someone other than the author; usually begins on recto page)
Preface (usually by the author; usually begins on recto page)
Acknowledgments (usually begin on recto page)
Introduction (usually by the author; usually begins on recto page)
Inside, or second, half-title (on recto page)
Prologue (comes immediately before chapter 1 and is usually considered the first element of the body matter)

GENDER-ACCURATE LANGUAGE

For several decades, an awareness of the subtle sexist messages in the English language has made writers and readers alike sensitive to the implications of common words. Writers strive for accurate, unbiased communication and avoid debasing terms, stereotypes, and language that expresses an inherent superiority of one gender over the other. Not only are the words themselves important, but so is the overall tone of the writing. Most writers and readers have become so attuned to these issues that they take the following guidelines for granted.

Simple Accuracy. Seek out gender-neutral words and phrases when the sex of a person is unknown or immaterial or when a group of people consists of both male and female. Good substitutes are usually not difficult to find. Gender-accurate language improves communication and should not result in awkwardness, inexactness, or obscurity. For example:

spokesperson (for a man or woman when the gender is immaterial to the context or unknown)
spokespeople (referring to a group of mixed-gender or possibly mixed-gender people)
spokesman (when it is important to specify that the spokesperson is male)
spokeswoman (when it is important to specify that the spokesperson is female)

"Man" as a Generic Term. The use of *man* as a generic term for both men and women is best avoided whenever possible. While most older readers are not confused by the generic *man*, after more than forty years of writers' avoiding its use, younger readers now often take the gender specification at face value. When a text reads, "Blessed is the man who does not walk in the counsel of the wicked" (Ps. 1:1, NIV 1984 version), many take it to refer to a specific unnamed male. Here are some outmoded terms and alternatives for them:

Instead of:	Use:
man, mankind	humanity, people, human beings, humankind
common man	the average person, the ordinary citizen
manhood	maturity, adulthood
manpower	workforce

spokesman	spokesperson, representative
forefathers	forerunners, forebears, ancestors

Vocational Terms. **Avoid vocational terms that unnecessarily focus on gender.**

Instead of:	Use:
fireman	firefighter
foreman	supervisor
housewife	homemaker
insurance man	insurance agent
pressman	press operator
steward, stewardess	flight attendant
waiter, waitress	server, serving person, waitron
watchman	guard

In the case of *firefighter*, firefighters' organizations themselves (for instance, the International Association of Fire Fighters, the IAFF) prefer the gender-neutral term. In most cases, the gender of the firefighter is immaterial. When gender specificity is necessary to a written passage, the terms *male firefighter* and *female firefighter* suffice.

Double Standards. **Avoid double-standard semantics, such as describing a behavior as acceptable for one gender but not for the other. Connotations as well as denotations must be carefully considered. For example, don't use the word *domineering* to describe a wife if a husband displaying similar behavior would be described as *authoritative*. Other examples:**

assertive businessman	pushy businesswoman
thrifty woman	miserly man
cautious woman	spineless man
spirited little boy	unruly little girl

Negative Overtones. **Select words carefully to show gender. Many widely used terms have negative overtones and are not appropriate for fine writing.**

ladies, gals, girls (for adults)	women
old maid, spinster	single woman
the little woman, my better half	wife, spouse
women's libber	feminist
my old man	my husband, spouse
little old lady	elderly woman
dirty old man, little old man	elderly man
man and wife	man and woman, or husband and wife

When Gender Is Significant. **Do not hide gender if it is significant.**

Grammar. Do not violate grammar rules just to avoid a gender-specific word or phrase.

Disclaimers. In certain works that do not allow for reediting, such as reprints of classics or other previously published works or quotations from such works, it may be advisable to place a disclaimer somewhere in the front matter, perhaps on the copyright page, though this is probably only needed when the quoted author's opinions are of such an inflammatory nature as to be offensive to a large number of readers.

Deliberate Sexism. Some "sexist" language may be appropriate to evocative communication in certain circumstances, such as when used to add color to a fiction writer's palette. Such language can be effective in dialogue to characterize the speaker's assumptions, values, and cultural background—as when the soldiers in *South Pacific* sing, "There is nothing like a dame." Use such language consciously and for a desired end.

Neutral Pronouns. Use neutral pronouns instead of the generic *he* whenever possible. Changing a phrase or recasting an entire sentence usually yields an acceptable alternative. Do not use such contrivances as *s/he*, *he/she*, *him/her* when a neutral pronoun is needed. These forms only distract the reader. (See also "*her, she.*") Here are some alternatives to the male generic:

1. *Alternate "he" and "she."* One solution is to alternate gender-specific pronouns (*he* and *she*) as they are needed in different contexts throughout a work.
2. *Use Third-Person Plural Pronouns.* Sometimes changing the pronouns from the singular to the plural remedies the problem: *He asked any student who knew the answer to raise their hand.* (Although that usage is still frowned upon by some, the majority of style manuals now list it as acceptable.)
3. *Change Entire Reference to Third-Person Plural.* By changing the neutral "he" to "they," the male-only reference can become inclusive without changing the meaning: *He asked the students who knew the answer to raise their hands.*
4. *Change to First-Person Plural.* Often, shifting a "he" to a "we" is a helpful solution.
5. *Use "he or she" and "him or her."* Although these wordy constructions grow tiresome after only a few uses, they can be used in place of a generic *he* to express that the discussion concerns both males and females. The problem with this solution is that it can quickly look stiff, formulaic, and distracting if used too often.
6. *Use Passive Voice.* Occasionally a sentence may be restructured into passive voice to avoid the male-only generic pronoun. Since

this is perhaps the least satisfactory of the solutions, use it only as a last resort.

7. *Use "one."* Curiously, English already has a long-standing generic pronoun, *one*, though it is seldom used now because it usually sounds stuffy. In the right context, it can be effectively used as long as it is not repeated too often. *One shouldn't judge too quickly.*

Here are some examples of these solutions:

[Original sentence] A Christian needs to be concerned about his witness before the watching world. [*Problem:* the neutral subject *Christian* is followed by the male pronoun *his*, presuming that Christians are invariably male.]

[Solution 1: alternate *his* and *her*] A Christian needs to be concerned about her witness before the watching world. [*She* is used. In the next instance, *he* would be used.]

[Solution 2: *their* with singular reference] Each Christian needs to be concerned about their witness before the watching world. [Acceptable.]

[Solution 3: third-person plural] Christians need to be concerned about their witness before the watching world. [Preferred, whenever possible.]

[Solution 4: first-person plural] As Christians we need to be concerned about our witness before the watching world.

[Solution 5: *his* or *her*] A Christian needs to be concerned about his or her witness before the watching world. [Acceptable, though *his or her* can become awkward if used frequently.]

[Solution 6: passive voice] A Christian's witness before the watching world should be a matter of concern. [Acceptable, though the passive construction can sound convoluted and artificial if not handled well.]

[Solution 7: *one*] As a Christian, one needs to be concerned about one's witness before the watching world. [Acceptable, though *one* can sound stiff in many contexts.]

Gender Self-Identification. Use the gender pronouns that individuals apply to themselves, whenever those preferences are known. This means that noted British writer Jan Morris is referred to with the pronouns *she* and *her* and American entertainment personality Chaz Bono is referred to with *he* and *his*. This applies both to those who simply identify with a gender other than their birth gender and to those who have had gender-reassignment surgery. (See also "*transgender, transsexual.*") This recommendation may seem controversial, but it accords with the major style books and follows the general principle of allowing all groups of people to identify themselves.

GENDER SELF-IDENTIFICATION

See "GENDER-ACCURATE LANGUAGE," specifically the section on "*Gender Self-Identification.*"

GENERATIONAL CATEGORIES

Authors and editors are sometimes imprecise about the informal names for recent generations and when they began and ended. This is understandable because firm dividing lines are hard to establish. The following rough list may help:

Informal Name	Born (about)
lost generation	1883–1900
greatest generation (builders generation, or GI generation)	1901–1924
silent generation	1925–1945
baby boomers	1946–1964
generation X (gen X)	1965 to early 1980s
millennial generation (gen Y or millennials)	early 1980s to early 2000s
generation Z (gen tech or gen next)	early 2000s to present

Except for the abbreviations *GI*, *X*, *Y*, and *Z*, lowercase generational names, though they may be capitalized in some contexts if it would help clarify their distinctions.

GENRE FICTION

The term *genre fiction* describes various types of fiction written with certain conventional premises or general plot formulas in mind. It is often distinguished from *literary fiction*, though that distinction is artificial and misleading because the line between the two is not a clear one. Among the kinds of genre fiction are *crime*, *detective*, *fantasy*, *historical*, *romance* (*historical* and *contemporary*), *science fiction*, *suspense*, *thriller*, *vampire*, *young adult*, and many more. Many genre novels are written as series with shared characters and plot elements. While Christians write in all these genres, some types of genre fiction are peculiar to the Christian market, including *Amish novels* (such as Amy Clipston's), *clerical novels* (such as Jan Karon's), *end-times novels* (such as Tim LaHaye's), and *spiritual thrillers* (such as Bill Meyers's). (See "CHRISTIAN BOOKS, TYPES OF.")

GERUNDS, POSSESSIVE WITH

See "POSSESSIVES," section on "*Gerunds.*"

GOD, NAMES FOR

See "TRINITY, NAMES FOR PERSONS OF THE."

"GOD" COMPOUNDS

When compound words are formed with the word *god*, they are usually set solid (without a hyphen) and lowercase: such as *godchild*, *goddaughter*, *goddess*, *godfather*, *godhood*, *godless*, *godlike*, *godliness*, *godling*, *godly* (and *ungodly*), *godmother*, *godparent*, *godsend*, *godson*, and *godward*. When God-as-deity is specifically referred to, then the compounds are usually hyphenated and the word *God* is capitalized: *God-fearing*, *God-forsaken*, *God-inspired*, and *God-given*. A few conventional compounds are exceptions: *god-awful* (colloquial), *godforsaken* (when colloquial in a nonreligious context), *Godspeed* (customarily capitalized but not hyphenated).

GOD SPEAKING

See "DISEMBODIED VOICES, CONVEYING IN DIALOGUE."

GRADES, ACADEMIC

See "LETTER GRADES."

GRAWLIX

Sometimes called *profanitype*, a *grawlix* is a series of random typographic symbols that represent swearing in text: such as ***#*†%!***. This visual convention is often seen in comic strips. It is commonly used in text messages and occasionally in blogs and social media, but in the context of book typography, it is much more difficult to recognize it as a stand-in for swearing. Many readers will think it is an error. Still, if it is used, be sure the reader has enough cues to know the intent of the symbols. In practice, it is often best to italicize the characters or even set them in boldface to set them apart from the ordinary text. The author and editor should also realize that its effect is always comic and that this device should not be used as a convenient way to get around a publisher's prohibitions against profanity, nor should it be used in fictional dialogue as a replacement for profanity. It simply draws too much attention to itself and distracts from the narrative. (See also "PROFANITY.")

H

HALF-TITLE PAGE

The *half-title page* (sometimes called the *bastard title*) is a holdover from an earlier era of printing when books were often sold without covers. It identified the book, protected the interior pages, and was disposable and easily reprinted whenever the book needed a fresh binding. A half-title page is usually the first page of a book after the flyleaf, though in some elegant settings, it may be preceded by a blank leaf or two. Only the title of the book, without the subtitle, appears on a half-title page. In some books, it may be eliminated in favor of endorsements, quotations from reviews of earlier editions of the book, descriptive copy, or the author's biography. If space is a consideration, the half-title page may be dropped. (See also "SECOND HALF-TITLE PAGE.")

HARD COPY

Hard copy is a publisher's term for any manuscript or book printed out on paper, as opposed to digital, or electronic, copy.

HEAD AND BODY COVERINGS, WORDS FOR

Western Christianity. Both men and women in Roman Catholic and Anglican orders wear *habits*, which usually consist of a *tunic* (shirt) overlaid with either a *scapular* (an apronlike shoulder covering, which can be short or long) or a *cowl* (monk's robe) or both. Monks and friars often add a *hood* to their cowls. The long robe of Catholic priests is a *cassock*. The most common head covering for a Catholic nun is called a *coif*, to which is added a *veil*. A larger and more elaborate *coif*, once common in Europe, is called a *cornette* (think of the 1960s TV series *The Flying Nun*). In the US and Canada, Amish women and some Mennonite women wear what is called simply a *head covering*, also often called a *bonnet* or *cap*, sometimes spelled *kapp*. Some old-style Quaker women wear a similar bonnet called simply a *head covering*.

Other Cultures. One of the most common mistakes Western writers make is to confuse terms for various head and body coverings worn by people of other cultures. The following list clarifies a few of the most common.

Covering	Function	Culture
abaya	loose black body cloak, buttons up the front	Muslim
burka	covers head and entire body, female, often with mesh covering over the eyes	Muslim
chador	covers head and shoulders or entire body, female; similar to burka, but leaves face open	Muslim, Iranian
chunni	black scarf-like head covering, female	Sikh
dastar	head covering (turban), male and female	Sikh
hijab	generic term for head covering or for modest female dress in general	Muslim
kaffiyeh (also keffiyeh)	loose male head scarf, held in place with a cord; sometimes worn by women; symbol of Palestinian solidarity	Arab
kapp	female head covering; US/Canada	Amish/Mennonite
kippah (Hebrew)	covers top of head, male (plural is *kippot*)	Jewish
niqab	body and face covering, female, with only a small space for eyes to look through	Muslim
pagri	hand-wound head turban, male	Sikh
patka	small head covering, young males	Sikh
sheila	rectangular scarf covering the head, female	Muslim
snood	covers hair portion of head, female	old European
tallith, or shawl	shawl covering head and shoulders, male	Jewish
turban	wound head covering, male or female	Middle Eastern and Asian subcontinent
yarmulke (Yiddish)	covers top of head, male, same as *kippah*	Jewish

HEADINGS AND SUBHEADINGS

Written text is often divided into sections, each with its own *heading*, and sometimes these sections are themselves broken down into subsections, each of which bears its own *subheading*. There is no precise difference between the terms *heading* and *subheading*, other than the notion that a *heading* is applied to the first or primary divider, while a *subheading* is applied to all subsidiary dividers.

Levels. The various levels of headings are referred to by letters: *A-heads*, *B-heads*, *C-heads*, and so on. Since readers may have difficultly recognizing the fine typographic distinctions between the various levels of headings and subheadings within a chapter, authors and editors should minimize the number of levels. A book with too many subheadings can resemble an annotated outline.

Spacing. Place more white space over a heading than under it so the heading clearly appears to be part of the text that follows it.

Breaking over Lines. Ideally, headings and subheadings should be short enough to fit on a single line. If a heading or subheading is long enough to break over a line, break it by sense, that is, at the end of a phrase, whenever possible.

HIDDEN ENDNOTES

See "NOTES," section on "*The Hidden Endnote Style for Nonacademic Books.*"

HOLY SPIRIT, NAMES FOR THE

See "TRINITY, NAMES FOR PERSONS OF THE."

HOURS, BIBLICAL

Because the NT writers conceived of timekeeping differently, readers today often have questions. For example, exactly what time is *the ninth hour*? One advantage of the NIV, following its stated goal of dynamic equivalence, is that it translates the biblical hours of the day into modern "clock times," according to this scheme:

Biblical Time	Modern "Clock Time" (NIV)	Biblical Time	Modern "Clock Time" (NIV)
first hour	7:00 a.m.	seventh hour	1:00 p.m.
second hour	8:00 a.m.	eighth hour	2:00 p.m.
third hour	9:00 a.m.	ninth hour	3:00 p.m.
fourth hour	10:00 a.m.	tenth hour	4:00 p.m.
fifth hour	11:00 a.m.	eleventh hour	5:00 p.m.
sixth hour	12:00 noon	twelfth hour	6:00 p.m.

This scheme is only roughly accurate because it misleadingly suggests that biblical time was as rigidly measured as modern time is. By convention, the NT writers divided the daylight portion of each day into twelve hours, but as the days grew longer or shorter with the seasons, the length of those hours expanded or contracted. Thus, the *third*, *sixth*, and *ninth hours* (the three most often used in the Bible) suggest "midmorning," "midday," and "midafternoon" respectively. No clocks struck the hour in Bible times, and to say "the ninth hour" meant an approximate time, give or take about half an hour either way. Also, *the first hour* usually implies sunrise itself (rather than one hour after sunrise), which in the earth's temperate zones is closer to 6:00 a.m. in the summer than to 7:00 a.m.

By a curious coincidence, the term *the eleventh hour* had the same metaphorical implications for the Bible writers as it does for us today—that is, a final, critical moment of decision—but for different reasons. In our time, *the eleventh hour* suggests the hour before midnight, a crucial time when Cinderella, for example, must return home, or when Dr. Faustus, in Christopher Marlowe's play, knows he has "but one bare hour to live." In Bible times, *the eleventh hour* was late afternoon, one hour before sunset, when a field worker's usable daylight was soon to expire (see Matt. 20:9 KJV). The day's urgent business had to be concluded, and the traveler needed to find shelter. Similar symbolism, but quite different times of the day.

HOURS, CANONICAL

Confusion exists regarding the names and times of the canonical hours of the Divine Office, that is, the assigned daily prayers that priests, monks, and laity of some branches of Christianity (Roman Catholic, Anglican, and Eastern Orthodox) are encouraged to pray throughout the day. This confusion arose because (1) the hours of the Roman Catholic Church have changed over time; (2) the number of hours differs among the various traditions; and (3) the *matins* is the last prayer of the day in Roman Catholic tradition, while it is the first prayer of the day in the Anglican tradition. From about the fifth century until the Reformation, there were eight traditional hours of the Roman Catholic Church. The first seven were considered the day hours; the last one, *matins*, the night hour.

Hour	Description
lauds	prayer upon rising
prime	the first hour, or 6:00 a.m.
terce	the third hour, or 9:00 a.m. (pronounced like *terse*)
sext	the sixth hour, or 12:00 noon
none	the ninth hour, or 3:00 p.m. (pronounced like *known*)
vespers	late afternoon or early evening
compline	late evening (pronounced *CAHMP-lin*)
matins	late night/early morning

This system was later simplified, and the modern Roman Catholic hours specified in the official Breviary of 1971 are *lauds, a midday prayer* (either *terce, sext,* or *none*), *vespers*, and *compline.* The Church of England simplifies this even further, including only a morning prayer (called *matins*, though spelled *mattins* in England) and an evening prayer (*evensong*). The Eastern Orthodox round of canonical hours, called the *Horologion*, is as follows, beginning with sunset, since that is considered the beginning of the day:

Hour	Description
esperinos	vespers, sunset
apodepnon	compline, bedtime
mesonyktikon	midnight
orthros	matins, before dawn
prote ora	prime, about 6:00 a.m.
trite ora	terce, about 9:00 a.m.
ekte ora	sext, noon
ennate ora	none, about 3:00 p.m.
typika	follows either sext or none

Lowercase the names of the hours, though they are sometimes capitalized within their own traditions, especially in liturgical and monastic use. If a book's readership is confined to a specific tradition, follow the most common style for that tradition.

HYMN METERS

When quoting hymn lyrics and other old or traditional songs from musical tablature, authors and editors sometimes need to determine where the lines are to be broken, how to indent the lines, and which words are capitalized as the first words of lines of poetry. Even in those hymnals that capitalize the first letter of each line—and they are becoming fewer—indentation patterns can still be difficult to interpret. The examples in this entry show the most common stanza forms, with line breaks and indentation patterns noted.

Meter Abbreviations. Many hymnals used in churches or by choirs provide meter abbreviations (such as *CM* for *Common Meter*) for every hymn. Those abbreviations are found either on the page with the hymn itself or in a "Hymn Meter Index." Each abbreviation corresponds to a particular line-length scheme, designated by numbers—one number for the number of syllables in each line. The periods (dots) between the numbers (as in *86.86*) show the most common caesuras, that is, the strongest breaks between the lines, usually where the singers are meant to draw a breath. A solidus (slash) is sometimes used between the verse and chorus (as in *8888/88*).

Interchangeability. The lyrics to any song can be sung to the tune of any other song with the same metrical form—a favorite trick of church music directors. For instance, the words of "Amazing Grace," in Common Meter, can be sung to the tune of "All Hail the Power of Jesus' Name," whose tune, "Coronation," is also in Common Meter, as well as scores of other tunes. This interchangeability is especially easy for traditional hymns because nearly all of them are iambic.

Indentations. In hymns with lines of varying lengths and whose lines vary by two or more syllables (as in *86.86* or *66.86*), the shorter lines are usually indented. Differences of one syllable between varying lines (as in *87.87*) do not usually result in any indentation. Rhyme schemes can also be a factor in determining indentation. While hymns with series of repeating couplets (*aabb*), as in Long Meter, are usually aligned left, many Long Meter songs with alternating rhymes (*abab*) or alternating unrhymed and rhymed lines (*abcb*) indent the even-numbered lines (as in the Long Meter Double example in the list).

Capitalization. Once line breaks are established, the first letter of every line is usually capitalized, as in traditional poetry. The names for the meters, such as *Common Meter* and *Long Meter*, are capitalized by convention and set in roman type.

The following examples, taken from the classic *Sacred Harp* hymnal (1860), show the most common metrical forms of hymnody.

Common Meter (CM—86.86)

Amazing grace! (how sweet the sound)
  That saved a wretch like me!
I once was lost, but now am found,
  Was blind, but now I see.

("Amazing Grace")

Common Meter Double (CMD—86.86.86.86)

As on the cross the Savior hung,
  And bled and wept and died;
He poured salvation on a wretch
  That languished at his side.
His crimes, with inward grief and shame,
  The penitent confessed;
Then turned his dying eyes to Christ,
  And thus his prayer addressed.

("Converted Thief")

Long Meter (LM—88.88)

Lift up your hearts, Immanuel's friends,
And taste the pleasure Jesus sends;
Let nothing cause you to delay,
But hasten on the good old way.

("The Good Old Way")

Long Meter Double (LMD—88.88.88.88)

The busy scene of life is closed,
    And active usefulness is o'er;
The body's laid in calm repose,
    And sin shall ne'er distress it more.
The happy soul is gone to rest,
    Where cares no more shall spoil its peace:
Reclining on its Savior's breast,
    It shall enjoy eternal bliss.

("Paradise Plains")

Short Meter (SM—66.86, rhymes abcb)

He wept that we might weep,
Each sin demands a tear;
In heav'n alone no sin is found
And there's no weeping there.

("Jesus Wept")

Other Forms

Determining the line breaks and indent patterns for the following meters is a matter of common sense and applying the principles listed in the foregoing discussion.

Common Proper Meter (CPM—886.886)
Short Hymnal Meter (SHM—66.86; same as Short Meter but rhymes *abab*)
Hallelujah Meter (HM—66.66.88)
Long Proper Meter (LPM—88.88.88)
Proper Meter (PM—irregular or no pattern. The Geneva Psalter had a different meter for nearly every psalm; thus, each had its own "proper" meter.)
Miscellaneous: All other stanza forms are shown by syllable counts alone: for instance, 664.6664 ("My Country 'Tis of Thee"), 77.78 ("Just a Closer Walk with Thee), and 87.87 ("In the Cross of Christ I Glory").

HYMN TITLES AND TEXTS

Titles. Put hymn titles in quotation marks and capitalize them as you would the title of any short poem. Whenever possible, use the common title rather than the first line of the hymn: "Take My Life and Let It Be" not "Take my life and let it be consecrated, Lord, to thee." Also be aware that many hymns have two titles: one for the words and one for the tune. This is often an indication that the verse and the music were created separately. (See "HYMN METERS.") For instance, William C. Dix's nineteenth-century Christmas carol "What Child Is This" is set to the sixteenth-century traditional tune "Greensleeves," and the carol is even occasionally referred to as "Greensleeves." Similarly, John Newton's "Amazing Grace" is set to a tune called "New Britain." In most cases, refer to a hymn by the title its text is known for, and leave the tune names to choir directors and musicians.

Hymnals and scholarly works on hymnody often print tune names in cap-and-small-cap style to distinguish them from the titles of the texts, as in IDUMEA, which is the tune name for the hymn "And Am I Born to Die?" When the cap-and-small-cap style is used for a tune name, do not put it in quotation marks.

Texts. In formal writing, refer to hymns as having *texts* rather than *lyrics.*

For an outstanding resource for information about hymn tunes and texts, see the *Cyber Hymnal* online at http://www.hymntime.com/tch/index.htm.

HYPHEN

A hyphen (-) is used for word division (that is, to show that a single word is continued from one line of type to the next), compound adjectives, syntactical purposes, adding certain prefixes and suffixes, noun pairs, and other situations.

Word Division. One of the most common conundrums in print-book typography is that of correct hyphenation (that is, how to break words over two lines of type). This is usually not a problem in ebooks and online copy, which often don't break words at all but opt to keep them whole. One problem that does arise with an ebook is when its text has been drawn from the same file as the print version where hard hyphens (the manual character) may have been inserted by the compositor to solve copy-fit problems. The hard hyphens, as a result, can carry over into the ebook, appear-ing in the mid-dle of lines (like *appearing* and *middle* in this sentence). So take care when converting print files to e-files.

Merriam-Webster's Collegiate Dictionary, 11th Edition is an authoritative, accessible standard for proper word division, which is not to say that all word breaks shown with a small bullet character in *Webster* are legitimate for end-of-line purposes in typesetting, but a high proportion of them are. (For more details about word division and the exceptions to *Webster*, see "WORD DIVISION.") Beyond that, the most complete analysis is given in *CMoS* 7.31–7.43.

Compound Adjectives. When two or more words form an adjectival unit, called a *compound adjective*, preceding a noun, hyphens are placed between the words (*a well-timed anecdote, a ninety-two-year-old artist*). Compounds that are so familiar as to preclude the possibility of misreading need not be set with hyphens (*high school prom, Sunday school class, Old Testament translation*). When the compound adjective is used as a predicate, it is often set with no hyphens (*the anecdote was well timed*), though many familiar compound adjectives are always hyphenated (such as *full-time, old-fashioned, well-known*) whether they come before the noun or are set as a predicate. Always check the dictionary. A hyphen is never used when an adverb ending in *-ly* is combined with an adjective (*a previously unknown work, a barely visible star*). (For more detail, see "ADJECTIVES, COMPOUND.")

Syntactical Use. Hyphenation frequently depends on the syntactical use of a phrase or expression. Compare *Has he been born again?* with *Is he a born-again Christian?*

Prefixes and Suffixes. Some common prefixes, like *all-*, *ex-* (meaning "former"), *half-*, and *self-*, usually use hyphens (*all-terrain vehicle, ex-pastor, half-moon, self-sacrifice*). Some exceptions exist (like *halfhearted* and *halfway*), so check *Webster*.

Other common prefixes, like *anti-*, *co-*, *counter-*, *mid-*, *non-*, *out-*, *over-*, *post-*, *pre-*, *pseudo-*, *re-*, *semi-*, and *super-*, are usually set without hyphens (*antipope, counterculture, midweek, outpreach, prekindergarten*), but be aware that hyphens are inserted in some circumstances (*anti-Darwinian, counter-Reformation*, or *"out-Herods Herod"* [Shakespeare], *pre-K*). (For more detail, see "PREFIXES" or check *Webster*.)

Suffixes like *-fold* and *-like* are usually set without a hyphen. (See "SUFFIXES" and "*-like*" for exceptions.)

Changes in Meaning. Note that the meanings of some words change depending on the hyphen; for example, *coop* and *co-op*, *recover* and *re-cover*, *recreation* and *re-creation*.

Noun Pairs. When two nouns of equal importance are temporarily yoked, hyphenate them (like *poet-priest, pastor-activist*). Using a solidus (slash) is discouraged because it may create ambiguity. For instance, does the term *parent/guardian* mean that a person is both a parent and a guardian, or does it imply that the person is either one or the other? The hyphen makes it clearer that the person is both: a *parent-guardian.* (Clearest of all is to say either *parent and guardian* or *parent or guardian*).

"Great." A hyphen is used after the *great* in terms for family relationships, such as *great-grandmother, great-nephew.* (See "FAMILY RELATIONSHIPS, TERMS FOR," section on "*Great.*"

Spelling Out Words. A hyphen is used to spell out words in text or dialogue, as in, *"I can't remember; is Niebuhr spelled N-I-E or N-E-I?"*

I

IMPRIMATUR

The Roman Catholic Church's 1983 Code of Canon Law (Book III, Canons 822–32) spells out the guidelines by which Catholic publishers are to use an *imprimatur* (Latin, "let it be printed"). An imprimatur is the official notice, placed on a blank front-matter page (usually facing the title page) or on the copyright page, that declares that a bishop or his representative (called the *local ordinary*) has reviewed the book and found nothing contrary to Catholic doctrine or morals. The word is most commonly lowercase. In its most common form, the entire Latin phrase *Nihil obstat quominus imprimatur* ("Nothing stands in the way of allowing this to be printed") is given, along with the date and the bishop's name and full title, often also rendered in Latin.

General Use. The word *imprimatur* can also refer to an official government license granted to a publisher in those countries in which government review and approval are required whenever a book is published. The word, set in roman type, is also used metaphorically to mean "an official stamp of approval."

INCLUSIVE LANGUAGE

See "GENDER-ACCURATE LANGUAGE."

INDEXES

Though various types of indexes exist, they all serve the same function: to make a book's information more accessible. Not all books need an index. Fiction, devotional, gift, and inspirational books do not contain the kind of information that would necessitate an index, though exceptions exist even among those genres. Any work that contains names, references, facts, or data that the reader might want to locate quickly can benefit from an index. Two principal types are common to religious publishing: the subject–proper-name index and the Scripture index.

Who Prepares an Index? Any book's ideal indexer is the author. No one else has such a comprehensive understanding of the contents. In some cases, the author is contractually responsible for preparing the index, though the author may opt to hire a professional or have the publisher hire a professional. In either case the expense is usually borne by the author when the author is the one who is requiring an index. An index is prepared from a clean set of final galleys provided by the publisher. (For indexing methods and guidelines, refer to *CMoS*, chapter 16.)

Subject–Proper-Name Index. This kind of index lists references and page numbers to all major subjects and proper names discussed in the text of the book itself. In some cases, there may be an advantage to splitting the index into separate indexes: a subject index and a proper-name index.

Typographic Considerations. Indexes are commonly set in two columns per page (even three columns in some larger formats) to conserve space, but specific designs may differ. An even white vertical column of space (from 1 to 1½ picas wide) rather than a rule line should separate the columns. Two typographic styles are common: the paragraph style and the column style. Paragraph style is convenient when space is a consideration; column style tends to make the entries easier to read. In both styles, commas are used before page numbers. In paragraph style, a colon separates the main heading from the subentries, while in column style, no additional punctuation is used. The following examples show the two styles.

Paragraph Style

Heaven: NT conceptions of, 28–32; OT conceptions of, 32–33; pagan views of, 20–25; theological implications of, 33

Helen, St. (mother of Constantine): abandonment of, 133; advocacy of Christianity, 160, 167, 180–84; birth of Constantine, 126; marriage, 120; restoration under Constantine, 150–52, 160

Column Style

Heaven
  NT conceptions of, 28–32
  OT conceptions of, 32–33
  pagan views of, 20–25
  theological implications of, 33
Helen, St. (mother of Constantine)
  abandonment of, 133
  advocacy of Christianity, 160, 167, 180–84
  birth of Constantine, 126
  marriage, 120
  restoration under Constantine, 150–52, 160

(For issues of alphabetization in indexes, see “ALPHABETIZATION.”)

Subentries in Indexes. Subentries under each heading may be listed in three ways: (1) alphabetically, the most common and versatile way; (2) chronologically, used mainly for indexes of predominantly biographical or historical information; and (3) numerically by page number, which is reserved for simple indexes that do not contain a large number of subentries. Only one style is used in any given book. If the index is set in paragraph style, a colon separates the entry heading from the subentries, and semicolons separate subentries from each other.

Cross-references. Cross-references are an important element in any thorough index. They indicate where alternate entries or additional information might be found under other headings. In a paragraph-style index, a cross-reference that includes the whole entry is placed at the end of the entry; in column style, such an inclusive reference is placed after the main entry heading. In both styles, when only a subentry is being cross-referenced, the cross-reference appears immediately after the subentry. The word *see* indicates that an entirely different heading should be referred to, and the words *see also* indicate that additional information may be found under another entry. The word *see*, whether alone or in the phrase *see also*, is usually capitalized (because it will usually follow a period) and set in italic. In paragraph style, the cross-reference is placed in parentheses and the word *see* is lowercase when only the subentry is being cross-referenced.

Paragraph Style

Bird, William. *See* Byrd, William
Bishop's Bible, the, 182, 188. *See also* Bibles: before 1611
Blake, William: paintings of, 228–30; poetry of, 233–39 (*see also* Religious Poetry); his visions, 211. *See also* Artists; Painters

Column Style

Bird, William. *See* Byrd, William
Bishop's Bible, the, 182, 188. *See also* Bibles: before 1611
Blake, William. *See also* Artists; Painters
  paintings of, 228–30
  poetry of, 233–39. *See also* Religious Poetry
  his visions, 211

Scripture Indexes. A Scripture index lists all the Bible quotations used in a book. Most often it only contains references to those verses that are actually quoted, though for some scholarly works the index may also include those verses that are mentioned but not quoted. The Scripture index is usually set in two to four columns per page and is arranged in the same order as the books of the Bible themselves. Within each book of the Bible, entries are listed numerically by chapter and verse numbers; a chapter-only reference precedes any chapter-and-verse references for that same chapter. When continuous references begin with the same verse number, the one with the lower ending number precedes one with a higher ending number. Although leader dots are no longer commonly used for tables of contents and subject–proper-name indexes, they are still common in Scripture indexes. The most common form is as follows:

Genesis		**Exodus**	
1	113–14	6	27
1–3	71	6:14–25	28
1:1	7, 12, 117	15:21	33
1:1–13	189	20:1–17	98, 100–101
1:1–19	7, 18		
2:4–7	60–61		

An Index of Citations. An index of citations is similar to a Scripture index but may include works other than the Bible. It is usually reserved for ancient and classic works in cases when the reader is likely to be interested in looking up references to those works alone. Such works might include the writings of the early church fathers, the Apocrypha, deutero- and noncanonical books, Greek and Roman classics, and so on. In the context of literary studies, an index of citations will reference the works of the author being studied.

Other Kinds of Indexes. Among other kinds of indexes are the title-and-first-line index (for books of hymns and poetry), the concordance (common to Bibles; see "CONCORDANCE"), the index of place names (common to atlases), and the author or contributor index (for compilations, reference works, and anthologies). An index can be tailored for almost any kind of book in which information needs to be organized for accessibility.

INDIRECT DISCOURSE

See "QUOTATION MARKS," section on "*Direct Discourse*."

INITIALISMS

See "ACRONYMS AND INITIALISMS."

INSIDE HALF-TITLE PAGE

See "SECOND HALF-TITLE PAGE."

INTENSIFIERS

Use common intensifiers with caution. Adjectives like *absolute*, *complete*, and *total*, and adverbs like *absolutely*, *completely*, *very*, and so on, often undercut—even trivialize—the word they modify rather than intensifying it. You can describe a poor musical performance as "a complete disaster," but when describing a devastating earthquake, calling it simply "a disaster" is stronger and more direct than calling it "a complete disaster." Intensity is often heightened by compacting rather than expanding the language. (See also "*literally*" and "*very.*")

INTERJECTIONS OF EXPRESSION

An interjection of expression is a specialized part of speech, often independent of other grammatical constructions, that is used as an exclamation or a sudden expression of emotion. There are also interjections of salutation and farewell, such as *hello*, *hi*, *good-bye*, *bye*, and *good night*. (See "*goodbye, good-bye, goodby, good-by*" and "INTERJECTIONS OF GREETING AND PARTING.") The Bible and the church use many special interjections that are termed *liturgical interjections*, such as *amen* and *alleluia*. (See "*amen*," "*hallelujah, alleluia*," and "*hosanna, hosannah.*") Interjections of expression differ from minced oaths in that interjections are usually not euphemisms for other words. (See "MINCED OATHS" and "PROFANITY.")

Uses. Interjections that express exclamation or emotion are particularly useful in dialogue, where they lend immediacy and realism. While a nonfiction writer can spice up the exposition with an occasional authorial interjection, be selective in using interjections, since they call attention to themselves and can make the writing seem self-conscious or overly dramatic.

Repetition of Letters. Some writers tend to repeat letters (*Ahhhhh*, *hmmmm*, or *oh-hoooo*), which is acceptable when a comic effect is intended. In nonhumorous writing, such extended words not only draw attention to themselves but also do not communicate well to readers, who may perceive such spellings as errors. Overlong interjections can also be distracting and focus the reader on orthography rather than content. Most style books advise that the letters not extend beyond three repetitions (*Ahhh*, *h'mmm*, or *oh-hooo*). Using no repetition at all usually suffices (*Ah*, *h'm*, or *oh-ho*).

Conjugating. In rare instances, interjections are used as verbs, as in *The department-store Santa ho-ho-ho'd all day.* Probably the most common instance is the phrase *oohing and aahing.* Other verb endings, which can be used as models for other interjections, would be *he oohs and aahs* and *they ooh'd and aah'd*, but these are not invariable. In most instances, common sense will usually dictate a solution to difficult usages. As always, it is better to rewrite rather than risk confusing the reader.

Spelling. Since the spelling of interjections varies from dictionary to dictionary, the following list, which accords with *Webster* (though it includes some not found in *Webster*), offers a standard styling for some of the most common conversational interjections in English.

aah, ah—expression of satisfaction, delight, content; can have negative connotations of regret or longing
aha—exclamation of discovery, contempt, triumph, irony
ahem—clearing the throat; drawing attention to oneself; interrupting
ai, aie, aiee—expression of grief, despair, pain
alas—expression of grief or woe; now considered comically melodramatic and antiquated
argh, aargh—expression of despair, often mock or exaggerated frustration (one of Charlie Brown's favorites)
aw—expressing sympathy (either feigned or sincere), incredulity, disgust, or disappointment
ay, ay me—expression of regret or sorrow. Not *aye*, which is an affirmative vote (as in *aye* and *nay*)
bah—expression of disdain or contempt (as in Scrooge's "bah, humbug")
brr—a whirring sound with the lips; the state of being cold
duh—expression of dim-wittedness; used as a mocking accusation of stupidity
eek—a shriek or scream of fright, usually comic ("Eek! A mouse!")
eh—used as a question, "Is that right?" or to beg the listener's agreement; often used as Canadian locution
er—expressing a pause, searching for words, inarticulateness. Be careful not to double the *r*, since it will be misread as the verb *to err* (to commit an error)
glub—sound of drowning or of water in a drain; sometimes repeated, usually comic in effect
gulp—the act of swallowing, usually expressing anxiety or fear
ha, hah—expression of contempt, surprise, triumph, joy, or discovery
ha-ha—laughter, derision, or amusement
harrumph—communicates indignation, a dissatisfied turning away, a certain self-righteousness, a blustering clearing of the throat
hee, hee-hee—laughter or giggling
h'm, hmm—thoughtful pondering, musing
ho—surprise, calling attention to something (as in *land ho*)
ho-ho—expression of discovery or laughter (used by Santa Claus)
huh—expression of surprise, doubt, disbelief, confusion; also an expression of wondering; usually followed by a question mark
humph—expression of disdain or disgust, doubt or uncertainty
hup—shout of a marching cadence
hurrah, hurray—cheer; expression of joy, excitement, etc.; also *huzzah*, which is an antiquated form of *hurrah*
hut—a marching cadence or a football quarterback's directive
ick—expression of disgust

mm—expression of content with taste of food or drink, like *yum*; also can express a state of pondering, similar to *h'm*

oh—expression of surprise, pain, abashment, or understanding; used often in direct address

oh-oh—taunting, discovery, contempt

ooh, oo—(rhymes with *who*) wonder, joy, satisfaction, or sometimes concern

oops—dismay or surprise, usually involving a mistake or accident

ouch—usually followed by exclamation point; expression of sudden pain

ow—intense pain

oy, oy vey—Yiddish expression of a sigh

pew—expression of disgust, as with a bad odor

phew—expression of relief, fatigue; sometimes an expression of sensing an unpleasant smell

rah, rah-rah—a cheer, a shout of encouragement

sh, shh—request for someone to be quiet

tee-hee—laughter or giggling

tsk-tsk, tsk—expression of scolding; "For shame!"

ugh—expression of disgust, aversion, or fright

uh—expression of pause, filling time, searching for words

uh-huh—positive; saying yes; also mock agreement

uh-oh—same force as "Oh no!"; favorite expression of toddlers when something falls

uh-uh—negative; saying no

um—hesitation, doubt, searching for words

whew—expression of relief after a close scrape

whoa—"stop" or "slow down"; usually said to horses

woo-hoo—a celebratory cry, similar to *hurrah* or *yippee*

wow—expression of being impressed; powerful emotion, either good or bad

yahoo—a triumphal cry, similar to *yippee*

yay—a cheer, similar to *hurrah* (*Webster* prefers *yea*)

yech, yecch—expression of disgust

yippee—a triumphal cry, similar to *hurrah*

yo—getting someone's attention

yoo-hoo—a call to attract someone's attention

yow—expression of pain or dismay

yuck, yuk—expression of disgust, distaste

yum, yummy—expression of content with taste of food or drink

zz—suggesting sleep or snoring; is considered comic no matter how many times the letter is repeated

INTERJECTIONS OF GREETING AND PARTING

Most common interjections of greeting and parting (*ahoy*, *aloha*, *hiya*, *hello*, *howdy*, *shalom*, *yo*, and so on) offer little difficulty, but some can be tricky, especially if they are made of two words or are colloquially condensed. Here are some recommendations for handling them consistently: *bye* (not *by*), *bye-bye*, *goodbye* (or *good-bye*), *good day*, *good evening*, *good morning*, *good night*, *night-night*, *nighty-night*, *so long*, *ta-ta*. (Also see "*goodbye, good-bye, goodby, good-by*.") Hyphenate them as compound adjectives, as in *a good-night kiss*.

INTERNAL CAPITAL LETTER

See "MIDCAP."

INTERNATIONAL STANDARD BOOK NUMBER (ISBN)

An International Standard Book Number (ISBN), which is a standard part of the CIP data, is obtained for every publication. (See "CATALOGING-IN-PUBLICATION DATA [CIP].") If no CIP is used in a particular book or if the CIP is located elsewhere in the book, then the ISBN is still shown on the copyright page. The ISBN also always appears somewhere on the cover or flap of the book (customarily in the EAN, or barcode).

Cloth, Paper, and Ebook Editions. Each separate format of any book—whether cloth, paper, audio, or ebook—has its own ISBN.

Series. Each book in a series has its own ISBN. If a multivolume set is to be sold only and invariably as a unit, then a single ISBN may be assigned to the set, though this is rare. An example would be when volume one contains a text and volume two contains the annotations to that text, or when two or more closely related books are available only as a boxed set.

Reprints and Revisions. If a book is reprinted in a new format or binding style or has been heavily revised (as opposed to only simple corrections being made), a new ISBN is assigned. Usually, if more than about 10 percent of the content is new, then the book is considered a revision, though this guideline is not universally recognized. If the book cover is to be redesigned without changing the format and content of the original, the original ISBN is retained. (See also "REPRINTS AND REVISIONS.")

Obtaining. Commercial publishers as well as self-publishers may obtain ISBNs for their publications by writing R. R. Bowker Co., 1180 Avenue of the American, New York, NY 10036 or by applying online at http://www.isbn-us.com/home1/?gclid=CKTE2Y7PtcgCFUyAaQodTE0NMQ.

Note: It is redundant to say "ISBN number," since the N in the abbreviation already stands for "number." Just "ISBN" suffices.

INTRODUCTION

When present, an *introduction* is the final element of a book's front matter. The introduction is usually written by the author but can, on occasion, be written by someone else. If a well-known person has written the introduction, it is best to place that writer's name at the beginning of the introduction, right after the title, where it will be noticed. Otherwise, the author's name and a dateline (if used) come at the end of the piece. If the introduction is written by the book's author, no signature or dateline is needed unless the writer requests it (see "EXPLICIT"). If two or more introductions are reprinted from various editions of the book, the original introduction appears closest to the text itself.

What distinguishes an introduction from a foreword or a preface is the degree of relatedness to the text itself. An introduction has a closer thematic connection to the content and is more crucial to an understanding of the text than a foreword or a preface, both of which can often be left unread without limiting the reader's appreciation of the book. (See also "FOREWORD" and "PREFACE.")

INTERRUPTED DIALOGUE

See "DIALOGUE, INTERRUPTED."

ISBN

See "INTERNATIONAL STANDARD BOOK NUMBER (ISBN)."

ISLAMIC RELIGIOUS TERMS

Of the three great monotheistic faiths, all of which claim Abraham as their authority, Islam is the second largest. According to Pew Research (June 2013), about 1.6 billion Muslims live in the world, which is 23% of the world's population, compared to 2.18 billion Christians, or about a third of the world's population; and 14 million Jews, or .2% of the world's population. Christians and Jews alike owe it to themselves to know more about Islam's history, culture, and customs. The following list shows only a few of the more common Islamic religious terms, with recommended spelling, capitalization, and styling, as well as some rudimentary definitions. (Also see "*Islam, Islamic, Islamist*," "JEWISH RELIGIOUS TERMS," and "*Muslim*.")

adhan—call to prayer

AH—the abbreviation of *anno Hegirae* ("in the year of the Hegira"); the beginning of the Islamic calendar, which began on July 16, 622 CE. Like AD, BC, CE, and BCE, it is usually set in full caps without periods.

Islamic scholars often use the abbreviations BCE (before the Common Era) to specify dates before the birth of Christ and CE (Common Era) to specify dates between the birth of Christ and 622. See *Hegira*.

alim—an Islamic scholar; the plural is *ulama*

Allah—means "the one true God"; always capitalized; used interchangeably with *God*

ayatollah—the most learned and respected among various Shiite teachers and interpreters of the law; capitalize the term as a title when it precedes a proper name

fakir—a Muslim religious mendicant or, by extension, a Muslim or Hindu holy man noted for asceticism

fatwa—an opinion rendered by a religious leader on a matter of interpretation of the law; it is a recommended opinion but not necessarily legally binding on believers; occasionally spelled *fatwah*

five pillars of Islam, the—(sometimes capitalized) the five essentials of the Muslim faith: (1) *shahada*: belief that "there is no god but God, and Muhammad is his prophet"; (2) *salat*: praying five times a day, facing Mecca; (3) *zakat*: giving alms; (4) *saum*: fasting during Ramadan, the ninth month of the Islamic year; and (5) *Hajj*: making at least one pilgrimage, or *hajj*, to Mecca.

hajj—a pilgrimage to Mecca. Most Muslims try to make at least one pilgrimage to Mecca in a lifetime. This pilgrimage is called a *hajj*, while the pilgrim is called a *hajji*.

halal—ritually approved food according to Islamic law

Hegira—Arab word meaning "flight"; always capitalized when referring specifically to Muhammad's flight from Mecca to Medina, 622 CE. The Muslim calendar begins with that event; hence, AH (*anno Hegirae*, "in the year of the Hegira") for dates. Sometimes spelled *Hejira*. When lowercase, it means any escape from a dangerous situation, somewhat similar in sense to the Hebrew idea of *exodus*.

imam—the prayer leader in a mosque; can also mean one who claims descent from Muhammad and serves as a religious leader with responsibility over a given region

Injeel—(capitalized) the NT Gospels

Islam—(always capitalized) the term that means "submission to God"

Islamic calendar—a lunar calendar that retrogrades in thirty-year cycles and is reckoned in terms of years since the Hegira (622 CE, which is termed 1 AH by Muslims)

jihad—"the struggle along the path toward God," often implying one's personal struggle in the faith, though it is also used to mean violent conflict with one's enemies

Koran—see *Qur'an*, in both this list and the Word List

Muhammad—(c. 570–632) the founder of Islam and the receiver of the faith's holy scriptures, the Qur'an, in about 610. He is considered by Muslims to be the final prophet in a line of prophets that stretches back to Abraham.

mujahideen—one who carries out a jihad; a holy warrior

mullah—an interpreter or teacher of Islamic law; capitalize the term as a title before a proper name

Qur'an (Koran)—the holy book, written in Arabic, believed by Muslims to be Allah's direct revelation to Muhammad; see "*Qur'an, Koran*" in the Word List

Ramadan—the ninth month of the Islamic calendar, during which the faithful are required to fast

sharia—the term, literally meaning "the path to the water hole," that refers to Islamic law as a whole, the body of law applicable to all Muslims; see "*sharia law*" in the Word List

sharif—a person of influence or importance in Muslim countries; originally referred to any descendant of Muhammad through his daughter Fatima

sheikh—a learned Muslim leader or chief; sometimes spelled *sheik*; capitalize the term as a title before proper names

Shia (n.), Shiite (n. and adj.)—the branch of Islam that believes Ali and the imams were Muhammad's legitimate successors; see *Sunni* in this list

Sufism—a mystical branch of Islam, often stressing meditation and eremitism; an adherent is a *Sufi*

Sunna—the customary practices of Islam based on the extraqur'anic teachings of Muhammad

Sunni—the branch of Islam that adheres to the orthodox traditions and believes that the first four caliphs after Muhammad were his legitimate successors; see *Shia* in this list

talib—a student of Islamic law

ulema (or ulama)—a group of Muslim scholars

Zabur—(capitalized) the Psalms of the Hebrew OT

ITALIC

Italic type (*right-leaning letters like these*) was devised by Venetian Renaissance printer Aldus Manutius for his series of Roman classics. Said to be inspired by the elegant handwriting of the Italian poet Petrarch, italic type took up less space than ordinary roman type and allowed Aldus to produce readable, compact editions at a reasonable price, which helped fuel the Renaissance. Although Aldus set entire books in italic, italic type is used with discretion in our time. Not only are extended passages in italic difficult to read, but tests have shown that they slow the reader somewhat, causing distraction, fatigue, and, at times, misreading.

Italic type is indispensable in the following, fairly well-defined situations.

Words as Words, Phrases as Phrases. **A word or phrase referred to as a word or phrase is set in italic. When such a word or phrase is defined (for instance, when translating a foreign phrase), the formal definition is usually set in quotation marks and roman type. Use italic even when the word or phrase in question is quoted from another source.**

Early Methodist ministers used the word *liberty* to describe an openness to God's Spirit in their preaching. [A word referred to as a word]

The words that do the most political work are simple ones—*jobs and growth, family values*, and *color-blind*, not to mention *life* and *choice*. [From Geoffrey Nunberg, *Going Nucular*, 124–25; phrases and words referred to as phrases and words]

By *feretory*, hagiographers mean "a shrine in which a saint's bones are deposited and venerated." [A word referred to as a word, accompanied by a formal definition in quotations marks]

When Philautus says, "so unkinde a yeare it hath beene ...," "unusual" would cover all he need mean by *unkinde*. [From C. S. Lewis, *Studies in Words*; the word *unkinde* is italicized because it is discussed as a word, even though it is drawn from a quoted source; *unusual* is in quotation marks since it defines *unkinde*.]

To refine this last point: if it is important to signal to the reader that the word-as-word or phrase-as-phrase is intentionally quoted from another source, then quotation marks rather than italic may be used, often with a said reference.

That is why [Augustine] took Paul's words "Welcome him whose belief is weak" as aimed at him personally. [From Garry Wills, *Augustine's* Confessions, 74; the phrase is referred to as a phrase, but the quotation marks signal that it is quoted from a specific source.]

Specialized Vocabulary. **Technical terms or words likely to be unfamiliar to the reader, especially when accompanied by a definition, are usually set in italic in the first reference and in roman type thereafter.**

Medieval theories of *impanation* asserted that the elements of Communion could be both the real presence of Christ and bread and wine at the same time. Impanation was condemned as heresy and is no longer propounded.

Titles. Italic is used for titles of certain works and for some names. (Compare the following list with the one given in "QUOTATION MARKS," section on "*In Titles*.") Italicize the titles of:

Artworks, including art exhibitions, installations, paintings, photographs, sculptures: *The Bayeux Tapestry*; *David*; *The Gates of Hell*; *Self-Portrait in a Convex Mirror*

Audio recordings, including collections of songs, music albums, spoken-word recordings: *Dylan Thomas Reads His Own Poetry*; *Mississippi Mass Choir: The First Twenty Years*; *Shadows in the Night* (individual song titles are set in roman and quotation marks)

Blogs: *A Holy Experience*; *Rachel Held Evans*; *Red Letter Christians*; *ReNew* (titles of individual blog entries are set in roman and quotation marks)

Books, ebooks, and enhanced ebooks: *The Dawn Mistaken for Dusk*; *Letters from the Land of Cancer*; *The Lion, the Witch and the Wardrobe*; *One Thousand Gifts*; *The Pioneer Woman Cooks: Food from My Frontier*

Computer games (specifically named): *Grand Theft Auto*; *Minecraft*; *Singing Monsters*; *Trivia Crack* (names of general computer and smartphone application sites are usually set in roman: Fitbit, Google Play, Instagram, Spotify Music)

Curricula, whether in print, digital, or multimedia formats: *Marketplace AD 29*; *What's So Amazing about Grace Groupware*

Feature-length films: *The Apostle*; *The Hobbit*; *The Man Who Would Be King*; *Philomena*; *The Return of Martin Guerre*

Legal cases: *Brown v. Board of Education*; *Citizens United v. Federal Election Commission*; *Roe v. Wade*

Long poems or collections of poems: C. D. Wright's *One with Others*; John Milton's *Paradise Lost*; John Leax's *Remembering Jesus: Sonnets and Songs*; William Blake's *Songs of Innocence and Experience*

Musical compositions, including ballets, musicals, operas, printed collections, and any performance-length composition: *Amahl and the Night Visitors*; *The Bay Psalm Book*; *Godspell*; *The Nutcracker*; *Sports et Divertissements*; *The Well-Tempered Clavier*; *The Symphony of Sorrows*

Newspapers, journals, magazines, and newsletters, whether in print or online (do not italicize the initial *the* in ordinary text): the *Christian Century*; the *Christian Science Monitor*; the *Faith and Imagination Newsletter*; *Gadfly Online*; the *Hightower Lowdown*; *Rock and Sling*; *Salon.com* (names of web-based companies are set in roman type like any company name: Amazon.com, eBay)

Plays: *The Cocktail Party*; *The Producers*; *Shadowlands*; *The Shoemaker's Holiday*

Ships and aircraft: USS *Constitution*; the space shuttle *Challenger*; the *Spirit of St. Louis*; RMS *Titanic* (the designations USS, SS, HMS, and RMS are not italicized)

Television and radio series, shows, and programs: *All Things Considered*; *Breaking Bad*; *Freaks and Geeks*; *Wait Wait ... Don't Tell Me!* (titles of individual episodes are set in roman and quotation marks)

The word *magazine* is set lowercase and in roman type when it is not part of the official name of a publication: *Eternity* magazine; *Time* magazine; but *Parents Magazine*.

Also, the initial article of a title may be dropped when syntax warrants it, such as following a possessive noun or pronoun. Omit an initial article if another article or an adjective precedes it.

They planned on reading Tolkien's *Lord of the Rings* aloud. [The word *The* omitted]

The powerful *Jesus I Never Knew* by Philip Yancey ... [The word *The* omitted]

For Titles of Specific Modern Editions of the Bible. Specific modern editions of the Bible are set in italic, especially when they appear in many editions and formats, unlike the names of general versions of the Bible, which are set in roman type.

Specific Editions:

Good News Bible: The Bible in Today's English Version
The King James 2000 Edition
The Message
The New Testament in Modern English (J. B. Phillips)
The NIV Study Bible
The Oxford Annotated Bible: Revised Standard Version
Scofield Reference Bible: King James Version
Young's Literal Translation of the Bible

General Versions:

Breeches Bible
Jerusalem Bible
King James Version
New International Version
J. B. Phillips's paraphrase of the New Testament
Revised Standard Version
Today's English Version
Vulgate

For Emphasis. While it is best to minimize the use of italic to indicate emphasis, a word or phrase may occasionally be italicized when a specific emphasis will not be clear otherwise. A dependence on italic for emphasis is a sign of weak writing.

Emphasis Added in Quotations. When an author, quoting another source, uses italic to emphasize words that are not italicized in the original, the reader should be notified. Place an ascription, like *emphasis added*, in parentheses immediately after the quotation.

> Note the contrast in David's parallelism: "When we were overwhelmed by sins, *you* forgave our transgressions" (Ps. 65:3, emphasis added).

Foreign Words and Phrases. Foreign words and phrases are set in italic only when they are likely to be unfamiliar to the reader. Foreign expressions that appear among the main entries of *Webster* do not require italic, while those not listed in the main entries of *Webster* or those only listed in its "Foreign Words and Phrases" section are, in most cases, unfamiliar enough to require italic. If an unusual foreign word or phrase is introduced as a way of conveying a specialized or technical meaning, italicize it when first defined. Thereafter it may be set in regular type. (See also "FOREIGN WORDS AND PHRASES COMMON TO CHRISTIAN LIFE AND WORSHIP.")

Scholarly Terms and Abbreviations. Except for *sic*, which is usually italicized, scholarly Latin terms and abbreviations (like *e.g.*, *et al.*, *q.v.*) are set in roman. When in doubt, consult *Webster* or *CMoS*. (See also "ABBREVIATIONS: SCHOLARLY.")

Thoughts. We no longer recommend that a person's thoughts, imagined words, and unspoken prayers, when expressed in the first person, be set in italic—for two reasons. First, long stretches of italic can be difficult to read, and second, italic can be mistaken for emphasis. Italic may be used when such thoughts are infrequent or cannot be conveyed without italic. Otherwise, thoughts are expressed in roman type, with or without quotation marks, according to the author's preference. (See "THOUGHTS" for more detail.)

> "Dear Father," prayed Augustine silently, "make me pure—but not quite yet!" [Quotation marks used for unspoken prayer]
>
> Ananias looked at the blind man and thought, Surely I have not been called to heal him! [Roman type, without quotation marks, used for thought]
>
> *I will lay my weapons upon the altar of Christ*, thought Ignatius as he rode toward Montserrat. [Italic for occasional use]

Dream Sequences, Flashbacks, and Other Narrative Devices in Fiction. Sometimes in fiction, italic may be used to distinguish typographically between the simple past tense, in which the story is being told, and such things as dream sequences, flashbacks, and other fictional devices. If such devices are frequent or highly extended, the editor and author may want to consult with the book's designer so that either an alternate typographic setting may be sought or a typeface with a highly readable italic face may be chosen. (See also "DISEMBODIED VOICES, CONVEYING IN DIALOGUE.")

Italic in the KJV and NASB. In most editions of the KJV, italic is used to highlight words for which no corresponding words exist in the original. The translators often added words to make sense of elliptical passages or to fill in words that were only implied. In most cases, the KJV's italicized words are set in roman when quoting from that version. (For more discussion, see "QUOTING THE BIBLE," section on "*Italic in the KJV and NASB*.") The New American Standard Bible follows the style of the KJV; in addition, it uses italic whenever the OT is quoted in the NT. Again, the NASB's italicized words are set in roman when quoting that version.

> "And Pharaoh said unto his servants, Can we find *such a one* as this *is*, a man in whom the Spirit of God *is*?" [Gen. 41:38, as it appears in the KJV]
>
> "And Pharaoh said unto his servants, Can we find such a one as this is, a man in whom the Spirit of God is?" [The same passage as it would ordinarily be quoted]

J

JARGON, RELIGIOUS

Every religion has its own vocabulary, words that help the faithful communicate with each other but can also leave those outside feeling excluded—at which point the words become a code that only the initiated understand. Even the subgroups within a religion often develop their own exclusive lingo.

Evangelicals have developed a vocabulary that is often opaque to non-Christians and even many Christians outside evangelicalism. While much of this vocabulary may be appropriate when communicating to a targeted readership, writers should be wary of using such Christian jargon when writing for a broader audience. Unconsciously, some writers allow the outdated rhetoric of sermons, hymns, and devotional literature to shape their prose, resulting in indefiniteness, lack of originality, and at worst, insincerity.

Jargon, like clichés, anachronisms, and archaisms, can prove valuable in the skilled writer's hands, but it is an obstacle to good communication when used unthinkingly. Religious writing is strengthened when writers find innovative, contemporary ways of expressing ideas. Here are some examples of evangelical jargon to be used with discretion, if at all. Most approach the level of cliché.

abundant life
after God's own heart
alive to the Spirit
believe on (the name of the Lord)
born again
brothers and sisters in the Lord
burden of (on) my heart
carnal desires
cast a vision
Christian walk
crossed over (died)
daily walk, one's
den of iniquity
depths of depravity (or despair)
desires of the flesh
desires of your heart
devout Catholic
epitome of evil
eternal refuge
eternal resting place
eternal reward
fervent prayer
fleshly desires
forever and ever
from on high
get into the Word
giant of the faith
God-fearing man (or woman)
God made known (or revealed) to me
God-shaped vacuum
good Christian

groanings of the spirit
grounded in the faith
grounded in the Word
heart of the gospel
heathen, the
heavenly angels
heavenly anthems
heavenly host
hellfire and damnation
highest heavens
hopeless sinner
host of angels
inspired Word of God
just pray (just ask)
laid upon my heart
let go and let God
life abundant
life-changing experience
life everlasting
life of sin
lift [someone] up in prayer
lift up the Lord
lusts of the flesh
meet his [or her] Maker
moved by the Spirit
of old [as in "Abraham of old"]
passions of the flesh
pearly gates
person/people of faith
poor sinner
prayer warrior
precious blood of Jesus
prepare our hearts
primrose path
prodigal ways
real Christian
realms of glory
rooted in the faith
rooted in the Word
saving knowledge of Christ
seventh heaven
share a verse [of Scripture]
sins of the fathers
snares of the devil
sorely tempted
soul of humility
spiritual high
spiritual state
spoke to my heart
stand before the judgment seat
stars in one's crown
storms [tempests] of life
straight and narrow
take captive every thought
take it to the Lord
throughout eternity
time immemorial
traveling mercies
trials and tribulations
trophies of grace
trust and obey
turn it over to God
unrepentant sinner
unspoken needs
unto eternity
unto the ends of the earth
uphold in prayer
urgings of the Spirit
vale of tears
victorious living
wait on the Lord/God
walk by faith
walk in the Spirit
walk with God
watch and pray
weeping and moaning
wicked ways
wiles of the devil
wondrous ways of God
word of faith
word of prayer

JESUS, NAMES FOR

See "TRINITY, NAMES FOR PERSONS OF THE."

JEWISH HOLIDAYS AND FEASTS

To those unfamiliar with them, Jewish holidays and feasts can seem baffling. The following descriptions of the seven major seasons and holy days of the Jewish calendar offer some clarification. These are largely movable feasts, so the months in parentheses are only general time frames.

Hanukkah (Feast of the Dedication) is an eight-day festival commemorating the victory of Judas Maccabeus over the Seleucids and the rededication of the temple in Jerusalem. It starts on the twenty-fifth day of Kislev (December) and incorporates the Festival of Lights, in which the eight candles of the menorah are lit by a ninth. Sometimes spelled *Chanukah* or *Hanukah*.

Passover (Pesach) commemorates the exodus of the Jews from Egypt. It is celebrated from the fourteenth to the twenty-second days of Nisan (March–April).

Purim (Feast of Esther, or Feast of Lots) is a joyous festival commemorating the deliverance of the Persian Jews from a massacre as recounted in the book of Esther. It is celebrated on the fourteenth day of Adar (February–March).

Rosh Hashanah (Jewish New Year) falls on the first and second days of the Hebrew month Tishri (September–October). After ten days of penitence, Yom Kippur is observed. Together, Rosh Hashanah and Yom Kippur are termed the *High Holy Days*.

Shabuoth (Pentecost, or Feast of Weeks) takes place on the sixth and seventh days of Sivan (May–June) around the world, though only on the sixth in Israel. It is an agricultural festival during which the story of the grain harvest in the book of Ruth is recounted. Secondarily, the festival commemorates the receiving of the Ten Commandments.

Sukkoth (Feast of Tabernacles) is the annual harvest celebration. This eight-day festival begins on the fifteenth day of Tishri (September–October). The day after the end of Sukkoth is Simhath, which celebrates the completion of the annual reading of the Torah. Also spelled *Sukkot*.

Yom Kippur (Day of Atonement) is a day of praying for forgiveness for the sins of the past year and of fasting, observed on the tenth day of Tishri (September–October).

JEWISH RELIGIOUS TERMS

Since Judaism, along with Christianity and Islam, is one of the three great monotheistic faiths, it is important for Christians to understand the Jewish roots of their faith. The following list of modern Jewish religious terms provides some basic information. While inevitably incomplete, such a list offers a few of the most common terms, along with their recommended spellings, capitalization, and definitions, using *Webster* as a guideline whenever possible.

bar mitzvah—at age thirteen, a Jewish boy is considered a morally responsible adult; he is then called a *bar mitzvah* (Hebrew, "son of the law"), as is the initiation ceremony that takes place at that time.

bas mitzvah—at age thirteen, a Jewish girl, like a *bar mitzvah*, is considered a morally responsible adult; she is called a *bas mitzvah* (Hebrew, "daughter of the law"), or sometimes a *bat mitzvah*, which is also the name of the initiation ceremony that takes place.

B'nai B'rith—the largest international Jewish service organization, founded in 1843 by Henry Jones, committed to training, charity, and education

cantor—the prayer leader and singer for a congregation

congregation—a group of Jews who meet regularly is called a *congregation*.

Conservative Judaism—one of the three forms of Judaism, alongside Orthodox and Reform, practiced in the US, though it is called Masorti Judaism worldwide. It started in the mid-nineteenth century as a reaction against the more liberal Reform Judaism.

"El Malei Rachamim"—"Lord, full of mercy"; the title of a Jewish prayer of remembrance

Gemara—the part of the Talmud that is the commentary on the traditions (Mishnah)

Haggadah—the passage from the Hebrew Scriptures about Passover that is recited at a Seder meal. The plural is *Haggadot*.

Halacha—(also spelled *Halakha*) the part of the Talmud dedicated to unwritten laws based on oral interpretations of the Scriptures

Hallel—Ps. 113–18, selections of which are chanted at Passover and other feasts

Hanukkah—the Festival of Lights, or the Feast of Dedication, also spelled *Chanukah*

Hasidism—a Jewish religious movement founded c. 1750, tending toward mysticism and stressing personal devotion over scholarly interpretation of Scriptures; capitalized. Related to a Jewish movement of the second century CE, which rejected Hellenism

Kabbalah—a mystical method of interpreting the Hebrew Scriptures. Usually capitalized and used without an article. Sometimes spelled *Cabala*

Kaddish—the Jewish prayer for the dead, recited in Aramaic (not Hebrew); always capitalized

kippah—(also spelled *kipa*) a yarmulke, or skullcap. The plural is *kippot.*

kittel—a white ceremonial robe in which the dead are wrapped; sometimes worn by worshipers during Yom Kippur; pronounced so that it rhymes with *little*

kosher—food prepared in accordance with the Hebrew Scriptures and ceremonial law

menorah—a ceremonial candelabra, accommodating seven, eight, or nine candles depending on use

mezuzah—a small scroll on which is written the texts of Deut. 6:4–9 (beginning "Hear, O Israel: The LORD our God, the LORD is one"); 11:13–21 (beginning "So if you faithfully obey the commands . . ."); and the name *Shaddai.* In Jewish custom, this scroll is attached to the doorframe of a house as a reminder of one's faith. The word *mezuzah* means "doorpost."

midrash—stories told, sometimes with elaborations, from the Hebrew Scriptures; to teach a lesson in the Law or a moral principle

Mishnah—(also spelled *Mishna*) a collection of traditions and incorporated into the Talmud

mitzvah—a commandment in Jewish law. The plural is *mitzvoth,* though *mitzvahs* is also common.

Orthodox Judaism—one of the principal movements within Judaism, teaching that the Law is divinely given and therefore immutable and without exception throughout history

patriarchs—Abraham, Isaac, Jacob; the founders and forefathers of the Jewish faith

Pesach—Passover

phylactery—one of two small, leather, square boxes that contain passages from Scripture and are worn by Jewish men on the head and forearm during certain prayers

rabbi—the spiritual head of a congregation

Reform Judaism—a movement within Judaism that believes the faith should adapt to and participate in contemporary culture

Seder—a Jewish ceremonial meal served at the beginning of Passover as a commemoration of the exodus from Egypt. The term is sometimes lowercase.

shalom—"peace"; used as a salutation in both greeting and bidding farewell

shofar—the ram's horn trumpet used on Jewish holidays. The plural is *shofroth*.

Talmud—Jewish traditions, made up of the Mishnah (traditions), the Gemara (commentaries), and Halacha (laws)

tetragrammaton—the four letters of the Hebrew alphabet that stand for God's personal name: YHWH, or JHVH. Some Jewish publishers capitalize this term.

Torah—narrow reference to the Five Books of Moses (the first five books of the Hebrew Scriptures) but may also mean all Jewish learning and law

Yahweh—the name by which God is known (Ex. 3:14); used in place of his proper name, which is unknowable; how the letters of the tetragrammaton are pronounced

yarmulke—(pronounced YAH-mul-kuh) Yiddish term for the skullcap. In the US the Hebrew term *kippah* is more often used. To avoid confusion, the English *skullcap* is the most convenient fallback.

JOGGING AND FANNING

Jogging and *fanning* have nothing to do with running and cooling off afterward. They are two bits of age-old publishing-house practice that are worth sharing with anyone who works with stacks of paper (like writers, editors, and proofreaders). First, manuscripts that are "jogged" (all edges even) are easiest to work with. Since thick stacks of paper don't jog easily, here's a trick: stand the stack on its side and loosely bend the ends toward you. Then grip the ends tightly as you straighten the stack. The back part of the stack will bow outward, allowing air between the pages. Now you can jog the stack firmly on the table, and the pages will fall evenly into place. It is a courtesy to jog stacks of paper before passing them on to the next person in the production process.

If you need to turn the pages quickly or flip through the stack with your thumb, then *fanning* is the best method. Simply jog the paper stack so all edges are even. Firmly grasp the top of the stack. Carefully bend the bottom part of the stack up, toward you, allowing the bottom edge to fan out evenly at an angle. Then firmly grasp the bottom edge to maintain the angle, loosening your grip on the top edge as you do so. Lay the stack on the desk. With the bottom edges now angled toward you, you can easily turn each page quickly with the thumb or flip speedily through the entire stack. All this may seem senseless to those who don't work with paper, but it is a timesaver for those who do.

K

KEYS ON ELECTRONIC DEVICES

See "BUTTONS (OR KEYS) ON ELECTRONIC DEVICES."

KING JAMES VERSION, SPELLINGS IN THE

Different editions of the KJV follow different rules of spelling. The 1769 edition, on which most of our modern editions are based, differs significantly in spelling from the 1611 original, and a number of "contemporized" KJVs now available do not even agree with each other in matters of spelling, capitalization, and syntax.

Unless you have a compelling reason to use the antiquated and often confusing spellings of the 1611 KJV (such as *powred* for *poured* and *Sonne* for *Son*) or a special reason to use a modern-spelling edition of the KJV, stick with the most universally available, most familiar, and bestselling version, based on the 1769 update. The following commentary concerns that version.

Caution is required when using a computer's spell checker or autocorrect feature on a text that contains quotations from the KJV. Spell-checkers will flag the odd Jacobean verb endings for the second- and third-persons singular, such as *makest* and *taketh* (see "KING JAMES VERSION, VERB ENDINGS") and sometimes recommend hilarious alternatives (suggesting *breadth* for *readeth*, for instance). Spell checkers also flag such KJV words as *vail* (Ex. 34:33) for *veil*, *subtil* (Prov. 7:10) for *subtle*, *instructer* (Gen. 4:22) for *instructor*, and *intreat* (Gen. 23:8) for *entreat*. Spell-checkers set to default to US style also flag all those Briticisms not usually seen in the US: *favour*, *honour*, *neighbour*, *odour*, *rigour*, *Saviour*, *savour*, *valour*, and so on. Be especially aware that autocorrect programs will change some KJV spellings to modern American English *without* notifying the writer or editor.

Several classes of words exist that spell checkers, autocorrect programs, and flesh-and-blood proofreaders are often tempted to modernize but are actually correct in the KJV. The KJV often spells several common adverbs and pronouns as two words instead of one: *any more* (Gen. 8:12), *any one* (Matt. 13:19), *any thing* (John 1:3), *every one* (John 6:40), *every thing* (Matt. 8:33), *every where* (Gen. 13:10), *for ever* (Ps. 23:6), *to day* (Matt. 16:3), and *to morrow* (Josh. 11:6). Spell checkers invariably flag those spellings as incorrect. Still, the KJV is not always consistent, for it will occasionally set the following solid: *anything* (Job 33:32), *everything*

(Num. 18:7), *today* (Luke 23:43), and *tomorrow* (Num. 14:25). At the opposite extreme, the KJV sometimes uses a single word where we would use two words today: for example, *kneadingtrough* (Ex. 8:3), *snuffdishes* (Num. 4:9), and *stumblingblock* (1 Cor. 1:23).

Other quirks include the KJV's occasional use of an apostrophe in such possessives as *our's* (Titus 3:14), *their's* (2 Tim. 3:9), *her's* (Job 39:16), and *your's* (1 Cor. 3:21), though it often uses the modern *ours*, *theirs*, *hers*, and *yours* elsewhere. It universally lowercases the word *sabbath* and seems to randomly shift from *always* in some passages (Luke 21:36) to *alway* in others (John 7:6). In the last sentence, Microsoft Word's autocorrect feature automatically capitalized *sabbath* and changed *alway* to *always* without notification.

For syntactical reasons the KJV occasionally lowercases a word following a question mark or an exclamation point, which autocorrect programs will capitalize. For instance, in the quotation "What? know ye not that your body is the temple of the Holy Ghost" (1 Cor. 6:19), the *know* is lowercase; and in "But woe unto you that are rich! for ye have received your consolation" (Luke 6:24), the *for* is lowercase. In both cases, autocorrect automatically capitalized *know* and *for.* Also note that the KJV capitalizes *Holy Ghost* but lowercases the *h* in *holy Spirit* (except in Luke 11:13).

In short, double-check the accuracy of all quotations from the KJV, and whenever that version is quoted more than a few times in a book, use the spell-checker cautiously and turn off the autocorrect feature entirely while writing or editing.

KING JAMES VERSION, VERB ENDINGS IN THE

The rules behind those Elizabethan and Jacobean *-st* and *-th* verb endings (*dost/doth*, *lovest/loveth*, *makest/maketh*, and so on) are not complex and certainly should not be an impediment to reading the KJV (or Shakespeare, for that matter). The rules are these:

- The *-st* endings are used only for the second-person singular ("thou") for most verbs, as in "Thou lovest righteousness" (Ps. 45:7).
- The *-th* endings are used only for the third-person singular ("he," "she," or "it"), as in "For he that loveth his life shall lose it" (John 12:25).
- The first-person singular ("I") and *all* the plural persons ("we," "ye" [since the KJV uses "you" only as the object of a verb, never a subject] and "they") are exactly the same as our modern English forms:
  - "The world may know that I love the Father" (John 14:31)—first-person singular

- "We know that we love God" (1 John 5:2)—first-person plural
- "If ye love them which love you" (Matt. 5:46)—second-person plural
- "They love to pray standing in the synagogues" (Matt. 6:5)—third-person plural

A few common exceptions exist, such as the verb *to be* and the auxiliary verbs *will* and *shall*. Those verbs in the KJV are inflected like their modern counterparts except for the second-person singular, the forms of which are, respectively, *thou art*, *thou wilt*, and *thou shalt*.

L

LARGE-PRINT BOOKS

The average reader, either with no visual impairment or with adequate vision correction, is able to read 9-point type with 2 points of leading comfortably, whether print or digital, provided that the line lengths are not too long and the type is a standard text face. With age, most readers suffer some degree of visual impairment. According to Lighthouse International, an advocacy organization for the visually impaired, about 17% of Americans older than forty-five have trouble reading, even with correction. That increases to 21% among adults sixty-five years of age and older—more than one in five.[2]

Whether book publishers are up to the challenge of aging readers remains to be seen, though with the advent of tablets and e-readers offering customizable text as well as the expanding print-on-demand technology, the options for producing texts with larger typefaces, euphemistically called *comfort editions*, are becoming less expensive.

Standards. The American Printing House for the Blind, Inc. (APH) has established stringent standards for large-print books, and any publisher that wishes to obtain its imprimatur needs to review that organization's helpful parameters.[3] Sadly, many publishers either are unaware of large-print standards or find them economically unviable, with the result that many so-called large-print books do not meet basic standards.

Publishers often photographically enlarge the pages of a book, in a process called *shooting up*, deeming it large print even though such enlargement may not bring the type up to most large-print standards. Some publishers license their large-print editions to specialty printers, some of which "shoot up" inexpensive editions that are not adequate in size, leading, or type density.

While neither the government nor publishing-industry associations have established clear guidelines for large print, several organizations for the visually impaired have. Most guidelines suggest that 14-point text type is the bare minimum for a book to be considered "large print," though a 16- or 18-point type size is preferable. (APH states that 14–16-point types are "enlarged" and that only 18-point type is "large print.") Some advocates prefer sans-serif types, which many readers feel are less blurry, though some scientific research suggests that the perceptual differences between serif and sans-serif are minimal. (Some studies marginally endorse serif typefaces as more readable for readers without visual impairment.)

The following recommendations are adapted from a variety of sources and offered only as a broad guideline. While not all are feasible for every book, they offer a yardstick against which large-print books can be measured.

1. *Type Size and Font.* The size of the text type should be at least 14 points—though 16- or 18-point type is recommended. Century, Times New Roman, and Garamond are good serif typefaces for large-print reading. The contrast between the thick and thin strokes is minimal, and serifs are not too thin. Verdana, Tahoma, and Helvetica are popular sans-serif faces. With all typefaces, medium should be used, not condensed or fine, and bold is appropriate only for captions, titles, and other display type.
2. *Density.* Density is important for both print and digital type. Type that appears gray is unacceptable for large-print purposes. For most print types, at least 400 dots-per-inch is best. If the text is photographically enlarged, it should not result in letters that are faded, broken, or fuzzy. If type must be "reversed out" (for instance, white type on a black or gray background) for display or graphic purposes, boldface is commonly used to make the type more readable.
3. *Spacing.* The leading (the space between lines) is as important as type size in readability and should be slightly larger than in normal books. Most standards recommend a leading of at least one and a quarter to one and a half times the measurement of the type itself. That is, a 20- to 24-point leading for a 16-point type. Although the leading should be larger than normal, it is important that the letter and word spacing remain standard.
4. *Setting.* Ragged right setting is preferred whenever a large-print is being planned. This minimizes the breaking of words over lines.
5. *Page Size.* The ideal trim size is between 6" x 9" and 8½" x 11". Books with larger pages are too unwieldy.
6. *Paper.* Although one might think pure white paper (called *blue-white*) would offer the best contrast for black type, slightly off-white, natural vellum, or matte stock is recommended because it creates less glare when viewed under the bright reading light often recommended for those with visual impairments.
7. *Margins and Words per Line.* The margins between the body text and the spine of a print book (the "gutter margins") should not be smaller than 7/8". The outside margin between the text body and the three trimmed edges should not be smaller than 1/2". Ideally, the text width should be such that the average line of type contains no more than twelve to fourteen words. This helps the eye "track back" to the next line easily.

8. *Binding.* A flexible binding is helpful so that the book can easily lie open on a flat horizontal or slightly inclined surface.
9. *Columns.* A bold vertical line should be used to separate columns in multiple-column settings.
10. *Numerals.* Numerals should be used for all numbers over ten. Research has shown that numerals are more easily assimilated than numbers that are spelled out. Also, set a phone number without parentheses around the area code, since a parenthesis can be mistaken for the numeral *1*.

LATIN CHARACTERS AND ABBREVIATIONS

See "ABBREVIATIONS: SCHOLARLY" and "SCRIBAL LATIN CHARACTERS AND ABBREVIATIONS."

LCCN

See "LIBRARY OF CONGRESS CONTROL NUMBER (LCCN)."

LEGAL DEPOSIT

See "MANDATORY DEPOSIT."

LETTER GRADES

When conveying an academic letter grade in text, capitalize it (*A*, *B*, *C*, *D*, or *F*) and set it in roman with no quotation marks. An apostrophe is added to *A* to make it plural (*She earned all A's*), since otherwise it would look like the word *As*. The other letter grades are set with apostrophes in the plural when used in proximity to *A's*: that is, *B's*, *C's*, *D's*, and *F's*. Otherwise, those plurals may be set without apostrophes: *Bs*, *Cs*, *Ds*, and *Fs*. If a plus or minus is added, the symbols + and – may be used (using an en dash for the minus sign): *A*–, *B*+, and so on; or they may be spelled out with a hyphen between the elements: *A-minus*, *B-plus*, and so on. When used as an adjective, the spelled-out form is preferred: *an A-minus student*. When grades with a plus or minus need to be made plural, spell them out: *A-minuses*, *B-pluses*, and so on.

LETTERS AS LETTERS

When a letter is referred to as a letter, italicize it unless the reference is a common expression. (See also "WORDS AS WORDS.")

> The unknowns were shown by the letters *x*, *y*, and *z*.
> *A* and *B* in this instance represent the first and the last.
> mind your p's and q's [common expression]

LETTERS AS SHAPES

Single letters are sometimes used not as abbreviations but to suggest shapes. Capitalize or lowercase them according to the shape evoked. A *T square* is in the shape of a capital *T*, so lowercasing it (*t square*) does not make sense. By the same token, the *f-hole* on a violin is shaped like the lowercase letter, not the capital. In most cases, the reference is to the capitalized form. The following is a list of a few common words that use letters for their shapes.

A-frame
C-clamp
E-wing Escort Starfighter
f-hole—lowercase (*f* may be italicized)
I beam—no hyphen
J-bar
L-bracket, L-brace
O-ring
T-bone steak
T-shirt
T square—no hyphen
U-lock
U-turn
V-eight, V-six (engines)
V-neck
Y-back tank top

LETTERS AS WORDS

Sometimes the letters of the alphabet need to be spelled out as words, as in the phrase *to drop one's aitches*. Apart from such typographic terms as *em dash* and *en dash*, we seldom use the spelled-out forms since the letters alone (usually italicized) suffice in most contexts (see "LETTERS AS LETTERS"), but when a careful writer needs to distinguish between *tea* and the letter *tee*, for instance, or *are* and the letter *ar*, the following list might be helpful. Note the vowels are usually spelled with the letter alone, but if further differentiation is required, the forms in parentheses may be used.

A—a (ay)
B—bee
C—cee
D—dee
E—e (ee)
F—ef
G—gee
H—aitch
I—i (eye)
J—jay
K—kay
L—el
M—em
N—en
O—o (oh)
P—pee
Q—cue
R—ar
S—ess
T—tee
U—u (you)
V—vee
W—double-u
X—ex
Y—y (why)
Z—zee (*zed* in UK)

LIBRARY OF CONGRESS CONTROL NUMBER (LCCN)

The Library of Congress Control Number helps librarians and researchers find the "bibliographic record" for books in databases. The number represents the record for the book in all its formats, though books available only as ebooks are not included. After receiving an LCCN, a publisher submits a "best edition" of a book to the Library of Congress (usually a hardcover when both hard- and softcover editions are available). Librarians often prefer this system because an LCCN, unlike an ISBN, does not change when a book's format does or when a new edition appears. (See "INTERNATIONAL STANDARD BOOK NUMBER [ISBN].") LCCNs are a standard part of a book's CIP information. (See "CATALOGING-IN-PUBLICATION DATA [CIP].") For an explanation of how LCCNs are constructed, see http://www.loc.gov/marc/lccn.html.

LIGATURES

A *ligature* is the visual tying together of two or more letter characters into one. In English, the most common are Æ, æ, & (for *et*), *ﬃ*, *ﬄ*, *ﬁ*, *ﬂ*, *ft*, Œ, and œ. Some editors perceive them as especially elegant and will sometimes request that ligatures be used for certain kinds of books, such as classics or books with high design or literary values. Otherwise, such decisions are best left to the book's designer or compositor, who best know the capabilities of their fonts and programs.

One argument against the use of some ligatures is that they can look odd or fuzzy in digital settings—or even be unavailable in the font. Also, when book files are converted or copied, the destination software will sometimes not recognize the ligature character and will replace it with a garbage character. Many typesetting programs automatically convert some appropriate letter combinations into ligatures, but a few fonts do not include them. In any case, an author or editor may recommend the use of ligatures but should not presume to add ligature characters to a manuscript before typesetting.

LIMITED EDITION, CERTIFICATE OF

A *certificate of limited edition*, also called a *limit notice*, sometimes appears in gift books, deluxe editions, and other print books to indicate that the print run of the edition is limited to a specific number of copies. This often increases the value of such books to collectors. It is usually only done for first printings of the first edition, and only when the print run is relatively small (usually less than a thousand copies). Often, the limit information is provided in a colophon at the back of the book (see "COLOPHON"). Otherwise, it can appear in the front matter on its own page, which is called a *limit page*; or, less commonly, it can be given on the copyright page (see "COPYRIGHT PAGE"). The phrasing of the notice is not standardized but may take either of two forms. First, the notice may specify how many copies were printed and provide a space or rule line for an individual copy number to be written in.

This edition was printed in a limited edition of ____ [NUMBER OF COPIES IN THE FIRST PRINTING], of which this copy is number ____ [NUMBER OF INDIVIDUAL COPY].

Second, a limit notice may simply specify how many copies of the book were printed. This is more cost-efficient because it saves hours of tedious hand numbering.

This volume is one of a limited edition of ____ [NUMBER OF COPIES IN THE FIRST PRINTING] copies.

Extra copies of such editions that do not bear a limited edition number are referred to as *out of series*—and *OS* is sometimes written in the space instead of a number.

LITURGICAL INTERJECTIONS

See "INTERJECTIONS OF EXPRESSION" as well as "*amen*," "*hallelujah, alleluia*," and "*hosanna, hosannah*."

LIVE COPY

See "DEAD COPY, LIVE COPY."

LOGO STYLE

As obvious as it may seem that a corporation should dictate the style of its own company's name, such styles may occasionally be overruled in written text for clarity or for reasons of common sense. Some odd stylings are the result of corporate logos, which often take liberties with company names, sometimes unconventionally lowercasing, capitalizing, bolding, italicizing, or eliminating spaces. J. C. Penney, Inc., for instance, refers to its stores as *jcpenney*, in accord with the company signage. Since this may cause confusion for readers, the writer or editor is justified in using the more recognizable *J. C. Penney* or simply *Penney's* in text. Otherwise, when logo styling offers no obstacle to understanding (*Procter & Gamble*, *Jell-O*, *7Up*, for example), honor the company's preferred styling. (Also see "BRAND, PRODUCT, AND COMPANY NAMES: COMMONLY MISSPELLED" as well as "*the, The* [BEFORE NAMES OF ORGANIZATIONS].")

"LOREM IPSUM"

See "DUMMY COPY."

M

MALE PRONOUNS FOR GOD

When a pronoun for God or the Holy Spirit is needed, the traditional male pronouns are most commonly used (see also "DEITY PRONOUN, THE" as well as "*Holy Spirit*," section on "*Gender Pronoun*"). In all cases, use the male pronoun in reference to Jesus.

Still, in deference to God's inclusiveness, some authors are uncomfortable using male pronouns for the Deity, and their opinion should be respected. These writers usually opt either to minimize the use of pronouns for God or to avoid the pronoun completely, repeating the word *God* (or a synonym such as *the Holy One*) as needed. This style can work surprisingly well and is acceptable as long as it doesn't become stilted or artificial, as it does, for instance, in a sentence like *God alone knows God's plans for God's people*, or when a phrase like *God himself* gets transformed into *God Godself*. When that style draws too much attention to itself, the author should rewrite or revise. Such solutions as alternating male and female pronouns for God or using the contrived *he/she* or *s/he* are unacceptable and confuse the reader.

MANDATORY DEPOSIT

The term *mandatory deposit*, sometimes called a *legal deposit*, refers to the legally mandated provision of copies of books and other materials published in the US to the Library of Congress. Every publisher is required, as a condition of copyright protection, to provide two copies of every copyrightable work to the Copyright Office of the Library of Congress within three months of publication. This also applies to foreign works that are published in the US by means of either distribution of imported copies or a new edition printed in the US. Materials should be mailed to:

Library of Congress
Copyright Office CAD 407
101 Independence Avenue SE
Washington, DC 20559-6607

Further information can be found at http://www.copyright.gov/. This website also provides a means of searching copyright registrations from 1978 to the present. Phone: Public Information Office (202) 707–3000; Forms and Publications Hotline (202) 707–9100.

MANUSCRIPT PREPARATION: AUTHOR GUIDELINES

Most contracted manuscripts are submitted electronically to the publisher in a standard word-processing format, such as Microsoft Word. In most cases, the data should be styled as *flat* as possible (that is, free of unusual or special formatting) so that the publisher can most easily convert the data for typesetting. Authors should resist the temptation to design and format their manuscript to simulate a printed book. A standard 12-point Times New Roman (or comparable font), double-spaced with one-inch margins, is a convenient and common format, one that helps the publisher calculate the length of the finished book. When a printout is also contractually required, the hard copy should be printed on one side only of standard 8½-by-11-inch white paper, double-spaced, with about one-inch margins on all sides.

Preparing Artwork. When the book includes artwork (or any graphic matter reproduced from another source), a digital scan or a clean photocopy of the original should accompany the manuscript. In the electronic version, the artwork, if already digitized, should be segregated in a separate graphics file and not embedded in the word-processing document along with the written text. Inclusion of graphics files in a word-processing document will increase the likelihood of an inaccurate conversion of the data. Note that graphics copied off the internet may not be usable for book purposes; first, they are likely to be copyrighted, and written permission from the original copyright holder will be needed; and second, their resolution may not be high enough to reproduce well either in a printed book or ebook.

Preparing Tables and Charts. Simple tabular material such as charts and graphs may be inserted directly into the document. If the material is complex or involves nontype elements (such as line art, curved figures, or three-dimensional graph-bar formatting), then it should be placed in a separate file to be inserted later. If you can easily type the table, graph, or chart using the basic keys on the keyboard (letters, numbers, tabs, symbols), it should be included in the text. Anything more complex than that is considered art and will need to be freshly created by the compositor, digitally scanned, or submitted in a separate graphics file.

Matters of Style. Once a book is contracted, the author should request the publisher's style guidelines, or "house style" document. The author will then communicate to the editor all matters of preference, especially when they conflict with the publisher's style, and distinctive features that may require the editor's attention. The author's responsibility for obtaining permission to quote from published sources, for ensuring the accuracy of quoted material, for providing complete and detailed references, and for other such matters are delineated in this manual. (See "PERMISSION GUIDELINES: GENERAL," "NOTES," and "SOURCES.")

Quoting from the Bible. The author is responsible for checking the accuracy of all Bible references and the wording of quotations from the Bible before submitting the manuscript to the publisher. The author should also state the predominant Bible version used and indicate in the manuscript whenever any alternate version is used. When no translation is preferred, this manual recommends the New International Version as an accurate and accessible modern translation. (See "PERMISSION GUIDELINES: THE BIBLE" and "QUOTING THE BIBLE.")

Quoting from Other Sources. The author is responsible for checking the accuracy of all quotations from other sources. (See "QUOTATIONS, GENERAL" and "QUOTING ONLINE SOURCES.") The quotations should be reproduced exactly as they appear in the source, with no style changes to make it conform with either the author's or the publisher's style. The primary exception is when antiquated spellings might confuse the reader. In those cases, the modern spelling may be substituted. In the course of writing and researching, authors should be careful to note the sources for the borrowed material to save having to retrace their steps later. This is especially important if the quote will require a written permission. (See "PERMISSION GUIDELINES: GENERAL," "PERMISSION GUIDELINES: QUOTING READER REVIEWS FROM A WEBSITE," and "WRITERS, TEN COMMANDMENTS FOR.")

Using Greek and Hebrew. Since religious books often contain words and quotations from Greek and Hebrew, whose characters are not found on all word processors, the author is responsible for indicating such characters and any accompanying diacritical marks in their correct positions—by hand if necessary. (For a list of convenient Greek and Hebrew transliterations, see *The SBL Handbook of Style, 2nd Edition*, sections 8.3.13 and 8.3.4.)

Avoiding Bias and Insensitivity. Authors should eliminate gender bias and any insensitive language in regard to racial, ethnic, disability, religious, and other groups. Such biases are often unintentional and the result of anachronistic forms, obsolete terms, stereotyped assumptions, and unnecessary labeling. (For guidelines and examples, see "DISABILITY DESIGNATIONS," "ETHNIC, NATIONAL, AND RACIAL DESIGNATIONS," and "GENDER-ACCURATE LANGUAGE.")

MEASUREMENTS

Use numerals to indicate precise measurements: *a 12-inch ruler, 10-point type, 1 x 4 pine boards.* When measurements are used in a casual or general sense, they may be spelled out: *a one-gallon jug of milk, a two-ton truck, the castle's sixteen-foot ceilings.* (See "NUMBERS, SPELLING OUT VERSUS USING NUMERALS" for more detail.)

With Fractions. When a measurement is fractionally larger than one but less than two, use the plural noun: *1½ cups of flour, one and a quarter miles from home.* Similarly, use the singular noun for any measurement fractionally less than one (*¾ teaspoon salt*). When a fractional number is spelled out, use the plural denominator and a plural verb when the numerator is more than one (*three quarters of a teaspoon are added* or *only two thirds of the students attend class*).

Dimensions. A plain lowercase letter *x* is commonly used in expressing dimensions: *8½ x 11 stationery.* This is acceptable in casual contexts, especially because the mathematical times sign may not be available in all fonts. Whenever possible in formal or scientific copy, opt for the times sign: *12 × 12 × 15.* When stating dimensions, it is customary to state length, width, and height in that order.

MID-ATLANTIC STYLE

Most publishers cannot afford to issue separate editions of a book for US and UK markets, each with its own style. The following guidelines blend aspects of US and UK style in an attempt to outline a unified style that minimizes discomfort for readers in both cultures. This approach, called mid-Atlantic style or world-English style, should not be confused with "International English," which is a stripped-down form of basic English, intended for foreign speakers.

Mid-Atlantic Style Begins with the Author. When a book is likely to be sold in both the US and the UK, the author should be aware of the extent to which his or her own vocabulary, regional dialect, local references, and topical allusions might confuse readers in one market or the other. Celebrities, retail chains, television shows, and magazines in one country are often unknown in another; and some anecdotes or illustrations may be limited by geography. While most Americans recognize *Stonehenge* and *Westminster Abbey*, for example, few would understand a British reader's associations with *Iona* or *Blackpool*. By the same token, British readers who know *the Grand Canyon* and *the White House* might not be familiar with *the Twin Cities* or *the Delta*.

Vocabulary. Many common objects have different names in the British Isles and the United States, and many shared words have different meanings. This can't be avoided. The best path is to adhere to the author's own vocabulary, whether US or UK. Often, more damage is done by trying to rewrite around a difficult word than by simply leaving it as it is. Editors, copyeditors, and proofreaders should respect the intelligence of readers who, in most cases, know how to interpret the meaning of an occasional unfamiliar word in context.

Phrasing, Syntax, Cadence, and Voice. Editors and proofreaders need to be sensitive to the author's voice as well—whether American or British. Writers should be free to phrase sentences, order their words, establish rhythms in their speech, and choose words in conformity with their unique voice. Unless an editor is certain that a specific usage is wrong in both US and UK style, and that both readerships are likely to be confused, then the editor should not make the change.

Spelling. Like vocabulary and phrasing, an author's national spelling should be retained. Few spelling differences between the US and the UK cause problems; the British *centre* is clearly understood to be *center* by US readers, just as the American *inflection* is understood to be *inflexion* by UK readers.

Quotation Marks. UK publishers conventionally use single quotation marks where US publishers use double quotation marks, though some UK publishers are now adapting the US system. Readers of English worldwide have little difficulty reading either system, and both are workable. While the US style takes up slightly more space than the UK style, this manual recommends US double-quotation-mark style as marginally more useful for a mid-Atlantic style if only because, worldwide, more books in English are actually published in the double-mark style than the single.

Punctuation with Quotation Marks. Use the UK style of punctuation in mid-Atlantic style, especially when the readership is likely to be predominantly or at least half British. The British style has a certain inherent logic that makes it effective and easy to remember. If the readership is certainly going to be predominantly American, then the American style may be used. Ultimately, the two systems only differ in a couple of instances, so this should not be a major change. (See "UK STYLE.")

The Dash. Use the UK spaced en dash instead of the US em dash. This is less obtrusive, breaks more easily over lines, and is more pleasing to the eye.

Dates. For books styled in mid-Atlantic English, use the UK style of spelling out dates (day/month/year, without commas) as the most universally understood: *28 August 1953.*

Abbreviations. Use the British system of abbreviation, that is, avoiding periods wherever possible, especially when the missing letters are from the interior of a word and not the end (as in *Dr*, *Ltd*, *Mr*, *Mrs*, and so on).

Footnoting. Either the UK or the US style of footnoting can be employed; that is, beginning with *1* on every new page (UK) or beginning with *1* only at the beginning of every new chapter (US). Neither is more accessible to most readers than the other, so the author's preference is retained. Using the author's style also minimizes the busywork of converting styles.

Summary. In short, once the author has written the book with an awareness of the international readership, the publisher should:

- Use the author's style in all matters of vocabulary, spelling, phrasing, syntax, footnoting, etc.; query the author when important references seem wholly opaque
- Use US style for quotation marks
- Use UK style for dashes (spaced en dashes), punctuation, dates, and abbreviations
- Use numerals for all numbers over 100, even large rounded ones

(See also "UK STYLE.")

MIDCAP

The last three decades have seen a trend toward using a capital letter in the middle of a product or company name, a usage called a *midcap*. Midcaps commonly occur in two kinds of words: (1) personal and commercial names with a capital letter both at the beginning and in the middle (such as *McCarthy*, *YouTube*, *MasterCard*, *HarperCollins*), and (2) commercial product and company names with a beginning lowercase letter followed by a capital letter (such as *eBay*, *iPad*, *eReader*).

Capitalization. When a midcap of the latter kind falls at the beginning of a sentence or in a title, the current convention is to leave the name as is. For instance, if the name *eBay* is the first word of a sentence, it should appear like this: *eBay managed to sell . . .*; and *not* like this: *EBay managed to sell* . . . The same holds true for titles and headings; for instance, the title of this magazine article: *"iPads, iPods, and iTunes Establish Apple's Dominance."* The reasoning is that the internal capital letter already informs the reader that the word is a proper noun, so no further capitalization is needed. This is why common nouns for electronic products should not contain internal caps; an *e-reader* is a generic term, whereas an *eReader* is the name of a specific commercial product (such as *Sony's Touchscreen eReader*). In that case, the midcap distinguishes the specific from the generic in the same way that an initial capital does. (See also "*ebook*.")

MILITARY TITLES

When it precedes a full name, a military title is usually abbreviated; for instance, *Adm. David Glasgow Farragut*, *Col. Strong Vincent*, *Gen. Ulysses S. Grant*. When it precedes a surname only, spell the title out: *Admiral Farragut*, *Colonel Vincent*, *General Grant*.

MINCED OATHS

A minced oath is a form of euphemism for words or phrases that are considered profanity, swearing, or taking God's name in vain, such as *dang* in place of *damn*, or *heck* in place of *hell*. While a minced oath is not usually considered profanity in itself, some Christians feel it should be treated as profanity and never uttered or written under any circumstances. This is problematic because many readers are unaware of the profanity behind some common minced oaths; for example, *by gum*, *doggone*, *drat*, *for crying out loud*, *gee*, *golly*, *good grief*, *gosh*, *land sakes*, *my goodness*, *phooey*, *shoot*, *shucks*, or *what in Sam Hill*, to name a few. The Christian bestseller *The Shack* uses *gosh* several times, and Charlie Brown would hardly be Charlie Brown if he never said, "Good grief"—which has a long history in English as a euphemism for *good God*. Some terms, like *land o' Goshen* ("God") or *tarnation* ("damnation"), are even considered quaint and nearly *de rigueur* in Western fiction.

Other minced oaths, like *freaking*, *frigging*, *gawd*, *jeez* (and others), are more closely related to the word they represent and would be unacceptable in many Christian publications. But a large gray area exists between the extremes. All this is further complicated by the fact that it is not clear whether some old expressions are minced oaths or not. For instance, etymologists disagree about whether *great Scott* is a minced oath for "[by the] grace of God" or a reference to an overweight Civil War general—or both. The term *my stars and garters* is thought to have its origins in British honors and awards, but many etymologists believe that its distant root is in the phrase *I swear*.

Whatever one thinks of minced oaths, it is hard to imagine fictional dialogue without them. They add realism and color to a novel. Finding the balance between expressions that are too strong and those that are too mild can be difficult. Mild minced oaths are unrealistic in many contexts and risk unintentional humor, as when a fictional detective arrives at a murder scene and says, "Golly." Fictional characters in extraordinary circumstances should be allowed to respond like real human beings.

Each publisher must decide what level of expressiveness they will allow in the use of minced oaths. No rule exists other than what the publisher and author believe a book's readership would feel comfortable with.

The editor's role is particularly important. Each author and editor needs to have an acute sensitivity to the book's ideal readership and a thorough grasp of the publisher's guidelines. (See also "PROFANITY.")

MISNAMING, INTENTIONAL

Some writers intentionally use a slightly incorrect name for anyone they wish to mock or diminish. This is a form of pejorative labeling, or *dysphemism*. Some people in England, for instance, humorously refer to their neighbors to the north as *the Scotch* rather than *the Scots*. Likewise, some American Republicans relish using the name *the Democrat Party* in lieu of *the Democratic Party*, while some Democrats mockingly call the Republicans *the Publican Party*. Intentional misnaming is an old and sometimes useful rhetorical device, but it should be used with care since, as a form of premeditated rudeness, it often reveals more about the author than the intended target.

MOVEMENTS AND ERAS, HISTORICAL

Lowercase broad cultural and historical movements and eras (like *the classical era*, *the monastic movement of the fourth century*, *romanticism*) unless they are based on a proper name (like *Aristotelianism*, *the Arminian movement*, or *the Calvinist era*), or unless they need to be distinguished from generic uses of the words (like *the Civil Rights era*, *the Holiness movement*). Lowercase the terms *movement* and *era*. Still, a great deal of flexibility is allowed. Lowercase terms may be capitalized consistently throughout a work with a special focus on that era or when it would be helpful to the reader to do so (for instance, *the Sixties* could be capitalized in a work specifically about that era). If one movement or era is capitalized in a work, other comparable terms for movements and eras are capitalized as well.

N

NAMES FOR THE BIBLE

See "BIBLE, NAMES FOR THE."

NAMES FOR PERSONS OF THE TRINITY

See "TRINITY, NAMES FOR PERSONS OF THE."

NAMES FOR SATAN

See "SATAN, NAMES FOR."

NATO PHONETIC ALPHABET

The NATO phonetic alphabet is sometimes used in novels about the military or espionage. The system is a communications alphabet that uses words in place of letters and is especially helpful in distinguishing between letters that might otherwise be easily confused in radio or other aural communications (such as the letters *b* and *p*, *d* and *t*, *f* and *s*, *m* and *n*, and *s* and *x*). The letters of the NATO phonetic alphabet are as follows: *Alpha*, *Bravo*, *Charlie*, *Delta*, *Echo*, *Foxtrot*, *Golf*, *Hotel*, *India*, *Juliet*, *Kilo*, *Lima*, *Mike*, *November*, *Oscar*, *Papa*, *Quebec*, *Romeo*, *Sierra*, *Tango*, *Uniform*, *Victor*, *Whiskey*, *Xray*, *Yankee*, *Zulu*. (See also "PHONETIC ALPHABETS.")

NIV STYLE (NEW INTERNATIONAL VERSION)

The translators of the New International Version (NIV) have established a style that is largely compatible with this manual and *CMoS* but differs in a few significant ways. These style exceptions are used for the text of the Bible and any ancillary material, and they are recommended for publications tightly tied to the NIV text. In general, these guidelines also apply to the New International Reader's Version (NIrV).

Omit the Serial Comma. The NIV text omits the comma before *and*, *or*, and *nor* in a series unless the comma is required for clarity or to avoid misreading.

Capitalize Prepositions of Four or More Letters in Titles. While this manual and *CMoS* lowercase all prepositions in titles regardless of length, the NIV capitalizes those of four or more letters.

The Deity Pronoun. The NIV does not allow for any exceptions to its lowercasing of the deity pronoun, whether in the NIV text or in supporting material.

"Lord" and "God" with Small Caps. The cap-and-small-cap forms *LORD* and GOD should be retained in all quotations, regardless of context, when they appear in the NIV.

Spelling Out Numbers. The NIV spells out numbers through ten in ordinary text. This includes numbers indicating people's ages. Use numerals for all numbers over ten except for large round numbers.

Abbreviation of "Chapter(s)." The NIV annotations and ancillary materials abbreviate the words *chapter* and *chapters* as *ch.* and *chs.*, respectively.

Punctuation with Bible References. While the NIV uses an en dash between continuous verse numbers (*Matt. 4:8–10*), it uses an em dash between continuous chapter numbers (*Matt. 4—8*) and continuous verses spanning separate chapters (*Matt. 4:8—5:10*). The NIV does not insert a space after a comma in nonconsecutive verse numbers (*Matt. 4:6,8,10*).

Capitalization. By and large, the NIV accepts most of the capitalized forms of religious terms shown in this manual (see "CAPITALIZATION OF BIBLICAL AND RELIGIOUS TERMS"), though the NIV is less inclined to capitalize occasional epithets for persons of the Trinity, Satan, and some biblical characters, events, and locations. Note the exceptions in the following list, which shows the preferred forms of the editors and translators of the NIV and its ancillary materials:

NIV tends to lowercase occasional epithets for persons of the Trinity

advocate
bread of life (Bible or Christ)
bridegroom
defender
door
eternal God; Eternal God (used both ways; see Rom. 16:26 and Gen. 21:33)
firstborn
great high priest
head
high priest (Christ)
King of glory
King of kings
light of the world
Lord of hosts
Lord of lords
man of sin
man of sorrows
Passover lamb
shepherd (though *Shepherd* in Heb. 13:20 and 1 Peter 5:4)
victor
vine
water of life
way

NIV tends to lowercase epithets for Satan

antichrist	dragon	evil one	wicked one
beast	enemy	serpent	

NIV tends to lowercase some biblical events, people, things, and places

book of life (book of judgment)	patriarch, the (Abraham)
celestial city (abode of the redeemed)	promised land (Canaan or heaven)
Christ-child	sun of righteousness
false prophet (of Revelation)	tower of Babel
high priestly prayer	tree of life (in Garden of Eden and Revelation 22)
Lamb's book of life	word of life
land of promise	word of truth
new Jerusalem (heaven)	

Though some epithets for biblical events, people, things, and places are capitalized

Advent (Christ's first coming)
Battle of Armageddon (final battle)
Children of Israel
Garden of Eden
Garden of Gethsemane
Holy City, holy city (used both ways; see Rev. 21:2, 10 and Rev. 22:19)
Holy Place, holy place (used both ways; see Ez. 45:3 and Ez. 45:4)
Last Judgment, the
Magi
Millennium, the
Nativity, the
Rapture, the
Sheol (italicize when referred to as a Hebrew word)
Tent of Meeting (use lowercase when talking about the construction of the tabernacle but capitalize when the context refers to the finished tabernacle)
Triumphal Entry, the
Virgin Birth, the

NIV tends to capitalize descriptive terms for the Bible and portions of the Bible

Apocryphal	Book of the Law	Mosaic Law
Biblical	Canon, the (Scripture)	post-Biblical
Book of the Covenant	Gospel (John's, et al.)	Scriptural
	Law of Moses	

Miscellaneous

Catholic church (*but* Roman Catholic Church)
Christianize (-ization)
Christology (-ical)
faith-healing
Gentile laws (adj.)
Gnostic (generic)
Good News, the (the gospel)
Judge, judge (used both ways; see James 4:12 and Heb. 12:23)
living word (Bible)
Messiahship
Messianic
Neo-Pentecostalism
Rock, the (Christ); rock, the (used both ways; see 2 Sam. 22:2 and Ps. 92:15)
Satanism
Savior (depends on usage; note on 1 Sam. 8:7: "Lord, who was pledged to be their savior")
twenty-third psalm

NOTE FROM THE AUTHOR

See "AUTHOR'S NOTE."

NOTES

Textual annotations, variously called *citations*, *endnotes*, *footnotes*, *references*, or *text notes*, commonly appear in any of four places: (a) in parentheses in the text itself (called *parenthetical notes* or *in-text notes*); (b) as footnotes at the bottom of the text pages (called *footnotes*, or *bottom-of-page footnotes* to clarify); (c) as chapter endnotes at the back of each chapter (called *chapter endnotes*); or (d) as book endnotes at the back of the book (called *endnotes*, or *book endnotes*). Notes are of two general types: *narrative notes* and *source notes*.

Narrative notes, sometimes called *substantive notes*, are used for any explanatory comments that could not be conveniently incorporated into the text itself. They can define words or points, comment or expand on the text, provide explanations, refer the reader to other parts of the text, or provide information peripheral to the text. Narrative notes are usually provided when the information contained within them would prove disruptive to the reading if it was incorporated into the text.

1. Such was Jeremy Taylor's reputation that he was later referred to as the "Shakespeare of divines."
2. *Euphuistic* is used here to refer specifically to the ornate style of Elizabethan prose.

Source notes, also called *bibliographic notes* or *citations*, inform the reader of the precise sources of quotations, facts, statistics, data, credit lines, or other information; they can also refer the reader to works that might be of related interest.

3. A. C. Cawley, ed., *Everyman and Medieval Miracle Plays* (New York: Dutton, 1959), 79–108.
4. See also Leland Ryken, *Triumphs of the Imagination* (Downers Grove, Ill.: InterVarsity Press, 1979), and Walter Kaufmann, ed., *Religion from Tolstoy to Camus* (New York: Harper & Row, 1961).

Narrative notes and source notes are not mutually exclusive, for a single note can serve both purposes.

5. In many of his books Martin E. Marty tries to get an overview of these tensions in the modern church. Perhaps the most representative of his works on this topic is Martin E. Marty, *Modern American Religion* (Chicago: Univ. of Chicago Press, 1986).

In Popular and Academic Books. Authors of popular books are encouraged to keep the number of narrative notes to a minimum, since such annotations intrude upon the reader's attention and detract from the flow of the reading. In scholarly works narrative notes are often essential to clarify important and complex information, although when possible, the author should still try to keep the number of notes to a minimum. Source notes, of course, are common in both kinds of books whenever quotations or other information has been quoted or taken from another source, although the presentation of such notes can differ greatly in each kind of book.

Parenthetical Notes. The simplest way of including a note is in parentheses within the text itself. These are called ***parenthetical notes***, or ***in-text notes***. This is commonly done with Bible references. These should be short so as not to distract the reader unnecessarily. Some academic disciplines prefer all citations to be inserted, in an abbreviated fashion (usually showing only author last name, date of publication, and page number) within the text itself. Then a more complete source list is given at the end of the book or article with the complete bibliographic references. Refer to the style guides of those disciplines for more detail about the formats the disciplines prefer.

James says that dehumanizing speech stokes the fires of hell (James 3:6), and I assume we all want to avoid that place. [From Preston Sprinkle, *People to Be Loved*; Bible citation in text]

Shakespeare seems to quote the Bible from memory since his quotations don't precisely match either of the popular Bible versions of his time. (Most of the plays were written before the publication of the King James Version.) [Narrative note in text]

"A single behavior/choice/action can result from a combination of motives." (Turvey 2012, 131) [Shortened in-text bibliographic reference]

Citing in Text. A reference is usually pinpointed in text by a superscript number next to the sentence or word to which the note refers. Where possible, place the superscript number at the end of a sentence to minimize distraction. While reference numbers are always set in superscript numerals, the corresponding numerals attached to the note may be set in either superscript with no period or in regular type followed by a period. (Examples of both kinds are found in this entry; see page 250, for example.) Symbol reference marks may be preferred to numerals in some cases (see "*Symbol Reference Marks*" section later in this entry).

The Superscript Number. Whether the notes appear as footnotes, chapter endnotes, or book endnotes, begin superscript citations in the text over again at 1 in every new chapter (or every page in UK style) whenever such citations are numerous. If relatively few notes appear in the book, they may be numbered consecutively throughout. Superscript numbers follow all punctuation marks except a dash and are placed at the end of a sentence or a clause whenever possible. Place them at the end of a block quotation rather than with the statement that introduces the block quotation. Do not italicize them even if they are adjacent to italic text. The use of symbols instead of numerals should be reserved for bottom-of-page footnoting only.

Superscripts in Display Type. Avoid superscript citation numerals in lines of display type or after subheadings. Find an alternative location.

Unnumbered Footnote. If a general note applies to an entire chapter and not to a specific word or passage, it should be unnumbered and appear on the first page of the chapter as a footnote, whether or not the rest of the book is annotated in a footnote style.

Headings for Book Endnotes. In the endnotes section in the back matter of a book, the number and title of each chapter should appear as a heading for notes from that chapter so that those notes will be easier to locate. These section markers can be eliminated if there are relatively few notes throughout the book.

The Hidden Endnote Style for Nonacademic Books. A *hidden* (or *blind*) *endnote style* may be used for those books in which it is desirable to avoid the academic appearance of superscript footnote or endnote callouts. Hidden endnotes are arranged at the back of the book like ordinary endnotes, but instead of being linked to superscript numbers in the text, the note itself is listed by the page number and the first word or words of the sentence or phrase to which it refers. Thus, no superscript numbers are given in the text at all. Like an index entry, the hidden endnote makes its own reference by using the page number and an associated word or words. Also like an index, this style of endnoting has to be done at the end of the production process when the pages have all been correctly set and flowed. Any change in pagination, obviously, would cause the page references of the hidden endnotes to shift.

Here are some examples of the hidden endnote style:

[page] 33. *This child is destined . . .*: Luke 2:34.

38. *The prayer-book exiles during the Commonwealth . . .*: Alan Jacobs, *The Book of Common Prayer: A Biography* (Princeton: Princeton University Press, 2013), 96.

136n. *Muggeridge.* Malcolm Muggeridge, "Books," in *Esquire*, April 1972, 39. [The *n* indicates that the name is referenced in a footnote on that page.]

Footnoting Often Discouraged. Although some academic writers view footnotes as more scholarly than endnotes, many publishers discourage the use of footnotes for two reasons: (1) footnotes often unnecessarily distract the reader from the main argument of the book, and (2) the small type and narrow leading are often unattractive. Endnotes, it may be countered, are more of a distraction in that they force the reader to turn to the back of the book each time a superscript citation appears. But ideally, endnotes are less distracting, because the reader can look up only those notes that are of special interest. Still, whenever the author or editor expects readers to scrutinize the sources extremely closely—as in polemics or books dealing with major controversies—footnotes are the best option.

Footnotes and Endnotes Together. In some cases, footnotes and endnotes may be used in the same work. If narrative notes are so closely related to the text that it is not appropriate to set them as endnotes, set them as footnotes instead. In such cases, cite the footnote references in the text by using the symbol reference marks (*, †, ‡, and so on). Cite endnote references with superscript numbers.

Symbol Reference Marks. Symbol reference marks are used in the following sequence only if more than one note appears on a particular page. Otherwise, the sequence begins with the asterisk on each new page.

* asterisk or star	‡ double dagger	‖ parallel lines
† dagger	§ section mark	¶ paragraph mark

(then the same marks doubled: **, ††, ‡‡, and so on)

Titles and Degrees of Authors. Titles and degrees are usually not given with authors' names in source notes and are only included in narrative notes if that information is pertinent.

Referencing Books. The following information is normally included, as appropriate, in a source note that cites a book as the source:

Full name of author(s) or editor(s)
Title and subtitle of book
Full name of editor(s) or translator(s), if any
Name of series, and volume and number in the series
Edition, if other than the first
Number of volumes
Facts of publication: city (and state if city is not well known), publisher, and year of publication (all in parentheses)
Volume number
Page number(s) of the citation

6. Winthrop S. Hudson, *Religion in America*, 2d ed. (New York: Charles Scribner's Sons, 1973), 154.
7. John Calvin, *Institutes of the Christian Religion*, ed. John T. McNeill, 2 vols. (Philadelphia: Westminster, 1960), 2:1016.
8. Ruth A. Tucker and Walter Liefeld, *Daughters of the Church* (Grand Rapids: Zondervan, 1987), 100–102.

Including State Names in Sources. For well-known cities, state names need not be used in notes or bibliographies. When in doubt, use the state abbreviation.

Using the Shortened Form of the Publisher's Name. Delete such words as *Publisher, Inc., Co., Press*, and *Books* after the names of publishers in citations. Retain such words as *Press* and *Books* whenever a publisher's name might be confused with its parent organization or another institution; for instance, the university presses or such publishers as Moody Press or InterVarsity Press. Use the longer form for university presses, though drop the article *the* and shorten the word *University* to *Univ.* Thus, *the University of Chicago Press* could be rendered *Univ. of Chicago Press.*

References to Classical and Scholarly Works. References to classical and some scholarly works appearing in many editions may be designated by division numbers rather than page numbers. This enables citations to be located regardless of the particular edition an author uses. Different levels of division (such as book, section, paragraph, line) are indicated by numerals separated by periods. Commas, en dashes, and semicolons are used for multiple references just as they are in citing page numbers.

Numerals are usually arabic. Using division numbers eliminates the need for volume and page numbers, but notes may contain both forms of notation if desired.

[9] Saint Augustine, *Confessions* 9.23–31. [Book 9, sections 23 through 31]
[10] Eusebius, *The History of the Church* 1.2.15, 18. [Book 1, section 2, paragraphs 15 and 18]
[11] William Langland, *Piers Plowman* 5.136–89; 15.1–49. [Canto 5, lines 136 through 189; and canto 15, lines 1 through 49]
[12] John Calvin, *Institutes of the Christian Religion*, ed. John T. McNeill, 2.1.5. [Book 2, chapter 1, paragraph 5]
[13] *The Didache*, 2.9.1 [Part 2, section 9, line 1]

Referencing Periodicals. The following information is normally included in citing an article from a periodical as the source:

Full name of author(s)	Volume and issue numbers
Title	Date (in parentheses)
Name of periodical	Page number(s)

Note that not all of this information is available for every periodical. Popular newspapers and magazines often do not carry discernible volume and issue numbers (though most of them have such numbers), and many articles do not carry a byline. In such cases, as much of the information as possible should be provided. Some manuals, like *CMoS*, recommend that the date information of popular magazines, as opposed to scholarly journals, be separated with commas rather than parentheses. That style is perfectly acceptable as long as it is consistently applied throughout a work. But since the line between scholarly journals and popular ones is sometimes thin, and since many works contain a mix of both kinds of references, we recommend staying with parentheses in all cases. Note also that a colon precedes page number(s) if volume and/or issue numbers are given; otherwise, a comma is used.

14. James Johnson, "Charles G. Finney and a Theology of Revivalism," *Church History* 38 (September 1969): 357.
15. Mark Edmundson, "Test of Faith," *American Scholar* 64, no. 4 (Autumn 2015): 83.
16. Tom Carson, "Baring the Celtic Soul of U2," *Los Angeles Times Book Review* (March 27, 1988), 15.
17. "Bruce Cockburn: Singer in a Dangerous Time," *Sojourners* 17, no. 1 (January 1988): 28–35.

Referencing Websites. Several styles of referencing websites exist. This manual recommends a style modified from that proposed by the Modern

Language Association, which is also compatible with the general principles laid out in *CMoS*. We recommend the style outlined here for a number of reasons, not the least of which is that this format resembles that already used for books and periodicals. This manual does not insist on providing access dates, though an author may provide them if they will be helpful.

The following elements are included where available or applicable.

Full name of author(s), first name, then last name

Title of page, entry, or article

Title of the larger work of which the entry or article may be a part (if applicable) (in italic)

Version or file number (if available)

Publication, posting, or last-revision date (if available)

The website's name (in italic)

The website's URL (in italic)

Access date (in parentheses) (if known)

18. Cal Thomas, "Have We Settled for Caesar?" *Is the Religious Right Finished? Christianity Online*: *www.christianity.net/ct/current/* (September 21, 1999).
19. John Bunyan, "The Author's Apology for His Book," *The Pilgrim's Progress*. Last updated May 27, 1999. *Christian Classics Ethereal Library*: *ccel.wheaton.edu* (August 4, 1999).

The Use of "Ibid." For both book and periodical references, *Ibid.* takes the place of the author's name, the title, and page number when all that information is identical to the information in the immediately preceding note. If the author and title are the same but the page reference has changed, *Ibid.* may be used with the new page reference. In books for a general or popular readership, authors are encouraged to repeat short-form references instead of using *Ibid.*, especially in endnotes. (See next paragraph for the proper elements of a short-form reference.) In academic and scholarly books, *Ibid.* is used primarily in bottom-of-page footnotes, while short-form references are preferred for repeated endnotes. If many endnotes are repeated consecutively, they may be condensed into a single endnote listing all the various page numbers. (See also "*ibid.*")

[20] Nicholas Wolterstorff, *Art in Action* (Grand Rapids: Eerdmans, 1980), 45.

[21] Ibid., 47.

[22] Ibid.

Note that *Ibid.* is not italicized when used in references. (It was only italicized here to show that it was a word being used as a word.)

Using Short-Form References. For second references to a work within a single chapter, a short-form reference is used in both scholarly and popular works. This is preferred over the older system of using "op. cit." or "loc. cit." A short-form reference includes the author's last name, a shortened form of the title (if it is more than five words), and a page reference.

23. James Samuel Preus, *From Shadow to Promise: Old Testament Interpretation from Augustine to Young Luther* (Cambridge, Mass.: Belknap, 1969), 50.
24. Wolterstorff, *Art in Action*, 97.
25. Preus, *From Shadow to Promise*, 58.

Using Page Citations for Books and Periodicals. Whenever possible, exact page references are given in lieu of using a single page number followed by *ff.* Such abbreviations as *vol.* and *p.* or *pp.* are unnecessary unless their omission will result in ambiguity.

State Abbreviations in Notes. Most manuals prefer two-letter postal abbreviations for state names with publishers' locations in notes and bibliographies. The older, conventional state abbreviations may be used at the discretion of the author and as long as they are used consistently. (See "STATE AND PROVINCE ABBREVIATIONS.")

NUMBERS, BRITISH

See "UK STYLE," section on "*British Numbering.*"

NUMBERS, INCLUSIVE (ELISION)

To show a range of numbers, use an unspaced en dash. These are called *inclusive numbers*. The second number may be elided (shortened) in some combinations, especially in year designations and page references. The most common elisions are listed here:

For date references:

2000–2004 [do not elide when first number ends in 00]	1910–14
	1914–18
2000–2014 [do not elide when first number ends in 00]	1897–1901
	AD 374–79
1904–8	379–374 BC [do not elide year dates that are BC or BCE]
1905–13	

For page numbers and bibliographic references:

2–3	101–5
22–23 [not 22–3]	110–25
100–107 [do not elide when first number ends in 00]	151–58
	1081–87
100–119 [do not elide when first number ends in 00]	12,483–515

Remember that such numbers are inclusive. If a person lived in China from 2000 to 2004, that is usually considered a five-year stay, not a four-year stay. (See also "PAGES, COUNTING.") Also, if a range of numbers is introduced with the word *from*, then the word *to* is used between the numbers instead of an en dash: *from 1914 to 1918*, not *from 1914–1918*.

In Titles. Do not elide numbers in a book title: for instance, *The Impending Crisis, 1848–1861* or *T. S. Eliot: Collected Poems, 1909–1962*.

NUMBERS: SPELLING OUT VERSUS USING NUMERALS

Spell out numbers of one hundred or less (*six* or *seventy-one*) and round numbers in hundreds (*two hundred*), thousands (*nine thousand* or *thirty-two thousand*), millions (*three million*), billions (*nine billion*), and so on. When a million or a billion (or higher) is preceded by a two- or three-digit number (or decimal combination of two or more digits), it may be expressed with a combination of numerals and words (such as *2.4 million, 130 billion, 14.9 trillion*). Use numerals for all other numbers (for example: *195*; *1,876*; *385,000*). (For an alternate method of spelling out numbers, see the next-to-last section of this entry: "*Journal Style.*")

Ordinal Numbers. The preceding guidelines also apply to ordinal numbers (for example, *twenty-first century*, *tenth grade*, but *the 115th person to receive the award*). The forms for ordinal numbers that combine numerals and superscript letters are: *1st*, *2nd*, *3rd*, *4th*, *5th*, *6th*, *7th*, *8th*, *9th*, *10th*, and so on.

Groups of Numbers. If several numbers are given for similar items in a group, style all the numbers in the same way, whether as numerals or spelled out. If any of the numbers contain three or more digits, use numerals for them all.

> With a choir of fifty people and a worship committee of more than thirty, why can't we get more than two people to take care of infants on Sunday?
>
> There are 61 graduate students in the religion department, 14 in the classics department, and 93 in the romance languages, totaling 168 in the three departments.

Percentages. Use numerals with percentages in nearly all contexts (*he graduated in the top 10 percent of his class*). For most nontechnical purposes, use the word *percent* with the numeral rather than the percent symbol (%), but in technical, statistical, or frequent usage, use the % symbol (*recent polls show that only 10% of the people polled favor the new policy*). Also use the percent symbol in tables and charts. Note that when the symbol is used, a word space should not be placed between the numeral and the symbol. In dialogue, a number may be spelled out in any percentage that could be considered informal: as in *"I'll bet you not five percent of the people know that."*

Idioms and Common Expressions with Numbers. A handful of idiomatic expressions using numbers has gained currency. It is not always possible to formulate guidelines for such expressions, but the following list offers a few of the most common.

Catch-22—usually capitalized; hyphen is always used

eight ball, behind the

eighteen-wheeler

800 number, an

800-pound gorilla—sometimes "900-pound gorilla." (These are curious expressions since even the largest gorillas don't weigh much more than 500 pounds.)

eleventh hour, the

fifty-fifty—even odds

five-star hotel

4x4—four-wheel drive car; use numerals

4-H Club

Fourth of July holiday, the Fourth

forty-niner, a—California gold miner

hundred-and-fifty percent, to give a—to work exceptionally hard; spell it out

million, to look (or feel) like a

9/11 attacks—spoken as "nine-eleven" or "the events of September eleventh"

nine-to-five job, to work nine-to-five, a nine-to-fiver

n^{th} degree, to the—*n* stands for an unknown number

ninety-nine percenter, a—income bracket

one percenter, a—income bracket

666—the antichrist; spoken as "six, six, six"

ten-gallon hat

3-D—three-dimensional; use numeral when abbreviated

Twelfth Night

twentysomething, thirtysomething, and so on

20/20 vision, or twenty-twenty vision—either is acceptable, though numerals slightly preferred

24/7, or twenty-four/seven—"night and day, seven days a week"; either numerals or spelling it out is acceptable

two-by-four, two-by-six, etc.—lumber; spell out in casual references, but use numerals for precise measurements

Measurements. Use numerals for precise measurements in scientific, statistical, or technical contexts: *47 percent*, *98° Fahrenheit*, *the 45th parallel*. Even in nontechnical contexts, use numerals with objects or devices that are defined by exacting measures: *a .22mm rifle*, *a 60mm camera lens*, *a 24k-gold ring*, *an 18-horsepower engine*. Objects defined by casual measurements use numbers that are spelled out according to the common guidelines: *a two-ton boulder*, *a twelve-foot ladder*, *a two-liter bottle*, *an eight-foot-deep swimming pool*. In some cases, numbers may be either spelled out or set as numerals according to the context (*three-by-five card*, or *3 x 5 card*). The multiplication symbol × or the letter *x* may replace the word "by" in technical works (*an area of 12 × 12 centimeters*), though *x* is sufficient in nontechnical writing (*an 8½ x 11 sheet*).

Parts of a Book. Use numerals referring to the parts of a book. This is one of the more common exceptions to the rule that recommends spelling out words under one hundred: as in *The author makes four points in chapter 6; as indicated in table 3 on page 97.*

The Beginning of a Sentence. Customarily, a number at the beginning of a sentence is spelled out. If that cannot be done without causing clumsiness, then the sentence should be rewritten.

First Corinthians 1:27 introduces what Paul calls "the foolishness of God."

Nineteen seventy-eight marked the five hundredth anniversary of the birth of Sir Thomas More.

The five hundredth anniversary of the birth of Sir Thomas More was observed in 1978.

Dialogue. Except for year dates, most numbers are spelled out in dialogue as long as it can be done with clarity. Numerals may be used whenever the numbers are so large that it would be impractical or awkward to spell them out.

"On October thirty-first, 1517," said the tour guide, "more than four hundred and ninety-nine years ago, Luther affixed his Ninety-Five Theses to this very door."

Money. Monetary references are spelled out or set in numerals according to the general guidelines for numbers. If several dollar amounts are given in close context, set them as numerals. When fractional and whole dollar amounts appear near each other, place zeros after the decimals in the whole dollar amounts for consistency.

> Hundreds of people paid fifty dollars each to hear the candidate in person. [Spelled out]
>
> The deacons collected $413. [No decimal point or *00* is needed.]
>
> The agent received $9.50, $22.00, and $28.00 for the three sales. [Because of the first *.50*, decimals and *00*s were added to the other numbers for consistency.]

Age. Always spell out numbers indicating ages of people, even if they are older than one hundred. Note the correct hyphenation of the following: *a class full of five-year-olds, a twenty-five-year-old woman, he was sixty years old, she lived to be one hundred and eleven.*

Street Addresses. When a street bearing a number for its name is mentioned in text, the name is usually spelled out (*Ninth Street*). (For more detail, see "ADDRESSES, STREET.") House numbers or other numbers used with that name should always be given in figures: *Fifth Avenue, 21 Forty-Second Street, Fifty-second Street, 221b Baker Street.*

Route Numbers. In both formal and informal writing, road and highway route numbers should always be shown in numerals: *Highway 61, M-21, Interstate 75* or *I-75, Route 66.* Note that hyphens are used with route numbers, not en dashes.

Journal Style. An alternate system of spelling out numbers is found in newspapers. Basically, journalists commonly spell out numbers of a single digit (that is, *one* through *nine*) and set all numbers *10* and higher in numerals. This is convenient even for some non-newspaper contexts. Some writers of nonfiction for children and young adults, for instance, use newspaper style because studies have shown that numerals are more quickly understood than spelled-out numbers. Whenever space or speed of reading are considerations, journal style should be considered.

Webpage Style. Use journal style (previous entry) for numbers on webpages.

NUMBERS, TELEPHONE AND CELL PHONE

See "PHONE NUMBERS IN TEXT (TELEPHONE AND CELL PHONE)."

NUMERAL PREFIXES

The following list shows the common, correct prefixes indicating numeric values, such as those found in such words as *monotheism*, *deuterocanonical*, *triptych*, or *tetragrammaton*.

Numeral	From Latin	From Greek
one	uni-	mono-
two	du-, *or* duo-	deuter-, *or* deutero-
(twice	bi-	di-)
three	tri-	tri-
four	quadr-	tetra-
five	quin-, *or* quinque-	penta-
six	sex-	hexa-
seven	sept-	hept-
eight	oct-, *or* octo-	oct-, *or* octo-
nine	nona-	nove-, *or* novem-
ten	dec-, *or* decem-	deca-
hundred	cent-	deca-
thousand	mill-, *or* mille-	kilo-

NUMERALS, COMMAS WITH

Use a comma in numerals of four or more digits: *1,000*; *1,476*; *9,000*; *9,500*; *31,928*; *5,000,000*. The main exceptions are page numbers of four numerals in cross-references and bibliographic references and in year designations:

> See page 1125.
>
> C. S. Lewis, *The Collected Letters of C. S. Lewis: Narnia, Cambridge, and Joy, 1950–1963* (San Francisco: HarperSanFrancisco, 2007), 1305.
>
> Most historians date the Cold War from 1947 to 1991.

O

OMNIBUS EDITION

The term *omnibus edition* refers to a book that contains several reprinted works, usually by one author, in a single volume.

ORPHANS (TYPOGRAPHIC)

See "WIDOWS AND ORPHANS (TYPOGRAPHIC)."

OUTLINES AND LISTS

An outline explains and organizes information systematically and hierarchically. Two major systems of multilevel outlining are recommended: the *traditional system* and the *decimal system*.

The Traditional System. This system is appropriate for short, informal outlines that might appear in popular or trade books. It is the one most readers have been familiar with since primary-school days. Such outlines follow this format:

I. C. S. Lewis [capital roman numeral with period]
  A. Writings [capital letter with period]
    1. Fiction [arabic numeral with period]
      a. The *Narnia* books [lowercase letter with period]
        (1) *The Lion, the Witch and the Wardrobe* [arabic numeral in parentheses]
          (a) Characters [lowercase letter in parentheses]
            (i) Aslan [lowercase roman numeral in parentheses]

The Decimal System. The decimal system is so-called because it uses a period between numbers, though they aren't truly decimals; they merely separate the levels of information. Decimal style is used in formal presentations in which a strict hierarchy needs to be maintained, for instance, in scholarly, reference, and textbook settings. That said, the decimal system is most accessible when it does not go beyond two or three levels, since the multiplication of levels can be quite confusing. A decimal outline follows this pattern:

1. C. S. Lewis
  1.1 Writings
    1.1.1. Fiction

1.1.1.1. The *Narnia* books
1.1.1.1.1. *The Lion, the Witch and the Wardrobe*
1.1.1.1.1.1. Characters
1.1.1.1.1.1.1. Aslan

Runover Lines. **Runover lines in outlines should begin under the first letter of the first word in the previous line.**

1. Gregory contributes his support and energies to the formation of the papal states.
2. Gregory becomes a leading advocate of the missionary work in England.
3. Taken as a whole, Gregory's writings earn him the status of "Doctor of the Church."
    a. *The Book of Morals* is his most extensive commentary.
    b. To this day, his *Dialogues* continues to be considered his most influential work.

At Least Two Points. **Each level of an outline should have at least two points.**

Informal Outlines. **In popular books where outlining is minimal, less formal, or not carried beyond the third level, it is acceptable to begin the outline with *A.* or *1.* rather than the roman numeral.**

OXFORD COMMA (SERIAL COMMA)

See "COMMA," section on "*With a Series of Elements.*"

P

PAGES, COUNTING

One doesn't think of counting pages as tricky. After all, a chapter that runs from page 22 to page 34 is twelve pages long, right? One simply subtracts the smaller number from the larger. *Wrong.* That chapter actually runs 13 pages because the numbers must be calculated inclusively, and therein lies the potential for miscommunication among authors, editors, typesetters, and printers. This is often a problem, for instance, when unnumbered blank pages are present at the back of a printed book. Some companies insert promotional materials or discussion questions on those pages, so an exact count is helpful. The printer also usually needs to know the exact number of blanks to account for, since being off by one page can cause confusion or even misprinting. (See also "PHOTO SECTIONS" for other problems with counting pages.)

As a rule, whenever you use subtraction to calculate the number of pages, ask yourself whether the page count is inclusive. If so, add one to the answer.

PAIRED CONJUNCTIONS

See "*both ... and*" and "*either ... or, neither ... nor.*"

PARAGRAPHING DIALOGUE

When writing dialogue in fiction or nonfiction, set each speaker's words as a new indented paragraph (a custom formalized by the French writer Balzac and his contemporaries because they were paid for their fiction by the line). Although it may violate our sense of propriety, occasionally good reasons exist to run dialogue together. In some cases, it may be unavoidable because of sentence structure. There is no reason, for instance, a writer should not be able to write:

> When Polyphemus asked, "Who are you?" Odysseus replied, "Nobody," and when the other Cyclopes later asked Polyphemus, "Who was it who blinded you?" Polyphemus replied, "Nobody."

Sometimes a writer runs dialogue into a single paragraph to communicate a sense of hurry, humor, or repetitiveness.

> "Are you sure?" "Yes." "Absolutely?" "Yes." "Beyond a doubt?" "Yes." "Yes?" "Yes!"

It is also common in children's picture books and books for beginning readers to make no distinction between paragraphs at all, so that all kinds of text are run together. By and large, children's writers and editors feel that paragraphing, as a typographic device, is lost on young readers. To avoid confusion, the *said references* in such books need to be carefully managed to clarify who the speaker is. (See also "SAID REFERENCES.")

The disadvantage of running dialogue together is that it may confuse readers accustomed to the traditional method. But if it can be done with no loss of clarity, then it is a legitimate, and often useful, device. The paragraphing of dialogue is no different from any other rule of grammar and style: if there's a good reason to break it, do so. "Really?" "Yes!"

PARENTHESES

Text inside parentheses expands, comments on, explains, defines a point, or makes an aside. While commas and em dashes can also be used to set apart parenthetical thoughts and statements, commas are best used when an extremely close affinity exists between the inserted element and the rest of the sentence. By contrast, using dashes to set off a parenthetical idea conveys a heightened sense of energy, urgency, interruption, or immediacy.

> William of Ockham (after whom the term "Ockham's Razor" was coined) left Avignon in 1328. [Makes an aside]
>
> Lancelot Andrewes, who was said to have kept Christmas all the year, was noted for his hospitality. [Close affinity]
>
> "For only love—which means humility—can cast out the fear which is the root of all war." [From Thomas Merton, *Seeds of Contemplation*; sense of energy and urgency]

Numbered Lists. When lists are run into the text, parentheses are used around the numbers or letters: *(1)*, *(2)*, *(3)*, and so on. Do not use just a closing parenthesis: *1)*, *2)*, *3)*,...

> Historians are usually careful to distinguish between (1) Macarius Magnes, (2) Macarius of Alexandria, and (3) Macarius of Egypt.

With Other Punctuation. Periods, question marks, and exclamation points are placed outside a closing parenthesis when the parenthetical statement is inserted in a larger sentence, though a question mark or exclamation point is placed inside the closing parenthesis when it is part of the parenthetical statement itself. Periods, question marks, and exclamation points are placed inside the closing parenthesis when the entire sentence is enclosed in parentheses.

Elizabeth Fry's activities reflected the many social concerns of her time (such as slavery, mission work among the Indians, and the poor).

Dorothy Sayers published her first detective novel (could she have guessed how popular they would become?) just after establishing her teaching career.

The Ephesus that Paul knew was the major trade center in the Roman province of Asia. (By 950 CE it had become a ghost town.)

With Font Changes. **Set parentheses in the same font as the main text and not necessarily in the font of the material contained within the parentheses. Ordinarily this means that parentheses are set in roman type unless they are used in an italic title, heading, or display line or in a text sentence that is entirely italic.**

The Latin form (*sacire*) ultimately comes from a Hittite word, meaning "to make sacred." [Parentheses in roman]

The title of the book was *How to Make (and Lose) a Million*. [Parentheses in italic as part of title]

With Bible References. **When a parenthetical Scripture reference immediately follows a Scripture quotation, place any needed punctuation after the parenthetical reference. If the quotation itself requires a question mark or exclamation point, it should be placed with the text regardless of what punctuation follows the closing parenthesis.**

"Jesus wept" (John 11:35), the shortest verse in Scripture, is often quoted out of context.

"In the beginning God created the heavens and the earth. Now the earth was formless and empty" (Gen. 1:1–2).

"Lord, are you going to wash my feet?" (John 13:6).

PAST TENSE OF THE PAST TENSE

See "PLUPERFECT."

PERCENTAGES

See "NUMBERS: SPELLING OUT VERSUS USING NUMERALS," section on "*Percentages.*"

PERFORMANCE SYMBOL

The *performance symbol*, sometimes called the *p-in-the-circle*, is used to indicate copyrighted sound recordings, including audio books. The performance symbol does not serve as a copyright notice for any of the material that accompanies the recording, whether in print or ebook format. A copyright symbol with a complete copyright notice should be provided to protect

any material that accompanies a sound recording, though, conversely, it should be understood that the © symbol does not protect the audio recording. (See also "COPYRIGHT NOTICE." For a detailed discussion of how the performance symbol is used, see William S. Strong, *The Copyright Book: A Practical Guide*, 6th edition [Cambridge, Mass.: MIT Press, 2014].)

PERIOD

As an End Stop. The most common use for a period is as an end stop, that is, to signal the end of a declarative or imperative sentence.

In Initials and Abbreviations. The period is also used in initials (*J. I. Packer, E. F. Hutton*) and abbreviations (*a.m., Mr., 1 Thess.*), though some abbreviations do not commonly use periods (*OT, BA, JFK*). (For guidelines, see "ABBREVIATIONS," section on "*With or Without Periods.*")

In Vertical Lists with Numbers or Letters. When items are listed vertically using numerals or letters, a period should follow each numeral or letter.

1. Susannah Wesley
2. Hannah More
3. Phoebe Palmer

In Vertical Lists of Sentences. In a vertical list, a period is used after each item only if at least one of the items is a complete sentence.

Among Whitefield's favorite themes were the following:

The boundlessness of God's love.
Man's misery without God.
Repentance is necessary for salvation.

With Captions and Legends. A period is used after photo captions and other descriptive copy attached to charts or graphic illustrations only when such copy forms a complete sentence.

Illustration: Thomas Cromwell [No period]

Table 1: This chart traces the evolution of the reprints of the King James Version. [Complete sentence uses period.]

When Not to Use a Period. No period should follow titles, running heads, display type, bylines, chapter heads, or subheads that are set off from the text, even if they form a complete sentence. When a sublevel head is run into the text, it should be followed by a period.

For Emphasis. The popular blogger's device of using periods to emphasize words in a sentence (as in *Best. Style. Manual. Ever.*) is so overused as to become a cliché. (See "BLOG STYLE AND TURNING BLOGS INTO BOOKS.")

PERMISSION GUIDELINES: GENERAL

Under most contracts, the author is responsible for obtaining permissions to reprint materials quoted or reproduced from other sources.[4] The author should write for such permission as soon as he or she decides to quote or reproduce any copyrighted material. If the author waits too long and permission is denied, the author may be forced to delete the quoted material or find suitable replacements, or the book's release date may have to be delayed until the permission is granted. Also, if the permission fee required by the copyright owner is too high, the author may wish to delete the material or substitute other material. The author is also responsible for including full credit information in the manuscript whenever credit is required as a condition of the permission license.

Payment. A request for permission is not a commitment to use or pay for the material. If, after permission has been granted, the author decides not to use a given passage, the author simply informs the copyright holder that the material will not be used. Only when it is certain that the quote will actually be used in the book does the author need to pay the fee.

Address. If, as occasionally happens, the source publisher's address is not given in the book from which the author is quoting, that address can probably be found online. Most publishers provide the permission contact information at their company's website. A volume called *The Literary Market Place*, available at many libraries, is also an excellent resource for finding publishers' addresses.

Online Sources. Writers need to be aware that the necessity to obtain permission to quote material from printed sources applies equally to internet sources. The fact that a quotation has appeared online, even if it appears thousands of times, does not imply that it is in the public domain or that it can be quoted without obtaining a permission or paying a fee. Also note that frequent or extended use of passages from modern Bible versions or translations usually requires permission. (See "PERMISSION GUIDELINES: THE BIBLE" and "QUOTING ONLINE SOURCES.")

Obtaining Permission. When writing for permission to quote from an outside source, the author needs to provide the publisher of the quoted material with the following information:

The title and author(s) of the work from which the quote is taken

A description or copy of the material quoted, along with an explanation of how the quotation will be used (a copy of the relevant page might be included)

An approximate total of the number of words quoted

The title and author(s) of the work in which the quote will be used
The projected publication date
The projected number of copies to be sold in the first year
The projected retail price
A one-sentence synopsis of the work's subject

If the author has any difficulty finding any of this information, the book's editor can help.

Accuracy. The author is responsible for reproducing the quoted material exactly as it appears in the original, with no reworking of the spelling, punctuation, grammar, or general style. Occasionally, in works from the public domain, antiquated spelling, syntax, grammar, and punctuation may be modernized, though a declaration of such modernization, either as a footnote or as a notation on the copyright page, should be provided as a courtesy to the reader.

Public Domain. In 1976 Congress passed a new Copyright Act, which took effect on January 1, 1978. The new law recognized two methods of measuring the duration of a copyright, depending on when the work was first published. Works first published in or before 1922 are now in the public domain, and no permission is required to reproduce them in the US. Works first published in or after 1923 are protected for ninety-five years from the date of their initial publication. Works created and published after January 1, 1978, are copyrighted for the life of the author plus seventy years. In addition, scientific and historical facts, general ideas and concepts, titles, names, common short phrases and slogans, and most US government publications are also considered to be in the public domain. Written permission must be obtained to copy or closely paraphrase all copyrighted material unless the privilege of "fair use" can be invoked. (See "FAIR USE.")

Ownership of Copyrighted Material. Bear in mind that for a permission to be valid, it must be granted by the copyright owner, who controls the rights to the use the author wishes to make of the material. Most often, the author or original creator of the material is considered the copyright owner and usually holds the permission rights unless those rights have been assigned to another individual or entity, usually the publisher. In the majority of cases, the author assigned the publisher the right to grant permission to reprint or quote material. The owner of a photo negative or print, for instance, does not necessarily control the copyright, even though he or she may possess the only original copy of that photograph; the owner may have assigned permission to reprint to the first publisher of the photo. Authors should be sure to secure permission from the proper party.

Quotations within the Cited Material. In reprinting articles or long portions of a book (such as material in an anthology or a compilation), it is easy to overlook internal quotations from other sources. If reprinted material has been taken from another original source and it requires permission according to guidelines outlined here, the compiler or author must obtain separate permission for that material. This applies even to public domain material that contains copyrighted material within it. Thus, an author may need several permissions to reprint one passage or article.

Territories. Whenever the publishing house that plans to publish the author's book controls world rights to the book and plans to exploit any rights outside of the US and Canada, permissions should be cleared for use throughout the world. If the author's publisher will not be exploiting the work beyond North America, permissions may be cleared for the US and Canada only.

No Reply. If the author receives no reply within a reasonable period of time (usually about three weeks) from the publisher from whom he or she is seeking permission, a second request should be sent by registered mail, return receipt requested. If after several weeks the request is still outstanding, the author should try to call the publisher by phone or contact them by email. In some cases, the publisher will give a verbal permission over the phone or in an email and will tell the author the proper credit line to use. This may be acceptable, provided the author provides his or her publisher written confirmation of the permission granted within a short period of time after the phone call. If, despite the author's best efforts, permission still is not granted, the material should not be used without further advice from the legal department of the company publishing the author's book. In summary, "no reply" does not translate into a grant of permission.

Credit Lines and Source Notes. The author should provide the precise credit line as provided by the copyright owner as part of the grant of permission. If the copyright owner does not specify the exact wording, then a standard credit line should be shown in the source note or on a permissions page, giving the following information: author, book or article title, publisher or publication source, a copyright notice for the publication, and the notation "Reprinted by permission." The author should remember to provide a proper source note for material that constitutes fair use even though permission did not need to be obtained.

Keeping Permissions Records. When the permissions are complete, the author should send copies of the original documents and correspondence to the editor along with the final manuscript. The author should keep a copy of the complete file.

The Publisher. The publisher is responsible for applying for and securing proper copyright for new publications, and the publisher usually also retains the privilege of granting permission for the reprinting of excerpts as requested for use in other publications.

PERMISSION GUIDELINES: THE BIBLE

Most Bible organizations and their publishers allow their Bible texts to be quoted within certain parameters without a fee, though a credit line is usually required. Some publishers allow unlimited use of their Bibles, and those versions already in the public domain have no restrictions at all. The following list details some of the major versions and translations, along with the parameters for quoting them.

AMP and AMPC

The Amplified Bible (AMP, 2015*)* and *The Amplified Bible, Classic Edition* (*AMPC*, 1987). Published by Zondervan and the Lockman Foundation. The publisher's policy states:

> Up to 500 verses may be quoted without permission as long as the verses quoted do not amount to a complete book of the bible, do not comprise 25 percent or more of the total text of the work in which they are quoted, and the verses are not being quoted in a commentary or other Biblical reference work.

The correct credit lines for *The Amplified Bible* and *The Amplified Bible, Classic Edition* read respectively:

> All Scripture quotations, unless otherwise indicated, are taken from *The Amplified® Bible*, Copyright © 2015 by The Lockman Foundation. Used by permission. (www.Lockman.org.) All rights reserved.
>
> All Scripture quotations, unless otherwise indicated, are taken from *The Amplified® Bible*, Copyright © 1954, 1958, 1962, 1964, 1965, 1987, by the Lockman Foundation. Used by permission. (www. Lockman.org.) All rights reserved.

Permission requests for commercial use that exceeds the above guidelines must be directed to and approved in writing by:

> Zondervan
> Attn: Amplified Bible Permission Director
> 3900 Sparks Drive
> Grand Rapids, MI 49546
> Or visit www.Zondervan.com.

Permission requests for noncommercial use that exceeds the above guidelines must be directed to and approved in writing by:

Director of Rights and Permissions—*Amplified* NT
The Lockman Foundation
PO Box 2279
La Habra, CA 90632–2279
Or visit www.Lockman.org.

CEV

Contemporary English Version (CEV). Published by the American Bible Society. The publisher's policy states:

> The CEV text may be quoted in any form (written, visual, electronic or audio) up to and inclusive of five hundred (500) verses without written permission, providing the verses quoted do not amount to 50% of a complete book of the Bible nor do the verses account for twenty-five percent (25%) or more of the total text of the work in which they are quoted.

Use whichever of the following credit lines is most appropriate:

1. The following notice for the CEV may be used on each page where material quoted from the CEV appears:

   Scripture taken from the Contemporary English Version © 1991, 1992, 1995 by American Bible Society, Used by Permission.

2. When the CEV is identified at the end of each Scripture quotation from the CEV, the following notice may be used on the title page or verso thereof of each copy:

   Scripture quotations marked (CEV) are from the Contemporary English Version Copyright © 1991, 1992, 1995 by American Bible Society, Used by Permission.

3. If appropriate, the following notice may be used on the title page or verso thereof of each copy:

   All scripture quotations in this publication are from the Contemporary English Version Copyright © 1991, 1992, 1995 by American Bible Society, Used by Permission.

Permission may be obtained by writing to:

The American Bible Society
1865 Broadway
New York, NY 10023

ESV

English Standard Version (ESV). Published by Crossway Books. The publisher's policy states:

> The ESV text may be quoted (in written, visual, or electronic form) up to and inclusive of one thousand (1,000) verses without express written permission of the publisher, providing that the verses quoted do not amount to a complete book of the Bible nor do the verses quoted account for 50 percent or more of the total text of the work in which they are quoted.
>
> The ESV text may be quoted for audio use (audio cassettes, CDs, audio television) up to two hundred fifty (250) verses without express written permission of the publisher providing that the verses quoted do not amount to a complete book of the Bible nor do the verses quoted account for 50 percent or more of the total text of the work in which they are quoted.

An appropriate credit line reads:

> Scripture quotations are from The Holy Bible, English Standard Version® (ESV®), copyright © 2001 by Crossway, a publishing ministry of Good News Publishers. Used by permission. All rights reserved.

When more than one translation is in printed works or other media, ESV should be credited as follows:

> Unless otherwise indicated, all Scripture quotations are from The Holy Bible, English Standard Version® (ESV®), copyright © 2001 by Crossway, a publishing ministry of Good News Publishers. Used by permission. All rights reserved.

Or

> Scripture quotations marked (ESV) are from The Holy Bible, English Standard Version® (ESV®), copyright © 2001 by Crossway, a publishing ministry of Good News Publishers. Used by permission. All rights reserved.

The "ESV" and "English Standard Version" are registered trademarks of Crossway. Use of either trademark requires the permission of Crossway.

Permission requests that exceed the preceding guidelines must be directed to:

> Crossway
> Attn: Bible Rights
> 1300 Crescent Street
> Wheaton, IL 60187, USA

Or email https://www.crossway.org/support/esv-bible-permissions/.

Permission requests for use within the UK and EU that exceed the preceding guidelines must be directed to:

HarperCollins Publishers
Attn: Collins Bibles
77–85 Fulham Palace Road
Hammersmith, London W6 8JB, England

KJV

King James Version (KJV). The KJV is in the public domain in the US and may be reproduced without restriction for publication in that country only. Otherwise, in the UK the KJV is owned by the English crown and published by Cambridge University Press. The publisher's policy states:

> The reproduction by any means of the text of the King James Version is permitted to a maximum of five hundred (500) verses for liturgical and non-commercial educational use, provided that the verses quoted neither amount to a complete book of the Bible nor represent 25 percent or more of the total text of the work in which they are quoted.

An appropriate credit line reads:

> Scripture quotations from the Authorized (King James) Version. Rights in the Authorized Version in the United Kingdom are vested in the Crown. Reproduced by permission of the Crown's patentee, Cambridge University Press.

Rights or permission requests that exceed the preceding guidelines must be submitted to:

Permissions Department
Cambridge University Press
The Edinburgh Building
Shaftesbury Road
Cambridge CB2 8RU, United Kingdom

Or submit the "Permission Request Form" found at www.cambridge.org/rights/corporate/permission.htm.

MSG

The Message (MSG). The full title of this periphrastic translation, which is the work of author and scholar Eugene H. Peterson, is *The Message: The Bible in Contemporary Language*. It is published by NavPress Publishing Group. The publisher's policy states:

The text of *The Message* may be quoted in any form (written, visual, electronic, or audio) up to and inclusive of five hundred (500) verses without written permission of the publisher, provided that the verses quoted do not account for more than 25 percent of the work in which they are quoted, and provided that a complete book of the Bible is not quoted.

You must include copyright information for *The Message* on the title page or copyright page of the project in which verses are quoted.

Appropriate credit lines vary:

When multiple translations are being used in the same project, each verse quoted must be followed by "*(The Message)*" or "(MSG)" and the following reference credit must be included:

> Scripture quotations from *The Message*. Copyright © by Eugene H. Peterson 1993, 1994, 1995, 1996, 2000, 2001, 2002. Used by permission of Tyndale House Publishers, Inc.

When *The Message* is being used exclusively:

> All Scripture quotations in this publication are from *The Message*. Copyright © by Eugene H. Peterson 1993, 1994, 1995, 1996, 2000, 2001, 2002. Used by permission of Tyndale House Publishers, Inc.

When multiple translations are being used but the majority will be taken from *The Message*:

> Unless otherwise indicated, all Scripture quotations are taken from *The Message*. Copyright © by Eugene H. Peterson. 1993, 1994, 1995, 1996, 2000, 2001, 2002. Used by permission of Tyndale House Publishers, Inc.

For permission, complete the "Permissions Questionnaire" at www.tyndale.com/00_Home/permissions-form.php.

Or write to:

Tyndale House Publishers, Inc.
351 Executive Drive
Carol Stream, IL 60188

NAB

The New American Bible (NAB). Published by the Confraternity of Christian Doctrine, whose policy states:

> No permission is required for use of less than 5,000 words of the NAB in print, sound, or electronic formats provided that such use

comprises less than 40% of a single book of the Bible and less than 40% of the proposed work.

Permission must be requested for use of more than 5,000 words from the NAB (or when the use comprises more than 40% of a single book of the bible or more than 40% of the proposed work).

A credit line should contain the basic information:

Scripture texts in this work are taken from the *New American Bible, revised edition* © 2010, 1991, 1986, 1970 Confraternity of Christian Doctrine, Washington, D.C. and are used by permission of the copyright owner. All Rights Reserved. No part of the New American Bible may be reproduced in any form without permission in writing from the copyright owner.

For permission write to:

Associate Director, Permissions CCD
3211 Fourth Street, NE
Washington, DC 20017–1194

NASB

New American Standard Bible (NASB). Published by the Lockman Foundation, whose policy states:

The text of the New American Standard Bible® may be quoted and/or reprinted up to and inclusive of one thousand (1,000) verses *without express written permission of The Lockman Foundation*, providing the verses do not amount to a complete book of the Bible nor do the verses quoted account for more than 50% of the total work in which they are quoted....

When quotations are primarily from the NASB text on an Internet webpage (Scripture quotations not from the NASB must be identified), instead of the full copyright notice on the title page, this notice must be placed somewhere on the webpage containing the quotations: "Scripture quotations taken from the NASB."

One complete copy of the work using the quotations from the NASB®, if published for sale, must be sent to The Lockman Foundation within 30 days following the publication of the work.

For requests that exceed the permissions granted above, please use the "Permission to Quote Request Form," which can be found at www.lockman.org/tlf/pqform.php, to request express written permission.

The standard credit line for "fair use" quotations from the NASB reads:

> Scripture quotations taken from the New American Standard Bible®, Copyright © 1960, 1962, 1963, 1968, 1971, 1972, 1973, 1975, 1977, 1995 by The Lockman Foundation. Used by permission.

The address is:

The Lockman Foundation
PO Box 2279
La Habra, CA 90632-2279
http://www.lockman.org/mail/index.php
(714) 879-3055

NCV

New Century Version (NCV). Published by Thomas Nelson, Inc. The publisher's policy states:

> Scripture from any of the Thomas Nelson translations may be quoted in any form (written, visual, electronic, or audio) up to two hundred fifty (250) verses or less without written permission, as long as the Scripture does not make up more than 25% of the total text in the work and the Scripture is not being quoted in commentary or another Biblical reference work. If an entire book of the Bible is being reproduced, regardless of verse count, written permission is required.

An appropriate credit line reads:

> Scripture taken from the New Century Version®. Copyright © 2005 by Thomas Nelson. Used by permission. All rights reserved.

To officially submit a permissions request, download and complete the "Thomas Nelson Permission Request Form" that can be found at http://www.harpercollinschristian.com/permissions/.

NET

New English Translation (NET). Published online by Biblical Studies Press. The publisher's policy states:

> The NET Bible® verse text (no Notes) can be used by anyone and integrated into your non-commercial project or publication upon condition of proper Biblical Studies Press copyright and organizational acknowledgments. However, for the full NET Bible® verse text and NET Bible® notes, you cannot change the format of the NET Bible® data file(s) or integrate it into or bundle it with any other software e.g. display program or Bible study tool without expressed permission. For

> distribution of the full NET Bible® in any form other than paper, e.g. electronic, CD, DVD, you must obtain written permission and comply with our guidelines for content control and include current copyright and organizational acknowledgments.

The publisher's credit line reads:

> Scripture and/or notes quoted by permission. Quotations designated (NET) are from the NET Bible® copyright © 1996–2006 by Biblical Studies Press, L.L.C. All rights reserved.

For permission requests that exceed the guidelines, email "Permissions" at https://bible.org/contact?category=Permission.

NIrV

New International Reader's Version (NIrV). Published by Zondervan for Biblica, Inc. The publisher's policy states:

> The *NIrV* may be quoted in any form (written, visual, electronic, or audio), up to and inclusive of five hundred (500) verses or less without written permission, providing the verses quoted do not amount to a complete book of the Bible, nor do verses quoted account for 25% or more of the total text of the work in which they are quoted, and the verses are not being quoted in a commentary or other biblical reference work. This permission is contingent upon an appropriate copyright acknowledgment.
>
> *One* complete copy of the work using quotations from the New International Reader's Version must be sent to Zondervan within 30 days following the publication of the work.
>
> Rights and permission to quote from the NIrV text in printed or electronic media intended for commercial use within the US and Canada that exceed the above guidelines must be directed to, and approved in writing by, Zondervan Publishing House.
>
> Rights and permission to quote from the NIrV text in printed or electronic media intended for commercial use within the UK, EEC, and EFTA countries that exceed the above guidelines must be directed to, and approved of in writing by, Hodder & Stoughton, Ltd., 338 Euston Road, London, NW1 3BH, England.
>
> For rights and permissions to quote from the NIrV text in printed or electronic media intended for commercial use outside the territory of the US and Canada (North America), your permission request must be directed to:
>
> Biblica, Inc.™
> 1820 Jet Stream Drive

Colorado Springs, CO 80921–3969
http://www.biblica.com/en-us/
RightsPermissions@Biblica.com

Works using NIrV quotations must include one of the following copyright notices (whichever one is most appropriate):

1. Scriptures taken from the Holy Bible, New International Reader's Version®, NIrV® Copyright © 1995, 1996, 1998 by Biblica, Inc.™ Used by permission of Zondervan. The "NIrV" and "New International Reader's Version" are trademarks registered in the United States Patent and Trademark Office by Biblica, Inc.™
2. Scripture quotations marked (NIrV) are taken from the Holy Bible, New International Reader's Version®, NIrV® Copyright © 1995, 1996, 1998 by Biblica, Inc.™ Used by permission of Zondervan. All rights reserved worldwide. The "NIrV" and "New International Reader's Version" are trademarks registered in the United States Patent and Trademark Office by Biblica, Inc.™
3. All scripture quotations, unless otherwise indicated, are taken from the Holy Bible, New International Reader's Version®, NIrV® Copyright © 1995, 1996, 1998 by Biblica, Inc.™ Used by permission of Zondervan. All rights reserved worldwide. The "NIrV" and "New International Reader's Version" are trademarks registered in the United States Patent and Trademark Office by Biblica, Inc.™

Note the use of the registered ® symbol after both the complete and abbreviated titles.

If quotations exceed the preceding guidelines, written permission may be obtained by downloading and completing the "Zondervan Permission Request Form" that can be found at www.harpercollinschristian.com/permissions/ and emailing it to zPermissions@zondervan.com.

NIV

New International Version (NIV). Published by Zondervan for Biblica, Inc. The policy states:

> Text from the *NIV* ... may be quoted in any form (written, visual, electronic, or audio, up to and inclusive of 500 verses or less without written permission, providing the verses quoted do not amount to a complete book of the Bible, nor do verses quoted account for 25% or more of the total text of the work in which they are quoted, and the verses are not being quoted in a commentary or other biblical reference work. This permission is contingent upon an appropriate copyright acknowledgment.

Please note that Zondervan is granting permission for the latest edition of the NIV text only (2011). They are not granting permission for use of the earlier editions or versions of the NIV text.

One complete copy of the work using quotations from the New International Version must be sent to Zondervan within 30 days following the publication of the work.

Rights and permission to quote from the NIV text in printed or electronic media intended for commercial use within the US and Canada that exceed the above guidelines must be directed to, and approved in writing by, Zondervan Publishing House.

For rights and permissions to quote from the NIV text in printed or electronic media intended for commercial use outside the territory of the US and Canada (North America), your permission request must be directed to:

Biblica, Inc.™
1820 Jet Stream Drive
Colorado Springs, CO 80921–3969
http://www.biblica.com/en-us/
RightsPermissions@Biblica.com

Rights and permission to quote from the NIV text in printed or electronic media intended for commercial use within the UK, EEC, and EFTA countries that exceed the above guidelines must be directed to, and approved of in writing by, Hodder & Stoughton, Ltd., 338 Euston Road, London, NW1 3BH, England.

Appropriate credit lines read:

All scripture quotations, unless otherwise indicated, are taken from the Holy Bible, New International Version®, NIV®. Copyright © 1973, 1978, 1984, 2011 by Biblica, Inc.™ Used by permission of Zondervan. All rights reserved worldwide. www.zondervan.com. The "NIV" And "New International Version" are trademarks registered in the United States Patent and Trademark office by Biblica, Inc.™

Or

Scriptures taken from the Holy Bible, New International Version®, NIV®. Copyright © 1973, 1978, 1984, 2011 by Biblica, Inc.™ Used by permission of Zondervan. All rights reserved worldwide. www.zondervan.com. The "NIV" and New International Version" are trademarks registered in the United States Patent and Trademark Office by Biblica, Inc.™

Or

> Scripture quotations marked (NIV) are taken from the Holy Bible, New International Version®, NIV®. Copyright © 1973, 1978, 1984, 2011 by Biblica, Inc.™ Used by permission of Zondervan. All rights reserved worldwide. www.zondervan.com. The "NIV" and "New International Version" are trademarks registered in the United States Patent and Trademark Office by Biblica, Inc.™

Note the use of the registered (®) symbol after both the complete and abbreviated titles. In addition, if *NIV* or *New International Version* is to be used in a title or on the cover of a book, special written arrangements must be made with Biblica, Inc.

Permission requests for Zondervan may be directed to:

> HarperCollins Christian Publishing
> Attn: Permissions Manager
> P.O. Box 141000
> Nashville TN 37214
> zPermissions@zondervan.com

(For more information, see http://www.harpercollinschristian.com/permissions/#2.)

NKJV

New King James Version (NKJV). Published by Thomas Nelson, Inc. The publisher's policy states:

> Scripture from any of the Thomas Nelson translations may be quoted in any form (written, visual, electronic, or audio) up to two hundred fifty (250) verses or less without written permission, as long as the Scripture does not make up more than 25% of the total text in the work and the Scripture is not being quoted in commentary or another Biblical reference work. If an entire book of the Bible is being reproduced, regardless of verse count, written permission is required.

The publisher's credit line reads:

> Scripture taken from the New King James Version®. Copyright © 1982 by Thomas Nelson. Used by permission. All rights reserved.

To submit an official request, download and complete the "Bible Permission Request Form" at www.harpercollinschristian.com/permissions and email it to permissions@thomasnelson.com.

NLT

New Living Translation (NLT). The NLT began as a revision of TLB but evolved into an all-new translation from the original languages. It is published by Tyndale House Publishers, whose policy states:

> The text of the *Holy Bible, New Living Translation (NLT),* may be quoted in any form (written, visual, electronic, or audio) up to and inclusive of five hundred (500) verses without express written permission of the publisher, provided that the verses quoted do not account for more than 25 percent of the work in which they are quoted, and provided that a complete book of the Bible is not quoted.
>
> When the *Holy Bible, New Living Translation,* is quoted, one of the following credit lines must appear on the copyright page or title page of the work:
>
> When multiple translations are being used in a project:
>
> Scripture quotations marked (*NLT*) are taken from the *Holy Bible, New Living Translation,* copyright © 1996, 2004, 2007, 2013 by Tyndale House Foundation. Used by permission of Tyndale House Publishers, Inc., Carol Stream, Illinois 60188. All rights reserved.
>
> When the NLT is being used exclusively in a project:
>
> Scripture quotations are taken from the *Holy Bible, New Living Translation,* copyright © 1996, 2004, 2007, 2013 by Tyndale House Foundation. Used by permission of Tyndale House Publishers, Inc., Carol Stream, Illinois 60188. All rights reserved.
>
> When multiple translations are being used in a project but the majority will be taken from the NLT:
>
> Unless otherwise indicated, all Scripture quotations are taken from the Holy Bible, New Living Translation, copyright © 1996, 2004, 2007, 2013 by Tyndale House Foundation. Used by permission of Tyndale House Publishers, Inc., Carol Stream, Illinois 60188. All rights reserved.
>
> For permission to quote in excess of the preceding guidelines, please fill out the "Permissions Questionnaire" at www.tyndale.com/00_Home/permissions-form.php, or write to:
>
> Tyndale House Publishers, Inc.
> 351 Executive Drive
> Carol Stream, IL 60188

Tyndale House Publishers can also be contacted via fax or phone at:

Fax: (800) 684–0247
Phone: (800) 323–9400

NRSV

New Revised Standard Version (NRSV). Published by Augsburg Fortress for the National Council of Churches. The NCC's permissions policy states:

> The [New] Revised Standard Version Bible may be quoted and/or reprinted up to and inclusive of five hundred (500) verses without express written permission of the publisher, provided the verses quoted do not amount to a complete book of the Bible or account for fifty percent (50%) of the total work in which they are quoted.

An appropriate credit line reads:

> New Revised Standard Version Bible, copyright 1989, Division of Christian Education of the National Council of the Churches of Christ in the United States of America. Used by permission. All rights reserved.

Direct permissions inquiries to:

NRSVcopyright@aol.com

RSV

Revised Standard Version (RSV). Published by the National Council of Churches, whose policy states:

> Up to 500 verses of the RSV or NRSV may be quoted in any form (written, visual, electronic, or audio) without charge and without obtaining written permission provided that all of the following conditions are met:
>
> The total number of verses quoted is:
>
> - less than an entire book of the Bible, and
> - less than 500 verses (total), and
> - less than 50 percent of the total number of words in the work in which they are quoted.
> - No changes are made to the text. All quotations must be accurate to the text, including all appropriate punctuation, capitalization, etc. unless specifically approved to the contrary prior to publication.

Credit lines for the various RSV editions are as follows:

Revised Standard Version:

Scripture quotations are from the Revised Standard Version of the Bible, copyright © 1946, 1952, and 1971 National Council of the Churches of Christ in the United States of America. Used by permission. All rights reserved.

Revised Standard Version Bible, Catholic Edition:

Scripture quotations are from The Catholic Edition of the Revised Standard Version of the Bible, copyright © 1973 National Council of the Churches of Christ in the United States of America. Used by permission. All rights reserved.

Revised Standard Version Apocrypha:

Scripture quotations are from the Revised Standard Version of the Bible, Apocrypha, copyright © 1957; The Third and Fourth Books of the Maccabees and Psalm 151, copyright © 1977 National Council of the Churches of Christ in the United States of America. Used by permission. All rights reserved.

Revised Standard Version Common Bible:

Scripture quotations are from Common Bible: Revised Standard Version of the Bible, copyright © 1973 National Council of the Churches of Christ in the United States of America. Used by permission. All rights reserved.

Revised Standard Version, Second Catholic Edition:

Scripture quotations are from the Revised Standard Version of the Bible—Second Catholic Edition (Ignatius Edition) Copyright © 2006 National Council of the Churches of Christ in the United States of America. Used by permission. All rights reserved.

For requests to publish a print or electronic edition of the entire RSV Bible (or the Old Testament only or the New Testament only) that will be distributed anywhere other than in the UK, contact HarperOne at NRSVBibles@harpercollins.com.

For all other requests, contact NRSVcopyright@aol.com. This includes requests to use all or portions of the RSV in an audio product, to publish the RSV in the UK, and to use RSV excerpts that in any way exceed the guidelines.

TLB

The Living Bible (TLB). Published by Tyndale House Publishers and created by Kenneth N. Taylor, *The Living Bible* is a paraphrase first published in 1971. The publisher's policy states:

> *The Living Bible* text may be quoted in any form (written, visual, electronic, or audio) up to and inclusive of five hundred (500) verses without express written permission of the publisher, provided that the verses quoted do not account for more than 25 percent of the total work in which they are quoted, and provided that a complete book of the Bible is not quoted.

One of the following credit lines must appear on the copyright page or title page of the work.

When multiple translations are being used in a project:

> Scripture quotations marked (TLB) are taken from The Living Bible copyright © 1971. Used by permission of Tyndale House Publishers, Inc., Carol Stream, Illinois 60188. All rights reserved.

When TLB is being used exclusively in a project:

> Scripture quotations are taken from The Living Bible copyright © 1971. Used by permission of Tyndale House Publishers, Inc., Carol Stream, Illinois 60188. All rights reserved.

When multiple translations are being used in a project but the majority will be taken from TLB:

> Unless otherwise indicated, all Scripture quotations are taken from The Living Bible copyright © 1971. Used by permission of Tyndale House Publishers, Inc., Carol Stream, Illinois 60188. All rights reserved.

If quotations are in excess of the guidelines, complete and submit the "Permissions Questionnaire" that can be found at www.tyndale.com/00_Home/permissions-form.php, or write to:

> Tyndale House Publishers, Inc.
> 351 Executive Drive
> Carol Stream, IL 60188

PERMISSION GUIDELINES: QUOTING READER REVIEWS FROM A WEBSITE

Authors often ask, "May I use reader reviews posted at Amazon, Facebook, or Twitter or from my own personal website as endorsements for my book, either on the cover or on an endorsements page?"

Amazon's terms of use specify that Amazon has the nonexclusive right to allow others to reproduce reader reviews. So, whenever quoting more than a few words, the author should obtain permission from Amazon. Whether quoting a few words or many, neither the reviewer's user name nor actual name should be revealed, though using a first and last initial is acceptable. It is also possible to obtain permission directly from the reviewer, and in obtaining the rights to reprint the review, the author can request to use the reviewer's full name, though the reviewer is under no obligation to grant the request.

Facebook's and Twitter's policies state that the user owns the rights to any original work posted on the user's sites but does not own the rights to the work of others who post there. So, again, it is best to obtain permission from either Facebook or Twitter directly (and not use the reviewer's full name or user name) or to obtain permission from the reviewer directly.

Many authors do not establish legal terms and conditions for readers who post on their personal websites. Because of that lack of legal clarity, the author is advised to obtain permission from the reviewer before quoting a portion of that person's review of the author's book.

PERMISSIONS NOTICE

Any credit lines for permissions granted for materials quoted or used in the book should appear on the copyright page. If such permission notices are numerous or long, then they may be listed on a separate acknowledgments page either in the front or at the back of the book. If the permissions are moved to a separate page, it is considered courteous to readers and researchers to place a note on the copyright page stating where the full list of permissions may be found.

PERMISSION-TO-COPY NOTICE

A permission-to-copy notice is a short statement, placed on the copyright page, detailing the conditions under which the reader is allowed to copy portions of the book for personal or classroom use. It is useful in such books as:

workbooks intended for study groups
books of charts or tables that might be useful in educational situations
certain Bibles or Bible studies

books with content already in the public domain
reference books containing material required to be copied by students
fill-in-the-blank books, so that the reader doesn't need to mark the book itself
books of copyright-free images, quotations, templates, or forms
books containing financial or other worksheets

A permission-to-copy notice specifically states which pages are free for copying, under what conditions, and if needed, how many copies may be made. Restrictions might include:

the number of copies the publisher will allow to be made of any given page
the maximum number of pages that can be copied from a single work
whether a credit line should be included on the copied text pages
how many graphic images may be used and how the credit line should read

For instance, the notice for a Sunday school curriculum guide might read: "Up to thirty copies of each 'Questions for Reflection' page may be made for distribution in a classroom setting."

A permission-to-copy notice is sometimes used in conjunction with a *warning notice* (see "WARNING NOTICE"), in which case the notice might read as follows:

> No part of this publication may be reproduced, stored in a retrieval system, or transmitted in any form or by any means—electronic, mechanical, photocopy, recording, or any other—without the prior permission of the publisher, except as follows: individuals may make a single copy of a page (or a single transparency of a page) from this book for purposes of private study, scholarship, research, or classroom use only. Teachers may make multiple copies of a page from this book for classroom use only, not to exceed one copy per student in the class. Copies made for classroom use should provide the title of the book, the author's name, and the publisher's name on each copy.

PERSONAL NAMES, ADJECTIVES DERIVED FROM

Many well-known people embody concepts so strongly that their names have been adapted as adjectives. The most common way to do this is to add an *-ian* to names ending in consonants (*Lewisian*—C. S. Lewis; *Barthian*—Karl Barth) and an *-an* to most names ending in vowels (*Blakean*—William Blake; *Joycean*—James Joyce; *Tolstoyan*—Leo Tolstoy). With ancient Greek and Roman names, the suffix *-an* is often added to the root form of the name (*Aeschylean*—Aeschylus; *Lucretian*—Lucretius). The ending *-ic* is also common but unpredictably applied. (See the list in this entry.)

Some names become adjectives by having an *-esque* added to the end (*Lincolnesque*—Abraham Lincoln; *Kafkaesque*—Franz Kafka). The *-esque* ending can suggest the ideas embodied by the person, but it can also imply that something is simply similar to, or "like," the person in question (as in *his brushstrokes were Rembrandtesque*). The *-esque* ending is especially common with artists' names (*Cézannesque*—Paul Cézanne; *Leonardesque*—Leonardo da Vinci), though many artists' names take the traditional form (*Duchampian*—Marcel Duchamp; *Warholian*—Andy Warhol). When in doubt, check *Webster*. If no reference to a preferred form can be found, an author or editor may formulate his or her own according to euphony and the guidelines stated in the foregoing discussion.

Many exceptions to these forms exist, as the following list shows.

Aaronic—Aaron (descended from Aaron)
Abrahamic, or Abramic—Abraham (in Genesis; descended from Abraham)
Adamic, or Adamical—Adam (in Genesis)
Aquinian—Thomas Aquinas; see also *Thomistic* in this list
Bernardine—Bernard of Clairvaux
Byronic—Lord Byron
Calvinist, or Calvinistic—John Calvin
Ciceronian—Cicero
Daliesque—Salvador Dalí (note: no accent used in the adj. form)
Dantesque—Dante Alighieri
Demosthenic—Demosthenes
Eliotian, or Eliotic—T. S. Eliot
Goyaesque, or Goyesque—Francisco de Goya
Homeric—Homer
Huxleian, or Huxleyan—Aldous Huxley
Johannine—John (apostle)
Lucan—Luke (gospel writer)
Markan, or Marcan—Mark (gospel writer)
Marlovian—Christopher Marlowe
Matthean, or Matthaean—Matthew (gospel writer)
Miltonic, or Miltonian—John Milton
Mosaic—Moses
Napoleonic—Napoleon Bonaparte
Neronic—Nero
Ockhamistic, or Occamistic—William of Ockham, or Occam
Pauline—Paul (apostle)
Petrine—Peter (apostle)
Quixotic—Don Quixote, but *quixotic* as a common adjective

Rimbaldian—Arthur Rimbaud

Shavian—George Bernard Shaw (humorously contrived by the author himself)

Socratic—Socrates

Thomistic—Thomas Aquinas; usually refers to his theology in general, or Thomism; *Aquinian* is often used to refer to the man

Thoreauvian—Henry David Thoreau

PERSONAL NAMES, COMMONLY MISSPELLED

Many personal names, some of which are common to religious books, are often misspelled. Note the spelling, alphabetical order, diacritical marks, and particles of the following:

Addams, Charles—American cartoonist; *The Addams Family*; note double *d*

Addams, Jane—American social worker; note double *d*

Ælfric—note the capital ligature (called an Old English *ash*); *Aelfric* also acceptable

Andersen, Hans Christian—note *-en*

Andrewes, Lancelot—note *-es*

Bartók, Béla—note acute accents

Bashô, Matsuo—note circumflex mark; if mark is not available in the font, set simply as *o*

Becket, Thomas à—grave accent; alphabetize under "Becket" (unlike Thomas à Kempis, who is alphabetized under "Thomas")

Beckett, Samuel—note *tt*

Berkouwer, Gerrit

Bernanos, Georges—note the *s* in the first name

Beyoncé (Knowles)—pop singer; note acute accent

Bonhoeffer, Dietrich

Brontë, Charlotte, Emily, and Anne—note umlaut

Buechner, Frederick

Bustanoby, André—note acute accent

Chardin, Pierre Teilhard de—alphabetize under "Chardin"

Crouch, Andraé—note acute accent

Cummings, E. E.—capitalize; the poet himself signed it that way, and the E. E. Cummings Society recommends adhering to that usage in all references

de Gasztold, Carmen Bernos—alphabetize under "de Gasztold"

de Gaulle, Charles—alphabetize under "de Gaulle"

de Hueck, Catherine—alphabetize under "de Hueck"

de Vil, Cruella—Disney character, *101 Dalmatians*; not *de Ville*

DiMaggio, Joe—note midcap *M*

Dostoyevsky, Fyodor—among the variant spellings, this one is preferred by *Webster* and *Webster's Biographical*

Dvoøák, Antonín—note diacritics

Eiseley, Loren—note all the vowels

Eliot, John—Bible translator; note *l* and *t*

Eliot, T. S.—poet; note *l* and *t*

Elliot, Elisabeth—Christian author; note *ll* and *t*

Elliott, Ramblin' Jack—folksinger; note *ll* and *tt*

Fénelon, François—note acute accent and cedilla

FitzGerald, Edward—English poet (*Rubaiyat of Omar Khayyam*); note internal capital *G*

Foxe, John—martyrologist; note *-e*, though some old editions spell it *Fox*

Gilliland, Glaphré—note acute accent

Gogh, Vincent van—note lowercase *v*; alphabetized under "Gogh"

Gutenberg, Johannes—commonly misspelled *Gutenburg*

Guyon, Madame (Mme)

Hammarskjöld, Dag—note umlaut

Héloïse—of Abelard and Héloïse; note acute accent and umlaut; the *H*, by the way, is silent when pronounced

Jabba the Hutt—*Stars Wars* character; note *tt*

Kierkegaard, Søren—note Danish *ø*

Küng, Hans—note umlaut

LaHaye, (Dr.) Tim and Beverly—note midcap *H*

Li'l Abner—cartoon character; note position of apostrophe

MacDonald, George—Scottish writer; curiously, *Webster* and *Webster's Biographical* lowercase the *d*, but the author himself signed his name with a capital *D* (per Wade Center, Wheaton College, Wheaton, Illinois)

March, Fredric—actor; no final *k* in first name

M'Intyre, David M.—*M'* is a contraction of *Mac*. In England the form used to be rendered with an apostrophe (*M'*) but no longer. This Christian writer's name is still traditionally given in the contracted form.

Möbius, August F.—deviser of Möbius strip; umlaut over *o*

Moltmann, Jürgen—note double *n* and umlaut over *u*

Mother Teresa—not *Mother Theresa*

Müller, George—note umlaut; the umlauted form is preferred to *Mueller*, which is occasionally seen. The evangelist himself used the umlaut in his publications.

Niebuhr, Reinhold and Richard—not *Neibuhr* or *Niebhur*

Poe, Edgar Allan—not *Alan* or *Allen*

Salome—literary and biblical character; spelled without an accented *e* in English; only in French is the name spelled *Salomé*

Schaeffer, Francis, Edith, and Frank

Scooby-Doo—cartoon character; name is hyphenated

Selassie, Haile

Sindbad (the sailor)—not *Sinbad*

Solzhenitsyn, Aleksandr—per *Webster* and *Webster's Biographical*

Spock—*Mr. Spock* is the *Star Trek* character; *Dr. (Benjamin) Spock* is the pediatrician

Ten Boom—with first name, *ten* is lowercase (Corrie ten Boom); capitalize it as a family name (the Ten Boom family)

Teresa of Ávila—acute accent over the capital

Thomas à Kempis—grave accent; alphabetize under "Thomas" (unlike Thomas à Becket, who is alphabetized under "Becket")

Tolkien, J. R. R.—often mistakenly rendered *Tolkein*; note space between initials, which, by the way, stand for *John Ronald Reuel*

Tolstoy, Leo—sometimes spelled *Tolstoi* in the UK

Truman, Harry S.—US president; though *S* was his full middle name, not an abbreviation, Truman himself put a period after it

Virgil—Roman poet; preferred to *Vergil*

Wesley, Susannah—note spelling of first name

Wolfe, Thomas—American writer; final *e*

Wolfe, Tom—American writer; final *e*

Wolff, Tobias—American writer; double *f*

Woolf, Virginia—British writer; double *o*

Wycliffe, John—*Wyclif* is preferred in UK, but use *Wycliffe* in US; more than a dozen other spellings have been used throughout history

PHONE NUMBERS IN TEXT (TELEPHONE AND CELL PHONE)

The following template is used when setting telephone and cell phone numbers in text: *123-456-7890*; that is, place hyphens between the groups of numbers (not en dashes), and do not use parentheses around the area code. Do not use periods between the groups of numbers, though that style is becoming more common online. If an extension is used, the number may be set either *123-456-7890, ext. 123* or *123-456-7890, x123*.

This hyphenated setting is a change from the previous system that used parentheses around the area code: *(123) 456-7890*. Not only is there little reason to distinguish area codes by putting them in parentheses, but advocates for the visually impaired rightly argue that a parenthesis can be too easily mistaken for a numeral *1*.

International Phone Numbers. The same hyphenated setting also facilitates the setting of international numbers: *011-44-20-1234-5678*.

Fictional Phone Numbers. Often in the course of a novel a telephone or cell phone number must be given. It is possible that any randomly chosen number is a real one, which could prove inconvenient for the person who owns that number and even result in litigation. In one popular movie, a seven-digit number was given as God's personal call-line, and people in several area codes were harassed by unwanted calls.

The safest and most considerate way to fictionalize a US phone number is to give *555* as the first three digits, followed by any combination of four numbers between 0100 and 0199. Those numbers (*555-0100* through *555-0199*) are officially reserved for fictional use. Other number combinations following *555* are available as working numbers, including *1212*, which is reserved for directory assistance in the US. If you look for it, you'll see the *555* solution popping up in movies quite often, from *Ghostbusters* in 1984 to *Toy Story 3* in 2010.

Emergency 9-1-1. The numerals *9-1-1* are used for the US and Canadian emergency telephone number. Often this is rendered *911*, which is acceptable for occasional use, but the hyphenated setting is preferred in frequent use or whenever other phone numbers are listed. Audio producers should note that this phone number is pronounced *nine one one*, not *nine eleven*, since the latter might be confused with the attacks of September 11, 2001. In text, this is correctly set with hyphens rather than en dashes between the numbers.

Fiction writers concerned with accuracy should take note: *9-1-1* is not used throughout the world for emergencies: *9-9-9* is the equivalent number in the UK, Ireland, Poland, Hong Kong, Kenya, Malaysia, Singapore, and other places. The number *1-1-2* is used in most other EU nations, *0-0-0* is used in Australia, *1-1-1* in New Zealand, and *0-6-5* in Mexico. Beyond that, writers should check the internet for the correct numbers, especially for Africa, Asia, and Central and South America, which have widely varying numbers from country to country.

PHONETIC ALPHABETS

How often do you find yourself saying to someone on the phone, "That's *b* as in *boy*"? Without realizing it, you are using the 1913 US military phonetic alphabet. The need to distinguish between similar letters (*m* and *n*; *f*, *s*, and *x*; or *b*, *c*, *d*, *g*, *p*, *t*, *v*, and *z*) in spoken communication comes up occasionally in fictional dialogue. Because it so often occurs in espionage and military novels, the NATO phonetic alphabet, commonly known as the "Alpha, Bravo" system, is given under the heading "NATO PHONETIC ALPHABET."

Several phonetic alphabets have been devised. One often hears the "Abel, Baker" alphabet used in World War II novels and films, but that system seems to have been devised in 1952 (in what is known as the British military phonetic alphabet). During World War II, the Americans and British used different systems, both of which started with "Affirm, Baker," though a few letters differed slightly. These and other phonetic alphabets are accessible online by searching "phonetic alphabets."

PHOTO SECTIONS

When, in a printed book, a higher resolution is needed for photographs than can be printed on a standard book page, photographs can be segregated into photo sections, which can be printed in higher-resolution black-and-white or color on glossy photo paper. These sections are usually printed in one or more signatures of eight pages (four leaves).

Placement. Although it is not always possible, photo sections are ideally placed close to the text material to which they relate. Since photo sections have to be inserted between signatures of the printed book, the designer or editor should look for a convenient signature break in which to insert the photo section so that it will not disrupt the reader. An ideal place is between chapters whenever the chapter breaks correspond to the signature breaks.

Referencing. The photographs (sometimes called *plates*) in the photo section should be marked so that they can easily be cross-referenced from the text (such as *Plate 1*, *Plate 2*, and so on, or *See Photo 1*, *See Photo 2*, and so on).

Counting Pages. Does an eight-page photo section imply eight leaves (totaling sixteen face-pages) or four leaves (totaling eight face-pages)? (By *leaves* we mean a two-sided sheet of paper, and by *face-pages* we mean one side of a sheet of paper.) Unless otherwise specified, an eight-page photo section implies the latter, that is, four sheets of paper containing eight pages (or face-pages) of photos.

PHRASES AS PHRASES

See "WORDS AS WORDS."

PLAGIARISM

We think of a plagiarist as someone who deliberately steals some portion of another's work and publishes it as his or her own. It is an ethical taboo akin to both stealing and lying. So why does this manual feel compelled to exhort Christian writers to avoid this particular sin? The answer is that in the age of the internet, much, if not most, plagiarism is unintentional and afflicts even the most morally scrupulous.

Plagiarism in Research. Many writers now do the bulk of their research online, where everything from simple statistics to entire books can be accessed and downloaded instantaneously. An author can copy a relevant bit of information, or even an entire article, from a website and paste it into a document on the computer's hard drive. Later, at the writing stage, the author may open the research document, and if the extract's source has not been carefully annotated, the writer may mistakenly assume it to be original. Then the extracted passage is cut-and-pasted into the manuscript as the writer's own. It happens time and again, as many recent legal cases have shown.

Guidelines. Ignorance, though understandable, is no defense. It is now more important than ever to keep accurate references for all materials used in research and writing, whether from print or online sources. These guidelines should help:

1. *Annotate.* When gathering notes, information, and extracts, keep detailed annotations of the author and source. Be sure to copy the publication's title, author, date, publisher, and page number for all print sources and the web address and access date for all online sources. Keep the annotations *with* the extracted material, not in a separate file. This will save you or your assistant countless hours of having to track down the references later.
2. *Keep a Dedicated Research File.* Keep all downloaded materials in a computer file exclusively reserved for those materials and separate from any documents of original writing.
3. *Put It in Quotation Marks.* Make a habit of putting all downloaded material in quotation marks as soon as it's inserted into the document. Put an open quotation mark at the beginning of each new paragraph just as you would in a printed quotation. Coupled with careful author-date-publisher annotations, this should help the writer avoid mistaking the extract for original work. Let the quotation marks be a visual signal that the material is borrowed.
4. *Transfer with Care.* When digitally copying a quotation or passage from the research document to the body of the book, make sure that the quotation marks and correct citations are always attached. Don't assume you'll remember to attach the annotations later. You won't.

How Much Is Too Much? Some writers wonder how many words "borrowed" from another source actually constitute plagiarism, as though it were a matter of a simple word count. Is it plagiarism to steal a sentence, a phrase, two or three words? The answer is simple: If it is enough to cause the writer to ask the question in the first place, then it is probably too much. Taking as little as two words of a highly unique coinage from another author and crediting it as one's own can constitute, ethically and legally, plagiarism. It can be a special problem if the originator of that coinage has trademarked it. The author's conscience should be the yardstick, and erring on the side of caution is advised.

Common Knowledge. While leaving even a short phrase from another author uncredited may be considered plagiarism, using facts or ideas that are common knowledge is not. In your research, for instance, you might have found the diameter of the earth or the dates of Shakespeare's plays. In those cases, the information is considered common knowledge, and you need not credit the source. When academic writers are occasionally unsure if something is common knowledge, they often use the "Rule of Five": If you can find five independent sources (print or online) for the information, then it is most likely common knowledge and defensible as such in a court of law. Be advised that online sources often simply reproduce each other's information, so be sure that those sources are truly independent.

Paraphrasing. Some writers think of paraphrasing as a way to avoid plagiarism. Sometimes this is the case, sometimes it isn't, depending on the content and context of the original. For instance, if you paraphrase the Greek myth of Perseus as found in Robert Graves's *Greek and Roman Myths*, then your own paraphrase is an original retelling of a traditional myth that is considered common knowledge and in the public domain. But if you closely paraphrase another author's retelling of that myth in which both you and that author transform the characters into farm animals, then your paraphrased version may well be considered plagiarism since the uniqueness of the barnyard retelling belongs to the original author. In that case, credit should be given to the author, and if the telling does not fall under the fair use guidelines (see "FAIR USE"), then permission should be obtained as well.

Another example: If you write a detailed, two-page paraphrase of the plot of a particular episode of a television comedy, then, even though it is a paraphrase, permission should be obtained and proper credit given to the original writer because you have taken that author's original storyline. When in doubt, consult a legal advisor.

Self-Plagiarism. An author may sometimes wish to reproduce a passage from one of his or her own previous books. If this is done without informing the reader or the publishers involved, it can constitute plagiarism. In most cases, the original publisher is the legal copyright holder, and the author should ask for permission before reproducing the passage. It may be better to rewrite the passage entirely, in essence making it new. Otherwise, the publisher who owns the copyright to the previous book may request that the passage be quoted verbatim and provided with a citation and credit line. If the number of words exceeds the standards of the usual fair use defense, the publisher may even ask that the author request legal permission to quote the passage and perhaps pay a fee. (See "FAIR USE.")

Conclusion. Writers need to be careful when handling the intellectual property of others. The guidelines of the American History Association formerly defined *plagiarism* as a deliberate act but have now amended that to say: "It's plagiarism whether you intended to do so or not." (And to credit our source, that quotation was found in Geoffrey Nunberg's *Going Nucular*, 28.) In 1938, American playwright Wilson Mizner famously said, "When you take stuff from one writer it's plagiarism, but when you take from many writers it's called research." Had he lived in the computer age, he may well have revised that to say, "... but when you take from many writers it's called the internet." (See also "PERMISSION GUIDELINES: GENERAL," and "QUOTATIONS, GENERAL," and "QUOTING ONLINE SOURCES.")

PLAIN STYLE (AMISH)

The following points of style relate specifically to books by and for those who identify as Amish or Mennonite.

"Plain." Capitalize the word *Plain* in reference to Amish, some Mennonite, and some Quaker communities: *Plain clothing, the Plain community, the Plain People, Plain lifestyle.* (See "*Plain, plain (Amish).*")

Deity Pronoun. Amish writers commonly capitalize the deity pronoun. Mennonite publishers tend to lowercase it. (See "DEITY PRONOUN, THE.")

"Kapp." Amish and some Mennonite women wear a head covering that is usually called a *bonnet* or sometimes a *kapp*. In the US and Canada the latter word is pronounced like *cap*, though the original German pronunciation is more like *cop*. (See "HEAD AND BODY COVERINGS, WORDS FOR.")

PLURALS

As a conglomeration of languages, English has acquired some unusual plural nouns, which can be maddening for people trying to learn the language.

Regular Plurals. Most plurals are formed by adding an *s* to the noun (*cats, seas, trucks*) or an *es* to the noun if it ends with a sibilant *s, z, ch*, or *sh* sound (*tresses, buzzes, churches, bushes*). These are *regular plurals*.

Other Regular Plurals. While still ending in *s*, certain nouns require more modification in forming the plural, as seen in the following list:

words ending in *-y*, when preceded by a consonant, change *y* to *ie*, and add an *s* (*candies, countries, mercies*)
words ending in *-uy* replace *y* with *ie* and add *s* (*colloquies, obloquies*)
some words ending in *-f* or *-fe* replace with –*ves* (*elves, lives, selves*)
some words ending in *-o* add *-es* (*echoes, heroes, potatoes, tomatoes*), though some simply add an *-s* (*banjos, pianos, solos, zeros*)

Irregular Plurals. Irregular plurals follow their own rules. The following is a list that includes some of the most common forms as well as some less common but helpful ones:

Singular	**Plural**
attorney general	attorneys general
auto-da-fé	autos-da-fé (*s* is pronounced)
axis	axes
beau	beaux (or beaus)
Bedouin	Bedouin *or* Bedouins
bourgeois (s not pronounced)	bourgeois (same, but s is pronounced)
bulla	bullae
cherub	cherubim, but see *"cherub, cherubim, cherubims, cherubs"*
child	children
corps (s not pronounced)	corps (same, but *s* is pronounced)
court-martial	courts-martial
ellipsis	ellipses
erratum	errata
faux pas (s not pronounced)	faux pas (same, but s is pronounced)
foot	feet
genus	genera
goose	geese
Haggadah (Jewish Seder prayer)	Haggadot
hoof	hooves
[no common singular form]	dos and don'ts
jack-of-all-trades	jacks-of-all-trades
keeshond (breed of dog)	keeshonden
kibbutz	kibbutzim
man	men
man-of-war (warship)	men-of-war
mongoose	mongooses (*not* mongeese)
mother-in-law (father-in-law, etc.)	mothers-in-law (fathers-in-law, etc.)

mouse (animal)	mice
mouse (computer)	mouses
notary public	notaries public
ox	oxen
passerby	passersby
précis (s not pronounced)	précis (same, but s is pronounced)
prie-dieu	prie-dieux (both pronounced the same)
radius	radii
rendezvous (s not pronounced)	rendezvous (same, but s is pronounced)
right-of way	rights-of-way
seraph	seraphim
shofar	shofroth
stratum	strata
surgeon general	surgeons general
tooth	teeth
woman	women

Plural Form Same as the Singular. For some words, the plural is the same as the singular. These are referred to as *zero plurals*. Examples: *bison, cattle, deer, elk, fish, grouse, moose, salmon, sheep, shrimp, swine, tuna*. The word *fish*, by the way, uses *fishes* as a plural only when different kinds of fish are being referred to. Often nationalities take the zero plural as well: *Chinese, Japanese, Norse, Taiwanese, Sioux*.

Latin Plurals. Some familiar words rooted in Latin have two common plural forms, a Latin plural and a common English plural. In a few cases, there is a distinction in meaning between the two forms (for instance, see "*stigmas, stigmata*"). In most instances, there is no distinction in meaning between the two: for instance, *cacti/cactuses, compendia/compendiums, indices/indexes, matrices/matrixes, memoranda/memorandums*, and many more. Editors will usually follow the author's preference as long as that preference does not sound stilted in context. Otherwise, most editors lean toward the Latin plurals for technical or highly academic books (for instance, *foci* and *formulae* for scientific contexts rather than *focuses* and *formulas*) and toward the English plurals for all other books (for instance, *gymnasiums* and *referendums* rather than *gymnasia* and *referenda*).

Plurals Commonly Construed as Singular. In actual usage, both written and spoken, certain plural forms are construed as singulars. This is especially found with some Latin plurals that have become common in English, such as *agenda, criteria*, and *data*. For example, sentences such as *The agenda is enclosed* or *The data is ready for review* are acceptable in informal writing. Sometimes, using the correct Latin singular forms or using a plural noun can sound stilted or pedantic: *The agendum is enclosed* or *The agenda are enclosed.* Stick with the common, colloquial forms. Still, in books of a high literary or academic standard, the precise formal forms may be used: *The researchers' data are of three types* ...

Plurals of Single Letters. The plural forms of lowercase letters end in *'s*, as in *watch your p's and q's* or *dot your i's and cross your t's.* The plurals of capital letters end only in *s* unless that would lead to misreading: *Ps and Qs*, but *A's, U's.* In most ordinary text, the *'s* or *s* is set in roman, even when the single letter is set in italic.

Plurals of Abbreviations. An *'s* is used when forming the plurals of abbreviations with periods (*ibid.'s, Ph.D.'s,*), and an *s* alone for abbreviations with all capital letters and no periods (*DVDs, UFOs*). (See also "ABBREVIATIONS," section on "*Plurals of Abbreviations.*")

Plurals of Proper Names. These are formed simply by adding an *-s* in most cases (*two Toms, several Sarahs*), or an *-es* when a name already ends in an *s, x,* or *z* (*the Warnerses, the Blixes, the Bozes*). Add just an *-s* to names ending in *y* (*two Gregorys*, not *two Gregories*) and *o* (*the Munros*, not *the Munroes*).

PLUPERFECT

The pluperfect is the verb form that describes an action in the past that takes place before another action in the past. It is, in a sense, "the past tense of the past tense." It is usually formed by using *had* before the preterit, or past participle. Example: *Even before going to college I had decided to take a year off.* In that sentence, *had decided* is the pluperfect. That much is simple.

Sometimes a series of events needs to be described as having taken place before some specified action in the past. So the question arises whether every verb in that series of earlier events should be in the pluperfect. The answer is no. In most cases, a long series of pluperfect verbs sounds awkward and detracts from the narrative. Once the "past tense of the past tense" has been established, the writer can subtly shift back to using the simple past tense without confusing the reader. When the writer needs to revert back to the initial past tense (that is, the action closer to the present), then a strong signaling word or phrase is used to convey to the reader that the "past tense of the past tense" is no longer being used. As a simplified example, consider the following:

> In April he went to the hospital for tests [past tense]. In the four years before then, he had had two heart attacks and a stroke [shift to pluperfect using *had* to establish "the past of the past"]. At one point the doctors had simply recommended exercise and a healthy diet [a second

verb in the pluperfect using *had*, firmly establishing the time frame]. But despite modifying his diet, he found little time for exercise [subtle shift to using a verb in the simple past tense, even though we're still in the time before going to hospital]. But that changed when he discovered Richard Watson's *Philosopher's Diet* and was newly motivated to work out [still in the time before going to the hospital, and still using a verb in the simple past tense]. So after seeing his new hospital test results [a strong signaling statement to return the reader to the original time frame], the doctors were astonished by his progress [the shift back to the time when the story began is complete].

POETRY

Titles. The titles of most poems are set in roman and quotation marks, though the titles of book-length poems are italicized and not set in quotations. Capitalize most poem titles according to the guidelines for titles, but when a poem does not have a formal title and is identified only by its first line, then the title is set sentence style.

"God's Grandeur"—Gerard Manley Hopkins [ordinary poem]
Paradise Lost—John Milton [book-length poem]
"Because I could not stop for death"—Emily Dickinson [first line as title]

Quoted in Text. When poetry is quoted and set as an extract (block quotation) within a prose text, set it in the same typeface as the text, either the same size or, more customarily, one point smaller in size. The smaller size is recommended to minimize the number of long lines that might need to be broken if the full text size were used.

Traditionally, and unless the designer has a different intention, the longest line of the poem is centered on the page and the rest of the poem is allowed to align accordingly. If a lot of poetry is quoted, or when more than one poem appears on a single page, the verses can all be aligned on a preestablished indent (usually one or two picas) to avoid the appearance of a ragged left margin. If the lines are especially long (as with Whitman's verse), the poetry can even begin at the left margin and runover lines set at a preestablished indent, though in such cases the poetry should be set in a different font or type size to distinguish it from the prose. Secondary leading before and after the extract is also recommended.

In books meant to project a high literary value, extracted poetry can be set in italic—another way to squeeze long lines onto the page, because italic is more condensed than roman in many typefaces. Since italic fonts often slow the reader down, some designers like to set poetry in italic, feeling that poetry should be read more slowly than prose. Other designers either avoid italic setting of poetry or limit its use to those instances when poetry is quoted only sparingly.

As appropriate, two lines of quoted poetry may be either set as a block quotation or run into the text, using a spaced slash (/) to show the line breaks. Three or more lines of quoted poetry may also be run into the text with spaced slashes whenever the context requires it.

POLITICAL CORRECTNESS

Writers sometimes accuse editors of paying too much attention to political correctness, even though the definition of that term varies with one's point of view. What is politically incorrect for one person is plain-spokenness for another. While editors need to be sensitive to authors who are provocative and challenging, they also need to be aware that some writers, a relative few who strongly assert their First Amendment right to be politically incorrect, are actually asserting their right to be uncivil. But there is a point at which incivility is simply unchristian. Proverbs 12:18 says, "The words of the reckless pierce like swords, / but the tongue of the wise brings healing." Derogatory terms, ethnic and racial slurs, stereotyping of groups of people—none of that has any place in Christian publishing. (See "DISABILITY DESIGNATIONS," "ETHNIC, NATIONAL, AND RACIAL DESIGNATIONS," and "GENDER-ACCURATE LANGUAGE.")

POSSESSIVES

Adding an *'s* to a noun is the most common way to show possession. This is true for most singular nouns (*the author's manuscript, that person's answer, the tiger's stripes*) as well as for plural nouns that do not already end with *s* (*the children's school, the oxen's field, the women's meeting*). When a plural noun ends in an *s*, as most do, only an apostrophe is added (*the dogs' kennel, the schools' custodians*).

Personal Names and Proper Nouns. The same rules apply to personal names and proper nouns, both the singular (*Adrian's car, Chicago's new stadium, Keats's poetry*) and the plural (*the Lewises' letters, the Smiths' house*).

Proper Names Ending with Sibilants. Grammarians have proposed various methods of forming possessives of personal names and proper nouns ending in *s* or *z* sounds. To establish consistency, *CMoS 16* recommends that all such singular personal names and proper nouns add an *'s* to show possession (*Bliss's hymns, John Rogers's Bible, Dickens's novels*). This also applies to names from classical literature, ancient history, or the Bible—including those that end with *eez* or *ez* sounds or with an *x* or a *z*, whether pronounced or not.

Achilles's heel
Ananias's house
Augustus's reign
François's poetry
Jesus's disciples
Judas's betrayal
Moses's staff
Perez's escape
Proulx's novels
Ramses's dynasty
Socrates's method
Thales's philosophy
Thomas's doubt
Xerxes's throne
Zacchaeus's tree

This near universal adding of *'s* to all words and names in the singular is in contrast to an older rule of possessives, which adds an *'s* only if the extra *s* is actually pronounced. Since few people pronounce the extra sibilant in *Xerxes' Anabasis*, the extra *s* is not added. The problem is that people often differ in their pronunciation. Some people pronounce the extra *s* in *Jesus's three-year ministry*, and some do not. So the spell-it-as-you-pronounce-it rule is unreliable, and the rule of adding of *'s* to all singular words and names at least offers a welcome consistency.

Are there no exceptions? Not quite. Though nearly all exceptions have now been eliminated, a few common phrases, for the sake of euphony and tradition, continue to use an apostrophe only: *for conscience' sake* and *for goodness' sake*.

Still, if an author has a strong preference for *Jesus'* or other similar forms, then that should be honored.

Gerunds. The possessive *'s* is usually added to any noun that is linked to a gerund, as in *the minister's leaving the church* or *God's having gathered his people to himself*. While this rule is still used, avoid it if the result sounds stilted: *they heard Harold singing in the wings* is more natural than *they heard Harold's singing in the wings*. Note the subtle shift in meaning between the two.

Feast Days. The names of feast days of saints are formed as possessives, using an apostrophe: *All Saints' Day, St. Patrick's Day, Saint Michael's Eve, St. Valentine's Day.*

With Italicized Words. When added to an italicized noun, a possessive *'s* is most often set in roman:

> Timmer explains how the riches of the kingdom can be found in the *anawim*'s very poverty.
>
> Sandy joined the *Banner*'s staff in 1980.

To Show Joint Possession. When a possessive needs to be formed for two or more persons in the same context, use the following guidelines: (1) if a single object is possessed mutually by all the people listed, only the final name needs to be in a possessive form; (2) if separate objects are possessed, each name should be in the possessive form. In some cases, rewriting may be called for if the distinctions are not otherwise clear.

Keil and Delitzsch's study [the book they wrote together]
Vaughan's and Herbert's poetry [their separate poetry]
my aunt and uncle's library [their joint library]
my aunt's and uncle's books [their separate books]
my aunt's books and my uncle's books [their separate books; rewritten for clarity]

With Phrases. Phrases or epithets of two or more words form possessives as long as they are not more than three or four words in length and no ambiguity results. Otherwise, rewrite the sentence.

the Evil One's devices
the Good Shepherd's promises
the Apostle to the Gentile's writings [ambiguous]
the writings of the Apostle to the Gentiles [rewritten]

Collective Possessives. The plural possessive form is used when an object is described by the group of people who commonly control, own, or possess it. When the group uses an object but no possession is implied, then it is called an *attributive form*. In both cases, use an apostrophe since a strict distinction cannot always be made between possessive and attributive forms; for example: *the bishops' letter, the nurses' station, the parents' association, writers' guidelines*. Note that many organizations and publications drop the possessive apostrophe in their official names; in these cases, adhere to the group's preference; for instance, *American Booksellers Association, FaithWriters Magazine, Michigan Teachers Association.*

Possession by Things. An antiquated grammar rule states that only people, not things, may possess an object and that it is improper to say "the book's cover." In modern usage this rule may be ignored, and possessives may be used with inanimate objects.

PRAYERS

Designers have much leeway in the setting of prayers in text. If the prayers are short, italic might be used; if longer, they might be set like extracts, or block quotations. In most cases, the setting should be such that the reader will be able to distinguish between the prayer and the text. In some cases they may be treated like thoughts or unspoken discourse. (See "THOUGHTS.")

PREFACE

Unlike a foreword, a preface is usually written by the author (see "FOREWORD"), and a preface differs from an introduction in the way each relates to the book's content. A preface's content is usually only peripherally related to the main argument or content of the book, often explaining either the author's background or how the book came about in the first place. An introduction is more integral to the content, often outlining what to expect or explaining concepts essential to the reading. If two or more prefaces are reprinted from various editions of the book, the original preface is placed closest to the text itself. (See also "INTRODUCTION.")

PREFIXES

The challenge of prefixes (letters added to the beginning of a word to alter its meaning) is in determining whether a hyphen should be inserted between the prefix and root word. Among the most common prefixes that are set "solid" (with no space or hyphen) when forming compound words are *anti-*, *co-*, *counter-*, *mid-*, *non-*, *out-*, *over-*, *post-*, *pre-*, *pseudo-*, *re-*, *semi-*, and *super-*. Exceptions are made when the prefix (1) precedes a numeral (*pre-1939*, *the mid-1400s*), (2) precedes a capital letter (*to out-Herod Herod*, *anti-Christian*), (3) precedes an already compounded term (*non-returnable-item receipts*), (4) duplicates a letter, especially a vowel (*anti-intellectual*, *re-enumerate*), (5) or forms a new word that might cause misreading (*co-op*, *re-create*, *re-sent*). In those cases, a hyphen is used, though an en dash is inserted when a prefix defines an entire unhyphenated compound term rather than just the first word in that term (*pre–Civil War*).

Since many exceptions exist (words like *co-payment*), it is always best to check *Webster* when in doubt. If the word does not appear there, then use common sense. The following examples may help.

codirector, coworker, cowriter—*but* co-colonize, co-edition, *and* co-op [all to avoid misreading]

counterculture, counterespionage, counterintuitive—*but* Counter-Reformation [precedes a capital letter], counter-counterintelligence

midday, midcareer, midlife, midterm, midwinter—*but* mid-1900s [precedes a numeral], mid-nineteenth century [precedes a compound term]

multifaceted, multitalented, multivolume set—*but* multi-international *and* multi-instrumentalist [to avoid duplicated vowel]

postdated, postelection, postmodern—*but* post-9/11 [precedes numeral], post-Christian [precedes a capital letter], post-traumatic stress disorder [precedes compound term], post–Desert Storm [precedes compound term; note en dash]

predate, predestination, preschool—*but* pre-presentation [to avoid *prepre-*], pre-engineered [to avoid duplicated vowel], pre-Socratic [precedes a capital letter], pre–World War II [precedes compound term; note en dash]

The prefixes *all-*, *ex-* (meaning "former"; see also "*ex-*" for more details), *half-*, and *self-* most often use hyphens: *an all-faiths meeting, all-weather protection, ex-missionary, half-pint, half-smile, self-sacrifice.* Exceptions (like *halfway, selfhood*) are common. Again, check *Webster.*

PREPOSITIONS, ENDING SENTENCES WITH

The mistaken notion that it is always unacceptable to end a sentence with a preposition is common. (Winston Churchill is credited, probably wrongly, as having said, that it is "a rule up with which I will not put.") In practice, feel free to end a sentence with a preposition whenever it sounds more natural to do so. Avoid hypercorrection.

PREPOSITIONS IN TITLES

Lowercase a preposition of any length in a title or subtitle unless the preposition is used adverbially or otherwise emphasized: for instance, *The Crusades through Arab Eyes* and "Comin' through the Rye," but *The Prayer of Jabez: Breaking Through to the Blessed Life* and "All Through the Night."

PRESENTATION PAGE

A presentation page is a commemorative page included in any Bible or book meant to be given away on special occasions, such as confirmations, weddings, and graduations (there's one in the front of *Webster*, for instance). It provides prompts and blank rule lines on which the purchaser may write personal information. It is usually printed either on the flyleaf (most often the recto) or on the first recto page following the flyleaf, and it can include any elements appropriate to the occasion, usually including:

Presented to ____________________
on this day ____________________
on the occasion of ______________

A short prayer or an appropriate message or quotation, as well as a decorative border or other graphic elements, can also be provided.

PRINTER'S ORNAMENTS

See "DINGBATS."

PROFANITY

The reason most Christian publishers avoid profanity in their books is simple: their readers don't like it. If you want to touch the hearts of Christian readers, four-letter words are not your friends. Beyond that, this manual can't answer all authors' and publishers' questions about taboo language, though the following guidelines are offered as a discussion starter.

Consider these issues, for instance: Does an author sin when her fictional character uses vulgarity? Does an editor sin by allowing an author to use a four-letter word in a book? How honestly or explicitly should sinful behavior be described in a book? Is all offensive language forbidden in Christian writing? If so, what about offensive ideas? At what point does violence become obscene and as offensive as profanity? And who is to judge?

Most Christian writers and editors take seriously the biblical admonitions against coarse jokes (Eph. 5:4), filthy language (Col. 3:8), and the misuse of God's name (Deut. 5:11), but when it comes to using such language in writing, the issues are not always clear cut. No human language is devoid of fringe speech, that is, words used largely to express pain, surprise, anger, and other emotions; create coarsely humorous or grotesque effects; or startle—even shock—the listener or reader. They are all part of an author's rhetorical tool kit.

Authors and editors alike should recognize not only the existence of "taboo words and phrases" but also their occasional appropriateness in effective communication. As many readers have noted, even some of the writers of the Bible used the taboo language of their time. While such language offends some readers, individual words are, from a linguistic standpoint, objective signifiers and morally neutral. Thomas Aquinas said that things are neither good nor evil in themselves—only in the uses to which they are put by fallen humans.

Preferring not to alienate prospective buyers, most religious publishers require their authors to avoid taboo speech. If authors use those terms, editors routinely eliminate them at the editorial stage. This is wise whenever a strongly negative reaction among the book's target readership can be anticipated. Alienating readers is always counterproductive. If a moral consideration is at issue, it is usually not so much in the words themselves as in the desire to avoid offending those who have paid money for the book.

This tacit censorship runs up against the author's First Amendment right to free speech, though, in a larger sense, editors at all publishing houses, general and religious alike, make decisions that are tantamount to censorship in an effort to accomplish the publisher's goal of helping the author communicate effectively to a given market. Ironically, many general publishers censor an author's religious opinions (though they may euphemistically call it "toning it down") if they are apt to offend a more nonsectarian readership. The nature of publishing is imbued with implicit censorship, beginning with the fact that some manuscripts are accepted for publication and others are not. These conflicting rights of authors and publishers are serious matters, and it is best for the publisher and author to discuss them ahead of time.

For practical purposes, taboo and fringe speech can be roughly divided into six categories:

Profanity: using the names of persons of the Trinity in inappropriate ways, commonly termed "cursing" or "taking God's name in vain."

Scatology: narrowly defined as insensitive or coarse, slang terms for bodily functions and waste.

Venery: obscene words and expressions explicitly describing reproductive organs, body parts, or sexual acts.

Vulgar Interjections: taboo words used as expressions of sudden emotion. These are often drawn from profanity, scatology, or venery.

Vulgar Epithets: often colorful but socially unacceptable terms used pejoratively to describe individual people.

Social Insensitivity: words and expressions that inherently communicate a derogatory attitude toward groups of people because of their race, gender, ethnic background, religion, physical or mental challenge, sexual orientation, and so on. This category runs the gamut from "politically incorrect language" to "hate speech." (See "DISABILITY DESIGNATIONS," "ETHNIC, NATIONAL, AND RACIAL DESIGNATIONS," and "POLITICAL CORRECTNESS.")

Authors and publishers must decide for themselves where they stand on these issues, and publishers should clearly state their policy and expectations in their contracts and author guidelines so that authors won't be blindsided later.

The following guidelines outline a middle path adopted by Zondervan, which may be helpful to other producers of religious materials:

Zondervan does not allow its authors to use the most offensive examples from any of the six categories listed above—that is, those words and phrases recognized as strictly taboo by the largest proportion of Christian readers. The word *largest* is important here, because there exists a sizable "second tier" of language—sometimes referred to as *euphemisms* or *minced oaths*—that might offend some readers but not others (see "MINCED OATHS"). In such cases, our editors employ the criteria of *appropriateness*, of which two aspects should be considered.

First, is the language appropriate to the work itself? Is the taboo word or minced oath necessary to convey a mood or an idea that cannot be conveyed otherwise? In fiction, particularly, strong language can be helpful in characterizing people, providing a sense of realism, and describing the true nature of sin and evil.

Second, is the language appropriate to the intended readership? Not all books are for all readers. So we ask: Will the language be acceptable in its context by the largest number of readers for whom this book is intended? Judgment needs to be exercised, though the publisher needs to accept that it may be impossible—to say nothing of useless—to produce a book that is wholly inoffensive to every possible reader. Often an over-delicate social propriety, not a biblical mandate, is at stake.

No book can please every reader. Nor should an author or publisher's goal be to produce a perfectly inoffensive book. Since definitive guidelines for the use of profanity, vulgar speech, and frank portrayals of evil are difficult to formulate, the best procedure is for the author and publisher to confer and ask: Who will read the book? What are the costs of using offensive language in terms of reader trust and sales? Can effective alternatives be found for the offensive language?

A common solution practiced by some authors and publishers, though rejected by others, is to state, without using the actual words, that taboo language has been used. For instance, a fiction writer might say, "The detective let out a string of profanity," or a nonfiction writer might say, "After the tumble, I couldn't help swearing under my breath."

Beyond specific words and phrases, some readers are offended by mature situations and discussions of sensitive topics. Issues of immorality and sin are central themes in many Christian books and cannot be addressed effectively without allowing for realistic portrayal. Again, the criteria of appropriateness to the work and to the intended audience are applied, and judgment must be used.

Ideally, such decisions cannot be made unilaterally by the editor or author alone. They are best discussed with the publisher's marketing and sales people, who have more direct contact with retailers. Such decisions might also be discussed with readers themselves, by way of focus groups or marketing surveys.

These are difficult issues, but they must be confronted for the sake of the health of religious communication.

(See also "GRAWLIX.")

PROFANITY, MISPERCEIVED

Many ordinary words resemble profanity but aren't. Some readers complain, for instance, that *asinine* is a vulgarity (it isn't; it is derived from *ass*, "donkey"), that *niggardly* is a racially charged epithet (the word, which simply means "stingy," predates the racial epithet by more than two hundred years), and that *dastardly* is a euphemistic adverbial form of *bastard*. In none of these cases is the accusation true, but a sensitive writer may want to avoid them anyway, knowing that some readers will be offended by the perception of profanity. A judgment call needs to be made, and the specific readership should be taken into account.

PROLOGUE

When present, a book's *prologue* is the first element of the body matter (and not part of the front matter), usually coming immediately before the first chapter. It is commonly reserved for works of fiction, drama, biography, history, and nonfiction narratives. Its purpose is to show what came before the main action of the book and, in that way, serves to complement an epilogue, which informs the reader of what came after the main action of the book, though an epilogue need not be present if a prologue is used, and vice versa. A prologue should be distinguished from prefaces and forewords, which have different functions and are counted among the book's front matter. A prologue is often written in the same voice as the rest of the book, that is, in the narrator's voice rather than the author's, when those voices are distinct. (See also "FOREWORD," "INTRODUCTION," and "PREFACE.")

PROMO PAGE

See "promotional page."

PROMOTIONAL PAGE

A promotional, or promo, page is an advertisement placed in the back of a book to alert readers to other works by the same author or other books in the same series. Publishers should inform an author of their intention to insert such a page. It is considered bad form for a publisher to advertise any other books without the permission of the author. The layout and design are usually determined by the publisher, but some ministries and major authors have ready-made promotional pages, which they provide to the publisher. An author's or ministry's website can also be promoted in this fashion. (See also "SOCIAL MEDIA PAGE.")

PRONUNCIATION GUIDE FOR AUDIO BOOKS

Since audio downloads are a key part of electronic publishing, audio producers have more questions than ever about pronunciation. The following guidelines and lists offer some help.

Pronunciation of Words in the Bible. This topic is too large to cover in this manual, but every audio producer for religious books should own a copy of William O. Walker's *The HarperCollins Bible Pronunciation Guide* (New York: HarperCollins, 1994).

Ghost Words. Some common phrases, especially those involving numerals, contain words that are not actually present on the printed page but are meant to be spoken when read aloud. For instance, anyone who reads the words *Henry VIII* for an audiobook will know to supply the ghost word *the* and pronounce it *Henry the Eighth*, not *Henry Eight*. The same is true for dates and times. In text, a date might appear as *February 21*, but the audio voice talent should speak it as *February the twenty-first*. The time designation *8:00* is usually read aloud as *eight o'clock*, not just *eight*. And most Bible readers know that *2 Corinthians* is spoken as *Second Corinthians*.

Foreign Words and Names. Avoid affecting a foreign pronunciation when a foreign name already has a common English pronunciation. For instance, *Volkswagen* is *VOHKS-WA-gun* (not *VOLKS-VAH-gun*); *Paris* is *PAIR-iss* (not *par-EE*), and *Van Gogh* is *van-GO* (not *van-GOK*, with the guttural final consonant). Also, avoid using a foreign accent when foreign words common to English are used; for instance, speak words like *maître d'* (MAY-truh DEE) and *coup de grace* (COO duh GRAHSS) without slipping into a French accent. Foreign accents may be used for extended passages in a foreign language but only if the voice talent can do so accurately.

Ecclesial Latin. Students studying classical Latin learn how the language was pronounced in ancient Rome. The Roman Catholic Church has developed its own pronunciation over the centuries, which is still used whenever the Vulgate is read aloud or when liturgical Latin is used. The following chart outlines the primary rules for ecclesial Latin pronunciation. Note that the consonants *b, d, f, l, m, n, p, q, t, v, x* are pronounced as they are in English.

a = "ah" like *father* (ex. *anno*)
e = "eh" like *led* (ex. *credo*)
i = "ee" like *seem* (ex. *sic*)
o = "o" like *more* (ex. *ora*)
u = "oo" like *moon* (ex. *urbs*)
y = "ee," same as *i* (ex. *hymnus*)
ae, oe = "eh," same as *e* (ex. *Caesar*)
c = "k" like cut, before consonants, *a, o, u*, and at end of words (ex. *contra*)
c = "ch" before *e* and *i* (ex. *pace*)
cc = "tch" like *hatch* (ex. *ecce*)
ch = "k" like *chrome* (ex. *Christus*)
g = "g" like *gold*, before consonants, *a, o*, and *u* (ex. *virgo*)

g = "j" like *gem*, before *e, i, y, ae, oe* (ex. *genuit*)
gn = "ny" like *canyon* (ex. *angus*)
h = silent, except pronounced like "k" in the words *mihi* and *nihil*
j = "y" like *yet* (ex. *Jesu*)
r = slightly rolled almost like "dd" (ex. *miserere*)
s = "ss" like *hiss*, never "z" (ex. *sola*)
sc = "sk" like *scare*, before consonants, *a, o,* and *u* (ex. *scriptum*)
sc = "sh" as in *share*, before *e, i, y, ae, oe* (ex. *ascendere*)
sch = "sk" as in *school* (*schola*)
th = "t" like *thyme* (ex. *Thomas*)
ti = "tsee" like *tsetse fly* (*gratia*)
z = "zd" like *beads* (ex. *Lazurus*)
double consonants = slightly lengthened (ex. *bello*)

Pronouncing Latin Abbreviations in Scholarly Books. The person directing an audio recording session should guide the voice talent in handling scholarly Latin abbreviations correctly. If the author is reading the text, then he or she makes those decisions, since they know the readership best. If the author is not reading the text, we recommend (1) that common sense be used, and (2) that English translations and equivalents be used for both general and academic audiences. Here are a few of the common abbreviations and their English equivalents:

Abbreviation	To Be Spoken
c., or ca.	about (the date) *or* around (the date)
cf.	compare with *or* compare to
e.g.	for example *or* for instance
et al.	and others
etc., or &c.	et cetera *(the Latin phrase is okay) or* and so on
ff.	and following; *rarely used—avoid it*
ibid.	*use the Latin* ibid *or* ibidem; *rarely used in text*
id.	*use the Latin* idem; *rarely used in text*
i.e.	that is
N.B.	note, *or* note well
op cit.	the work cited; *rarely used*
p., and pp.	page, pages
q.v.	see *(the Latin* quod vide *translates literally to* "see which")
sic	*if the error is audible to the listener, say* sic *(pronounced SICK); if it is inaudible, drop the* sic
v., or vs.	*always pronounce as* versus
viz.	that is, namely, *or* precisely

Chinese Transliteration. See "CHINESE TRANSLITERATION" for a pronunciation guide to Chinese words in English (pinyin).

"A" and "An" Before Vowels and the Letter "H." See "*a, an*" for a full discussion of this.

Commonly Mispronounced Words and Names. Although this manual can't foresee all possible difficulties (we recommend *Webster* as well as online sources for standard pronunciations), the following list gives a few of the more common problem words and names found in Christian life and worship.

Common and Occasional Words

9-1-1—(US emergency phone number) "Nine one one," not "Nine eleven." (See also "PHONE NUMBERS IN TEXT [TELEPHONE AND CELL PHONE]," section on "*Emergency 9-1-1.*")

9/11—(terrorist attacks of September 11, 2001) "Nine eleven." (See also "*September 11, 2001.*")

666—("number of the Beast," Rev. 13) "six six six," not "six hundred sixty-six" or "six sixty-six."

accidie—(noun, meaning "sloth") OX-uh-dee

aegis—(noun) EE-jiss

Aéropostale—(clothing brand) air-uh-poe-STALL

al-Qaeda—the Arabic pronunciation is too difficult for most Americans; sufficient for audio book purposes is the English approximation el-KIE-duh (*not* el-KAY-duh); the second syllable rhymes with *eye*. In Arabic, the second syllable is two syllables, closer to el-KIE-uh-duh, though that is still inaccurate.

amen—AH-MEN (most common, and sung form); AY-MEN is also okay; usually both syllables are equally accented, like a poetic spondee. (See "*amen.*")

apartheid—(noun) uh-PAR-tate, or uh-PAR-tight; avoid both the *th* sound in the middle and the *d* sound at the end.

Appalachia, Appalachian—*Webster* prefers APP-uh-LAY-chuh and APP-uh-LAY-chun (the *a* in the third syllable being long), though people in the southern part of that region itself pronounce the words APP-uh-LATCH-uh and APP-uh-LATCH-un (the *a* in the third syllable sounding like the *a* in *lad*). Use *Webster*'s pronunciation for general audiences, but if the book is about Southern Appalachia or the South, or is meant to appeal to readers in that region, use the regional pronunciation.

Baal—(pagan god in Bible) pronounced BAY-ul (preferred), as if pronouncing the word *bail* as two syllables; BAH-ul is also acceptable.

Babel—(Tower of . . . , in Gen. 11:1–9) BAY-bul (preferred, esp. in academic references); or pronounced the same as *babble* (common in spoken American English and in trade books)

Beelzebub—(devil) pronounced bee-EL-zuh-bub (preferred), though BEEL-zuh-bub is also acceptable

blessed—pronounce this as two syllables, BLESS-ud, when used as an honorific title (*the blessed martyrs*) or as a minced oath (*the blessed bad weather*). Pronounce it as one syllable, BLEST, to describe the possession of blessings (*we have been blessed*). (See also "*Blessed, blessed.*")

bona fides—as a plural noun, this can be pronounced either BONE-uh FIE-deez or BONE-uh FIDES. The adjective is BONE-uh FIDE.

bourgeois—*s* not pronounced as singular; the s is pronounced in the plural but spelled the same.

cache—pronounced the same as CASH, *not* cash-AY

caveat—(Latin for "beware") KAH-vee-YAHT

Celtic (church, culture)—KEL-tick (not SELL-tick) in general usage; the Boston basketball team pronounces their name "the SELL-ticks."

chasm—KA-zuhm (rhymes with *spasm*), (not CHA-zuhm)

chimera—(noun) kye-MEER-uh

collect—(liturgical prayer) when referring to a short liturgical prayer, this word is accented on the first syllable: KAHL-ect. Otherwise, the common verb is pronounced kuh-LECT.

compline—(canonical hour) CAHM-plin. (See "HOURS, CANONICAL.")

corps—*s* not pronounced as singular; the *s* is pronounced in the plural but spelled the same.

cuneiform—(ancient wedge-shaped writing) CUE-nee-uh-form or cue-NEE-uh-form (four syllables), not CUE-nuh-form (three syllables)

daemon—(Greek mythology) pronounced the same as *demon*

Daesh—(terrorist organization) two syllables: DA-ish, though often sounding like one syllable: DAHSH

dais—(noun) DAY-us is preferred, but DIE-us is also acceptable.

Dalai Lama—(Tibetan Buddhist leader) DOLL-eye LAH-mah

deity—DEE-uh-tee is most common, but DAY-uh-tee is also acceptable

divisive—the first pronunciation in *Webster* has this rhyming with *incisive* (long *i* in the second syllable) rather than *dismissive* (short *i* in the second syllable).

ergo—(Latin for "therefore") either AIR-go or UR-go is acceptable.

electoral—(adj) ee-LECK-tuh-rull

err—(verb) traditionalists pronounce this UR (rhymes with *her*), as in "to err is human," though *Webster* lists the more common AIR (rhymes with *hair*) as the first option. While both are correct, UR is more formal and proper, but say AIR in informal contexts.

et cetera, or etc.—pronounced ett-SET-ur-uh, *not* eck-SET-ur-uh

faux pas—*s* not pronounced as singular; the *s* is pronounced in the plural but spelled the same.

feng shui—(Chinese geomancy) FUNG-SHWEE or FUNG-SHWAY

forte—(meaning *strength*) FOR-tay is common in the US, though for-TAY and FORT are also acceptable. *Webster* says, "Someone somewhere will dislike whichever variant you choose" (493).

Grosvenor—(square and street in London) *s* not pronounced: GROVE-ner

gyro—(noun) as a wrapped Greek sandwich, it is correctly pronounced *YEE-roe* (though it is sometimes pronounced JEE-roe in US); when used as a shortened form of *gyroscope*, pronounced it JIE-roe.

Hanukkah—(holiday) In Hebrew this word begins with a mild guttural *k* sound, but in most contexts, pronounce it with a standard English *h* sound

Hiroshima—heer-roe-SHEE-muh is preferred to heer-ROE-shee-muh

I Ching—(Chinese classic) EE CHING

imprimatur—(noun) IM-prim-AH-toor

Jesu—(Latin for *Jesus*) YAY-zoo

kapp—(Amish/Mennonite head covering) even though this is often pronounced with a German *a*, almost like *cop*, the Amish themselves pronounce it like the American *cap*.

Kilns—the Oxford home of C. S. Lewis and his brother, Warnie, is pronounced as it is spelled: KILNS, not with a silent *n*, as the word is sometimes pronounced in English. Even for the common noun *kiln*, pronouncing the *n* is preferred. (See also "*Kilns, the*.")

koine—(Greek) COY-nay

larvae—(noun, pl. of *larva*) LAR-vee

larynx—LAIR-inks (commonly mispronounced LAIR-nix)

liable—in formal speech, it's three syllables: LIE-uh-bull, *not* LIE-bull.

Logos—(Greek, "Word") when used to mean personified Wisdom or the Word as Christ, use Greek pronunciation: LAW-GAWSS. Pronounce it LOH-GOHSS (long *o*'s) for the Christian bookstore chain and the Bible software.

Lourdes—(town in France) LOORD (pronounced like *lured*)

Louvre—(museum in Paris) LOOV-ruh

Magdalen College (Oxford) and Magdalene College (Cambridge)—both colleges are pronounced MAWD-lin, sounding identical to *maudlin*.

Marquis—(title of nobility) mar-KEY in US and France but MAR-kwiss in UK

Moleskine—(notebook company brand name) the company rather coyly says everyone may pronounce it as they wish; but the company's president says that MOLE-skin is the English pronunciation (it was originally a UK product) and MOLE-uh-SKEEN is the French. The company, now in Italy, is pronounced MOLE-uh-SKEEN-uh in its home country.

Nag Hammadi—(site of ancient manuscript discovery) NAHG huh-MAH-dee

niche—NEESH, *not* NITCH; it rhymes with *quiche*

Noel—(sometimes spelled *Nowell*) no-EL, meaning Christmas, but as a person's name, NO-ul is often the male form and no-EL is often the female form. (See "*Noel.*")

none—(canonical hour) pronounced like *known*, not NO-nay or NUN (See "HOURS, CANONICAL.")

nuclear—(adj.) NEW-klee-ur

nuptial—(noun and adj.) NUP-shul

Pauline—(adjective form of *Paul*) PAW-line (second syllable rhymes with *mine*). Though some pronounce this PAW-leen, that is less common and can be mistaken for the common personal name pronounced that way.

Pilates—(exercise system) puh-LAH-teez

précis—(noun) *s* not pronounced as singular; the *s* is pronounced in the plural but spelled the same.

primer—(noun) as an elementary spelling book, it is pronounced PRIM-ur; as a base coat of paint, it is pronounced PRIME-ur.

prophecy—(noun) PRAH-fuh-see. (See also "*prophecy, prophesy.*")

prophesy—(verb) PRAH-fuh-sigh. (See also "*prophecy, prophesy.*")

Pulitzer (Prize)—PULL-it-zur, not PEW-lit-zur

Qur'an—(Muslim scriptures) kuh-RAHN is preferred, but it may also be pronounced kur-ANN. (See also "*Qur'an, Koran.*")

rendezvous—*s* not pronounced as singular; the *s* is pronounced in the plural but spelled the same.

sacerdotal—SASS-ur-DOE-tul is the preferred pronunciation, but SAK-ur-DOE-tul is commonly heard as well.

São Paulo—(city in Brazil) SOW POW-lo; the first two syllables rhyme with *cow*; or, more accurately, the first syllable ends with a lightly sounded nasal *n*.

short-lived—the first pronunciation given in *Webster* shows *lived* with the short *i* of *give* rather than the long *i* of *five*.

Sikh—(follower of Sikhism) adherents pronounce it similar to SICK but are usually okay with Americans pronouncing it SEEK, since the idea of "seeking" is closer to the original meaning of the word itself.

slough—SLUE (rhymes with *clue* in US); SLAOU (rhymes with *cow* in UK)—as in Bunyan's "Slough of Despond" in *The Pilgrim's Progress*, and meaning "a swamp or bog." When the same word means "to shed" (as a snake's skin), *slough* is pronounced SLUFF.

suite—pronounced SWEET, *not* SUIT

tenet—pronounced TEN-ett, not TEN-ent

terce—(canonical hour) pronounced like *terse*. (See "HOURS, CANONICAL.")

victuals—the *c* is silent: VITT-uls; an alternate spelling of *vittles*

Weltanschauung—(German, meaning "worldview") VELT-un-SHAH-oong

wreak—(as in *to wreak havoc*) REEK is preferred, though RECK is sometimes heard.

Yahweh—(the spoken form of the abbreviation for God's name) both YAH-way and YAH-vey are common, though the former is more so.

yarmulke—(Jewish skullcap) YAH-muh-kuh (preferred), or YAR-mul-kuh

yea—(meaning "yes" or "indeed," as in "Yea, though I walk through the valley of death ...") pronounced the same as *yay*; rhymes with *day*

Names of People

Augustine—(saint) AWE-gus-teen, though some in UK pronounce it uh-GUS-tin

Barth, (Karl)—(theologian) BART

Bede, (the Venerable)—(medieval Christian writer) BEED

Bernstein, (Leonard)—(musician) BURN-stine, not BURN-steen

Boethius—(sixth-century philosopher) boe-EE-thee-us

Böhme, Jacob—(medieval mystic) BURM, YAH-cub

Bonhoeffer, Dietrich—(theologian) BAHN-haw-fur, DEE-trick

Bono—(U2 lead singer) BAH-no, *not* BOE-no

Brontë, (Charlotte, Emily, and Anne)—(English writers) BRON-tee is correct, though BRON-tay is also commonly heard.

Brueghel—(Dutch painter) BREW-gull (sometimes spelled *Breughel*)

Buber, (Martin)—BOO-ber, not BYOO-ber

Buechner, (Frederick)—(writer) BEEK-ner

Caedmon—(medieval writer) CAD-mun, not CAYD-mun

Camus, Albert—(French writer) CAH-moo, ahl-BARE

Chardin, Teilhard de—(theologian) char-DA(N) (ends with the French nasal *n*), tay-YAR duh

Chrysostom—(early Christian writer) KRIS-us-tum (accent on first syllable)

Cockburn (Bruce)—(musician) COE-burn

Columba—(Celtic saint) kuh-LUM-buh (accent on second syllable); also known as Colum (KUH-lum), Colm (CULM), or Columcille (kuh-LUM-kill)

Comenius (John Amos)—(theologian) koh-MEEN-ee-us (accent on second syllable)

Cynewulf—(medieval writer) KIN-uh-wolf

Danaë—(mythological character) DAY-nuh-ee

Dives—(rich man in Luke 16:19–31) DIE-veez

Eusebius—(early church historian) you-SEE-bee-us

Fiennes, Ralph—(actor) FINES, RAFE

Gandhi, Mohandas—(Indian leader) GAHN-dee, moe-HAHN-dus

Gibran, Kahlil—(Lebanese poet) juh-BRAHN (rhymes with *LeBron*), kuh-LEEL

Goethe, (Johann Wolfgang)—(German writer) GU(R)-tuh (pronounced as if an *R* is just barely sounded)

Groening, (Matt)—(cartoonist) GRAY-ning

Hammarskjöld, Dag (writer, UN chief)—HAHM-ur-shuld, DAHG

Héloïse—(medieval writer) AY-luh-weez (the *H* is silent)

Iraneaus—(early church father) eye-ruh-NAY-us

Jordan, (Clarence)—(author) JUR-den (rhymes with *burden*, not *Gorden*)

Kempe, (Margery)—(medieval mystic) KEMP (one syllable), not KEMP-ee

Kuyper, Abraham—(theologian) KY-purr, AHB-ruh-hahm

Le Carré, (John)—(writer) luh car-RAY; do not pronounce this with a French accent.

Lao-tzu—(ancient Chinese philosopher) LAU-dzuh (first syllable rhymes with *pow*)

Lucado, (Max)—(writer) loo-KAY-doe, not loo-KAH-doe

Marquis, (Don)—(humorist) MAR-kwis, not mar-KEY

McGrath (Alister)—(writer) muh-GRATH; last syllable rhymes with *math*. Note this writer's first name is correctly spelled "-ter," not "-tair." Also note that some people with this surname in the UK and US pronounce it "muh-GRAW."

Milosz, Czeslaw—(poet) pronounced *MEE-wosh, CHESS-lauv*

Moltmann, Jürgen—(theologian) MOLT-mahn, YER-gun

Nabokov, (Vladimir)—(writer) nuh-BOE-cawv

Nietzsche, Friderich—(philosopher) NEE-chuh (*not* NEE-chee), FREED-rick

Oz, Amos—(writer) OHZ, AHM-ohss; last name rhymes with *froze*, not *rahs*.

Proulx, (Annie)—(writer) PRU, rhymes with *true*

Ralph—(common first name) occasionally men in the UK (composer Ralph Vaughn Williams and actor Ralph Fiennes, for example) pronounce it RAFE. Otherwise, pronounce it as normal.

Rand, Ayn—(philosopher) first name is pronounced INE, rhyming with *mine*.

Rawlings, Marjorie Kinnan—(writer) middle name is accented on the second syllable: kuh-NAN; rhymes with *a man*.

Rowling, J. K.—(writer) ROE-ling; rhymes with *bowling*, not *howling*

Salome—(literary and biblical character) suh-LOH-mee (preferred) or SAL-oh-may. The daughter of Herodias is not named in the NT, but her name is provided by Josephus; the only Salome named in the Bible was one of the women who accompanied the two Marys at Jesus's crucifixion and resurrection.

Shaw, George Bernard—(writer) the middle name is BURN-urd, not bur-NARD

Thielicke, Helmut—(theologian) TEA-luh-kuh, HELL-moot

Thoene, Brock and Bodie—(novelist team) TAY-nee, BRAHK and BOH-dee

Thoreau, (Henry David)—(writer) though you are unlikely to be corrected if you accent the second syllable (in the French style), thuh-ROE, it is correctly accented on the first syllable, THUH-roe. New Englanders pronounce it the same as the word *thorough*, or to rhyme with *burrow*.

Tolkien, (J. R. R.)—(writer) Though Americans commonly pronounce this TOLL-kun, it is correctly pronounced TOLL-keen (long *e* in the second syllable).

Waddell, (Helen)—(writer) wah-DELL

Wangerin Jr., (Walter)—(writer) WAHNG-rin, *not* WAYNG-rin

Weil, (Dr. Andrew)—(writer) WHILE

Weil, Simone—(writer and activist) VEY, SEE-moan

Weill, Kurt—(composer) WHILE, CURT in English, but VILE, KOORT in German

Whitefield, (George)—(English evangelist to America) WITT-feeld, *not* WHITE-feeld

Wycliffe, (John)—(Bible translator) WICK-liff, *not* WHY-cliff

PROOFREADERS, TEN COMMANDMENTS FOR

1. *Use Standard Markup.* On hard copy, nothing is more counterproductive than inaccurate markup. (See "PROOFREADING MARKS, STANDARD" or *CMoS* 2.116–2.129.) Make *two* marks for every correction: one simple mark (caret, slash, strike-through, or so on) in the text, and one explanatory mark in the right margin. Only use the left margin (1) when the right margin has become overloaded with corrections or (2) when the text is set in two columns (use the left margin for corrections in the left-hand column). At the bottom right corner of every page, sign your initials, which are like a signed contract that states, "I guarantee this page is error-free."
2. *When in Doubt, Use the Dictionary—Even When You Don't Think You're in Doubt.* If you're only 99.9 percent sure, look it up. After plain old misspellings, proofreaders commonly miss the correct setting of compound words. Are they set solid, hyphenated, or spaced? Is it *shut eye*, *shuteye*, or *shut-eye*? *Wool gathering*, *wool-gathering*, or *woolgathering*? *Nightcrawler*, *night-crawler*, or *night crawler*? (The correct answer, according to *Webster*, is the last option in each of those cases.) Also be sure to use the publisher's preferred dictionary.
3. *Circle Anything Not Meant to Be Set in Type.* All proofreader queries, reference callouts (for checking endnotes), sources, comments,

and so on should be circled. This is not a quaint custom. Assume that if it is not circled, it will find its way into the final copy—an embarrassment for the proofreader, the author, and the publisher. Write reference callouts (if used for double-checking the endnotes) in a different color, and place them as close to the edge of the paper as possible; otherwise they might be mistaken for corrections.

4. *Keep Queries Short.* Do not provide "chapter-and-verse" from a dictionary or style manual to prove the validity of any correction—and do not provide pages printed from the internet to prove a point. The editor will understand without your writing "Per Webster" every time you correct a misspelling. Again, be sure to use the publisher's recommended dictionary and house style guide.
5. *After Correcting an Error, Back Up Five Lines Before Resuming.* Studies show that a high percentage of missed errors are found near an error that was caught. Back up and read—and be doubly vigilant.
6. *Read "Syllabically."* Reading word-for-word makes the context clearer but makes small typos easier to miss. Reading letter-for-letter is too slow and doesn't allow for contextual reading. Letter-for-letter reading should be used for proper names and technical terms and for any new or difficult words. For standard copy, read syllable by syllable as a happy medium, to verify that all letters are present and that the word is correct in context.
7. *Study the Style Sheet.* As carpenters say, "Measure twice; cut once." Read the editor's style sheet twice *before* beginning a project. Remember that a style sheet overrules the publisher's preferred dictionary and house style. Query only if you think a style decision is counterproductive or demonstrably wrong. Otherwise, assume the style sheet is correct.
8. *Check Formatting.* Most casual readers don't realize that proofreading is more than catching typos. It involves a thorough check of the book's format: folios, running heads, indents, runovers, orphans, widows, margins, word and line spacings, coordination of the contents page with the chapters, consistency of design elements, and so much more.
9. *Don't Correct the Grammar in Dialogue.* Most people speak ungrammatically—splitting infinitives, ending sentences with prepositions, using *who* instead of *whom* and *like* instead of *as*, not using the subjunctive, saying things like "between you and I," and so on. Ideally, the editor should provide a style sheet with some examples and include a note to "allow ungrammatical and colloquial speech." When in doubt, query the editor. This commandment also applies to any fictional narrator or nonfictional writer whose voice is distinctly personal or colloquial.

10. *Take a Five-to-Ten-Minute Break Every Hour.* Not only does this give your eyes a rest, it also sharpens your accuracy. Get up, stretch, walk outside, do jumping jacks or pilates—whatever activity keeps you alert.

PROOFREADING MARKS, STANDARD

Insert Copy

Insert lettr. e

Insert a word

Insert new copy. (see p. x)

Insert endin letter. g

Insert eginning letter. b

Insertspace. #

Insert period ⊙

Insert comma ^,

Insert semicolon ;/

Insert colon ⊙

Insert hypen, as in "bornagain." =/

Insert em dash or long dash. 1/m

Insert en dash, as in 1898 1963. 1/n

Insert parentheses called "brackets" in the UK (/)

Insert brackets called "square brackets" in the UK [/]

Insert ellipsis. (...)

Insert quotation marks. "/"

Insert solidus slash. (slash)

Insert apostrophe, as in Freds. '

Insert accent, as in cliche. (accent) ´

Insert question mark (set) ?

Insert exclamation mark (set) !

Insert superior number. 2

Delete Copy

Deletee character. e

Deleete and close up.

Delete word word. e

~~Delete line.~~ e

Replace Copy

Replace latter. e

Replace ~~term.~~ word

Mark in text	Margin mark
Lowercase letter or Word	lc
capitalize letter or word.	cap
SET IN CAPS AND LOWERCASE.	c/lc
Set in italic.	ital
Set in boldface.	bf
Set in *roman*.	rom
Set in small caps.	sc
Set in caps and small caps.	c/sc
Spell out abbrev, number, symbol.	sp

Move Copy

Mark in text	Margin mark
Transpose charactre.	tr
words Transpose	tr
Indent one em space.	□
Move copy left.	[
Center copy.	][
Move copy right.	]
Align copy.	align
Close sp ace.	⁀‿
Less space.	less #

Mark in text	Margin mark
¶Start new paragraph.	¶
Run lines together.	run-in
Break. Start on new line.	break

Fix Copy

Mark in text	Margin mark
Fix defective character.	x
Correct wrong font.	wf
Equalize uneven spacing.	eq #

Other Symbols

Mark in text	Margin mark
Let it stand as set.	stet
Author or editor query.	?
Indicate correct word division, called "bad break."	division bb
Circle notations not meant to be set.	Note

Slashes Are Used to /

Mark in text	Margin mark
Separate corections In an single line.	r/lc/e
Rpeat sam corrction in a single line.	e///

PSALMS, ALTERNATE NUMBERING OF

Two numbering schemes exist for the book of Psalms, one based on the Hebrew Bible and the other on the Septuagint. Care must be taken when quoting some Jewish and classic Christian authors' writings about a given psalm because they may be referring to a different psalm. Throughout history, many Roman Catholic Bibles took their cue from the Vulgate, which followed the Septuagint's numbering, in which all but twelve of the psalms are assigned a number one less than the number assigned to those same psalms in most Protestant Bibles, such as the KJV and NIV. Many contemporary Roman Catholic Bibles, such as the JB, list both numbers: the Hebrew number first, followed by the Vulgate's number in parentheses.

Psalms 10 through 147. The psalms in question are Pss. 10–147 (as they are numbered in most modern Bibles). Pss. 9 and 10 are separate in the Hebrew Bible (from which most Protestant Bibles take their numbering), but they are regarded as a single psalm, simply Ps. 9, in the Septuagint and Vulgate. The scholarly arguments in favor of the Septuagint's numbering are strong. Ps. 10 is the sole psalm among the first thirty-two that does not bear its own heading, suggesting it may have been intended as part of the preceding psalm. Also, Ps. 9 begins an acrostic pattern that is continued in Ps. 10, and the two psalms possess a continuous theme and tone. Ps. 9 may have been split into two psalms in the Hebrew Bible to facilitate its use in liturgical settings. When Pss. 9 and 10 are considered a single unit, the psalms that follow it bear a different number, which is one less, according to Septuagint and Vulgate numbering. The famous Ps. 23, for instance, is actually Ps. 22 in the Septuagint and the Vulgate and in many Bibles based on them.

Psalms 114 through 116. Another shift occurs in Pss. 114–116 (as numbered in most modern Bibles). The Hebrew Bible considers Pss. 114 and 115 as two separate psalms, while the Septuagint folds them into a single psalm, which is numbered 113. Conversely, the next psalm, 116 in the Hebrew Bible, is separated into two in the Septuagint, where they are numbered 114 and 115. After those three psalms, the alternate numbering system continues until Ps. 147, which the Septuagint again divides into two, thereby reverting to the numbering system most familiar to Protestant readers for Pss. 148–150.

Other Differences. The Septuagint also contains Ps. 151 (which begins "I was small among my brothers ...," NRSV), which does not appear in the Protestant Bible or the Vulgate but is included as canonical in Eastern Orthodox Bibles. The Septuagint also has different verse numberings in many cases because it numbers the titles and headings that precede some of the psalms as verse number 1, which none of the later Bibles do, not even the Vulgate. So in many cases, the verse number of the Septuagint Psalms is one off from later versions of the Bible. What is true of all quotations from the Bible is especially true of Psalms: take no quotation for granted. Careful writers check their sources. The following chart should help.

Hebrew Bible *(& Protestant Bibles)*		**Septuagint** *(& Vulgate & Some Roman Catholic Bibles)*
1–8	=	1–8
9	=	9a
10	=	9b
11–113	=	10–112
114	=	113a
115	=	113b
116a	=	114
116b	=	115
117–146	=	116–145
147a	=	146
147b	=	147
148–150	=	148–150
(omitted)	=	151 (though omitted in Vulgate)

PSALMS, TRADITIONAL GROUPINGS OF

Certain groupings of the Psalms have acquired their own names, which are capitalized as titles and set in roman. Here are a few of the major ones. Note that many of the groupings overlap, and sources often disagree on exactly which psalms belong to any particular group.

the Alphabetic Psalms—Pss. 9, 10, 25, 34, 37, 111–112, 119, and 145. So called because they use an alphabetic device in their poetic structure.

the Asaphite Psalms—Pss. 73–83. Also called the Psalms, or Songs, of Asaph, so called because Asaph and possibly his descendants are attributed as the author(s). Ps. 50 may also have been included in this group.

the Great Hallel—in Jewish tradition, Ps. 136

the Hallel—Pss. 113–118, which are customarily chanted at such Jewish festivals as Passover; also called the Egyptian Hallel. Sometimes Jewish tradition also refers to the Songs of Ascents, 120–134, as the Hallel.

the Halleluja Psalms—Pss. 146–150. The last five psalms, which all begin with "Praise the Lord."

the Penitential Psalms (or Psalms of Penitence)—Pss. 6, 32, 38, 51, 102, 130, 143. These are psalms expressive of contrition, often spoken in times of illness and suffering. They are commonly used as texts for Ash Wednesday services. Unlike the other groupings, this set of psalms was compiled for Christian liturgical use and is not a grouping organic to the Septuagint.

the Prayer of Moses—Ps. 90. This title does not mean that the patriarch Moses wrote the psalm but that it is imitative of his style.

the Psalm of Ethan—Ps. 89

the Psalms of David (or the Davidic Psalms)—Pss. 3–9, 11–32, 34–41, 51–65, 68–70, 86, 103, 108–110, 122, 124, 131, 133, 135–145. These psalms are ascribed to David.

the Psalms of Imprecation (or the Cursing Psalms, or the Imprecatory Psalms)—Pss. 7, 35, 55, 58, 59, 69, 73, 79, 109, 137. These are so called because they call on the Lord to take vengeance on Israel's enemies. Other psalms, such as 5, 6, 11, 12, 40, 52, 54, 56, 83, and 139, are sometimes included in this list because they contain imprecatory elements.

the Psalms of Solomon—Pss. 72 and 127. Like the Psalm of Moses, this ascription most likely means that these psalms imitate Solomon's style rather than asserting his direct authorship.

the Psalms of the Sons of Korah—Pss. 42–49, 84–85, 87–88

the Songs of Ascent—Pss. 120–134. Also called the Gradual Psalms or the Songs of Degrees (KJV). They are probably so called because they were sung by Jewish pilgrims on their way to Jerusalem as they ascended Mount Zion.

PUBLISHER'S ADDRESS

See "ADDRESSES OF PUBLISHER, MAILING AND WEB."

Q

QR CODES

QR code is short for "quick-response code." It is a matrix-based, machine-readable barcode for many types of products, including books. This code can be read by dedicated scanners as well as smartphones. Scanning a QR code takes the consumer to a website where more information can be found. When a QR code is placed on the jacket of a book or in its interior, it is advisable to display a standard URL nearby, so that those users who don't link to the internet by phone can still find the website referenced.

QUAKER STYLE

Those within the Religious Society of Friends refer to themselves as *Friends* (capitalized) but often represent themselves as *Quakers* to the world. When used as an adjective in such terms as *Friends meeting* or *Friends school*, do not use the possessive. An individual member of the society is called a *Friend* (capitalized). In traditional Quaker dating, months and days of the week are numbered and capitalized: *First Month*, *Second Month*, and so on; *First Day*, *Second Day*, and so on. This system of referencing dates is called *Plain style* (see also "*Plain, plain (Amish)*"), though it is seldom used today. For more detail see "TIMES AND DATES," section on "*Quaker System of Dating.*" Quakers also attend *meeting* rather than *church*, and the children attend *First Day school* rather than *Sunday school*. (*First Day* is capitalized as the Quaker term for Sunday.) (See also "*Quaker*" and "*thou, thee, thy, thine.*") An excellent glossary of contemporary Quaker terminology can be found at http://www.nyym.org/?q=glossary.

QUESTION MARK

The question mark was developed by early printers from the first and last letters of the Latin word *questio* (with the *q* atop the *o*) and later simplified to the modern form. In usage, a question mark follows a direct question and, like the period and the exclamation point, is considered an *end stop*, that is, a punctuation mark found at the end of a sentence, though exceptions exist.

Questions within Sentences. Even though the question mark usually falls at the end of a sentence, it is sometimes used within a sentence, for instance in fiction, to show a character's thought-but-not-spoken question, or in quoted dialogue.

Why would she have said that? she thought.
"Where are they hiding?" he said.

Sometimes a series of questions occurs within a sentence, and a question mark can appropriately be used with each: *A good reporter asks who? what? where? when? and how?* Also, the KJV frequently places question marks within sentences without capitalizing the phrase after the question, as in Ps. 39:7: *"And now, Lord, what wait I for? my hope is in thee."* Use caution in quoting the KJV because autoformatting and grammar-checking programs will automatically capitalize the first letter after all question marks.

Indirect Questions. Do not use a question mark with an indirect question (as in *We all wondered who the new archbishop would be*).

With Other Punctuation. A question mark is considered a "strong" punctuation mark and usually has precedence over any other mark of punctuation that might logically fall in the same location. Only the exclamation mark is as strong, and to determine whether the question mark or exclamation mark takes precedence, the sense of the sentence should be considered. If the querying nature of the question is stronger than its surprise, or if the question is clearly asked in anticipation of an answer, then the question mark is used. If a strong declamatory question is meant to be largely rhetorical, then an exclamation point is used.

In his fright, he yelled, "Who's there?" [An answer is expected.]
With utter incomprehension, she shouted, "What do you people expect!" [Declamatory and rhetorical]

In Titles. When a book, movie, or other title ends in a question mark, that question mark may be followed by a comma if the title is part of a list:

Philip Yancey's books include *Where Is God When It Hurts?*, *The Jesus I Never Knew*, *What's So Amazing about Grace?*, *What Good Is God?*, and *Prayer*.

Spanish Question Marks. In Spanish-language publishing worldwide, an inverted question mark (¿) precedes a question, and an upright question mark (?) follows it. You do not need to reproduce this device when translating a Spanish quotation into English, but retain it when a quotation is given in the original language.

QUESTIONS, INTERNAL

An *internal question*, sometimes referred to as an *embedded question*, is a question placed within a declarative sentence but not set apart with quotation marks. Formerly, the first word of an internal question was capitalized, just as it would be if it were a direct quotation, but it is now more common to lowercase the first word, especially when the question is short or consists of a single word. A comma should precede the question. Longer or proverbial questions, or questions that have a formal tone or internal punctuation, may be capitalized as appropriate. Do not mistake simple wonderings (which are not set off with a comma and do not end with a question mark) for internal questions.

She wondered, why haven't they called yet?

They shivered to think, what would Mrs. Grundy say?

The committee wanted to know: What did the president know and when did he know it? [Capitalized because the question is longer and has a more formal sense]

The committee wanted to know what the president knew and when he knew it. [Not an internal question]

QUOTATION MARKS

For Direct Discourse. Quotation marks set off material quoted from another source or indicate spoken words in dialogue. These uses, called *direct discourse*, are distinguished from *indirect discourse*, which is not set off with quotation marks.

"Few individuals have done as much as St. Francis to show Christians the way of peace," wrote Morton Kelsey. [Written source]

The pastor responded, "In witnessing, remember that we are only beggars advising other beggars where to find food." [Dialogue]

G. K. Chesterton once referred to coincidences as spiritual puns. [Indirect discourse]

Quotes within Quotes. In the US, double quotation marks are used for most purposes (though see "UK STYLE," section on *"Use Single Quotation Marks for Quotes"*). Single quotation marks are used almost exclusively to indicate quotes within quotes. If a further level of interior quotation is needed, double quotation marks are reverted to. Although single quotation marks are then placed within those, if needed, and so on alternately, such multiples levels of quotes within quotes should be avoided for obvious reasons.

"The angel said to them, 'Do not be afraid' " (Luke 2:10).

John read Job 42:1–2, 4 aloud, "Then Job replied to the LORD, 'I know that you can do all things.... You said, "Listen now, and I will speak." ' "

For Irony, Slang, and Emphasis. Writers sometimes use quotation marks when a word or phrase is meant to be ironic (called *irony quotes*), though this technique can lead to ambiguity since readers may not understand the writer's intention. Whenever possible, the careful writer should convey irony by some other means. Slang words and jargon are placed in quotation marks only when the author is trying to convey that they are not part of his or her normal vocabulary. Quotation marks are best used with slang words or colloquial expressions when a strong emphasis is desired; even then they should be used cautiously.

> He resented the church's insistence on a "free-will" offering. [Ironic]
>
> She could not be sure to what extent he had been "born again." [Jargon]

For Thoughts. Quotation marks may be used to convey a person's unspoken thoughts. (See "THOUGHTS.")

With Other Punctuation. When other punctuation marks are used with quotation marks, correct placement depends on the context. In direct discourse, for instance, periods and commas usually go inside a closing quotation mark; question marks and exclamation points usually go inside closing quotation marks, although they may go outside if the sentence structure calls for it. As a general rule, colons and semicolons are placed outside. To summarize: single marks go inside, double marks go outside, except for exclamation points and question marks, which can vary according to the context.

> As he read the creed he hesitated before saying, "... the quick and the dead"; a more modern translation would read, "... the living and the dead."
>
> " 'Why were you searching for me?' he asked. 'Didn't you know I had to be in my Father's house?' " (Luke 2:49).
>
> Why did he refer to the 1560 Geneva Bible as the "Breeches Bible"?

With "Yes" and "No." Except in direct discourse, the words *yes* and *no* do not need to be enclosed in quotation marks. For example: *Although saying yes to Jesus doesn't solve all of life's problems, saying no can be a bigger problem in itself.*

In Titles. Certain titles of short works and pieces of larger works are set in quotation marks. Be sure to contrast this list with that found in "ITALIC," section on "*Titles*."

- articles in periodicals
- blog entries
- chapters in books
- essays
- hymns
- individual television and radio programs (series are set in italic)

short musical compositions	short stories
short poems (anything less than small book length)	songs

He referred to the "Speaking Out" column in last month's *Christianity Today.*

PBS broadcast Muggeridge's television show "God's Spies" from his series *The Third Testament.*

Nicknames. Only set people's nicknames in quotation marks when the full name is given. Otherwise, set them without quotation marks. For instance, *Christopher "Kit" Smart* but *Kit Smart*; *G. A. Studdert "Woodbine Willie" Kennedy* but *Woodbine Willie*; *William Ashley "Billy" Sunday* but *Billy Sunday.*

Adjective Phrases. Quotation marks can be used to create adjectives out of extended phrases, as in *She was a "nobody's happy if Mama ain't happy" kind of character.* (See "ADJECTIVES, COMPOUND," section on "*Adjective Phrases.*")

With Display Caps. At the beginning of a chapter, do not use an opening quotation mark before an initial display capital that is larger than text size, though the closing quotation mark should be retained. This custom developed in English and American typesetting because oversized quotation marks look awkward.

Foreign Quotation Marks. European-style quotation marks are often seen on the internet, though rarely in English-language publishing. Although famed typographer Jan Tschichold once lobbied for modified French guillemets to be used in English publishing, his recommendation was universally ignored. When a quotation is in a European language but in an English context, convert all quotation marks, internal and external, to the American style.

For information purposes, here are the two most common alternate quotation-mark styles. (1) French quotations marks are called *guillemets.* The opening and closing double quotation marks (which are primary) are « / », and the opening and closing single quotation marks (secondary) are ‹ / ›. *Guillemets* are also used in Italian, Swiss, and Spanish publishing. Note that some French publishers use the English system. (2) German quotation marks are called *Anführungszeichen*. The opening and closing single quotation marks (primary) are ‚ / ‘ (the opening mark looks like an English comma and the closing mark looks like a single opening quotation mark), while the opening and closing double quotation marks (secondary) are the same marks doubled: „ / “.

QUOTATIONS, GENERAL

To prove a point, support an opinion, muster an argument, reference an authority, inject humor, or gloss the content of a chapter or book with an appropriate thought—all these can be accomplished with an appropriate quotation. As the writer of Proverbs somewhat unappetizingly says, "A word aptly spoken is like apples of gold in settings of silver" (25:11).

Accuracy. Authors are responsible for reproducing all quotations in wording, spelling, capitalization, and punctuation exactly as they appear in the original sources. Do not force the style of a quoted passage to conform to the style of the book in which it will be used. Idiosyncrasies of spelling and capitalization in older works, for example, should be preserved; the word *sic*, enclosed in brackets, may be used after an obvious misspelling but should be used sparingly. (See "*sic.*") In the case of works in the public domain, outdated spelling and punctuation may be modernized for the sake of clarity, though a note (usually on the copyright page) should inform the reader that this has been done.

The Pitfalls. Note to authors: Take care to avoid the common pitfalls of quoting from copyrighted sources. First and most importantly, do not quote so much from a single source as to infringe upon that work's legal copyright protection unless you are prepared to write for permission and possibly pay a fee. (See "PERMISSION GUIDELINES: GENERAL" and "FAIR USE.") The fair use defense can only be invoked when the total number of words of all the quotations from a single source falls within the guidelines. For instance, if you quote a source ten times, the total number of words of those quotes may well exceed the commonly accepted limit even if no single quote exceeds it.

Second, don't overquote. Resist the feeling that you cannot express an opinion without offering supporting quotations from other sources. Using too many quotations can be a distraction, even an annoyance. Have faith in your own ability to convince the reader without having to depend on the authority of others.

Third, do not use quotations as a way of avoiding the task of putting an idea into your own words. (Dorothy Sayers once wrote, "I always have a quotation for everything—it saves original thinking" [*Have His Carcase*].) Even if a quotation is within the fair use guidelines, its use may be questionable when another author's wording is used simply to avoid expressing the same idea in a fresh and original way. This last pitfall is more subtle. Take heart in knowing that most readers are interested in your own words and opinions, not those of others.

Allowable Changes. In most books, an initial letter in a quotation may be changed to a capital or a lowercase letter to conform to the quotation's context within the new work, and a final punctuation mark may be changed to suit the syntax of the larger context. In some highly formal academic works, indicate such minor changes in capitalization or punctuation by using brackets.

> As John Donne wrote in *Devotions upon Emergent Occasions*, "What a giant is man when he fights against himself." [In the original quotation, the word *what* is lowercase and a comma follows *himself*, but these changes are allowed to conform to the context.]

> Augustine challenged this notion by reminding believers that "[i]t is human to err; it is devilish to remain willfully in error." [from Augustine's *Sermons*; in the original quotation, *It* is capitalized. In this highly formal style, any change to the original material is noted in brackets.]

Run-In versus Block Quotations. A short quotation is run into the text (called a *run-in quotation*). A longer quotation is set off from the text (called a *block quotation*, or *extract*) and is usually set in smaller type (usually one point smaller than text type) and with a narrower width. A prose quotation of more than eight typed lines (five or six typeset lines) or more than a hundred words should be set as a block quotation. Any quotation shorter than that should also be set in block style if it runs to two or more paragraphs. If a series of short quotations are separated by text, then those quotations may be best set off as individual block quotations. Block quotations of a single paragraph need not have a paragraph indent in the first line, but if more than one paragraph is included in the block quotation, provide paragraph indents for the rest of them.

Three or more lines of poetry are usually set as a block quotation. Two lines of poetry may be either set as a block quotation or run into the text with a spaced slash (*/*) indicating the line breaks (though see also "POETRY"). More lines of poetry may be run in with spaced slashes whenever an extract setting might look odd or cause distraction. Books written for a popular audience should err on the side of running quotations into the text rather than setting them as extracts. This is done to avoid an overly academic appearance. (See "SCHOLARLY APPEARANCES.")

Block Quotations and Quotation Marks. Block quotations do not normally begin or end with quotation marks. Block quotations should retain any and all quotation marks that appear in the original. Also, epigraphs (whether on a separate page or at the beginning of a chapter) and other quotations used for display should not be enclosed in quotation marks. Only those quotation marks that appear in the original should be retained in epigraphs.

Block quotations, whether prose, poetry, or song, are set in quotation marks when they are part of an ongoing dialogue. If the block quotation is preceded by a spoken lead-in phrase or other words spoken by the same speaker, the block quotation begins with a new opening quotation mark, just as if it were a new quoted paragraph.

Introductory Phrases for Block Quotations. When a block quotation is introduced by a word or phrase like *thus* or *the following*, that word or phrase should be followed by a colon. When a verb-of-saying introduces the block quotation, a comma is used. If it is introduced by a complete statement, a period is used. When the introductory phrase forms a grammatically complete unit with the block quotation that follows it, no punctuation is used at all. In other words, the syntax of the introductory phrase will determine the correct punctuation.

The role of the pastor has been described as follows: "…" [Uses a colon]

In his letter to Queen Ethelberga, Pope Boniface said, "…" [Uses a comma]

O'Connor tells the legend of Saint Francis and the wolf of Gubbio. "…" [Uses a period]

William Jay said in his book on prayer that "…" [Run in without punctuation]

Crediting Block Quotations. The source of a block quotation may be credited in a footnote, a chapter or book endnote, or a parenthetical reference after the quotation. (See "SOURCES.") In some cases, as in epigraphs, an em dash may be used to inform the reader of the source. (See "EPIGRAPH.")

… I felt my heart strangely warmed.* [Foonoted]

… I felt my heart strangely warmed.[1] [Reference to chapter or book endnote]

… I felt my heart strangely warmed. (John Wesley, *Journals*, Wednesday, May 24, 1738) [An in-text reference using parentheses]

… I felt my heart strangely warmed.—John Wesley [As used in an epigraph; only an author name is needed, though see "EPIGRAPH."]

Accurate Indenting of Poetry, Hymns, and Songs. It is the author's responsibility to make sure that quoted poetry is indented line-for-line as in the original. Sometimes, when a manuscript's data is converted from one software to another, indents can get scrambled. It is especially important in these cases for the author to provide the publisher with a hard copy of the manuscript so that the indents may be double-checked. Like poetry, hymns and other songs should also be indented correctly. (See "HYMN METERS," section on "*Indentations.*")

Centering Poetry and Songs on the Page. When poetry, verse, or song lyrics are set as block quotations, they are traditionally centered on the page according to the width of the longest line. In some books, the designer may have reasons to vary the setting; for instance, if a lot of poetry is quoted amid blocks of prose, the designer may opt to set all the poetry left to avoid a shifting appearance of the quoted material on the page.

Tenses for Verbs of Saying. Sometimes the question of tense arises with verbs of saying used with quotations. In most cases, logic and the context will dictate the tense. When in doubt, the best guideline is this: An author spoke or wrote the work in the past, but the work itself speaks to us in the present.

> Solomon said, "Remember your Creator in the days of your youth" (Eccl. 12:1).
> As Ecclesiastes says, "Remember your Creator in the days of your youth" (12:1).

Quotations in Passing. Do not use quotation marks for individual words used in an informal or general sense, or only in passing, and do not set them off with commas; for instance, *Only half of the people said yes to the agreement* or *Next time I'll be prepared to say okay*. If such quoted material is more than a single word, especially if it could be confusing or misread, quotation marks may be used around the phrase, but a comma need not be used with the verb of saying: *Countless couples say "I do" every June* or *Once again it was as if the voters were saying "never again" to themselves.* Don't capitalize the first word in such phrases even though the phrase is in quotation marks.

QUOTING ONLINE SOURCES

Writers commonly quote poems, songs, bits of humor, Facebook postings and email vignettes, people's personal stories, text messages, tweets, anecdotes, articles, reviews, and other material from online sources as if there were no ethical strings attached. "After all," some writers argue, "a hundred sites on the internet quote it without permission; why can't I?" But remember this: Treat online sources just as you would treat print sources. The fact that it is circulating online in no way implies that it is in the public domain. Usually these oft-repeated and uncredited internet writings have been reproduced without their original authors' permission, and to repeat them once more is to compound the theft.

Unless an internet quotation falls under the fair use guidelines (see "FAIR USE" and "PERMISSION GUIDELINES: GENERAL"), plan on tracking down the source and obtaining written permission to use the quote from the author's publisher or (if no other copyright owner is available) from the author. Be even more reserved with private emails, tweets, text messages, and comments from chatroom discussions. Treat them just as you would treat unpublished letters, which means don't quote them unless you have written permission from the original author. Remember that fair use does not usually apply to unpublished correspondence. (For quoting reader reviews on retail websites like Amazon.com, see "PERMISSION GUIDELINES: QUOTING READER REVIEWS FROM A WEBSITE.")

It is painful for a writer to see his or her work exploited for another's financial profit. So keep the Golden Rule in mind: Get permission from others just as you would expect them to get permission from you—whether online or in print. (Also see "PLAGIARISM.")

QUOTING THE BIBLE

Authors are responsible to reproduce quotations from the Bible accurately and, in most cases, to indicate which version is being referenced.

Notice on Copyright Page. Any book containing Bible quotations should inform the reader which version has been predominantly used. This notice is usually provided on the copyright page since, in many cases, extensive use of modern translations requires a permission notice, or credit line, which is most conveniently placed on the copyright page. The following form is acceptable, though the granting copyright holder may prefer a different form, in which case that form should be adhered to. (For specific permission notices and limitations on use for the most commonly quoted Bible, see "PERMISSION GUIDELINES: THE BIBLE.")

> Unless otherwise noted, all Scripture references in this book are taken from the [Version], copyright © [year and copyright holder]. Used by permission of [permission grantor].

When Alternate Bible Versions Are Used. When a note regarding a predominant Bible version has been provided on the copyright page, the author should not indicate that version when references to it are made in the text. The reader should only be informed of the source of an in-text reference when an alternate version is used. This is done by placing the abbreviation of the alternate version next to the in-text reference. These abbreviations are usually set in full caps without periods. (See "BIBLE VERSIONS IN ENGLISH" and "BIBLE VERSIONS NOT IN ENGLISH" for a list of abbreviations.) When used in combination with the Bible reference itself, these abbreviations are not preceded by a comma. Abbreviations of Bible versions may be used in text as well as in footnotes and endnotes.

> "Love is patient, love is kind. It does not envy" (1 Cor. 13:4). [No version is cited because the predominant version in this case is the NIV, and a notice to that effect has been provided on the copyright page.]
>
> "Caritas patiens est benigna est caritas non aemulatur" (1 Cor. 13:4 Vulg.)

"Loue is pacient & curteous, loue envyeth not" (1 Cor. 13:4 Coverdale).
"Charity suffereth long, and is kind; charity envieth not" (1 Cor. 13:4 KJV).
"La charité est longanime; la charité est serviable; elle n'est pas envieuse" (1 Cor. 13:4 JB).

One can appreciate the differences in musicality and rhythm among the NIV, Vulg., Coverdale, KJV, and JB translations. [In text]

Personal Translations or Paraphrases. When an author creates his or her own translation or paraphrase, this should be indicated in a note at the beginning of the book (if it is the predominant version) or in a note attached to each specific reference if there are only a few. In the latter case, the phrase *author's translation* or *author's paraphrase* should suffice. Such a phrase is best preceded by a comma.

"Love is content to wait and is always considerate. It's never envious" (1 Cor. 13:4, author's paraphrase).

Arabic Numerals for Books of the Bible. Use arabic rather than roman numerals for books of the Bible: *2 Corinthians* rather than *II Corinthians*, even if that specific version uses roman numerals. It is preferable to write out the number if it begins a sentence: *First John 4:7 tells us …*

Chapter Only. When an entire chapter is referenced, it may be spelled out, though a numeral may be used if no confusion will result: *In the first chapter of Genesis …* or *In Genesis 1 …*

Dialogue. Numerals may be used for Bible references in dialogue, though frequently the syntax will require that they be spelled out.

"I'm sure," said the minister, "everyone here could recite John 3:16 by heart."
"Amanda Smith overcame her fear by remembering the third chapter of Galatians and the twenty-eighth verse."

Abbreviation Styles. Three styles of abbreviating books of the Bible are commonly used: the *General Style* for trade and some academic books; the *SBL Style* for scholarly works; and the *NIV Style* for references closely keyed to the NIV. (For complete lists, see "ABBREVIATIONS: BIBLE BOOKS AND RELATED MATERIAL.")

Spelling Out Versus Abbreviating. Names of the books of the Bible may be either spelled out or abbreviated in text. For trade and popular books, it is common to spell out all references, whether in text or in parenthetical references. When references are especially numerous, as in academic books, it is preferable to use abbreviations in the parenthetical references. In highly technical works, books of the Bible may be abbreviated in all text and parenthetical references. (See "ABBREVIATIONS: BIBLE BOOKS AND RELATED MATERIAL" for complete lists.)

With Block Quotations. **In a reference following a block quotation from the Bible, the name of a Bible book may be spelled out or abbreviated within parentheses at the author's or editor's discretion, but the same form should be used consistently throughout a manuscript. No period follows the reference itself.**

> No, in all these things we are more than conquerors through him who loved us. For I am convinced that neither death nor life, . . . nor anything else in all creation, will be able to separate us from the love of God that is in Christ Jesus our Lord. (Rom. 8:37–39 NIV)

Punctuation with Run-in Quotations. **For run-in quotations that require a chapter-and-verse reference, place the period or other punctuation after the closing parenthesis containing the reference. If the quotation contains a question mark or exclamation point, place it with the quotation and place any other needed punctuation after the closing parenthesis.**

> "Here is your king" (John 19:14).
>
> "Take him away! Take him away! Crucify him!" (John 19:15), was heard through the crowd.

The Abbreviations "v." and "vv." **The abbreviation for *verse* is *v.*, and for *verses, vv.* Use these abbreviations only in parenthetical references or in text and only when the repetition of the whole book and chapter reference would be cumbersome.**

> Later in the eleventh chapter (v. 42) John wrote, "In that place many believed in Jesus."

The "a"/"b"/"c" System. **Distinguishing parts of a single Bible verse by using an *a* or other letter after the reference (for instance, *Job 21:11a* and *Job 21:11b*) is usually superfluous in books for general readers. This system is commonly used only in academic books where Bible references need to be extremely precise, and even there, the letter system is best reserved for only those occasions when a specific portion of a verse is being singled out for discussion. In other words, in a book for a lay readership, it is acceptable to reference "The LORD is my shepherd" as "Ps. 23:1." But in an academic book, say, where the idea of God-as-shepherd is being discussed, it would be appropriate to reference that verse specifically as "Ps. 23:1a" because only that part of the verse is relevant to the discussion.**

The Colon in Scripture References. **A colon separates chapter from verse: *Mark 2:17; 1 Peter 3:12*.**

Semicolons in Scripture Citations. Use a semicolon in Bible citations to separate references from different books or to separate chapter-and-verse references within one book: *Acts 16:31; John 3:3; 10:10.*

When to Use Spaces. No space should precede or follow a colon in a Bible reference (*Ps. 23:1*). There should be a space following but not preceding a comma or a semicolon (*Ps. 23:1, 4–5*).

The En Dash in Bible References. An en dash is used between consecutive verse numbers. A comma separates nonconsecutive numbers of the same chapter: *John 3:1–6, 15–16; Acts 1:1–8, 13, 16.* An en dash is also used to indicate two or more chapters of a Bible book inclusively or to indicate that a citation begins in one chapter and ends in another: *Gen. 1–11; Gal. 5:26–6:5.*

Obadiah, Philemon, Jude, 2 John, 3 John. These little books pose a special problem in references: each contains but a single chapter. Often the first verse of Jude is referenced as *Jude 1:1*, which has the disadvantage of implying that other chapters exist. Some writers opt to reference the verse as *Jude 1*, which ambiguously suggests either the first chapter of Jude or its first verse. The clearest way to reference them in text is either *the first verse of Jude* or *verse 1 of Jude*. If the reference is parenthetical after a quotation, then use this form: (*Jude v. 1*). If the reference falls in a Scripture index or in some other place where columnar appearance needs to be maintained, then revert to the form *Jude 1:1*. Most readers will understand.

Familiar Phrases. Christian writers and publishers have tended to overreference quotations from the Bible, as though a Bible quotation needs the authority of a chapter-and-verse reference to legitimize it. Avoid this tendency when possible. Casually rendered or familiar phrases from the Bible need not be set apart by quotation marks or referenced in every instance, especially in books intended for a general audience. For instance, you can write, *We too can share the shepherds' wonder at hearing the good tidings of great joy,* without either using quotation marks or referencing a specific Bible verse, because the reader understands that the writer is echoing a biblical phrase.

When it is important to communicate exactly which words are being quoted, then use quotation marks: *When the Bible says, "God so loved the world ...," it means all the world.* The phrase is so common that no reference is needed, even though the phrase is in quotation marks. It is not wrong to reference such familiar quotes, but it is often unnecessary.

It is also superfluous to annotate Bible quotations in fiction, especially fictional dialogue. Parenthetical references in those cases distract from the reading. For example, a character might say, *"Have you not read that God is love?"* In that case, again, the reader understands that a biblical phrase is being referenced.

Using Brackets. If the author needs to change an occasional word for clarity's sake when quoting the Bible, square brackets are used to specify the change. This should be done with fidelity to the original meaning of the quote; for instance, *"We love because [God] first loved us" (1 John 4:19).* The bracketed word here has replaced the word *he*.

Noting Repeated Changes in Style. The author may wish to change a particular word or words of a given translation throughout an entire manuscript. This may be done without brackets as long as a note informing the reader of this change is given in the front matter or on the copyright page. For instance, an author may want to replace the words *thee*, *thou*, *thy*, and *thine* of the KJV with *you* and *your*. Provide a note informing the reader of this change. Such a note is also useful when the author wishes to change the capitalization style of the deity pronouns in the predominant Bible version or translation used. Do not globally alter the style of a copyrighted version of the Bible without the permission of the publisher, which is unlikely to be granted. Modern Bible translators usually request that their given style preferences be honored.

With Ellipses. In most cases, do not place an ellipsis before or after a quoted Bible verse or a portion of a verse, though an ellipsis should be used whenever an interior portion is not included in the quotation. If the quotation is a sentence fragment, begins or ends with a fragment, or might otherwise cause confusion, insert an ellipsis as appropriate. Introductory words such as *And*, *Or*, *For*, *Therefore*, *But*, *Verily*, and so on may be omitted from the beginning of any Bible verse without inserting an ellipsis. In a sense, the reader is already aware, without the aid of an ellipsis, that other words precede and follow any given quotation. (See also "ELLIPSIS.")

> "The God of all comfort . . . comforts us in all our troubles, so that we can comfort those in any trouble" (2 Cor. 1:3–4). [Ellipsis needed because interior words are dropped.]
>
> "He that is not against us is on our part" (Mark 9:40 KJV). [The original reads: "For he that is not against us is on our part," but no ellipsis is needed at the beginning.]

"Lord" and "God." In some versions of the Bible, the words *Lord* and *God* appear in small caps with an initial capital (LORD, GOD). In books written in a familiar or popular vein, such as fiction, this cap-and-small-cap style need not be followed. In scholarly works and serious nonfiction, quotations from Scripture should reflect the typographical rendering of the version cited. (See "*LORD*, *GOD* [CAP-AND-SMALL-CAP FORMS].")

Italic in the KJV and NASB. Words italicized in the King James Version (KJV) and the New American Standard Bible (NASB) are not italicized when quoted. The translators used italic to show "supplied" words that have no exact parallels in the original Greek or Hebrew. (See "ITALIC," section on "*Italic in the KJV and NASB*.") These italicized words only confuse the modern reader who might mistake them for words meant to be emphasized. Some editions of the KJV, such as *The New Cambridge Paragraph Bible* (2006), dispense with italic for supplied words. In rare instances the italic may be retained when it is important for the reader to know which words are the "supplied" in the given translation, such as in an academic discussion of Bible translating or in a scholarly work on interpreting the passages in the original languages.

Small Caps and Italic in the NASB. When passages from the OT are quoted in the NT of the NASB, the quotation is set in caps-and-small-caps, and the NASB also follows the KJV device of setting supplied words in italic. When quoting from the NASB, all cap-and-small-cap quotations and italicized words should be rendered in regular text type, since the reasons for those faces will be unclear to the reader and, again, may be mistaken for emphasis. (See "ITALIC," section on "*Italic in the KJV and NASB*.")

Pronunciation Marks in the KJV. Some editions of the KJV and other versions provide pronunciation marks (diacritics) with proper names. Do not reproduce these marks when quoting from that version unless you have a specific reason to do so.

Correct Paragraphing. Some Bible versions, most notably many editions of the KJV, set each numbered verse as though it were a separate paragraph. Since this is merely a typographic convention, these verses, when quoted, are not set as separate paragraphs but run together. Actual paragraph breaks in the KJV are shown by the paragraph symbol (¶), or pilcrow. When quoting the KJV, simply indent each paragraph rather than providing the ¶ symbol.

Verse Numbers. In most contexts, do not include the small or superscript verse reference numbers within the quotation. The primary exception is Bible studies in which it is important to distinguish where each verse begins.

Spelling of Proper Names. In a written text, biblical proper names should accord with the spelling of the primary Bible version used. When no primary translation is used, this manual recommends that proper nouns follow the style given in the New International Version.

Hezekiah [NIV]	Jehoshaphat [NIV]
Ezekias [KJV]	Josaphat [KJV]

Ligatures. Because of the limitations of many typesetting systems, ligatures (such as *æ*) should be set as separate letters (*ae*) when quoting from Bible versions that use such ligatures. Ligatures tend to look antiquated, may cause confusion, and are often garbled in web settings.

Setting Bible Poetry as Poetry. The default is this: If a passage is set as poetry in the Bible version you're using, then set it as poetry when quoting it. The translators of the NIV and other Bibles prefer that their work be reproduced line-for-line as shown in the text. At least three exceptions exist.

First, do not set a single line of poetry as a poetry extract by itself. Run it into the paragraph as appropriate. The exception to this exception might be when quoting short sections of a psalm, a few lines at a time. If a single line is quoted and discussed in that series, it might be appropriately set it as a single line of poetry to keep the same format as the other quoted sections.

Second, in nonacademic texts, run in a poetry quotation if it is quite short and runs fluidly into the text. For instance: *"Job assures even modern people that God will never 'willingly bring affliction or grief to the children of men.'"* (A line break actually falls between "affliction" and "or.") This rule can be extended to three or four lines, but if the quotation is much longer than that, it is best to revert to setting it as poetry, even when the introductory phrase "runs in." It is even preferable to show each line division with a spaced solidus (/) with a word space on either side: *". . . God will never 'willingly bring affliction / or grief to the children of men.'"*

Third, setting poetry as prose is sometimes required for space reasons, as in a page-a-day devotional (that is, when trying to fit a devotional entry into a specific limited space). Though this is not preferable, it is sometimes unavoidable. If at all possible, use a spaced solidus (/) to show the line divisions, unless that will be distracting or confusing for the reader.

R

READABILITY

Readability, which is different from legibility, is essential for both print books and ebooks. Most books are legible, that is, their basic letter forms are clear and distinguishable—but not all are readable. Readability has more to do with the book's impression on the reader's eye, the extent to which a book can be comfortably read for extended periods of time or for a particular purpose, and the extent to which the type and design prevent fatigue. Critics and researchers have pointed out that online reading tends to be done is short spurts, which is probably because websites usually do not adhere to the same readability standards that traditional print books have.

Three Rules of Print and Digital Readability

1. *Most classic serif text faces are inherently more readable than most sans-serif.* Serifs (the small strokes added to a letter) are not just ornamental; they serve a purpose. Since they are mostly horizontal, their lateral emphasis increases reading efficiency. Without that emphasis, sans-serif type can force the eye to read more slowly. Sans-serif faces are popular for display purposes (noncontinuous reading) when speed is not a factor. In text, sans-serif faces can be the typographic equivalent of someone speaking too slowly. Most of us, when forced to listen or read slowly, lose interest.

   One study showed that the average reader can read serif type 7 to 10 words per minute faster than sans-serif type. This may not seem like much, but over a two-hour reading session, that amounts to a short chapter. Coupled with the fact that research also found that serif faces are more aesthetically pleasing to most readers than sans-serif faces, this would suggest that traditional serif faces are most often a better choice for continuous text reading.

   Not all reading is continuous, which is why reference books and other books of short readings are sometimes set in sans-serif faces. Note that some sans-serif faces are specifically designed for continuous reading and tend to be less problematic than other sans-serifs.

2. *Regular roman type is intrinsically more readable than italic, bold, expanded, or condensed.* By design, regular roman type contributes to the lateral flow. Other fonts, such as italic and bold, are used intentionally for emphasis because they disrupt lateral flow, causing the reader to pause. This is why many designers prefer not to set large blocks of type in italic

or bold. Though roman type is the norm, there has been a temptation among some designers to "copy-fit" text by electronically condensing the font. This practice is inadvisable for any but the most experienced typographer for the simple reason that types were designed with a certain visual proportion, and to alter them electronically is to change their character.

3. *Tight-to-moderate word spacing is more readable than loose word spacing.* Despite exceptions to this rule, lateral flow is again the ideal. Wide spacing causes the eye to stop and start—the visual equivalent of stuttering. Also, when word spaces are too large, the likelihood of "rivers" (blotches of white space spanning two or more lines) increases (see "RIVERS, TYPOGRAPHIC"). Rivers add an unattractive vertical element and distract the reader from lateral eye movement. When you have a choice between setting a line too tight or too loose, a too-tight line is usually preferable. Editors often resist tight lines, but in continuous reading, a tightly spaced line is less likely to cause problems for the reader than a loose line.

Additional Factors

Type Size. Many people assume that type size is the most important factor in readability, but it is not. While important, size is not as significant in readability as typeface, font, line spacing, and line length. The average reader with normal or corrected eyesight can comfortably read even 6-point type as long as the line widths are within the optimal 10-to-12-words-per-line range (that is, about 60 to 72 characters per line, counting spaces) and the leading (line spacing) is sufficient to keep the text from looking splotchy. It is usually an overlong line length and a too-tight leading that cause problems.

For average trade books, body types in sizes of 9 to 11 points are the norm. Those are the sizes that most often approach the ideal 10-to-12-words-per-line average for the line widths. A few faces (like Bembo) tend to be smaller than other faces in comparable size, so in those cases, a 9-point type may be too small and 10 to 12 may be preferred.

Line Length. For type sizes in the 9- to 12-point range, an average of 10 to 12 words per line is ideal (assuming the average word is 5 characters plus a word space), or an average of 60 to 72 characters per line (including spaces). Studies have shown that 72 characters per line is the threshold beyond which the reader begins to have trouble finding the next line of text ("tracking back"). When line lengths must run longer than an average of 72 characters per line, then an extra point or two of leading should be added to all text lines to give the reader more space and a better chance to find successive lines. Every character beyond 72 characters per line significantly decreases the readability of a text. Everyone has had the experience of trying to read a text online in which the line lengths are too long and the leading too small. It causes eyestrain and can force the reader to give up.

Text that averages fewer than 7 words per line also poses problems. First, if the copy is justified, there is more chance of frequent word division and wide word spacing, and second, since the reader has to shift the eyes back to the beginnings of lines more often, fatigue can set in. Such narrow widths are more legible when set ragged right and with perhaps a little more than standard leading. Many people adjust their ebook readers to the maximum font size only to find fatigue setting in quickly. This is because their eyes have to track back more often than if the font size were smaller.

Line Spacing (Leading). Ideally, the average space between lines (leading) should always appear larger than the average word space. If the word spaces are larger than the leading, then "rivers" (jagged lines of white running down the page) are most likely to form, and reading will become more difficult. Overly wide leading can be as much of an eyestrain as too little, though it is best to err on the side of slightly too much than too little. Reference works and other works intended for short piecemeal reading do not need this extra leading.

READER RESPONSE CARD

A publisher or author sometimes provides a separate page, usually the last one in the book, asking readers for their thoughts on the book they just read. The publisher or author usually provides their street address, email address, or website URL. This common marketing practice is used to build email lists to alert readers to other products of interest.

READING-LEVEL CALCULATION

Several formulas exist for determining the reading level (by grade or age) of written texts. Among the most common are the Gunning "FOG" Readability Test and the Flesch-Kincaid Formula. Those two and a third one, the Powers-Sumner-Kearl Formula, which is chiefly used for primary-school-age readers, are briefly outlined here. These tests offer only general guidelines, and their results can vary, depending on the samples chosen. Still, they allow an editor and author to calculate whether a piece is broadly written at the level of the intended readership. The conventional publishing wisdom is that books written for the general reader should aim at about an eighth-grade reading level. Academic and literary works are expected to rate much higher, since their specialized vocabularies will already be familiar to the intended readership. But for the general trade, these tests may be helpful.

The Gunning "FOG" Readability Test. This test is most accurate when measuring older elementary- and secondary-school-age groups. To find the reading level:

1. Select three samples of a hundred words each.
2. Determine the average length of each sentence (that is, the total number of words divided by the number of sentences).
3. Then, in each sample, count the number of words containing three or more syllables, and find the average over the three samples.
4. To calculate grade level, add the average sentence length to the average number of words of three or more syllables. Multiply that sum by 0.4.
5. To calculate reading age in years, add 5 to the total in step 4.

The Flesch-Kincaid Formula. This standard test was devised by the US Department of Defense and is appropriate for secondary school and adult reading. To find the reading level:

1. Take a single sample of text from one hundred to three hundred words.
2. Determine the average number of words per sentence (total number of words divided by the number of sentences).
3. Determine the average number of syllables (total number of syllables divided by the total number of words).
4. To calculate grade level, multiply the average number of words per sentence by 0.39; then multiply the average number of syllables by 11.8. Add those two numbers together and subtract 15.59.
5. To calculate reading age, subtract 10.59 years instead of subtracting 15.59 as in step 4.

The Powers-Sumner-Kearl Formula. This is most accurate for primary-school-age students, up to about age ten. To find the reading level:

1. Select one or more samples of a hundred words each.
2. Find the average number of words per sentence and divide that by the number of total sentences (rounding to the nearest tenth).
3. Count the number of syllables in each hundred-word sample, and average them.
4. To calculate grade level, multiply the average number of words per sentence by 0.0778; then multiply the average number of syllables (per hundred-word sample) by 0.0455. Add those two numbers together, then subtract 2.2029.
5. To calculate age level in years, add 2.7971 instead of subtracting 2.2029 as in step 4.

RECTO VERSUS RANDOM SETTINGS OF PAGES

Recto (right-hand) pages have odd folio numbers and *verso* (left-hand) pages have even numbers. (See "FOLIO.") Recto pages are considered the dominant page in any spread. Ordinarily, most elements of a book's front and back matter start on recto pages, except for the copyright page, which is intentionally set as the verso of the title page. When space is a consideration, most any element of a book may be set verso, though it can sometimes diminish the aesthetic appeal and even the accessibility of the book. The first chapter of the book begins on a recto page. Ideally, each subsequent chapter should begin on a recto page (called *recto setting*), but the design and available space may require that subsequent chapters begin on the next available blank instead, whether a recto or verso (called *random setting*). Part-title pages are invariably set recto. In ebook settings, where fixed right- or left-hand pages are often absent, these preferences do not apply.

By and large, no recto page should be blank, other than the flyleaf and any unused pages at the end. Similarly, no page of an ebook has any reason to be blank.

RECYCLED-PAPER STATEMENT

The Book Industry Environmental Council's 2013 survey found that only about a quarter of the books printed in the US are printed on recycled paper. Although it is by no means mandatory, a notice is usually shown on the copyright page when recycled paper is used. The standard industry formula, preceded by the recycled symbol, is

♲ Printed on recycled paper.

Eliminate this statement from any ebook edition or if the print version is later reprinted on nonrecycled paper.

RED-LETTER EDITIONS OF THE BIBLE

In more than half of the Bibles printed each year, the words spoken by Jesus appear in red type. These are called *red-letter editions*. The device (sometimes called *rubrication*) was first used in 1899 and is considered an aid to Bible study, especially in the KJV, which contains no quotation marks with spoken passages. A few *red-letter* Bible concordances also exist, as well as some rare editions in which all the words of God in the Old and New Testaments are printed in red. Note the following style issues regarding red-letter editions of the Bible.

Punctuation, Verse Numbers, and Annotations. In red-letter editions, not only the words of Jesus but all punctuation (including quotation marks)

associated with them are printed in red. As with punctuation, all verse numbers and superscript numbers or letters used as callouts for footnotes or cross-references are set in red type when they are within or immediately precede the red-letter text. Red type is not used for any words of Jesus that are quoted in footnotes, introductions, or other ancillary matter.

Said References. Said references attached to the words of Jesus, such as *he answered* or *he said*, are not set in red.

The Epistles and Revelation. In several places—for instance, in Acts 9:4 and following as well as throughout Rev. 1–3—Jesus is quoted as speaking words that do not appear in the four gospels. Those words too are usually set in red type, though some red-letter editions include only those words that Jesus spoke during his lifetime on earth.

Printing Registration. In some older printing processes, inks of different colors have to be printed in separate passes through the press, which can result in slight misalignments, called *poor registration*. It is common to see Bibles in which the red words of Jesus seem to be fractionally higher or lower on the baseline than the rest of the text. Anytime a red-letter edition is printed, the publisher and printer should spot-check to ensure that the registration is accurate and consistent from signature to signature.

REFERENCING THE BIBLE

See "QUOTING THE BIBLE."

REPRINTS AND REVISIONS

A *reprint* is a fresh printing of an existing book in which no major or substantive changes have been made. Ordinarily, reprints are an opportunity to correct the errors (called *reprint corrections*) of the previous edition. New copyright dates are not needed in the copyright notice for such reprints, even if the corrections are extensive. A reprint is sometimes called a *new impression* or a *new printing*. If no bibliographic information (title, number of pages, author, publisher, ISBN) other than the year of publication has changed in the new printing, then a new CIP need not be applied for. (See "CATALOGING-IN-PUBLICATION DATA [CIP].")

A book is considered a *revision* when major substantive corrections are made or when new material is added. In other words, anytime anything *new* is added that requires the protection of copyright, a new date should be added to the copyright notice on the copyright page. A revision is considered a *new edition*. A fresh CIP and ISBN are required for all revisions.

RIVER, TYPOGRAPHIC

A *typographic river* is a white line, composed of word spaces in adjacent lines of type, that runs, like a river on a map, through a block of text. It was once thought to be distracting, a sign of poor composition and of word spacing that was too generous. This was especially common in the days when typographers usually put double spaces between sentences. (See "SPACE, DOUBLE.") Remarkably, rivers are easier to spot when holding a book upside down.

Rarely will a proofreader or editor in our time check for rivers, and even more rarely would they be expected to. The reason is that with digital typesetting and modern fonts, distracting rivers occur much less frequently. Still, in settings that are too narrow (too few words per line) and in display copy (like advertising or back-cover copy), rivers can make the typography look awkward and amateurish. A trained proofreader should spot them in such instances.

With Typographic Orphans. The concept of *typographic rivers* is also useful when determining whether a broken word on a line by itself at the end of a paragraph is acceptable or not (see "WIDOWS AND ORPHANS [TYPOGRAPHIC]"). If the partial word extends beyond the point where the first indented word of the next paragraph begins, then it is most likely acceptable. If a visual river exists, then the paragraph containing the broken word should be reconfigured to fix the problem. (See "WORD DIVISION.")

ROMAN CATHOLIC ORDERS, ABBREVIATIONS OF

Set the abbreviations of Roman Catholic religious orders without periods, though some publishers retain the periods since many of the abbreviations also contain lowercase letters (such as O. *Cart.*). When used after a name, set the abbreviation apart with commas: for instance, *Brother Patrick Hart, OSCO, attended the conference.* A short list follows, showing some of the more common orders with their abbreviations and common names. For a comprehensive list, see http://www.catholicdoors.com/misc/abbrev.htm.

Abbreviation	**Order**	**Common Name**
AA	Augustinians of the Assumption	Assumptionists
CRL	Canonici Regulares Lateranenses	"Canons Regular of the Lateran"
OCC	Ordo Carmelitarum Calceatorum	Carmelites
OCart, or O. Cart.	Ordo Cartusiensis	Carthusians

Abbreviation	Order	Common Name
OCD	Ordo Carmelitarum Discalceatorum	Discalced Carmelites
OCist, or O. Cist.	Ordo Cisterciensium	Cistercians
OFM	Ordo Fratrum Minorum	Observant Franciscans
OM	Ordo [Fratrum] Minimorum	Minims of St. Francis of Paul
OMC	Ordo Minorum Capuccinorum	Capuchins
OP	Ordo Praedicatorum	Dominicans
OPraem, or O. Praem.	Ordo Praemonstratensium	Premonstratensians, Norbertines
OSA	Ordo [Eremitarum] Sancti Augustini	Augustinians
OSB	Ordo Sancti Benedicti	Benedictines
OSC	Oblati Sancti Caroli	Oblate Fathers of St. Charles
OSCO	Order of the Cistericians of the Strict Observance	Cistercians
OSD	Order of Saint Dominic	Dominicans
OSFC	Ordinis Sancti Francisci Capuccini	Order of Franciscan Capuchins
OSFS	Oblati Sancti Francisci Salesii	Oblates of St. Francis de Sales
OSH	Ordo [Eremitarum] Sancti Hieronymi	Hieronymites
OSM	Ordo Servorum Mariae	Servites
OSSC	Ordo Sanctissimae Trinitatis	Trinitarians
SJ	Societas Jesu	"Society of Jesus," Jesuits
SM	Societas Mariae	Society of Mary

ROMAN NUMERALS

Even without a clear concept of zero as a number, the ancient Romans devised a complex numbering system that has survived, surprisingly, into the modern world for specialized uses. One minor advantage of the Romans' system is that it employs fewer basic characters (only seven) than our familiar arabic system (sometimes referred to as the Hindu-Arabic system), which uses ten. The Romans could render all the numbers between 1 and 100 with only five characters. The disadvantage of roman numerals is the long and often confusing strings of characters that can result. The year *1998*, for instance, is *MCMXCVIII* in roman numerals, more than twice as long as the same number in arabic numerals. By contrast, the year *2000* is a simple *MM*, half the length of the arabic.

The Characters. The basic characters of the Roman numbering system are:

I (or i) = 1	VM (or vm) = 5,000
V (or v) = 5	XM (or xm) = 10,000
X (or x) = 10	CM (or cm) = 100,000
L (or l) = 50	MM (or mm) = 1,000,000
C (or c) = 100	*Note:* In the Middle Ages, the character Z was added to represent 2,000.
D (or d) = 500	
M (or m) = 1,000	

How to Form Roman Numerals. When a smaller numeral appears to the right of a larger one, the smaller is added to the larger. Thus, *VI* is 6 (5 plus 1). When a smaller numeral appears to the left of a larger one, the smaller is subtracted from the larger. Thus, *IV* is 4 (1 subtracted from 5), though that form was introduced during the Renaissance since the ancient Romans actually rendered the number *4* as *IIII*. This method of subtraction-according-to-position is called the ***subtrahend system.*** With those basic rules, all the numbers can be formed except, as stated before, zero. A line over the characters *V*, *X*, *C*, and *M* multiplies the value of that character by one thousand.

With Names. Roman numerals are commonly used with the names of kings, other royalty, and popes: for example, *Henry VIII*, *James I*, *Pope John XXIII*. This practice is extended to ordinary family names, usually the child of someone who is already designated a *Jr.* Thus, the son of John Doe Jr. is John Doe III, who might name his son John Doe IV. As with *Sr.* and *Jr.*, do not allow the roman numeral to be separated from the name over a line break, and do not insert a comma. Though rare, some families prefer *II* to *Jr.*: as in *John Doe II.*

With World Wars. A common place to find roman numerals is in references to the two major wars of the twentieth century: *World War I* and *World War II*. By extension, futurists also refer to *World War III*, *World War IV*, and so on.

Paginating Front Matter. Another common place to find roman numerals is in the front-matter pagination of some scholarly books. The reason is partly the flexibility it offers in indexing a book even before the front matter has been completed. It is even recommended that roman numerals be used for the front matter in any book that has an index. In this way, once the main body of the text has been indexed, the folios on the text pages and page numbers in the index will still align, no matter how many changes are made to the front matter. Then, once the front matter is finalized, its references can be added to the index as well. In such books, the front matter is paginated with roman numerals, while the main text of the book is paginated with arabic numerals (starting with 1). (See "FOLIO.") When front matter is paginated with roman numerals, only lowercase letters are used (*i, ii, iii, iv, v,... x,* etc.).

For Year Dates. A Roman Catholic imprimatur, displayed either across from the title page or on a book's copyright page (see "IMPRIMATUR"), commonly bears a year date in roman numerals. Official pronouncements, especially religious ones, sometimes bear roman numeral dates, and though the practice is waning, the film industry for many years made it a tradition to display the release dates of their films in roman numerals—causing viewers to squint and frantically calculate as the credits roll by. (Metro-Goldwyn-Mayer, for instance, released *The Wizard of Oz* in MCMXXXIX.)

On rare occasions one still sees the year of a book's publication shown on the title page in roman numerals. In some older books, *D* (the roman numeral for 500) was actually rendered *IↃ* and *M* (1,000) was *CIↃ* as stylized variants of those characters. They were printing conventions only, the primary result of which seems to have been to further confuse those who were already baffled. In the twenty-first century, using roman numerals for publication dates is an ill-advised affectation.

For Numbering Chapters and Parts. The use of roman numerals for numbering chapters of a book is discouraged by contemporary designers unless a certain classical or elegant mood is required. Even in that case, use them only when the book contains fewer than ten chapters. A reader should not have to puzzle out the numerals beyond X (10). More commonly, parts of a book are designated with roman numerals, though that practice too has declined in popularity. Again, do not use roman numerals if the book has more than ten parts.

For Acts in Plays. Roman numerals are still occasionally used in referencing the number of an act in a theater piece, though *CMoS* recommends a newer style of using arabic numerals only. If the older style is used, in which acts are referenced with roman numerals, capitalize the word *Act* and set scene numbers in arabic numerals, with the word *scene* lowercase: as in *The wedding masque in Act IV, scene 1 of Shakespeare's* The Tempest *suggests the play was written for a royal wedding.* Either the old or new style may be used, as long as it is used consistently within a publication.

For Books of the Bible. Do not use roman numerals for referencing books of the Bible (such as *I Samuel* or *II Corinthians*), even when they are used in the version of the Bible being quoted. Use arabic numerals instead. While many older editions of the KJV use roman numerals, most recent editions have dropped that style.

For Appendixes. Formerly, roman numerals were often used to number book appendixes. Though this use is still acceptable, we recommend against it unless there is a specific reason for doing so. Again, roman numerals are best used when only the numbers one through ten are needed.

In Outlines. Roman numerals are used for the primary levels in an outline, though that traditional system has in many places been supplanted by the so-called decimal system (1, 1.1, 1.1.1, etc.). (See "OUTLINES AND LISTS.")

In Columns. If roman numerals are set in a vertical column, as in a chart or a table of contents, align them on the right, not the left.

RUBRICATION

See "RED-LETTER EDITIONS OF THE BIBLE."

RUNNING HEADS AND FOOTERS

A *running head*, which is the line of type set at the top of text pages (though usually omitted on chapter opening pages), can include such information as the book title, part title, chapter title or section head, folio, and sometimes the author's name. A *running footer* appears at the bottom of the page. In some designs, in textbooks, for instance, the running head may appear in the side margin and incorporate several lines of type as well as the folio (page number). Running heads and footers do not ordinarily appear on pages without text type, that is, on title pages, copyright pages, tables of contents, dedication pages, and so on. Running heads and footers may be eliminated in popular fiction and mass-market books to conserve space and to contribute to the narrative flow. Folios may appear on the same line as the running heads or separately.

Formatting. Traditionally, running heads display the book title on the verso pages and the chapter title on the recto pages, though this format is less common than it once was. Any number of combinations of book title, chapter title, part title, section heads, author name, series title, or other elements may be used in the running heads. The element with the greater weight or importance is placed in the left (verso) running head.

Since different types of books have different needs, the formatting and positioning of the running heads are flexible and should be determined by the designer, sometimes with recommendations from the editor. Running heads are usually not set flush left unless sufficient line space is provided to ensure that the head won't be mistaken for the first line of type on the page.

With Fiction. Many works of fiction dispense with running heads. Novels often have only chapter numbers with no chapter titles, which would leave only the book title to be included in the running head. It is too repetitive to have the book's title appear twice on every spread, and most authors would be abashed to have their name included in every spread (though some authors actually insist on having their name on every spread as a sort of subliminal marketing technique). Also, some novels tend to run long, and running heads eat up valuable space. Finally, running heads can prove a distraction to the experience of reading fiction, disrupting the flow of the narrative with uselessly repeated material.

S

SAID REFERENCES

A *said reference* is a phrase containing a "verb of saying" (such as *ask, answer, respond, say, shout,* and so on) that connects the subject of a sentence to a direct quotation.

Alternatives to "Said." Some writers, wary of overusing *said*, resort to a wide array of other words. In 1948, two teachers, J. I. Rodale and Mable F. Mullock, even wrote a hundred-page book called *The "Said" Book,* which is nothing but a list of alternatives (Emmaus, Pa.: Rodale Press). But many alternatives are counterproductive. Some said references are redundant, such as: *"I beg you!" she pleaded,* or *"Why?" he queried.* Some can seem so unnatural as to distract from the quotation: *"Never!" he countermanded,* or *"I believe so," she cogitated aloud.*

Other words look like said references, but it is hard to imagine anything actually being spoken in the specified way, such as: *"What?" he giggled* or *"I suppose there's nothing to do but get it over with," she groaned.* In the first instance, *what* is a single syllable and giggling implies a series of repeated sounds. In the second instance, groaning implies a short low sound, so it would actually be hard to "groan" such a long string of words.

Writers do not need to be overly inventive in finding alternatives to *said.* Most often, *said* is itself the ideal said reference. The late William Zinsser wrote that *said* is so common as to be nearly invisible, and it takes an extraordinary number of them in a small space to become distracting. The goal, rather, is to keep all said references from drawing too much attention to themselves. Ideally, the quotation itself will convey the mood and emotion of the words and will not have to depend on any attached verbs or adverbs.

Remember also that said references can be minimized in closely written dialogue: *"That's how it will be," he said. "Why?" "Because I said so!"* Whenever the speaker is unambiguous, as in most two-person dialogues, few said references are needed at all.

Saying a Question. Some grammarians insist that one cannot *say* a question. They find a sentence like *"Who cares?" she said* to be substandard. But grammatically, there is no reason why a question cannot be *said. To say* simply means "to speak," and questions can be spoken like any other spoken words. So use *ask* or other interrogative verbs as long as they don't seem awkward or redundant, but don't shy away from *say* for questions.

SAINTS' DAYS

Saints' days, found chiefly in the Roman Catholic, Eastern Orthodox, and Anglican traditions, commemorate days on which noted saints died. While those traditions share some saints, each tradition has its own roster, and many countries commemorate national saints' days not found on other calendars. A saint's day is sometimes called a *dies natalis* ("day of birth") because it is the day on which a saint was "born into heaven."

Saints' days use the possessive form (such as *Saint Nonnus's Day* or *All Saints' Day*). Those saints' days that have become popular holidays usually abbreviate the word *Saint* (*St. Patrick's Day, St. Valentine's Day*, which is further shortened to *Valentine's Day* or *St. Valentine's*), while less widely observed days from the liturgical calendar often spell it out (*Saint Stephen's Day*). When a descriptive phrase follows the saint's name, use "the Feast of" to avoid awkwardness; for instance, instead of saying *Saint Thérèse of the Child Jesus's Day*, say *the Feast of Saint Thérèse of the Child Jesus*. The same "Feast of" formula applies to days that are named for two saints: *the Feast of Saints Peter and Paul*. (See also "CHRISTIAN HOLIDAYS, FEASTS, AND THE LITURGICAL YEAR.")

SCARE PARAGRAPH

See "WARNING NOTICE."

SCHOLARLY APPEARANCES

A scholarly editorial style can give an academic book an air of added authority, but that same scholarly appearance can be a turn-off to readers of a popular trade book. Editors and book designers are responsible for making the look of each book suitable for the book's unique readership. Some of these recommendations might help.

Scholarly Abbreviations. Avoid scholarly abbreviations like *e.g., etc., ibid., i.e., op cit.*, and so on in books for general readers. Reserve them for scholarly books and, even then, only when they are essential. (See "ABBREVIATIONS: SCHOLARLY.")

BC, AD, BCE, CE. In books for general audiences, stick with *BC* and *AD* for designating year dates before or after the birth of Jesus. For academic books, use either the *BC/AD* system or the slightly more scholarly *BCE/CE* system. (See "*BC, AD*" and "*BCE/CE*.")

Abbreviating Books of the Bible. When citing the sources of Bible quotations in works for a general audience, use the general style of abbreviation for books of the Bible; or, if there are relatively few references, spell out the names of the books of the Bible in full in both the text and the citations.

In scholarly works, use the SBL style of abbreviation in all citations, or use SBL abbreviations in both the text and citations when such references are extremely frequent. (See "ABBREVIATIONS: BIBLE BOOKS AND RELATED MATERIAL.")

Quotations. Ordinarily, short quotations are run into the text, and long quotations are set as block quotes, or extracts. But the boundary between short and long is flexible. In books for a popular or lay readership, allow quotations on the longish side to run into the text to avoid the academic appearance of too many block quotations, or extracts. Most general readers are more apt to read a longish quotation when it is run into text and to scan or skip quotations set as extracts. (See "QUOTATIONS, GENERAL," section on "*Run-in versus Block Quotations.*")

Notes. Minimize footnotes and endnotes in books for a popular readership. If endnotes cannot be avoided, consider using the hidden endnote style outlined in the "NOTES" entry of this manual. That eliminates distracting superscript references in the text.

SCRIBAL LATIN CHARACTERS AND ABBREVIATIONS

Medieval scribal church Latin, which continued to be used in print from the time of Gutenberg to about the eighteenth century, used distinctive characters and abbreviations. This was sometimes done as a way to justify lines of calligraphy or type. One of the most familiar though confusing characters is the "long *s*." It looks like an *f* in form but without the crossbar. It is used only at the beginning or in the middle of a word, never at the end. Should two *s*'s come at the end of a word, it would read *fs*. Here is a list of the most common scribal Latin abbreviations and characters. With these, one could start to make sense of the Latin in the Gutenberg Bible.

â	letters *am*
æ	Latin feminine plural
ɔ	*contra* ("against")
ð	*de* ("half") or *dedit* ("he gave") or letters *di*
ç	letters *em*, *en*, or *est*
ê	*est* ("is") or letters *æ* or *œ*
î	*in* ("in") or letters *in* or *im*
ñ	*non* ("nor") or *nunc* ("now")
ô	letters *on*
œ	dipthong
p̄	letters *pro*, *pra*, *per*, *pur*, *pre*
q̄	*quam* ("whom")
qꝫ	*quippe* ("that is"), *que* ("that"), or letters *que*
ſ	letter s (the "long s")
ſi,ſſi	"long s" ligatures: letters *si*, *ssi*
ß	letters *s* or *sz*
û	letters *um* or *us*
ꝰ	letters *us*, *ius*, *eus*
†	blessing, benediction
&	ampersand; et ("and")
¶	pilcrow; main topic or paragraph
§	section(al) symbol; subtopic

SECOND HALF-TITLE PAGE

Like the half-title page, the second half-title page (sometimes called the *inside half-title page*) bears only the title of the book, but it is placed immediately before the main body of the text and immediately following the front matter. (See also "HALF-TITLE PAGE.") The half-title and the second half-title are identical in appearance and can both be used in any given work. In a sense, the second half-title provides a psychological threshold, a subtle announcement that the preliminaries are over and the actual book is about to begin. Such a page is common in fiction and memoir and can add an elegant touch to almost any book where space allows. While its use is encouraged for such books, a second half-title page can be easily discarded for space reasons.

SEMICOLON

Despite the late William Zinsser's disparagement of the semicolon (;), which he felt had a certain "19th-century mustiness" about it (*On Writing Well*), the semicolon is still commonly used because it serves some needful, if limited, functions.

With Compound Sentences. A semicolon may be used in place of a conjunction between two independent clauses of a compound sentence.

> Mary Slessor knew the hardships of the mission field; she would have been appalled by the romantic image that eventually surrounded her work.
>
> One aspect of things strikes us and we talk of the "peace" of Nature; another strikes us and we talk of her cruelty.—C. S. Lewis, *Miracles*

With Internal Punctuation. When items enumerated in text are particularly long or contain internal punctuation, substitute semicolons for the commas in those cases when commas alone would not clarify the relationship of one item to another.

> Hannah More knew many of the famous people of her day: Samuel Johnson; Horace Walpole; David Garrick, who produced her plays; William Wilberforce, the abolitionist politician; and John Newton, who eventually became a major influence in her life.

With Transitional Adverbs. Such words as *also*, *consequently*, *hence*, *however*, *indeed*, *moreover*, *then*, *therefore*, and *thus* are thought of as transitional adverbs when used between independent clauses; therefore, these words are customarily preceded by a semicolon (like the last *therefore* in this sentence).

> Wilberforce thought of himself as a Christian rather than a politician; moreover, he saw his abolitionist views as an outgrowth of his faith.

The words *so* and *yet*, although also transitional adverbs, are customarily preceded by a comma when used between independent clauses.

I always find, however, that I am either too busy or too lazy to write this fine work, so I may as well give it away for the purposes of philosophical illustration.—G. K. Chesterton, *Orthodoxy*

God warned Adam and Eve about the consequences of sin, yet they disobeyed him.

Commas, rather than semicolons, are used in a series of short, closely related clauses with no conjunction. Also, short antithetical clauses are separated by a comma instead of a semicolon.

He got up, he took his mat, he walked away. [commas okay here for short parallel sentences]

The opposite of faith isn't doubt, it's certainty. [quote from John Fugelsang; don't use a semicolon for short, contrasting independent clauses]

With "Namely," "That Is," and Other Expressions. Use a semicolon before such expressions as ***namely*** and ***that is***, and before the abbreviations ***i.e.*** and ***e.g.***, depending on the context and the degree to which the continuity of thought is interrupted. Note that the use of scholarly abbreviations such as ***i.e.*** (***id est***, Latin for "that is") and ***e.g.*** (***exempli gratia***, Latin for "for example") is discouraged in nonacademic writing.

Lewis wrote Greeves that he had crossed a major threshold in his life; that is, he had passed from "believing in God to definitely believing in Christ." [quotation from C. S. Lewis, *They Stand Together*]

Until the last half of the twentieth century, Southern religious music was dominated by the popular shape-note hymnals, e.g., *The Sacred Harp*, *Southern Harmony*, and their imitators. [no semicolon used in context]

In Bible References. In Bible citations, place a semicolon between references to different books and between references to different chapter-and-verses within one book. Use a comma to separate verse references within chapters.

Luke 1:46–55; 2:14; and Acts 1:7–8.

John 1:1–13, 15, 29–34.

If chapter numbers within one book are referenced without verse numbers, use commas to separate them.

Psalms 19, 20, 23.

Matthew 8, 9, 12, 15, 17, 20.

SENTENCE FRAGMENTS

Sentence fragments are of two kinds: effective or ineffective. The effective ones are those used judiciously for a specific reason, such as to heighten drama, create a mood, emphasize a point, make dialogue more realistic, suggest a spoken or intimate style, or introduce a definition, as in Ambrose Bierce's "Saint, n. A dead sinner revised and edited" (*Devil's Dictionary*). Well-written fragments make for powerful writing. Consider this example from *Bleak House* by Charles Dickens, a master of the sentence fragment:

> Fog everywhere. Fog up the river, where it flows among green aits and meadows; fog down the river where it rolls defiled among the tiers of shipping, and the waterside pollutions of a great (and dirty) city. Fog on the Essex marshes, fog on the Kentish heights.

So, editors and proofreaders should not dismiss fragments out-of-hand. Not by a long shot. Still, ineffective or unintentional fragments need to be challenged because they cause problems; they create confusion by obscuring antecedents, prompting the reader to ask, "What's going on?" Even intentional fragments cause problems when they occur so often as to become distracting or when their use is perceived as gimmicky. (*No. Seriously. For sure.*)

SERIAL COMMA

See "COMMA," section on "*With a Series of Elements.*"

SIGNATURE BREAKS

Most people realize that book pages are not printed separately but amassed and printed together on large sheets, after which the sheets are folded and trimmed into sections called *signatures*. So large are these sheets that it takes only a few to print a single copy of an average book. In former times, a single sheet folded once, so as to create two leaves, or four pages, was called a *folio* (as in the 1623 First Folio of Shakespeare's plays). Once they were printed, they were nested together and bound. Modern presses commonly accommodate sheets of paper that can contain sixteen pages (octavo) or thirty-two pages (sextodecimo), and some mass-market books are even printed on signature sheets of sixty-four pages (trigesimo-secundo). As a result, the total number of pages in nearly every book that is printed will be a multiple of eight (a half signature) or sixteen. (There are also less common printing methods that render a twenty-four-page, or duodecimo, signature as well as a thirty-six-page, or octodecimo, signature.)

The science of arranging the pages on large sheets or paper so that they appear in the correct order when gathered and folded is called *imposition*. In the world of ebooks, the terms *signature* and *imposition* are meaningless since ebooks contain any number of pages with no blanks. The following chart shows the common page lengths for most print books, based on multiples of sixteen. Printers and publishers refer to these as the "signature breaks."

16	208	400	592	784	976	1168	1360
32	224	416	608	800	992	1184	1376
48	240	432	624	816	1008	1200	1392
64	256	448	640	832	1024	1216	1408
80	272	464	656	848	1040	1232	1424
96	288	480	672	864	1056	1248	1440
112	304	496	688	880	1072	1264	1456
128	320	512	704	896	1088	1280	1472
144	336	528	720	912	1104	1296	1488
160	352	544	736	928	1120	1312	1504
176	368	560	752	944	1136	1328	1520
192	384	576	768	960	1152	1344	1536

Legend:
Standard signature = 16 pages (octavo)
Half signature = 8 pages (also common quarto)
Underscores = 32-page signatures (sextodecimo)

SLANG

See "JARGON, RELIGIOUS" and "DIALOGUE SLANG."

SMALL CAPS

Small capital letters (A, B, C, D, ...) have the form of regular capitals but are only as tall as the letter *x* (the *x-height*) in most fonts. They are common in display type of all kinds and have some specific uses in text, though they are becoming less common than they once were. They are no longer recommended for the abbreviations for historical eras (use *AD, BC, BCE, CE*) or for time designations (use *a.m., p.m.*), though the small-cap abbreviations may still be appropriate to convey an elegant or formal tone. When small caps are used, apply them consistently throughout the project.

For "Lord" and "God." See "LORD, GOD (CAP-AND-SMALL-CAP FORMS)."

For Display Purposes. Some print-book designs call for small caps to be used for the opening word (after an initial capital), phrase, or sentence at the beginning of a chapter. Unless otherwise noted by the designer, all punctuation marks and ordinarily capitalized letters remain in regular type.

PHILLIP BLISS'S HYMNS WERE POPULAR AT D. L. MOODY 'S CAMPAIGNS.

In Phonetic Spellings. Small caps may be used to show an accented syllable in informal renderings of phonetic pronunciation. For instance, *Eusebius (pronounced you-SEE-bee-us) is the father of church history.*

For Special Emphasis. Small caps are sometimes used to show emphasis in text, similar to the way italic is used, though perhaps more emphatic. In most cases, italic is preferred. In traditional typography, designers tend to avoid all-cap words in text, so small caps are sometimes used in their place for aesthetic reasons. All caps tend to look overbold and too spread out when used together, drawing too much attention to themselves on the page. This manual recommends the use of small caps rather than all caps for occasional emphasis in works of an academic or artistic nature, or where accuracy or an unusually high-quality page appearance is desired. In works of a popular nature, especially books of humor or fiction, all caps may be used for emphasis instead.

> From the bell tower of the cathedral, Quasimodo shouted, "SANCTUARY! SANCTUARY!" [Cap-and-small-cap style used here, though cap-lowercase italic would probably be preferable]
>
> In bold letters, the notice on the back gate of the Compassionate Heart Church read, "NO TRESPASSING." [To indicate capital letters on a sign, though all caps could have been used instead]

Web Design. Because of readability issues, avoid small caps in copy intended to be read online.

SOCIAL MEDIA PAGE

A social media page is a specialized promo page (see "PROMOTIONAL PAGE") on which the author invites readers to follow him or her on Facebook, Twitter, or other social-networking sites. This page is usually set in regular text and not heavily designed. A plain statement of invitation is sufficient, such as "Please join me on Twitter at [the author's Twitter hashtag]." It can also include a reference to the author's website, especially if reader comments about the book are solicited. Although some authors prefer such a page to appear at the front of a book, this manual recommends placing it at the back of the book since more readers are likely to read the invitation there. Ideally, after finishing the book, readers will be so interested in the content that they will want to seek out the author online.

SOLIDUS (FORWARD SLASH)

An unspaced solidus, (/), also called a *slash*, a *forward slash*, a *diagonal*, or, infrequently, a *virgule*, is most often encountered as part of internet URLs (uniform resource locators), as in *zondervan.com/interactive.* In such cases, it is referred to as a *forward slash* so as not to confuse it with the *back slash* (\ ), which is used in computer programming.

For Numerals, Dates, and Times. The solidus is found in such common numerical terms as *9/11* and *24/7*. It is occasionally used for dates, especially in online forms: *8/28/53*, though keep in mind that in the US such dates are rendered *month/day/year*, while in the UK they are rendered *day/month/year*. An unspaced solidus or an en dash may be used to show that a season or other period of time spans two consecutive years, though the en dash is preferred: for example, *winter 1620/21* and *fiscal year 2015/16*, though *winter 1620–21* and *fiscal year 2015–16* are preferred.

For Alternative Words. An unspaced solidus is occasionally used to link a pair of alternative or combined words or phrases, as in *he/she* or *and/or*. The solidus should be word-spaced when one or both elements are compounds: for instance, *a late Romantic / early Modernist*. Note that in most formal writing the use of a solidus in such combinations is discouraged since most concepts can be more concisely expressed without them. For instance, *a hunter-gatherer* is preferable to *a hunter/gatherer* because it is not clear whether those terms are parallel or mutually exclusive.

In Poetry. If two or more lines of poetry are run into the text, a solidus (with a word space on both sides) is used to show line breaks, as in *He quoted Blake: "Little fly, / Thy summer's play / My thoughtless hand / Has brushed away."* A poetry solidus may fall at either the end or the beginning of a line of type that has been broken, though it is less distracting if the solidus is set at the end of the first line rather than the beginning of the second. (See also "POETRY.")

SOURCE LISTS, SOURCES

See "BIBLIOGRAPHIES AND SOURCE LISTS." For footnotes and endnotes see "NOTES."

SPACE, DOUBLE

As far as putting two spaces between sentences—*don't*. Inserting a double space was common in Victorian typesetting and twentieth-century typewriting, and it is still sometimes required for papers in a classroom setting. The extra space has no place in printed material. A single word space is sufficient.

SPELLING OUT WORDS IN TEXT

Occasionally, a writer needs to show how a word, or words, are spelled. This happens most frequently in dialogue. The common practice is to use capital letters separated by hyphens, for instance: *"The name is Psmith, spelled P-S-M-I-T-H."* If the capital letters look too heavy in the font, then small caps may be used: *P-S-M-I-T-H*. (See also "DIALOGUE, SAYING WORDS SLOWLY IN.")

SPLIT INFINITIVE

The headmaster of an English school in P. G. Wodehouse's novel *The Gold Bat* (1904) was known to "sit up in his chair stiff with horror" whenever he encountered a split infinitive—that is, any word coming between *to* and its accompanying base verb. Nonetheless, good reasons exist for splitting infinitives, not the least of which is to indicate emphasis. To say *We expect our presidents to faithfully execute the duties of their office* places the emphasis squarely on the word *faithfully.* To reposition the adverb elsewhere diminishes its force. In some instances, splitting an infinitive simply sounds more natural: *We can never hope to fully understand the mysterious ways of God* or *The call to holiness ought to profoundly shape and inform our private and public posture.* The alternatives run the risk of sounding stilted or weak.

In Dialogue. Editors and proofreaders need to resist the temptation to eliminate split infinitives in dialogue unless the fictional speaker is portrayed as being precisely that kind of person who would "sit up in horror" if caught splitting an infinitive (and such people are rare). Split infinitives are common in everyday speech: *"I'm ready to completely take Broadway by storm!"* That's simply how people talk.

Exceptions. Good reasons also exist for not splitting infinitives, the main one being that they sometimes sound odd. No one is comfortable with sentences like *He learned to smoothly and consistently play his scales* or *They promised to every year cut the deficit by 10 percent.* Those are awkward and should be fixed.

Writers from Geoffrey Chaucer to John Updike split infinitives boldly and effectively when needed, and few style manuals prohibit them wholesale. In short, fix them whenever they cause awkwardness or lack of clarity, and also fix them in formal, academic writing when the author is likely to be accused of not knowing "proper English."

STACKS, TYPOGRAPHIC

When the same word falls at the beginning or end of three or more consecutive lines of type, it is called a *stack*. The same word appearing twice consecutively is not a problem, but a sequence of three or more should be fixed since it could distract the reader. In most cases, a line or two can be rebroken to avoid such stacks.

STATE AND PROVINCE ABBREVIATIONS

Whenever possible, spell out the names of US states and territories and Canadian provinces in text. In lists, footnotes, endnotes, indexes, bibliographies, and charts, those names may be abbreviated, using either standard abbreviations or two-letter postal abbreviations at the author's and editor's discretion. The following list shows state, territory, and province abbreviations in both standard and postal style. Note that a few names are traditionally not abbreviated.

State	Standard Abbrev.	Postal Abbrev.
Alabama	Ala.	AL
Alaska	Alaska	AK
Arizona	Ariz.	AZ
Arkansas	Ark.	AR
California	Calif.	CA
Colorado	Colo.	CO
Connecticut	Conn.	CT
Delaware	Del.	DE
Florida	Fla.	FL
Georgia	Ga.	GA
Hawaii	Hawaii	HI
Idaho	Ida.	ID
Illinois	Ill.	IL
Indiana	Ind.	IN
Iowa	Ia.	IA
Kansas	Kans.	KS
Kentucky	Ky.	KY
Louisiana	La.	LA
Maine	Me.	ME
Maryland	Md.	MD
Massachusetts	Mass.	MA
Michigan	Mich.	MI
Minnesota	Minn.	MN
Mississippi	Miss.	MS
Missouri	Mo.	MO

State	Standard Abbrev.	Postal Abbrev.
Montana	Mont.	MT
Nebraska	Neb.	NE
Nevada	Nev.	NV
New Hampshire	N.H.	NH
New Jersey	N.J.	NJ
New Mexico	N.Mex.	NM
New York	N.Y.	NY
North Carolina	N.C.	NC
North Dakota	N.Dak.	ND
Ohio	Ohio	OH
Oklahoma	Okla.	OK
Oregon	Ore.	OR
Pennsylvania	Pa. or Penn.	PA
Rhode Island	R.I.	RI
South Carolina	S.C.	SC
South Dakota	S.Dak.	SD
Tennessee	Tenn.	TN
Texas	Tex.	TX
Utah	Utah	UT
Vermont	Vt.	VT
Virginia	Va.	VA
Washington	Wash.	WA
West Virginia	W.Va.	WV
Wisconsin	Wis.	WI
Wyoming	Wyo.	WY

Canadian Province	Standard Abbrev.	Postal Abbrev.
Alberta	Alta.	AB
British Columbia	B.C.	BC
Manitoba	Man.	MB
New Brunswick	N.B.	NB
Newfoundland and Labrador	N.L.	NL
Northwest Territories	N.W.T.	NT
Nova Scotia	N.S.	NS
Nunavut	Nunavut	NU
Ontario	Ont.	ON
Prince Edward Island	P.E.I.	PE
Québec	Qué. or P.Q.	QC
Saskatchewan	Sask.	SK
Yukon Territory	Y.T.	YT

STATE AND PROVINCIAL RESIDENT NAMES

A *demonym* (pronounced DEEM-uh-nim) describes a person in terms of geographic location. Entire dictionaries of demonyms have been written (see Paul Dickson's *Labels for Locals: What to Call People from Abilene to Zimbabwe* [HarperCollins, 2006]). The following list provides demonyms for people in the fifty US states and thirteen Canadian provinces. In some cases, especially when the state or province has not designated an official name, the recommended name is listed first, followed in parentheses by a common alternative. When in doubt, use the first option.

State	Demonym
Alabama	Alabamian (Alabaman)
Alaska	Alaskan
Arizona	Arizonan (Arizonian)
Arkansas	Arkansan (Arkansawyer)
California	Californian
Colorado	Coloradan (Coloradoan)
Connecticut	Connecticutter
Delaware	Delawarean (Delawarian)
Florida	Floridian
Georgia	Georgian
Hawaii	Hawaiian (Islander)
Idaho	Idahoan
Illinois	Illinoisan (Illinoisian, Illini)
Indiana	Indianan (Hoosier, Indianian)
Iowa	Iowan
Kansas	Kansan
Kentucky	Kentuckian
Louisiana	Louisianan (Louisianian)
Maine	Mainer
Maryland	Marylander
Massachusetts	Massachusettsan
Michigan	Michiganian (Michigander)
Minnesota	Minnesotan
Mississippi	Mississippian
Missouri	Missourian
Montana	Montanan
Nebraska	Nebraskan
Nevada	Nevadan

State	Demonym	State	Demonym
New Hampshire	New Hampshirite	South Carolina	South Carolinian
New Jersey	New Jerseyan (New Jerseyite)	South Dakota	South Dakotan
		Tennessee	Tennessean
New Mexico	New Mexican	Texas	Texan
New York	New Yorker	Utah	Utahan
North Carolina	North Carolinian	Vermont	Vermonter
North Dakota	North Dakotan	Virginia	Virginian
Ohio	Ohioan	Washington	Washingtonian
Oklahoma	Oklahoman	West Virginia	West Virginian
Oregon	Oregonian	Wisconsin	Wisconsinite
Pennsylvania	Pennsylvanian	Wyoming	Wyomingite
Rhode Island	Rhode Islander		

Canadian Province	Demonym
Alberta	Albertan
British Columbia	British Columbian (informal: BCer)
Manitoba	Manitoban
New Brunswick	New Brunswicker
Newfoundland and Labrador	Newfoundlander Labradorian
Northwest Territories	Northwest Territorian
Nova Scotia	Nova Scotian
Nunavut	Nunavummiuq (pl. Nunavummiut)
Ontario	Ontarian
Prince Edward Island	Prince Edward Islander
Quebec	Quebecer (French: Quebecois)
Saskatchewan	Saskatchewanian
Yukon	Yukoner

STYLE MANUALS, RELIGIOUS

Various denominations and religious presses have their own specific house styles; here is a representative sampling.

Catholic: *Stylebook on Religion 2000*. Washington, D.C.: Catholic News Service, 2000. Updated electronic version (Kindle) available as *CNS Style Book on Religion: Reference Guide and Usage Manual*, 2013.

Catholic (OSB): *Style Guide*. Collegeville, Minn.: Liturgical Press, Order of Saint Benedict, 2008. https://www.litpress.org/Authors/PDFs/style_guide.pdf.

Episcopal: *Style Guidelines for the Episcopal Church.* New York: The Episcopal Church, Office of Communications, 2014. http://www.episcopalchurch.org/files/the_episcopal_church_guidelines.pdf.

Lutheran: *ELCA Style Guide/Alphabetized Word List.* Chicago: Evangelical Lutheran Church in America, n.d. http://ltsp.edu/wp-content/uploads/2014/05/elcaeditorialstyleguide-042014.pdf.

Mennonite: *Supplement to* The Chicago Manual of Style. Scottdale, Pa.: Mennonite Publishing Network, Inc., Herald Press, 2006. http://www.heraldpress.com/pdf/0410_mpn_manual_of_style.pdf.

Methodist: *Author Guidelines and Submission Instructions.* Atlanta: Methodist Review: A Journal of Wesleyan and Methodist Studies, 2009. https://www.methodistreview.org/files/MR_Author_Guidelines.pdf.

Mormon: *Style Guide for Publications of The Church of Jesus Christ of Latter-day Saints*, 4th ed. Salt Lake City: The Church of Jesus Christ of Latter-day Saints, 2013. http://mormonnewsroom.org/style-guide

Orthodox: *Saint Vladimir's Seminary Press House Style.* Crestwood, N.Y.: Saint Vladimir's Orthodox Theological Seminary, 2015. http://www.svspress.com/content/files/SVS-Press_House-Style.pdf.

Southern Baptist: *The Southern Seminary Manual of Style.* Louisville: The Southern Baptist Theological Seminary, 2014. http://digital.library.sbts.edu/handle/10392/4041.

STYLE SHEET

A style sheet lists an editor's decisions regarding grammar, spelling, capitalization, punctuation, and word style, especially when those decisions (sometimes requested by the author) run contrary to the publisher's house style or are not covered in standard references. A style sheet also includes any unusual proper names with their correct spelling and capitalization. The style sheet accompanies the book at every stage of editing and proofreading so that everyone is, as the saying goes, "reading off the same page." Other people in the content development process may add to it, but they should not overrule the original style decisions without consulting its creator. The following blank style sheet is appropriate for a typical book.

Style sheet for [Author and Title] ______________________

Editor ______________

Bible version used: __________ Other versions used: __________

Deity pronoun: lc ___ cap ___ Spell out numbers over: 100 ___ 10 ___

Special style notes: ______________________________

Word List:

ABCD	MNOP
EFGH	QRST
IJKL	UVWXYZ

SUBHEADINGS

See "HEADINGS AND SUBHEADINGS."

SUBJUNCTIVE

A verb in the subjunctive mood defines circumstances that are contrary to fact, are as yet unrealized, or express a strong wish or emotion about something yet to occur. The phrase *If I were you …* is one of the most common phrases using the subjunctive. The subjunctive is in contrast to the indicative mood (the most common), which defines circumstances as they exist. A "mandative subjunctive" also exists, which indicates a strong recommendation for something to happen that is not presently happening: as in *I suggest that everyone be quiet now.* The subjunctive is more complex than outlined here, but this discussion at least introduces its appropriateness in various circumstances.

Some editors and proofreaders view themselves as staunch advocates of the subjunctive and often revise authors' verbs accordingly. This impulse should be resisted whenever the subjunctive sounds overly formal or stuffy, which is fairly often the case. Other than a few common phrases (such as *If I were you …* and *If wishes were horses …*), most people seldom use the subjunctive in ordinary speech, which means it is appropriately avoided in most dialogue. For instance, a prizefighter in a novel is far more likely to say the ungrammatical "If I was world champ …" rather than the correct "If I were world champ …" The latter simply sounds out of character. As stated elsewhere (see "EDITORS, TEN COMMANDMENTS FOR"), don't make characters speak like English professors unless they actually are. Similarly, any book written in a colloquial or highly personal voice should probably not use a lot of verbs in the subjunctive mood, unless the author has a particularly erudite tone that demands it. Trust the author's voice in most cases.

What good, then, is the subjunctive? Formal or academic writing can benefit from using the subjunctive, though always take the author's preference into account. It is also useful when precision is demanded and for distinguishing fact from fantasy. For example, *If he is the perpetrator, we'll soon find out* implies that *he* may well be the perpetrator (it may be factual), while *If he were the perpetrator, we would have already found out* implies that *he* has been ruled out as the perpetrator (contrary to fact). Still, the line between the two may be thin at times, and even many educated readers are not aware of the nuances. As a result, some language experts predict the subjunctive in English is destined for extinction.

SUBSIDIARY RIGHTS

The publisher pays the author for the right to publish the first edition of the author's book, but a number of other rights are often included in the author-publisher contract. These subsidiary rights usually include audio rights (CD, audio download), book-club rights, educational rights (curriculum), electronic rights (ebook, download, or related software), film rights, foreign-publication rights, paperback rights, reprint rights, serial rights, theater rights, and translation rights. In most cases, the publisher is in the best position to capitalize on the subsidiary rights in the author's interest, but an author may wish to retain some of those rights when he or she feels more capable of exploiting them.

SUFFIXES

Common suffixes such as *-fold* (as in *tenfold*) and *-like* (as in *Christlike*) are usually set without a hyphen. (See also "*-like*" and "*-ology*.")

SUSPENSION POINT

A suspension point (…) is a punctuation mark that signals a trailing off of or an indecisiveness in thought or speech. It is often used in fictional dialogue as a device to heighten the drama or introspective quality of a character's words. (For the use of the same three-dot character to show an intentional omission in a quotation, see "ELLIPSIS.")

For Trailing Off of Thought. A suspension point is commonly used to signal a trailing off of thought, daydreaming, or hesitation, though its overuse is discouraged. Do not use suspension points to show a sudden interpolation or an interruption of thought or speech; in those cases, use an em dash. (See "EM DASH.")

"I'd be glad to buy another for you if you wanted it replaced … I thought … I don't know … I thought …" His voice died away. [From Charles Williams, *War in Heaven*; to show hesitating speech in fictional dialogue]

It came down on him in an instant: he was … an … unusual … child. [From Flannery O'Connor, "The Turkey," *The Complete Stories*; to show hesitation in narration]

If only people would read the Bible … if only …, thought Frelinghuysen, then God would bring about revival. [To show trailing off of thought]

Niebuhr—Reinhold, that is, not Richard—was a pastor in Detroit in the twenties. [Em dashes, not suspension points, used here for interpolated thought]

Note that a suspension point, unlike an ellipsis, is never to be used with a period, either preceding or following, but it may be used with other punctuation.

Split over Line. A suspension point may fall at the end or the beginning of a typeset line, though most typographers prefer to set a suspension point at the end of a line of type. In any case, it should never stand on a line by itself at the end of a paragraph.

SYLLOGISTIC WORDS AND PHRASES

Words and phrases like *actually, as a result, certainly, clearly, evidently, however, in fact, moreover, obviously, of course, therefore, undoubtedly* are commonly overused by writers who want to give their writing an air of inevitability—of incontrovertible logic—sometimes when no such inevitability has been shown. They can be a verbal sleight of hand. It is the kind of language that Thomas Merton criticized in G. K. Chesterton's writing: "Everything is 'of course' 'quite obviously' etc. etc." (*A Search for Solitude*). Actual logical sequences (*Fact 1 plus Fact 2 leads to Fact 3*) are often stronger when these syllogistic words and phrases are avoided. Readers can be trusted to follow the logic without the pointers, which often feel condescending. Syllogistic words and phrases are sometimes inserted for rhythmic purposes or to help place emphasis on a certain portion of a sentence, but again, it's surprising how often the rhythm and emphasis are improved when such words are deleted. Obviously. (See also "WORDY WORDS.")

SYNDROMES, DISEASES, AND DISORDERS

Do not use the possessive for names of syndromes, diseases, and disorders. Most medical journals and style manuals prefer this as a way to indicate that a particular disease was named for a researcher or scientist and usually not for someone who actually had that disease; for instance, *Charles Bonnet syndrome* rather than *Charles Bonnet's syndrome.* An exception is *Lou Gehrig's disease*, which was named for the patient, though even that is now sometimes referred to as *Lou Gehrig disease*; the more accurate name is *ALS* ("amyotrophic lateral sclerosis"). Other examples that formerly used the possessive: *Alzheimer disease, Asperger disorder, Cushing syndrome, Down syndrome, Hodgkin lymphoma*, and *Parkinson disease.* (See also "*Down syndrome*" and "*syndrome.*")

T

TABLE OF CONTENTS

A *table of contents*, or *contents page*, not only helps the reader find specific parts of a book but also may provide a snapshot outline of the book's content, a fact the author and editor should keep in mind when devising chapter and part titles for nonfiction.

Placement. The table of contents is customarily placed on the next recto after the title page (across from the copyright page) or on the next recto after the dedication page, though the location can shift to accommodate space limitations or special designs. When a table of contents runs to two pages, they may be set on facing pages (a spread), which keeps the reader from having to turn the page to get a one-glance overview of the book.

Elements and Setting. A table of contents lists all the major divisions of a book, usually parts and chapters, along with their numbers and titles. All elements of front and back matter are listed, though they are often shown in a contrasting font (for instance, in italic when the chapter titles are in roman). Usually, the word *chapter* does not appear before the chapter numbers on the contents page. They are superfluous in most cases. In the same way, the word *page* should not appear at the top of the column of page numbers or before the numbers themselves.

Style Considerations. Usually, the table of contents is set in the same type style as the book's text, and the title *Contents* should echo the treatment of the chapter openers. Leader dots were once used to connect chapter titles with their appropriate page numbers but are now considered eyesores, though they can still be used whenever a tight line setting makes it difficult to ascertain which page reference goes with which title.

Unnumbered Part- and Chapter-Title Pages. Since part-title pages as well as full-page chapter-title pages usually do not bear folios (page numbers), how does one reference those pages in a table of contents? The table of contents should not list the page number of the part- or chapter-title page but the number on which the actual text of that part or chapter begins. That may seem odd, but readers are less likely to be confused when this is done. It is counterproductive for the table of contents to suggest that Part One begins on page 15 when the number *15* is not printed on the actual page. It is better for the table of contents to state that Part One begins on page 17, the first page of text.

TERMS OF ENDEARMENT, CAPITALIZATION OF

Lowercase a term of endearment (*honey*, *sweetie*, and so on) unless used regularly as a nickname for that person. (See "CAPITALIZATION: GUIDELINES," section on "*Terms of Endearment.*")

TEXT BREAKS

In writing, the most convenient way to signal the passage of time, a scene change, a new point of view, or some other shift in the narrative is the *text break*. Such shifts are usually not so strong or sudden as to warrant a new chapter or the insertion of a subheading.

In Manuscripts. In preparing a manuscript, the author should use three spaced asterisks (* * *), also called an *asterism*, to show the text break. (See "ASTERISM.") Another form of *asterism* is three pound signs (# # #). An extra line space, or two returns, should not be used, because that space often gets lost or discarded when the data is uploaded to the publisher's computer, since some editing programs delete multiple returns.

Levels of text break. Text breaks are either *primary* (or *strong*) or *secondary* (or *weak*). Primary text breaks indicate a major shift in setting, time frame, or point of view. Secondary text breaks signal less emphatic shifts, such as a point-of-view change within a single scene, the passage of only a short time, or a minor shift in setting. If two levels of text breaks are needed, the author should inform the editor of his or her system of distinguishing between the two (such as an asterism for a primary text break and a small rule line for a minor text break). Never go beyond two levels of text breaks.

At the Tops and Bottoms of Pages. A problem sometimes occurs when only an increased amount of line space (called *extra leading*) is used to signal a text break. If the break falls at the top or bottom of a page, it may not be clear that the scene has shifted. In those instances, a small rule line or asterism is used at the top or bottom of a page (whichever has more space available). It is okay to use an occasional graphic signal in those cases—even if the other text breaks are indicated with only line spaces.

THOUGHTS

In fiction (and some nonfiction), a person's thoughts, imaginings, and silent prayers, when expressed in the first person, are called *unspoken discourse*. (See also "DISEMBODIED VOICES, CONVEYING IN DIALOGUE.")

Roman, Quotation Marks, or Italic? Until recently, unspoken discourse was commonly set in italic. Because of the slightly reduced readability of italic, which can appear even less readable on some electronic devices, authors and publishers are increasingly using roman for thoughts, or even placing them in quotation marks. *CMoS* now recommends both of those methods as an alternative to italic. Since it is usually clear from whose point of view a given scene is written, it should be obvious who is thinking any first-person thoughts within that scene without resorting to italic.

Nevertheless, this manual acknowledges the usefulness of italic type for thoughts. The convention is widely recognized by readers, and many authors prefer it, arguing that it clarifies why a passage has suddenly shifted from the third person to the first. Also, quotation marks strongly suggest speech, even when such signaling phrases as *he thought* are present; it is as if the character, while alone, is speaking thoughts aloud, which is often not the writer's intent.

The choice of which style to use is a matter of author preference in consultation with the editor. As with nearly every style issue, the question is: What will be most easily understood by the greatest number of readers? Also note that a niggling consistency need not be maintained throughout the book. Even when italic is used for thoughts in some places, quotation marks may be more appropriate in others, for instance, when the thoughts have an identifiably spoken tone:

He kept lecturing himself, "Don't be such a dunce!"

First Word Capitalized. Whether using roman, quotation marks, or italic, a capital letter begins the first word of the unspoken discourse itself if the word falls in the middle of a sentence.

She wondered, Why didn't he tell me this before?
She wondered, "Why didn't he tell me this before?"
She wondered, *Why did he not tell me this before?*

Avoid Redundancy. Finally, don't use *to himself* or *to herself* with the verb *to think*. It is redundant to write, *She thought to herself* . . . No other person exists to whom one can think.

TIMES AND DATES

Numerals versus Spelling Out. The time of day is usually set in numerals (as in *Sunday school begins at 9:30*). Numerals are especially helpful whenever a precise time is given (*7:21*) or when ***a.m.*** or ***p.m.*** is used (*7:21 a.m.*). The time of day may be spelled out when the term *o'clock* is used, which is always with whole-hour references (as in ***he arrived at two o'clock***, but never *two thirty o'clock*). The time of day is also spelled out with such conventional idioms of time as ***half past***, ***quarter past***, ***quarter to*** (as in ***half past ten*** and ***quarter to twelve***). The same guidelines apply to specifying times of day in fictional dialogue.

If, for whatever reason, a precise time needs to be spelled out, do not place a hyphen between the hour and minute designations (for example, *two thirty*, not *two-thirty*); this is to avoid confusion with times of day in which the minute designation is already hyphenated (for example, *two thirty-two* rather than *two-thirty-two*).

"a.m." and "p.m." This manual recommends setting the abbreviations *a.m.* and *p.m.* in lowercase with periods. Small caps were formerly used but are no longer recommended. (See "*a.m., p.m., noon, midnight*" for more detail.)

Daylight-Saving Time. This term is hyphenated, with no *s* at the end of the word *saving*. As a phrase, lowercase it: *daylight-saving time*.

Eras. References to millennia, centuries, and decades are spelled out and lowercase: *the second millennium BC, the sixteenth century* (rather than *the 16th century*), *the eighties and nineties*. If numerals are used for centuries or decades, add an *s* with no apostrophe: *the 1600s, the 1990s*.

Abbreviated Years. In informal contexts, a year designation may be abbreviated by using an apostrophe, for instance, with automobiles and graduating classes: *a '57 Studebaker, the class of '19*.

Months. Do not abbreviate the names of the months in text, though they may be abbreviated in references or charts: *Jan., Feb., Mar., Apr., May, June, July, Aug., Sept., Oct., Nov., Dec.*

Days of the Week. Do not abbreviate days of the week in text. If a special situation, such as a chart or list, calls for an abbreviation, use: *Sun., Mon., Tues., Wed., Thurs., Fri., Sat.*

Seasons. Lowercase the names for the seasons, solstices, and equinoxes: such as *spring, summer solstice, fall* (or *autumn*) *equinox, a winter festival, a harvest fair*. Capitalize names for seasons when they appear in periodical references: *James Galvin, "River Edged with Ice,"* Orion 21, *Winter 2002*.

BC and AD. The abbreviations *BC* and *AD* are set in capital letters with no periods (though the small-cap style may still be used when appropriate). Place *AD* before a specific year reference, though it should follow a reference to an entire century. The abbreviation *BC* always comes after a century or year reference. (See "*BC, AD*.")

BCE and CE. In recent years the abbreviations *BCE* ("before the Common Era") and *CE* ("Common Era") have gained currency. (See "*BCE/CE*" for details.)

Calculating Centuries and Millennia before Christ. No one disputes that the eighteenth century is roughly the 1700s (1701 to 1800). This applies to centuries and millennia before Christ as well. For instance, the eighth century BCE (when Rome is said to have been founded, when Homer wrote *The Iliad* and *The Odyssey*, and when the Assyrians conquered Israel) ran from the year 800 BCE to the year 701 BCE (that is, roughly the 700s BCE).

AH. In Islamic scholarship, *AH* (*anno Hegirae*, "in the year of the Hegira") designates the era after Muhammad's flight from Mecca in 622 CE.

Rendering Dates in Text. This manual recommends the "month day, year" style of rendering dates (the month and day are separated from the year by a comma): for instance, *On May 30, 1934, the Barmen Declaration was signed.* Another common ordering is the "day month year" style, which is common in many scholarly and reference works and is also the preferred style in the UK. Note that no commas are used in this style: *Wesley's conversion took place on 24 May 1738.* When necessary, the number of the day may be spelled out as an ordinal: *On the first day of September 1670, William Penn's trial began.*

Ordinals. In text, do not use the ordinal abbreviations *st*, *nd*, *rd*, or *th* with numerals after month designations: *December 25 was etched in his memory* rather than *December 25th was etched in his memory.* If an ordinal must be used, spell it out: *December twenty-fifth was etched in his memory.* An exception is made for some street names; spell out numbered street names under eleven (*Fourth Street*, *Fifth Avenue*), but use ordinal numerals for street names eleven and higher (*19th Street*, *39th Avenue*). (See "ADDRESSES, STREET.")

Month and Year Only. Do not use an intervening comma when a month or season designation alone is followed by a year: *Booth's East End tent ministry began in July 1865* or *It all began in winter 1941.*

Web Style. In web copy, never use numeral abbreviations for dates, like *7-4-04*, because international readers will not know whether that is *July 4, 2004* or *April 7, 2004.* Always spell out the month.

Old Style and New Style. Some historical references distinguish between dates from the Julian calendar (established in 46 BCE) and those from the Gregorian, or Western, calendar by using the abbreviations *OS* (Old Style) and *NS* (New Style) respectively. Unless otherwise specified, all modern references to historical dates are in New Style. The Gregorian calendar was first officially established in 1582, though many Western countries did not adopt it until many years later. The Eastern Orthodox Church still dates its holy days by the older Julian calendar.

Dates in and around the year in which a specific country adopted the

Gregorian calendar should be checked carefully, especially when precise dating is essential. For instance, when Great Britain and the American colonies adopted the New Style system in 1752, two important changes took place. First, eleven days were dropped from the calendar (the day after September 2, 1752, was considered September 14, 1752). Also, January 1 was officially considered the first day of 1752, whereas before that time March 25 (the Annunciation) had traditionally been regarded as New Year's Day in England. This is further complicated by the fact that many people at that time already considered January 1 to be New Year's Day. In referring to the years immediately before 1752 in English history, dates between January 1 and March 24 are sometimes listed with a double-year designation, with a solidus between the elided year numerals. Again, if no such designation is given, it can usually be assumed that a New Style date is being referenced.

The storm at sea that led to Newton's conversion took place on March 21, 1748 NS (March 10, OS).

The service took place on Epiphany, January 6, 1720/21.

When Does a Day Actually Begin? Although most modern cultures consider one second after midnight to be the start of the new day, both Jewish and Christian traditions have informally regarded sunset as the start of the new day, which is why the eve of feast days are celebrated; they are the beginning of the holy day itself. So, Christmas Eve, Halloween (the eve of All Saints' Day), John Keats's famous "Eve of Saint Agnes," Twelfth Night (the eve of Epiphany), and other eves are singled out for special celebration because they mark the beginning of the holiday. Inherent in this Jewish and Christian tradition, perhaps, is the idea that God brings light out of darkness, so that daylight always follows night, a symbol of hope and new life. Curiously, the ancient Babylonians, Syrians, and Persians began the day at sunrise, while the ancient Egyptians began the day at noon. (See also "HOURS, BIBLICAL" and "*watches of the night.*")

Quaker System of Dating. The founders of the Religious Society of Friends (the Quakers) felt that the names of the weekdays and months, rooted as they are in pagan mythology, should be avoided. In old-style Quaker dating, the days and months, referred to numerically, are spelled out and lowercase (*first month*, *second month*, and so on). This system is not used today but is common in Quaker writings of the past. Also note that before 1752 the Society of Friends considered March the first month of the year.

the twelfth day of the first month, 1814 [January 12, 1814, New Style]

Nineteen-year-old George Fox left home on the ninth day, the seventh month, 1643. [September 9, 1643, Old Style]

TITLE CHANGES

If the title of a book changes in a later reprint or edition (regardless of who the original publisher was), the publisher is required by the Federal Trade Commission (FTC) to give a notice of the original title on both the front cover (or jacket) and the title page of the book. It should be displayed in a relatively prominent manner so that it may readily come to the attention of the reader. The phrasing of such a notice is up to the publisher, but any of the following are appropriate:

Originally published in [YEAR] under the title ...
Previously published as ...
Originally published in [COUNTRY] under the title ...

The FTC also mandates that such notice of the change of a title be mentioned in promotional copy (meaning primarily catalog copy) for the book. Such change-of-title notice is not required in consumer or trade advertising unless it would benefit the marketing of the book to mention the original title. If a foreign work is appearing in English for the first time, the FTC regulations do not require that the original foreign-language title appear on the cover or title page, though it is a courtesy to mention the original title on the copyright page.

TITLE PAGE

A book's *title page* (which is the third page in most print books) can vary widely according to the design. At the designer's discretion, it can even be spread across two facing pages. A title page usually carries these elements:

1. The complete title and subtitle
2. The name(s) of the author(s), as well as the name(s) of any translators, compilers, series editors, etc.
3. Whether the book is an unnumbered revised edition or a newly numbered revised edition
4. Whether the book was previously published with another title
5. The name of the publisher(s) and sometimes the publisher's city or full address
6. The publisher's logo

Sometimes other elements are also appropriate, such as an epigraph, especially if it is closely related to the title, or such short taglines as "Author of the Bestselling ..." or "Winner of the ____ Award." No running head or folio should appear on the title page. Designers often strive for typographic simplicity, elegance, and cleanness on a title page because it is, in a sense, a formal invitation to the book. Typographically, it may echo the design of the cover but may be independent of the cover design as well.

TITLES, MILITARY

See "MILITARY TITLES."

TITLES OF COMMON TEXTS OF THE WORLD'S RELIGIONS

Like the Bible, the names of the most common sacred and venerated texts of the world's religions are set in roman type. As with the Bible, specific editions of such works are italicized as ordinary book titles: for instance, *The Essential Chuang Tzu* or *The Tao Te Ching: An Illustrated Journey*.

Unless an author has a different preference, use the unaccented and unhyphenated forms of such titles (*Tao Te Ching*, rather than *Tao Tê Ching* or *Tao-te-ching*, for instance). Although pinyin is recommended for most Chinese words, an exception is made for Chinese authors and religious works whose names are already long established in an anglicized form; for instance, *Tao Te Ching* rather than *Daodejing* (pinyin) and its legendary author *Lao Tzu* rather than *Laozi* (pinyin). (See "CHINESE TRANSLITERATION.") Though once again, honor the author's preference.

Here is a list of the most common titles in their preferred anglicized forms. Some alternate titles are also given.

Akaranga Sutra—Jain

Anelects, the—Confucian; also called the Lun Yü

Atharva-Veda, the—Hindu; part of the Samhita, or Vedas

Avesta, the—Zoroastrian; sometimes wrongly called the Zend-Avesta

Bhagavad-Gita, the—Hindu; part of the Mahabharata

Blue Cliff Record, the—Zen Buddhist

Book of Changes, the—Confucian; also called the I Ching, or the Classic of Changes; one of the Five Classics

Book of Filial Piety, the—Confucian; also called the Hsiao Ching

Book of History, the—Confucian; also called the Shuh Ching; one of the Five Classics

Book of Mormon, the—Mormon; subtitled Another Testament of Jesus Christ

Book of Rites, the—Confucian; also called the Li Ki; one of the Five Classics

Book of Songs, the—Confucian; also called the Shih Ching; its two parts are two of the Five Classics

Book of the Dead, the—Buddhist; also called the Tibetan Book of the Dead

Brahmanas, the—Hindu

Chuang Tzu—Taoist; the writings of Chuang Tzu

Dhammapada, the—Buddhist

Doctrine of the Mean, the—Confucian; also called the Chung Yung

Doctrines and Covenants, the—Mormon

Egyptian Book of the Dead, the—Egyptian; also known as the Papyrus of Ani

Five Classics, the—Confucian

Gemara, the—Jewish; part of the Talmud; a commentary on the Mishnah

Granth Sahib—Sikh; or Shree Guru Granth Sahib

Great Learning, the—Confucian; also called the Ta Hsueh

Hadith, the—Muslim; usually capitalized, even though it is an oral body of work rather than a written document

Haggadah, the—Jewish; also spelled Aggada; the legends and stories section of the Talmud

Halakah, the—Jewish; the legal section of the Talmud

I Ching, the—Confucian; also called the Book, or Classic, of Changes; one of the Five Classics

Inner Chapters, the—Taoist; the oldest section of the writings of Chuang Tzu

Kalpa Sutra—Jain

Kojiki, the—Shinto

Koran, the—Muslim; see *"Qu'ran, the"* in this list

Lao Tzu—Taoist; the Tao Te Ching and other writings attributed to Lao Tzu

Lotus Sutra, the—Mahayana Buddhist

Mahabharata, the—Hindu

Mishnah, the—Jewish; part of the Talmud

Nihongi, the—Shinto

Papyrus of Ani, the—Egyptian; also known as the Egyptian Book of the Dead

Pearl of Great Price—Mormon

Pentateuch, the—Jewish

Qur'an, the—Muslim; also spelled Koran and Quran, though this manual recommends Qur'an as the preferred English form; see *"Qur'an, Koran"* for discussion

Rig-Veda, the—Hindu; part of the Samhita, or Vedas

Sama-Veda, the—Hindu; part of the Samhita, or Vedas

Samhita, the—Hindu; the four Vedas together

Spring and Autumn Annals, the—Confucian; one of the Five Classics

Sunna, the—Muslim; usually capitalized, even though it is an oral body of work rather than a written document

Sun Tzu—Taoist; also called the Art of War

sutra—Buddhist; generic; capitalized only if a specific one is named

Talmud, the—Jewish

Tanak, the—Jewish

Tao Te Ching, the—Taoist; attributed to Lao Tzu

Torah, the—Jewish

Tripitaka, the—Buddhist
Upanishads, the—Hindu; the final portion of the Vedas
Veda, or Vedas, the—Hindu
Vimalakirti Sutra, the—Mahayana Buddhist
Wen Tzu, the—Taoist; later writings attributed to Lao Tzu
Yajur-Veda, the—Hindu; part of the Samhita, or Vedas

TRADEMARK SYMBOL

See "BRAND NAMES, TRADEMARKED," section on "*Trademark Symbol.*"

TRIM SIZES, STANDARD, FOR PRINT BOOKS

Although books can be trimmed to almost any dimension, a few sizes are standard in the book industry. These tend to be the least expensive to produce since many printers have preset their presses and production equipment to handle them. These trim sizes apply to print-on-demand books as well. The following chart shows the common book-trim sizes in the US and their common descriptions and purposes.

Common US Trim Sizes

Width x Height (in inches)	Type of Book
4-3/16 x 6-3/4	mass-market size; pocketbooks
5-5/16 x 8	standard trade-paper size; small softcovers and hardcovers; some gift books and small novels
5-3/8 x 8-3/8	trade-paper and hardcover size; standard hardcover fiction size
6 x 9	blockbuster hardcover fiction and some lengthy nonfiction; history
7-3/8 x 9-1/8	slightly larger than average book; workbooks, "lifestyle" books; some references and textbooks
8 x 9-1/8	large "square" format; "coffee table books," oversize

TRINITY, NAMES FOR THE

Just as names for persons of the Trinity are capitalized (see "TRINITY, NAMES FOR PERSONS OF THE"), so too are names for the Trinity itself, such as *the Trinity, the Holy Trinity*, or *the Three in One*. Lowercase them whenever they seem primarily descriptive, such as *our triune God* or *the three persons of the Trinity.*

TRINITY, NAMES FOR PERSONS OF THE

When a word or phrase is used as a name for one of the persons of the Trinity, capitalize it. Be especially sensitive to phrases that seem as if they could be names but are really descriptors, which are lowercase. For instance, *Holy God* is a name when God is addressed as such, but the *holy* in *he is a holy God* is a descriptor and therefore lowercase. Also lowercase the generic phrases *the first person of the Trinity* (though *Trinity* is always capitalized), and so on. Here are some common examples of names for persons of the Trinity with some common descriptive phrases in parentheses:

God

Creator, the (*but* the creator of the universe)
Deity, the
Designer, the
Divine Providence
Divinity, the
El
El Shaddai
Father
God Almighty (*but* he is an almighty God)
Holy God (*but* he is a holy God)
Jehovah
Lord Almighty, the
Lord of Hosts, the
Most High, the
One, the (*but* the one God of creation)
Providence (*but* the providence of God)
Sovereign Lord, the (*but* he is a sovereign Lord)
Yahweh

Jesus

Bread of Life, the
Bridegroom, the
Door, the
Galilean, the
God's Son
Good Shepherd, the
High Priest, the
Immanuel
Incarnate Word of God
Intercessor, the
King of Kings
Lamb of God, the
Light of the World, the
Logos (Christ)
Lord of Lords
Lord's Anointed, the (*but* the Lord's anointed Savior)
Man of Sorrows, the
Messiah, the
Only Begotten, the (*but* the only begotten of God)
Passover Lamb, the
Prince of Peace, the
Promised One, the
Redeemer, the
Rock, the
Son, the
Son of God, the
Son of Man, the
Suffering Servant
Way, the
Word, the

The Holy Spirit

Advocate, the	Holy Ghost, the	Spirit of Life, the
Comforter, the	Intercessor, the	Spirit of Truth, the
Counselor, the	Mediator, the	Teacher, the
Eternal Spirit, the	Paraclete, the	
God's Spirit	Spirit, the	

TYPOGRAPHIC SYMBOLS, COMMON

The following typographic symbols are common online and in contemporary publishing. Although some seem antiquated, their presence persists in most type fonts. Some, like @, sometimes called the *at symbol*, have found a new life in digital communication. In the following list, an asterisk means that a more complete discussion can be found in this manual under a separate heading for that symbol. (Also see individual punctuation marks: "COMMA," "PERIOD," and so on.)

Symbol	Name	Function
&	ampersand* (also called the *tironian sign*)	sign for "and"; a typographic form of the Latin *et*
§	section(al) mark or symbol	shows the beginning of a section and is also the fourth footnote symbol; it is a stylized double *S*, for the Latin *signum sectionis* ("sign of a section"); also called a *hurricane* or a *double s*
☞ or ☝	fist (or *index hand*)	printer's symbol meaning "note this"
¶	paragraph symbol (also called *blind P* or *pilcrow*)	shows the beginning (or end) of a paragraph and is the sixth footnote symbol; also denotes paragraphing in the KJV
( )	parentheses* (or *round brackets*)	to show parenthetical thought or statement
[ ]	brackets* (or *square brackets*)	to show parenthetical statement within parentheses
{ }	braces* (or *curly brackets*)	to group consecutive lines together
*	asterisk*	the first footnote symbol; also used for itemizing elements in a list, similar to a bullet
* * * *or* # # #	asterism* (or *triple asterisk*)	to show minor breaks in text
✓	check mark	to note special items in a list or to fill in selected boxes (as on ballots); verb is *to checkmark*

Symbol	Name	Function
†	dagger (or *obelisk*)	the second footnote symbol
‡	double dagger	the third footnote symbol
‖	parallel lines	the fifth footnote symbol
#	number sign (called *pound sign, hashtag,* or *octothorp*)	still occasionally used for numbers, but now mostly used as a select key on phone keypads and a grouping tag for social networking; also used as the seventh footnote symbol
$	dollar sign	US currency
€	euro sign	European currency
¥	yen sign	Japanese currency
%	percent* sign	for percentages; abbreviation of the Latin *per centum* ("per one hundred"); used in scientific or statistical contexts
/	solidus*	see "Solidus (Forward Slash)"
<	less-than sign	mathematical
=	equal sign	mathematical
>	greater-than sign	mathematical
+	plus sign	mathematical
−	minus sign	mathematical
÷	divide, or division, sign	mathematical
×	times sign	mathematical or to show dimensions
±	plus-or-minus sign	mathematical
^	caret*	for insertions in copy intended for print
@	the *at* symbol	formerly used as an abbreviation to mean *at* or *approximately*; now almost exclusively used to designate an email address
\	back slash	used primarily in computer programming and URLs
™	trademark symbol	shows that a trademark is legally protected
©	copyright symbol	shows that material is legally copyrighted
®	registered trademark symbol	shows that a trademark is legally registered

U

UK STYLE

In *The Canterville Ghost* (1882), Oscar Wilde wrote that England has "everything in common with America … except, of course, language." The main difficulties are spelling and vocabulary. The first Harry Potter book, for example, contained more than seventy words that had to be "translated" into American for the US edition, beginning with changing the title from *Harry Potter and the Philosopher's Stone* to *Harry Potter and the Sorcerer's Stone*, since most American readers would be unfamiliar with the legend of the philosopher's stone.

Still, publishers often export books across the Atlantic without any "translation" at all. For example, Americans usually expect British detective novels to *read* like British detective novels, unfamiliar words and all. So, while it is a mistake to overemphasize the differences, a few guidelines may help editors navigate the contrasts between American English and British English (the latter term is disliked by many in England, by the way, who prefer the term *standard English*). At the end is a short vocabulary list that will offer a few common words in both styles. (See also "AMERICANIZING UK PUBLICATIONS" and "MID-ATLANTIC STYLE.")

Spelling. Many spelling differences between common British and American words can be attributed to lexicographer Noah Webster (1758–1843) and his *American Dictionary of the English Language* (1828). Some of those differences can be loosely categorized as follows:

Type	British	American
our / -or endings	colour, honour, labour	color, honor, labor
re / -er endings	centre, spectre, theatre	center, specter, theater
ce / -se endings	defence, offence	defense, offense
ize / -ise endings	analyse, criticise, paralyse (though *-ize* endings are gaining ground in the UK)	analyze, criticize, paralyze
double l / single l	counsellor, jeweller, travelling	counselor, jeweler, traveling
ae and *oe*	anaemia, anaesthetic, oedema	anemia, anesthetic, edema
augh and *ough*	draught, plough	draft, plow

Type	British	American
t / *-ed* for some verbs	burnt, dreamt, learnt	burned, dreamed, learned
xion	connexion, inflexion	connection, inflection

Exceptions exist to the patterns in the preceding list. The word *glamour* is *not* spelled *glamor* in the US, for example, and American orthography has retained such British *-re* words as *acre*, *euchre*, *lucre*, and *mediocre*. Also note the British are increasingly using *-ize* endings for such words as *organize* and *agonize*, and the Americans have never discarded the British *-ise* ending in such shared words as *advertise*, *chastise*, *compromise*, *enterprise*, *exercise*, and *supervise*. The British have also largely shifted toward the American *inflection*, *connection*, and so on.

American Episcopalians spell the word for morning prayer *matins*, while those in the Church of England spell it *mattins*. (See "HOURS, CANONICAL.") For religious publishers, probably the most noticeable spelling difference is the word *Saviour*, which is usually spelled *Savior* in the US, though many writers, basing their preference on the KJV, use *Saviour* when referring to Christ but revert to *savior* for all other uses. (See "*Savior, Saviour*.") Also note the difference between *baptise* (UK) and *baptize* (US).

Other spelling differences follow no clear pattern. In general these pose no cross-cultural confusion because most American readers have little trouble comprehending *catalogue*, *cheque*, *enquire*, *fulfil*, *gaol* (for "jail"), *kerb* (for "curb"), *mum* (for "mom"), *programme*, *skilful*, *storey*, *tyre*, *waggon*, and others.

The words *towards* and *afterwards* tend to be the forms preferred in the UK, whereas both those forms and *toward* and *afterward* are used interchangeably in the US. In either case, maintain consistency. (See "*toward, towards*.")

Collective Nouns with Plural Verbs. Although not always consistent, the British tend to view organizations and other collective nouns for groups of people as plural, whereas Americans usually view them as singular.

> The corporation are braced for a takeover. [British, though sometimes *is*]
> The government have issued checks. [British, though sometimes *has*]

The Serial Comma. The British often drop the serial comma—called the *Oxford comma*—in lists.

A Spaced En Dash in Place of an Em Dash. It is common in UK typography to use an en dash, with spaces on either side, where American typography uses the em dash.

Ellipses and Suspension Points. British publishers do not use an ellipsis or suspension points in combination with a period and always set a word space (or 3-to-em space) between those and any adjacent punctuation mark. This contrasts with the American style, which sometimes uses a period with an ellipsis, though not with suspension points, and will close both of those up to other punctuation. (See also "ELLIPSIS" and "SUSPENSION POINT.")

Hyphens for Some Prefixes. When a prefix ends with the same letter as the word it precedes, the British insert a clarifying hyphen: *co-ordinate, no-one, pre-eminent, re-evaluate.* This was often done in the US until the mid-twentieth century, at which time such words began to be run together (like *coordinate*) or separated (like *no one*).

Single Quotation Marks for Quotes. The British often use single quotation marks (called *inverted commas*) where Americans would use double quotation marks, most commonly in direct quotations, dialogue, and some titles. The British also use single quotation marks for primary quotations and double quotation marks for "quotes within quotes." Still, some UK publishers use the US system as a matter of house style

Punctuation with Quotation Marks. In UK style as in US style, if a complete sentence is set in quotation marks, the periods (called *full stops*) and commas are placed inside the quotations marks. Likewise, in dialogue, the punctuation goes with the spoken words in quotes. When a fragmentary quotation or a single quoted word is run into a larger context, the punctuation is set outside the quotation marks:

> The publisher said that 'Adrian is our best-selling author.' [Full quote]
> The publisher said, 'Adrian is our best-selling author.' [Dialogue]
> The publisher said that Adrian is 'our best-selling author'. [Fragmentary quote]
> The publisher referred to it as a 'best-seller'. [Single word]

Fewer Periods in Abbreviations. The British rule is not to use a period in abbreviations when only internal letters are eliminated (like *Ltd, Mr, Mrs, Revd*). Like the Americans, the British retain the periods when the final letters of the word have been cut off (such as *Corp., Gen., Inc., Prof., Rev.*) and for personal initials (such as *C. S. Lewis* and *J. R. R. Tolkien*). UK stylists, like those in the US, avoid periods in abbreviations of organizations, famous people referred to by initial, terms of scholarship, units of measurement, acronyms, and computer-related terms; but in addition, the British also tend to eliminate the periods in time designations (such as AM and PM) and scholarly abbreviations (such as *eg, ie, cf*).

Authorized Version. The Bible issued by King James's printers in 1611 is called the Authorized Version in the British Isles and the King James Version in the US. A strict adherence to these uses is not essential since readers in each country are likely to be familiar with the other's terminology, but the difference is usually observed whenever possible.

Books of the Bible. The names of books of the Bible are nearly always spelled out in British publications rather than abbreviated.

Periods in Expressions of Time. The British use a period (*full stop*) rather than a colon in expressions of time: *3.30 am*, for instance. Also, they tend to drop the zero (*nought* or *cipher*) before a single-digit designation for minutes: *7.5 pm* rather than the American *7:05 p.m.* Also note the British use the twenty-four-hour clock more often than Americans do: *15.00* rather than *3:00 p.m.* Also note the British preference for *AM* and *PM* (small caps) in contrast to the American *a.m.* and *p.m.*

Dates. The British use the European style of referring to specific dates by giving the day of the month first, followed by the month and the year with no internal commas: *12 February 1953.*

Footnotes. The British system of academic footnoting uses superior numbers, with no periods, for both the callout and the bottom-of-page reference. The style of both the Oxford and Cambridge Universities presses is to begin the numbering of footnotes with *1* on every new page, unlike the US system that begins the numbering with *1* with every new chapter or, more rarely, sometimes numbering consecutively throughout the book. Alternatively, if footnotes are relatively few, the asterisk-dagger system is used as in American publishing. (See also "NOTES," section on "*Asterisk-Dagger System*" and "FOOTNOTE SYMBOLS, BOTTOM-OF-PAGE.")

British Numbering. In 1975, because of confusion in the financial industry, the British abandoned their old names for large numbers and adapted the American system. Nearly all modern references are the same in the two cultures. Before 1975, American and British terms were identical through the millions but differed in numbers more than a million as follows:

British	American
one milliard, or one thousand million	one billion
one billion	one trillion
one thousand billion	one quadrillion
one trillion	one quintillion
one thousand trillion	one sextillion
one quadrillion	one septillion
one thousand quadrillion	one octillion

one quintillion
one thousand quintillion

one nonillion
one decillion

Zero. The American *zero* (*0*) is referred to as a *cipher* or *nought* in the UK.

Vocabulary. Many common objects have different names in the UK and the US. While many Americans know that the British *lift* is the American *elevator*, fewer realize that the British *vest* is not part of a three-piece suit, but what would be called an *undershirt* in the US. If a British play is a *bomb*, it is a success, while an American theatrical *bomb* is a failure. Entire dictionaries have been compiled to list the differences between the two vocabularies (see Norman W. Schur's *British English A to Zed* [2007]), and their entries run into the thousands. The following list contains only a few of the most common.

UK	US
aerodrome	airfield
berk	jerk
biro	ball-point pen
biscuit	cracker or cookie
bonnet	hood (car)
boot	trunk (car)
brackets	parentheses
candy floss	cotton candy
caravan	trailer
car-boot sale	trunk sale
carriage	railroad car
chemist	druggist
chips	French fries
clothes-peg	clothespin
cookery book	cookbook
crisps	chips
drawing pin, push-pin	thumbtack
dustbin	garbage can
engage	hire
first floor	second floor
flyover	overpass
football	soccer
Girl Guide	Girl Scout
headlamp	headlight
interval	intermission
inverted commas	quotation marks
jumble sale	rummage sale
knock-on effect	side effect
larder	pantry
lead, or flex	electric cord
lift	elevator
loo	toilet
lorry	truck
mince	ground meat
motorway	highway
nappy	diaper
overdraft	bank loan
petrol	gasoline
plaster	bandage
post	mail (verb)
pram	baby carriage
queue	line (of people)
return	round trip
roadway	pavement
charity	junk shop
spanner	wrench
tarmac	asphalt
tea towel	dish towel
tinned	canned
torch	flashlight
tram	streetcar
trolley	shopping cart
tube	subway

turn-ups ....cuffs
underground ....subway
vacuum flask.....thermos bottle
vest ....undershirt
Wellingtons......rubber boots
windscreen......windshield
winge............whine or cry
zed..............the letter z (zee)

UNSPOKEN DISCOURSE

See "THOUGHTS."

UNSPOKEN PRAYERS

See "PRAYERS" and "THOUGHTS."

V

VOCATIVE O, THE

See "*oh, O.*"

W

WARNING NOTICE

The *warning notice*, usually included on a book's copyright page, is a statement that notifies the reader that reproducing material from the book, in whatever form, is illegal. Its inclusion is by no means mandatory since the current copyright laws are sufficient to protect the book. Still, its use is recommended. (See "COPYRIGHT PAGE.")

The following formula is standard throughout the publishing industry:

> All rights reserved. No part of this publication may be reproduced, stored in a retrieval system, or transmitted in any form or by any means—electronic, mechanical, photocopy, recording, or any other—except for brief quotations in printed reviews, without the prior permission of the publisher.

Notice that the all-rights-reserved notice is often incorporated into the warning notice. (See "ALL-RIGHTS-RESERVED NOTICE.")

If space is a problem, a shorter warning notice may be used:

> No part of this publication may be reproduced, stored in a retrieval system, or transmitted in any form or by any means except for brief quotations in printed reviews without the prior permission of the publisher.

Or the even simpler notice:

> No part of this publication may be reproduced without the prior permission of the publisher.

Publisher's Address. Whenever a warning notice is given, the company's address should appear on the copyright page so readers and researchers will know where to write if they wish to obtain permission to quote or reproduce portions of the text legally.

Permission to Copy. For some books, the publisher may want to qualify the warning notice so that the copying of certain pages is allowed in clearly defined situations. This is done by adding a permission-to-copy notice to the warning notice. (See "PERMISSION-TO-COPY NOTICE.")

WEBSITE NAMES

Names of websites are set in roman (for instance, Amazon.com, Bible Gateway, and Wikipedia) in both references and ordinary text. Names of online journals, magazines, news sites, and periodicals are set in italic (for example, *Salon.com*, *Lark News.com*, or *the Huffington Post*) as print periodicals are. Admittedly, differentiating between website and journal names can be difficult.

A domain extension (*.com*, *.edu*, *.org*, and so on) may or may not be included according to the website's own preference (check the masthead on the homepage) as well as common usage; for example, both *Amazon* and *Amazon.com* are acceptable. If it is important for the reader to know that a less-familiar name is a website, then the domain extension may be inserted as a hint.

WEB STYLE

Here is a short guide for styling text on webpages.

Keep It Short. Keep sentences short and punchy, and break up the text with subheads. Keep web articles and personal blog entries between about three hundred and a thousand words.

Avoid Culture-Specific References. Remember that the web reaches a vast international readership.

Do Not Use Small Caps. Some web-management systems don't allow for small caps. Set such words as *Lord* and *I Am* in all caps instead: *LORD* and *I AM*.

Use Informal Style. Use informal style on webpages rather than formal. For instance: allow contractions and use general abbreviations for Bible books.

Spell Out Abbreviations. Because of the web's global reach, many abbreviations will not be familiar to international web users. Spell out abbreviations on first use.

Use Boldface for Emphasis. As long as it conforms to the overall design of the webpage, bold can be used for emphasis. Italic can often look weak and deemphasized onscreen.

Bullets Need Not Be Indented or Followed by a Space. Because of the limitations of some web-management systems, allow bullets to set in the most convenient manner, with or without a space after the bullet.

En Dash. Use a hyphen in place of an en dash whenever a true en dash is not available.

Em Dash. Two hyphens may be used in place of an em dash whenever a true em dash is not available.

Ellipses. Avoid ellipses if possible. The dots sometimes break over lines of text since webpages usually set ellipses as three word-spaced periods. When an ellipsis is needed, set it as three periods with nonbreaking spaces before the first one and between the second and third. That keeps the dots together.

Minimize Lists of Source Materials. Provide source lists only when necessary, with hyperlinks as appropriate.

Use Numerals for All Numbers 10 and Higher.

Spell Out Months in Dates. Never use all-numeral date indicators. Some international readers assume that 7-10-15 is July 10, 2015, while others assume it's October 7, 2015.

Include Such Prefixes as http:// and www. in All Hyperlinks.

Web Typography. Web typography differs from print and ebook typography in some significant ways:

- Widows are inapplicable and orphans unavoidable.
- End-of-line word division usually does not occur on the web.
- Web text is usually ragged right.
- Webpages often use internal and external links in place of citations.
- Paragraphs are often block style and distinguished by line spaces rather than indents.

WIDOWS AND ORPHANS (TYPOGRAPHIC)

As typographic terms, *widow* and *orphan* are often used interchangeably, though they describe distinct situations.

Widows. A *widow* is any last line of a paragraph that is allowed to stand apart from the rest of the paragraph, for instance, on the top of the following page or after an inserted graphic. Most typesetting systems are programmed with preset widow conditions that calculate the lines per page so that a single line is not allowed to carry over to the next page by itself.

The term *widow* also applies to the ends of chapters where one or two lines stand alone on an otherwise blank page. Three- or four-line widows are strongly discouraged but may be allowed if no other typographic solution is available. Ideally, the last page of any chapter should have at least five lines of type.

Note that the first line of a paragraph that appears by itself at the bottom of a page (with the rest of the paragraph appearing on the following page) is not considered a widow and is acceptable in standard typesetting.

Orphans. A typographic *orphan* is a broken word or a short word of four or fewer characters that is allowed to stand alone on a line by itself at the end of a paragraph. Usually a typographic fix exists, either by reducing the word space in the previous lines to bring the short word up or by expanding the word spaces to force more characters down to the last line. In most cases, avoid reducing (kerning) or expanding the letter space in the previous line or lines, since the resulting appearance usually draws more attention to itself than the original orphan. As a last resort, the editor has the option of editing out a nonessential word or rewriting a portion of the paragraph to eliminate the problem. This should be done with caution and only when the orphan is likely to be a distraction. Some editors and book designers have an informal rule that orphans need only be fixed when the orphan is smaller than the paragraph indentation at the beginning of the next line, giving the impression of an extra line space between the paragraphs. (See "RIVER, TYPOGRAPHIC.")

WORD CHOICE, TEN TIPS

1. *Write the Way You Speak (at Your Best).* Always begin there. Use the words and syntax that are natural to you. After that, revise your writing by availing yourself of the standard tools—structure, organization, pacing, and so on.
2. *Put Yourself in the Reader's Place.* That is, choose words that will resonate with your ideal reader. Each word needs to be familiar to that readership as well as evocative and precise.
3. *Read Aloud What You Write.* Gerard Manley Hopkins once wrote, "Read it with the ears" (*Selected Poems*). Weak word choices and garbled syntax become evident when you read your own writing aloud during revision. This is the best self-editing tip ever devised.
4. *Avoid "Thesaurus-itis" and Keep It Simple.* Use a thesaurus the way you would dress for church—that is, neatly but avoiding

ostentation. When an inexperienced writer throws in words like *ochlocracy* to mean "mob rule" or *gracility* to mean "elegance," readers instinctively know the writer has been trolling through *Roget's* in a misguided effort to dazzle the reader. Avoid fancy ways of saying simple things. Don't write "implement" when "tool" will do, or "initialize" when you mean "begin," or "sent an electronic communication" when "emailed" or "texted" is more precise.

5. *Look for Old English Roots.* English often has two words for basic concepts, one rooted in Old English (like *ghost, home, free, walk*) and one from Latin through French (like *spirit, domicile, liberate, perambulate*). Old English–related words are often simpler and punchier. There is a reason that *I shall dwell in the house of the Lord forever* sounds better than *I shall inhabit the residence of the Master eternally.*
6. *Appeal to the Senses.* Help the reader touch, taste, smell, hear, see, and feel. Whenever possible, choose specific sense-related words. *Gritty* is better than *rough*; *gamy* better than *smelly*; *racket* better than *noise.*
7. *Choose Lively Verbs.* This is the one of the oldest writing tricks around. Juice up your writing with verbs rather than adjectives or adverbs. Fictional characters don't always just *walk*; they can *creep, march, sashay, saunter, stagger, strut, traipse, tread*, and *wander.* Read through your manuscript looking *only* at the verbs (but don't fall into "thesaurus-itis"—see number 4). Major exceptions are the "said references." Usually a plain and simple *said* is better than a self-conscious *articulated, elucidated, enunciated, opined,* or *verbalized.* (See "SAID REFERENCES.")
8. *Jettison Jargon and Clichés.* Even the old one-liner about *avoiding clichés like the plague* is a cliché. Think of jargon and clichés as something really stinky at the back of your manuscript's vegetable drawer. Serve fresh. (See "JARGON, RELIGIOUS.")
9. *Eradicate Redundancy.* Ministers do us no service with phrases like *dearly beloved* and *gather together.* So familiar are such phrases that we don't notice the redundancies. Avoid common ones like *evolve over time, natural instincts, nostalgia for the past, an old proverb, past history, revert back, surrounded on all sides,* or *an unexpected surprise.*
10. *Avoid "Wordy Words."* See "WORDY WORDS."

WORD DIVISION

When a word must be split over two lines of type, the division takes place between syllables. A hyphen is inserted to show that the word has been broken (though see the guidelines later in this entry for breaking proper names, numerals, and compounds). That much is simple. The execution is often more complex.

Legitimate Breaks for Typesetting. Most English dictionaries show syllabification; that is, they break multisyllabic words into their basic syllables, but not all syllable divisions are legitimate for typographic word division. Dictionaries differ on their rules. For instance, *Merriam-Webster's Collegiate Dictionary, 11th Edition* (our preferred dictionary), breaks words according to pronunciation, while *The Random House College Dictionary* tends to divide them according to etymological derivation, or root word. Furthermore, word-processing programs often generate their own divisions either from a programmed dictionary or, when stumped, from a logic program, neither of which may correspond to the publisher's preferred style. The following guidelines may help. (See also *CMoS* 7.31–7.43.)

1. *Single Letters.* Never allow a single letter to stand alone. Neither *a-/while* nor *distopi-/a* is acceptable. *Webster* actually does not show single-letter syllable divisions.
2. *Two-Letter Breaks.* Avoid two letters on a second line (*enchant-/er*) whenever possible. In many cases, the two letters can be brought up to the previous line without causing a too-tight line. Two letters standing alone on a first line (*en-/chanter*) is acceptable as long as it doesn't cause misreading or constitute a common word by itself. For instance, *bi-/furcated* would be no problem, but *do-/minion* might cause misreading.
3. *Breaks over a Page.* Do not allow a word to break from a recto (odd-numbered) page to a verso (even-numbered) page. Verso-to-recto breaks are permitted as long as they are not too frequent and don't cause misreading.
4. *Orphans.* Allow a three- or four-letter portion of a word to stand alone on a line by itself at the end of a paragraph as long as it extends beyond the point where the indented word begins in the next paragraph. In other words, no typographic "river" should run between the two paragraphs. (Also see "WIDOWS AND ORPHANS" and "RIVERS, TYPOGRAPHIC.")
5. *One-Syllable Words.* Do not divide a one-syllable word, no matter how long it is. (The word *brougham*, by the way, is thought to be the longest uninflected one-syllable word in English.)
6. *Abbreviations.* Do not divide abbreviations or contractions.
7. *Acronyms and Initialisms.* Do not divide acronyms and initialisms unless they have passed into use as common nouns. For instance, *fu-/bar* is acceptable, but *UNI-/CEF* is not. (See "ACRONYMS AND INITIALISMS.")

8. *With Hyphenated Words.* If possible, avoid breaking words that already contain hyphens. If that is not possible, break such words at the existing hyphen; for instance, *self-/parody* rather than *self-par-/ody* or *Counter-/Reformation* rather than *Coun-/ter-Reformation.*
9. *With En and Em Dashes.* To avoid loose lines or lines that are too tight, compounds already containing an en dash or words adjacent to an em dash may be divided; for instance, *Gold Medallion Award–win-/ling author* or ... *such misstatements—delib-/lerate or otherwise* ...
10. *Prefixes and Suffixes.* For clarity, break words after a prefix or before a suffix whenever possible: *dis-/equilibrium* rather than *diequi-/librium,* and *random-/ness* rather than *ran-/domness.*
11. *Compounds.* Words that are clearly compounds of two other elements are best broken between the root elements: *foot-/dragger* rather than *footdrag-/ger* and *proof-reading* rather than *proofread-/ing* (though the latter break is acceptable if it would prevent a too-loose or too-tight line).
12. *Misreading.* Avoid any break that might cause misreading, such as *adam-/ant* or *Anti-/gone.* And especially avoid any breaks that will cause embarrassment. For instance, imagine the problem caused by misbreaking the KJV's *shittim wood* (Ex. 25:5 and elsewhere), which the NIV fortunately renders *acacia wood.*
13. *Liquid l Breaks.* Formerly, syllables containing an *-le* (in words that are called "*liquid l*" *words*), as in *people* and *article,* were not allowed to be broken from the rest of the word. Both *CMoS* and this manual now accept "liquid l" word divisions. For example, *peo-/ple* and *arti-/cle* are okay.

Allow for Flexibility. You'll note the phrase *whenever possible* in those guidelines. Take that to mean that a slightly awkward word division is usually preferable to a line of type that is noticeably too loose or too tight. Use common sense, and always ask: What will cause the least disruption for the reader?

As long as the general guidelines are met, some publishers accept word divisions that conform to the style of any major dictionary. For instance, *righteous* may be broken either *righ-/teous* (*Webster*'s "pronunciation" style) or *right-/eous* (*Random House*'s "root word" style), and a publisher may accept both as legitimate. This liberality is often a compromise and should be avoided in high-quality, literary editing. But in many cases, such flexibility is necessary since even a slight adjustment in line length at late proof stages can cause a paragraph, a chapter, or even an entire book to reflow. Small adjustments can snowball into expensive changes. Also, many computer spell-checkers and even human proofreaders don't differentiate between the styles of various dictionaries. The fact is, most readers will survive an occasional inconsistency.

Proper Names. Avoid dividing names whenever possible, unless they are quite long and would result in a loose or tight line. Always keep a middle initial with the first name, and never separate personal initials; for instance, do not allow *C. /S. Lewis*. By the same token, do not allow designations such as *Jr., Sr., II, III*, etc. to be separated from the name; for instance, *Henry /VIII* is unacceptable.

Numbers. Sometimes unusually large numerals need to be broken over two lines of type. Break large numerals after a comma as long as that comma does not follow a single digit. Never break a numeral after a decimal point. Do not use a hyphen to break a numeral over a line. Simply drop the rest of the number to the next line. For instance, *A trillion is* 10^{12}*, or 1,000,000,000,000.*

Webpage Addresses. As described in the entry "ADDRESSES, WEB," break a webpage address (a URL) after a back slash whenever possible. Otherwise, break the address before any other internal punctuation, such as a dot. As with numerals, do not add a hyphen to show where the URL is broken since the hyphen can be mistaken for part of the address. Simply drop the rest of the URL down to the next line.

Keep Style Sheets. Freelance editors and proofreaders should be thoroughly familiar with the publisher's preferred style of word division. The proofreader, especially the one who reads the first set of typeset proofs, should keep a style sheet listing any problematic word divisions encountered.

WORDS AS WORDS

When a word or phrase is referred to as a word or phrase, italicize it. When a definition is also provided, put quotation marks around it.

A surprising number of people confuse *hoard* with *horde*. [Word as word]

He explained to us what *that dog won't hunt* means. [Phrase as phrase]

Targum is from Aramaic and means "translation." [Word as word with definition]

WORDY WORDS

Check for wordiness. You may even want to search your work for some of the "wordy words" in the following list. (See also "SYLLOGISTIC WORDS AND PHRASES.")

Wordy	More Direct
a large part of	many, most
all of	all
along the lines of	like
altogether	[often redundant]
and so	so
and then	then
approximately	about
as a matter of fact	in fact
at all times	always
at the present time	now
a total of	[usually redundant]
attempt	try
be a blessing to	bless
conceptualize	picture, envision
concerning	about
currently	now
demonstrate	show
different	[sometimes redundant; see "*different*"]
due to	because
due to the fact that	because
elucidate	explain
endeavor	try
few in number	few
first and foremost	first
for me	[redundant when *me* is already implied]
for the most part	mostly
for the purpose of	for
for the reason that	because
gather together	gather
generally	[often used to avoid being emphatic]
however	[often unnecessary]
illustrate	show
inasmuch as	since, *or* because
in close proximity	near
in fact	[often not needed]
in need of	need(s)
in order that	so (that)
in order to	to
in spite of	despite
in terms of	[often a useless phrase]

Wordy	More Direct
in the event that	if
in the near future	soon
it should be noted that	[often a useless phrase]
just	[often unnecessary]
located in	in
necessary	needed
numerous	many
oftentimes	often
on the grounds that	because
on the occasion of	when
optimal	best
past history	history
previously	before
previous to	before
prior to	before
subsequently	later
subsequent to	after
technique	method; way
terminate	end
that	[often unnecessary]
therefore	[often unnecessary]
there is, there are	[avoid these if possible]
to be	[sometimes unnecessary]
to himself, to herself	[often redundant, as in "thought to himself"]
to the tune of	[usually redundant when used with numbers]
until such time as	until
utilize	use
very	[often unnecessary]
whether or not	whether
with regard to	about
with the exception of	except

WORLD-ENGLISH STYLE

See "MID-ATLANTIC STYLE."

WRITERS, TEN COMMANDMENTS FOR

The following dos and don'ts for authors are compiled from an editor's perspective rather than a writer's. These are things to keep in mind while researching and writing a manuscript.

1. *Do Not Succumb to Jargon.* To influence culture, Christians need to write in the language of the culture, not the church. (See "JARGON, RELIGIOUS.") To write for contemporary Christians means to write contemporary English, not some echo of older, pulpitized English.
2. *Do Not Argue.* Lead the reader gently. John Henry Newman once said, "It is as absurd to argue men, as to torture them, into believing" (*Fifteen Sermons*). Personal anecdotes, humor, humility, accurate facts, persuasion, and well-crafted prose accomplish more than polemical grandstanding.
3. *Do Not Get Clever with Type.* It is always counterproductive. The reader should be so engrossed in the content that the words virtually disappear. For instance, using a *script font* to simulate handwritten letters in a novel only makes the text harder to read and breaks the spell of the story. The reader may not understand what your **boldface** or oversize letters mean or what your
   stair-
   stepping
   single-
   word
   paragraphs
   are supposed to convey. The reader may simply think, *Something weird's going on!* Unless comedy is intended, don't use too many letters to show prolonged sounds, as in *Her only response was, "Waaaaaaaaaaaaaah!"* Don't use the already overused and outdated single-words-with-periods device for emphasis, as in *Don't. Do. This.* (See "BLOG STYLE AND TURNING BLOGS INTO BOOKS.")
4. *Do Not Overcapitalize.* The great Era of Victorian Devotional Literature is over, and we are Eternally Grateful. (See "DEITY PRONOUN, THE" and "DEVOTIONAL CAPS.")
5. *Keep Track of Your Sources.* Unintended plagiarism creates anxiety for editors and embarrassment for authors. It is too easy to copy passages from the web only to forget later that those words are someone else's. Be scrupulous in keeping track of every reference, whether from a print or an online source. (See "NOTES" and "PLAGIARISM.")
6. *Do Not Assume That Just Because It's on the Internet, It's Free or in the Public Domain.* Because a poem, anecdote, devotional thought, or joke is copied a thousand times on the internet with no attribution does not mean you can drop it into your book without credit or permission. The rules for print sources also apply to the internet. (See "QUOTING ONLINE SOURCES.") The same is true for

graphics, charts, emails, tweets, blog entries, people's personal stories, songs, extended quotations, videos, reader reviews, and so on. Somebody holds the copyright to most of those things and would appreciate credit if not a small fee as well. (See also "PERMISSION GUIDELINES: QUOTING READER REVIEWS FROM A WEBSITE.")

7. *Do Not Design Your Book for the Publisher.* Most of the things you do to gussy up your manuscript—inserting decorative capitals, using special fonts, adding fancy graphics, and so on—will only get stripped out when the publisher designs your book. Use the plainest styles and simplest formatting that will allow you to account for all the elements in your manuscript. You're providing the content, not the container.
8. *Do Not Assume Your Experience Is Universal.* Just because an hour of prayer every day healed your depression doesn't mean it will work for everyone. Be sensitive to the reader's perspective and limitations.
9. *Do Not Assume That Writing about Spiritual Maturity Is the Same as Achieving It.* Writing as though you've already scaled the heights of spiritual living is usually a form of dishonesty that can cause frustration for readers who are struggling to grow. Do not assume you have all the answers. Humility and sincere confession are the best ways to help others. (Read Philip Yancey's *Vanishing Grace* to learn more about this subject.)
10. *Find Your Favorite Writers on Writing.* Scores of great books are available about the craft of writing—from classics like Brenda Ueland's *If You Want to Write* and William Zinsser's *On Writing Well* to more contemporary books like Anne Lamott's *Bird by Bird* and Verlyn Klinkenborg's *Several Short Sentences about Writing.* (All of those are highly recommended.) Every writer should adopt at least two or three favorite "writers about writing." Seek them out; reread them often.
11. *A Bonus Commandment: Find Joy.* If you don't find joy in your writing, in your characters (even the villains—maybe especially the villains), in your ideas, or in your research, then the reader won't either. Joy is a gift from God. (Read C. S. Lewis's *Surprised by Joy* on this topic.) Revel in it. If you do, no reader in the world will be able to put your book down.

Y

YEAR OF PUBLICATION

An accurate statement of the year of a book's publication is needed at two points. It is required in the copyright notice on the copyright page, where it is placed between the © symbol (or word *copyright*, or both) and the name of the copyright holder. Also, it is needed when the book is officially registered with the Library of Congress and the US Copyright Office. (See "COPYRIGHT HOLDER AND COPYRIGHT OWNER," "COPYRIGHT NOTICE," and "COPYRIGHT PAGE.")

Ends of Years. At both points, care needs to be taken at year's end. For instance, a book may arrive in the publisher's warehouse in December but not actually filter out to the bookstore shelves until January. So which year is the publication date? The best rule is to go by the actual in-stock date, that is, the year the book actually arrives in the warehouse.

While no serious problem arises if the date is off by a year one way or the other in the copyright notice, the US Copyright Office should be notified of the correct date when registering the copyright itself. If a wrong date was given to the Library of Congress when applying for CIP information (for instance, if the book is delayed), it should be notified of the corrected date as soon as possible.

PART 2

The Word List

Words are a pretext. It is the inner bond that draws one person to another, not words.

Rumi, *The Discourses*, trans. A. J. Arberry

A

a, an

The correct use of the indefinite articles *a* and *an* is second nature to most speakers of English, but a word of caution might be helpful for written copy. The occasionally stated rule is that *a* is used before consonants and *an* before vowels—which is wrong. We say *a one-time fee* and *a universal solution*, the *a* being used because *one* is pronounced as if it began with *w* and *universal* as if it began with *y*. The sound is what matters. If it *sounds* as if it begins with a consonant, *a* is used. (A *y* at the beginning of a word is nearly always a consonant, except for such exotic nouns as *ylang-ylang* and *yttrium*.) If it *sounds* as if it begins with a vowel, *an* is used. The same applies to words beginning with the letter *h*. If the *h* is pronounced, or aspirated, use *a* as the article (*a historic event*, *a helpful clue*), but if silent, use *an* (*an herbal remedy*, *an honest answer*). For abbreviations, use the common pronunciation to determine which article is appropriate: for instance, *a UN charter* but *an mp3 player*.

abbot, abbess, abbé

Many words describing job functions have gender-neutral forms (see "GENDER-ACCURATE LANGUAGE"), but a few, like *abbot* and *abbess*, retain their gender distinction. *Abbot* is the title given to the male superior at a monastery, or abbey (*Abbot Frederic Dunne*), though an abbot is addressed in conversation as *Father*. Do not confuse the English word *abbot* with the French *abbé*; an *abbé* is simply a younger member of the French clergy. *Abbess* is the title given to a woman in charge of a convent (*Abbess Hildegard of Bingen*), though an abbess would be addressed as *Mother*. In the modern Roman Catholic Church, the term *mother superior* is now more common than *abbess*.

Forms of Address. The address line of a letter to an abbot reads, "The Right Reverend [first and last names], Abbot of [name of monastery]," which also serves for formal introductions in public. The salutation reads, "Dear Reverend Father [last name]" or "Dear Father" (or "Dear Father Abbot"). For a Catholic abbess, the address line reads, "The Reverend Mother [first and last names], Abbess of [name of monastery]," which is also how she is introduced in public. The salutation reads, "Dear Reverend Mother."

ABC's, ABCs

Refer to the English alphabet as either *the ABC's* (preferred by *Webster*) or *the ABCs*, but not *the abc's*, *the A-B-Cs*, or *the A B C's*. The related noun and adjective *abecedarian* can imply either "related to the alphabet" or "basic or rudimentary." (See also "LETTERS AS WORDS.")

abiblical

See "*nonbiblical, abiblical, extrabiblical, unbiblical.*"

above, below

Avoid the terms *above* and *below* when referring to other parts of a book's content. Readers don't necessarily conceive of a text as a top-to-bottom construct; or, more simply, why is page 51 *below* page 49? When the book stands upright, page 51 is actually beside page 49. In such references, specific page numbers are preferable (such as *see page 51*). If the material referred to immediately precedes or follows the reference, use such phrases as *the preceding list* or *the following chart*.

Abrahamic, Abramic

These adjectives are synonymous, and both are acceptable, though *Abrahamic* is more common (as in *the three Abrahamic religions*).

a cappella

This is spelled *a cappella* (preferred) or *a capella*, not *acappella*. It means "sung without instrumental accompaniment." Although from the Italian meaning "in the chapel," the term is familiar enough in English that it need not be italicized as a foreign term.

accident

See "*on accident, by accident.*"

AD

See "*BC, AD.*"

Adam's apple

Adam is capitalized; *apple* is not.

adherent

In religious contexts, an *adherent* is the broadest catchall term for those who believe in the tenets of a specific religion but who may not be formal members or attenders.

Advent, advent

Capitalize *Advent* in reference to the traditional holy season before Christmas, as in *Advent, the Advent season, Advent Sunday, an Advent calendar*, and so on. (For determining the dates of Advent, see "CHRISTIAN HOLIDAYS, FEASTS, AND THE LITURGICAL YEAR," section on "*Advent*.") Lowercase *advent* as a common noun, as in *the advent of digital media*, and in general references to the historical birth of Jesus, as in *his advent, a century after the advent of Christ*, or *Christ's second advent*. (See "EVENTS IN THE LIFE OF JESUS, LOWERCASING.")

ae

The letter combination *ae* is in the process of becoming simply *e* in many English words; for instance, *et cetera, ether*, and *medieval* used to be spelled *et caetera, aether*, and *mediaeval*. The words *aetiology, anaesthetic*, and *encyclopaedia*, as they are still spelled in the UK, have become *etiology, anesthetic*, and *encyclopedia* in the US—though the American publishers of *The Encyclopaedia Britannica* retain the *ae* in their name. Other examples of the transition are found in the words *aeon* and *aesthetic*, which, though still the preferred spellings in *Webster*, are occasionally seen as *eon* and *esthetic*. Then again, the *ae* is consistently preserved in such words as *aerial, aerobics, Aesop, Caesar, Zacchaeus*, and others. When in doubt, check *Webster*.

Ligature. When encountering an *ae*, some compositors wonder whether the ligature (tied-together) character representing those letters should be used: *æ* (as in *Cæsar*) and *Æ* (as in *Æsop*). This particular ligature is never mandatory and is much less common than other ligatures. (See "LIGATURES.")

Old English. While most *ae* words are Latin or French in origin, an identical character was used in Old English and seen in such proper names as *Ælfric* or *Ælfred*. For whatever reason, *Ælfric* has retained the *ae* (though often spelled *Aelfric*) while *Ælfred* is rendered *Alfred*.

Afghan, afghan, afghani

Someone from Afghanistan is an *Afghan*, not an *Afghani*. *Afghan* is also the adjective (as in *the Afghan government* or *an Afghan hound*). While the country uses a currency called *the afghani* (lowercase), no language called *Afghani* exists. The two main languages of Afghanistan are Pashto and Dari. To mean "a small blanket," *afghan* is lowercase.

African American, black

The following guidelines are based on both *CMoS* and the style guide of the National Association of Black Journalists (NABJ). As an adjective, both *black* and *African American* are acceptable, though do not hyphenate *African American* either as a noun or an adjective. Although *Webster* hyphenates it, *CMoS* does not, since not hyphenating it causes no misreading. As a noun, the NABJ prefers *African American* to *black*, though it recommends *black* as a shorthand in headlines. The NABJ further notes that not all black people are from Africa, so be sensitive to a person's self-identification, such as *Haitian American*, *Jamaican American*, and so on. (See also "*black*" and "ETHNIC, NATIONAL, AND RACIAL DESIGNATIONS.")

agnostic, atheist, unbeliever

Although sometimes used synonymously, *agnostic* and *atheist* are distinct. *Agnostic* was coined by nineteenth-century biologist T. H. Huxley, based on the reference to the "unknown god" in Acts 17:23, to describe the belief that humans cannot conclusively know whether a deity exists. By extension, it has come to mean that belief in a creator is irrelevant to living. It is often used metaphorically (*an agnostic in matters of taste*). An *atheist*, by contrast, is proactive in asserting a divine being cannot exist. As broad philosophies, lowercase *agnosticism* and *atheism*. (See "*New Atheism, the New Atheists.*") An *unbeliever*, or *nonbeliever*, may well believe God exists but simply does not adhere to any specific religion.

air force

See "*army, navy, air force, marines.*"

alleluia

See "*hallelujah, alleluia.*"

All Hallows' Eve

See "*Halloween, Hallowe'en, All Hallows' Eve.*"

all right, alright

Both words have long pedigrees in English, but most writers use *all right* in formal writing, reserving *alright* for fictional dialogue or when a slangy tone is intended. In dialogue, *alright* is sometimes made even more slangy by spelling it the way many people actually say it: *awright.*

All Saints' Day, All Souls' Day

These two holy days are often confused. Capitalize both names and use the plural possessive. *All Saints' Day* is celebrated on November 1 in Western churches and on the Sunday after Pentecost in the Eastern churches. It commemorates the great saints of the faith. *All Souls' Day*, celebrated primarily in the Roman Catholic Church, commemorates all believers who have died and is the day on which Catholics pray for the souls of deceased family members and friends. It takes place on November 2, the day after All Saints' Day. Some Protestant denominations celebrate them together on the Sunday closest to November 1, calling it *All Saints' Day* or *All Saints' Sunday.*

Almighty, almighty

Capitalize *the Almighty* and *God Almighty* (as in *We have come here to worship God Almighty*), but lowercase *almighty God* (as in *our almighty God*). In the first two instances, *Almighty* is part of an epithet that has the force of a proper name. In the last instance, *almighty* is a descriptive adjective. When the last example is meant to appear more like a proper name, especially when it is not qualified, then capitalize it: *Almighty God* (as in *Hear us, Almighty God*). (See also "TRINITY, NAMES FOR PERSONS OF THE.")

alms

Although the word *alms* can be both singular and plural, it nearly always takes a plural verb: *The alms were distributed by the bishop.* Note the article is sometimes dropped: *to give alms to the poor.* An obscure but interesting adjectival form is *eleemosynary.*

al-Qaeda

Variant spellings for the name of this terrorist group are common, but for most uses we recommend *al-Qaeda*, which accords with *CMoS*. Other spellings commonly found are *al-Qaida* (*AP, Guardian UK, UPI*), *al Qaeda* (*National Geographic* and *Reuters*), *Al Qaeda* (*NYT* and US Government Printing Office), and *Al-Qaeda* (*Christian Science Monitor* and *Wikipedia*). Also occasionally seen is *al-Qa'ida* (*The Independent UK*). In all cases the word is pronounced al-KIE-duh, not al-KAY-duh.

although, though

As conjunctions, *although* and *though* are interchangeable. A slight distinction is that *although* is sometimes used in more formal contexts, while *though* is more common in speech and casual writing. *Although* tends to be more emphatic and usually precedes a main or independent clause; *though* usually introduces a subordinating clause that follows a main clause. For example, *Although the weather was bad, a good time was had by all*, but *The weather was bad, though a good time was had by all.* Only *though* can be used as a terminal adverb, meaning "however," as in *He failed the exam; he tried hard though.*

altar

The word *altar* has its origin in the Latin word for "burn up" and means "the place where burnt sacrifices are offered." In Christian liturgical settings, *on the altar* suggests the Communion table itself: as in *The bread and wine were placed on the altar.* Since the Reformation, many less liturgically oriented churches have referred to the place where Communion is offered as *the table*, or *the Communion table*, rather than *the altar*, and the phrase *on the altar* often simply suggests the raised portion of flooring at the front of the sanctuary, whether a Communion table is present or not: as in *The acolytes stood on the altar.* The phrases *at the altar* and *before the altar* suggest something that happens in front of the Communion table: *The groom waited at the altar* (which simply indicates a place, often called *the chancel*, in the sanctuary) or *They laid palm branches before the altar* (which suggests both a place and the sacrificial meaning). Lowercase the term *the altar of repose*, which is a side altar in some Roman Catholic churches where a consecrated Host is stored between Maundy Thursday and Good Friday.

a.m., p.m., noon, midnight

The abbreviations *a.m.* (*ante meridiem*, "before noon") and *p.m.* (*post meridiem*, "after noon") were once commonly set in small caps with periods (A.M. and P.M.). That style is not as widely used as it once was, but it may be retained if applied consistently throughout a publication. Publishers in the UK often use the small-cap style. In accordance with *CMoS*, this manual recommends lowercasing those abbreviations and using periods: *a.m.* and *p.m.*; those forms are often more easily adapted to ebook and online formats.

With Numerals. The abbreviations *a.m.* and *p.m.* are customarily used with numerical time designations that use a colon; for instance, *11:00 p.m.* rather than *11 p.m.* The words *morning*, *afternoon*, *evening*, and *o'clock* obviate the need for *a.m.* or *p.m.*: as in *10:45 in the morning* or *four o'clock in the afternoon*.

In Fiction. In fictional dialogue, the time of day is usually spelled out while including the abbreviation: *He told them, "I'll be back before eight p.m."* If the numeral were used (*"I'll be back before 8:00 p.m."*), an ambiguity would exist as to whether the character was saying "eight p.m." or "eight o'clock p.m."

Noon. Noon, sometimes called the *zero point*, is neither *a.m.* nor *p.m.* In precise scientific writing, it is marked with an *m.*, which stands for the Latin *meridies*, meaning "midpoint." Avoid the abbreviation in ordinary contexts; few readers are familiar with it and some may mistake it for "midnight." Such combinations as *twelve noon, twelve o'clock noon*, or *12:00 noon* are redundancies; noon is most simply referred to as just *noon*.

Midnight. Technically, midnight is *12:00 p.m.* and is considered the final moment of the day just ending. One second after midnight is the start of the new day. To put it another way: *12:00 p.m. on Friday* is one minute before *12:01 a.m. on Saturday*. Avoid any ambiguity by simply referring to it as *midnight* or *twelve o'clock at night*.

amen

This solemnizing Hebrew word means "may it be so." When used to conclude a prayer, it usually stands alone as an interjection (as in ... *we pray in Jesus's name. Amen.*), though some writers prefer to incorporate it into the concluding statement (as in ... *we pray in Jesus's name, amen*). Either is acceptable, though logic would dictate a preference for the former because *amen* concludes the entire prayer, not the final statement alone.

Apart from prayer, *amen* is used to express strong affirmation. Since it often stands alone (*"Amen!"*) or as a complete conclusion to a prayer, many writers assume it is always capitalized. There is no reason to capitalize it when used as an ordinary noun (as in *They only mumbled the amen at the end of the hymn*) or when incorporated into the concluding statement of a prayer (as in ... *in Jesus's name we pray, amen*).

Pronunciation. The word, whether sung or spoken, can cause consternation in liturgical settings because it can be pronounced *ah-men* (short *a*) or *ay-men* (long *a*). Both are correct, though *ah-men* (short *a*) is more common in liturgical prayer and is how the word is pronounced in the UK. The *ah-men* pronunciation is also the one most often used when the word is sung, since diphthongs (two vowel sounds masquerading as one) such as *ay* (a long *a* and long *e* together) tend to be avoided in singing. One exception is the word's use in those churches where spontaneous shouts of "amen" tend to be pronounced with the long *a* (*ay-men*) and the accent, spoken or sung, is sometimes on the second syllable (*ay-MEN*) for emphasis.

As a Verb. In those rare instances when *amen* is used as a verb, the past tense is *amened* (not *amenned*); as in *The congregation hooted and amened throughout the service.*

Amen Corner. This nineteenth-century phrase jokingly refers to the most vocally responsive part of a congregation. In modern usage it is antiquated and humorous, most often used metaphorically to mean the most ardent supporters of a person or cause, as in *that news network became the candidate's most vocal amen corner.* Lowercase the phrase.

amendments to the Constitution

Capitalize the names of the current twenty-seven amendments to the US Constitution (only the first ten of which are referred to as the Bill of Rights) when they are referred to by number—*The Fourteenth Amendment* or *to plead the Fifth*—and do not hyphenate them as compound adjectives—*our First Amendment right to free speech.* Lowercase the word *amendment* when referring to one or more of them: *Citizens are protected by the Constitution's amendments*, or *the amendment that gave women the right to vote.* (See also "*Constitution, constitutional.*")

amid, amidst

Amid is preferred, though it can usually be replaced with *among* or *in*. *Amidst* is handy in fictional dialogue to convey an old-fashioned impression but is otherwise less common.

amoral, immoral

Increasingly, the word *amoral* has come to mean "evil" or "knowingly defying moral norms" in popular usage, even though the word *immoral* already covers that territory adequately. In a strict sense, *amoral* means "outside the bounds of moral consideration." The study of mathematics, for instance, is *amoral*, but that does not imply any deliberate evil on the part of mathematicians. For some writers, *amoral* seems to be a mincing way of saying *immoral*, suggesting someone is bad without actually saying it outright. Honor the distinction, and avoid equivocation.

Anabaptist, Anabaptism

The term *Anabaptism* is nearly always capitalized to mean the broad Christian movement, beginning in the sixteenth century, that advocated nonviolence, adult baptism, and government noninterference in church affairs.

Anabaptist is both a noun, referring to an adherent of that movement, and an adjective. In rare instances, *anabaptism* may be lowercase to refer to the concept of adult baptism after someone has been baptized as a child.

and/or

Avoid this contrivance whenever possible. It not only sounds stuffily precise, but how is a reader to know whether it means *"and* and *or"* or *"and* or *or"*? Perhaps it means *"and* and/or *or"*! Although rare exceptions may be found, usually a simple *and* or *or* adequately conveys the intended meaning.

angel

Do not capitalize *angel* before names; for instance, *the angel Gabriel.* It is a descriptor, not a title. It is capitalized in theophany, that is, when the angel is a manifestation of God or specifically represents one of the persons of the Trinity.

Anglican Church, Church of England

The Church of England is the more formal term used for that church as it exists in the UK today and in most historical references. The term *Anglican Church* is less formal. *The Anglican Communion* connotes the worldwide body of churches that are associated with the Church of England, including the Anglican Church of Canada and the Episcopal Church in the US. The term *Anglican* alone can refer to any of those denominations. (See also "*Episcopal, episcopal, Episcopalian.*")

Anglo-Catholic

The term *Anglo-Catholic* is distinct from both *Anglican* and *Catholic.* It refers to that portion of the Church of England that emphasizes the church's Roman Catholic rather than Reformation origins, and it was influenced by such seventeenth-century writers as Archbishop William Laud, Lancelot Andrewes, John Cosin, and Jeremy Taylor, as well as the later Oxford, or Tractarian, Movement of the mid-nineteenth century. Today Anglo-Catholics tend to stress liturgy, including some traditionally Roman Catholic worship practices.

Annunciation, the; annunciation

Capitalize *Annunciation* to mean the holy day observed in some churches on March 25. As for the word for the event itself (the announcement of the incarnation to the Virgin Mary as described in Luke 1:26–38), lowercase it.

antichrist, Antichrist

The term *antichrist*, coined in the epistles of John (1 John 2:18, 22; 4:3; 2 John 7), can mean either "a person who opposes or denies Christ" or "a false Christ." Lowercase it to mean someone who possesses a spirit of evil and opposition to Christ. When used to mean the specific individual referred to in Revelation who will be defeated by Christ at the second coming, capitalize the term. Throughout Christian history, many people, from the Emperor Nero to Mikhail Gorbachev, have been identified as generic antichrists or the biblical Antichrist himself.

anti-Christian

This simply means "in opposition to whatever is Christian" and does not refer to *the Antichrist*. Note it is spelled with a hyphen and capital *C*, unlike the term *unchristian*, which dispenses with the hyphen and capital letter. (See also "*unchristian, non-Christian.*")

anticommunist

Lowercase *anticommunist* to mean opposition to the philosophy of communism as well as opposition to the Communist party. (See also "*communist, Communist, communism, Communism.*")

anti-Semite, anti-Semitic, anti-Semitism

Capitalize *Semite* and its related forms even when preceded by a prefix; for instance, *non-Semitic*. (See also "*Semite, Semitic, Semitism.*")

anymore, any more

Anymore is an adverb meaning "any longer" and is usually used in the negative: as in *I can't take it anymore*. The adjective (or adjective-noun) combination *any more* is an indicator of extent or quantity; as in *I can't eat any more chocolates* (or *I can't eat any more*). Always double-check the context. For instance, consider this typo from an actual manuscript: the author wrote, "God cannot love us anymore" (meaning "God is no longer able to love us"), when the author meant, "God cannot love us any more" (meaning "God already loves us to the fullest possible extent"). A word space makes a world of difference.

A-OK

See "*okay, OK.*"

Apocrypha, apocryphal

The writings known as the Apocrypha are part of the Roman Catholic and Eastern Orthodox OT canon but not the Protestant (though considered "profitable" or "edifying" by some denominations). As the title of a specific group of writings, the name is printed in roman type and capitalized. Because the adjective *apocryphal* means "writings or stories whose authority is doubtful," it is best to avoid the adjective in references to the OT writings. The Apocrypha was included between the OT and NT in the original 1611 KJV but is absent in most modern editions. The books of the Apocrypha largely overlap but are not identical to what are called the deuterocanonical books; for instance, the King James Apocrypha adds three books not found in the Catholic Apocrypha. Catholics, Protestants, and Eastern Orthodox believers differ on which books are included in the Apocrypha and which are among the deuterocanonical writings. (See "BIBLE, THE—WHAT IS IT?" for a list of the commonly accepted books of the Apocrypha.)

apostate

The term *apostate* describes a person who once accepted but later rejected the Christian faith. (For more, see "*heresy, schism*.") The etymology of *apostate* links it to the Greek word meaning "to revolt," or "to stand against," while the similar word *apostle* goes back to a different Greek word meaning "to send out" (as on a mission) or "a messenger."

apostle, Apostle

The word *apostle* (from the Greek *apostolos*, "messenger") is usually lowercase (as in *the apostle John* or *the apostle Paul*) unless part of a common epithet that has the force of a proper name (as in *the Beloved Apostle* or *the Apostle to the Gentiles*). In some devotional contexts, *the Apostle* is understood to refer to Paul. (See also "*apostles, twelve*" and "DEVOTIONAL CONTEXTS.")

Apostles' Creed, the

This title is capitalized but not italicized: the Apostles' Creed. Note also the plural possessive. In passing references to *the creed*, lowercase it, as in *The creed's influence on our understanding of doctrine ...*

apostles, twelve

Sunday school pupils have long puzzled over the twelve apostles because they actually number fourteen or more. After the death of Judas, a man named Matthias was chosen by lot to replace him (Acts 1:18–26), and

Paul also applied the term to himself (Rom. 1:1 and 11:13 among others). The NT labels several other people *apostles*: among them, Barnabas (Acts 14:14); Jesus's brother James (Gal. 1:19); Levi (Luke 5:27, who may be Luke himself); Judas, son of James (Luke 6:16 and John 14:22, not Judas Iscariot); and possibly Andronicus and Junias (Rom. 16:7). Finally, the term *apostle* is sometimes loosely used in the pulpit to describe any follower of Jesus.

Meticulous writers use the unqualified phrase *the twelve apostles* (lowercase) to refer to Jesus's original disciples before the crucifixion:

Andrew
Bartholomew
James (son of Alphaeus, also called James the Less)
James (son of Zebedee, also called James the Great)
John
Judas Iscariot (replaced by Matthias well after the resurrection)
Matthew
Philip
Simon (Peter)
Simon (the Zealot)
Thaddaeus
Thomas (Didymus)

When using the word *apostles* alone, the writer may need to further clarify the intended meaning. In all cases, lowercase the phrase *the apostles*. (See also "*disciple, apostle*" and "*Twelve, the; twelve disciples*.")

apostolic fathers, Apostolic Fathers

The term *apostolic fathers* (lowercase) is sometimes mistakenly used to mean Jesus's apostles, though it actually refers to the generation of Christian writers immediately after the original twelve (though see "*apostles, twelve*"). They are called *apostolic* because they most likely knew the apostles personally. They are Clement of Rome, Hermas, Ignatius, Papias, Polycarp, and the anonymous writers of 2 Clement, Didache, Barnabas, and Diognetus. The writings of these individuals are corporately referred to as the Apostolic Fathers (capitalized, in roman type, as the formal title for that group of writings).

arabic numeral

Lowercase *arabic* in this term, despite the fact that most autoformatting programs will override the lowercase *a* and capitalize it. (Similarly, see "*roman numeral, roman type*" and "*italic, roman, arabic*.")

archbishop

Archbishop is an Eastern Orthodox and Roman Catholic clerical title. An archbishop leads an archdiocese or ecclesiastical province. It is also a title of honor in the Roman Catholic Church for the head of an important ecclesiastical see. Lowercase *archbishop* in references to *the archbishop of Canterbury,* though capitalize it as a title preceding a name: as in *Archbishop Welby.*

Forms of Address. The address line of a letter to a Catholic archbishop reads: "The Most Reverend [first and last names], Archbishop of [name of archdiocese or see]"; the salutation reads: "Your Excellency" or "Dear Archbishop [name of archdiocese or see]"; when addressing an archbishop in person, say, "Your Excellency" or "Archbishop [last name]"; when introducing an archbishop, say, "His Excellency" or "Archbishop [last name]."

The address line for the archbishop of Canterbury reads: "The Most Reverend and Right Honourable the Lord Archbishop of Canterbury [first and last name]"; the salutation reads, "Your Grace" or less formally, "Dear Archbishop"; when addressing the archbishop in person, say, "Your Grace" or "Archbishop."

archdeacon

This is a clerical title in the Roman Catholic and Anglican churches. An archdeacon is the assistant to a diocesan bishop.

Arche, L'

L'Arche (French for "the Ark") is a network of socially active Christian communities founded in 1972 by Jean Vanier. It is spelled with a capital *L* and a capital *A* and alphabetized under *A*. Do not put an English article in front of it since *L'* is the French article *the*.

ark

Lowercase it in all contexts: *Noah's ark, the ark of the covenant, the ark of the testimony.*

arm's length

Only one arm is implied. Do not write *arms' length.*

army, navy, air force, marines

When using these terms generically, lowercase them: *Joining the army is an option for high school grads.* In that sentence, *army* stands for the military services in general. When specifying branches of the US military (or other national militaries), capitalize them: *The president secured additional funding for the Air Force and the Navy.*

AS, AC

In the unlikely event that you run across the abbreviations *AS* and *AC*, they stand for *Anno Salutis*, "year of our salvation," and *ante Christum*, "before Christ," respectively. They are synonymous with *AD* and *BC* but have not been used since the eighteenth century. *AC* is particularly worth avoiding because it was also formerly used to mean "after Christ," the opposite of *ante Christum*. They are mentioned here because they are sometimes encountered in genealogical references and in some classic Christian writings.

ascension, the

Lowercase this in most contexts when referring to Jesus's ascension. (See also "EVENTS IN THE LIFE OF JESUS, LOWERCASING" for a fuller discussion.) Capitalize it in reference to the holy day on some church calendars: *Ascension Day*.

ascetic, ascetical

In the context of Christianity and some other religions, an *ascetic* is a person who practices self-denial, often living as a hermit or recluse. The philosophy is called *asceticism*, not to be confused with *aestheticism*, which is the study of beauty or the arts. Both *ascetic* and *ascetical* are correct adjective forms, though *ascetic* is the more common in the US.

Asian, Asia

In reference to a person from an Asian country, the word *Oriental* is neither accurate nor acceptable. Use the term *Asian*, or, preferably, state the specific nationality when known. Avoid the term *Asiatic*, as it is often perceived as pejorative. Similarly, *the Orient* smacks of colonialism; refer to the region as *Asia*.

atheist

See "*agnostic, atheist, unbeliever.*"

aureole

In religious art and iconography, *aureole* is sometimes misused as a synonym for *nimbus* or *halo*. *Aureole*, instead, is the golden sheenlike background that surrounds the entire body of a figure, as opposed to the *nimbus* or *halo*, which is the luminous circlet over the head. All those symbols denote sanctity and holiness.

auxiliary bishop

A clerical title. In the Roman Catholic Church the auxiliary bishop assists an archbishop or bishop.

a while, awhile

The phrase *a while* is a noun preceded by an indefinite article. *Awhile* is an adverb. That much is simple. The harder task is using them correctly in specific contexts. In most cases, the phrase *for a while* can be substituted for the word *awhile* (*I thought for a while* or *I thought awhile*). Often, *a while* is used with a preposition, most commonly *for* or *in*, or with a word indicating relative time, like *after*, *ago*, *before*, *since*, and so on (*I sold it a while ago*). Another way to approach it is this: if you can't decide whether *awhile* is being used correctly as an adverb, try replacing it with another adverb (*I listened awhile/I listened intently*). If an alternate adverb can be dropped in, then use *awhile*.

aye

As a response to a question, both *aye* and its doubled form, *aye, aye* (as in "*Aye, aye, Captain!*"), mean "yes" and are pronounced like the word *eye*. *Aye* can also be a noun meaning "an affirmative, or yea, vote": as in *the ayes have it*. An *aye-aye* (with a hyphen) is a small nocturnal primate in Madagascar. The antiquated poetic adverb *aye*, rhyming with *hay*, means "always" and is now only seen in old poetry and hymns, as in the line "For His mercies aye endure" from "Let Us, With a Gladsome Mind."

B

Baal, Ba'al

Baal is the spelling found in nearly all Bible translations. *Ba'al*, in which the internal mark stands for the Hebrew *ayin* character, is used primarily in Hebrew transliteration. The word, by the way, is most often pronounced BAY-ul, though BAH-ul and BAHL are acceptable.

baby boomer

Baby boomer, *baby boom*, and *baby boomlet* are spelled lowercase and without hyphens, though hyphenate them as adjectives (*the baby-boom generation*). (See also "GENERATIONAL CATEGORIES.")

baby Jesus, infant Jesus

Lowercase *baby* and *infant* in the phrases *the baby Jesus* and *the infant Jesus*, except, perhaps, in some Christmas devotional contexts, such as hymns, poems, or pageants. (See "DEVOTIONAL CONTEXTS.")

bacteria, bacterium

In scientific writing, treat *bacteria* as a plural (*bacteria are found in warm conditions*), the singular of which is *bacterium*. In trade writing, *bacteria* is commonly treated as a singular (*the specific bacteria isn't known*), and it is sometimes even pluralized as *bacterias*, though this manual recommends sticking with *bacteria* as the plural.

bah, humbug

Insert the comma in this phrase made famous by Charles Dickens's Scrooge (*Every year grandpa grumped, "Bah, humbug."*), though a hyphen could reasonably be inserted for the rare adjective (*bah-humbug attitude*). Surprisingly, Dickens never places those words side by side. The closest he comes is " 'Bah!' said Scrooge, 'Humbug' " (*Christmas Carol*). So if you need to quote Scrooge with absolute precision, use *Bah! Humbug* or, even more precisely, *Bah!… Humbug*.

banns of marriage

The term *banns of marriage* is lowercase and takes a plural verb. Although *banns* is sometimes mistakenly thought to mean "bands" or "bonds," it means the announcement of an intention to marry and has its origin in a Middle English word meaning "proclamation." It is plural because of the former English custom of posting in the church an announcement of an impending marriage for three consecutive weeks. It is usually used with the verbs *to post* or *to publish*, which are usually passive in construction: *the banns were posted.*

baptismal name

See "*Christian name.*"

barista

A *barista* can be either male or female. Some people mistakenly think a barista, because of the *-a* ending, can only refer to a woman, and some writers have even invented the awkward *baristo* to refer to male dispensers of coffee. Stick with *barista* for both genders.

bated breath

Bated breath, not *baited breath.*

BC, AD

Since *BC* is the abbreviation for "before Christ" in dates, it logically comes after references to a year, century, or millennium: *Augustus was born in 63 BC* (that is, sixty-three years before Christ). Year dates before Christ are never elided, whether *BC* is used or not: *Sophocles (496–406 BC) lived in Athens* or *Rome's quest for expansion resulted in the First Punic War (264–241).* Note that for spans of years, *BC* is used only after the second date, not both.

AD, the abbreviation for *anno Domini* ("in the year of the Lord"), is used to demark the historical era after the birth of Jesus. Grammatically, *AD* precedes single-year dates: *AD 90* ("in the year of our Lord 90"). While it was once considered incorrect to use *AD* with any but single-year dates (since "in the year of our Lord the twelfth century" is nonsensical), it is now acceptable to use *AD* with century designations, though the abbreviation follows the century: *the first century AD.* It is also acceptable to use the abbreviation with a range of dates: *AD 396–430.* Still, many scholars prefer the older style of using *AD* with single year dates only.

Until recently, *AD* and *BC* were commonly set in small capitals with periods (B.C., A.D.), a style that is no longer common in the US but is still used when a feeling of elegance or high artistic quality needs to be conveyed. The small-cap forms are common in the UK.

Use *BC* with all year dates before the time of Jesus, but it is best to reserve *AD* for year dates limited to two numerals (*AD 78*) or when the reader might be confused as to whether the year referred to is *AD* or *BC* (*The Roman senate's role changed significantly in AD 300.*)

Note that many writers in the general market now prefer *BCE* ("before the Common Era") to designate the time period before the birth of Jesus and *CE* ("Common Era") for dates after. (See "*BCE/CE*.")

BCE/CE

For references to year dates, many academic and general publishers prefer the scholarly abbreviations *BCE* ("before the Common Era") and *CE* ("Common Era"), which are synonymous with the older forms *BC* ("before Christ") and *AD* (*"anno Domini"*—"in the year of our Lord"). As with *BC*, year dates given with *BCE* are not be elided: *Euripides (484–406 BCE) died the same year as Sophocles.*

Although some Christians believe the BCE/CE system is a secularist attempt to expunge Christianity from history, the reasons for the shift toward the BCE/CE system are not nearly so pernicious. The use of the phrase *Common Era* and its abbreviation *CE* originated in the early eighteenth century among Jewish scholars who wished to adopt the Gregorian calendar but not appear as if Christ were the central focus of their own history. Authors and editors now use the BCE/CE system when they feel their readers—whether Jewish, Muslim, or general—may be offended by the christocentric forms.

Disadvantages of the BC/AD System. The older BC/AD system has inherent weaknesses. Both *BC* ("before Christ") and *AD* ("*anno Domini*") imply that year dates can be precisely measured as being before or after the year of Jesus's birth, and yet many scholars (including Christian scholars) have long suggested that less-than-perfect accuracy exists about the year Jesus was born. For instance, since it is fairly certain that King Herod died in 4 BC, Jesus is likely to have been born somewhat earlier—somewhere between four and seven years before the year we now assign as year AD 1. Further inaccuracy was introduced when sixth-century monk Dionysius Exiguus, who instituted our system of dating, may have miscalculated the year of Jesus's birth. Add to all that the fact that even if the BC/AD system were entirely accurate, the first year of Jesus's life would have been AD 1, since there was no year 0; this adds another element of imprecision, because Jesus, in that case, would have died at age thirty-three in the year AD 34.

The BC/AD system has a further disadvantage. *BC* can be used logically with both year dates and spans of years (for instance, *96 BC* as well as *83–30 BC*). *AD* has traditionally been used with single-year dates only (since *anno Domini* means "the *year* of our Lord"), making century designations and spans of years illogical. While it has become acceptable to use *AD* with centuries and year spans, that doesn't make its use any less clumsy. (See "*BC, AD*.")

Advantages of the BCE/CE System. *BCE* and *CE* are consistently placed after the year date, thereby avoiding the confusion caused by *AD*. Additionally, *BCE* and *CE* can be used unambiguously with single-year dates, spans of years, centuries, or even millennia.

To avoid imprecision, scholars use *BCE* and *CE* ("before the Common Era" and "Common Era") as a way of referring to the commonly accepted dates regardless of the actual date of Jesus's birth. The word *Common* in these phrases refers to the way in which dates have "commonly" been recorded in the West, that is, the BC/AD system. In a sense, it is actually an endorsement of the Western system of dating while acknowledging the variables. Otherwise, *AD 476* and *476 CE* are identical except that the latter does not imply that it is exactly 476 years after the birth of Jesus.

One disadvantage of *BCE* and *CE* is the number of people who mistakenly believe the abbreviations stand for, respectively, "before the Christian era" and "the Christian era." But by the same token, a surprising number of people believe that *AD* stands for "after death" (that is, after the death of Jesus), which would lead to an even greater mistaken assumption in dating any particular event.

With Year Dates before the Time of Christ. Like *BC*, *BCE* is used with all year dates before Jesus's time, and, like *AD*, *CE* is best used for one- or two-numeral year dates after the time of Jesus or in those cases when a reader might be unsure if the date is *CE* or *BCE* (for instance, *The emperor Trajan was born in 53 CE*).

Author Preference. This manual recommends that the author determine which system to use, though we encourage authors and publishers alike to consider seriously the BCE/CE system since it is becoming more common and is not inherently anti-Christian. Increasingly, an insistence upon the older form may raise issues of credibility for Christian publishers who wish to compete in the general academic market.

Beast, the

Although the NIV does not capitalize *the beast* in the book of Revelation (chapter 13), whenever the term is used as a name for Satan in general writing, it is usually capitalized as an epithet with the force of a proper name. Also capitalize *the Beast of the Apocalypse*.

Beatitudes, the; beatitude

Capitalize the term *the Beatitudes* as the title of a specific portion of the NT (Matt. 5:3–11), sometimes called *the Eight Beatitudes.* Lowercase it to mean a general state of bliss or any statement similar to those contained in the Beatitudes (often beginning with the KJV phrase "Blessed are ..."). The phrase *His Beatitude* is also an honorific title used before the names of some Roman Catholic patriarchs and Eastern Orthodox metropolitans.

Beelzebul, Beelzebub

The name *Beelzebul* (from Hebrew "lord of the house") is identified with Satan, or "the prince of demons," in Matt. 12:24 (NIV) and elsewhere in the Gospels. A similar name, spelled *Beelzebub* (pronounced either bee-EL-zuh-bub or BEEL-zuh-bub, meaning "lord of flies"), is used in the KJV. Note that in Milton's *Paradise Lost,* this figure is not Satan but a subordinate "next himself in power" (I:79).

believer

In recent decades the term *believer* has come into vogue as a synonym for *Christian.* It is common in Christian writing since, for many writers, it seems an inoffensive way of distinguishing practicing Christians from nominal ones. Still, in some contexts, it has acquired an air of Christian cant. The term is also limited by its generality, since it can refer to a believer of any religion, so use caution when targeting a readership made up of both Christians and non-Christians or when trying to distinguish between Christians and the faithful adherents of other religions. Note the term *true believer* often carries a hint of zealotry. (See also "*Christ follower.*")

believers baptism

Those churches that stress the concept of *believers baptism* usually use the term without a possessive apostrophe.

beloved, belovèd

In ordinary usage, *beloved* is pronounced as two syllables, especially when used as an adjective: for instance, *Wodehouse's beloved Pekinese.* Often, when used as a noun in liturgy, classic literature and poetry, and especially when quoting the Song of Songs, the word is pronounced as three syllables (*belovèd*): "*Dearly beloved, we are gathered here today ...*"; "*Beloved, thou hast brought me many flowers ...*" (E. B. Browning, "Sonnets from the Portuguese 44"); "*My beloved is mine and I am his*" (Song 2:16). In the case of tightly metered English poetry (like the example from Browning), one can determine whether *beloved* is two or three syllables by how it scans, usually in the iambic meter. Many writers, like Shakespeare, always considered it three syllables and indicated the two-syllable version by contracting it: *"Grant, if thou wilt, thou are belov'd of many . . ."* (Sonnet 10.3).

benediction, Benedictus

A *benediction* (lowercase) is a short blessing at the end of a worship service. It is sometimes capitalized in references to the specific portion of a Protestant liturgy or to that part of the Roman Catholic Eucharistic Mass. The *Benedictus* is the Latin title of a canticle (a sung portion of the Bible used in Roman Catholic and other liturgies) based either on Luke 1:68 or Matt. 21:9.

Benjamite, Benjaminite

Some English Bibles use the word *Benjamite* (KJV, NASB, and NIV) to describe someone from the ancient Hebrew tribe of Benjamin, while others use *Benjaminite* (Eugene Peterson's *The Message*, the recent ESV and CEB, and the UK version of the NIV). The earliest translation, Wycliffe's, uses both, though it favors *Benjaminite*. Both words are correct, though writers usually choose the variant used in their preferred translation.

bestseller, bestselling

Set these as single words, without space or hyphen. This is contrary to *Webster*, which lists *best seller* (noun) and *best-selling* (adj.). *The New York Times Manual of Style and Usage* agrees with *Webster*, and yet in the pages of the paper itself, the famous list on which all publishers wish their books to appear is referred to as the "Bestseller List." This is simply one of those combinations that are destined for closure.

Sometimes an author is referred to as a *bestseller*, as in *She is a* New York Times *bestseller*. For clarity's sake, reserve the noun *bestseller* for books rather than people. Use *bestselling author* to refer to a person: *She is a* New York Times *bestselling author*.

Bible Belt

No precise boundary can be drawn around the geographical region referred to as the *Bible Belt*. It is broadly identified with the American South—extending as far west as Texas and as far north as Kentucky, Virginia, and Maryland—and portions of the Midwest. The term, which is capitalized, seems to have been coined by journalist H. L. Mencken in a column in 1924 and is used derogatorily to describe conservative fundamentalists or those who hold an uncritical view of biblical literalism, regardless of geographic location.

Bible, bible

Capitalize the word *Bible* except for those instances when it is used metaphorically, as in *The Audubon guide is the bird lover's bible.* In the UK, the word *bible* is often lowercase in generic references, as in *How many bibles do you own?* (See also "BIBLE, THE—WHAT IS IT?")

Bible, Scripture

Though most Christians view them as synonymous, the terms *Bible* and *Scripture* are subtly different. *Bible* is the more plainspoken and the more commonly used both inside and outside the Christian subculture. For many general readers, *Scripture* has an overtone of religious cant. Additionally, the word *scripture*, lowercase, can refer to the sacred writings of other faiths (the Qur'an and the Book of Mormon, for instance). Even within Christian circles, the Latinate *Scripture* (from *scriptura*, Latin for "writing") can have a slightly artificial ring, since it has long been associated with the language of Victorian devotional literature and preaching. Both words are perfectly acceptable in most contexts, but the careful writer will be aware of their different shades of tone and the audience to which they are addressed. (See also "BIBLE, THE—WHAT IS IT?," "*Holy Bible, the*," and "*Scripture, the Scriptures, scripture, scriptures.*")

Bible study

Do not hyphenate this either as a noun or an adjective: *to conduct a Bible study* or *a Bible study group.* (See also "*biblical studies, Bible study.*")

Bible-thumper, Bible-thumping

Hyphenate both.

biblical

To the consternation of many, this adjective, as well as its synonym *scriptural*, is always lowercase, and it has been the most common style in English for many decades. Keep in mind that the word *bible* finds its origin in a Greek word meaning "book," and it was only when the word *holy* was added that it took on its special meaning: *The Holy Bible.*

biblical studies, Bible study

Despite their similarity, these terms are distinct. *Biblical studies* is the name of an academic discipline, usually involving the study of the original biblical languages and intended for seminarians, university students, or others studying to become scholars or religious professionals. A *Bible study* is a genre of book that discusses specific Bible passages, with the goal of leading lay readers to a better understanding of the Bible. Also, a group of lay people studying the Bible is termed *a Bible study*. A writer should not send a proposed series of Bible studies to a publisher that specializes in biblical studies and vice versa.

Biblicism, Biblicist

Biblicism and *Biblicist*, which are older terms meaning "biblical literalism" and "biblical literalist," are usually capitalized.

bibliolatry, bibliolater

The term *bibliolatry*, which is lowercase, usually means an excessive veneration of the Bible, as though the contents were themselves divine, or an exaggerated legalism regarding its tenets. For Christians, it can also imply a belief that the Bible or specific doctrines are more important than the persons of the Trinity in determining one's faith. Since the term can also mean "an excessive devotion to books," make sure the definition is clear in context. The term is sometimes awkwardly spelled *Bible-olatry*, perhaps to specify the Bible as the object of adoration as opposed to books in general. Most readers would be confused by that spelling. The word for a person who practices bibliolatry is *bibliolater* (not *bibliolator*), and it can mean a person excessively devoted either to the Bible or to books in general.

Various common Bible superstitions are rooted in bibliolatry; for example, the custom of never placing a Bible facedown on a table or never placing it next to certain nonreligious books on a shelf. Some sources describe procedures for properly disposing of old Bibles, stating they must be buried, burned, or even shredded rather than thrown in the trash. Most people, whether superstitious or not, would feel hesitant to toss an old family KJV in a Dumpster.

bibliomancy

Lowercase the term *bibliomancy*. It refers to the questionable practice of randomly selecting a Bible passage for spiritual direction or as an answer to prayer. One of the most famous instances was when Augustine of Hippo heard a child chanting, "Take up and read" (*Confessions*, 8:12). He did just that and opened his Bible to Rom. 13:13–14. Historically, bibliomancy has been practiced with other books as well, a favorite being Virgil's *Aeneid*. The *biblio-* in *bibliomancy* refers to books in general, not just Bibles.

bi-, semi-

What exactly do the prefixes *bi-* and *semi-* mean? It is clear that *bi-* suggests "two" (as in *bicycle* and *binary*) and *semi-* means "half" or "partly" (as in *semicircle* or *semiarid*). *Webster* reminds us that readers are often confused by such phrases as *a biweekly newspaper*, since some readers think it means "once every two weeks" and others think it means "two times a week," since the idea of "two" is inherent in both. Linguists agree that *a biweekly newspaper* is published every two weeks and *a semiweekly newspaper* is published twice a week. The same ambiguity exists for the terms *bimonthly* and *triweekly*. Although *biennial* means "every two years" and *biannual* means "twice a year," again, many readers confuse them. A gap lies between what readers *should* understand and what they actually *do* understand. The solution is for the writer and editor to clarify any terms that might cause confusion.

bishop

This is a clerical title, though the responsibilities of a bishop change from church to church. In the Eastern Orthodox, Anglican, and Roman Catholic churches, a bishop heads a diocese. In those Protestant denominations that have bishops, such as the Methodist, that title is given to those who supervise other clergy in a specific region. In the Mormon Church a bishop heads a ward.

Forms of Address. When writing to an Anglican bishop, the name in the address reads, "The Right Reverend [first and last names], Bishop of [name of diocese]," and the salutation reads, "Right Reverend Sir" or "Dear Bishop [last name]." When speaking to an Anglican bishop in person, say, "Bishop [last name]," and say, "The Right Reverend [first and last names], Bishop of [name of diocese]" when formally introducing a bishop.

When writing to a Roman Catholic bishop, "The Most Reverend [first and last names], Bishop of [name of diocese]" appears in the address and "Your Excellency" or "Dear Bishop [last name]" is used as the salutation. When addressing a bishop in person, say, "Your Excellency" or "Bishop [last name]," and say, "His Excellency" or "Bishop [first and last names]" when introducing him.

black

Lowercase this as a racial designation, though it may be capitalized in some contexts, such as a sociological study in which different races are formally highlighted. Although the term *African American* was the preferred adjective form for many years, the term *black* has recently come to supersede it, especially in journal style. (For more detail, see "*African American, black*" and "ETHNIC, NATIONAL, AND RACIAL DESIGNATIONS.")

Black Death

Black Death, capitalized, refers to the devastating pandemic that took place in Europe in the middle of the fourteenth century. Other, later episodes of the bubonic plague are sometimes referred to as the Black Death, though many of those episodes have their own historic names, such as *the Great Plague of London* (1665–66) and *the Russian Plague* (1770–72). In other words, *the Black Death* is a specific historical event rather than the name of disease.

Blessed, blessed, blessèd

In Roman Catholic tradition, *Blessed* is sometimes used as an honorific title before the names of those who have been beatified (that is, those for whom one miracle has been confirmed), as in *the Blessed Catherine of Saint Augustine*, or deserving of special veneration, as in *the Blessed Virgin Mary*. It is also used as a title in many formal epithets for groups of the venerated: *the Blessed Martyrs of Compiègne*. It is capitalized to distinguish it from the general use of the word, such as *the blessed fathers of the church*. This last usage is less common because it can be mistaken for the humorous use of *blessed* as a minced oath: *the blessed dog ate my sandwich* (in which *blessed* is a euphemism for its opposite). While the form *blest* is given as a secondary spelling in *Webster*, it is usually avoided.

Pronunciation. Note that when *blessed* is used in the senses described in the previous section, it is nearly always pronounced as two syllables (BLESS-ud), as in the Beatitudes, which begin "Blessed are . . ." (Matt. 5:3–12). Wycliffe's 1395 Bible made this two-syllable pronunciation clear by spelling the word *blessid*. If it is essential, in a poem, for instance, that the reader understand that it should be pronounced as two syllables, it may be spelled *blessèd*, though some readers may find the accent confusing. When the word is used broadly to describe the possession of spiritual or material blessings, the word is pronounced as one syllable: *As a nation, we've been blessed*. Many classic English writers, such as Shakespeare, spelled the word *bless'd* when specifying the one-syllable form: as in *The heavens have bless'd you with a goodly son (Richard III*, 1.3.9).

Blessed Sacrament, the

This term, meaning either the consecrated Host or the Eucharistic rite itself, is usually capitalized. *Blessed* here is pronounced as two syllables. (See also "*Blessed, blessed, blessèd*" and "*sacraments.*")

blog post

Spelled as two words. *Blog* is short for *web log*. (See also "BLOG STYLE AND TURNING BLOGS INTO BOOKS.")

blond, brunet

Use *blond* and *brunet* as the ordinary noun or adjective, whether referring to a male or a female. The feminine nouns *blonde* and *brunette* are more common in British English, but are often used in the US. To say *the blonde* or *the brunette* is acceptable in most writing, though some readers will consider those terms vaguely sexist—not because of the spellings so much as the defining of a woman by her hair color.

body and blood, Body and Blood

This term is lowercase (as in *The saving power of Christ's body and blood*), though it may be capitalized in liturgical contexts or when it is used as a synonym for Communion elements or the Eucharist, as in *We partook of the Body and Blood.*

book of . . . , Book of . . .

In references to books of the Bible, lowercase the word *book*, as in *the book of Genesis*, unless the version of the Bible being referenced capitalizes the entire phrase as a title, as does the KJV and some of its derivative translations: *the Book of Genesis*. Always follow the style of the translation being used.

Book, the

Capitalize this expression when used as a name for the Bible: *Pa would read from the Book every night*. The term carries an overtone of cant, piety, or old-time religion.

Book of Common Prayer, the

The title of this book, which exists in many editions, is set in roman type in text, and, as with *the Bible*, the article is lowercase: the Book of Common Prayer. It was originally written and compiled by Archbishop of Canterbury Thomas Cranmer and published in 1549, with Cranmer's revision being published three years later.

born again, born-again

This term, which finds its origin in John 3:3, is hyphenated as a compound adjective preceding a noun (*a born-again Christian*) but set as two words otherwise (*he was born again*). While this well-worn term still has credibility among evangelicals, it has been tarnished through overuse. For many readers, both inside and outside the church, it smacks of religious jargon. Since the 1970s, the popular press has used it sarcastically to describe anyone who has adopted a new creed or enthusiasm with zeal, as in *a born-again fiscal conservative* or *a born-again vegetarian.* For these reasons, use the term with care if the target readership is broader than the evangelical subculture. (See "JARGON, RELIGIOUS.")

both ... and

The formula *both ... and* is what is termed a paired conjunction, akin to *either ... or* and *neither ... nor.* The main problem with paired conjunctions is knowing whether they take singular or plural verbs. In the case of *both ... and* it's easy. Always use a plural verb, as in *Both Layali and Molly are first-year students.* (See also "*either ... or, neither ... nor.*")

boy

Apply the term *boy* only to males seventeen years of age or younger. Use *man* or *young man* for those eighteen or older.

brethren

Although *brethren* is often used as a gender-neutral way of saying "fellow believers" or "members of the church," most readers see it as male-specific. The more inclusive *brethren and sistren* is sometimes used, but it is awkward and sounds colloquial; *Webster* does not acknowledge the word *sistren* (though *Webster's Unabridged* does). When a gender-neutral word is needed, opt for an alternative to *brethren* such as *members, fellow worshipers, the faithful,* and so on.

Britain

An abbreviated form of *Great Britain.* (For details, see "*United Kingdom, Great Britain, England, British Isles.*")

Briticism, Britishism

To mean "characteristic of the people or language of England," these words are synonymous and acceptable, though *Briticism* is the older of the two and slightly preferred in some references.

British Isles

See "*United Kingdom, Great Britain, England, British Isles.*"

brother, Brother

The word *brother* is sometimes used informally before a proper name to indicate a fellow member of a church or congregation, as in *Let's ask Brother Raymond for a song.* In that usage the term is capitalized, though in general references (as in *It's good to see all the brothers and sisters here today*), it is lowercase. If used as an affectionate form of address for a sibling, it is capitalized: *How do we explain this to our parents, Brother?* (See also *"sister, Sister."*)

Monastic Use. The term *brother* is also used to refer to a friar or monk of the Roman Catholic Church and is capitalized before a proper name: *Brother Lawrence.* Some monks are also ordained priests and are addressed as *Father* by those outside the monastery, even though many of their fellow monks would still refer to them privately as *Brother.*

Forms of Address. When addressing a letter or email to a Roman Catholic brother, use "Brother [first name or first and last names]" in the address line, followed by the abbreviation indicating which order he is in (*"Brother Raymond Sykes, SJ"*). "Dear Brother" or "Dear Brother [first name]" serves as the salutation. When speaking, say, "Brother [first name]" or simply "Brother" and introduce him as "Brother [first name or first and last names]."

brunet

See *"blond, brunet."*

bulrush

Spelled *bulrush* (Ex. 2:3 KJV and some other versions), not *bullrush.*

by and by, by-and-by

As an adverbial phrase, *by and by* means "eventually," as in the gospel song, "We Will Understand It Better By and By." The noun form, also common in gospel songs in such phrases as "in the sweet by-and-by," is lowercase and hyphenated. This phrase, which is synonymous with "heaven" or "God's kingdom," is inconsistently rendered in hymnbooks as *by and by, By and By, bye and bye, Bye and Bye, bye-and-bye, Bye-and-Bye*, and so on. If it is important to quote a specific source accurately, then use the style of the original. Otherwise, *by and by* is the standard adverbial form ("eventually") and *by-and-by* the standard noun form ("heaven"). Avoid any combination that uses the spelling *bye*, since that is likely to evoke leave-taking, as in *goodbye.*

bye

See *"goodbye, good-bye, goodby, good-by."*

C

cabala

See "*Kabbalah, cabala.*"

call, calling

The words *call* and *calling* have a special meaning in Christian usage, and while the two are similar, a small distinction is observed. *Call* is more specific and temporal, often synonymous with one's specific job. A seminarian, for instance, receives a call (a more or less formal invitation) to become a pastor. This term is often rendered as a passive verb: *The seminarian was called to be the church's pastor.* (This is one instance where a passive construction is acceptable; *to be called to.*) By contrast, a *calling*, as a noun, has larger implications and is most often synonymous with one's life path or core identity. This is the sense of the word as used by Paul when he advises the Ephesians to "live a life worthy of the calling you have received" (4:1). That same seminarian, for instance, may have realized early in life that his calling was to serve as a pastor someday, but he had not yet received a specific call.

callous, callus

The adjective *callous* means "hard-hearted" or "uncaring" (or as Ambrose Bierce defined it, "Gifted with great fortitude to bear the evils afflicting another" [*The Devil's Dictionary*]), for instance, "*It is a callous age*" (L. Frank Baum, "Julius Caesar"). In precise usage, no such adjective as *calloused* exists since *callous* without the *-ed* already performs that function. The word *callused* does exist. It is an adjective describing someone who actually has *calluses*, or "hardened or thickened skin," as in *Her fingers were callused. To callus* (as a verb) means "to cause to have calluses," as in *The mandolin callused her fingers.*

Cambridge, University of

See "*Oxford and Cambridge, the Universities of.*"

canon (title)

A clerical title in the Anglican Church. A canon is connected with a chapter, a cathedral, or a collegiate church, or sometimes assists a bishop.

Canon, canon, Canonical, canonical

When used alone to mean "the Bible," capitalize *the Canon* as an alternate title. (Though see "BIBLE, THE: WHAT IS IT?") Lowercase it when it is used descriptively in such phrases as *the canon of Scripture.* Capitalize *Canonical* as part of a formal title for a portion of the Bible, as in *the Canonical Epistles.* Otherwise, lowercase *canon* and *canonical*: as in *the canonical hours* or *canon law.* A common mistake is to misspell *canon* ("accepted writings") as *cannon* ("large gun").

canoness

A clerical position in the Roman Catholic Church given to a woman who lives in a religious community but is not under binding vows.

Canticles

In some older references, the Song of Songs is referred to as Canticles (not *the* Canticles) or the Book of Canticles or the Canticle of Canticles, the last of these being used in English as early as the Wycliffe Bible in the fourteenth century. Though the use of *Canticles* is now largely outdated, it is still often found in literary contexts or when the plainer *Song of Songs* doesn't convey the exotic tone of the text itself. Like *Psalms*, the title *Canticles* has the form of a plural but takes a singular verb since it refers to a single book: as in *Canticles is part of the Old Testament canon.* One argument for avoiding the term is that other portions of the Bible are occasionally referred to as *canticles* (lowercase), notably those poetic portions that have been transformed into common liturgical songs, such as the Magnificat (Luke 1:46–55) and the Psalms.

carat, karat, caret

These three words are often confused. *Carat* is the measurement for diamonds; *karat* is the measurement for gold. *Caret*, as used by proofreaders and editors, is the " ^ " symbol used for inserting matter into type copy (see "TYPOGRAPHIC SYMBOLS, COMMON.") And none of them has anything to do with *carrot* ("a root vegetable").

cardinal

In the Roman Catholic Church, *cardinal* is a clerical title given to a high-ranking bishop appointed by and ranking just below the pope. Capitalize it before a proper name.

Forms of Address. When writing to a cardinal, use "His Eminence, Cardinal [first and last names], Archbishop of [location]" in the address block, and "Your Eminence" or "Dear Cardinal [last name]" as the salutation. When speaking to a cardinal, address him as "Your Eminence" or "Cardinal [last name]," and introduce him as "His Eminence, Cardinal [first and last names]." Until recently it was common to place the title *cardinal* between the person's given name and surname, as in *John Cardinal Newman*, but the Roman Catholic Church no longer sanctions this practice.

carol

In the US, the term *carol* has become synonymous with *Christmas song*, though the term can be appropriately applied to a song for any seasonal celebration. Only about half of the nearly two hundred songs in *The Oxford Book of Carols* (1965) relate to Christmas. A carol is defined as any song, often with traditional words or lyrics, used ceremonially or as part of a traditional seasonal celebration, though not necessarily religious; "May Day carols" are common in the UK, for instance. While "White Christmas" and "Frosty the Snowman" are sometimes regarded as Christmas carols in the US, they are more accurately Christmas songs. In its earliest meaning, *carol* described a specific poetic form, consisting of four lines, rhymed AAAB, and often the last line was either short or one of two repeating refrain lines.

catalog, catalogue

Catalog rather than *catalogue*. (But see "*dialogue, dialog.*")

catechism

Many churches, both Protestant and Catholic, offer religious education in the form of a *catechism*, which often takes the form of questions and answers that must be memorized. Classes of instruction, called *catechism classes*, are offered to coach prospective members in the *catechism*. The related terms are *catechist* (the instructor), the *catechumen* (the person being instructed), *catechesis* (the process of instruction), *catechetics* (the study of religious education), and *to catechize* (the verb teacher of a catechism class).

catholic, Catholic

Many a Protestant eyebrow has been raised over the line "I believe in the holy, catholic, and apostolic church" in the Apostles' Creed. The word *catholic*, when lowercase, means "universal, or general." The NT epistles of James, 1 and 2 Peter, 1 John, and Jude are known as the Catholic Epistles, because they are not addressed to any individual or church. Otherwise, *Catholic*, when capitalized, refers to the Roman Catholic Church.

CAT scan

Spelled *CAT scan* (for "computerized axial tomography"), not *cat scan* or *CAT-scan.*

CBA (The Association for Christian Retail)

Established in 1950, the CBA is the largest Christian retail association in the Western hemisphere. The abbreviation *CBA* originally stood for "Christian Bookseller's Association," but since its member retailers deal in more than books, the name was changed to the Association for Christian Retail, though the original acronym has been retained.

CE/BCE

See "*BCE/CE.*"

celebrant

In general usage, *celebrant* means "one who celebrates." A reveler at a party, for instance, may be referred to as a *celebrant*, though *celebrator* is the term more often used. In Protestant ecclesial contexts *celebrant* may refer to any worshiper at a religious service, though *attendee* or *congregant* would be the more common terms (see "*congregant*"). Be careful when using *celebrant* in the context of the Roman Catholic Mass, in which the word refers specifically to the priest who officiates at the celebration of the Eucharist, not those in the congregation. If more than one priest celebrates the Mass, they are *concelebrants*, not *co-celebrants.*

Celestial City

Even though *heaven* is usually lowercase, capitalize *Celestial City*, which comes from John Bunyan's *Pilgrim's Progress*, where it is used allegorically as a geographic place name, along with other allegorical place names from that work like the *City of Destruction* and the *Delectable Mountains.* (See "*heaven, Heaven.*")

celibate, chaste, chastity

Someone who is *celibate* has chosen to refrain from both marriage and sex (as Roman Catholic priests, monks, and nuns do). Someone who is *chaste* refrains from sex outside of marriage or refrains from sex entirely if they are not married. In other words, a *celibate* is also *chaste*, but a *chaste* person need not be *celibate. Chaste* can be applied to both males and females, though it is most commonly applied to females. Note that Christian readers will understand the words *chaste* and *chastity* quite differently from general readers, who may even consider them terms of derision, or at least antiquated. This makes using those words problematic outside a strictly Christian context.

cell phone

Spell *cell phone* as two words until otherwise notified by *Webster* at some point in the future. They spell it as two words, perhaps, on the model of *mobile phone* and *pay phone*. Still, *cell phone* seems destined to become one word, and some style guides are already listing it that way. (See also "*smartphone*.")

censer, censor, censure

These words are occasionally confused. A *censer* is a container, often suspended from a chain, for burning incense during religious worship. A *censor* is someone who prohibits something from being released to the public or who eliminates the objectionable portions of a larger work. It can also be a verb, *to censor*. The word *censure* is also both a noun and a verb, meaning *condemnation* and *to condemn* respectively.

century

Lowercase *century* in date designations, and hyphenate it as part of a compound adjective: *the fourth century, twenty-first-century evangelicalism*.

chaplain, chaplaincy

A *chaplain* is a clergyperson who conducts services in a chapel or for a particular organization. The word is usually used alone as a noun (*The chaplain led the prayer*) and not as a title before a proper name. The person's actual title is used instead: as in *Reverend Browne led the prayer.* The office itself is referred to as a *chaplaincy*, not a *chaplainship*. Avoid the common misspelling *chaplin*.

charismatic

In common usage *charismatic* means "relationally attractive and compelling." In its modern religious sense, it has come to mean "characterized by an emphasis on the gifts of the Holy Spirit." Most contexts will clarify the meaning without much difficulty. Lowercase the word in both senses. The reason that *charismatic* is lowercase while *Pentecostal* is capitalized is that *Pentecostal* is derived from a proper noun (*Pentecost*), while *charismatic* is not. Also lowercase such terms as *the charismatic church* and *the charismatic movement*.

cherub, cherubim, cherubims, cherubs

A biblical *cherub* is a winged, angel-like being, first referred to in Gen. 3:24. The plural is *cherubim*, though be careful when quoting the KJV, which uses the double plural *cherubims*. Angelology distinguishes between *cherubim*, who have multiple roles, and the *seraphim*, who are more closely connected to the throne of God and who surround it with praises. (See also "*seraph, seraphim, seraphims, seraphs*.") A biblical *cherub* is not to be confused with the pudgy, winged baby, also called a *cherub*, depicted in Western art, sometimes mistakenly called a *cupid*. The correct plural of that kind of *cherub* is *cherubs*, though art historians' term for them is *putti* (Italian for "small boys").

chrish

Lowercase this contemporary slang word (pronounced KRISH), which is short for *Christian* and derogatorily refers to certain Christians, especially those who used to be referred to by the pejorative term *goody-goody*.

chrismation

This term, referring to the sacrament in the Eastern Orthodox Church in which new members are anointed, is correctly lowercase. It is sometimes capitalized because the root word is mistakenly thought to be *Christ*, but both *Christ* ("the Anointed One") and *chrismation* ("the act of anointing") go back to earlier Latin and Greek roots meaning "ointment" or "oil." The term is properly capitalized whenever a publisher's house style is to capitalize all words for the sacraments.

Christ, Jesus

Some writers use the name *Jesus* when referring to him during his time on earth or when stressing his human characteristics, and they tend to use *Christ* when referring to his messianic role as savior or when discussing his divinity. This is not a rule, for following it too strictly would lead to verbal woodenness. As an occasional guideline, it may be helpful, since it can seem slightly off-kilter to say, "The baby Christ, lying in a manger" or "Glory to the ever-living Jesus, at the right hand of the Father."

Christendom, Christianity

Writers commonly use *Christendom* and *Christianity* synonymously to mean the Christian faith. In precise usage, *Christianity* is applied to the Christian faith as practiced around the world, but *Christendom*, which has become a largely antiquated term, is more limited to those parts of the world where Christianity has been a dominant historical and cultural force. Christianity, for instance, is widely practiced in Asia and Africa, but those continents as a whole are not usually considered part of Christendom, though that is rapidly changing as the demographic weight of the Christian faith shifts toward Asia and Africa. The term *Christendom* also has geopolitical overtones, and some writers, including Malcolm Muggeridge, use it to mean nominally Christian Western culture in contrast to genuine Christian faith worldwide. In using this term, which can have such different meanings, a writer should clarify his or her definition.

Christ follower

Christ follower has been adopted by some writers for whom the word *Christian* seems overly identified with a particular branch of the faith or with nominal Christianity. *Christ follower* defines those who, no matter what branch of the faith they belong to, are serious about obeying Christ's admonitions. The term is common especially among the young and those who identify with the emerging church. Whether this term will be outdated within a few years remains to be seen. It is usually set open, but hyphenating it—*Christ-follower*—is acceptable whenever the author has a strong preference. (See also "*believer.*")

Christianism, Christianist

Originally, the terms *Christianism* and *Christianist* were neutral (and little used), referring to the Christian faith and its believers worldwide, but in recent years, the terms have been redefined as parallels for the terms *Muslimism* and *Muslimist*, and all these terms imply a militant, even violent fundamentalism. The terms are pejorative.

Christianize, Christianization

Capitalize these terms.

Christian name

Although the term *Christian name* has been common in English since the sixteenth century, most contemporary stylists discourage its use. Like the synonymous *baptismal name*, which implies that a person has been baptized, *Christian name* presumes that a person is a Christian. Use the terms *first name*, *forename*, *given name*, or *personal name* instead, unless specifically referring to a ceremony of baptism at which a child receives a name or at which an adult receives a saint's name. These terms are not to be confused with *surname*, which is synonymous with *family name*, or *last name*. Note the terms *first name* and *last name* are increasingly being avoided because they are reversed in many cultures.

Christ Jesus, Jesus Christ

Both forms are correct. *Christ Jesus* seems more formal and appropriate for prayer and liturgy, while *Jesus Christ* seems less formal and appropriate for general expository writing. *Christ* (meaning "anointed one") is not a name but a title, so it can be appropriately placed before the personal name. *Jesus Christ*, which is short for *Jesus, the Christ*, is the form most commonly seen, though it has misled generations of Sunday school children into thinking that *Christ* is Jesus's last name.

Christlike, Christlikeness

These are commonly misspelled with a hyphen between *Christ* and *like*. Close these up.

christo-, Christo-

Should we capitalize words that begin with *christo-*? *Webster* recommends capitalizing them (*Christocentric, Christogram*), while this manual has long recommended lowercasing them. It may seem strange that a Christian style manual would lowercase words so closely associated with Jesus, but as is pointed out elsewhere, capitalization is not used to confer respect or grant importance. It is used as a way to distinguish specific things from general things.

Technically, the word *Christ* is not a proper name, but a title. When it is used as if it were a proper name for Jesus, capitalize it as you would capitalize *Messiah*. But lowercase both of those terms when they are used in a general or adjectival sense: *he foretold of false christs to come* or *they studied messianic prophecies*. In a sense, *Christ* and *Messiah* are capitalized in reference to Jesus for the same reasons that *the Boss* is capitalized in a book about Bruce Springsteen. The title comes to have the force of a name for those specific people.

The following terms, though they reference Jesus, are more general than they are actual names, so we recommend lowercasing them: *christocentrism*, *christogram*, and *christophany*. One exception to this rule would be the word *Christology*—the formal study of Jesus's life and work. The reason is largely precedent and convention in academic circles—though note that the adjective *christological* is lowercase.

church, Church

The word *church* is capitalized when used in the name of a specific denomination or congregation's meeting place: as in *the Church of England, the Church of Rome*, or *Saddleback Church*. When used to mean believers as a whole, the historical church, the body of Christ, the church universal, or organized religion in general, the term is usually lowercase: *the church age, church and state, the church in all times and places, the church in America, the church invisible, the church militant, the church triumphant, the church visible, the first-century church*, and so on. Avoid the feminine pronoun in referring to the church unless it is clearly in the metaphorical context of the church as the Bride of Christ. (See also "*her, she.*")

church fathers

See "*fathers of the church, church fathers.*"

churchgoer, churchgoing

Don't hyphenate these words.

churchianity

This derogatory term dates from the first half of the nineteenth century and refers to an excessive adherence to one's denomination or individual fellowship. It also suggests a belief that mere church attendance is an adequate display of one's faith.

Church of England

See "*Anglican Church, Church of England.*"

circa

Meaning "about" or "approximately," the Latin word *circa* is abbreviated as either *ca.* or *c.* (Older references sometimes use *circ.*) Academics lean toward *ca.*, so as not to confuse it with the abbreviation for *century*, which is *c.* Popular writers and those who bridge the gap between scholarship and popular readerships tend to use *c.* Both options are acceptable. *SBL* recommends only *ca.* for scholarly writers. *CMoS* lists both but states that *ca.* offers more clarity. *MLA* and *Oxford* list only *c.* The word *circa* and its abbreviations are used primarily with year dates, as in *Saint Ambrose (ca. 340–397 CE)*. The word is often spelled out in narrative text, as in *Ambrose Bierce disappeared in Mexico circa 1914*.

Use of Question Mark. Some trade-books writers, concerned that readers will not know what *c.* means, use a question mark, as in *Sundar Singh (1889–1929?)*. This is acceptable but not ideal; the reader doesn't know whether scholars in general or only the author is unsure of the date. Reserve the question mark to express authorial doubt, as in *He left for Europe about a decade later (1962?)*.

With Precise Dates. Although *circa*, *ca.*, and *c.* are often used with year dates rounded to the nearest five or ten, they may be used with more precise year dates. For instance, Athanasius of Alexandria is sometimes noted as having been born *ca. 297.* This indicates that the birth year is fairly certain, give or take a year or so. This is perfectly acceptable.

With or Without Space. US style is to put a space after the abbreviation (*c. 1300*); UK style is to close it up (*c.1300*).

With a Range of Dates. Do not use *ca.* or *c.* for a range of year dates; use it before each date that is uncertain.

> Papias of Hierapolis (ca. 70–163) [only the birth year uncertain]
> Tertullian (ca. 155–ca. 240) [both birth and death years uncertain]

cleave, to

We think of the verb *to cleave* as a particularly biblical word because of its use in Gen. 2:24 (KJV): "Therefore shall a man leave his father and his mother, and shall cleave unto his wife." But as we do today, the KJV also uses the word to express a nearly opposite meaning: "Thou didst cleave the fountain and the flood" (Ps. 74:15).

As an intransitive verb, *to cleave* means "to adhere." As a transitive verb, it means "to split or divide." This odd state of affairs came about because the two meanings of *to cleave* stem from distinct etymologies. *To cleave* ("adhere") comes from the High German *kleben*, meaning "to stick"; whereas *to cleave* ("divide") comes from Latin and Greek roots through the Old Norse word *kljûfa*, meaning "to split." Fortunately, the words are used seldom enough to cause much confusion, and the context usually makes the meaning clear.

clergy

Clergy is a collective noun, so it is as awkward to say *many clergy attended the conference* as it is to say *many flock grazed in the field.*

Use *clergyman* or *clergywoman* for individuals only when it is essential to specify gender; otherwise, *clergy* is the standard non-gender-specific form. (See also "GENDER-ACCURATE LANGUAGE.") This can also be expanded as needed to *member(s) of the clergy*, as in *many members of the clergy attended the conference*. If a non-gender-specific form is required for an individual, *clergyperson* is acceptable, though awkward, and this manual suggests using *member of the clergy* instead. The correct plural form of the collective *clergy* is *clergies*, as in *the clergies of several denominations attended.*

clerical title, clerical position, lay position

A *clerical title* is a formal title given to a member of the clergy, by which that person is addressed. For instance, *Pastor Charles Stanley, Archbishop Fulton Sheen, Presiding Bishop Katharine Jefferts Schori.* A *clerical position* refers to an official job or duty within the church, such as *a minister* or *a priest*, but the terms themselves are not used as formal titles. A minister, for instance, is referred to as *Reverend [Name]* rather than *Minister [Name]*, and a priest is usually referred to as *Father [Name]*. Be aware that some terms are titles in one denomination while being simply a position in another. A *clerical position* usually implies that the person has had special training for that position and is considered a member of the clergy; a *lay position* implies that the person has not had formal training.

coauthor

See "*cowriter, coauthor.*"

coheirs, co-heirs

The NIV spells it *co-heirs*, though it is used only once (Rom. 8:17: "heirs of God and co-heirs with Christ"). Spell it *coheirs* in text, to accord with *Webster.* The hyphenated form may be useful in copy that quotes that particular passage from the NIV Romans, though the divergence from *Webster* should be noted on a style sheet. Other Bible versions translate the word as *joint-heirs* (KJV) or *fellow heirs* (ESV, NASB). Only the Holman Christian Standard Bible uses *coheirs*.

coliseum, Colosseum

The lowercase word *coliseum* means "a large amphitheater." The *Colosseum* is the ancient amphitheater in central Rome, also called the Flavian Amphitheater. In the context of early church history, many Christian martyrs were killed "in the Colosseum," not "in the coliseum," though one may wish to clarify such references since historical evidence suggests that more early Roman Christians were martyred in the Circus Flaminius than in the Colosseum. Note that *coliseum* is often spelled *colosseum* in the UK.

collect, Collect

When referring to a short liturgical prayer (common in Anglican and Lutheran worship, when congregants are asked to "collect" their thoughts), this word is accented on the first syllable (KAHL-ect). When listed as the title for that part of a formal worship service or liturgy, it is commonly capitalized: *The Collect came after the Invocation.*

come-to-Jesus meeting

In a *come-to-Jesus meeting*, one person confronts another with hard truths or calls that person on the carpet. The Southern-sounding phrase does not necessarily imply a religious context and has become an overused catchphrase.

commandments, the

The term *the commandments* usually refers to the Ten Commandments, though in some Jewish contexts, it can refer to the 613 individual commandments given in the Torah. In either case, the term is usually lowercase when unqualified (*The commandments specifically proscribe such behavior*). (For more detail, see "*Ten Commandments, the*.")

Common Era

See "*BCE/CE*."

common sense, commonsense

The noun is *common sense*; the adjective is *commonsense*, as in *Reaching a commonsense solution often takes more than common sense.*

Communion

Capitalize *Communion* in all references to the sacrament, as in *The church offers Communion only twice a year.* (See also "*Holy Communion*" and "*Last Supper, the*.")

communist, Communist, communism, Communism

Capitalize *Communist* when the Communist Party is invoked either directly (*a card-carrying Communist*) or indirectly (*he was interrogated for alleged Communist activity*). Also capitalize it when referring to nations with Communist governments (*Communist China, Communist North Korea*). If the philosophy of communally owned property is meant, lowercase it (*The early church practiced a form of communism*). When in doubt, lowercase it (*The West's struggle against communism*). The derogatory epithet *Commie* is usually capitalized, implying that a person is, or is alleged to be, a member of an official Communist organization.

completed Jew

This term is highly offensive to Jews as well as many Christians. It refers to a Jewish person who embraces a form of Messianic Judaism that views Jesus as the Messiah. Avoid it.

comprise, compose, consists of

Comprise and *compose* are found in nearly every usage manual because they are so commonly confused. Remember: the whole *comprises*, or *contains*, the parts, and the parts *compose, constitute*, or *make up* the whole. Some pedants insist that the passive *comprised of* (as in *The denomination is comprised of sixty-eight churches*) is an error and should never be used, but it has been part of English since at least the 1700s. Both *The Bible is comprised of sixty-six books* and *The Bible comprises sixty-six books* are correct. The phrase *consists of* is often a wordy way of saying *has*: for instance, *The book has five chapters* is more efficient than *The book consists of five chapters.*

confession

Largely because of Saint Augustine's revelatory autobiography, *The Confessions* (ca. 400), the term *confession*, as a literary genre, has come to mean a personal narrative in which the author admits to misdeeds and indiscretions. We forget that Augustine actually used the word to mean "praise," "proclamation," and "thanksgiving," a series of declarations of his faith in God. This sense of the word is found in the titles of such documents as the *Augsburg Confession* and is still with us when we say that someone is a "confessing Christian" or "confesses faith in Christ," even though many people believe that to "confess one's faith" means to "admit to being a Christian" or "owning up to one's faith," as if it were a secret.

The word was eventually applied to the admission of sin as part of the Catholic penitential process, and as a modern literary genre it came to imply an author's usually self-justifying moral self-assessment, as in Jean-Jacques Rousseau's seminal *Confessions* (1781, 1788). In that sense, *confession* has come to mean the "confessing of sin," as a criminal might give a "confession" to the police. Confession is one of the rites of the Roman Catholic Church, in which the person confessing a sin is absolved by a priest. When the *rite of confession* is being referenced, lowercase the term, though some Roman Catholic publishers prefer to capitalize it. (See "*Rite, rite.*") Note that in the Roman Catholic rite of confession, *the confessor* is the priest who hears the confession. The person confessing is *the penitent.*

Although the context will usually make the meaning clear, care should be taken when the older meaning of *confession*, that is, "proclaiming one's faith," is intended. Many general readers do not understand the way Christians have historically used the term.

Congo

This region of West Africa, largely the Congo River basin, is referred to as *Congo*, not *the Congo*. If referring to a country, the term *Congo* alone (again, no article) specifies the easternmost of two adjacent countries, the Democratic Republic of the Congo (which was called Zaire from 1971 to 1997, the capital of which is Kinshasa). The term *Congo Republic* refers to the Republic of the Congo (formerly called Middle Congo, the capital of which is Brazzaville). If precision is needed, reference to the capital city is helpful: *The diplomatic mission arrived in Congo (capital, Kinshasa).*

congregant

Although the word *congregant* may seem unambiguous, it can mean either "a member of a church or congregation" or "someone attending a worship service." The context will clarify the meaning. Most Christian readers assume that those two meanings are the same, but to specify only those who are in attendance at a particular worship service, as opposed to members, the words *attendee* or *attender* would be clearer.

Congress, congressional

Capitalize *Congress* when referring to the US Congress, but lowercase the adjective *congressional* unless it is part of the name of a specific legislative district (*the Tenth Congressional District*). Like other titles, *congressman* and *congresswoman* are lowercase unless they immediately precede a proper name (*Congresswoman Huizinga*). The gender-neutral terms *congressperson* and *congresspeople* are acceptable.

In references to the US government, the terms *Congress* and *congressional* encompass both the Senate and the House of Representatives (though *congressional committees* are further subdivided into *Senate committees* and *House committees*), whereas the terms *congressman* and *congresswoman* refer only to members of the House of Representatives. A senator serves in Congress but is not considered a "congressperson."

Using an Article. Unmodified, *Congress* does not use an article, as in *Congress blocked the president*. Otherwise, when *Congress* is modified, use the article, as in *the 113th Congress* or *the US Congress*.

conservative

As an ideological approach to theology or politics, lowercase *conservative* as both an adjective and a noun (*conservative Christianity* or *the modern conservative movement*). (William F. Buckley once defined a conservative as someone who "stands athwart history, yelling Stop" [*National Review*,

Nov. 19, 1955]). *Conservative* is capitalized in the term *Conservative Judaism.* (See "*Judaism.*")

Constitution, constitutional

When *Constitution* refers to the US Constitution, capitalize it. Lowercase the adjective *constitutional* (as well as *unconstitutional*).

continual, continuous

Use *continual* to mean "something repeated or done at regular intervals" (*the continual interruptions to answer the phone*), and *continuous* means "ongoing, without break or interruption" (*the continuous ringing in his ears*). Apply the same rules for *continually* and *continuously.* It is a useful distinction for those aware of the difference.

convert, conversion

The terms *convert* and *conversion* are used to describe someone who moves from one religion or from atheism to another religion or belief system entirely. It is not used to describe someone who moves from one form of Christianity or denomination to another. A Roman Catholic, for instance, does not convert to Protestantism or Orthodoxy. Still, because of the Christian sense of this word, it is now commonly used metaphorically, as in ... *her conversion from classical music to jazz.*

convict, to

The verb *to convict* has a specific theological meaning for evangelicals that may be opaque to readers outside the Christian subculture. For evangelicals, it means "to pique the conscience of," so that a phrase like *the sermon convicted the congregation* means that God, through the sermon, made the listeners aware of some sin or shortcoming in their lives. *Conviction* of sin, in this sense, leads to repentance and salvation. When used in this religious sense, the terms *to convict*, *to be convicted*, and *conviction* may need to be defined for a general readership. Additionally, these terms are sometimes used so loosely by Christians that they amount to jargon.

copastor

Set solid; no hyphen.

copyeditor, copyedit

Although *Webster* presents *copy editor* and *copyedit* as their preferred forms, this manual recommends spelling both of them solid: *copyeditor*, *copyedit*. This conforms with *CMoS* and *Garner.*

corporal, corporeal

The noun *corporal* is the military rank above a private. As an adjective, it is often confused, especially in religious contexts, with *corporeal* because both relate to the idea of "bodies." *Corporal*, as an adjective, which is most commonly found in the phrase *corporal punishment*, means "affecting or relating to a body." *Corporeal* is usually used when emphasizing the tangibility, or physicality, of the body in contrast to something spiritual or less tangible (as in *the corporeal presence of Jesus*). Note that *corporal* is sometimes used as a noun in the Roman Catholic Mass, referring to the cloth on which the Eucharist is placed.

Counter-Reformation

Contrary to the rule that most words combined with the prefix *counter* are set solid (as in *counterculture* or *counteroffer*), the term *Counter-Reformation* (which, during the last half of the sixteenth and first half of the seventeenth centuries, was the Roman Catholic response to the Protestant Reformation) is hyphenated. Both elements are capitalized. It is sometimes referred to as *the Catholic Reformation*.

couple

Purists insist that *couple* should always be followed by *of* in phrases like *a couple of pastors*. While this rule is valuable—even preferred in formal writing—it is not mandatory. Dropping *of* after *couple* has not only been part of English for centuries but is required when used with such modifiers as *less* or *more* (*a couple more invitations*). The *of* is commonly dropped in fictional dialogue and informal writing ("*He disappeared a couple months ago*"). Note that *of* is necessary when specifying two items out of a larger group (*I need a couple of you to volunteer*).

Singular or Plural? As a noun meaning "two," *couple* can be singular or plural, depending on the context. When two people are spoken of as a unit, a singular verb is usually used (*the couple is into bluegrass music*), but when the context references the two as individuals, a plural verb may be preferred (*the couple always give each other lots of encouragement*). This is not a rigid rule, and the author's preference should prevail. Note that when *couple of* is used, a plural verb is used (*a couple of clerks are quitting*).

Who or That? Use *who* rather than *that* for modifying phrases with *couple* whenever people are involved; as in *the couple who moved in next door*.

court

See "*Supreme Court, court.*"

covenant, old or new

Lowercase *covenant* in most references to the covenants of God: *the old covenant*, *the new covenant*, *the covenant of grace*, *the covenant of the Lord*. Also, don't be fooled by the adjective form; it is *covenantal*, not *covenental*.

cowriter, coauthor

Webster does not hyphenate these words, which are extremely common to publishing, and *Webster*'s judgment, as usual, is sound. Some writers feel that the initial *cow-* of *cowriter* could cause misreading, but few readers are likely to stumble over the word. Stick with *Webster*, and don't be cowed by those who think otherwise.

creation

Lowercase it when referring to either God's act of creating the physical world or the physical world itself.

Creator, creator

When the word is used as an epithet—that is, a name—for God, capitalize it: *the Creator*. When it is used descriptively for God's creative acts, lowercase it: *the creator of the world*, *he is an all-powerful creator*, *the creator God*, and so on.

crèche

Crèche is from an Old French word meaning "manger." Note that the grave accent is usually retained in English. The word is usually pronounced with a short *e* sound (rhyming with *flesh*), but it is also alternately pronounced with a long *a* sound (rhyming with the first syllable of *patient*).

crosier

Usually called a *pastoral staff*, this word is spelled *crosier*, not *crozier*.

cross, the

Lowercase this word both as the wooden object itself and as referring to the event of the crucifixion of Jesus. (See also "*crucifix*.")

crossroad, crossroads

Although *crossroad* is perfectly correct, *crossroads* is more commonly used since the word implies more than a single road (as in *my life was at a crossroads*). *Crossroads* is usually construed as a singular noun, despite looking like a plural; as in *the crossroads is empty.* Only construct *crossroads* as a plural when more than one such intersection is implied: *both of the town's crossroads are without traffic lights.*

crucifix

In precise usage, *crucifix* is not synonymous with *cross.* A *crucifix* is an art object (often a sculpture) showing Jesus on the cross, while such an object without the figure of Jesus is referred to as a *cross.*

crucifixion, resurrection

Lowercase such terms as *the crucifixion* and *the resurrection* in most writing for general readers. Capitalizing them is a holdover from a time when devotional books capitalized many religious objects, ideas, and events. While capitalization is used to distinguish specific things from general ones, the article *the* does enough to define which crucifixion and which resurrection are being referred to. When writing of "*the* crucifixion," little doubt exists as to whose crucifixion is meant.

An added disadvantage is that the capitalized terms may appear to hold special meanings for the author that are not understood by all readers, especially those who may not be Christians. For instance, in a popular book that tries to argue for the historicity of the crucifixion of Jesus or an apologetic that tries to make an objective case for the resurrection, capitalizing those terms may make the reader feel that the writer has a preconceived bias toward one point of view. Typographic style should not suggest partisanship in a book purporting to be objective.

Like most rules in this manual, this one may be broken when appropriate. The terms may be capitalized when the author and editor agree that they should be, for instance, in scholarly works in which *the crucifixion* and *the resurrection* are discussed largely as abstract theological concepts, or, like the deity pronoun, in devotional works intended to have a somewhat classic or antiquated feel. (See also "EVENTS IN THE LIFE OF JESUS, LOWERCASING.")

crusade, crusades

The terms *crusade* and *crusades* are legitimate words in many contexts, though they are best avoided when used figuratively for Christian evangelism, modern military campaigns, or any effort to promote beliefs or values cross-culturally. The terms have acquired negative overtones in the popular press, suggesting extremism or zealotry, as in *the parents' crusade to ban the book from the library.* More importantly, the terms are an affront to Muslims worldwide. The terms still strongly evoke the Crusades (capitalized only in reference to the historical event) of the eleventh, twelfth, and thirteenth centuries because they were specifically coined to describe those wars (from the French *croisade* and Spanish *cruzada,* meaning "blessed by, or marked with, a cross"). In that sense, it means "holy war" and is comparable to the Arabic term *jihad.* Even the Billy Graham Evangelistic Association at one point distanced itself from the term *crusade.* When in doubt, find another word. Such words as *outreach, event, appeal,* and *campaign* (though that last term may be overly warlike in some contexts) can usually be substituted, as in *a city-wide evangelism outreach* or *a spiritual appeal to nonbelievers.*

cult

Be careful—or even seek legal advice—before derogatorily labeling any contemporary religion or movement a *cult.* It could constitute libel in some cases.

curate

Although this title describes a member of the clergy who is in charge of a parish, it is an informal title and does not precede a proper name. The person's regular title is used instead: for instance, *Reverend Beefy Bingham, curate of Market Blandings.* (See "*clerical title, clerical position, lay position.*") Although Catholic parish priests are sometimes referred to as *curates,* the title is mostly associated with parish priests or their assistants in the Anglican Church.

cursed, cursèd

Like its counterpart *blessed,* the word *cursed* has two common pronunciations: one syllable and two syllables. As an adjective preceding a noun, the word is usually two syllables, as in John Ruskin's "the cursed animosity of inanimate objects" (pronounced CURSS-ud, optionally spelled *cursèd*). As an adjective following a verb or as the past tense of the verb *to curse,* the word is pronounced as one syllable: as in *"Their portion of the land is cursed" (Job 24:18).* (See also "*Blessed, blessed, blessèd.*")

cyber

The word *cyber* has been a stand-alone adjective since the early 1990s to mean "relating to computer, internet, or social media"; for instance, *cyber warfare* and *cyber marketplace*. The trend has been to close up *cyber* to its companion word: *cyberattack*, *cyberbullying*, *cyberchurch*, *cybercrime*, *cyberlink*, *cyberspace*, *cybertech*. No rule exists to distinguish the adjective from the prefix, but few readers will be confused by either form. Consult standard references and trust author preference. The word *cyber* is fading as a prefix because it is often irrelevant; *cybercrime* is *crime* and *cyberpoetry* is *poetry*, whether it's digital or not.

D

Daesh

In September 2015, even before the November terrorist attacks on Paris, the French government began using the name *Daesh* (pronounced DAH-ish) in reference to the terrorist organization known as *ISIS*, *ISIL*, or *the Islamic State*. (See "*ISIS, ISIL*.") *Daesh* is a rough acronym of the Arabic version of those names, although unlike *ISIS* and *ISIL*, it is spelled cap-and-lowercase. Though the name *Daesh* will become more common, *ISIS* and *the Islamic State* will probably remain the forms used most often in the media.

Dalai Lama, the

Since it is used like a proper name, the title for the head of Tibetan Buddhism is always capitalized, with an article: *the Dalai Lama*.

damn, damned

Some writers argue that *damn*, when used expletively as an adjective or adverb, should actually be *damned*. But the casual use of *damn* goes back to the 1700s and is firmly established in English in such common phrases as *damn Yankees* and *damn lies*. While most Christian publishers discourage the use of *damn* and *damned* as casual profanity (see "PROFANITY"), they are acceptable in their literal sense, as in "*Sooner or later, nearly everyone is surprised at some kind of rich man being damned*"—*Charles Williams*. Note that *damned* was formerly pronounced as two syllables, *damnèd*, but is only humorously done so now. Avoid the mincing *dam* as a euphemism.

Dark Ages, the

This problematic term is used less often than it once was. First, *Dark Ages* usually refers only to the first portion of the Middle Ages, from the fall of Rome to about 1100, but many people mistakenly think of it as synonymous with the entire span of the Middle Ages. Second, the era was only considered "dark" because Rome had fallen, but scholars have shown that the era was one of great artistic and cultural innovation and experimentation. For these reasons, use *medieval era* (lowercase) or *Middle Ages* (capitalized) instead. If only the early portion is being referred to, use *early Middle Ages* or specify the time span: *the first five centuries after the fall of Rome*. (See "*medieval*" and "*Middle Ages*.")

Still, *the Dark Ages* abides as a useful metaphor. For instance, one might refer to the 1950s as *the Dark Ages of Rock 'n' Roll* or as one's youth being *back in the Dark Ages*. In such usage, the term is still capitalized.

D-Day

Even though *Webster* spells this *D-day*, referring to the Allied invasion of Nazi-occupied France on June 6, 1944, General Eisenhower himself spelled it *D-Day*, as do most other references and history books. *Webster* gets overruled in this case.

deacon

Deacon is a formal clerical title in the Anglican and Roman Catholic churches. A deacon is one step on the way toward becoming a priest. Some deacons do not advance farther and serve in the church in unpaid positions. Deacons are usually addressed as "reverend" in the Anglican Church. In the Mormon Church, a deacon is the lowest grade of the Aaronic priesthood.

Deacon is also a clerical position in many Protestant churches, usually referring to a lay officer, sometimes elected, who performs pastoral care or administrative duties or oversees ministries or maintenance duties in a church. This seems to be the sense in which Paul uses the term in 1 Tim. 3:8–13, where he carefully outlines the traits required of a good deacon. (See also "*clerical title, clerical position, lay position*.")

Dead Sea Scrolls, Dead Sea scroll

When referring to the collections of ancient texts discovered in Qumran, capitalize this term; otherwise, lowercase *scroll* for individual documents or scrolls.

dean

In the Anglican Church, *dean* is a clerical title commonly given to the head of a cathedral or seminary, and such a person is usually addressed in person and in written salutations as *Dean* (*Dean Wallingham*) and in the address line of letters as *The Very Reverend* (*The Very Reverend Theresa Wallingham*). Beyond that, the function and forms of address for deans of other denominations vary.

debts, trespasses, sins

See "*trespasses, sins, debts*."

Decalogue, the

See "*Ten Commandments, the.*"

decimate

Although purists insist that *decimate* should stay true to its linguistic roots and mean *only* "to destroy one tenth," the word has come to mean "to destroy in part or large part." This is the contemporary meaning given in *Webster* and nearly every other dictionary. Even the NIV uses it in this general sense: "We have been decimated and have no place anywhere in Israel" (2 Sam. 21:5). So there's no going back to the old meaning. In general usage, the term implies devastating though not complete destruction. If one needs to specify that only one-tenth of something was destroyed, it is better to say "one-tenth was destroyed."

defrock

This curious verb, dating from the sixteenth century, means "to remove someone from an ecclesiastical position," though its literal meaning is "to remove vestments." The term is used of clergy in most branches of Christianity who have had their ecclesial privileges revoked. The term *laicization* is the term used in the Roman Catholic Church, though *defrock* is often used casually, as in news reports. Laicization is not necessarily a punishment in the Catholic Church, since some priests request to be returned to the laity. It is also different from a *suspension*, which takes away only some of the priest's privileges. In both the Roman Catholic Church and the Eastern Orthodox Church, defrocking is not to be confused with excommunication, which is the removal of a person from the church body.

deist, deism

Some scholars argue that *deist* and *deism* should be capitalized since they refer to *the Deity*. (See "*deity, Deity.*") This manual recommends that, like *theist* and *theism*, *deist* and *deism* be lowercase to indicate a broad philosophy, unless the author has a strong preference otherwise. (For the distinction between *deism* and *theism*, see "*theism, deism.*")

deity, Deity

Capitalize *Deity* when used as a name for God: *the Deity*; or without the article, as in Charles Williams's quotation: "a high eternal flavour which savoured of Deity Itself" (*War in Heaven*). Otherwise, lowercase it: *the deity pronoun, a deity, the deity of Christ.*

democrat, Democrat, democratic, Democratic

A *democrat* (lowercase) believes in democracy but is not necessarily a member of the Democratic Party, though that person may be a *Democrat* (capitalized) as well (that is, a member of the party). Remember that the adjective in both cases ends in *-ic*. To say *the Democrat Party* is as wrong as it is to say *the Republic Party*. (See also "MISNAMING, INTENTIONAL.")

Deo gratias, Dei gratia

These two Latin phrases are often confused. *Deo gratias*, found in the Vulgate (1 Cor. 15:57), means "thanks be to God" and is commonly used as a spoken response in Roman Catholic liturgy. *Dei gratia* means "by the grace of God" and is a formula, usually abbreviated as *D. G.*, seen on coins and in documents as a way of stating that a monarch has been established by God's authority. The legend *D. G. Regina* ("[she is] queen by the grace of God") still appears on some British and Canadian currency.

desert, dessert

Most people know the difference between the nouns *desert* ("an arid expanse") and *dessert* ("a sweet treat at the end of a meal"). They are even pronounced differently. The confusion comes because the verb *desert* ("to abandon or vacate") is pronounced the same as the noun *dessert*. More confusion arises when the phrase *just deserts* is used. Proofreaders occasionally change that to *just desserts*, which is incorrect. The old form of the noun *deserts* is pronounced like *desserts* but is related to the word *deserve*. Someone who gets their *just deserts* gets what they *deserve*—and it usually isn't sweet. As Charles Williams once wrote: "It is as pleasant as it is unusual to see thoroughly good people getting their deserts" (*James I*).

Deus, deus

Deus, the Latin noun for God, and its related forms *deo* (dative) and *dei* (genitive or plural) are used in many common phrases in church life and liturgy. (See, for instance, "*Deo gratias, Dei gratia*" and "FOREIGN WORDS AND PHRASES COMMON TO CHRISTIAN LIFE AND WORSHIP.") Because early Latin did not distinguish between capital and lowercase letters, the question arises: Should *deus* be capitalized? The common practice is to capitalize or lowercase the terms by the same rules used for the words *God* and *god*. In references to a generic god, lowercase it, as in *a deus ex machina* ("a god out of the machine"). In reference to the God of the Bible, capitalize it, as in *Deo volente* ("God willing"), unless it is quoted from a source that lowercases it.

deuterocanonical books

The phrase *deuterocanonical books* refers to those writings accepted as part of the OT canon by the Roman Catholic and Eastern Orthodox Churches but not by Protestants or Jews. The deuterocanonical writings (which means "the books of the secondary canon") share much of the same material as the Apocrypha (see "*Apocrypha, apocryphal*"), but the two are not identical. Also note that while a few Roman Catholic theologians use the term *deuterocanon* to refer to these writings, it is considered an arcane grammatical back formation. Use *deuterocanonical books*, *works*, or *writings* instead.

devil, Devil

Lowercase *the devil* in most references to Satan. This accords with *CMoS* 8.90 and *SBL* (40), both of which recommend that style. This is a departure from previous editions of this manual. It may be capitalized whenever an author has a strong preference. In all cases, lowercase the word in casual references to the general spirit of evil or to demons, as in *the devil is in the details* or *tormented by devils*.

devout

Enough ambiguity exists in the adjective *devout* to make it tricky to use. Is a *devout churchgoer* a person who is faithful in going to church or a deeply religious person who goes to church as well? Like *pious*, the word *devout* is used ironically so often as to drain it of some of its religious meaning, as in *a devout listener of talk radio*. Often, *devout* is simply a one-word cliché. Use it with caution. (See "*devout Catholic*.")

devout Catholic

Though this pairing is usually innocuous (as in *The pope's appeal to devout Catholics everywhere is enormous*), it is sometimes troublesome, and not only because it's a cliché. The phrase is often a sort of code. Protestant evangelical writers occasionally use it as a way of distinguishing conservative, evangelical Catholics from others who are deemed nominal or otherwise less acceptable in their view. A hint of condescension lurks in that phrase, as in *Mary Higgins Clark, a devout Catholic, often has religious characters in her novels*. It is fair to query authors as to what they really mean.

dialogue, dialog

Go with *dialogue* rather than *dialog*. (But see "*catalog, catalogue*.")

Diaspora, diaspora

The word *Diaspora* refers specifically to the dispersion of the tribes of ancient Israel at the time of the Babylonian exile. It can refer both to the event and to the dispersed people themselves. The term is usually capitalized for both of those senses, and, like the term *Holocaust*, it is an exception to the rule of lowercasing most historical and biblical events. In modern times, the term has been appropriated to mean the dispersion of populations, sometimes implying that the dispersion was imposed under threat of harm. When the term is used in this general sense, lowercase it.

different

While the common word *different* is helpful in making distinctions (*the two siblings were as different as night and day*), it is redundant in situations when a distinction is already implied: *The chemicals could be divided into five different categories* or *Two different people stood up to complain*. The word *different* can be deleted from those phrases with no loss of meaning. (See also "WORDY WORDS.")

different from, different than

Different from is preferred in most instances except when *from* is clearly ungrammatical, as in *Their results are different for solids than for liquids* or *The worship was different than I had expected*. Use *from* unless your ear tells you otherwise.

dis

As a shortened slang form of the verb *to disrespect*, spell this as *to dis*, not *to diss*, though the inflected forms are *dissed* and *dissing*.

disc, disk

Opinions vary as to the difference between *disc* and *disk*, but a common rule is to use *disc* in reference to sound and video recordings (*compact disc, disc jockey, vinyl discs, digital video disc, a ten-disc set*) and *disk* (and *diskette*) for computer applications (*disk drive, disk cleanup, backup disk, disk storage*) and for ordinary objects (*an unidentified disk-shaped object, a flying disk*).

disciple, apostle

Disciple can refer to any follower of Jesus, ancient or modern, while *apostle* is usually restricted to the original twelve called by Jesus, as well as Matthias and Paul, though it is occasionally used metaphorically for modern believers. (See "*apostles, twelve*.")

discreet, discrete

Discreet means "subtle" or "quiet" (*God's discreet promptings*) and is related to the word *discretion*, which implies "tact." *Discrete* means "separate, distinct, or noncontinuous" (*five discrete processes*). They are pronounced the same, and of the two, *discreet* is used more often.

dive, dived

Use *dived* rather than *dove* as the past tense of *to dive*. Though *dove* is common in speech, *dived* is preferred for formal writing.

Dives

The name of the rich man in Jesus's parable (Luke 16:19–31) is sometimes given as *Dives* in literature, and authors from Chaucer to Melville have referred to the story as that of "Dives and Lazarus." While the name of the beggar, Lazarus, is given in Luke, the name *Dives* is not found in any English Bible; the phrase *a rich man* is used in most translations. The word *dives* comes from the Vulgate, where it is not a proper name but the Latin word meaning "a rich man." The word is pronounced *DIE-veez*.

divine, divinity

As an adjective describing persons of the Trinity, as well as their actions or attributes, lowercase *divine*, as in *divine guidance, divine intervention, divine providence*, and so on. Capitalize *Divine* in the phrase *Divine Liturgy* when referring to a Eucharistic service, especially in the Orthodox Church. As a noun, *the Divine* is sometimes used as an epithet for God and is capitalized in that sense. Occasionally, a theologian is referred to as *a divine*, though that usage is now rare. The word *divinity* is usually lowercase (*the divinity of Christ*), unless it is used as if it were another name for God: *the Divinity*. The word *divinity* was once synonymous with *theology*, meaning "the study of divine things," and that meaning is still present in such terms as *a doctor of divinity* or *a divinity student*.

DJ, dee-jay

Either *DJ* (short for *disc jockey*) or *dee-jay* is acceptable, though you might want to opt for *dee-jay* if it will be used as a verb elsewhere: *dee-jayed, dee-jaying, dee-jays*.

doctor of the church

While this term is used loosely to mean any of the earliest Christian theologians (a group of about thirty individuals), only eight are considered the true *doctors of the church*. In the Western tradition they are Jerome, Ambrose of Milan, Augustine of Hippo, and Gregory the Great; in the Eastern tradition they are Athanasius of Alexandria, Basil the Great of Caesarea, Gregory of Nazianzus, and John Chrysostom. The writings of these individuals proved important in the forging of Christian doctrine. Always define whether the term is being used in the strict or broad sense. (See also "*fathers of the church, church fathers.*")

dogma

In its narrowest sense, a *dogma* is one item on a list of tenets deemed essential for faith by the Roman Catholic Church. The preferred plural is *dogmas*, though the Greek-based *dogmata* is sometimes seen. Since the Reformation, Protestants have largely avoided the term, though the formal study of essential doctrines is still called *dogmatics*. In common usage, *dogma* (and related words like *dogmatic*, *dogmatism*, and *dogmatist*) is often pejorative, meaning "a strong but usually uninformed opinion or belief," as in *When it came to science, he was dogmatic in his skepticism.*

Dome of the Rock

Use *Dome of the Rock*, not *Dome on the Rock*, in reference to the Muslim shrine on the Temple Mount in Jerusalem. Capitalize the term as the name of a specific building.

dos and don'ts

These are simple plurals. Don't add unneeded apostrophes (*do's and don't's*).

double-check, double check

Double-check is the verb; *double check* is the noun.

double-click, double click

Hyphenate the verb *to double-click*. The noun is *a double click*.

Down syndrome

Advocacy organizations prefer the form *Down syndrome* to the once-common *Down's syndrome*. Also note that *syndrome* is lowercase. (See also "SYNDROMES, DISEASES, AND DISORDERS.")

doxology, Doxology

Lowercase, the term *doxology* (from the Greek *doxa* for "glory") refers to any short expression of praise and glory to God in a liturgical setting. Capitalized, it is the title of any specific composition of such expression. Most doxologies are addressed to God, in contrast to blessings and benedictions, which are addressed to worshipers. People often refer to "The Doxology" as though there were only one, though many are commonly used. Among Protestants, "The Doxology" usually refers to what is formally known as the *Lesser Doxology* or, in Roman Catholic tradition, the *Gloria Patri*. Another, called the *Greater Doxology*, is known to Roman Catholics as the *Gloria in Excelsis*. Two other common biblical doxologies are found in Rom. 16:27 and Jude 25.

each other's

Do people *value each other's opinions* or *value each others' opinions*? The singular form, *other's*, is correct. The same applies to *one another's*.

Earth, earth

Lowercase *earth* (with or without the article *the*) in all contexts except scientific or astronomical ones. Thus: *The Lunar Orbiter took the first photos of Earth from the Moon.* (Note that *moon* is capitalized or lowercase according to the same rules). But: *Jesus walked the earth for thirty-three years.* Also, whenever the word *earth* is preceded by the word *planet*, both words are usually capitalized, even when the context is not scientific or astronomical: *Nearly seven billion people now inhabit Planet Earth.*

Easter, Easter Sunday

Some editors and proofreaders object to the phrase *Easter Sunday*, seeing it as a redundancy since Easter is always on Sunday. But because *Easter* alone can refer to the entire liturgical season as well as the week preceding the Sunday of Easter, usually called Holy Week, using *Easter Sunday* to specify the actual day is perfectly okay.

Eastern Orthodox, Orthodox

When capitalized, the term *Orthodox* refers to those Christian groups listed under *Orthodox and Oriental Orthodox Churches* in the *Handbook of Denominations in the United States* (Abingdon, 2010). Since some readers may miss the capital letter and assume the term simply means "conforming to established religious teaching," a writer should use the term *Eastern Orthodox* in a first reference. Otherwise, the terms *Eastern Orthodox* and *Orthodox* are used interchangeably. The terms cover the eleven national churches and four patriarchs of those churches, which came into being after the Great Schism of 1054. Some writers mistakenly refer to only one of the national churches, usually Greek Orthodox or Russian Orthodox, to mean Eastern Orthodoxy as a whole. This is an error. It is also a mistake to refer to Orthodox groups as Protestant. Orthodoxy predates Protestantism by many centuries. (See "*catholic, Catholic*" and "*Protestant.*")

Eastern Rites, Western Rites

Broadly, the rituals observed by the Eastern Orthodox Church and the Roman Catholic Church are distinguished by the terms *Eastern Rites* and *Western Rites* respectively, though the actual rituals within each category differ over time and in various subgroups. The terms are capitalized. (See also "*Eastern Orthodox, Orthodox*" and "*Rite, rite.*")

ebook

Is this best spelled *ebook* (as in *Publisher's Weekly* and *Wired*, as well as at Amazon.com and in the UK), *e-book* (as in *Webster* and *CMoS* and in the US), or *eBook* (as Apple does for its e-readers)? Some bloggers have suggested *e.book*. This manual opts for *ebook* (preferred in the UK) since it seems destined to be spelled closed and obviates the need to hunt for that pesky hyphen.

The form *eBook* is less common than it once was. The internal capital (see "MIDCAP" and "E-COMPOUNDS.") signals that it is a brand name, like *iPad* and *eReader*. Already the commercial midcap style is looking dated.

Ecclesiastes, Ecclesiasticus

Few Protestants are familiar with the book of Ecclesiasticus in the Apocrypha, but when it is referenced, it should not be confused with the OT book of Ecclesiastes. Ecclesiasticus, better known under the title Sirach, or the Wisdom of Sirach, is a second-century BCE collection of wise sayings, similar to Proverbs, which was part of the Greek Septuagint but not part of the Hebrew Bible. It is canonical in Roman Catholic and Eastern Orthodox Bibles.

ecclesiastical, ecclesiastic, ecclesial

The words *ecclesiastical*, *ecclesiastic*, and *ecclesial*, when used as adjectives, are synonymous, all meaning "relating to the church." *Ecclesiastical* is the most commonly used term and preferred for most writing. *Ecclesiastic*, while occasionally used as an adjective, is most often used as a noun, indicating a person who works in an official position at a church (as in *a conference of ecclesiastics*). The least frequently used term *ecclesial* carries a hint of old-fashioned formality and is more common in the UK and in some academic contexts.

e-church

The word *e-church*, like most other *e* combinations, is hyphenated. Odds are the *e-* prefix will become closed over time—*echurch*—if the *e* doesn't disappear entirely. (After all, "e-banking" is now part of "banking.") Like *ebook* and *email, e-church* may be next to drop its hyphen. (See also "E-COMPOUNDS.")

E. coli

Short for *Escerichia coli*. The *E* is capitalized; the *c* is lowercase. Although this scientific name for an enterobacteria is a plural, treat it as a singular noun (as in *E. coli causes serious illness*) in all contexts except technical scientific writing. (See also "*bacteria, bacterium*.")

ecumenical

The word *ecumenical* is commonly used to mean one of three things. First, it has been used in the Roman Catholic Church to mean "worldwide Catholicism" (from the Latin *oecuminicus*). A convocation of Catholic bishops from around the world is thus considered an *ecumenical convocation*. Second, the term has also come to mean "worldwide" in the sense of "interdenominational," or representing all the Christian faiths. A worldwide *ecumenical movement* exists, seeking to promote dialogue and unity among Christian traditions. Finally, the word has also come to imply "interfaith," or representing the various major religions. Often an *ecumenical conference* might be attended by Christians, Muslims, Jews, Buddhists, and Hindus alike. The careful writer will make sure that the context clarifies the meaning.

e.g., i.e.

The abbreviations *e.g.* and *i.e.* are used primarily in books with a scholarly readership since many lay readers will not understand them, let alone distinguish between them. Writers of popular nonfiction should resist the temptation to appear more scholarly by using such abbreviations. (See "SCHOLARLY APPEARANCES.") When they are used, they should be used correctly. Although both are set primarily within parentheses to present additional information, and both are always followed by commas, their similarities end there. Since *e.g.* (for the Latin *exempli gratia*) means "for example" or "for instance," it is used to introduce a sampling of representative items, as in *Some of Lewis's students became well known in their own right (e.g., actor Robert Hardy)*. The abbreviation *i.e.* (for the Latin *id est*) means "that is to say" or "namely" or "that is" and is used when the information in parentheses is equivalent to or the same as the information it refers to but is stated in a different way. For instance, *He grew up in the era most highly suspicious of left-wing involvements (i.e., the 1950s)*.

either ... or, neither ... nor

Using the paired conjunctions *either ... or* and *neither ... nor* can be tricky because they can use either singular or plural verbs, depending on the number of the element closest to the verb; for instance, *Either candy or flowers are good Valentine's gifts*, but *Either candy or a card is a good Valentine's gift*. But notice how the verb changes when it is placed next to the single noun: *Is candy or flowers a better Valentine's gift?* (See also "*both ... and*.") Also remember that *nor*, not *or*, is paired with *neither* in formal writing; for instance, *He is neither one or the other* is unacceptable.

eke, eek

You *eke out a living* or *eke by on an exam*. You cry *eek* when you see a mouse or encounter commonly confused homophones. (See also "INTERJECTIONS OF EXPRESSION.")

elder, Elder

In many Protestant churches an elder is a lay officer whose duties are set forth in 1 Tim. 5:17. Two kinds of elder are common: a *ruling elder*, who assists a pastor in administrative functions, and a *teaching elder*, who has pastoral and educational duties. Though the term is a clerical position and usually not a formal title, capitalize it when it is used before a proper name: *Elder Cunningham*. An *elder* in the Church of Jesus Christ of Latter-day Saints is a formal position in the priesthood requiring ordination.

elegy, eulogy

An *elegy* is a poem or song, usually reflective and melancholy. A *eulogy* is a speech delivered at a funeral.

Eleven, the; eleven disciples

See "*Twelve, the; twelve disciples.*"

email

Although both *email* and *e-mail* (the latter preferred by *Webster*) are common, this manual prefers the unhyphenated form. Since the point of email is quick communication, it simply seems more rational to save a keystroke and not force people to hunt for the hyphen every time they type the word. (See "E-COMPOUNDS.")

Some experts insist that *email* should be treated as a collective noun, like *mail*, and is its own plural. They suggest that we can't say *I received twenty emails* any more than we can say *I received twenty mails.* They insist that the correct form is *I received twenty email messages.* This is frankly absurd. Actual users of this relatively recent coinage are the ones who determine its usage, and these users have already spoken. While *email* can indeed be a collective noun like *mail* (it is a contraction of *electronic mail*, after all), it can also be used as the electronic equivalent of the word *letters*, as in *I sent more than forty emails before they acknowledged the problem.* The plural *emails* is perfectly okay in our book. It is part of our changing language.

emerging church, emergent church

The phrase *emerging church* refers to a movement largely within American Christianity (from the 1990s through the first decade of the twenty-first century), spanning denominations and traditions and characterized by an emphasis on lived spiritual experience, a de-emphasis on traditional church hierarchy and doctrine, a receptivity to multiculturalism, and an openness to new technologies. Though the issues important to the *emerging church* are still present, the phrase is not used as often as it once was, largely because the movement has splintered and evolved into other groups and directions.

The phrase *emergent church* describes one of the subsets of that larger movement, namely those people associated with the Emergent Village, a group that grew out of the Leadership Network. Some within those organizations capitalize *Emergent Church* to suggest its more specific meaning, but this manual recommends lowercasing it since it is not the official name of an organization (whereas *Emergent Village* and *Leadership Network* are).

Emmanuel, Immanuel, Emanuel

See "*Immanuel, Emmanuel, Emanuel.*"

empathic, empathetic

Although the word *empathic* is slightly older than the word *empathetic*, they are functionally synonymous and equally acceptable. The adjectival form of *empathy* was originally *empathic*, but *empathetic*, in a linguistic process called back formation, came into existence as a parallel to *sympathetic*. Those who insist that *empathetic* should be forever banished in favor of *empathic* are, to put it bluntly, pathetic.

empire, Empire

When historical empires are defined by a proper adjective—*the Babylonian Empire* or *the Roman Empire*—capitalize the word *Empire.* But lowercase it when referring to any such empire as *the empire* alone: for example, *While the Roman Empire may not have been built in a day, much of the empire's infrastructure was built during the reign of two Caesars.* Capitalize *Empire* when it stands for two or more empires in a series: as in *Both the Byzantine and Carolingian Empires considered themselves the heirs of Rome.* (See also "*period.*")

end times, end time

Though both forms are acceptable, the plural *end times* is more common. In most cases, lowercase it: *He felt we were living in the end times.* Hyphenate it as an adjective preceding a noun: *an end-times novel.*

England

See "*United Kingdom, Great Britain, England, British Isles.*"

ensure, insure

Experts distinguish between *ensure* and *insure,* stating that *to ensure* is "to guarantee" and *to insure* means either "to guarantee by taking precautions beforehand" or "to indemnify" as an insurance company would do. While it is good to observe the distinction when it is clear, most writers and readers consider those terms synonymous.

Episcopal, episcopal, Episcopalian

Episcopal is the adjective, *Episcopalian* the noun; as in *The Episcopalians welcomed the new Episcopal minister.* Capitalized, the terms refer to the Protestant Episcopal Church, which is the name given in the US to the Anglican Church. Lowercase (as in *an episcopal letter*), the word refers to bishops or the governing authority of bishops, which is usually called the *episcopacy.* Note that such bishops exist in many churches and denominations, not the Episcopal Church only.

Episcopalianism, episcopalism

Episcopalianism (capitalized) is a belief in the tenets of the Episcopal Church, while *episcopalism* (lowercase) is an espousal of a system of church governance in which authority is placed in bishops. (See also "*Episcopal, episcopal, Episcopalian.*")

epistle, Epistle

Lowercase *epistle* in references to the letters of the NT, as in *Paul's epistle to the Corinthians*, unless the version of the Bible being used capitalizes it. Capitalize it when it is used as a formal title for a specific section of the Bible: *the Catholic Epistles, the Pastoral Epistles, the Pauline Epistles, the Prison Epistles*. Also capitalize it as a title when referring to the epistles as a group: *the Epistles*. Apart from its biblical context, *epistle* often has an elevated or archaic tone—and sometimes even a humorous one, as in *the editor didn't see fit to publish my lengthy epistle on the economic situation*.

etc.

Etc. is the abbreviation for the Latin *et cetera*, or *etcetera*, and is a condensed way of saying "and so on" or "and other things." It is usually preceded by a comma, even in lists when no serial comma is used. It is more appropriate in scholarly texts than in popular ones, the phrases *and so on* and *and so forth* being the common substitutes in books for a general readership. It was once commonly abbreviated *&c*, but that form is rarely used today.

ethics

The word is construed as a singular noun when referring to the academic subject (*ethics is offered at most universities*) but as a plural when referring to personal values (*his ethics are appalling*).

Eucharist, eucharistic

Capitalize *Eucharist* (noun); lowercase *eucharistic* (adj.). (See also "*Communion*.")

evangel

Though now infrequently used as a noun, *evangel* can mean either "the gospel message," "one of the four gospels," or "one of the four gospel writers." The word is also the root for such words as *evangelical, evangelist, evangelize* and comes from a Greek word meaning "happy message" or "good messenger"—what Christians now call "the good news" of Christ.

evangelical, evangelicalism

Lowercase the term *evangelical* (as in *evangelicalism, evangelicals*, and so on), though capitalize it as part of the name of a specific church, denomination, organization, or, in the case of the *Evangelical Church in Germany*, to specify the Lutheran Protestants as opposed to the Calvinists.

Although those who describe themselves as *evangelicals* do not always agree on its definition, it is most often used to mean those Protestants since the Reformation, and especially since the time of John Wesley, who stress the importance of (1) the four gospels, (2) the inerrancy of the Bible, (3) personal conversion, and (4) salvation by faith in the atoning death of Christ. Their worship tends to focus on preaching rather than ritual, and they emphasize each believer's responsibility in evangelization.

Use the term *evangelical* with caution when writing for general readers. People outside the church often view *evangelical* as synonymous with *fundamentalist* or *the religious right.* Some readers think *evangelical* means any Christian who evangelizes, sometimes in insensitive ways. People inside the church accept the term more as a more general description of a personal theological viewpoint.

evangelist, Evangelist

Lowercase *evangelist* unless it is used as an epithet for one or more of the four gospel writers or their writings as a whole: *the evangelist John* or *the four evangelists*, but *John the Evangelist, the Evangelists.* (See also "*televangelist, televangelism.*")

evangelistic, evangelical

As an adjective to mean "with fervor," use *evangelistic*, as in *the evangelistic zeal with which they canvassed the neighborhood.* Use *evangelical* when referring to the gospel message, as in *the pastor's powerful evangelical preaching.*

evangelize, proselytize

Although *evangelize* and *proselytize* are often used synonymously, some writers observe a difference. While *evangelize* can mean "to attempt to convert others," it can also mean simply "explaining, or sharing, one's faith." *Proselytize* implies more forcefulness in the use of strong and active persuasion.

evildoer, evildoing, evil-minded

Evildoer and *evildoing* are not hyphenated; *evil-minded* is.

ex-

When *ex-* is used as a prefix to mean "former," hyphenate it: *ex-boss, ex-husband, ex-president*, and so on. It usually only refers to people; most writers would write *former company*, not *ex-company*, and some would even suggest that *former* is slightly more proper than *ex-* when referring to people: *former president*, and so on. The use of *ex* alone as a noun to mean "a former spouse" is a common and acceptable slang though it has a dismissive tone. As odd as it may seem, the plural of *ex* is *exes*.

examine, examen

These two words are pronounced the same but differ in meaning. *Examine* is the verb meaning "to test or question." *Examen* is a noun synonymous with *examination* or with a critical study of a given subject (as in *They provided an examen of the committee's findings*). In Christian practice, *examen* refers to the ancient spiritual practice of examining one's conscience or meditating to discern God's will, usually involving prayer, Scripture, and devotional reading. The term *daily examen* is used in Roman Catholic spirituality for this practice and was developed by Saint Ignatius of Loyola (sixteenth century) in his *Spiritual Exercises*. Also note that *examen* should not be confused with *exam*.

Exodus, exodus

Capitalize *Exodus* as the book that comes after Genesis in the Hebrew Bible. Lowercase it to mean the event described in that book or to mean any mass emigration of people.

expatriate

The noun and adjective to describe someone living outside their home country is *expatriate*, not *expatriot*. The abbreviated slang form is *expat*.

extrabiblical

See "***nonbiblical, abiblical, extrabiblical, unbiblical.***"

extreme unction

See "***last rites.***"

ezine

Although it can be alternatively spelled *e-zine* (as in *Webster*), this manual recommends spelling it without the hyphen, like *email* and *ebook*. (See "E-COMPOUNDS.") In the past few years, the word *ezine* has been largely replaced by *online magazine*.

F

faith

In Christian jargon, a number of phrases use the word *faith* as an adjective: *faith commitment*, *faith journey*, *faith walk*, and so on. Do not use a hyphen in these combinations unless they are themselves compound adjectives: *a faith-based organization*, *a faith-healing service*, *his faith-walk testimony*. When referring to Christianity (or any other religion) as *the faith*, lowercase the term.

fall, the

Lowercase *the fall* in reference to the events depicted in Gen. 2–3. Also lowercase it in such phrases as *the fall of Rome* or *the fall of Troy.*

farther, further

The standard rule is to use *farther* for physical distances (as in *he ran farther than the marathoners*) and *further* for abstract or metaphorical distances (as in *nothing could be further from my mind*). In practice the distinction is fading, and it is sometimes difficult to distinguish between physical distances and metaphorical ones (as in *Never had he felt farther/further from the heavenly city* or *The events receded farther/further into the past.*). In the UK, *further* is often used to mean physical distances, and in the US we often use *farther* idiomatically to mean abstract distances, as in the gospel song, "Farther along, we'll all understand it." The same rules apply to *farthest* and *furthest.* Always use *further/furthest* when the idea of "more of something" is implied (as in *we need further evidence* or *we should discuss this further*). As long ago as 1977, *New York Times* stylist Theodore Bernstein, in *The Careful Writer*, predicted the imminent demise of the distinction. Honor it for now, but, as Bernstein says, expect the distinction to be "mowed down by the scythe of Old Further Time" (181).

father, Father

In the Eastern Orthodox and Roman Catholic churches, *father* is the clerical title given to most priests, and it is capitalized when used before a name—*Father Zosima*—and in direct address—*Hello, Father.* Some priests in the Anglican Church also prefer to be addressed as *Father.*

fathers of the church, church fathers

The terms *fathers of the church* and *church fathers* are used loosely to mean those theologians who forged the early doctrines of the Christian faith, especially in the first twelve centuries after Christ. (See also "*doctor of the church*.") In stricter usage, the *fathers of the church*, or *church fathers*, were not only those who forged the doctrines but those, especially of the first six centuries, whose lives were of exceptional holiness and orthodoxy. The primary early and later fathers of the church are:

Early Fathers

first century: Clement of Rome
second century: Cyril of Jerusalem, Ignatius of Antioch, Justin, Irenaeus, Polycarp
third century: Cyprian, Dionysius
fourth century: Hilary, Ephrem the Syrian, Optatus, Epiphanius
fifth century: Peter Chrysologus, Pope Leo the Great, Cyril of Alexandria, Vincent of Lérins
sixth century: Caesarius of Arles

Later Fathers

seventh century: Isidore of Seville
eighth century: John the Damascene, the Venerable Bede
eleventh century: Peter Damian
twelfth century: Anselm, Bernard

The Fathers may be capitalized when the term is used alone to stand for *the church fathers*, but for clarity and precision it is preferable to use the more extended phrases: *fathers of the church* and *the church fathers*. And the terms *the Church Fathers*, *the Early Church Fathers*, and *the Later Church Fathers* are usually only capitalized when referring collectively to the writings of those historical figures.

fellowship, to

Despite the fact that *to fellowship* has been used as a verb since the fourteenth century (both Chaucer and Wycliffe used it that way), it sounds like evangelical jargon to most contemporary ears (*we plan to fellowship at the new church*). It is acceptable when writing for Christians; avoid it for a wider readership.

Festschrift

This word of German roots, meaning "a multi-authored memorial volume dedicated to a noteworthy individual," is usually capitalized. The preferred plural is *Festschriften*. Among noted Christian Festschriften is *Essays Presented to Charles Williams*, edited by C. S. Lewis, and including essays by J. R. R. Tolkien, Dorothy Sayers, and others (Oxford University Press, 1947).

fiancé, fiancée

A *fiancée* is a woman engaged to be married; a *fiancé* is the male counterpart. The major dictionaries adhere to the French gender-specific forms and retain the acute accent.

first husband, first gentleman

See "*first lady, First Lady.*"

first lady, First Lady

When *First Lady* is used before a proper name, capitalize it as an honorific title: *First Lady Michelle Obama*. When using the term alone, lowercase it: *The boy shook hands with the first lady*. In some political and journalistic contexts, the first lady is referred to as the *FLOTUS* (*first lady of the United States*), all the letters of that acronym being capitalized. (See also "POTUS, FLOTUS, SCOTUS" and "*President, president, presidential*.") The husband of a female president would be called either *first husband* or *first gentleman* (the latter is preferred by the *Guardian UK*). Some authorities lean toward the first option because the initialism can be pronounced more easily: *FHOTUS*, pronounced *FO-tus*, whereas *FGOTUS* might end up being awkwardly pronounced *fuh-GO-tus*.

flak

Flak (an acronym for the German *Fliegerabwehrkanonen*) is preferred over *flack*, as in *flak jacket* and *flak catchers*.

flannelgraph

The term for this now outmoded, low-tech staple of Sunday school teaching is set as one word, lowercase.

flood, the

Lowercase it when referring to the flood of Gen. 6–8.

flounder, founder

To flounder is "to thrash around" or "to be awkward or ineffective." *To founder* is "to become lame," "to sink, as in shallow or rough water." People flounder when lost in a thicket; they founder when they're sinking in a boat.

font, typeface

See "*typeface, font.*"

foolhardy

Not *fool-hearty.*

footwashing

This is one word as both a noun (*a footwashing*) and an adjective (*a footwashing ceremony*). Note that Brethren Churches refer to the footwashing ceremony as *feetwashing.*

forever, for ever, forevermore, for ever and ever

The word *forever* is always spelled as two words in the KJV: *for ever.* Many autocorrect programs will, without asking, close up those two words, so take care when quoting the KJV (see "KING JAMES VERSION, SPELLINGS IN"). Note that some writers commonly misspell *forevermore* as *forever more*, and to complicate matters, the KJV spells it *for evermore* (which should be retained when quoting the KJV). The NIV spells *forever* as one word except in the formulation *for ever and ever*, where it is two words. So, again, care must be taken. Other Bibles, such as AMP, CEV, NASB, NRSV, HCSB, and WEB, spell it *forever and ever* and also spell *forever* closed. Needless to say, be forever alert to such variations.

forgo, forego

The common verb *to forgo* means "to give something up." The less common verb *to forego* means "to go before." Forms of *forego* are usually only seen in the common idiom *a foregone conclusion* and in such academic phrases as *see the foregoing material.*

Fortune 500

Although *Fortune* magazine is italicized as a title, the name is not italicized in references to its famous list of top businesses: Fortune 500 companies.

founder

See "*flounder, founder.*"

Founding Fathers, founding fathers

Capitalize *Founding Fathers* in reference to those who laid the foundations for the United States of America; the term is often limited to those men who attended the Constitutional Convention of 1787 or those who signed the Declaration of Independence in 1776. Otherwise, *founding fathers* and *founding mothers*, lowercase, refer to those people who founded any organization or movement; *founders* is the generic form.

four cardinal virtues, the

Lowercase the phrase *the four cardinal virtues* in most contexts. The virtues, which are also lowercase unless used as personifications, are, in order, (1) prudence, (2) justice, (3) temperance, and (4) fortitude. (See also "*seven deadly sins, the.*")

Fourth Estate

In England, society was said to be composed of three "estates": the First Estate was the "Lords Spiritual" (the church); the Second Estate was the "Lords Temporal" (the king and nobility); and the Third Estate was the "Commons" (the people). Capitalize each of those terms. Edmund Burke once claimed a Fourth Estate, more powerful than the others, existed—it was called the press. In our time, only the Fourth Estate is referred to, and any attempt to refer to the church as the First Estate or to the government as the Second Estate will only be met with blank stares. Occasionally, a Fifth Estate is mentioned, which is a catchall for any powerful group not covered by the other estates, and recently the blogosphere is occasionally dubbed the Fifth Estate.

frack, fracking, fracked

Some who think language must always be logical insist that the shortened forms related to the term *hydraulic fracturing* must, of necessity, be *frac*, *fraccing*, and *fracced*. Even assuming that the word *fracture* would be shortened to *frac* (without the *k*), one would still render the related gerund and past participle as *fracking* and *fracked*—for the same reason that *panic* and *picnic* become *panicking* and *panicked*, and *picnicking* and *picnicked*. Since the gerund *fracking* is used four times more often than the uninflected verb (according to the number of hits on the internet), the linguistic tail gets to wag the linguistic dog in this case. So, by a process called back formation, the widely used *fracking* renders its base word as *frack*. The logicians can complain, but that is how language works. Most references already list *frack*, *fracking*, and *fracked* as the preferred forms.

freewill, free will

Freewill (one word) is an adjective meaning "voluntary" or "not coerced." It is seen in such phrases as *a freewill offering*. *Free will* (two words) is a noun referring to the concept of humans being able to make choices apart from environmental or divine influences. In scientific discussions, "free will" is contrasted with "determinism," and in religious discussions, "free will" is contrasted with "predestination."

Webster mistakenly states that Baptists who believe in free will are called *Freewill Baptists*, but nearly every national and state organization of such Baptists refer to themselves as *Free Will Baptists* (such as the National Association of Free Will Baptists). Many individual churches use the term in the names of their meeting places, regardless of precise form, so be sure to note their particular usage; for instance, *the First Free Will Baptist Church (of Albany, Georgia)*, but *the Pleasant Hill Freewill Methodist Church (of Colbert County, Alabama)*.

Capitalize *Free Will* when referring to a specific church or denomination that uses the term in its title. Lowercase *free will* (with no hyphen) as an adjective in general references to those who believe in free will (such as *a conference of free will Christians of all stripes*).

free world

By and large, lowercase *free world*. It refers to "the noncommunist nations," but since the end of the Cold War, the term is harder to define and more susceptible to the assumptions of the writer using it. (See also "*Third World*.")

fundamentalism, fundamentalist

The term *fundamentalism* has come to describe uncompromising theological conservatives of nearly any faith, including Islam and Hinduism—which is curious because the term originated with a movement within Protestant Christianity. Early in the twentieth century, a group of Christians formulated what they believed to be the five nonnegotiable "fundamentals" of the Christian faith: (1) the inerrancy of the Bible, (2) the divinity of Christ, (3) the virgin birth, (4) the atonement, and (5) the physical resurrection and imminent return of Christ.

As with so much Christian terminology, *fundamentalism* and *fundamentalist*, which are lowercase when not part of a formal name, should be used carefully and with an awareness of how any particular group of readers views those terms. Beyond a Christian readership, and often even within that readership, the terms imply zealotry, even extremism, and are often considered pejorative. Still, the terms can be safely applied to those who use it in reference to themselves.

Note that Christian fundamentalism is not synonymous with evangelicalism, nor with Christianity as a whole. It is a specific term that should be used precisely.

G

garden

In accord with *SBL*, the KJV, and most other Bibles, this manual recommends lowercasing *garden* in references to *the garden of Eden* or *the garden of Gethsemane*. The NIV (as well as *Webster*) capitalizes *Garden of Eden*, so when writing about Eden in the context of the NIV, *Garden* may be capitalized.

gay

See "*LGBT*."

gehenna

See "*hell*."

general market, secular market

Christian publishers once commonly used the term *secular market* to mean general bookstores and nonreligious channels of distribution. With the advent of online retailers and large superstores, the line between that market and the specifically Christian market has all but vanished. Most of those general outlets sell nearly as much specifically Christian product as the dedicated Christian stores, if not more. Sales outlets that sell both religious and general merchandise are now more accurately referred to as the *general market*, as contrasted with *the Christian market*, which are those outlets that sell exclusively Christian materials.

gentile

Lowercase the term *gentile* as both a noun and an adjective. It refers to anyone of a non-Jewish nation or faith, though the Mormons also use the term to refer to non-Mormons.

gibe

See "*jibe, jive, gibe*."

girl

Use *girl* only for females seventeen years of age or younger. Use *woman* or *young woman*, as appropriate, for those eighteen or older.

Gnostic, gnostic

Capitalize *Gnostic* and *Gnosticism* when referring to the specific religious sects of the first century BCE and first and second centuries CE, who believed that the *gnosis* (secret spiritual knowledge) is the basis for salvation. When referring to the general philosophy (the belief that knowledge is granted only to certain adepts), lowercase *gnostic* and *gnosticism*.

God, god, G-d

Capitalize *God* when referring to the God of the Bible or of the three monotheistic, Abrahamic faiths: Judaism, Christianity, and Islam. Lowercase *god* in general and metaphorical references (as in *he hoped the gods were with him* and *Chris Turner is a harmonica god*) or when referring to the gods of polytheistic or pagan faiths (*the Greek gods*).

Taking their cue from the vowelless, unspoken, abbreviated name for God, *YHWH* (see "*tetragrammaton, tetragram*"), some Jewish writers prefer to insert a hyphen in place of the vowel: *G-d*. They do this so that they will not show disrespect should they need to delete or erase the word. Although Christian writers do not use this device, they should retain it when quoting Jewish writers who do.

godhead, Godhead

Lowercase or capitalize this word according to the same rules by which *god/God* is lowercase or capitalized (see "GOD COMPOUNDS"). To refer to a general divine essence, *godhead* is correct. To mean God or the triune nature of God in Christian theology, then *Godhead* is preferred. Note that in either case, it is usually used with the article: *the Godhead*.

God's Word, God's word

Capitalize *God's Word* when referring to the Bible. Lowercase *word* when the reference is to God's promise. (See also "*Word of God, word of God*.")

golden age

Lowercase *the golden age*, meaning "an idealized era of great accomplishment."

Golden Rule, the

Capitalize the term *the Golden Rule* (which is usually formulated as "Do unto others as you would have others do unto you"). It is found in various forms in most of the world's religions and is not exclusively Christian. Its closest expression in the Bible is in Matt. 7:12 and Luke 6:31; it is also related to Jesus's Great Commandment (Luke 10:27) and to the parable of the good Samaritan (Luke 10:30–37). The negative phrasing of the rule ("Don't do to others ...") is sometimes called *the Silver Rule*.

Good Book, the

Capitalize this as an alternate, quaintly dated name for the Bible.

goodbye, good-bye, goodby, good-by

Webster and the *OED* prefer *good-bye*, with *Webster* adding *good-by* as a secondary spelling. *The American Heritage Dictionary*, as well as the *New York Times* and *Associated Press* style guides, prefer *goodbye*. The editors of this manual opt for *goodbye* on the principle that hyphens are pesky and rapidly disappearing, but *good-bye* is acceptable as long as consistency is maintained. We discourage the use of *goodby* and *good-by* (the latter from Noah Webster's 1828 dictionary) largely because they look odd in proximity to the derivative forms *bye* and *bye-bye*, which need to have the final *e* to avoid confusing them with the common preposition *by*. *Goodby* is also objectionable because at first glance it could be misread as if it were pronounced GOOD-bee.

good ol' boy, good old boy

For a Southern male of a certain kind, either *good ol' boy* or *good old boy* is acceptable, but since the context is usually colloquial, the former is preferred. *Webster* also lists *good ole boy*, but that is less common. (See also "*ol'*.")

Good Samaritan, Good Sam

Although the words *parable* and *good* are lowercase in reference to *the parable of the good Samaritan* (see "*parable, Parable*"), the term *Good Samaritan* is conventionally capitalized when referring to any modern person who performs good deeds: *this anonymous Good Samaritan changed the tire on the elderly man's car*. The official designation of the club whose name is a reference to this parable is the *Good Sam Club*, not the *Good Samaritan Club*. Any of its more than million and a half members may be referred to as either *a Good Sam* or *a Good Samaritan* (capitalized).

goodwill

One word: *we regularly depend upon the goodwill of others*. Goodwill Industries International also spells it solid.

Goody Two-Shoes

Capitalize all the elements of this phrase (as in *Don't be such a Goody Two-Shoes!*). It is meant to look like a proper name. As a compound adjective, lowercase it: *his unflappable, goody-two-shoes outlook on life.*

Google, google

Google (capitalized) is the name of the internet search engine and the company that owns it. When used as a verb, *to google*, it is commonly lowercase. This is similar to the word *xerox*, which is also capitalized as a company name but lowercase as a verb.

gospel, Gospel

The word *gospel* (from the Old English *godspel*, meaning "good tale" or "good news") has several common meanings: (1) the message of Christ's kingdom; (2) one of the first four books of the NT canon; (3) any of the noncanonical books about the life or sayings of Jesus; (4) a liturgical reading from one of the first four books of the NT; (5) any statement that is said to be infallible, as in *the gospel truth* or *if he said it, it's gospel*; (6) a specific style of religious music. As a result, the word is subject to imprecision and misreading. (As Scot McKnight once said in a lecture, "When 'the Gospel' ... means everything, it loses all meaning.") A careful writer makes the meaning clear whenever the term is used.

Many rules have been suggested for the capitalization of the word *gospel*, most of which are confusing and contradictory. This manual advises that the word *gospel* only be capitalized when contained in an actual title (*The Gospel According to Saint Matthew* [KJV] or *The Gospel of Thomas*), when used as a collective title for some or all of the canonical gospels (*the Gospels, the Synoptic Gospels*), or in subheadings and titles. This capitalization style is consistent with the KJV and the NIV, among others, and it will also keep authors, editors, and proofreaders from having to split hairs over the various shades of meaning.

Lowercase all other uses of *gospel*: for instance, *gospel music, gospel revival, the gospel of Christ, the true gospel, the gospel of salvation, to preach the gospel, a gospel writer, the gospel of John* and *John's gospel, the four gospels* (but *the Gospels*, as a title for a portion of the NT).

gospel side

The archaic term *gospel side* meant the place in a church or cathedral to the left of the altar as one faces the front. This was the side of the chancel from which the gospel was traditionally read.

gospeler

The term *gospeler* once referred to anyone who read from Scripture in a liturgical setting, a meaning that is now archaic. Though rare, the word is still occasionally used pejoratively to refer to an overly zealous evangelist.

Gothic, gothic, Goth, goth

Capitalize both *Gothic* and *Goth* when referring to the ancient Goths or Gothic style in art, architecture, or letter forms. Lowercase it when referring to the literary genre known as *gothic fiction*, or *gothic romance*, or when referring to modern *goth culture* or *gothic rock*.

gray, grey

Gray is the most common spelling in the US; *grey* in the UK.

great (in family relationships)

See "FAMILY RELATIONSHIP, TERMS FOR."

Great Britain

See "*United Kingdom, Great Britain, England, British Isles.*"

Great Commission, the

Capitalize the term *the Great Commission* as both the title of a specific portion of Scripture (Matt. 28:16–20) and one of the central mandates of the Christian faith ("Go and make disciples of all nations . . ."). (See also "BIBLE, NAMES FOR SPECIFIC PORTIONS OF THE.")

great Scott

Capitalize *Scott* in this exclamation and spell it with two *t*'s (not *great scott* or *great Scot*, as is sometimes seen). The term, dating from the last half of the nineteenth century, may have originated as a reference to Civil War general Winfield Scott, who weighed over three hundred pounds, but it was more than likely a minced oath for "[by the] grace of God." (See "MINCED OATHS.")

green card

Lowercase this term as the informal name for the US immigrant permanent-resident-status card, officially called the I-151 Alièn Registration Receipt Card.

guilt (as a verb)

It may be one of those inevitable changes in the language, but *to guilt* (meaning "to throw guilt, or to cause to feel guilty") is now commonly used as a verb (as in *Of course, she guilted me into paying*). Such slang is useful in fictional dialogue and is common on social media, though it is already sounding somewhat dated. For formal writing, use *to throw guilt* instead.

Gypsy, gypsy

See "*Roma, Romani, gypsy.*"

H

h, a or an before words beginning with

See "*a, an.*"

Hades, hades

See "*hell.*"

hagiography, Hagiographa

These terms are occasionally confused. The term *hagiography*, lowercase, is the study and compiling of what are commonly called *lives of the saints*. As a group, the literary genre is called *hagiology*. In ironic usage, *hagiography* also means any effusively positive biographical statement that tends to gloss over the subject's weaknesses.

Hagiographa, which is capitalized as a title and set in roman type, is sometimes simply referred to as the Writings, or Kethuvim. It is one of the three major divisions of the Hebrew Bible, the portion that is neither the Law (Pentateuch, or Torah) nor the Prophets (or Nevi'im). The Hagiographa includes Psalms, Proverbs, Job, Ruth, Lamentations, Song of Songs, Ecclesiastes, Esther, Daniel, 1 and 2 Chronicles, Ezra, and Nehemiah. Some traditions also include Tobit and other similar deuterocanonical books. (See "BIBLE, THE—WHAT IS IT?" section on "The Jewish Bible.") Though plural, Hagiographa takes a singular verb.

Both *hagiography* and *Hagiographa* are pronounced with a hard *g* (as in *hag*), not a soft *g* (as in *badge*), which is also true of any related words such as *hagiolotry*, meaning "excessive worship of the saints," or *hagiarchy*, "rule by saints."

Hail Mary

This is the name of the short Roman Catholic prayer that begins "Hail, Mary, full of grace ..." and is often said as part of the rosary. (See also "*rosary, Rosary.*") It is based on Luke 1:28–35, 42–48. Capitalize *Hail Mary* as the title of the specific prayer or portion of the Bible, and set it in roman type. Do not put a comma after *Hail*; for instance, *The priest intoned the Hail Mary.* The plural form is *Hail Marys*, as in *the standard penance was saying three Hail Marys.*

The phrase is popularly used to mean "a last-minute, desperate course of action." The metaphor, in this case, is football, not prayer (though overtones of prayer are implied)—a Hail Mary pass being a specific trick play often used in the final moments of a game. When used in this sense, it is styled the same way as the prayer and not hyphenated as an adjective: *the senator's decision to back the bill was a Hail Mary move.*

half (in family relationships)

See "FAMILY RELATIONSHIP, TERMS FOR."

half-mast, half-staff

In precise usage, a flag flown halfway up a pole is only *half-mast* when it is aboard a ship. Otherwise, it is *half-staff.* But *half-mast* is so commonly used metaphorically (*his eyelids were at half-mast*) that it is pointless to insist on a distinction between *half-mast* and *half-staff.* If you use them interchangeably in informal contexts, *Webster* will back you up.

hallelujah, alleluia

Confusion exists as to the preferred spelling of the Hebrew liturgical interjection *halelu-Jah*, "praise Lord Jehovah," which occurs throughout Psalms, where it is most often translated as "Praise the Lord," and four times in Revelation (19:1, 3, 4, and 6), where it usually appears either as *hallelujah* (NIV) or *alleluia* (KJV). Most authorities consider *alleluia* the more accurate rendering, relating most closely to the form used in the Greek Septuagint and Latin Vulgate. But that does not take into consideration the long-standing traditional use of *hallelujah* in English, dating back to the early sixteenth century. Though not invariably, *hallelujah* is used in most Protestant churches, while the Latin *alleluia* is preferred by the Roman Catholic, Eastern Orthodox, and some Anglican churches.

Within the context of a particular book, when in doubt, go with the spelling of the predominant Bible version being used. In the absence of that, use *hallelujah* as a spoken interjection (*"I may be a sinner but, hallelujah, I'm saved"*) and for dialogue and informal liturgical settings. Use *alleluia* in formalized liturgical settings (*"The congregation responded with rousing alleluias"*), since that is the form most often used in worship and liturgical song. Exceptions are Handel's oratorio *The Messiah*, in which the word is spelled *hallelujah* in the well-known chorus of that name, and the popular song "Hallelujah" by Leonard Cohen.

Here is a breakdown of which spelling is used by the major English Bible versions:

hallelujah—AB, ASV, CEB, Darby, ESV, HCSB, Message, MLB/NBV, NASB, NCV, NET, NIrV, NIV, NLT, NRSV, RSV, TLB

alleluia—JB, KJ21, KJV, NAB, NEB, NJB, NKJV, Tyndale, Wycliffe, YLT
neither—TEV (uses "praise God")

hallowed, hallowèd

This word is usually pronounced as two syllables, HAL-ode (as in *the college's hallowed halls*), though it is sometimes pronounced as three syllables, HAL-oh-ud, in liturgical recitations of the Lord's Prayer: "... hallowèd be Thy name ..." Three syllables sounds affected or jocular in all but the latter instance. (See also "*Blessed, blessed, blessèd*" and "*cursed, cursèd.*")

Halloween, Hallowe'en, All Hallows' Eve

Halloween (October 31) is the common spelling in the US. *Hallowe'en* is sometimes used in the UK, *e'en* being a contraction of *even* ("evening"). *All Hallows' Eve* (note the apostrophe) is the ecclesial name for the holiday in the UK. All Saints' Day (November 1) was formerly called Hallowmas ("the Mass of All Hallows"); so, the previous evening is All Hallows' Eve. (See also "*All Saints' Day, All Souls' Day.*")

halo

In the US, the plural is *halos*. In the UK, it's *haloes*.

hanged, hung

Hanged is the past tense of *to hang* when referring to a person who has been executed by being suspended by the neck with a rope. All other senses take *hung* as the past tense. Jesus was *hung*, not *hanged*, on the cross.

Hanukkah, Chanukah, Hanukah

The name for this Jewish festival (the Feast of Dedication) is most commonly spelled *Hanukkah*. Even though the initial consonant in Hebrew has a slightly guttural *k* sound (a voiceless fricative), for most purposes, pronounce it with a standard English aspirated *h*.

havoc, to wreak

See "*wreak, wreck.*"

he, He, him, Him

See "DEITY PRONOUN."

healthcare

Although *Webster* prefers *health care*, it is now more commonly seen as one word, both as a noun and as an adjective: as in *the need for good healthcare* or *our healthcare provider.*

hear, hear

This common phrase, often misspelled *here, here*, uses a comma—unless the exclamatory form is used: *Hear! Hear!* (each *Hear* being capitalized). This imperative was once used to command people to listen, as in 2 Sam. 20:16 (KJV): "Then cried a wise woman out of the city, Hear, hear ..." In English parliamentary tradition, it is the contracted form of "hear him, hear him," though in ordinary speech it is now almost exclusively used as a vociferous cheer of approval or as an encouragement to a speaker: *The crowd responded with a rousing "Hear! Hear!"*

heaven, Heaven

Lowercase *heaven* in most instances. Why don't we capitalize it as a place name? The answer is that a fine distinction exists between a place and a state of being—especially when it concerns the afterlife. While most conceptions of the afterlife draw on both place and state of being, most tend to put greater emphasis on the latter. For that reason, words like *nirvana* (in Buddhism) are lowercase. Conversely, names like *Elysium* and *Valhalla* are capitalized because, in Greek and Norse mythology respectively, they are largely portrayed as specific geographic locations more than as states of being. It is perfectly acceptable to capitalize *Heaven* whenever it is discussed in geographic terms or portrayed as a physical location, as C. S. Lewis does, for instance, in *The Great Divorce* (1946). (See also "*paradise, Paradise.*")

heavenlies, the

The Darby Translation (NT 1867; OT 1890) is the main source of the term *the heavenlies* (Eph. 2:6), which other translations render as "heavenly places" or "heavenly realms" or simply "heaven." The term is avoided in contemporary contexts because it is sometimes misunderstood to mean multiple mythological gods or "stars and planets." It is not a synonym for God.

heavenly host

Because of the common use of the phrase *heavenly host* (lowercase) in Luke 2:13 (NIV and KJV, a passage popularly read at Advent), *heav-*

enly is often paired with *host* to the point of being a cliché. We tend to think of *host* in terms of the angels being heralds or even a choir, since in Luke's passage they are praising God ("Glory to God in the highest . . . ," Luke 2:14), but in most instances in the Bible, a *host* of angels is a military image, *host* being a translation of the Hebrew *Sabaoth*, meaning "armies." (See also "*Host, host.*")

Hebrew, Yiddish

Two distinctly Jewish languages are common worldwide. *Hebrew* was the written and spoken language of the ancient Jews and, in its revived form, is a contemporary, spoken Semitic language, usually referred to as Modern Hebrew. *Yiddish*, developed in Central and Eastern Europe, is a dialect, rooted partly in German, which is spoken by many Jews throughout the world. Many common English words are derived from Yiddish, such as *bagel*, *chutzpah*, *glitch*, *klutz*, *kosher*, *nosh*, *schmooze*, and *shtick*.

Hebrews, Jews

The term *the Hebrews* refers to the people of ancient Northern Israel as described in the Hebrew Bible. They are also referred to as *the Israelites*. It is inappropriate to refer to a modern Jew as "a Hebrew" or "an Israelite." The term *the Jews* may be applied to the descendants of the patriarch Jacob in either biblical or modern times. (See also "*Israeli, Israelite*" and "*Jew, Jewish.*")

hell

Lowercase as a state of being or nonbeing in the afterlife (see "*heaven, Heaven*"). It may be capitalized, especially in fiction, when a specific geographic location is portrayed, as C. S. Lewis does in *The Great Divorce* (1946). Similarly, Milton, in *Paradise Lost*, consistently capitalizes both *Heaven* (often spelled *Heav'n* to make it one syllable for scansion purposes) and *Hell*. The Greek *hades* is usually lowercase as a general state of death, but capitalize it when referring to the mythological location of the underworld or as a personal name for the ruler of the underworld himself. The term *Gehenna* is sometimes used metaphorically to mean hell, but it is capitalized since it is the name of an actual place outside Jerusalem. The word *Gehenna*, which doesn't appear in either the KJV or the NIV, is translated as "the Valley of Ben Hinnom" in the NIV (Jer. 7:32) or simply as hell (Matt. 5:22). Note the NIV capitalizes *the Abyss* (Rev. 9:1 and elsewhere), and the NRSV and the NASB capitalize *Sheol* (Ps. 6:5 and elsewhere).

helpmate, helpmeet

Although accepted by modern dictionaries to mean "companion" or "wife," the antiquated-sounding words *helpmate* and *helpmeet* are based on a misreading of Gen. 2:18 (KJV): "I will make him an help meet for him." *Meet*, in the Jacobean English of King James, means "suitable"—not "mate." The main objection to these terms is that they seem like jargon and can have condescending overtones. Find other, more direct ways of saying the same thing.

her, she

For the Church. Avoid referring to the church, either historical or contemporary, as *her* or *she*. In contexts in which the church is specifically referred to as "the bride of Christ," the female pronoun may be appropriate, but in other references the church is either *it* (as an institution) or *they* (as the people themselves).

Ships, Aircraft, Countries. Also avoid referring to ships, aircraft, countries, and other such entities as *her* or *she*. Though once common, the usage is now frowned upon by most style manuals and is confusing to some readers. *(See also* "GENDER-ACCURATE LANGUAGE."*)*

heresy, schism

Although the line between *heresy* and *schism* is often thin in early church history, the terms are distinct. The reason for a heretic's break with (or dismissal from) the established church is usually doctrinal, whereas a schismatic's often is not. Heretics have unorthodox beliefs in the eyes of the orthodox but can, and often do, perceive of themselves as remaining within the main body of the church. Schismatics can be entirely orthodox in their beliefs while purposefully separating themselves from the church in an effort to seek an alternative to traditional faith, often for reasons other than doctrine. The line becomes blurred when a schism has its roots in heresy.

The term *apostate*, which differs in meaning from both *heretic* and *schismatic*, applies solely to a person who has willfully rejected the Christian faith. (See "*apostate*.") Heretics and schismatics usually perceive of themselves as followers of a specific faith, while an apostate does not. Although these terms were liberally applied to certain Christians as late as the Counter-Reformation, they are considered too harsh to apply to major historic branches of the Christian faith today. By and large, it is best to leave such terms to historians.

As a matter of consistent style, the names of important heretical movements and schisms in the early church are capitalized out of convention, whether or not they find their etymology in a proper name. Here is a brief list of a few major heresies and schisms of the first millennium of the Christian faith:

Heresies of the Early Church

Adoptionism—(eighth century) the doctrine that Jesus was not God's true son but adopted as an inspired human

Apollinarianism—(fourth century) the doctrine that Christ possessed a divine Logos rather than a human mind

Arianism—(fifth century) the belief that Christ was a superior but wholly created human being and not divine

Cainites—(second century) a sect that rejected the NT in favor of the Gospel of Judas, believed the earth to be the creation of an evil force, and identified with Cain of the Hebrew Bible

Docetism—(first century) a Gnostic doctrine rejecting the Hebrew Bible; it taught that Christ's sufferings were "semblent," not real

Ebionitism—(first century) a doctrine that denied the divinity of Christ and the virgin birth

Gnosticism—(late second century) a doctrine emphasizing an esoteric revealed knowledge as the way to salvation, maintaining that the material world was evil and that Christ's human and divine natures were separate

Macedonianism—(fourth century) the doctrine that denied the Holy Spirit as a fully divine part of the Trinity

Manichaeism—(second century) followers of Mani; actually a distinct religion, but its strong influence on Christianity was considered heretical. Their doctrine was dualistic, giving nearly equal weight to good and evil

Marcionism—(second century) a Gnostic offshoot that maintained that the God of the Hebrew Scriptures was different from the God of the Christian Scriptures and that Christ was not born of a woman

Millenarianism—(second century) also called the *Chiliasts*, who believed Christ would reign over the faithful on earth for one thousand years after his return; was revived in many forms throughout the nineteenth century

Monarchianism—(second century) a doctrine emphasizing the unity of God at the expense of the Trinity

Monophysitism—(fourth century) the doctrine that Christ's incarnate nature was purely divine

Montanism—(late second century) the apocalyptic personality cult of its leader, Montanus

Nazarenes (Notzerim)—(first and second century) a Jewish-Christian sect that asserted that Christ, while divine, still conformed to all Mosaic rites and customs

Nestorianism—(fifth century) the doctrine that Christ's human and divine natures were separate, not unified

Pelagianism—(fourth century) the theological system asserting that the human will seeks salvation apart from divine grace

Sabellianism—(early third century) the doctrine that Christ was identical in nature to God the Father, a later form of Monarchianism

Schisms of the Church

Donatist Schism—(fourth century) followers of Donatus, who believed their sect to be the true, uncorrupted church, and that only those achieving exceptional holiness could belong

Great Schism of 1054—the historical point at which Eastern Orthodoxy and Roman Catholicism officially split, though the origins of their differences considerably predate that era

Novatianist Schism—(third century) followers of a Roman presbyter Novatian, who was orthodox in doctrine but felt he could not accept the cultural and political compromises of the church at large

hermit, cenobite

Some Protestants mistakenly think of Roman Catholic and Eastern Orthodox monastics as being *hermits*. The accurate term is *cenobite* for those living in a community. Only those living alone, usually outside the monastery walls, are termed *hermits*.

High Church, Low Church, high church, low church

Webster prefers to capitalize these terms, especially when discussing historical issues of ceremony and liturgy within the Anglican Church, where the terms originated. (Example: *The Tractarians inspired the High Church faction in England.*) But to distinguish between the various levels of formality in contemporary Christian worship, lowercase the terms *high church* (to mean "more formal and liturgical") and *low church* (to mean "less formal and liturgical"). (Example: *Today's high-church emphasis on liturgy and sacrament . . .*).

Still, the terms *high church* and *low church*, when applied to modern churches, contain negative value judgments and should be avoided as being either derogatory or rooted in class distinction (much the way *upper class* and *lower class* are perceived). If this is likely to be a sensitive issue with a book's readership, then the terms *liturgical*, or *more liturgical*, and *nonliturgical*, or *less liturgical*, are appropriate alternatives.

High Holy Days, the

Capitalize this as a specific Jewish religious season, usually in October, consisting of Rosh Hashanah and Yom Kippur.

High Mass

See "*Mass, mass (Roman Catholic)*."

Hispanic

The term *Hispanic* ("of Spanish origin"), capitalized as both a noun and an adjective, is preferred to the less accurate *Latin American*. Whenever possible, it is helpful to the reader to use a demonym specifying a person's actual country of origin; for example, *Cuban*, *Mexican*, *Puerto Rican*, and so on.

historic, historical

These words are sometimes confused. The common rule is that *historic* refers to an event, past, present, or future, of major significance or momentousness (as in *Keble's "National Apostasy" sermon was a historic turning point*), while *historical* refers to an event that occurred in the past, whether significant or not (as in *Tolstoy's historical detail is astonishing*). The article *a* is used with both terms (as in *a historic document*).

But that doesn't answer the question: Do we defend and uphold *the historic Christian faith* or *the historical Christian faith*? Since *historic* implies "something significant" and *historical* implies "something in the past," it would seem that both of those meanings apply to *the Christian faith*. Because the word *historic* embodies those two meanings slightly better than the word *historical*, we recommend using *historic* in such combinations as *the historic Christian faith*, *the historic church*, *the historic faith*, *historic orthodoxy*, and so on.

HIV/AIDS

Set in all caps with a solidus: *the conference on HIV/AIDS*.

holier-than-thou

This phrase, which mockingly refers to those who feel morally superior to others, is always hyphenated. It finds its origin in the words of God in Isa. 65:5: "Stand by thyself, come not near to me; for I am holier than thou" (KJV).

Holocaust, holocaust

When capitalized and preceded by the article *the*, the word *Holocaust* (from the Greek "burnt whole") refers to the mass murder of Jews by the Nazis between 1941 and 1945, though the persecutions began years earlier. Lowercase, the term refers to any other genocide or mass destruction (as in *the Rwandan holocaust* or *nuclear holocaust*).

Note to Writers. If any term is to be used with delicacy, it is this one. Because of the horrendous nature of the Nazi Holocaust, the term, even lowercase, should not be used lightly, for humor, for rhetorical purposes, or inappropriately. It is unhelpful to any argument to use the Holocaust as a point of comparison since relatively few events in history are comparable. This is not a point of political correctness but of accuracy.

Holy Bible, the

We forget that the full title of the Bible in many English versions is *The Holy Bible* (Latin, *Biblia Sacra*, "sacred book"), though in ordinary writing, that full title tends to sound falsely pious. Use *the Bible* in most instances unless you occasionally need the ring of extra authority. The term is usually set in roman type—the Holy Bible—unless a specific edition is referred to, such as *The Holy Bible NIV, Large Print Edition*. In casual references, the article is not capitalized: *the Holy Bible, the Bible*. (See also "*Bible, Scripture*.")

Holy Book, the

The Holy Book is sometimes used as a synonym for "the Bible," though it can often sound overly pious or archaic. Set it in roman.

Holy City, the

In Jewish and Christian contexts, *the Holy City* (capitalized) is Jerusalem, though that term is applied not only to the actual city but also to the new Jerusalem, that is, heaven or the coming kingdom (as described in Rev. 21). To some Roman Catholic readers, the term may also suggest Rome, the seat of the papacy. Some classic Christian writers even use the term to mean "the church" broadly. In most cases, the written context will make the meaning clear. Also keep in mind that many other religious faiths have holy cities as well.

Faith	Sacred City
Christian, Protestant	Jerusalem or new Jerusalem
Christian, Roman Catholic	Jerusalem, new Jerusalem, or Rome
Hindu	Allahabad

Hindu.................... Banaras (also called Varanasi)
Incan, Ancient.............. Cuzco
Jewish .... Jerusalem
Muslim..................... Mecca (or Medina)
Western Arab .... Fez

Holy Communion

Capitalize *Holy Communion* to refer to the church service or ceremony that contains the sacrament: *We attended Holy Communion on Sunday.* (See also "*Communion*" and "*Last Supper, the.*")

holy day of obligation

Lowercase this as the name for those days on which Roman Catholics are required to go to Mass. When not specified, it does not refer to any particular day.

holy exchange of gifts

Catholic Mass and some sacraments are referred to as a *holy exchange of gifts*. The phrase is usually lowercase in Catholic writing.

holy family

Although some Roman Catholic writers capitalize this epithet, it is not a title, nor is it used like a formal name. Lowercase it.

Holy Father

The use of this epithet in reference to the pope is confined to Roman Catholic writers and publications and is always capitalized. (See "*pontiff, Pontiff*" and "*pope, Pope.*")

Holy Ghost

Synonymous with *Holy Spirit*, the phrase *Holy Ghost* comes from the Old English *Hâlga Gâst*, giving us the word *ghost* (comparable to the German *geist*) in contrast to the Latinate *spirit* (from the Latin *spiritus*). In contrast to the Vulgate's *Spiritus Sanctus*, Wycliffe's Middle English rendered it *Hooli Goost* (as in Luke 2:25). The KJV popularized the use of *Holy Ghost*, though even that translation uses *holy Spirit* a few times (for instance, Eph. 1:13). Most later translations settled on *Holy Spirit* exclusively. In most contemporary liturgical contexts, *Holy Spirit* is preferred, though churches that use the KJV as their primary translation are likely to use *Holy Ghost*. (Also see "*Holy Spirit.*") Note the KJV capitalizes both elements of *Holy Ghost* (used eighty-eight times and only in the NT) while it usually lowercases (except in Luke 11:13) the first element of *holy Spirit* (used six times). (See also "KING JAMES VERSION, SPELLING IN THE.")

Holy Grail

The term *the Holy Grail* describes the legendary bowl, or in some versions a wide-brimmed cup, which the pseudepigraphal Gospel of Nicodemus identifies as both the wine bowl of the Last Supper and the receptacle in which Joseph of Arimathea is said to have caught the blood of crucified Jesus. As such, it achieved mythical significance and was rumored to possess life-giving qualities. Even the remote possibility of such a relic existing fired the imaginations of many medieval writers, and stories of knights going on quests to recover it soon became symbols of the soul's quest for union with God. It plays an important part in many of the Arthurian stories. The term, which can be referred to, interchangeably, as *the Holy Grail* or *the Grail*, is capitalized when referring directly to the object but lowercase when used metaphorically: as in *An original Gutenberg Bible is the holy grail of book collectors*. Why this term is capitalized when other terms, such as *the cross*, are not is a matter of long-standing convention.

Holy Joe

As a slang term to mean an overly religious person, capitalize *Holy Joe*.

Holy Land, the

Capitalize the term *the Holy Land* as an epithet for the geographic region of roughly 14,000 square miles, bound on the south by the Sinai Desert, on the east by Syria and Jordan, on the north by Lebanon, and on the west by the Mediterranean Sea. Although many people think of the term as synonymous with Israel, the two are not the same. The Holy Land incorporates a geographic area almost twice the size of modern Israel.

In using the term *the Holy Land*, it is important to remember that the land is "holy" to each of the three great monotheistic religions—Judaism, Christianity, and Islam—for overlapping but not identical reasons. For Jews it is the land of Israel, as promised to them by God in the book of Exodus; for Christians, it is the place of Jesus's life and ministry; and for Muslims, it is the region from which Muhammad is said to have ascended to heaven. Always capitalize the term. (See also "*Levant, the*," as well as "*Palestine, ancient Palestine, the State of Palestine, the Palestinian State*.") When referring jocularly to other locations, lowercase the term, as in *He finally performed in Nashville—that holy land of country music*.

holy of holies, the

Lowercase this term.

holy orders

The term *holy orders* is usually lowercase to describe those who have been officially ordained in the Roman Catholic and Orthodox Churches. The word *holy* is usually attached so that *orders* will not be confused with other senses of that word. Holy orders are considered a sacrament in those traditions, whereas ordination is usually not considered a sacrament in Protestantism.

Holy Roller

Capitalize this term. It is pejorative and describes a kind of rustic revivalism (usually mixed with Pentecostalism) that was popular in the American South in the nineteenth and early twentieth centuries. An entire class of rugged Appalachian folk hymns is referred to as *Holy Roller hymns* (no hyphen).

Holy Saturday

Observed primarily in the Roman Catholic and Eastern Orthodox traditions, *Holy Saturday* is the final day of Lent and Holy Week. Capitalize the term as a holy day. It is also known as *Black Saturday* in the Roman Catholic Church and as *the Great Sabbath* in the Eastern churches (See also "*Lent, Lenten*" and "*Holy Week.*")

Holy Spirit

This term is capitalized except in the KJV, which lowercases the first element: *holy Spirit* (the one exception being in Luke 11:13). In contemporary liturgy and worship, the term *Holy Spirit* is almost universally preferred to the term *Holy Ghost.* (See "*Holy Ghost.*")

Gender Pronoun. Use male pronouns for the Holy Spirit when necessary. Some writers refer to the Holy Spirit with the gender-neutral *it* (as in *May the Holy Spirit in all its fullness descend upon us*), though this seems a misunderstanding of the personhood of the three persons of the Trinity. Since the gospel of John consistently refers to the Holy Spirit as male, it is best to use masculine pronouns when referring to the Holy Spirit, just as masculine pronouns are used (in most traditions) when referring to God. In addition, all major Bible translations use the male pronoun for the Holy Spirit. Some writers refer to the Holy Spirit using the female pronoun, equating the Holy Spirit to the Sophia (Wisdom) figure in traditional Jewish theology. But that usage is usually confined to the field of feminist Christology and theology. Many writers prefer to avoid specifying a gender for the Holy Spirit in the same way they avoid gender pronouns for God. (See "MALE PRONOUNS FOR GOD.")

Holy Thursday

Capitalize this term. Originally, *Holy Thursday* referred to Ascension Day, which was the day traditionally ascribed to the day, forty days after Easter (counting Easter Sunday itself), on which Jesus completed his post-resurrection ministry and "ascended into heaven" (Heb. 4:14). Eventually, the Roman Catholic Church moved Ascension Day to the following Sunday, at which time the term *Holy Thursday* began to be applied to what is now known as Maundy Thursday. (See "CHRISTIAN HOLIDAYS, FEASTS, AND THE LITURGICAL YEAR.")

Holy Trinity

Capitalize *Holy Trinity*. (See "TRINITY, NAMES FOR PERSONS OF.")

holy war

Lowercase this term to mean a religiously motivated war. *The Holy War* (1682) is also the title of John Bunyan's sequel to *The Pilgrim's Progress* (1678).

holy water

Lowercase this term. Water for the sacrament of baptism, by the way, is only considered "holy" after it has been blessed by a member of the clergy.

Holy Week

Capitalize *Holy Week* to mean the week before Easter. In liturgical terms, it is the period that begins on Palm Sunday and ends at sundown on Holy Saturday, the day before Easter, even though most laypeople think of Holy Week as including Easter Sunday. If it is important for the reader to distinguish one from the other, the writer should explain it. (See also "*Holy Saturday*" and "CHRISTIAN HOLIDAYS, FEASTS, AND THE LITURGICAL YEAR.")

Holy Word, holy Word

Capitalize *Holy* as an adjective before *Word* when it is meant to be read as a name for the Bible: *the Holy Word*, *the Holy Word of God*, and *God's Holy Word*. Lowercase *holy* in those rare cases when the emphasis seems to be on the word *holy* as a descriptor rather than as part of a title, as in *the very holy Word that God wants us to respond to.* (See "*Holy Writ.*")

Holy Writ

The capitalized term *Holy Writ*, referring to the Bible or God's laws, has a long history in English, dating from before the twelfth century, though it now has an antiquarian mustiness to it and is seldom used. It is occasionally used jokingly to refer to any writing that has undeniable authority; and when used in that sense, it is usually lowercase: *Although the First Folio contains errors, it is regarded as holy writ by Shakespeare scholars.*

homeschool, homeschooler

The words *homeschool* and *homeschooler*, coined in the 1980s, are set solid. *Homeschool* is usually a verb, as in *they homeschool their five children. Homeschooled* is the past tense. By itself, the term *homeschooler* is ambiguous. To say *she's a homeschooler* does not make clear whether *she* is the child-student or the parent-teacher. The context should clarify it. Seldom is *homeschool* used as a noun. It is smoother and perfectly acceptable to use the passive; *I was homeschooled* is better than *I attended homeschool.* The adjective form is common, as in *the homeschool materials.*

horde, hoard

Angels come in *hordes*, not *hoards.* Both are nouns, but *horde* means "crowd, or mass of people" while *hoard* (which is also a verb) means "a pile of things stored away." (See also "*heavenly host*" and "*Host, host*" in reference to angels.)

hosanna, hosannah

Hosanna and *hosannah* are variant spellings of a one-word biblical prayer meaning "save us" or "deliver us." Occasionally modern writers mistakenly use it as a synonym for *hallelujah*, that is, as an interjection of adoration and praise. This Aramaic word is found only five times in the Bible, exclusively in the gospel passages describing the crowd's reaction to Jesus's final entry into Jerusalem (as in Matt. 21:9). They are calling out to Jesus with the expectation that he can save them from their oppressors and from their sins. It is not a cheer so much as a hopeful plea. The word is lowercase, and the form without the final *h* is the first option given in *Webster* and is also the form used in the NIV and most other major Bible versions, including the KJV. (Wycliffe used *osanna.*) *Hosannah*, with the final *h*, seems to occur primarily in Lenten liturgies and Easter pageants and was the preferred literary form of such classic authors as John Milton. Stick with *hosanna.*

Host, host

In Christian worship the capitalized word *Host* means "the consecrated bread of the Eucharist," though the same word, lowercase, meaning "multitude," is found in such formulaic expressions as *heavenly host* and *a host of angels*. The context and the capitalization should make clear which meaning of the word is intended. (See also "*heavenly host*.")

House of Representatives, the House

Capitalize *House of Representatives* and *the House* when referring specifically to that chamber of the US Congress. Lowercase the word *representative* to mean a member of that body, unless it is used as a title directly before a person's name: *Representative Elijah Cummings.*

however

See "SYLLOGISTIC WORDS AND PHRASES."

humankind, mankind, womankind

When referring to all the world's people, the word *humankind* is preferable to the word *mankind*. This is not a recent concession to political correctness; *humankind* has been part of English since the 1600s. Since the word *womankind*, which dates back to the thirteenth century, refers only to women, the word *mankind* could be easily mistaken to refer only to men.

Humvee

This is the common acronym for the military vehicle referred to as an HMMWV (high-mobility multipurpose wheeled vehicle). Capitalize the term *Humvee* because it is now used as the trade name for a specific commercially available vehicle.

hymnbook, hymnal

Hymnbook is one word and is synonymous with *hymnal*, though *hymnal* has a slightly more liturgical formality to it. Even more liturgical and obscure is the synonymous *hymnary*.

I

I Am

Just as the cap-and-small-cap form *LORD* is used to translate the Hebrew *Yahweh* (*YHWH* or *Jehovah*) in the NIV (and some other Bibles), the term *I AM* is also set in the same cap-and-small-cap style. Those are the only two names for God in the NIV OT that use that style.

ibid.

Most manuals recommend against using *Ibid.* in book endnotes. It is frustrating to scholarly readers to flip to the back of the book only to find that the source for note 23 is identical to the source for note 22, which is identical to the source for note 21, and so on. Instead, try to consolidate as many repeated references as possible under one note: such as *This quotation and the following five quotations are all from [insert citation]*. In general, if citations do need to be repeated, use shortened citations instead. *Ibid.* should be reserved for bottom-of-page footnotes, and only when space is at a premium. Even then, consolidated references are recommended.

ichthus, ichthys

The letters of the Greek word *ichthys*, meaning "fish," form an acrostic for a Greek phrase meaning "Jesus, the Christ, God's son, savior." Consequently, a stylized fish (sometimes called a *Jesus fish* or *fish symbol*) became an early rebus-like symbol for Christ and is still popular today. In modern English, the word is variously spelled *ichthus*, *icthus*, *ikthus*, and *ichthys*. Since *Webster* does not list the word in any form, this manual recommends *ichthus* when referring to the fish symbol, since that spelling is the most common. To refer to the Greek word itself, the more Greek-looking *ichthys* may be used.

ID

ID (meaning "identity" or "identity card") is a commonly understood abbreviation as both an adjective and a noun: *an ID card* or *to carry an ID*. Avoid inflecting the abbreviation. The reader shouldn't have to puzzle out what *the security guard IDed her* means. Rewrite such sentences: *the security guard was able to ID her* or simply *the security guard identified her.*

i.e.

The abbreviation *i.e.* stands for the Latin *id est*, meaning "it is" or "that is." Avoid this and most academic abbreviations in books targeted at a general or popular readership. (For a full discussion, see "*e.g., i.e.*")

immaculate conception, virgin birth

Do not confuse the terms *immaculate conception* and *virgin birth*. In Roman Catholic theology, *the immaculate conception* refers to the doctrine that Mary, the mother of Jesus, was conceived without any stain of original sin. The feast commemorating this occurs on December 8. Even many Catholics are not aware that *the immaculate conception* refers to Mary's conception, not Jesus's. The *virgin birth* refers to the birth of Jesus. Both terms are sometimes capitalized in Roman Catholic writing as formal theological doctrines; otherwise, lowercase them.

Immanuel, Emmanuel, Emanuel

Although as names for Christ *Immanuel* and *Emmanuel* are interchangeable, being different Anglicized versions of the Hebrew word found in Isa. 7:14, *Immanuel* is preferred since it is the form common to the most widely used English versions of the Bible (NIV, KJV, NRSV, and others). *Emmanuel* (from the Septuagint's *Emmanouçl*) is acceptable in the many Christmas stories and carols (for instance, "O Come, O Come, Emmanuel") that use that form. When in doubt, use *Immanuel*. Be aware that many individual congregations spell the word *Emanuel*, with one *m*, such as the historic Emanuel AME Church in Charleston, SC, and the Emanuel Hispanic SDA Church in Charlotte, NC. Always verify the spelling whenever a reference is made to any church with that word in its name because all three spellings are common.

immoral

See "*amoral, immoral*."

in fact

See "SYLLOGISTIC WORDS AND PHRASES."

infant Jesus

See "*baby Jesus, infant Jesus*."

infinity, infinitude

Infinity is the preferred noun, though *infinitude* is sometimes seen in theological contexts in reference to *the infinitude of God.*

Inklings

The group of writers who clustered around C. S. Lewis and J. R. R. Tolkien from the mid-1930s to the 1960s used the term *Inklings* to describe themselves. Among those who attended were Owen Barfield, J. A. W. Bennett, Lord David Cecil, Nevill Coghill, James Dundas-Grant, Hugo Dyson, Adam Fox, Colin Hardie, R. E. "Humphrey" Havard, Warren H. Lewis (C. S. Lewis's brother), Gervase Mathew, R. B. McCallum, C. E. Stevens, Christopher Tolkien (J. R. R. Tolkien's son), Charles Williams, Charles Wrenn, and others. There was no official membership list, so scholars sometimes disagree about who was and was not one of the Inklings. The term *Inklings* is capitalized when referring to the group and is mostly used in the plural, as in *He was one of the Inklings*, rather than *He was an Inkling.*

Because some Christian bookstores include George MacDonald and G. K. Chesterton in their Inklings section, it is sometimes assumed they were themselves part of that group. They lived before the Inklings' time and were simply influences. Dorothy Sayers, Ruth Pitter, and Joy Davidman are also sometimes included, but as women, they were never invited to attend. Another common mistake is to refer to the Inklings as a group of exclusively evangelical Christians. While most of the Inklings would have described themselves as Christians, they varied widely in their theology. They bonded not so much over religion as over their mutual love of imaginative literature and their largely conservative social views.

inner city, inner-city

Inner city is the noun; *inner-city* is the adjective: as in *The church's inner-city ministry spread well beyond the inner city.*

in order to

This phrase can usually be reduced to simply *to*: *He lived to gamble* is snappier than *he lived in order to gamble.* See "WORDY WORDS" as well as other similar "wordy words" like "*to be,*" "*very,*" and "*prior to, previous to.*"

interfaith, interdenominational

These words are set solid, without a hyphen. *Interfaith* means "encompassing more than one religion," while *interdenominational* means "involving more than one Christian denomination." Protestants tend to use the word *interdenominational* while Roman Catholics, who don't view themselves as simply a denomination, use *ecumenical* or even *interfaith* to mean the various branches of Christian faith, though see "*ecumenical*" for more nuances.

internet, the

Lowercase it. Although some references capitalize it (*Webster* and *Garner*), the reasons are never quite clear. *The internet* is now the common noun for one medium among others, like *the television*, *the radio*, and *the telephone*. Linguist Geoffrey Nunberg points out that in the 1920s the new media of *the Radio* and *the Cinema* were capitalized but lost their initial capitals when they "receded into the cultural background" (*The Years of Talking Dangerously*, 126). While it is not wrong to capitalize *Internet* consistently, especially if that is the author's preference, no grammatical justification exists.

InterVarsity, Inter-Varsity

The US publisher and the Christian organization that go by this name in the US have standardized the spelling. Thus, *InterVarsity Press* and *InterVarsity Christian Fellowship*. In the UK, the publisher that goes by this name spells it with a hyphen, *Inter-Varsity Press*. While the organization that once went by that name in the UK also spelled it with the hyphen, they now go by another name: *UCCF—the Universities and Colleges Christian Fellowship*.

irreligious, nonreligious, unreligious, areligious

Though these terms are broadly synonymous, *irreligious* is often used to suggest a deliberate neglect of religion and religious practices or sometimes even hostile opposition. In written contexts, it is often specifically contrasted with *religious*. The noun form is usually *irreligion*. *Nonreligious*, the most common term, and *unreligious* are used to mean something that is simply irrelevant, or not applicable, to religion. The much less common *areligious* suggests an indifference to religious matters.

ISIS, ISIL

ISIS (Islamic State of Iraq and Syria) and *ISIL* (Islamic State of Iraq and the Levant) are acronyms for the same terrorist organization. *ISIS* is the form used by the British government, and *ISIL* is the form used by the UN and the US government, although the US media tend to use *ISIS*. To avoid confusion, some media (such as *USA Today*) do not use the acronyms and refer to the group as *the Islamic State*. (See "*Daesh*" for yet another name for this group.)

Islam, Islamic, Islamist

The word *Islam* can mean the religion itself, the worldwide body of Muslims, or the geographic locations where that religion predominates, but in all cases it refers to the faith as a whole, not the individual adherents. When referring to people, use *Muslim*, either as a noun or an adjective. (See also "*Muslim*.") Use *Islamic* as an adjective to define concepts that represent Islam as a religion, such as *Islamic art* or *Islamic culture*. Although the terms *Islamist* and *Islamism* used to imply the faith as a whole, they have more recently come to imply those who advocate the restructuring of societies and governments to adhere to Islamic law, sometimes through violent means.

Israeli, Israelite

An *Israeli* is a citizen of the modern state of Israel, though remember that *Israeli* is not synonymous with *Jewish*. About 25 percent of the population of modern Israel is made up of Arab, Muslim, Christian, and nonsectarian Israelis. An *Israelite*, by contrast, refers to any descendent of Jacob (whose name was Israel) living in ancient Israel, specifically the Northern Kingdom. (See also "*Jew, Jewish*.")

italic, roman, arabic

Although these typographic terms are derived from proper names, they are lowercase by convention, probably because the letter forms themselves no longer evoke Italy, Rome, or Arabia (the same reason we usually lowercase *french fries*, *lima beans*, and *india ink*).

J

Jehoshaphat

The name of the king of Judah in 1 and 2 Kings and 1 Chron. is sometimes misspelled *Jehosaphat* (possibly because the phrase *jumpin' Jehosaphat* was popularized in Loony Tunes cartoons), but *Jehoshaphat* is the spelling in nearly all Bibles except Douay-Rheims, which spells it *Josephat.*

Jehu, jehu

Capitalize *Jehu* as the name of the biblical king portrayed in 2 Kings 9–10. Lowercase it when used metaphorically to mean a reckless driver.

jeremiad

This noun, meaning a "lengthy lamentation or denunciation," is lowercase despite being based on the name of the biblical prophet Jeremiah.

Jesu

Jesu is a Latinized form of *Jesus* and is most often found in Roman Catholic liturgies and musical compositions presenting the Latin Mass. When spoken, it is usually pronounced in the church-Latin manner as YAY-zoo, not JAY-zoo or GEE-zoo.

Jesus, Christ

See "*Christ Jesus.*"

Jesus's, Jesus'

What is the possessive of Jesus? The short rule is: Opt for *Jesus's* unless the author has a strong preference for *Jesus'*. In all cases, be consistent. This manual prefers *Jesus's* because our two primary guides in these matters, *CMoS* and *SBL*, both prefer it. This form also helps in consistency with other biblical and ancient names that include the *'s*, and in which the final *s* is actually pronounced: for example, *Judas's*, *Thomas's*, and *Zeus's*. (See also "POSSESSIVES," section on "*Proper Names Ending with Sibilants.*")

Still, not only does *Jesus'* have a long tradition in English literature and scholarship, but it is the form used by nearly every Bible version except Weymouth. We're also used to seeing it in such common phrases as "for Jesus' sake" and in such popular hymns as "All Hail the Power of Jesus' Name," in which no additional *s* is pronounced at the end of the name.

When *Jesus's* is used, then apply the same rule for other ancient or biblical names ending in a sibilant, even if the final possessive *s* is not pronounced: *Moses's*, *Judas's*, *Xerxes's*, *Socrates's*.

If *Jesus'* is used for pronunciation reasons, then you're on your own when it comes to visual inconsistencies like *Edward Thomas's poem about Jesus' blessing* or *Achilles' fear of Zeus's judgment*, but strive for consistency.

Jew, Jewish

Some Christian writers, fearing that the terms *Jew* and *the Jews* are somehow politically incorrect, come up with convoluted formulas like "a Jewish believer" or "people of the Jewish faith" in an effort to avoid the terms. In some ways this avoidance only exacerbates the problem by implying that the terms are somehow odd or unacceptable. This anxiety stems from the fact that, historically (and sadly even now), some people have tried to transform *Jew* into a term of vilification. Still, as nouns, *Jew* and *the Jews* remain perfectly dignified and appropriate terms.

That said, the word *Jew* is highly offensive when used as an adjective (as in *a Jew politician*), amounting to anti-Semitic rhetoric. The correct adjective is *Jewish*. A number of related words should also be avoided as derogatory or racist. The verb *to jew*, for instance, meaning "to bargain," is unacceptable. The phrase *Jewish princess* is demeaning and should be avoided, as should the word *Jewess*. Use *Jewish woman* if gender needs to be specified. The term *completed Jew* (see "*completed Jew*") is especially offensive. Different sources have a mixed reaction to the word *Jew's harp* in reference to the musical instrument. In an effort to take the least offensive approach, this manual recommends that *jaw harp* be used instead. (See also "*Hebrews, Jews*" and "*Israeli, Israelite.*")

Jewish rabbi

Since all rabbis are Jewish, the term is redundant. Say *rabbi* without the qualifier.

jibe, jive, gibe

These words are often confused. *Jibe*, a verb, means "to be in accord with" (*his views jibed with hers*). In speech, people often mistakenly substitute *jive* for *jibe*, though *jive*, as a verb, means something quite different; it means "to kid, tease, or lie to" (as when B. B. King sings, "Nobody loves me but my mother, and she might be jiving me too"). As a noun, *jive* can mean a style of swing dance or a kind of verbal teasing, outright lying, or "trash talk" (as in *he talked a lot of jive*). This differs from the noun *gibe*, which means a "verbal attack" or "scoffing" (*his constant gibes hurt her feelings*). To further confuse things, *gibe* is sometimes spelled *jibe* and is also occasionally used as a verb (*he gibed the speaker with insults*).

Jr., Sr.

Jr., Sr., I, II, III, and so on should not be separated from a proper name by a comma: *Walter Wangerin Jr.* and *Pope Francis I.*

Judaism

Why are the words *conservative* and *liberal* lowercase before the word *Christianity* but capitalized before the word *Judaism*? The reason is that *Conservative Judaism* and *Liberal Judaism* are the names of organized sects rather than broad philosophies. If only the general philosophy is meant, then lowercase the terms, as in *a group of liberal Jewish friends.* The same is true for *Orthodox Judaism* and *Reform Judaism* (note the correct term is *Reform Judaism*, not *Reformed Judaism*) and for derivatives of those terms: *an Orthodox Jew, a Reform Jewish synagogue.* To say of a Jewish person that *his views are Orthodox* may be different in context than saying *his views are orthodox*.

Judeo-Christian

Avoid the term *Judeo-Christian* whenever possible. It smacks of Christian cant and is sometimes used as a political code word for "people like us." Many Jews find it offensive because it implies that those traditions are homogeneous, if not the same. The traditions and beliefs are quite different. If both the Jewish and Christian traditions need to be referenced, simply say *the Jewish and Christian traditions.*

judgment, judgement

Spell it without the *e* in the US: *judgment, judgmental, judgment day.* Even though it is commonly spelled *judgement* in the UK, legal documents in the UK spell it without the *e*.

K

Kabbalah, cabala

In Judaism, Kabbalah is a mystical method of interpreting the Hebrew Scriptures, originating in the eleventh century and referring to the body of written literature that has grown up around it. The term is usually capitalized as the title of a body of writing, set in roman, and used without the article *the*; related terms are Kabbalism and Kabbalistic. In general references to esoteric or mystical beliefs, the term is lowercase and often spelled cabala.

Kilns, the

When referring to the Headington, Oxford, home (now a study center) of C. S. Lewis and his brother, Warren Lewis, *the Kilns* is capitalized and always preceded by the article *the*. When spoken, the *n* is pronounced. Some people do not pronounce the *n* in the common noun (like *kill*), though *Webster* prefers pronouncing it.

kingdom

Lowercase *kingdom* in references to God's rule: *the kingdom of God*, *his kingdom*, *God's kingdom*, *the coming kingdom*, *the kingdom of heaven*, *the kingdom age*, and so on. This conforms with the texts of the NIV and the KJV, as well as with *SBL*, and fewer ambiguities arise when the word is lowercase.

King James Version, Authorized Version

In the US, the term *King James Version* (KJV) is more readily understood than the term *Authorized Version* (AV) as the name of the Bible translation commissioned by King James I of England. The term *Authorized Version* is used primarily in the UK and its Commonwealth.

King of Kings and Lord of Lords

Capitalize this term when it is used as a formal title, or name, for Jesus. When the individual elements of that phrase are used in a descriptive sense, *kings* and *lords* are lowercase, as in Rev. 17:14: "The Lamb will triumph over them because he is Lord of lords and King of kings" (NIV). This passage misleads some to argue that the words *lords* and *kings*, which refer to the earthly lords and kings over which Jesus is sovereign, should be lowercase in all uses. In Rev. 19:16, the terms, used in reverse order, are used not as descriptors but specifically as a name for Jesus: "On his robe and on his thigh he has this name written: KING OF KINGS AND LORD OF LORDS" (NIV). The NIV uses all small caps for the title, while the 1611 KJV uses caps and small caps.

Some people say that we should not honor the earthly lords and kings by capitalizing those words, but, as pointed out elsewhere, capitalization is not used to confer respect or honor. In this case, the entire phrase *King of Kings and Lord of Lords* is used as a name for Jesus. This is a matter of conventional English capitalization and style. The original offers little help because Koine Greek was written in all capital letters. In any case, lowercase *kings* and *lords* if they are descriptive, as in Rev. 17:14, but capitalize them when used as part of a title or name, as in Rev. 19:16.

L

L'Arche

See "*Arche, L'.*"

last days, the

Lowercase the term, as in *living in the last days.*

last judgment, the

Lowercase this in most references, as in *awaiting the last judgment.*

last rites

Lowercase the term *last rites.* This sacrament was formerly called *extreme unction*, but in 1972 the Roman Catholic Church changed it to *last rites.* It is also sometimes called *anointing of the sick.*

Last Supper, the

Unlike many terms for biblical events, *the Last Supper* is capitalized by convention, probably because of its association with Communion, or the Eucharist, terms that are regularly capitalized. Many Protestants prefer the term *the Lord's Supper*, and some Eastern Orthodox refer to it as *the Mystical Supper*; these terms can refer to both the biblical event and the liturgical rite of Communion. (See also, "*Communion*" and "*Holy Communion.*")

late, the (for deceased person)

How long may you refer to a deceased person as *the late so-and-so*? Some experts say fifteen years is the cut-off, while others say the expression can be used for someone who died as long as thirty years ago. In personal communications, it can be a tactful way of informing someone that a person, such as a spouse, is deceased, and it is often used that way in writing—as a way of informing a reader who may not otherwise know that someone has died. In formal writing, generally reserve *the late* for people how have died recently, however you define *recently.* (See also "DEATH DAGGER.")

Latter-day Saints, The Church of Jesus Christ of

The church itself styles *Latter-day* with the hyphen and a lowercase *d*. The name is abbreviated *LDS* or *LDS Church* with a capital *C*. While the official name of the church, which was founded by Joseph Smith in 1830, is the Church of Jesus Christ of Latter-day Saints, the group considers the terms *Mormon* and *Mormon Church* acceptable, informal nicknames, used even among members themselves. Members are referred to as either *Latter-day Saints* or *Mormons*, though, whenever possible, use the full formal name as a form of respect. The LDS Church is the largest denomination within what is called the Latter Day Saint movement (no hyphen, with capital *D*)—also called the LDS movement—which includes smaller groups that also trace their origins to Joseph Smith. Only those in the LDS Church are referred to as Mormons; other groups in the Latter Day Saint movement that have broken with the LDS Church are not considered Mormon. Among the latter are the Fundamentalist Church of Jesus Christ of the Latter-Day Saints (hyphen and capital *D*), which still practices polygamy.

Law, law

In a biblical context, the word *law* has several meanings. Lowercase it in most references to *the law* as opposed to *grace* and also when discussing *God's law, the law(s) of God, the law of Moses, the Old Testament laws*, and so on. Reserve the capitalized form, *the Law*, for references to the first five books of the Hebrew Bible (the Pentateuch).

layperson

The terms *layperson* and *laypeople* have largely replaced *layman* and *laymen* as non-gender-specific terms, though the older generic *laity* has made something of a comeback; *laity* can sometimes sound slightly more highbrow in some contexts, though it is less awkward than *laypeople*. Be aware that *laity* takes a singular verb (*The laity is* ...), whereas *laypeople* takes a plural (*Laypeople are* ...). Reserve the terms *laymen* and *laywomen* for those instances when it is important to specify that a group of laypeople consists entirely of members of one sex or the other, as in *the women-in-leadership conference was attended by two hundred laywomen*. Otherwise, opt for *laity* or *laypeople*. (See also "GENDER-ACCURATE LANGUAGE.") A *lay brother* in a Roman Catholic monastery is one who works for the order but has not been officially initiated into it.

lay position

See "*clerical title, clerical position, lay position.*"

lectionary, Lectionary

Lowercase *lectionary* unless the title of a specific volume is being referenced, as in *The Revised Common Lectionary, Episcopal Edition* (2007).

leaped, leapt

Both are acceptable, though *leaped* is more common. Allow author preference to determine which of these two to use.

Lent, Lenten

Lent is the noun; *Lenten* is the adjective; and both are always capitalized. These terms refer to the period of forty days (not counting Sundays) starting on Ash Wednesday and ending on Holy Saturday (see "*Holy Saturday*"), the day before Easter Sunday. In precise liturgical dating, Easter Sunday is not considered part of Lent. (See "CHRISTIAN HOLIDAYS, FEAST, AND THE LITURGICAL YEAR.")

leper, leprosy

The medical name for leprosy is Hanson's disease, which is the preferred name for the disease in modern contexts. Do not use the word *leper* or *leprosy* to describe any modern person with the disease. Reserve the terms only for ancient or older historical contexts or in direct quotations, for instance, from the Bible. The NIV uses the word *leper* only twice, strictly in reference to the name of Simon the Leper. Where the KJV commonly uses *leper*, the NIV often says *a man with leprosy*. (For a definitive discussion of this disease and the stigma attached to it, see Dr. Paul Brand and Philip Yancey's *The Gift of Pain* [Zondervan, 1997]).

lesbian

See "*LGBT.*"

Levant, the

The term *the Levant* has been used historically to define the Eastern Mediterranean region, roughly the same area covered by the biblical name *Canaan* ("the borders of Canaan reached from Sidon toward Gerar as far as Gaza, and then toward Sodom, Gomorrah, Admah and Zeboyim, as far as Lasha" [Gen. 10:19 NIV]). In modern usage, the term is usually avoided because of its colonialist associations. Since authorities differ as to what countries used to constitute the Levant anyway, use other, more specific terms. (See also "*Holy Land, the.*")

LGBT

This abbreviation is an acceptable shorthand for *lesbian, gay, bisexual, and transgender.* Use the terms *gay* for men or women and *lesbian* for women rather than *homosexual,* and as with all such designations, only provide them if it is relevant. The abbreviation is sometimes extended to *LGBTQ* (*lesbian, gay, bisexual, transgender, and queer* or *questioning*). Some references even extend that to *LGBTQA,* the *A* in this case standing either for *asexual, aromantic, allies, advocates, affirming,* or *all.* When using either of the last two abbreviations, define for the reader what the *Q* and *A* stand for in the specific context.

liberal

As a general theological or political philosophy, lowercase *liberal* as both an adjective and a noun (as in *a liberal church* or *a moderate liberal*). Capitalize it as part of an official party name (for instance, *the Liberal Democrats* of the UK) and in the term *Liberal Judaism.* (See "*Judaism.*")

libertarian, Libertarian

As a lowercase noun or adjective, *libertarian* refers to the general philosophy of minimal government (as in *the libertarian impulse*). Capitalized, it refers to the Libertarian Party (*an acknowledged Libertarian*).

-like

When the suffix *like* is added to a word, it is usually added without a hyphen: *childlike, Christlike, Godlike, heavenlike, weblike.* When *like* is added to a word ending in the letter *l* or to any personal name, then a hyphen should be added for clarity: *angel-like, bell-like, Jesus-like, Luther-like.*

like, as

Both *like* and *as* are used to make comparisons, and most grammar books suggest using *like* as a preposition introducing a simile with no attached verb (*she sings like an angel*) and using *as* as a conjunction when the following noun or pronoun is attached to a verb (*she phrases each line as a trained vocalist would*). No reason exists not to follow this rule, especially in formal writing, even though both *like* and *as* have been used as conjunctions introducing comparisons going back to Old English.

An exception is made any time *as* sounds stilted or illogical in context; for instance, whenever *like* is followed by *what*: *It would be funny if it wasn't so much like what all of us do.* Also, allow *like* in place of *as* whenever the style is colloquial, as in dialogue. (*"He runs like a camel trots!"*) Also, since *as* can indicate simultaneity, meaning "while," use *like* for comparisons whenever *as* might cause ambiguity; for instance, in this line from a Paul Verlaine poem: "It rains in my heart / like it rains on the town" (*Poèmes saturniens*). Using *as* in place of *like*, though grammatically correct, would imply that the two actions are taking place simultaneously rather than one being compared to the other.

As is also used to define a role played by a person or thing. Consider these two sentences: *Like an editor, I presume to break the rules* and *As an editor, I presume to break the rules. Like* in the first sentence sets up a comparison and implies that the speaker is not an editor but breaks rules like one. The *as* in the second sentence states that the speaker actually is an editor (and still breaks rules).

In Titles. When used in comparisons, both *like* and *as* are lowercase in titles and headings (as in *Talk like a Pirate* or *Wise as Serpents*) unless they come at the beginning (as in *Like Lambs before Wolves* or *As Big as a Whale*). Some editors capitalize *like* in titles and headings anyway (as in *Steal Like an Artist*). Our advice is to stick with lowercase, if only to make life easier for copyeditors and proofreaders.

lions' den

Daniel faced more than one lion. Make it *lions' den*, not *lion's den* (Dan. 6; also Bel and the Dragon 14:31–42).

litany, Litany

As a noun meaning "a prayer that presents a list of supplications to God" or "a responsive, repetitive prayer," lowercase *litany*. The formal part of a worship service reserved for such prayers is often referred to as *the Litany*, capitalized. Care should be taken because to people outside the church, *litany* often means "a long list of complaints or accusations" (as in *a litany of abuse*), even though some dictionaries do not define it in that negative way.

literally

People don't "literally die of embarrassment" or "literally hit the ceiling." Avoid the word as a casual intensifier. Reserve it for those rare occasions when you want to signal that you mean to say exactly what the words intend, with absolutely no double meaning or metaphor implied. Even then, use it rarely. (See also "INTENSIFIERS.")

liturgy, Liturgy, liturgical

Lowercase, *the liturgy* refers to what most Protestants call "the order of service" (as in *They liked the church for its liturgy*), which can include Communion. When capitalized, *the Liturgy* refers only to that portion of a worship service reserved for the Eucharistic rite itself (as in *They sang hymns while the bread and wine were passed during the Liturgy*). *A liturgical church* usually implies a church with a formalized order of service that includes Communion.

long-suffering

Hyphenate *long-suffering* in all contexts.

Lord

The term *Lord* originated in the Old English word *hlâford*, meaning "loaf herd," or "the herder (keeper) of the loaves (food source)." This implied a medieval landowner or someone with authority over others. While using *Lord* (always capitalized) to refer to God or Christ in contemporary writing is unobjectionable and time-honored, some writers see the term as an archaism expressive of medieval class structure and patriarchy. Editors should be sensitive to writers who avoid the term and opt instead for *God*, *Savior*, *Redeemer*, or other terms. (See also "LORD, GOD (CAP-AND-SMALL-CAP FORMS)" and "TRINITY, NAMES FOR PERSONS OF THE.")

Lord giveth, the (and the Lord taketh away)

Some references point out that the phrase *the Lord giveth and the Lord taketh away* is adapted from Job 1:21, which in the KJV actually reads, "The LORD gave, and the LORD hath taken away." The phrase indeed echoes Job 1:21 but is actually a direct quotation from the burial service found in the 1559 Book of Common Prayer, which is why the phrase is so common in the English-speaking world.

Lord, God (cap-and-small-cap forms)

Many English versions of the Bible (NIV, KJV, and RSV among them) use the cap-and-small-cap forms LORD and GOD to translate the Hebrew *Yahweh* (*YHWH* or *Jehovah*) and the regular cap-and-lowercase forms *Lord* and *God* to translate *Adonai* and other words denoting the deity. This is a useful distinction for readers insofar as *Yahweh* tends to suggest greater personal intimacy on the part of the Bible writer than *Adonai*, which is more formal. (Note in some editions of the KJV, all caps are used for *LORD* and *GOD* [*Yahweh*], though the original 1611 edition used caps and small caps, albeit in black-letter type.)

How strictly should a writer adhere to this distinction when quoting a short passage from one of these versions? The following guidelines should be adapted to the sensibilities and tastes of each publishing house.

Academic Use. In academic materials, Bible studies, works of theology, books of sermons, formal Bible exposition, and any writing that focuses on the Bible itself, the cap-and-small-cap style for *Lord* and *God* should be maintained when quoting from a Bible version that uses that style.

Nonacademic Use. In works of a highly popular or informal nature, such as devotionals, popular theology, fiction, biographies, and autobiographies, the cap-small-cap style is strongly encouraged, but it does not need to be maintained if no compelling reason exists to adhere to it, as in fictional dialogue when a character is quoting the Bible. The distinction between *Lord* and *LORD* is lost on most readers and can even lead to confusion. Many people think that the *LORD* form is simply used to give the word special emphasis, as italic or capital letters might do. In such popular works, its presence can be superfluous. Also, many readers mistakenly feel that the cap-small-cap form lends the words more, rather than less, formality.

> When Genesis 2:15 says, "The LORD God took the man and put him in the Garden of Eden," the Hebrew word for "man," *'adam*, is a pun on *'adamah*, which means "ground." [Academic usage]
>
> The old gardener looked up and said, "Yup, I believe it. 'The Lord God took the man and put him in the Garden.' " [Informal, dialogue use]

If the cap-and-small-cap style is used extensively in a nonfiction work for a popular audience, a note of explanation may be given on the copyright page:

> In the following pages, the forms *LORD* and *GOD*, in quotations from the Bible, represent the Hebrew *Yahweh*, while *Lord* and *God* represent *Adonai*, in accordance with the Bible version used.

Such a notice is not needed in academic works since the readership is likely to be familiar with the convention.

Web Use. On webpages, small caps are often not available. In these cases, the small-cap *LORD* and *GOD* should be rendered in all caps: *LORD* and *GOD*.

Lord of Lords

See "*King of Kings and Lord of Lords.*"

Lord's Day, the

The *Lord* in this instance is Jesus, so *the Lord's Day* refers to Sunday, the day on which Jesus rose from the grave, not Saturday, the Jewish Sabbath. Some writers use *the Lord's Day* specifically to distinguish the Christian from the Jewish Sabbath, the day of rest (Saturday). The word *Day* in that phrase is usually capitalized. (See also "*Sabbath, sabbath, sabbatical, Sabbatarian*" and "*Sabbath, Sunday.*")

Lord's Prayer, the

Matt. 6:9–13 gives the standard version of the Lord's Prayer, though Luke 11:2–4 gives a shortened version. In the Roman Catholic Church the prayer is often referred to as the Our Father or as the Pater Noster (Latin for "Our Father.") All these names are commonly given in roman without quotation marks. (See also "*trespasses, sins, debts.*")

lordship of Christ, the

Lowercase *lordship* in this formula.

Lord's Supper, the

Capitalized, *the Lord's Supper* can refer to either Jesus's final Passover meal with his disciples or the sacrament of Communion. (See also "*Communion,*" "*Holy Communion,*" and "*Last Supper, the.*")

Lord's Table, the

To refer to the Communion portion of a church service, capitalize *the Lord's Table.*

Low Mass

See "*Mass, mass* (*Roman Catholic*)."

M

MacDonald, George

The last name of Scottish minister and writer George MacDonald (1824–1905) is sometimes misspelled *Macdonald* (possibly because *Webster's 11th*, *Webster's Online*, and *Merriam Webster's Biographical Dictionary* [1995] misspell it that way). MacDonald himself unambiguously signed his name with the midcap: *MacDonald*.

Magdalen, Magdalene

The college at Oxford is spelled *Magdalen*; the college at Cambridge is spelled *Magdalene*. (See "*Oxford and Cambridge, the Universities of.*") Both were named for Mary Magdalene (ordinarily spelled with a final *e*). Even though the name is pronounced MAG-duh-lynn, the names of both colleges are pronounced like the modern word *maudlin*. The English word *maudlin* comes from Mary Magdalene's name since she is often depicted in Western art as weeping for her sins.

magi

While Matthew's gospel (the only one that mentions the magi) nowhere specifies how many magi, who were probably astrologers, came to visit the infant Jesus, three gifts are mentioned: gold, frankincense, and myrrh (Matt. 2:11). Out of that fact grew the unreliable tradition that the magi themselves were three in number, referred to as *the three wise men* or *the three kings*. The term *magi* is the plural of the Latin *magus*, meaning "magician," or "sorcerer."

Unless you are using the term in connection with the NIV, which capitalizes *Magi*, this manual recommends lowercasing *magi*, *the three wise men*, and *the three kings* as common nouns. The terms may be capitalized in the traditional manner in such seasonal literary works as pageants, poetry, sermons, and Christmas stories. Note that the KJV refers to them as *the wise men*, though the word *wise* was capitalized in the original 1611 version: *the Wise men*.

In the Middle Ages, legends grew around these figures, and they acquired names: (1) Melchior, king of Arabia, brought gold; (2) Caspar, king of Tarsus, brought frankincense; and (3) Balthazar, king of Ethiopia (depicted as having dark skin), brought myrrh. No historical basis can be found for them or their royal status, and the Eastern Orthodox tradition gives them different names and makes them twelve in number.

major prophets, Major Prophets, the

See "*prophets, Prophets, the.*"

Maker, the

Capitalize *the Maker* as an epithet for God in such phrases as *to meet one's Maker.*

mammon, Mammon

Derived from a Hebrew noun meaning "money," *mammon* is not, as sometimes suggested, the name of a pagan deity. It is correctly lowercase. Some writers capitalize the word when used to personify money, which is allowable as long as the context is clearly personification. Even so, the KJV personifies it twice (Luke 16:13; Matt. 6:24) and lowercases it both times—"God and mammon." Modern versions variously translate it as "money" (NIV, NLT, ESV, HCSB), "wealth" (CEB, NASB), or "riches" (NCV).

marines

See "*army, navy, air force, marines.*"

Mariology, Mariolatry

Capitalize these terms. The first is "the study of doctrines about of Mary"; the second is the "inordinate veneration of Mary."

-mas

The English suffix *-mas* indicates "the feast of" and is used in the names of certain holy days on the church calendar, such as *Candlemas, Christmas, Lammas*, and *Michaelmas*. It is spelled with one *s*, unlike its cognate *Mass*. (See also "*Mass, mass [Roman Catholic]*.")

Mass, mass (Roman Catholic)

Capitalized, the word *Mass* (the Latin root of which means "feast") refers to the liturgical ceremony of the Roman Catholic Church and some Anglican churches in which the Eucharist is celebrated. Some fine points in using the word should be observed. *High Mass* contains singing and is *sung* not *said*. By contrast, *Low Mass*, which contains no singing, is *said* not *sung*. Both are *celebrated* or *offered*, but it is considered substandard to say that a Mass "took place" or "was held." It is acceptable and common to use these terms in passive constructions: *Mass was sung, Mass was celebrated*. The terms *Mass, High Mass*, and *Low Mass* are usually capitalized, but they may be lowercase if the context is generic enough to warrant it, as in *We attended as many as three masses a week.* The names of special masses are capitalized: *Baccalaureate Mass, Funeral Mass.* Note that when *mass* refers to a genre of classical musical composition, lowercase it, though specific titles should be capitalized: for example, *Though written by a Lutheran, Bach's* Mass in B Minor *is one of the greatest masses ever written.*

matins, mattins

This term, meaning "morning prayer," is spelled *matins* in the US and *mattins* in the UK.

May Day, Mayday

May Day is the first day of May and is a holiday in many countries. *Mayday* is an internationally recognized distress call. Even though the term *Mayday* is based on the French *m'aidez* ("help me") and has nothing to do with the month of May, it is conventionally capitalized in English.

Mecca, mecca

The Saudi Arabian city of *Mecca* is the destination for Muslim pilgrims worldwide. Lowercase the word when it is used metaphorically, as in *Nashville is a mecca for songwriters.*

media, medium

Even though the noun *media* was originally the plural form of *medium*, it has become a collective singular to mean one or more of the various mass-communications outlets. Treat it as a singular noun, as in *the media is reporting the incident.* It is acceptable in formal and academic writing to treat *media* as a plural noun (*the media are reporting the incident* ...) or whenever the author prefers it. It may also be treated as a plural when the meaning is "multiple reporters" or "people from the media," as in *the media were filing into the briefing room.* In all cases, avoid *medias* as a plural. Note that when the word *medium* is used to mean "spiritual channeling practitioner," the correct plural is *mediums.*

medieval

Lowercase *medieval* unless part of a formally capitalized term, such as *Medieval Latin* or *the Department of Medieval Studies.* Also, avoid the older spelling, *mediaeval,* unless quoting from a direct source that uses that spelling. Usually *medieval era* is lowercase while *the Middle Ages* is capitalized. (See also "*Dark Ages*" and "*Middle Ages.*")

megachurch

Though often hyphenated, *megachurch* is most commonly spelled closed. It is defined as a large, rapidly growing Christian fellowship, though in some contexts it has pejorative overtones, implying that a fellowship has grown too large.

Messiah, messiah

Capitalize *Messiah* to mean Jesus or the prophesied savior of the Hebrew Bible. Lowercase it in metaphorical or general senses: *a messiah complex*, *the false messiah of regulatory reform.*

messianic

Lowercase the adjective *messianic* in both religious and nonreligious contexts: *Christ's messianic role* or *the soccer fans' messianic fervor.*

messiahship

The term is usually lowercase.

metropolitan

A clerical title in the Eastern Orthodox Church. A metropolitan is a bishop who ranks below patriarch and oversees an ecclesiastical province.

mic, mike

As shortened forms of *microphone*, both *mic* and *mike* are common. *Mike* is older, dating back to the 1920s and the advent of commercial broadcast and recording technology. *Mic* dates from the 1960s, when soundboard technology was rapidly improving. Each term has disadvantages. *Mic* looks as though it should be pronounced *mick*, while *mike* may be misleading because it doesn't retain the *c* of *microphone* and is also a proper name when capitalized.

In most cases, use *mic* when used only as a noun. It is the more commonly used of the two and the one preferred by recording engineers and microphone manufacturers. That said, if the term is also used as a verb in close context with the noun, *mike* is probably better, since the inflected forms of the verb, *miked*, *mikes*, and *miking* are more readily understood than *miced*, *mices*, and *micing*, which are incomprehensible. As always, choose the word least likely to confuse the reader in the given context.

mid-

Most often, set the prefix *mid* closed (*midafternoon*, *midbrain*, *midcentury*, *midcourse*, *midstream*, *midterm*, *midtown*), unless followed by a numeral, a compound that is already hyphenated, or a capital letter (*mid-1800s*, *mid-nineteenth-century literature*, *mid-April*). Hyphenate *mid* when used with eras and ages—*mid-fifties*, *mid-twenties*—though note that some authorities recommend setting them closed. (See also "PREFIXES.")

middle age, middle-aged

These terms are often confused. *Middle age* is a noun, referring to the span in a person's life from roughly the mid-forties to the mid-sixties (as in *having reached middle age* . . .). *Middle-aged* is the adjective describing that time span (as in *a middle-aged man*). (But compare this to "*teenage, teenaged.*")

Middle Ages, the

Synonymous with *the medieval era*. Most authorities treat *the Middle Ages*, which is always capitalized, as a collective noun that takes a singular verb: *The Middle Ages was not as unenlightened as most people think*. (See also "*medieval*" and "*Dark Ages*.")

midnight

See "*a.m., p.m., noon, midnight*."

millennium

In reference to the thousand-year period of Christ's reign (Rev. 20), lowercase the term *millennium*, or *the millennium*, and all words derived from it (including theological positions): *amillennial(ism)(ist)*, *millenarian(ism)(ist)*, *millennial kingdom*, *postmillennial(ism)(ist)*, *premillenarian*, *premillennial(ism)(ist)*. *Millennium* and its derivatives are occasionally misspelled with one internal *n* instead of two, but be aware that one family of derivatives is correctly spelled with a single internal *n*: *millenarian(ism)(ist)*, *millenary*, *premillenarian(ism)(ist)*, *postmillenarian(ism)(ist)*, and so on. Either *millennia* (common in the US) or *millenniums* (common in the UK) are acceptable plurals. Author preference should prevail.

mind-set

If ever a word was destined to lose its hyphen, that word is *mind-set*, which is hyphenated in *Webster*. Go with the hyphen for now.

minister

This term describes most Protestant clergy. It is a clerical position but is not used as a title; the term *reverend* is the form usually used as the title. (For forms of address, see "*reverend, Reverend.*")

minor prophets, Minor Prophets, the

See "*prophets, Prophets, the.*"

minus sign

Some Microsoft Word fonts (like Cambria Math) distinguish between a minus sign and an en-dash, but the difference is slight. For most purposes, an en-dash in any given font will suffice when a minus sign is needed in text: as in *She resigned herself to an A– in chemistry.* That can also be rendered as *She resigned herself to an A-minus in chemistry.* (See also "LETTER GRADES.") Don't use a hyphen as a minus sign.

Miranda rights, to Mirandize

The rights that are read to a person who has been arrested by the police are called *Miranda rights.* Although most grammarians prefer *to read him his Miranda rights* as the verb form, the simpler *to Mirandize* is common. Lowercase the word *rights*, though capitalize *Miranda* as the name of the 1966 legal case that established that precedent (*Miranda v. Arizona*).

mischievous

Although the alternate spelling *mischievious* has been common in English for centuries, it is considered a misspelling in most dictionaries. Use *mischievous.*

mission, missions

Which is correct: *a mission trip* or *a missions trip*? *A mission organization* or *a missions organization*? Based on internet hits alone (admittedly unscientific), *mission trip* is used nearly six times more often than *missions trip.* Logic dictates that a person who goes on a short-term mission is going on a "mission" (singular), not on "missions" (plural), and most mission trips are of the short-term kind. Editor Brian Phipps further speculates that fifty years ago, *missions* implied special organizations with specific people, that is, missionaries making multiple or long-term trips. As time went by, the idea of an ordinary church person doing a short-term mission project became more common. Hence, more people now participate in some *mission* or other. So, unless the author prefers *missions*, this manual favors *mission trip* and *mission organization* as the slightly more contemporary terms.

miter

In the US, the correct spelling of the word for peaked headwear worn by Roman Catholic and Anglican bishops as well as the pope is *miter*, not *mitre*. The latter spelling is common in the UK.

monsignor, monseigneur

Monsignor is a title given to certain Roman Catholic prelates. *Monseigneur* is a title given to certain French dignitaries—and also to Roman Catholic monsignors in France. Capitalize those titles before names.

Forms of Address. When writing to a Roman Catholic monsignor, the address line should read "The Right Reverend Monsignor [last name]," and the salutation is "Right Reverend Monsignor" or "Dear Monsignor [last name]." He may be addressed in person as either simply "Monsignor" or "Monsignor [last name]" and may be introduced the same way.

Mormon

See "*Latter-day Saints, The Church of Jesus Christ of.*"

Mother Earth, Mother Nature

Some writers argue that, as Christians, we should lowercase terms like *mother earth* and *mother nature* so that readers won't think we are venerating pagan deities. Those writers forget that we also capitalize *Zeus* and *Zoroaster*, and some people may have the mistaken notion that capitalizing a term is way of conferring honor. This manual capitalizes *Mother Earth* and *Mother Nature* on the principle that the names of mythological figures as well as personifications of abstract concepts are capitalized like any other name. Even most English translations of Saint Francis's "Canticle of the Sun" capitalize *Brother Sun, Sister Moon, Brothers Wind and Air*, and so on.

Mother Superior

See "*abbot, abbess, abbé.*"

Mount

Spell out and capitalize *Mount* before all biblical mounts, such as *Mount Carmel*, *Mount Hermon*, *Mount Hor*, *Mount of Olives*, *Mount Shapher*, *Mount Sinai*, and *Mount Zion*, as well as before all modern place names that include the word, such as *Mount Airy*, *Mount Rainier*, and *Mount Rushmore*. Although the KJV regularly lowercases *mount* (for instance, *mount Gerizim*, *mount Seir*, *mount Sinai*), capitalize *Mount* even in discussions of passages from the KJV, unless quoting directly. (See also "*Saint, saint.*")

Mount Zion

See "*Zion.*"

Muhammad, Mohammed

Despite the fact that *Mohammed* is the most common spelling in the US, we opt for the UK variant *Muhammad* because it is closer to the Arabic and is also the spelling preferred in *Webster*. Either is preferable to spelling the name of the founder of Islam as *Muhammed* or *Mahomet*. (See "ISLAMIC RELIGIOUS TERMS.")

multifaith

Set *multifaith* solid, not hyphenated.

Muslim

The spelling *Muslim* is preferred over the outdated *Moslem* and even more outdated *Mohammedan* and *Mussulman*. It is both a noun, referring to an individual adherent, and an adjective. Many readers are offended by the spelling *Moslem* because it harks back to colonial days. When referring to the religion as a whole and not to individual adherents, use the noun and adjective forms *Islam* and *Islamic*. For example, say *Islamic art* and *the Islamic calendar* rather than *Muslim art* or *the Muslim calendar*. (See "ISLAMIC RELIGIOUS TERMS.")

must-read, a

Though not in *Webster*, this is one of the most commonly used nouns in book endorsements, marketing copy, and jacket blurbs. Hyphenate it as you would *a must-have* or *a must-see*. Calling a book "a must-read" is as much a marketing cliché as calling it "a page-turner" or saying "I couldn't put it down." Also hyphenate *a can't-miss*. (See also "ENDORSERS, TEN COMMANDMENTS FOR.")

myriad, a myriad of

Both the adjective *myriad* (as in *myriad answers come to mind*) and the noun *myriad* (as in *a myriad of answers come to mind*) are correct. Some grammarians insist that the noun form is substandard, but saying *a myriad of* has a long and established history in English. It is not only acceptable but entirely correct. The plural noun *myriads* (as in *myriads of answers come to mind*) is also acceptable. There are myriad ways of saying *myriad.*

Mystical Supper, the

This is the Eastern Orthodox term for *the Lord's Supper*, or *the Last Supper.* It is capitalized. (See also "*Last Supper, the.*")

N

name of God, the; name of Christ, the; Name, the

Lowercase *name* whenever it is used in a general sense, even in references to God's name. The term *the Name* may be capitalized in devotional contexts when used as an epithet for the deity: as in *all praise and glory to the Name.* Similarly, common devotional formulas may be capitalized; for instance, *the Holy Name of Jesus* and *by his Holy Name.* (See "DEVOTIONAL CONTEXTS.")

namesake

Although ambiguity exists among dictionaries, the word *namesake* is most commonly used to describe the person who is named for, or in honor of, another person. For instance, if a grandson is given the same name as his grandfather, the grandson, not the grandfather, is the *namesake.* The term is often used with a possessive, which only adds to the confusion; for instance, in the sentence *Her cousin was her namesake,* it is vague as to who was named for whom. Avoid the possessive with this term.

Native American, native American

Native American (capital *N*) is an ethnicity (sometimes referred to as *American Indian* or, in Canada, *First Nation*). The term *native American* (lowercase *n*) refers to any person born inside the borders of the US. Because of the possibility of being misunderstood, it is usually best to find an alternative to the latter term, such as *native-born American.* Do not hyphenate *Native American* as an adjective (say, for instance, *Native American artifacts*). Note that while *Native American* was once the dominant term, *American Indian* is now preferred among some groups of First Nations people. The term *Native Canadian* is also common in Canada. (See also "ETHNIC AND RACIAL DESIGNATIONS.")

nativity

Lowercase *nativity* in most references to the birth of Jesus: *the nativity, the nativity of Jesus, a nativity display, a nativity play,* and so on. (See "EVENTS IN THE LIFE OF JESUS, LOWERCASING.") It is often capitalized in Christmas devotional contexts such as Advent hymns, services, or performances. (See "DEVOTIONAL CONTEXTS.") Also capitalize it in reference to specific holy days of the church calendar: *the Nativity of John the Baptist.*

Note that the word *nativity* is most often used in reference to Jesus's birth, not to other births, and even in the case of Jesus, saying "the nativity of Christ" is a slightly churchy way of saying "the birth of Christ." Check to make sure its use is not simply a case of Christian jargon.

navy

See "*army, navy, air force, marines.*"

never-never land, the Neverland, the Neverlands

The phrase *never-never land* (lowercase) is used for any place of general happiness or fantasy. It is often conflated with the home of the title character of J. M. Barrie's *Peter Pan*, which is called *the Neverland* (one word, capitalized, and always with the article *the*). Note also that Barrie occasionally refers to that place in the plural: *the Neverlands*.

New Atheism, the New Atheists

Capitalize these terms when referring to a specific group of writers and thinkers, such as Sam Harris and Richard Dawkins, who argue that all religions should be aggressively rejected. (See also "*agnostic, atheist, unbeliever.*")

New Testament

See "*Old Testament, New Testament.*"

New Year's Day, New Year's Eve

Note the apostrophe.

Nine-Eleven, 9/11, 9-1-1

See "*September 11, 2001*" in reference to the terrorist attacks. See "TELEPHONE AND CELL-PHONE NUMBERS IN TEXT," section on "*Emergency 9-1-1*" in reference to the emergency phone number.

Ninety-Five Theses, the

Martin Luther's Disputation of 1517 is commonly referred to as the Ninety-Five Theses (the *Five* is capitalized), and as an important historic document it is set in roman type rather than italic.

Noel

Noel is the preferred spelling of this word, which means "Christmas." The older variant *Nowell* is confined to certain Christmas carols, such as "The First Nowell," as it appears in some hymnbooks. *Noël*, with an umlaut, is occasionally seen in the UK but is outdated. In reference to Christmas, the second syllable is accented: no-ELL. When it is used as a man's name, the first syllable is usually accented—NO-ul—or the word is pronounced as a single syllable—NOLE. When used as a woman's name, most often spelled *Nowell*, the second syllable is usually accented.

no less, no more, nothing less, nothing more

No less and *nothing less* imply "at least," while *no more* and *nothing more* imply "at the most." To say *"It was nothing less than bribery"* means that it was a clear case of bribery and perhaps worse. To say *"It is nothing more than bribery"* implies that it was indeed bribery but no worse than that. As always, clarify.

nominal Christian

This pejorative term describes someone who is perceived as being a Christian "in name only" and is sometimes contrasted with *practicing Christian*. Both terms imply value judgments that may or may not be true, and they should be used cautiously.

non-

Non-, used as a prefix, is set without a hyphen (for instance, *nonbeliever, nonfiction, nonnative, nonproliferation, nontoxic*) except when the main word is capitalized (for instance, *non-American, non-Catholic, non-Darwinian, non-Hodgkin lymphoma*) or when the *non-* precedes an already hyphenated compound (for instance, *non-gender-specific language*). Note that *non*, when used in many common Latin phrases, is a separate word, as in *non compos mentis, non gratia*, and *non sequitur*. (See also "PREFIXES.")

nonbeliever

See *"agnostic, atheist, unbeliever."*

nonbiblical, abiblical, extrabiblical, unbiblical

These words are often used interchangeably even though subtle shades of difference exist in some contexts. *Nonbiblical* suggests something marginally related to but not actually found in the Bible or something directly contrary to the Bible, while *abiblical* suggests something entirely unrelated to the Bible. For instance, the legend of the apostle Thomas's ministry in India is a nonbiblical story, whereas yoga might be considered an abiblical practice. *Extrabiblical* is close in meaning to *nonbiblical* but can also suggest a commonly accepted doctrine, passage, or idea that is often thought of as biblical but actually has little or no basis in Scripture. For instance, the traditional marriage vows are extrabiblical, coming, as they do, from the Book of Common Prayer. *Unbiblical* implies that something is completely unsupported by the Bible or contrary to specific tenets, as in *The group was considered a cult because of its unbiblical practices.*

non-Christian

See "*non-*" and "*unchristian, non-Christian.*"

noncanonical

Some writers prefer *non-canonical*, but this manual opts for *noncanonical.* The closed form is unlikely to cause confusion and accords with *CMoS*'s rule of setting the prefix *non-* solid with most words that follow it. (See "*non-*.")

nonclerical

Set this solid. (See also "*non-*.")

nonreligious

See "*irreligious, nonreligious, unreligious, areligious.*"

noon

See "*a.m., p.m., noon, midnight.*"

not only ... but

The mistake most writers make with sentences containing *not only ... but* (or *but also*) is lack of parallelism; for instance, *He not only plays guitar but also keyboards* is not as concise as *He plays not only guitar but also keyboards.* Whatever element (noun, verb, adjective) immediately follows the *not only* should parallel whatever element immediately follows the *but.* Usually an *also* is used after *but*, though it may be dropped if it seems awkward. The phrase *as well* can often be substituted later in the sentence: *He plays not only guitar but keyboards as well.*

Some writers insist on placing a comma before the word *but* in sentences containing a *not only ... but* formula. The comma is justified if a new subject is introduced after the *but*, creating an independent clause, as in *Not only does she chair the committee, but her husband serves as its sole member.* Otherwise, a comma is unnecessary, as in *He is not only willing but also able* or *They not only cheated but also lost.* A comma may be added if the sentence is overlong or already heavily punctuated.

number of

Even though the word *number* is singular, construe it as a plural when using *a number of . . .*, as in *A number of people were present*. Note that *number* reverts to being construed as a singular noun when the article *the* is used in place of *a*: as in *the number of mistakes is distressing.*

O

Occupy movement

To refer to the populist anticorporate protest movement that began in 2011, capitalize *Occupy*, lowercase *movement*. (See "MOVEMENTS AND ERAS, HISTORICAL" and "*Tea Party*.")

offices

In the Roman Catholic Church the term *offices* refers to the prescribed duties to pray and worship throughout the day. (See "HOURS, CANONICAL.") When referring to *the offices* (as in *the monks chanted the offices*), lowercase the term. Capitalize it when referring to *the Divine Offices*, since that is the title of a group of specific observances. Also capitalized are the terms *Major Offices* and *Minor Offices*. The names of the offices themselves are usually capitalized in Roman Catholic style: *Lauds*, *Matins*, *Vespers*.

oh, O

The Exclamation. The exclamation *oh* is usually followed by a comma, especially when a slight pause would occur after the word when spoken, and lowercase it except when it begins a sentence or is in a title. The comma may be dropped in common expressions such as *my oh my*, *oh boy*, *oh brother*, *oh gosh*, *oh man*, *oh my*, *oh no*, *oh yeah*, and *oh yes*.

***The Vocative* O.** Most writers and editors know the difference between the exclamation *oh* and what is called the *vocative* O. *Oh* is used as an interjection of surprise or sudden emotion (*Oh, you startled me!*) or a filler word that indicates a pause or thoughtfulness (*Oh, I'll get to it sooner or later*). The vocative O, which is always capitalized, is used when calling upon or directly addressing someone, especially in an oratorical manner (as in "*O ye of little faith . . . ,*" Matt. 8:26 KJV), or invoking a deity, as in prayer (as in "*Thy name, O Lord, endureth for ever,*" Ps. 135:13 KJV). Note that it is used without a comma. Readers are increasingly unlikely to be familiar with the difference between *oh* and O.

Caution should be used because the vocative O, which suggests oratory, is rapidly disappearing from English. First, O conveys a melodramatic tone in modern writing and is often used for humor or exaggeration (as in *O ye muses of the blogosphere*). Second, and perhaps more tellingly, many readers simply mistake it for *oh*, that is, as an expression of heightened emotion, so that its oratorical sense is lost. Some recent Bible translations, like the NIV, have all but eliminated the use of O for these reasons. The KJV's "Examine me, O LORD" (Ps. 26:2) has become "Test me, LORD" in the NIV. Still, the NIV has not completely eliminated it; for instance, "I will sing the praises of your name, O Most High" (Ps. 9:2).

O is still appropriate in formal prayers (in daily devotional books, for example), though *oh* may be just as appropriate. An editor can defer to the author (assuming the author understands the difference). Use O in direct quotations where it appears. Otherwise, use it cautiously, or simply opt for *oh*, which still communicates its intended meaning unambiguously.

okay, OK

Should we write *OK*, *O.K.*, or *okay*? As a rule, use *okay* in text because its inflected forms—*okayed*, *okaying*, *okays*—are more comprehensible than *OKed*, *OKing*, or *OKs*. Still, *OK* is fine for most occasional uses, especially colloquial. The abbreviated form *A-OK* is also acceptable, with capital letters and no periods. H. L. Mencken referred to *OK* as "the most successful of all Americanisms" (*The American Language, Supplement One*, 269).

ol'

As a colloquial way of saying *old* (as in *good ol' boy*), use the contracted form *ol'* instead of *ole*, despite the fact that most dictionaries approve of both spellings. *Ole* can be too easily misread as the Spanish *olé* (though note the official spelling of *the Grand Ole Opry*).

Old City, the

In Jewish and Christian contexts, this phrase, capitalized, refers to the walled section of Jerusalem, though other cities (from Knoxville, Tennessee, to Florence, Italy) also have districts referred to as *the Old City*, also capitalized.

old-fashioned

Unlike some other compound adjectives that follow a noun, this one always sports the hyphen: *his manners were old-fashioned.*

Old Testament, New Testament

As familiar as these terms are to Christians, they are offensive to some readers outside the Christian faith. Jewish readers often resent what they know as *the Hebrew Bible* (or simply *the Bible*) being referred to as *the Old Testament*, which seems to them completely Christocentric, as does the use of the term *the New Testament* in place of *the Christian Scriptures*. Although this manual does not recommend discarding the traditional terms *Old Testament* and *New Testament*, especially when writing for a Christian readership, it does recommend being sensitive to other possible readerships that any particular book might have. In books about Judaism, anti-Semitism, or rabbinical literature, for instance, use the more accurate *Hebrew Bible* and *Christian Scriptures* to avoid subtly perpetuating the notion that Judaism is in some way no longer valid or vital. Even in books for an exclusively Christian readership, the terms *Old Testament* and *New Testament* can often be replaced with references to specific books being discussed. For example, instead of *In the New Testament, Paul reminds us ...*, write *In his letter to the Romans, Paul reminds us ...* This is more precise and less offensive to many readers.

As Adjectives. When *Old Testament* and *New Testament* are used as adjectives, do not hyphenate them: for instance, *Old Testament patriarchs* and *New Testament studies*.

old times' sake

Although *old time's sake* is frequently seen, most sources think of the "old times" as plural: *old times' sake* (plural possessive and no hyphen).

Old World, New World

Capitalize *the Old World* and *the New World* when referring to Europe and the Americas respectively. *Webster* suggests *old-world* as the adjective (*quaint old-world villages*) but suggests no parallel adjective form for *New World*. This manual recommends *Old World* and *New World* (capitalized and without the hyphen) as the adjectives (*the city's Old World charm, New World explorers*).

-ology

The suffix *-ology* means "the study of." The following list shows some of the more common "-ologies" in the field of religion.

angelology—the study of angels and their theological implications
anthropology—the study of humans and civilizations
archeology—the study of ancient ruins and artifacts
bibliology—the study of the Bible as the Word of God
Christology—the study of the person and work of Christ
cosmology—the study of the universe
demonology—the study of demons and evil spirits
ecclesiology—originally, the study of church architecture and ornament;

now, also the study of church history and the nature and function of the church

epistemology—the study of how things can be known

eschatology—the study of theories of how the world will end

hagiology—the study of saints' lives

hamartiology—the study of doctrines regarding sin and the fall

heortology—the study of the history and significance of holidays, festivals, and seasons of the church calendar

hymnology—the study of church hymns

Mariology—the study of the Virgin Mary

numerology—the study of numbers; often applied to the study of numbers in the Bible

pneumatology—the study of the doctrines regarding the person and work of the Holy Spirit

sacramentology—the study of the nature of God's presence in the world, specifically in the form of the sacraments

soteriology—the study of the doctrines of salvation, especially in regard to Christ's role in salvation

teleology—the study of first causes, especially arguments for the existence of God based on scientific observation

theology—the study of God and God's interactions with humans

typology—the study of types and symbols, especially as they relate to the Bible

on accident, by accident

A 2006 study by Leslie Barratt of Indiana State University (http://www.inst.at/trans/16Nr/01_4/barratt16.htm) found that people under the age of thirty-five tended to say *on accident*, while those older tended to say *by accident*. Neither phrase is incorrect, but the age of an author's intended readership should be a factor in deciding which form to use. As the population ages, *on accident* will most likely supersede *by accident*.

one another's

See "*each other's*."

One, the

Capitalize *the One* when used alone as a name for God: *all our prayers are heard by the One*. Otherwise, lowercase it in most other phrases referring to God, even if the cap-deity style is being used: as in *We affirmed that he alone is the one true God* or *We know that He is the one who hears our prayers*. (See "TRINITY, NAMES FOR PERSONS OF THE.")

only begotten Son

Some punctilious editors insert a hyphen between *only* and *begotten* in the phrase *only begotten Son*, arguing that it is a compound adjective. This overlooks the fact that most Bible translations that use the phrase (John 3:16) do not hyphenate it, the KJV and NASB being the most common. Only the outdated *Webster* and *Darby* versions hyphenate it. The phrase is unambiguous without the hyphen. If Jesus is referred to simply as *the Only Begotten*, capitalize it.

on the other hand

Many editors insist that the phrase *on the other hand* should never be used without the preceding, contrasting phrase *on the one hand* or *on one hand*. The rationale is thin. *On the other hand*, which is a dead metaphor to begin with, signals a strong and apparent contrast by itself, implying that *the one hand* has already been applied to whatever is being contrasted. For instance, *The arguments for his position seemed unusually strong to most of those present. The arguments against his position, on the other hand, seemed just as convincing.* The larger point is that there are more direct ways of indicating contrasts than by using *on the one hand* and *on the other hand*, which are hackneyed. *Though the arguments for his position seemed strong, the counterarguments were just as convincing.*

oral, verbal

See "*verbal, oral.*"

Oriental

See "*Asian, Asia.*"

original sin

Lowercase this term, referring to the fallen state of humanity because of Adam's sin. While it is occasionally capitalized in books of theology, both *Webster* and *SBL* recommend lowercasing it.

Orthodox, Eastern Orthodox

See "*Eastern Orthodox, Orthodox.*"

Our Father, the

See "*Lord's Prayer, the.*"

our Lady, Our Lady

Capitalize *Lady* but not *our* in most third-person references to Mary, mother of Jesus (as in *The nun prayed to our Lady for healing*). Capitalize the *Our* in direct address in prayers (as in *Our Lady, full of grace . . .*) and in institutional names (such as *the Abbey of Our Lady of Gethsemani*).

Oxford and Cambridge, the Universities of

In part because of the popularity of the Inklings (see "*Inklings*"), some of whose members were associated with the Universities of Oxford and Cambridge (jointly referred to informally as *Oxbridge*), the names of some colleges within those institutions are commonly referenced in Christian books. Oxford comprises forty-four colleges; Cambridge, thirty-two. The careful writer should be aware of a few quirks in the names of those colleges, some of which are referred to not as "colleges" but as "halls."

For instance, most readers familiar with C. S. Lewis's life and work know the difference in spelling between *Magdalen College* (Oxford) and *Magdalene College* (Cambridge) since Lewis worked at both, a spelling difference that reputedly originated with the British postal service in the nineteenth century as an effort to distinguish between the two colleges. Similar is the single-letter difference between *St. Catherine's College* (Ox.) and *St. Catharine's College* (Cam.).

Note *All Souls College* (Ox.) is spelled without an apostrophe, and the same is true for *Blackfriars* (Ox.). Cambridge has a *Queens' College*, but the college at Oxford is called *The Queen's College* (singular possessive, and usually with the article). Additionally, Oxford has a *New College* and a *St. Edmund Hall*, while Cambridge has a *New Hall* and a *St. Edmund's College*.

Some of the formal names do not include either of the words *college* or *hall*. Neither *Christ Church* (Ox.) nor *Peterhouse* (Cam.) is followed by the word *college* or *hall*, and *Blackfriars* (Ox.) is simply *Blackfriars*.

The universities also have colleges that share names: at both institutions you find a *Corpus Christi College*, a *Jesus College*, a *Pembroke College*, a *St. John's College*, a *Trinity College* (Cambridge also has a *Trinity Hall*), and a *Wolfson College*.

Note the correct formal names for these institutions are *the University of Oxford* and *the University of Cambridge*, though the terms *Oxford University*, or simply *Oxford*, and *Cambridge University*, or simply *Cambridge*, are common in informal contexts. The third oldest university in the UK is *the University of St. Andrews* (no possessive) in Scotland.

palate, palette, pallet, pallette

These words are often confused.

palate = "the roof of the mouth"
palette = "a board on which an artist mixes paints"
pallet = "a makeshift bed" or "a slatted platform for piling goods in a warehouse"
pallette = (rarely used; accented on second syllable) "the shoulder plate in a suit of armor"

Hope this palliates any confusion.

Palestine, ancient Palestine, the State of Palestine, the Palestinian State

As a place name, *Palestine* should be used with care, first, because it has meant different things throughout history, and second, because of the sensitive nature of its geopolitical overtones today. In Roman times, the region comprised what we now think of as Israel and the West Bank (broadly from Egypt to Syria and from the Mediterranean to Jordan). Today the Palestinian Territories, overseen by an entity known as the State of Palestine, comprise the West Bank, East Jerusalem, and the Gaza Strip. Palestinians themselves refer to these territories as the Occupied Palestinian Territories (capitalized and abbreviated OPT).

The Palestinian Territories were given observer status by the UN in 2012, but lacking full-member status means that Palestine has yet to be internationally recognized as an independent country. In 2015, the Vatican signed a treaty with "the State of Palestine," which was the first international legal document to recognize the territories using that name. About two thirds of its West Bank portion is under Israeli control, and the West Bank and the Gaza Strip are governed independently of each other.

Palestine is legitimately referred to as a region, and it is also shorthand for the West Bank and the Gaza Strip areas today, but no internationally sanctioned, independent nation called Palestine exists—at least, not yet to the extent that would require the relabeling of world maps. The situation is still fluid.

parable, Parable

Unless used in an actual title, the word *parable*, like the words *book*, *epistle*, *gospel*, *letter*, and *psalm*, is lowercase as a descriptive term, as are any descriptive words that accompany it; for example, *the parable of the prodigal son* or *the parable of the talents*.

parachurch

While the word *parachurch* has yet to appear in most dictionaries, its use is common among churchgoing people in the US and UK. Most often the word is used as an adjective, as in *a parachurch organization*, but it is also used as a noun, as in *the ministries of the nation's parachurches*. *Parachurch* refers to a religiously based organization, often independent of traditional denominations, that was created to involve Christians in ministry beyond the scope of most traditional churches and denominations. Usually, parachurch organizations are established to achieve a specific goal, such as providing wheelchairs to the world's poorest countries or funding local food kitchens. They have their roots in the early nineteenth century when groups of Christians would band together interdenominationally for a specific purpose, such as to promote moral reform (as in the various abolition and temperance leagues), to print tracts, or to fund missionary endeavors.

paradise, Paradise

Lowercase *paradise* to mean "heaven" or "a state of bliss in the afterlife." If referring specifically to the garden of Eden, capitalize *Paradise* as a place name. (For a discussion, see "*heaven, Heaven*.")

Paschal, paschal

Capitalize *Paschal* (from Hebrew *pesaḥ*, "Passover") in references to Passover or Easter: *a Paschal candle, the Paschal Feast, the Paschal Lamb, a Paschal service, the Paschal Vigil*. Lowercase it when only secondarily related to Passover or Easter: *the paschal full moon, the paschal new moon*. Be sure not to misspell it *Pascal*.

passion (of Jesus), the

Lowercase the word *passion*—as in *the passion of Jesus*—in most contexts. (See "EVENTS IN THE LIFE OF JESUS, LOWERCASING.") Note that *passion* is capitalized when referring to specific times or days on the church calendar—*Passion Sunday, Passion Week*—and also in reference to *a Passion play*, since such plays are performed during Passion Week.

pastor, Pastor

This is a common clerical title as well as the name of a clerical position. In most Protestant churches, *pastor* is a general term describing the person with the primary authority over a local church, congregation, or parish. In the Roman Catholic Church, a pastor heads a parish. The Episcopal Church uses the term *rector* instead of *pastor.* Priests and ministers are often pastors, but not in all cases. In ordinary usage, only capitalize *pastor* before a name; for instance, *Pastor Chuck Fromm* or *Pastor Fromm.*

patriarch, Patriarch

In the Eastern Orthodox Church, *patriarch* is the clerical title given to a high-ranking bishop who oversees other bishops. In the Mormon Church a patriarch is a member of the clergy of the Melchizedek priesthood and is able to perform certain prescribed duties. In the Roman Catholic Church a patriarch is next in rank to the pope and is the titular head of a given geographical region. Like most clerical titles, capitalize it only when it comes immediately before a name: *Patriarch Thomas.* Abraham is sometimes referred to as *the Patriarch.* (See also "*patriarchs, the; Patriarch, the.*")

patriarchs, the; Patriarch, the

The term *the patriarchs* (lowercase) may refer to any of the early theologians of the Christian church and is synonymous with *fathers of the church.* (See "*fathers of the church, church fathers.*") It may also refer to the progenitors of the Hebrew people (Abraham, Isaac, Jacob), though when *the Patriarch* is capitalized, it usually refers to Abraham alone. Such distinctions are often lost on readers unless the writer makes it clear in the first reference; for instance, *The Patriarch, Abraham, stands out among the other patriarchs.*

Paul, Saul

A common misconception is that Jesus somehow changed Saul's name to Paul on the road to Damascus (Acts 9:1–19), but Paul doesn't seem to use that name until he's on Cyprus much later (Acts 13:9). As a Jewish Roman citizen by birth, Paul had both a Jewish name, *Saul*, and Roman one, *Paul.* He most likely preferred *Paul* when preaching to gentiles, since that is the name they would be more accustomed to. Use *Paul* in most references except, perhaps, in discussions of his Jewish background. The following epithets are also used in references to him: *the Apostle* (when the context specifically refers to Paul), *the apostle Paul, the Apostle to the Gentiles, Paul the Apostle, Saul of Tarsus, Saint Paul.* (See also "*apostle, Apostle*" and "*Saint, saint.*")

pearly gates

Lowercase *pearly gates* unless used allegorically as a place name, as in fiction. The expression is a reference to Rev. 21:21 (KJV): "The twelve gates were twelve pearls: every several gate was of one pearl." The term is often used for humor or rhetorical effect in contemporary writing; otherwise, it is hackneyed. The term is sometimes used humorously in the singular (*the pearly gate*) to mean a person's mouth.

Pentecostal, Pentecostalism

Usually capitalized when referring to churches. Be alert to the common misspelling *Pentacostal*. Some readers ask, "Why is *Pentecostal* capitalized while *charismatic* is not?" The reason is that *Pentecostal* is formed from the proper noun *Pentecost*, a feast in the Jewish and Christian calendars.

percent

In nontechnical contexts, spell out the word *percent* (as in *I give my job 110 percent*). In dialogue and extremely informal contexts, even the number may be spelled out (as in *I bet only ten percent of my plants survived.*) In contexts where percentages are frequent or given in a technical or statistical manner, use the % symbol (as in *Pew reports that 68% of the general public believes climate change is real*). Note that a word space is not placed between the numeral and the symbol. (See also "NUMBERS: SPELLING OUT VERSUS USING NUMERALS," section on "*Percentages.*")

period

Lowercase *period* in reference to historical eras: *the Neo-Babylonian period, the period of the judges, the Roman period*, and so on. (But see "*empire, Empire.*")

persons, people

Formerly, a common journalistic style insisted that *persons* be used instead of people when writing about a specific number of individuals, as in *Thirty-three persons lost their lives*. That style is somewhat outdated. Use *people* for groups as well as numerically specified individuals in most cases. Reserve *persons* for those contexts in which "bodies" are implied, as in *No contraband was found on their persons*. Also, custom dictates the use of *persons* when speaking of *the three persons of the Trinity*.

pharaoh, Pharaoh

Capitalize *Pharaoh* like a proper name, which is, in most cases, when it is used without an article (as in *Moses was raised in Pharaoh's household*). When an article precedes it or it is used generically, lowercase it as a common noun (as in *At first he was afraid to address the pharaoh* or *Two pharaohs ruled the Middle Kingdom*). (Topical note: the winner of the 2015 Triple Crown in horse racing was named *American Pharoah*, with the *a* and *o* transposed. The horse was originally registered that way, but the owners decided to keep the misspelling, which is now trademarked and correct in references to that particular horse.)

Pharisee, Pharisaic, Pharisaical

Because the Pharisees were a formal Jewish sect at the time of Jesus, capitalize the terms *Pharisee*, *Pharisees*, and *Pharisaic* in that context. The plural form is usually preceded by the article *the*, and *Pharisaic* is preferred to *Pharisaical* as an adjective referring to the original Jewish sect. Lowercase the terms when they are used in modern nonreligious contexts to mean "hypocritical" or "legalistic." Although some authorities declare the adjective *pharisaical* invariably substandard, it is nevertheless common in such uses as *the student displayed a pharisaical attitude toward his classmates*. *Pharisaic* can sound stiff. In contemporary usage, these terms are pejorative, though they are not necessarily pejorative in the biblical context. (See also "*scribe*" and "*Sadducee*.")

Philistine, philistine

Capitalize *Philistine* only in reference to the people who lived in ancient Philistia, as in *"Goliath, the Philistine champion from Gath" (1 Sam. 17:23)*. Otherwise, lowercase *philistine* and *philistinism* to mean people who are uninformed, vulgar, or culturally insensitive.

Photoshop, photoshop

Photoshop (capitalized) is the trade name of a powerful graphic-design program made by Adobe. Like *Google* and *Xerox*, this trade name is often lowercase when used as an adjective or verb: *He photoshopped the two faces together.*

piety, pious, piousness

Some grammarians insist that *piousness*, as a back formation of the word *pious*, should not be used, the correct noun form being *piety*, though most dictionaries list *piousness* as a legitimate word. *Piousness* and *piety* can also have slightly different shades of meaning. What the dictionaries sometimes miss is that all three words—*piety, pious, piousness*—which used to suggest sincere devotion and assiduous faith, are now often used pejoratively. They hint at insincerity and self-conscious display in matters of faith. If anything, *piousness* may have a slightly more pejorative tone than *piety* in common usage. Although these terms are not exclusively negative in contemporary usage, the careful writer must be aware that those words could be misunderstood by the reader to have a double sense, for instance, when referring to the "piety" of a well-known person. A religious readership may understand these words differently than a general audience might.

Pilgrims, the; Pilgrim Fathers, pilgrim

In the context of Anglo-American history, *the Pilgrims* (capitalized) were the dissenting English Christians who founded the Plymouth Colony in Massachusetts in 1620. The term *Pilgrim Fathers* (also capitalized) refers narrowly to those men who made the voyage from England aboard the *Mayflower* and implies the first generation of Pilgrim leaders. When lowercase, *pilgrim* refers to any traveler, especially one whose motives for traveling may be religious, such as Chaucer's Canterbury pilgrims or Muslims on the hajj to Mecca. (See also "*Puritan, Puritanism, Pilgrim.*")

Pilgrim's Regress, The

The title of this 1937 novel by C. S. Lewis was spelled *The Pilgrim's Re-gress* (with a hyphen) when it was first published in the US in 1944 by Sheed & Ward; later editions reverted to the standard spelling without the hyphen.

pj's

Although *PJs* is a colloquial, shortened form of "pajamas," *Webster* recommends *pj's*. No reason exists to capitalize it, and it is always plural (a single *pj* is hard to imagine). The apostrophe is there to avoid confusion, which is the same reason many other abbreviations insert an apostrophe to form their plurals. (See "PLURALS," section on "*Plurals of Abbreviations.*")

Plain, plain (Amish)

When referring to the people or customs of the Amish and some Mennonite communities, capitalize *Plain*: *the Plain People, a Plain community, dressing in Plain style*. In some contexts, *Plain style* (capitalized) can also refer to Quakers (Religious Society of Friends), some of whom also adopt simple clothing. Be aware that *plain* can also be used in its usual sense even in those contexts: *Mennonites believe in a plain style of church architecture* or *Sherry Gore proves that Amish food may be plain, but it's delicious.* (See also "PLAIN STYLE [AMISH].")

playdate

Spelled as one word.

p.m.

See "*a.m., p.m., noon, midnight.*"

podcast

Set as one word, not hyphenated.

pontiff, Pontiff

The word *pontiff*, lowercase, refers exclusively to the pope of the Roman Catholic Church. It is from the Latin *pontifex maximus* ("supreme pontiff," with the Latin *pontifex* meaning "bridge maker"—the one who acts as a bridge between God and humans). In contemporary references, *pontiff* is less common than *pope*. Some Roman Catholic presses capitalize *the Pontiff* as they capitalize *the Pope*. While the Eastern Church has had popes at various times, they are never referred to as *pontiffs*. (See also "*Holy Father*" and "*pope, Pope.*")

pope, Pope

Lowercase references to the head of the Roman Catholic Church unless the full name is used: *the pope*, but *Pope John XXIII*. This is consistent with *CMoS*. While some Roman Catholic presses capitalize *the Pope* when used alone, the Catholic News Services *Stylebook on Religion 2000* follows the *CMoS* guidelines. Whenever the term is used metaphorically or in a general sense, lowercase it: *the undisputed pope of hip-hop* or *the popes of the last two centuries*.

Alternate Titles. Capitalize other titles for the pope when they have the force of a stand-in name: *the Bishop of Rome*, *His Holiness*, *the Holy Father*, *the Vicar of Christ*, *the Vicar of Peter*, and so on, though *pontiff* is an exception. (See "*Holy Father*" and "*pontiff, Pontiff.*")

Forms of Address. The address line of a letter to the pope should read, "His Holiness, the Pope" or "His Holiness, Pope [name]," and the salutation should read, "Your Holiness" or "Most Reverend Father." In speaking to the pope, address him as "Your Holiness" or "Most Holy Father" and introduce him in public as "His Holiness" ("Pope [name]" may be added) or "The Holy Father."

pore over

A common mistake is to write *pour over* instead of the correct *pore over*. *Pore* means "to gaze or to scrutinize" and is almost always used with the accompanying word *over*, as in *The scholar pored over the manuscript*.

post-Christian

See "*pre-Christian, post-Christian.*"

postconversion

See "*preconversion, postconversion.*"

POTUS, FLOTUS, SCOTUS

The common journalistic acronym for *the president of the United States* is *POTUS*. Although some manuals spell it *Potus*, this manual recommends making it all caps like most initialisms. Also, the word *Potus* may be unfamiliar to many readers and the all-cap form at least communicates that it is an abbreviation.

The same form applies to *FLOTUS* (*the first lady of the United States*), *SCOTUS* (*the Supreme Court of the United States*), *SOTUS* (*State of the Union Speech*), and *VPOTUS* (*the vice president of the United States*, pronounced VEE-POE-tus). Only once have we seen a reference to *SLOTUS* (*the second lady of the United States*, that is, the vice president's wife). The style manuals have not yet determined what acronym will be used for the first husband of a female president. *FHOTUS*? (See "*first lady, First Lady.*")

prayer book

Although *Webster* gives *hymnbook* as one word, it gives *prayer book* as two, as well as other "prayer" compounds: *prayer beads*, *prayer meeting*, and *prayer shawl*.

Preacher, the

When capitalized, the term *the Preacher* usually refers to the narrator of the book of Ecclesiastes (KJV), traditionally said to be Solomon. The NIV uses the term *the Teacher* instead, but the KJV's use of *the Preacher* is firmly established in English. For instance, the phrase *Vanity of vanities, saith the Preacher* is far more likely to be familiar to modern readers (despite the King James language), than the NIV's *"Meaningless! Meaningless!" says the Teacher.*

preachify

This derogatory verb means "to preach badly" and implies fakery, ineptitude, or overlong presentation. Although the word dates back to the eighteenth century, it carries a hint of Southernism about it. The jocular noun is *preachifying.*

pre-Christian, post-Christian

In historical contexts, these terms refer to the eras before and after the time of Christ or before and after the arrival of Christian missionaries in a given country (*pre-Christian Gaul*). In modern missiological contexts, *pre-Christian* defines those people who, being largely new to the gospel, are therefore receptive to it, whether they live in a Christian country or not. *Post-Christian* defines those who have heard the gospel so often, and so negatively, that they are hardened to its message. Writers should be sure to clarify the context.

preconversion, postconversion

While some writers prefer *pre-conversion* and *post-conversion*, both *Webster* and *CMoS* recommend that the prefixes *pre-* and *post-* be set solid with the word that follows (that is, without a hyphen): *preconversion* and *postconversion.* The unhyphenated forms are preferred.

present writer, the

Style books used to consider it improper for academic writers to reference themselves in the first person, so the pretentious phrase *the present writer* sprang up as a way self-referencing. Avoid it. The present writer hereby grants you permission to use *I, me, my, myself,* and *mine* as appropriate, even in scholarly and reference works. (See also "FIRST PERSON.")

President, president, presidential

As a title before a proper name, capitalize *President* (*President Barack Obama*); in other references, lowercase it (*the president and his advisors*), even if you are referring to a specific president (*she spoke with the president of the United States*). The adjective *presidential* is always lowercase (*presidential motorcade*). Despite arguments to the contrary, lowercasing *the president* (of the US) seems appropriately democratic. Before the American Revolution, it was customary to capitalize *the King* (of England), since the king, it was believed, was second only to God in authority. But such deference ended when the colonies declared their independence, so that Ben Franklin, in his *Autobiography*, unapologetically lowercases both *the king* and *the president* (though Franklin refers to the latter as *the president-general*).

presiding bishop

The presiding bishop is a clerical title given to the person who heads the Episcopal Church or another denomination, such as the Church of God in Christ and the Church of Jesus Christ of the Latter-day Saints.

priest

This is a clerical position in the Roman Catholic, Eastern Orthodox, and Anglican and Episcopal churches. A priest is authorized to perform religious rites and ceremonies, usually as an intermediary between God and the congregants. In rank, a priest is between a bishop and a deacon.

Forms of Address. In conversation or in the salutation of a letter, address a priest as "Father" (or "Mother" in the Anglican and Episcopal churches); the last name may be added, and it is always added when introducing a priest to another person (*"I would like you to meet Father Thomas"*). In letters, the address line should read, "The Reverend [first and last names]."

primate

This is a clerical position in the Roman Catholic and Anglican churches. A primate is a bishop who has special authority over other bishops or whose ecclesiastical area has primary importance. (For forms of address, see "*bishop.*") Because most readers define *primate* as "relating to humans, apes, and monkeys," make sure the context is clear.

prior to, previous to

Prior to is a perfectly acceptable phrase, though the slightly more direct word *before* can usually be substituted. In many contexts, *prior to* sounds stuffy (as in *they had a nice dinner out prior to taking in a movie*) and is an affected way of being overprecise. *Prior to* is used in legal briefs when it is important to establish a detailed, accurate sequence of events (as in *she had no symptoms prior to taking the medication*). Still, *prior to* is not nearly as stuffy as *previous to*, a phrase that's best left to the legal profession. (For other "wordy words," see "*very,*" "*in order to,*" and "*to be,*" as well as "WORDY WORDS.")

prodigal

Because of its association with the parable of the prodigal son, the word *prodigal* has come to mean "straying" or "disobedient" (as in *the child's prodigal nature*), even though the word in its original KJV context meant "excessive" or "lavish." In the latter sense, it can have positive connotations, suggesting "bounteousness," as in its close cognate, *prodigality.* It is okay to use it in its modern sense of "straying."

pro-family

Spell this word with a hyphen. It means "endorsing or encouraging traditional family structures and values," usually implying opposition to gay marriage, abortion, and, for some people, birth control.

pro-life, pro-choice

These terms are hyphenated and lowercase even in reference to the social movements associated with them: *the pro-life movement, a pro-choice candidate, They are pro-life.*

promised land, Promised Land

This familiar phrase does not occur in the KJV, which opts instead for "the land which he promised" (Deut. 19:8). The phrase *the promised land* occurs only once in the NIV: "By faith he [Abraham] made his home in the promised land" (Heb. 11:9). While it is lowercase in most devotional literature, it is sometimes capitalized in classic English literature and hymns by long-established convention to refer to the land promised by God to Abraham (Gen. 15:18–21). Lowercase it when used metaphorically, as in *California turned out not to be the promised land they'd expected.*

prooftext

This term is set solid and usually used as a noun: *The author leaned heavily on his prooftext*, or *prooftexts*. The verb and adjective forms, though inelegant, are occasionally used: *He prooftexted his way through seminary* and *his prooftext mentality.*

prophecy, prophesy

Prophecy is the noun and *prophesy* is the verb, as in *A false prophet may prophesy, but will his prophecy come to pass?* The substandard verb *to prophesize* should be shunned in formal writing, although it is acceptable in Southern and colloquial contexts.

prophet, Prophet

The word *prophet*, not being a formal title, is lowercase before a name: *the prophet Jeremiah.* It may be capitalized as part of a common epithet that has the force of a proper name (as in *the Weeping Prophet* or *the Prophet of Fire*). (See also "*prophets, Prophets, the*.") Note that *the Prophet* used alone and capitalized is most often a reference to Mohammad.

prophets, Prophets, the

The lowercase form, *the prophets*, refers to people; the capitalized form, *the Prophets*, is the title of the prophetic books of the Hebrew Bible as a group. The same distinction holds true for *the minor prophets, the major prophets*, and *the latter prophets*, meaning the people who prophesied, and *the Minor Prophets, the Major Prophets*, and *the Latter Prophets*, meaning those subdivisions of the Prophetic Books (also capitalized) of the Hebrew Bible.

proscribe, prescribe

Observe the distinction between these verbs. *Proscribe* is "to forbid or prohibit," while *prescribe* means "to dictate a direction or provide a remedy."

proselytize

Use the term *proselytize* carefully since it often has negative connotations. Use *evangelize* or *preach the gospel* instead. Though the word *proselyte* was used as a verb in former times to mean "proselytize," it is used only as a noun today, meaning "a new convert."

Protestant

Capitalize *Protestant* as an adjective referring to the denominations established during the Reformation to oppose the primacy of the pope or referring to any other later, non-Catholic denomination that believes in justification by faith, the priesthood of all believers, and the Bible as the primary source of revelation. Such denominations include Anglican (in general references, though some Roman Catholics still consider the

Anglican Church part of Rome), Baptist, Congregational, Lutheran, Methodist, Presbyterian, Quaker, and Reformed. *Protestant*, as a noun, refers to a member of such a denomination. The term *Protestantism* refers to that form of belief as a whole. The term *Protestant* should not be used simply to mean non-Catholic since that ignores the fact that Eastern Orthodoxy is both non-Catholic and non-Protestant. Note that the Church of Jesus Christ of Latter-day Saints and the Jehovah's Witnesses are not considered Protestant churches insofar as neither was protesting the Catholic Church. (See also "*Eastern Orthodox, Orthodox*" and "*catholic, Catholic.*")

proved, proven

Although *proven* is often used as the past participle of *to prove*, the form *proved* is preferred by most grammarians, as in *He had proved his point.* Reserve *proven* for use as an adjective: as in *a proven remedy.*

Proverbs, proverb

Proverbs is always plural in citations to a specific verse (for instance, *Proverbs 17:28*), to an entire chapter (*Proverbs 17*), or to the entire book (*the book of Proverbs*). Unlike the word *Psalm*, which drops the *s* in references to a single psalm, the word *Proverbs* as a reference is always plural, even though a single proverb is quoted. Lowercase *proverb* when used in a general sense: *My favorite proverb is "Even a fool, when he holdeth his peace, is counted wise" (Prov. 17:28 KJV).* (See also "*Psalm, psalm.*")

Providence, providence

When using *Providence* to mean "God," capitalize it, but lowercase it in such phrases as *the providence of God* and *by his providence.* Also lowercase the adjective *providential.*

Psalm, psalm

Lowercase *psalm* in general references, as in *The lector read a psalm to the monks* or *one of the psalms of David.* Capitalize it when referring to a specific psalm, as in *The lector read Psalm 139 to the monks* or *His favorite is the Twenty-third Psalm.* When the entire book of the Bible is referenced, capitalize it as a title: *Psalms* or *the Psalms* or *the book of Psalms* (NIV) or *the Book of Psalms* (KJV).

Care should be taken in citations to specific psalms. When quoting the Twenty-third Psalm, for instance, the reference should read: *Psalm 23*, not *Psalms 23*. (The same is true for quoting only part of a psalm: *Psalm*

23:1–2, not *Psalms 23:1–2*). Use the plural form in references to the entire book or when citing more than one psalm: *Psalms* or *Psalms 9–10*. This is the only book in the Bible that uses both a singular and a plural form in citations, depending upon the situation. (See also "*Proverbs, proverbs*.") Note that the uncommon adjective form *psalmic* is always lowercase.

psalmist

In most cases, lowercase *the psalmist*. Even though some writers argue that it is an epithet for David and should be capitalized as having the force of a proper name, it must be remembered that David is not the only psalmist represented in the book of Psalms. It is best to leave the word *psalmist* as a common descriptive. In some devotional settings, when it is clear that only David is referred to, it may be capitalized.

Psalter, the; psalter

The term *the Psalter*, capitalized and set in roman type, refers either to the book of Psalms, to a separate volume containing the Psalms, or to a selection from the Psalms, sometimes set to music and used for worship or liturgical purposes, as in *We read from the Psalter every Sunday*. When referring to collections of psalms as a genre, lowercase *psalter*, as in *The Bay Psalm Book was the first and most famous psalter in the New World*. Be sure to distinguish *psalter* from *psaltery*, an ancient musical instrument referred to throughout Psalms in the KJV. The NIV translates it as *harp*. The words *psalm* and *psalter* are both rooted in a Greek word meaning "a stringed instrument."

Pseudepigrapha

The plural term *Pseudepigrapha* (meaning "falsely inscribed writings") can refer either to various noncanonical NT-like writings of the early Christian centuries or to certain noncanonical books written between the completion of the OT writings but before the Christian era. *SBL* contains convenient lists of the NT and OT pseudepigraphal writings along with their abbreviations (8.3.13 and 8.3.4 respectively). Note that *Pseudepigrapha* has been blessed with no less than four related adjectives, which are synonymous and lowercase; the most common are *pseudepigraphic* and *pseudepigraphal*, but also seen are *pseudepigraphical* and the rare *pseudepigraphous*. The uncommon singular form of the noun is *pseudepigraphon*.

purgatory, Purgatory

The word *purgatory* is lowercase in most Protestant literature, though seldom used, though it should be capitalized in any context where *Heaven* and *Hell* are also capitalized. Some Roman Catholic devotional works and literary classics, such as Dante's *La Divina Comedia*, capitalize it as a place name. Dante's translators also refer to it as *Purgatorio* and *Mount Purgatory*.

Puritan, Puritanism, Pilgrim

While the colonial American Pilgrims (see "*Pilgrims, Pilgrim Fathers, pilgrim*") were Puritans, Puritanism predated the Pilgrims. In English history, the term *Puritan* (capitalized) came into use in the 1560s as a pejorative to describe those Protestant believers who dissented from the established Church of England because they felt the church had not expunged enough of its Catholic influence. To describe a certain strain of religious feeling in the contemporary US, the terms are still capitalized, as in *the Puritan work ethic* (which is also referred to as *the Protestant work ethic*). Note that the terms *Puritan* and *Puritanism* have widely different connotations for different readerships.

Q

Q&A, Q & A, Q and A

Short for "question and answer," all the abbreviations shown in the heading are acceptable, though *Q&A*, without spaces, is preferable because it cannot be broken over a line of type.

Quaker

In reference to the Religious Society of Friends, this term is acceptable, especially in representations to those outside the Society. Those within refer to themselves as *Friends* (capitalized). *A Friend* is an individual member of the society. (See also "QUAKER STYLE," "*thou, thee, thy, thine*" and "TIMES AND DATES," section on "*Quaker System of Dating.*")

Qur'an, Koran

Although *Webster* gives *Koran* as its first option, this manual recommends *Qur'an*, the form preferred by the editors of *SBL* as the spelling most commonly found in academic writing. *Qur'an* most closely approximates the Arabic form, with the apostrophe standing in for the Arabic *alef* character. By contrast, *Koran*, which is more common in journalistic style, is an early Anglicization, dating from the seventeenth century, and carries a hint of colonialism. In nonacademic books, either *Qur'an* or *Koran* is acceptable if used consistently. *Webster* and some other references allow *Quran* as well. The alternate version *Qu'ran*, with its misplaced *alef*, is a blatant misspelling and should not be used. As with most sacred works, the title is set in roman type. It can be pronounced either *kuh-RAHN* or *kuh-RAN*, though the first option is preferred. (See also "*qur'anic, koranic.*")

qur'anic, koranic

Although some references (*Webster*, for instance) capitalize these adjectives, this manual recommends lowercasing them, like the adjective *biblical*. (See also "*Qur'an, Koran.*")

R

Ra, Re

The name for the Egyptian sun god is variously given as *Ra* (*Webster* and *Wikipedia*) and *Re* (*Britannica* and *SBL*). In the absence of a strong author preference, use the more familiar *Ra* as the form appropriate for trade books, though opt for *Re* in academic writing. The forms *Rah* and *Pra* are also seen but not recommended.

rabbi, Rabbi

A Jewish clerical title given to the leader of a congregation. A rabbi is also a teacher qualified to expound and interpret Jewish law. Capitalize it only as a title before a name: as in *Rabbi Abraham Heschel*. Avoid the antiquated form *rabbin* as well as the redundant *Jewish rabbi*. The adjective form can be either *rabbinic* or *rabbinical*, and the plural is *rabbis*.

Forms of Address. When writing a letter to a rabbi, use "Rabbi [first and last names]" in the address line; "Dear Rabbi [last name or first and last names together]" in the salutation. When addressing a rabbi in person, use "Rabbi" alone or "Rabbi [last name]." Use "Rabbi [first and last names]" in formal introductions.

rack my brain

This idiom is variously seen as both *rack my brain* and *wrack my brain*. Either is acceptable, though *rack my brain* is most often endorsed by grammarians. Also, the plural *rack my brains*, though illogical, is also common and acceptable.

rapture, the

When *the rapture* is used in the eschatological sense, lowercase it.

realtor, Realtor

Although the National Association of Realtors trademarked the term *Realtor* in 1916 and insist to this day that it should be universally capitalized, their preference is seldom honored except in publications aimed at the professional realty market. Lowercase *realtor* to mean "real-estate agent" in ordinary usage.

rector

A clerical position in the Anglican Church. A rector (equivalent to a *pastor* in other Protestant churches) heads a parish.

regalia (Native American)

The ceremonial clothing worn by Native Americans is referred to as *regalia* not *costume*. Though *regalia* is a plural noun, as a collective it can take either a singular or plural verb depending on the number of objects referred to: *his regalia contains four eagle feathers* or *countless regalia are preserved in the First Nations museum*.

religionist

While the word *religionist* is now rare, it has a long history in English, dating back to the mid-seventeenth century. It is used to refer to any religious believer but often carries an overtone of zealotry. A *religionist* is anything but lukewarm about faith.

religiose

Although sometimes mistaken as a synonym for *religious*, the word *religiose* has a negative connotation. A person who is *religiose* is overly religious, self-consciously pious, or embarrassingly sentimental about his or her faith. It is a perfectly good word when used correctly.

religious (as a noun)

The word *religious* is sometimes used as a noun in Roman Catholic literature. It refers to a person in a monastic order and not to a religious person in general: *This religious wore the white habit of her order.* That usage is now rarely understood. When it is encountered, it is both the singular and plural form. More commonly today, the word is usually used only in the plural, meaning "religious people in general": *The religious of several faiths assembled for the ecumenical conference.*

religious right, religious left

Lowercase these terms.

Religious Society of Friends

See "*Quaker*."

Renaissance, renaissance

The European historical period, roughly from the fourteenth to seventeenth centuries, is capitalized: *the Renaissance.* To refer to a general cultural rebirth, lowercase it: *the Harlem writers brought about a renaissance in black poetry and fiction.*

republican, Republican

Like *Libertarian*, *Democrat*, and *Communist*, the word *Republican*, which can be either a noun or an adjective, is capitalized when referring to the Republican Party. It is only lowercase in references to someone who favors a republican form of government (*Caesar was killed by the republicans in the Roman senate*).

resurrection

Lowercase *resurrection* and most other events in the life of Jesus. Use the article *the* before *resurrection* if you need to distinguish between Jesus's resurrection and a more general use of that word. (For a full discussion of the issues involved, see both "CRUCIFIXION, RESURRECTION" and "EVENTS IN THE LIFE OF JESUS, LOWERCASING.")

Revelation

The final book of the Christian Scriptures is *Revelation* (NIV), or *The Book of Revelation* (KJV)—not *Revelations,* or *The Book of Revelations.* Even the book's author refers to it as a single, unified vision: "The revelation from Jesus Christ ..." (Rev. 1:1).

reverend, Reverend

Traditional grammarians assert that the term *reverend* is an adjective, not a noun, and, when paired with a proper name, should always be preceded by the article *the* (as in *the Reverend Billy Graham*). These grammarians point out that it is not a title but an "honorific" (like the term *the honorable* used with the names of judges and politicians) and that ministers should be addressed by first or last name or academic title without using the honorific (*"Hello, Bill"* or *"Hello, Mr. Jones"* or *"Hello, Dr. Jones"* instead of *"hello, Reverend Jones"*). We would never address a judge as "Honorable Jones," so why would we address a minister as "Reverend Jones"?

Those rules are useful in formal writing, but like a lot of grammar rules, they crumble in the face of popular usage. The *OED* states that *reverend* has been in use as both an adjective and a noun for more than three hundred years. Although it may feel colloquial to some, people all across the US are comfortable referring to their minister as "the reverend" and addressing him or her as "Reverend Jones." Many people are uncomfortable addressing a minister as "Mr. Jones" or "Ms. Jones" or by first name unless they know the minister extremely well. Still, it is inconceivable to prohibit a writer of Western fiction from saying something like, "How do, Reverend!"

In informal writing, the article may be dropped (as in *He introduced Reverend Wilkins to us*); *reverend* may be used as a noun (as in *We spoke to the reverend about our marriage plans*), but note that those informal, colloquial uses are more common in Baptist and Methodist circles than they are in Anglican or other more liturgical churches. By the way, Lutherans commonly address their ministers as *Pastor*. Writers should be sensitive to the minister's own preference and also to their own tradition and that of the intended readers. The colloquial uses of *reverend*, for instance, may strike an Episcopalian reader as substandard.

Reverend (used before a name) is usually spelled out at the first reference (*Reverend Jennifer Browne, Reverend Browne, the Reverend Ms. Browne*), and it may be abbreviated thereafter (*Rev. Jennifer Browne, Rev. Browne, the Rev. Ms. Browne*).

Forms of Address. In a formal letter to a Protestant minister, the address line should read, "The Reverend [first and last names]," and "DD" may be added after the name if the minister has a doctor of divinity degree. The letter's salutation would read, "Dear Dr. [Mr. or Ms.] [first and last names]," and "Dr. [Mr. or Ms.] [first and last names]" would be used for a formal spoken introduction. If the minister is a personal friend, the salutation may read "Pastor [last name]" or, in those cases in which the minister is comfortable with it, "Pastor [first name]" at the most informal level.

right-to-life

This phrase is hyphenated both as a noun phrase and as a compound adjective: *He lobbied for right-to-life, He is a right-to-life advocate.*

Rite, rite

The word *rite* has two distinct meanings. It can mean the unique cultural and spiritual heritage of individual churches and groups of churches within a larger tradition; for instance, any of the several Roman Catholic liturgical traditions: *the Roman Rite, the Coptic Rite, the Ambrosian Rite*, and so on. In that sense, *Rite* is usually capitalized when paired with a proper adjective. The term can also refer to a specific ceremony within a church tradition, in which case it is lowercase: *the rite of confession*, *last rites, the rite of marriage*. Often, though not always, *rite* in the latter sense is synonymous with *sacrament*. (See also "*sacraments*.")

Ritual Decalogue

See "*Ten Commandments, the*."

Roma, Romani, gypsy

In references to the dispersed ethnic group commonly known as *Gypsies*, the term *Roma* is preferred for the people (as in *the Roma of Europe* or *a Roma woman* or *a Roma man*) and the term *Romani* is preferred for the language and for the general culture (as in *he speaks Romani* or *Romani fortune-telling*). The latter term is also spelled *Romany* (preferred form in *Webster*), but either form is acceptable. Lowercase *gypsy* and *gypsies* when the terms refer metaphorically to free-spirited, bohemian types—*the rock band's gypsy lifestyle*—and in other usages such as *gypsy moth* and *gypsy cab*.

roman numeral, roman type

Lowercase them. (See also "*arabic numeral*," "*italic, roman, arabic*," and "ROMAN NUMERALS.")

rosary, Rosary

In casual contexts and occasional references, lowercase *rosary*. It is also commonly lowercase when the physical object alone is referred to: *He found an old rosary in his grandmother's drawer*. In writing for Roman Catholic readers, it may be capitalized, especially whenever it serves as the title for the traditional prayers associated with the object: *She was faithful in praying the Rosary three times a day*. In common usage the rosary is *prayed*, *recited*, or *said*, but it is not *read*. Devotional nicknames for the rosary are capitalized to show that the terms are being used in a specific, not a general, sense (*Mary's Crown, Holy Beads, Holy Rosary*), primarily in publications for a Roman Catholic readership.

Rule of Benedict, the

In general references to this work, set it in roman like other classic religious documents, though in references to specific modern editions, italicize it like any other title; for instance, *The Rule of Benedict: A Spirituality for the 21st Century* (by Joan Chittister, 2010). Other names for the same work: the Rule, Benedict's Rule, the Rule of Saint Benedict.

S

Sabbath, sabbath, sabbatical, Sabbatarian

In reference to the Jewish day of rest (from sundown Friday to sundown Saturday), capitalize *Sabbath* (from the Hebrew, meaning "rest," or "cessation") as a day of the week: *the Sabbath, the weekly Sabbath rest for God's people*. (But also see "*Sabbath, Sunday*.") Occasionally the word is lowercase when it refers to the practice in the Hebrew Bible of allowing agricultural land to lie fallow: *the sabbath rest for the land*. In that case it is lowercase like a season, much as we lowercase *autumn* or *winter*.

This distinction also applies to most books that quote from the KJV, which lowercases *sabbath* in all instances. The discrepancy between the modern usage and the KJV's should not be jarring to most readers, but if the editor fears it will lead to confusion, then the modern style can easily be conformed to the KJV's.

Even though adding the word *day* to *Sabbath* is redundant, since *Sabbath*, used alone, adequately conveys the meaning, both the NIV and the KJV commonly use the phrase *Sabbath day* (NIV) or *sabbath day* (KJV).

The general word *sabbatical*, whether meaning a day of rest or a season of rest, is lowercase. The word is used as both a noun and an adjective: as in *the professor's year-long sabbatical* or *her sabbatical month*. Also, some specialized OT terms using the word *Sabbatical* are capitalized in academic writing, such as *Sabbatical cycle* and *Sabbatical Year*. Capitalize the words *Sabbatarian* and *Sabbatarianism* (referring to a strict observance of the Sabbath).

Sabbath, Sunday

The Sabbath is not synonymous with *Sunday* in all contexts. For Jews, the *Shabbat* ("Sabbath") is from sundown Friday till nightfall on Saturday, as it is (with some slight variation) for the Seventh-day Adventists and a few other Christian groups. Sunday was officially adopted as the Christian Sabbath in 364 CE at the Council of Laodicea. Although Christians refer to Sunday as "the Sabbath," that usage, though correct within the Christian subculture, seems to be losing ground as sounding somewhat fusty. Other religions have specific days of weekly observance or rest, but they should not be referred to as Sabbaths. If a generic term is needed for that day, use *day of rest*, *day of worship*, or *day of religious observance*.

sacraments

As many as thirty rites and rituals have been deemed *sacraments* in the course of Christian history. Only seven are widely recognized, and they are traditionally listed in this order:

The sacrament of baptism, or baptism
The sacrament of confirmation, or confirmation; or chrismation in Eastern Orthodox Church
The sacrament of the Eucharist, or the Eucharist; also called Holy Communion, Communion, the Lord's Supper, the Lord's Table, Mass, or Blessed Sacrament, though this last term can refer to the service or the elements themselves
The sacrament of penance, or penance, or confession
The sacrament of extreme unction, or extreme unction; also called anointing of the sick, or unction of the sick. The term *last rites* is the popular term for this sacrament, but it is not one used by the clergy or theologians. The term *unction* is also commonly used, but there are other nonsacramental rites involving anointing with oil to which that term also applies.
The sacrament of orders, or orders, or ordination
The sacrament of matrimony, or matrimony; also called the sacrament of marriage, or marriage

For the majority of Protestant publications, the names of the sacraments should be lowercase except for those associated with Communion, or the Lord's Supper. Keep in mind that most Protestant churches recognize only baptism and Communion as sacraments (and sometimes not even those). If a publication is targeted for a Roman Catholic, a Church of England, or an Eastern Orthodox audience, capitalize the names of the sacraments according to their customs. The Eastern Orthodox Church recognizes those seven in addition to others, all of which are termed *mysteries*.

sacrilegious

This is one of the most commonly misspelled words in Christian books. It is the adjective form of the word *sacrilege* and is not etymologically related to the word *religious*.

Sadducee

As the name of a specific Jewish sect at the time of Jesus, capitalize *Sadducee*. It is often juxtaposed to the words *Pharisee* (capitalized) and *scribe* (lowercase). (See also "*Pharisee, Pharisaic, Pharisaical*" and "*scribe.*")

Saint, saint

The word *Saint* is usually spelled out in text when used in place names or before the names of Christian saints: *Saint Paul, Minnesota,* as well as *Saint Paul (the apostle).* It may be abbreviated (*St.*, singular, and *SS.*, plural) whenever custom recommends it (*St. Louis, Missouri*), wherever a lack of space requires it (as in a chart or table), or when the terms are repeated so often as to be distracting (as in a reference work). Capitalize it before proper names (*Saint John*) but lowercase it in general usage (*the prayers of the saints*).

Protestant Usage. Mainstream Protestant tradition tends not to use *Saint* before the names of NT figures and figures from church history, preferring *the apostle Paul,* for instance, to *Saint Paul* and *Augustine* to *Saint Augustine.* This usage may have something to do with Protestantism's emphasis on the sainthood of all believers and not singling out certain ones for special status. The Roman Catholic, Eastern Orthodox, and Anglican traditions tend to use *Saint* more often to describe NT figures, early church figures, and the saints from their traditions, and the word should be used appropriately when writing for those traditions. Author preference should be followed.

French Style. The French feminine form, *Sainte,* and its abbreviation, *Ste.*, are not used in English before the names of female saints (*Saint Edith of Polesworth*). The feminine form *Sainte* is retained in some personal names (*Charles Augustin Sainte-Beuve*) and geographical references (*Sainte-Foy*).

In Proper Names. When part of a person's name, *Saint* should be abbreviated or spelled out according to the person's preference: *Oliver St. John Gogarty,* but *Antoine de Saint-Exupéry.* When in doubt, check an online encyclopedia or biographical dictionary.

sanctimonious

Scholars credit Shakespeare for inventing this word, first used in *Measure for Measure* (1.2.7–9): "the sanctimonious pirate, that / went to sea with the Ten Commandments, but scraped / one out of the table." The word has come to mean "hypocritically pious" since then. Shakespeare probably didn't conceive of the word as negative, for he used it later, completely without irony, in *The Tempest* as a synonym for *holy*: "… all sanctimonious ceremonies may / with full and holy rite be minister'd" (4.1.16–17). Regardless of the original meaning, the word and its relatives, *sanctimony* and *sanctimoniousness,* are most often pejorative in our time.

sanction

The *sanct-* root of this word means "holy," as in the words *sanctify* and *sanctity*. The word *sanction* originally had origins in church law, and today the verb *to sanction* means "to allow" or "to approve," and the adjective *sanctioned* usually means "allowed" or "approved of." The noun *sanction* can mean one of two things: "permission" (as in *The school's new sanctions allowed prayers before sporting events*) or "a prohibition" (as in *The US established sanctions against Iran*), so care must be taken in its use. When *sanctions* are *imposed*, they are the prohibitive kind.

sarcophagus

The plural is *sarcophaguses* in ordinary writing. While *sarcophagi* is etymologically correct (like *hippopotami*), it comes off as snooty even in academic contexts.

Satan, satanic, satanism

Capitalize Satan as a proper name, but lowercase most words derived from it: *satanic*, *satanism*, *satinist*. Capitalize most other words and phrases that are used as though they are names for Satan: *the Enemy*, *the Evil One*, *the Father of Lies*, *Lucifer*, *the Man of Sin*, *the Prince of Darkness*, and so on. (See also "*devil, Devil.*")

Savior, Saviour

Taking their cue from the KJV, many American writers cling to the British spelling *Saviour* when referring to Christ. This is unnecessary and can even seem like an affectation unless the text is quite closely tied to the KJV. Some US editions of the KJV Americanize the spelling. For US readers, use *Savior* except for direct quotations from the KJV.

scribe

Lowercase *scribe* when referring to an ordinary Jewish scholar, teacher, or copyist at the time of Jesus. The word is often mistakenly capitalized because it is so commonly paired with the word *Pharisees*, which is capitalized ("scribes and Pharisees," Matt. 23:13 KJV). The NIV translates *scribe* as "teacher of the law." (Also see "*Pharisee, Pharisaic, Pharisaical*" and "*Sadducee.*")

scriptural

Even though the noun *Scripture* is capitalized when referring to the Bible, *scriptural* is usually lowercase. The opposite is *unscriptural*. (See also "*biblical*" for more discussion.)

Scripture, Bible

See "*Bible, Scripture*" and also "BIBLE, THE—WHAT IS IT?"

Scripture, the Scriptures, scripture, scriptures

Capitalize *Scripture* and *the Scriptures* in reference to the Bible but lowercase them when referring to holy books of other faiths (such as *the Hindu scriptures*) or when used metaphorically (as in *I wouldn't take his word as scripture*). This may seem culturally biased toward Christianity, but this is the common style among Christian publishers.

Some writers feel that the term *the Scriptures* borders on evangelical jargon when used in place of the more plainspoken *the Bible*. (See "*Bible, Scripture*.") This perception may be even more pronounced in the tendency to use *a Scripture* to mean a single verse from the Bible, as in *This Scripture came to mind*. That is common parlance in the evangelical subculture but may seem pietistic to those outside. Opt instead for *verse* or *Bible verse* when writing for a broader readership.

scripturist, scripturism

The terms *scripturist* and *scripturism* are lowercase and refer to an extreme legalism, sometimes found in the Jewish faith, in regard to OT law—for instance, a literal interpretation of "an eye for an eye."

secretary-general, general secretary

A *secretary-general* is the title given to the chief administrator of some organizations, such as the United Nations. It is hyphenated, and its plural is *secretaries-general*. The term *general secretary* (not hyphenated) is the clerical title given to the person who oversees the general assembly of the World Council of Churches. It is also the title given to the head of the Communist Party in the former Soviet Union. Capitalize these titles before proper names: as in *Secretary-General Ban Ki-moon* and *General Secretary Olav Fykse Tveit*.

secular market

See "*general market, secular market*."

selah

Although the word *selah* is used seventy-one times in the book of Psalms (spanning thirty-nine psalms) as well as three times in Habakkuk 3, its precise meaning is unclear. It seems to have been a liturgical direction, such as a shift in tune or tempo, or an indication of a poetic division, an inserted interlude, or a stanza break. It is sometimes mistakenly used as having the meaning "so be it," like the word *amen*. *Selah* is probably not useful for any purpose other than its inscrutable function in Psalms. For these reasons the NIV eliminates the word entirely but references each omission with a footnote.

Semite, Semitic, Semitism

Capitalize these words in all their forms, even when used with a prefix: *anti-Semite*, *anti-Semitic*, and *anti-Semitism*.

Senate

Capitalize *the Senate* when referring to that chamber of the US Congress. Lowercase *senator* in general references, and capitalize it before names (*Senator Elizabeth Warren*). Other derivatives are lowercase: *senatorial district*, *a senatorial seat*, and so on.

September 11, 2001

The news media has largely settled on the following form for referring to the terrorist attacks of September 11, 2001: *the 9/11 attacks*, using numerals and a solidus and lowercasing *attacks*. Also acceptable is *the attacks of September 11, 2001*, but it is best to avoid *the nine-eleven attacks* and *the 9-11 attacks*, as they are less likely to be immediately recognizable. Also avoid the completely misleading *nine-one-one attacks*. If the term comes at the beginning of a sentence as a noun, where numerals are conventionally spelled out, rewriting the sentence is recommended so that the numerals don't come first. Otherwise, beginning the sentence with the awkward numerals—as in *9/11 was a wake-up call*—is preferable to the even more awkward spelled-out version—*Nine/eleven was a wake-up call.* Better yet, opt for *September 11 was a wake-up call* or *The 9/11 attacks were a wake-up call.*

sepulcher, sepulchre

Although *Webster* shows the common UK spelling *sepulchre* as its first option, this manual and most US dictionaries prefer *sepulcher*. Automated spell checkers will often change the UK spelling to the US one.

The rarely seen variant *sepulture* is best reserved for its specific meaning, "a burial," if used at all.

seraph, seraphim, seraphims, seraphs

The singular for this six-winged angel is *seraph*. That said, the NIV only uses the term in the plural—*seraphim* (Isa. 6:2 and 6:6)—which is the most common and preferred plural form, though *seraphs* is also correct. The KJV uses the term only in the plural as well, but it uses the double-plural form, *seraphims*. Unless the KJV is being specifically discussed, avoid *seraphims*. Do not confuse *seraph* with *serif* (meaning "a stroke on a letter"), since they are pronounced the same. (See also "*cherub, cherubim, cherubims, cherubs*.")

serpent, Serpent

When referring to the serpent of Gen. 3, the term is lowercase in nearly every English Bible version (*the serpent* or *the serpent of Genesis*), though a couple of translations render it as *snake*. Although the serpent is referred to as "crafty," neither Genesis nor the rest of the Hebrew Bible directly identifies it with Satan. Still, when referring to Satan as *the Serpent*, capitalize it as an epithet that has the force of a name.

seven deadly sins, the

In the *Summa Theologica*, Thomas Aquinas identified *seven chief*, or *capital*, sins to which humans commonly fall prey. They are known as *the seven deadly sins*. (Lowercase the phrase.) They are traditionally ranked in this order: *pride*, *covetousness* (or *greed*), *lust*, *envy*, *gluttony*, *anger*, *sloth* (also called *acedia* or *accidie*). Lowercase the terms for the particular sins unless they are personified or used in an allegorical sense, as they often are in medieval literature. (See also "*four cardinal virtues, the*.")

seven sacraments, the

See "*sacraments*."

Seven Storey Mountain, The

The title of Thomas Merton's autobiography (1948) is frequently misspelled. *Seven Storey* is not hyphenated, and *Storey* uses the older UK spelling of that word, with an inserted *e*.

Seventh-day Adventist Church

Lowercase the *d* in *day* per the denomination's own style guidelines.

shalom, sholom

This interjection of greeting and parting (from the Hebrew, meaning "peace") is usually spelled *shalom*, but *sholom* is sometimes seen and is also correct. In either case, lowercase it.

sharia law

Since *sharia law* is a large body of laws based on the Qur'an, lowercase it as you would other large bodies of law, such as *civil law*, *corporate law*, or *criminal law*. The common alternate spelling *shari'a* is acceptable in scholarly contexts if used consistently.

she, her (for ships, nations, the church, etc.)

Avoid using feminine pronouns for ships, nations, the church and other institutions, and so on. Use *it* or *its* instead. (See "GENDER-ACCURATE LANGUAGE.")

sic

The word *sic* (Latin "thus") is used to indicate that the use of a mistaken or uncommon word or phrase is intentional; for instance, when an error is reproduced exactly as it was found in a quoted source or when certain words or phrases seem odd in a given context. Within a quotation, *sic* is usually set in italic to distinguish it from the quotation itself, and the word is surrounded by square brackets in roman type ("To be or to be [*sic*], that is the question"). Occasionally *sic* is used in contexts other than quotations, where it should be surrounded by parentheses and set in the same font as the surrounding text; for example, *A gentleman by the name of Psmith (sic) was waiting to talk to me.* In all cases, avoid using an exclamation point with *sic*.

since, because

Academic writers and grammarians prefer to restrict *since* to references of time, as in *Since leaving his job, he's had nothing but trouble.* In informal or colloquial contexts, *since* may be used like *because*: *Since he's an expert, he would know.*

sins, debts, trespasses

See "*trespasses, sins, debts.*"

sister, Sister

The term *sister* is sometimes used before a proper name to refer congenially to a female member of a church or congregation (*Sister Williams has a word for us*) or a member of some Catholic female religious orders (*Sister Agnes taught the children their catechism*). Capitalize the term in those usages, though lowercase it in references to fellow Christians (such as *all the sisters and brothers said amen* or *the Dominican sisters*). At times it is used as an affectionate name for a sibling, in which case, capitalize it: *Here, Sister, is your birthday gift.* (See also "*brother, Brother.*")

Forms of Address. In conversation, address a nun as "Sister [first name]." When introducing her to someone, use either the first name alone or the first and last names: *"Sister Helen"* or *"Sister Helen Carter."* When addressing a letter, the address line reads, "Sister [first name or first and last names], [followed by her order's abbreviation]." The letter's salutation is simply, "Dear Sister" or "Dear Sister [first name]."

sistren

See "*brethren.*"

-size, -sized

When used as a suffix or in a compound adjective, both *-size* and *-sized* are acceptable. Unless the author has a strong preference, go with *-size*, which is usually *Webster*'s first option: *bite-size*, *child-size*, *giant-size*, *oversize*, *outsize*, *pocket-size*, *supersize*, and so on.

skeptic

Rather than *sceptic*.

smartphone

Lowercase the term *smartphone* since it is generic and not a specific brand or product name. Also, it is usually spelled as one word. (See also "*cell phone.*")

sneak, sneaked, snuck

Although *Webster* shows *sneaked* as the preferred past participle for *sneak*, they also note that *snuck* has become common in dialectal and colloquial contexts, particularly in the US and Canada. Use *sneaked*, and your former English teacher will smile. But if there's a good reason to use *snuck*, go for it.

so-called

Do not put quotation marks around a word or phrase that follows the words *so-called*. For instance, *He refused help from his so-called supporters.*

social gospel, Social Gospel

When lowercase, *social gospel* refers to the broad philosophy of using Christian ethics (particularly drawn from the Sermon on the Mount) to tackle such social problems as poverty, lack of education, poor working conditions, and war. Capitalize the term in specific references to the *Social Gospel movement* of the early twentieth century, often associated with Walter Rauschenbusch's book *A Theology for the Social Gospel* (1917). The term is often used disparagingly by theological conservatives.

Socialist, socialist, socialism

A *socialist* believes in socialism as an economic system. A *Socialist* is a member of the Socialist Party (in any country). The related word *socialism* is nearly always lowercase.

Sodomite, sodomite

Use *Sodomite*, capitalized, to mean "an inhabitant of the city of Sodom." The use of the term in reference to any person in the LGBT community is inflammatory and should be avoided. According to Ezek. 16:49 (NIV), God judged Sodom because "she and her daughters were arrogant, overfed and unconcerned; they did not help the poor and needy." (See "*LGBT*.")

Song of Songs, Canticles

See "*Canticles*."

South, south

Although some usage manuals recommend capitalizing *the South*, *Southern*, and *Southerner* only in the context of the American Civil War, this manual recommends capitalizing those terms whenever that region of the US is referred to as a region distinct from other parts of the country (as in *They sweeten the iced tea in the South* or *A Southerner born and bred*). Always capitalize the term *the Deep South*. (See also "*West, Western, west, western*.")

Spirit, spirit

In references to the third person of the Trinity, capitalize *Spirit*: as in *God shall send his Spirit unto you* or *the Spirit who is constantly present*. The word may be capitalized when it is used as a personification, as in *the Spirit of the Woodlands* or *the Spirit of Christmas*; otherwise, lowercase it as a general concept (as in *a spirit of harmony*). (See also "*Holy Spirit*" and "*Holy Ghost*.")

stages of cancer

The International Union against Cancer has established the uniform TNM (tumor/nodes/metastasis) system to describe the stages of cancer: from *stage 0* (present only) to *stage IV* (metastasizing). Per the organization's style, the word *stage* is lowercase, and the accompanying number is set as a roman numeral: as in *He was diagnosed with stage II cancer.*

stained glass

This is spelled *stained glass*, not *stain glass*, and is hyphenated as an adjective: *Tiffany himself designed the stained-glass window in 1895.*

star of Bethlehem, Star of Bethlehem

Lowercase *star* in the phrase *star of Bethlehem* in most references. In works of an especially devotional nature, especially Christmas plays, Advent devotionals, and so on, *star* may be capitalized, even if used alone: *The Star still shone above the little stable.* Note that the flower that goes by this name hyphenates the elements: *star-of-Bethlehem.*

Star of David

The term *Star of David* is capitalized by convention as the common name for the six-pointed star that is a well-known symbol for Judaism. The star is also known as *the Shield of David* or *the Magen David*, or *Mogen David*.

Stars and Stripes, Stars and Bars

Both expressions are capitalized and can be construed either as a singular or plural. If one flag is referred to, use a singular verb, as in *The Stars and Stripes is the national flag* or *The Stars and Bars no longer flies above the capitol.* Otherwise, it may be construed as a plural, as in *Stars and Stripes are seen throughout the cemetery.* Note that these terms are not synonymous: *Stars and Stripes* is a nickname for the national flag of the US, while *Stars and Bars* refers to the battle flag of the Civil War–era Southern confederacy and is widely perceived as having racist associations.

states and commonwealths

Every first-grader knows that the United States is made up of fifty states. Four of those states officially refer to themselves as *commonwealths* rather than *states*: Kentucky, Massachusetts, Pennsylvania, and Virginia. In casual writing, those four are referred to as *states*, but the proper term may be required in formal or legal writing or when the need for precision is acute. Always honor an author's preference for *commonwealth* whenever that term is used correctly.

stations of the cross, the

This phrase, which is sometimes seen as *the way of the cross*, is commonly lowercase, though some Roman Catholic publishers capitalize it when referring to the spiritual practice of meditating on certain artistic renderings of Christ's passion and death. Of the fourteen stages, or stations (not all of which have biblical sources), the most famous are the portrayals of the crucifixion. The traditional stations are (1) the condemnation; (2) the giving of the cross; (3) Jesus stumbles the first time; (4) Jesus sees his mother; (5) Simon of Cyrene carries the cross; (6) Veronica wipes Jesus's face; (7) Jesus stumbles a second time; (8) Jesus encounters the daughter of Jerusalem; (9) Jesus stumbles a third time; (10) Jesus's garments are taken from him; (11) Jesus is nailed to the cross (the crucifixion); (12) Jesus dies on the cross; (13) Jesus's body is lowered from the cross (the lowering); (14) the body is laid in the tomb (the burial).

Stephen Ministries, Stephen Ministry

Stephen Ministries is the name of the lay caregiving and training ministry based in St. Louis. Use the capitalized and plural *Ministries* when referring to the national organization, but when referring to the program in local churches, refer to it in the singular as *Stephen Ministry* (as in *We have a Stephen Ministry in our church*). Those trained in this program may be referred to as *Stephen Ministers* (capitalized).

step (in family relationships)

See "FAMILY RELATIONSHIP, TERMS FOR."

stigmas, stigmata

These plurals of the word *stigma* have different meanings. To mean "stains" or "marks of shame," use *stigmas* (as in *the dual stigmas of sin and guilt*). The word *stigmata* is only used in reference to "the marks of Christ's crucifixion."

still, small voice

Note the comma in *still, small voice*. This phrase, from 1 Kings 19:12 (KJV) has caused confusion. In the KJV, no comma appears. In contemporary usage, the lack of a comma causes an odd misreading, suggesting "a voice that has been small in the past and is still small," and many readers mistakenly read it that way. The original intention was to refer to "a voice that is both still (quiet) and small." The NIV translates it as "a gentle whisper." So when referring casually to God's promptings as "a still, small voice," use the comma for clarity. When quoting directly from the KJV, quote it as in the original.

storytelling, storyteller

Set *storytelling* and *storyteller* solid.

straight and narrow

This noun phrase, meaning "the upright, or moral, way," is spelled *the straight and narrow* in Webster. It finds its origin in Matt. 7:14: "strait is the gate, and narrow is the way" (KJV). Note that the KJV spells the word *strait*. Do not hyphenate the phrase when used as a compound adjective: *the straight and narrow way.*

straitlaced

This is correctly spelled *straitlaced*, not *straightlaced*.

suffragan bishop

A clerical title given to the person who assists the bishop in the Anglican Church.

Sunday school

Do not hyphenate this either as a noun or an adjective: *the Sunday school teacher.* Note that *school* is lowercase.

super Christian

This term, often derogatory, is not hyphenated as a noun phrase, though it is hyphenated as an adjective; as in *He was a super Christian with super-Christian attitudes.* It means "a Christian who is an overachiever in spiritual matters or overzealous in evangelism."

super PAC

Media outlets spell the abbreviated form of "super political action committee" several ways, but this manual opts for *super PAC*. The plural is *super PACs*.

superspiritual

Though not in *Webster*, spell this solid.

supplicant

To mean "a person who supplicates," *supplicant* rather than *suppliant* is the preferred form.

Supreme Court, court

Capitalize *the Supreme Court*, but lowercase *court* when using that word alone in reference to that body: for example, *Each member of the Supreme Court was familiar with the court's previous ruling*. When referencing a particular Supreme Court bench using the name of the chief justice, capitalize *Court*, as in *the Warren Court* or *the Roberts Court*.

sweet by-and-by, the

See "*by and by, by-and-by*."

synagogue, temple

Those who are part of Orthodox Judaism and Conservative Judaism attend synagogues, not temples. Those who are part of Reform Judaism attend either temples or synagogues. (See also "*Judaism*.")

syndrome

Lowercase *syndrome* in medical terminology, even when it follows a word that is capitalized: *Down syndrome, Kawasaki syndrome*. (See also "SYNDROMES, DISEASES, AND DISORDERS.")

Synoptic, synoptic

The gospels of Matthew, Mark, and Luke are collectively known as the *Synoptic Gospels* or simply *the Synoptics*. Capitalize the terms as titles when they are used for a specific section of the Bible. Lowercase *synoptic* in references to the writers of those gospels: *the synoptic writers*.

T

Taizé Community

Although the name for this ecumenical community, founded in 1940, is commonly spelled in English without the acute accent, the accent is correct and should be retained: *Taizé prayer, a Taizé service.* Also, capitalize *Community* in *the Taizé Community.*

Taser, taser

A Taser, or Taser gun, is a handheld weapon, often called a stun gun, which delivers an incapacitating electric charge to its victim. As brands, the names of both the weapon and the company that makes it are capitalized. In the same way we lowercase such verbs as *to google* and *to xerox*, we can lowercase the verbs *to tase* and, less commonly, *to taser* (as in *They tased the protesters*).

Tea Party

The editors of one major style manual insist that this term should be lowercase (*a tea-party Republican, a member of the tea party*) in reference to the political movement that began in 2008, because, these editors argue, it is not a formal political party and has no central organizational headquarters as the Republican and Democratic Parties do. But based on the principle that capitalization is used to distinguish specific things from general things, we believe that *Tea Party* should be capitalized to distinguish it from the common meaning of *tea party.* The word *movement*, used in conjunction with it, should not be capitalized: *the Tea Party movement.* By this same reasoning, we capitalize *the Occupy movement* and *the Civil Rights movement.* These are specific mass movements, important in modern US history, and they should be distinguished from the common uses of those terms.

Teavangelical

A portmanteau word coined by CBN reporter David Brody in his 2012 book, *The Teavangelicals* (Zondervan), *Teavangelical* is the combination of *Tea Party* and *evangelical.* The term, which has gained some currency in the media, is capitalized, unlike the term *evangelical*, because it refers to *the Tea Party*, which is capitalized (see "*Tea Party*"). It is used as either a noun or an adjective: as in *a voting Teavangelical* and *a Teavangelical rally.*

teenage, teenaged

Both are acceptable, but opt for *teenage* since it is the first choice in *Webster*. (But see also "*middle age, middle-aged*.")

televangelist, televangelism

The terms *televangelist* and *televangelism* have acquired such negative connotations, both inside and outside Christian media, that it is probably best to use the term *religious broadcaster* and *religious broadcasting*—unless a negative tone is intended. When used before a name, *televangelist* is a descriptor, not a title, so lowercase it, as in *televangelist Joyce Meyer*. (See also "*evangelist, Evangelist*.")

temple, synagogue

See "*synagogue, temple*" and "*temple, Temple, the*."

temple, Temple, the

Lowercase *temple* in general references to the Hebrew temple in Jerusalem: as in *the ancient temple, the destruction of the temple*. Capitalize it when a specific historical embodiment of that structure is intended: such as *the First Temple, Herod's Temple, the Old Temple, the Second Temple, Solomon's Temple*. Always capitalize *the Temple Mount* as a geographic location.

temptation, the

When referring to Jesus's spiritual confrontation with Satan in the desert, or wilderness (Matt. 4:1–11; Mark 1:12–13; Luke 4:1–13), lowercase such terms as *temptation*: *the temptation in the desert, the temptation of Christ, the temptation*.

Ten Commandments, the

Capitalize the term *the Ten Commandments* and its synonym *the Decalogue*, even when used metaphorically, as in *the Ten Commandments of conflict management*. When one of the biblical commandments is singled out, lowercase it, as in *the fourth commandment* or *the commandment regarding the keeping of the Sabbath*. The terms *the commandments* and *God's commandments*, whether referring to the Ten Commandments or to God's laws, are usually lowercase as common nouns but may be capitalized in special cases or according to author preference.

The Ten Commandments are listed twice in the Hebrew Bible: Ex. 20:1–17 and Deut. 5:6–21, with some differences between the two. For instance, in the Deuteronomic version of the tenth commandment against covetousness, the "neighbor's wife" is listed first and separately, whereas in the version in Ex. 20, she is listed among the neighbor's possessions. Ex. 34:1–28 also lists a set of commandments, which God instructed Moses to write upon stone tablets, but that list differs considerably from the other two. It focuses largely on ritual and worship and is sometimes referred to as the Ritual Decalogue.

Care should be taken in referring to a specific commandment because not all denominations and translations agree in wording, emphasis, or even order. Also, assume that most readers will not remember any given commandment by its number alone. For instance, instead of referring to *the sixth commandment*, it is better to refer to *the commandment prohibiting murder.*

tenet, tenant

It is common, especially in broadcasting, to hear the word *tenant* when *tenet* is intended. A *tenet* is a belief or doctrine. A *tenant* is a renter or occupant of a building. It's hard to imagine who the "five tenants of Christian fundamentalism" might be.

Teresa, Thérèse (Saints)

The names of several well-known religious women are confused often enough to justify some clarification. Medieval mystic Saint Teresa of Ávila and twentieth-century nun and Nobel laureate Mother Teresa spell their names the same way—*Teresa*, not *Theresa*. Another woman, Thérèse of Lisieux, is also sometimes confused with the other two, occasionally mistakenly referred to as Saint Teresa of Lisieux. Several other saints are named *Teresa*, nearly none of whom use the *h* in their spellings.

Testament, testament

Capitalize *Testament* whenever it is used to mean one of the two major parts of the Protestant, Orthodox, or Roman Catholic Bibles, as in *the Old Testament*, *the New Testament,* or simply *the Testaments*, referring to the two together. (See "*Old Testament, New Testament*" for more discussion.)

tetragrammaton, tetragram

Both terms refer to the four letters (*YHWH* or *JHWH*, "Yahweh" or "Jehovah") that make up the unwritten and unspoken Hebrew name of God, though *tetragrammaton* is the more common of the two. The words are usually preceded by the article *the* and lowercase (per *Webster* and

Wikipedia) since they are not in themselves alternate names for God. Still, some Jewish publishers (as well as *SBL*) capitalize the terms. (See also "*YHWH, JHWH*.")

thank you, thank-you

Thank you is a verb with a pronoun. When hyphenated, *thank-you* is a noun phrase (*she expected a thank-you*). Also use the hyphenated form as a compound adjective (*a thank-you note*). The plural of *thank-you* is *thank-yous*.

that, which

Although the rules disentangling *that* from *which* go back to the early 1800s, Strunk's original *Elements of Style* (1920, revised by E. B. White, 1959) as well as Fowler (1926) helped raise those rules to the level of near fetish among writers, editors, and teachers of English. Those guides recommend the word *that* be used in relative clauses when the sense is restrictive and the word *which* when the sense is nonrestrictive; also, a clause beginning with a nonrestrictive *which* should be set off with a comma.

This manual recommends the that/which rules be observed when it is useful, but never slavishly. Few classic English writers honored the distinction, and few readers are able to distinguish between the two uses or are likely to be confused by a misplaced *that* or *which*.

Exceptions. First, the strict distinction between *that* and *which* is more common in the US (probably because of Strunk and White) than in the UK, where editors often allow *which* in a restrictive sense. Do not force a UK writer to conform to US style, especially when a work is intended for a UK or combined UK/US audience. (See also "MID-ATLANTIC STYLE.")

Second, linguists report that the word *that* is the tenth most frequently used word in English, which means an editor must be sensitive to how often the word is repeated in a passage before insisting on changing a *which* to a *that*. If many other *that*s already appear nearby, it is perfectly acceptable to allow a restrictive *which* (the fifty-first most commonly used word in the language) to stand.

The editor and proofreader should be sensitive to the kind of writing in which the rule is being applied. For instance, one should not presume to impose a strict that/which distinction on a poet. The same would hold true for fiction and essays, where the music and rhythm of the author's words are important to the sense. In those cases, query the author if the usage of *that* and *which* might possibly confuse the reader. Otherwise, leave them as they are.

In Fictional Dialogue. Few speakers of English, even highly educated ones, consistently observe the that/which rule. So it is best to trust the author's ear when he or she is constructing fictional dialogue. As stated elsewhere, don't force fictional characters to speak like teachers of English.

That Which. Even when the that/which rule is observed, allow for the phrase *that which* in formal writing, as in *Often we must trust in that which we cannot see. Which* is used as a restrictive in that sentence because doubling the *that* would sound awkward to most ears: ... *trust in that that we cannot see.* And to the ears of many editors, rephrasing the sentence as ... *trust in what we cannot see* may seem too informal.

the, The (before names of organizations)

Some organizations insist that the article *the* before their name be capitalized in text: *He attended The University of Michigan*, for instance. Although editors and proofreaders should try to reproduce proper names correctly, an exception is made in the case of the article *the* and organizations. By and large, lowercase the article, despite the organization's preference. First, it always seems odd to read a capitalized *the* in the middle of a sentence; *The first meeting of The Open Forum took place* .... Second, it seems self-aggrandizing in some contexts (*Please note that The Parking Committee will meet next Tuesday*). Third, it would take a prohibitively long list to determine, authoritatively, which organizations do or don't capitalize the article. The issue is further confused by the fact that some state universities insist that the article should be capitalized when referring to the entire state system but lowercase when referring to individual campuses, a distinction unlikely to be understood by the average reader.

In-House Publications. If you are editing or proofreading an in-house publication of one of those organizations, then their house style should be honored to the letter. Otherwise, for general consumption, lowercase the articles.

In Contracts. In publishing, one common exception to this rule is when a contract specifies how an organization's name should appear in a credit line, a copyright notice, or permissions notice on a copyright or credits page in a book. For instance, *published by The American Bible Society.* But in ordinary text, the article would be lowercase: *He worked for the American Bible Society for twenty years.*

In Initialisms. Also capitalize the article when spelling out the name of an organization that incorporates *The* into their initialism: *TEF (The Environmental Fund), TLB (The Living Bank).* Still, in ordinary text, it is acceptable to lowercase the article: *Both TNC (The Nature Conservancy) and the Environmental Fund endorsed the legislation.*

theism, deism

These terms are often confused. Believers in *theism* and *deism* agree that a God exists, but a *theist* believes that God is both transcendent to and immanent in the world (that is, both universal and personal), while a *deist* believes that God is more impersonal and remote from human affairs. Note that monotheism is not necessarily implied by either term; theoretically, both a theist and a deist could believe that many gods exist.

then

The word *then*, as an adverb, causes little confusion (as in *She didn't notice him till then*). Formerly, some grammarians frowned on the use of *then* as an adjective (as in *the then governor of the state*), though that usage is now widely accepted. Do not hyphenate *then* in such compounds.

More problematic is the use of *then* when it falls between two verbs connected to the same subject and without a conjunction, as in *He looked across the table, then realized the truth.* Some people have argued that the comma is not needed in that case because *then* is functioning as a conjunction. Others, who note it is still an adverb in that place and not a conjunction, insert the comma because, when spoken, a small audible pause would be heard. This manual recommends using the comma in those instances because it not only signals a spoken pause but also fills in for the actual missing conjunction, the word *and.*

theologian

Theologian is a descriptive term when used before a name, not a title, so lowercase it, as in *theologian Gregory Boyd.*

therefore

See "SYLLOGISTIC WORDS AND PHRASES."

they, their, theirs, them (for singular antecedents)

In the controversy between those who allow plural pronouns for generic singular antecedents (as in *Anyone who hands in their paper late will have their grade reduced*) and those who don't, Zondervan opts for allowing it whenever other solutions are awkward (as in *Anyone who hands in his or her paper*). Many reasons exist for allowing the plural pronoun, not the least of which is the usage's long and unquestioned acceptance in English (from Shakespeare and the KJV to the NIV). This grammatical construction, in which agreement is based on general sense rather than syntax, is called a *synesis.* The prohibition against this particular one was largely a contrivance of grammarians of the early twentieth century.

Third World

The term *Third World*, dating from the early 1950s and referring to the world's economically underdeveloped countries, is used less often than it once was, largely because it not only seems dismissive but is also a somewhat dated holdover from the Cold War. With the dissolution of the Soviet Union in 1991, the *Second World*, that is, the Communist bloc, was diminished.

Majority World. Some writers recommend replacing *Third World* with the term *Majority World* (that is, the majority of the world's population that lives in poverty), which is certainly more accurate but has not caught on widely, perhaps because many people perceive that term and its companion term, *the Minority World*, to mean exactly the opposite of what they are intended to mean. Still, *Majority World* is gaining ground and, if used, should be capitalized.

Other Options. Some use the terms *developed countries* and *undeveloped*, or *underdeveloped*, *countries*, but other writers deem those as culturally insensitive. Some writers refer to the *North/South divide* (or *the Global North* and *the Global South*), by which the wealthier industrial countries of the northern hemisphere are contrasted to the less wealthy countries in the southern hemisphere. This is often problematic since it does not account for the highly developed countries in the southern hemisphere, and vice versa.

Opting for Third World. The term *Third World*, for better or worse, still seems the most readily recognized by most readers. Also, since the *Second World* seems to be making something of a comeback, it may be premature to dismiss it as having disappeared completely. If you use the term *Third World*, capitalize it (on the pattern of *Free World* and *New World*), and do not hyphenate it as an adjective: *Third World countries*.

First World. The term *First World*, referring to Western capitalist nations of the Cold War era, has also made a resurgence in the phrase *First World problems*, which is used by some people to mock the petty concerns of those living in the wealthiest countries (as in *"It takes sooo long for my smartphone to recharge!" is a typical First World problem*).

thou, thee, thy, thine

Pseudo–King James English—or at least the tendency to address persons of the Trinity as *thou*—pops up in public prayers and evangelistic tracts with surprising frequency. Originally these forms—*thou*, *thee*, *thy*, and *thine*—were the singular second-person pronouns. *Ye*, *you*, and *yours* were the plural forms. Eventually, as *ye* and *you* became more common singular forms of address (during the fourteenth and fifteenth centuries), *thou* and *thee* were retained as intimate and informal singulars, used primarily to address one's family, closest friends, children, and inferiors (equivalent to the French informal *tu* and *toi*).

Many modern readers think *thou* and *thee* are the formal forms, believing them to sound more respectful and reverent, as though addressing royalty. The opposite is true. They are the informal forms of address. The formal form in King James's time was the plural *you*, not *thou*. The king of England was addressed as "your majesty," not "thy majesty," largely because the king was thought to embody all the people of the realm. The plural was the formal and respectful form, and the plural form was used whenever addressing a superior or a stranger.

From the KJV. Unlike their contemporary Shakespeare, the translators of the KJV dispensed with this formal/informal distinction and reverted, somewhat anachronistically, to the older use of *thou* and *thee* exclusively as singular second-person pronouns and *ye* and *you* as the plurals. This was a nod to their Greek and Hebrew sources, languages that don't make any formal/informal distinction in their second-person pronouns but do distinguish between singular and plural. It was also a nod to the style of the English translations that preceded the King James, notably Tyndale's. Those translations used *thou* when addressing God solely because it was the singular form. Still, many people of that time used *thou* when addressing God, not only because it was the singular form but also because it was the informal form. God was addressed not as a king, but as an intimate.

Incorrectly Used. Many casual users of the old-style *thou* forms today use them incorrectly, sometimes indiscriminately interchanging *thou*, which is the nominative ("Thou preparest a table before me" [Ps. 23:5]), *thee*, which is an object ("Unto thee, O Lord, do I lift up my soul" [Ps. 25:1]), and *thy*, which is the possessive ("thy rod and thy staff" [Ps. 23:4]). One popular singer, in his recorded rendition of "Be Thou My Vision," mixes up his pronouns when he sings, "Naught be all else to me save that thy art."

Possessives. The alternate possessive form *thine* is usually used before a word starting with a vowel sound or an *h* ("Incline thine ear unto wisdom, and apply thine heart to understanding" [Prov. 2:2]). (See "*a, an*" for a complete discussion of what constitutes a "vowel sound.") Still, the KJV is inconsistent; it occasionally uses *thy* with words beginning with *h* ("love the Lord thy God with all thy heart" [Luke 10:27]). *Thine* is also a pronoun ("The day is thine, the night also is thine" [Ps. 74:16]).

Avoid Using Today. Needless to say, one should avoid these forms except in quotations or for some special reason. *Thou* adds special inflections to its accompanying verbs, *-est*, *-st*, and *-t*, familiar to anyone who reads the KJV ("Thou anointest my head with oil" [Ps. 23:5]) or Shakespeare. To most ears even today, *thou* sounds particularly jarring when used with modern verb forms: for example, *Thou knows my inmost thoughts.* (See "KING JAMES VERSION, VERB ENDINGS.")

Lowercase When Used. Note that the KJV always lowercases *thou*, *thee*, *thy*, and *thine* when referring to the deity, just as it lowercases all other deity pronouns. Unless quoting from a source that capitalizes these terms, lowercase them when referring to God.

In Modern Usage. The *thou/thee* forms persisted in English literature and hymn writing well into the nineteenth century, long after they were uncommon in spoken English. Until relatively recently, the informal *thou* forms were used by some in the Religious Society of Friends (Quakers) as a way of emphasizing our equality in God's eyes, what Herman Melville once called "the stately dramatic thee and thou of the Quaker idiom" (*Moby-Dick*). The forms are also still used in such popular expressions as *holier-than-thou* (which finds its source in Isa. 65:5) and in some old hymns and songs, such as "Come, Thou Long Expected Jesus" and "My Country, 'Tis of Thee." Such uses should obviously be retained as the ones familiar to most ears.

In Hymns. Many modern hymnal editors have taken the fairly simple step of rewriting old hymns by replacing *thee* and *thou* with *you* (and modernizing the associated verbs), and *thy* and *thine* with *your* and *yours*. If the archaic forms are used to complete a rhyme, as in Frances R. Havergal's "Take my life, and let it be / Consecrated, Lord, to Thee," then such rewriting is usually not attempted. Note that Havergal, like many Victorians, capitalized the deity pronoun in her lyrics.

In the Qur'an. Also note that many older English translations of the Qur'an and some Muslim devotional literature in translation use these older familiar forms, usually capitalized, when addressing Allah ("We celebrate Thy praise and extol Thy holiness" [Qur'an, 2:4, 30], *The Holy Qur'an*, trans. Maulvi Muhammad Ali, 1917). When quoting these, always follow the style of the source.

till, 'til

As a shortened form of *until*, which is correct: *till* or *'til*? Grammarians have long debated this topic. The word *'til* probably entered the language as a contracted form of *until*, but *till* is actually far older than either *'til* or *until*. Some stylists insist that *till* is the more formal and more correct, and yet there has been a mild prejudice against *till* in the US. This manual takes a different approach. Both words are perfectly correct, but in the writer's box of tools, *'til* might be slightly more useful in conveying a sense of dialectal or colloquial speech (in fictional dialogue, for instance), where it might be used alongside such dialogue slang as *waitin'* or *sleepin'*. In formal writing, *till* may seem more appropriate. Note that *until* tends to be the preferred form at the beginning of a sentence in formal writing, but no absolute rule exists.

Time magazine, *TIME* magazine

Although this question is discussed in "BRAND, PRODUCT, AND COMPANY NAMES: COMMONLY MISSPELLED," it still deserves its own entry. Which is correct: *Time* magazine or *TIME* magazine? Time Warner Inc., the company that owns the magazine, has officially trademarked the magazine as *TIME* (all caps). Some style manuals recommend *Time* in bibliographic references. On the principle of what best communicates to the reader, this manual recommends that *TIME* be used in fiction and trade nonfiction books for casual references in text. But for citations and bibliographies, use *Time*. Note the word *magazine* is not part of the actual title, so it should not be capitalized or italicized. (See also "*USA Today, USA TODAY.*")

tithe

A *tithe* is usually understood to mean "one tenth," so in most cases it is redundant to say *a ten-percent tithe*. The word has acquired a secondary meaning of "any donation to the church," so when a different required percentage is mentioned, then that should be specified: *The church required a tithe of only five percent*. Even in that case, it would probably be less confusing to say, *The church required a donation of five percent*.

to be

This is a word pair that can often be dispensed with. *They found him arrogant* is more direct than *they found him to be arrogant*. (Also see "WORDY WORDS.")

too

Commas were once routinely placed around the word *too* whenever it occurred in the middle of a sentence (*I, too, have been in Arcadia*), much the way commas are still used for *therefore* or *however* (*I, however, have been in Arcadia*). With the adverbs *therefore*, *however*, and other similar words, a slight pause occurs on either side of the word when spoken, and that pause justifies the commas. But few people pause when speaking the word *too*, which makes the commas superfluous. When *too* is inserted at an unexpected place in a sentence (for such reasons as euphony, rhythm, or rhetoric), thereby causing a slight spoken pause, then commas should be placed around the word (*I have been, too, in Arcadia*). Another example: *We need a new birth; we need, too, to have our sins forgiven.*

At the End of a Sentence. Usually no comma should be used before *too* when it falls at the end of a sentence (*I have been in Arcadia too*). But a larger problem often exists. When *too* falls at the end of a phrase or sentence, it can sometimes be unclear whether *too* refers back to the subject, the verb, or the object. For example, *I have driven through Arcadia too* can mean "I, as well as others, have driven through Arcadia" or "I have driven through as well as flown over Arcadia" or "I have driven through Arcadia as well as other regions of Greece." Often the context of the sentence will make the meaning clear (*My dad once drove across Arcadia, and I have driven through Arcadia too*), but an editor should check to make sure that the context clears up the ambiguities. Most often the word *too* is best placed immediately adjacent to the word it is modifying unless it results in awkwardness.

touchscreen

Although dictionaries disagree, set this solid: *a touchscreen device.*

toward, towards

Both forms are used without awkwardness in American English, though this manual opts for *toward* unless the author has a strong and consistent preference for *towards*. The same rule applies to such words as *backward/backwards*, *downward/downwards*, *heavenward/heavenwards*, *upward/upwards*, and so on.

Towards is the preferred form in the UK because *toward* has an old-fashioned and vaguely biblical ring to it in that region. This is probably because the original KJV uses *toward* throughout rather than *towards*. To UK ears, *toward* sounds as antiquated as *unto* and *thine* sound to US ears.

transcript, transcription

Though the two are commonly used interchangeably, most manuals recommend using *transcript* for documents containing words and *transcription* for musical notation. This rule is often unsatisfactory because translations of ancient documents, like the Dead Sea Scrolls, are referred to as *transcriptions*, not *transcripts*. The best policy is probably to use *transcript* when the idea of a *script* (something to be read from) is intended (as in *a transcript of the president's address*) and *transcription* when the idea of translating or recasting is intended (as in *a transcription for two pianos* or *a transcription of the Gnostic texts*).

transfiguration

Lowercase *transfiguration* in most contexts. (See also "EVENTS IN THE LIFE OF JESUS, LOWERCASING.") Capitalize the word as a place name in references to *the Mount of Transfiguration.*

transgender, transsexual

These terms are often used inaccurately because their definitions have been in flux for several decades. *Transgender* is the broader term, referring to individuals who dress or otherwise present themselves in a way other than their current biological gender. This includes transvestitism and other styles of alternate gender or nongender presentation. *Transsexual* refers to individuals who feel they were born with a gender physiology that doesn't match their psychological gender, and in many cases, though not all, such a person may eventually seek gender-reassignment surgery. By and large, as terms, *transgender* encompasses *transsexual*, but not all transgendered people are transsexual.

Transsexual is used as an adjective (as in *a transsexual person*) rather than a noun. This manual advocates using whatever gender pronoun is preferred by the specific transgender or transsexual person being discussed whenever that preference is known. (See also "GENDER-ACCURATE LANGUAGE," section on "*Gender Self-Identification.*") This is simply part of self-identification, which is a way of showing respect to all individuals and groups of people.

trespasses, sins, debts

Most people who have visited a variety of churches have noticed the differing versions of the Lord's Prayer as given in Matt. 6:12, which use, variously, *debts*, *trespasses*, and *sins*. Wycliffe's translation (1395) first used *debts*: "forgive to us oure dettis, as we forgiven to oure dettouris," which the KJV famously echoed as "forgive us our debts, as we forgive our debtors." Most other major Bible translations use *debts*: NIV, ESV, NASB, NET, ASV, Douay-Rheims, Darby, ERV, and so on. Most Presbyterian and Reformed churches have traditionally used *debts* and *debtors* in their liturgies, and many international debt-relief organizations, such as Jubilee 2000 and the Catholic Great Relief movement, prefer *debt/debtors* as a reminder that, in their view, Jesus intended to imply monetary forgiveness as well as the forgiveness of moral offenses.

Trespasses became the predominant form in Christian worship for several centuries because of the influence of the Book of Common Prayer (1549)—"forgeve us oure trespasses, as we forgeve them that trespasse against us"—which it picked up from Tyndale's NT (1526). This liturgical version was commonly found in Catholic, Anglican, and traditional Methodist worship, despite the fact that no major translation, other than Tyndale's, used *trespasses*.

A third variant, found in the NLT, renders the verse as "forgive us our sins, as we have forgiven those who sin against us," which is similar to the ISV.

The story would end there except that a slightly altered Lord's Prayer is also found in Luke 11:4, for which nearly all major Bible versions use *sins*: "Forgive us our sins, for we also forgive everyone who sins against us" (NIV).

When referencing the Lord's Prayer, use Matthew's version in whatever translation the author prefers. Few people will be confused by the alternate versions, but you may want to select the version most familiar to the intended readership or denomination.

Trinity, the

Capitalize *Trinity* in reference to the three persons of the Godhead. (See also "TRINITY, NAMES FOR THE.")

try to, try and

Try to is grammatically correct in phrases like *I will try to do better.* But despite grammarians' objections, allow *try and* in colloquial and informal writing and especially in fictional dialogue (as in *I'll try and do better*), especially in imperatives (as in *Try and do better from now on*). The locution *try and* has a long history in English (since before Shakespeare), and only the tinniest of editorial ears would change a fictional mobster's snarl from *"Try and stop me, copper"* to *"Try to stop me, copper."*

T-shirt, tee

Since a T-shirt is shaped like a capital *T*, most references have a preference for *T-shirt* over *tee shirt* (the latter with no hyphen). If the shirt is referred to simply at a *tee*, spell it out (as in *They made twenty tie-dyed tees*).

TV

As an abbreviated form of *television*, *TV* is capitalized. Some editors recommend spelling out *television* in formal writing, but *TV* is appropriate for most contexts.

tweet, Twitter

Two issues here. First, when referring to short-form messaging (on Twitter), most style manuals agree that the verb form *to tweet* is lowercase. Second, some people prefer to use the verb form *to Twitter*, in which case most manuals agree that that verb is capitalized. Use either form of the verb you want, though lowercase *to tweet* and capitalize *to Twitter*. Also lowercase the noun *tweet*, as in *His tweets reach more than a million followers*; but capitalize *Twitter*, as in *He said so on his Twitter page*.

Twelve, the; twelve disciples

Capitalize *Twelve* when referring to the disciples of Jesus as *the Twelve*. Otherwise, lowercase the word in such phrases as *the twelve disciples*, *the original twelve*, or *the twelve apostles*. Also capitalize *the Eleven* when referring to the twelve disciples minus Judas. (See also "*apostles, twelve*.")

Twelve Steps

Capitalize *Twelve Steps* when referring to the stages of recovery discussed by support groups like Alcoholics Anonymous; for instance, *the Twelve Steps*, *a Twelve Step group*, *a Twelve Step program*. Do not hyphenate it as an adjective.

type A, type B

To describe personality types, the terms *type A* and *type B* were coined in the 1970s. Lowercase the word *type* in these formulations, capitalize the single letter, and hyphenate them when used as adjectives: *a type-A personality*.

typeface, font

In the venerable old days of printing, a *typeface* was a family of similarly designed letters, numbers, and symbols, such as Baskerville, Bodoni, or Gill Sans. Within each typeface family, the various weights and styles (such as boldface, demi-bold, condensed, heavy, italic, and so on) as well as the various sizes were all referred to as *fonts*. In the age of digital typography, in which everyone has access to a huge number of typefaces in a vast array of styles, the terms *typeface* and *font* have become synonymous. Though diehard purists may cringe, the two words are now commonly used interchangeably to mean a family of similarly designed characters or sets of letters of varying weights and style.

U

uber-

To mean "super" or "extraordinary," the prefix *uber-* has become a trendy slang word, as in *uberballad* ("a great song") or *uberslacker* ("someone good at inconsequential things"). Spell it solid, though add the hyphen to avoid a double *r*: *uber-radical, uber-relevant*. Also avoid the German umlauted version (*über-*), though that is listed first in *Webster*. Use the umlaut in words actually drawn from the German; for instance, *Übermensch* (Nietzsche's "Superman").

Ukraine

Western news media formerly referred to this country as *the Ukraine* (which was a shortened form of *the Soviet Republic of the Ukraine*), but since gaining their independence in 1991, the Ukrainian people refer to their country as *Ukraine* (without the definite article).

unbeliever

See "*agnostic, atheist, unbeliever.*"

unbiblical

See "*nonbiblical, abiblical, extrabiblical, unbiblical.*"

unchristian, non-Christian

The words *unchristian* and *non-Christian* are not synonymous. *Unchristian* implies "uncharacteristic of Christianity" or in some instances "uncharitable" (*His refusal was unchristian*). *Non-Christian* means "not a believer in Christianity." A person with road rage, for instance, may be unchristian but still not be a non-Christian. Some people argue that *unchristian* should be spelled *un-Christian*, but the lowercase, unhyphenated form is preferred by *Webster*. Why the word *non-Christian* retains the hyphen and internal capital while *unchristian* does not is simply one of the many vagaries of English.

unchurched

This term suffers from imprecision. Some writers use it to mean "non-Christian," while others use it to mean those who, Christian or otherwise, simply don't attend church. If defined well, then use the term as an adjective, as in *unchurched adults*, since the noun form, *the unchurched*, has an air of evangelical cant and marketing jargon to it. It can sound condescending in many contexts.

unforgivenness

Although not found in dictionaries, this word is common in evangelical writing and in the pulpit. Unlike *unforgiveness*, which means "a refusal to forgive," *unforgivenness* means "the state of being unforgiven oneself." The problem is that the two words, with quite different meanings, look so much alike that they can be easily misread. We recommend avoiding *unforgivenness* and its less common antonym, *forgivenness*, for those reasons. Use *unforgiven state* and *forgiven state* or similar phrases instead.

ungodly

See "GOD COMPOUNDS."

United Kingdom, Great Britain, England, British Isles

Although many Americans vaguely think of these terms as synonymous, they are distinct. The British Isles comprise all the islands—more than a thousand of them—immediately north-northwest of France, the two largest of these islands being Great Britain and Ireland. Great Britain comprises England, Scotland, and Wales; and Ireland comprises the Republic of Ireland and Northern Ireland. The United Kingdom, called the UK, is made up of Great Britain (that is, England, Scotland, and Wales) and Northern Ireland, and as a country is formally called the United Kingdom of Great Britain and Northern Ireland. The Republic of Ireland is not part of the UK.

The term *Great Britain* is sometimes shortened to simply *Britain*, which is fine in informal contexts, but the longer term should be used whenever precision is needed. And yes, there used to be a *Little Britain*; it is now Brittany, France, but that term is no longer used.

The English means those people who come from England. *British* usually means those who are from Great Britain only (England, Scotland, Wales), though some writers use it to mean those who are from the UK (that is, including Northern Ireland).

The term *the British Commonwealth* is sometimes still used, though the correct contemporary term is *the Commonwealth of Nations*. That is made up of fifty-three nations, some of which are incorporated into areas referred to as *realms*, and most of which were once formally part of the global British Empire.

Writers of history and historical fiction need to be especially careful in using any of these terms because the definitions of some of them have changed through the centuries; for instance, all of Ireland was part of the United Kingdom before 1922, and the term *the United Kingdom* was not used before the union of Ireland and Great Britain in 1801. Always check primary sources for accurate geographical terms.

unreligious

See "*irreligious, nonreligious, unreligious, areligious.*"

until, till, 'til

See "*till, 'til.*"

USA Today, USA TODAY

Like *TIME* magazine, *USA TODAY* (all caps) is the style preferred by the company itself and should be used in most casual references. Some typographers and designers recommend *USA Today* (caps and lowercase) because that style blends in better with a normal block of text, causing less distraction. That is acceptable for design purposes. Also, most academic citations to that newspaper use *USA Today*, and that is acceptable. Either form is fine as long as it is italicized as a title. (See also "Time *magazine*, TIME *magazine*.")

usher

In church contexts, an *usher* can be male or female. Do not use *usherette* for women.

V

v., vs., versus

The word *versus* is only abbreviated as *v.* when used in the names of legal cases: such as *Brown v. Board of Education*. The *v.* is also lowercase. It was once common to set the *v.* in roman type while the parties in the legal case were set in italic, but this manual recommends that the entire name of the legal case be set in italic: *Citizens United v. Federal Election Commission*. Note that *vs.* is also an acceptable abbreviation when legal cases are referenced in casual, nonlegal, or nonacademic contexts. As a common preposition, *versus* is lowercase and usually spelled out in headings and titles, as in *Myth versus Reality* or *The Pill versus the Spring Hill Mine Disaster*.

vacation Bible school

Used generically, *vacation* and *school* are lowercase, though they can be capitalized when used as a specific name of a church program, as in *First Church's "Tots and Tikes" Vacation Bible School program will begin next week*. Still, *vacation Bible school* is abbreviated as *VBS* (all caps).

Valentine, valentine

Capitalize *St. Valentine's Day* and its variants, but lowercase *valentine* to mean a card sent on that day or the person to whom the card is sent: as in *It is estimated that 145 million valentines are sent for Valentine's Day each year.*

venerate, worship

In religious contexts, especially Roman Catholic and Anglican, saints are *venerated* (that is, honored or shown special respect), not worshiped. *Worship* is reserved for God alone.

venial, venal

The words *venial* and *venal* are sometimes confused in religious writing, most often when "a *venial* sin" is mistakenly referred to as "a *venal* sin." *Venial* means that something is "forgivable." *A venial sin* is a relatively minor, pardonable offense as opposed to *a mortal sin*, which can threaten one's prospects for salvation. *Venal* means "corruptible," especially implying "able to be bribed or influenced by money." To say that someone's sins are "of the venal kind" means that that person will do most anything for money.

verbal, oral

A *verbal communication* contains words—written or spoken. An *oral communication* is spoken only.

verger

A *verger* is a lay position in the Anglican Church usually equivalent to a sacristan or an usher.

very

As an adjective and adverb, *very* is a common intensifier, but in most cases a statement is as strong, if not stronger, without it. *He's very angry* is slightly minced compared to *He's angry.* It is also fruitless to add *very* to words that are already absolute: for instance, phrases like *very correct*, *very exact*, *very final* are clumsy. If an intensifier is needed, be creative. *He was jaw-droppingly handsome* may be clichéd, but it is better than *he was very handsome.* The word *very* has a knack for subtly undercutting whatever it modifies, so use it very, *very* sparingly. So common was the problem of *very* being overused that J. I. Rodale and Mabel F. Mulock once wrote a 96-page reference book containing nothing but suggestions for alternatives to the word *very*, called *The Substitute for "Very"* (Emmaus, Pa.: Rodale Press, 1948). (See also "INTENSIFIERS.")

vespers, vesper

As a noun meaning "evening worship" or "late afternoon canonical prayers," the plural *vespers* is used, though any accompanying verb can be either singular or plural: *vespers ends at 9:00* (singular verb) or *vespers are sung in Latin* (plural verb). Euphony and author preference should dictate which form is used. The adjective is *vesper*, without the *s*: *the vesper service* or *the vesper bell.* Note that Roman Catholic style usually capitalizes *Vespers* as one of the canonical hours. (See "*offices*" and "HOURS, CANONICAL.")

Veterans Day

No apostrophe.

vicar

The term is specific to the Anglican Church and usually refers to a priest in charge of a specific church or chapel. Capitalize *Vicar* in direct address (as in *Yes, Vicar, you're correct*) but lowercase it otherwise.

victuals, vittles

Victuals and *vittles*, meaning "food," are pronounced the same, both rhyming with *skittles*. *Vittles* is the older form, but in a re-Latinizing era in English, *victuals* was declared more correct. So, in formal writing, use *victuals*. Since the word has a slangy tone and is often used humorously, it is probably best to use the more folksy *vittles* in such books as Westerns (*"Come git your vittles"*). In other words, if the target reader is likely to think the *c* in *victuals* is meant to be pronounced, use the more phonetic *vittles*.

Vietnam, Vietnamese

Spell *Vietnam* as a single word (not *Viet Nam*). Likewise *Vietnamese*.

Virgin, virgin, virgin birth

In formal references to the mother of Jesus, capitalize *Virgin*, as in *the Virgin Mary, the Virgin*, since those have the force of a name. But lowercase it in references to such doctrines as *the virgin birth*, though that term is often capitalized in Roman Catholic theological writings. (See also "*immaculate conception, virgin birth*.")

voice mail

Two words.

Vulgate, vulgate

When capitalized, *the Vulgate* refers to the Latin Bible. This fourth century translation is attributed to St. Jerome and used in the Roman Catholic Church. Lowercase, the word can mean either an ordinary people's version of a common text (as in *Disney's* The Lion King *is a sort of vulgate* Hamlet) or the speech of ordinary people (as in *He had to learn the vulgate of the Outback*).

W

wages

Many dictionaries, including *Webster*, suggest that *wages*, as a plural noun, can take either a plural or singular verb. While the plural verb is used in such phrases as *Workers wages are lower now than before*, for instance, the singular verb is used in the familiar phrase "the wages of sin is death" (Rom. 6:23). Otherwise, the singular verb sounds misplaced in nearly every contemporary context; few English speakers would say, "Her wages is taxed at a higher rate than mine." It seems the *only* place the singular verb sounds natural is in the phrase "the wages of sin is death," a formulation that goes back to the Middle English of the Wycliffe Bible (1395): "the wagis of synne is deth." That phrase sounds natural to our ears because it was picked up by the influential KJV and possibly also because the singular verb is nestled between two singular words: *sin* and *death*. The New International Version also translates that passage as "the wages of sin is death," but the NIV uses the plural form of the verb with *wages* in all other instances: "its wages are riches and honor and life" (Prov. 22:4) and "wages are not credited as a gift" (Rom. 4:4) and nowhere else uses it as a singular. So, except for "the wages of sin is death," *always* use the plural verb with *wages*.

Wailing Wall

See "*Western Wall.*"

Walmart

This is the correct spelling for the name of the individual stores (as in *He ran out to Walmart*). (See a more complete explanation in the list at "BRAND, PRODUCT, AND COMPANY NAMES: COMMONLY MISSPELLED.")

watches of the night

The term *watches of the night* (or less correctly, *watches in the night*) is archaic, though when used, it is often used incorrectly. In Bible times, the night hours were divided into *watches*, though they take slightly different forms in the Old and New Testaments. *Watch* refers to the assigned guards (for livestock) or soldiers whose duty was to keep watch during designated periods of the night. In the Hebrew Bible, the Israelites observed three watches of about four hours each (varying with the seasons), so that when Gideon blows his trumpet "at the beginning of the middle watch" (Judg. 7:19), it means about four hours after sunset. In the NT, the Romans observed four watches of about three hours each (varying with the seasons), so that when Jesus walks on the water "about the fourth watch of the night" (Mark 6:48 ESV), it means in the hours immediately before dawn. (Also see "HOURS, BIBLICAL.")

Israelite Watch (OT)	Modern Equivalent (approximate)
first watch	6:00 p.m. to 10:00 p.m.
second watch	10:00 p.m. to 2:00 a.m.
third watch	2:00 a.m. to 6:00 a.m.

Roman Watch (NT)	Modern Equivalent (approximate)
first watch	6:00 p.m. to 9:00 p.m.
second watch	9:00 p.m. to 12:00 p.m.
third watch	12:00 p.m. to 3:00 a.m.
fourth watch	3:00 a.m. to 6:00 a.m.

way of the cross, the

See "*stations of the cross, the.*"

web, website

Lowercase *web* and *website* as well as most other *web* combinations like *webcam, webinar, webmail, webmaster, webpage*, or *webview. The web* has become a medium as common as *the press* or *radio*. In most cases, close *web* up to whatever element follows it: *webadvisor, weblink, webtoon*, and so on. Keep it simple. Otherwise, capitalize only *the World Wide Web.*

Weltanschauung

Capitalize this German word, meaning "worldview," in conformity with the German custom of capitalizing all nouns. It is pronounced VELT-un-SHAH-oong. (See also "*worldview.*")

West, Western, west, western

When contrasting Asia with the rest of the world (or when referring to the American West, or the Old West), capitalize *the West* and *Western*, or, as *CMoS* suggests, capitalize such terms when "a cultural entity" is specified. When referring to people in those regions, lowercase *westerner* and *to westernize.* Also lowercase the term when used as a point on the compass (*a westerly wind*) or when referring to a genre of fiction (*he collected westerns*).

Western church. Capitalize *Western* in the phrase *Western church* when distinguishing it from either the Eastern church or the Asian or African churches.

Western Wall

Modern Israelis prefer the term *Western Wall* to *Wailing Wall* (both terms capitalized) for that portion of the Old Temple in Jerusalem to which it refers (once thought of as part of Solomon's original temple but actually of a later date). Honor this preference, which symbolizes the Jews' new hope after emerging from the tragedies of history.

whatever, what ever

Style manuals disagree about when to use *whatever* and *what ever.* The simplest rule goes back to Fowler (1926), who endorses *whatever* as one word in all instances except questions, in which case *what ever* is preferred: *What ever happened to Dad's Bible?* or Larry Burkett's book *What Ever Happened to the American Dream?* (1993). That doesn't negate the fact that far more book titles use the single-word option, such as Gerald Smith's compilation of A. W. Tozer's sermons, *Whatever Happened to Worship?* (1986) and C. Everett Koop and Francis Schaeffer's *Whatever Happened to the Human Race?* (1979). Some grammarians suggest that *what ever* is appropriate when the word *ever*, used adverbially, is emphasized; as in *What ever do you mean by that?* When confronted with this situation, be sensitive, let the traditional rules guide you, but do what seems right in the immediate context. The fact is that both the one- and two-word options are so common in questions that neither is technically wrong or likely to mislead readers. Or as teenagers would say: "Whatever."

while, although

In informal writing, *while* and *although* are interchangeable in a sentence like *While* [or *although*] *few people believe it, it's true nonetheless*. Still, academics and strict grammarians wisely recommend reserving *while* for references related to time and simultaneity, as in *While the guards stood at attention, the queen greeted the crowd.* (See also "*a while, awhile.*")

white

As a racial designation, lowercase it in most contexts.

Whitsunday, Whit Sunday

In the formal church calendar, the seventh Sunday after Easter is referred to as *Whitsunday* in the US and as *Whit Sunday* in the UK. *Whitsuntide* refers to the days immediately following *Whitsunday*, not the days preceding it.

who, whom

The most useful way to determine the correct use of *who* (subject) and *whom* (object) is to insert *he* or *him* as a test. If *he* would be correct in context, then use *who*. If *him* is correct, use *whom*. This manual recommends observing the distinction in formal and academic writing, though this observance is partly because academic readers would consider any deviation from time-honored rules of grammar to be substandard. As one professor said, "My colleagues *expect* my grammar to be flawless."

Exceptions. Many contexts demand a more colloquial usage. The distinction between *who* and *whom* is seldom honored in conversation, except among the most highly educated. So it is okay to opt for *who* in place of *whom* in fictional dialogue—unless the writer wants to convey that the speaker *is* highly educated. In informal and fictional contexts, the author's voice and readership should be honored. For example, consider a book of advice for teenagers titled *Who Should I Turn To?* It is hard to imagine a teenager wanting to read it if it were called *Whom Should I Turn To?* (or worse, *To Whom Should I Turn?*). Would the *Ghostbusters* movie have been as popular if their slogan had been "Whom are you going to call?" instead of "Who you gonna call?" It's a spooky thought.

Whoever and Whomever. Sometimes *whoever/whomever* (and occasionally *who/whom*) stands at the junction between two clauses and makes a determination difficult. For instance, *I would like to talk to whoever/whomever made that rule.* In that case, *whoever* is correct, because, though it is the object of the first clause, it is still the subject of the verb in the second clause—and subject usage predominates. Only when the word is the object of both clauses do you use *whomever*; as in *I will gladly hire whomever you recommend.*

"Who" versus "That" with Collective Nouns Referring to People. With collective nouns referring to people, use *who* if the group would be referred to as *they* elsewhere in the sentence (as in *the couple who visited ... they were from Portland*); use *that* if the group would be referred to as *it* elsewhere in the sentence (as in *the council that made the decision ... it comprises four members*).

who, whom, whose (the deity pronoun)

In references to God, lowercase *who* and *whom* even when used in a text that capitalizes the other deity pronouns. (See "DEITY PRONOUN, THE.")

whodunit

Stick with the spelling *whodunit* (though *Webster* also shows *whodunnit* as an alternative) for the word that describes this subgenre of murder mystery.

Wi-Fi

The word *Wi-Fi*, meaning "wireless fidelity," is most commonly capitalized (as a brand name) and hyphenated, which is the form preferred by *Webster* as well as many computer companies and trade organizations. *WiFi*, without the hyphen, is probably the next most common spelling. In Europe and other parts of the world, the term *WLAN* ("wireless local area network") is used in place of *Wi-Fi*.

Wisdom Literature

When capitalized, *Wisdom Literature* is the title of the section of the Hebrew Bible containing the books of Job, Psalms, Proverbs, Ecclesiastes, and the Song of Solomon (with the addition of the Book of Wisdom and Ecclesiasticus in the Roman Catholic Bible). When lowercase, *wisdom literature* refers to the genre of literature that includes the sacred texts of many religions as well as certain types of philosophical and religious poetry and prose, especially ancient. Still, few readers are going to recognize the difference between the capitalized and lowercase forms. So if the context does not clarify which one is meant, the writer should make the meaning clear.

wise men, the

Lowercase this term in reference to the magi from the east who visited the child Jesus (Matt. 2:1), even though the KJV 1611 capitalized the *Wise* in *Wise men*. (See "*magi*" for more detail.)

Woman's Christian Temperance Union (WCTU)

This temperance organization, founded in 1874, is still active. Note the singular possessive in the name: *Woman's*, not *Women's*.

Word, the

Capitalize *the Word* when referring to the Bible or to Jesus. (See "*Word of God, word of God*" and "TRINITY, NAMES FOR PERSONS OF THE.")

Word of God, word of God

When referring to the Bible, capitalize this term. Lowercase it when referring to God's general promise. (See also "*God's Word, God's word.*")

World War I, World War II

Use the roman numeral—*World War I* and *World War II*—rather than *World War One, World War Two.* Also, by extension, use *World War III* and so on. The events may also be referred to as *the First World War* and *the Second World War.* Also, the once-common term *the Great War,* referring to World War I, is likely to confuse most modern readers unless it is defined. Many will assume it refers to World War II.

worldview

Formerly two words, *worldview* is now commonly set solid. (See also "*Weltanschauung.*")

world's fair

Note the possessive. Lowercase it in general references (as in *We went to the world's fair*), but capitalize it for specific fairs (as in *the Chicago World's Fair* or *Expo 2015 World's Fair Milan, Italy*).

worship

See "*venerate, worship.*"

worshiper, worshiping, worshiped

Use a single *p* in these words, which is the common US style. The double *p* is common in the UK.

wrack

See "*rack my brain.*"

wreak, wreck

The confusion between these words most often occurs with the phrase *to wreak havoc*, and the problem may arise from the pronunciation. *Wreak* is most often pronounced REEK, but it is occasionally pronounced *RECK*, which is how *wreck* is pronounced. To *wreak* is to "inflict"; to *wreck* is "to ruin" or "be cast ashore." So havoc is *wreaked*, not *wrecked*, and it is most definitely not *reeked*!

X

Xerox, xerox

Capitalize *Xerox* when referring to the company. Lowercase it as a verb to mean "make a copy." (See also "BRAND NAMES, TRADEMARKED.")

Xmas

The abbreviation *Xmas* (occasionally seen as *Exmas*) for Christmas should be avoided. It is offensive to many since it literally "takes Christ out of Christmas." It may be appropriate for compact advertising copy but is usually considered substandard even there. Curiously, that contraction dates back to an Old English form used in the Anglo-Saxon Chronicle of the twelfth century. The *X* is actually the Greek letter *chi*, which has been used as a symbol (and abbreviation) for the name of Christ (*Christos*) since the first century.

X-ray, x-ray

This manual conforms to *Webster*, which recommends *X-ray* (capitalized) as the noun and adjective, and *to x-ray* (lowercase) as the verb. Note the hyphen is always present except when using NATO's "Alpha Bravo" code-word system, where the verbal cue for the letter *x* is the word *Xray* with no hyphen or space. (Remember that when playing Scrabble. See also "NATO PHONETIC ALPHABET.")

xtian, Xtian

In text messages, social media, and online communications, *xtian* and *Xtian* are sometimes used as abbreviations for *Christian*. As with most such abbreviations, it is useless to dictate a style, such as whether it should be capitalized. In the unlikely event that it is used in print, this manual would opt for the capitalized version, insofar as the *X* is short for *Christ*.

Y

yea, yay, yeah

These three words are often confused. *Yea* is an affirmative response ("yes") and often used in roll-call voting, as in *the chair tallied the yeas and nays*. *Yea* can also be a formal or Bible-echoing way of saying "indeed": as in Ps. 18:48 (KJV): "Yea, thou liftest me up above those that rise up against me." *Yea* can also be a cheer or shout of rejoicing, similar to "hurray," though it is becoming more commonly spelled *yay* (though that spelling is not yet found in *Webster*). Both *yea* and *yay* are pronounced the same, rhyming with *way*. Use either *yea* or *yay* to represent cheering, as in *Yea, team*, or *Yay, team*.

Yeah (which is sometimes spelled *yah* in texting, or even *ya*) is a casual or slangy version of "yes." *Yeah* is pronounced like "yak" without the final *k*.

ye

The archaic *ye* (now rarely seen outside the KJV and Shakespeare) was originally the second-person plural pronoun, which complemented *thou*, the second-person singular (familiar) pronoun. Both were used as subjects of sentences, while *you* and *thee* were the respective objective cases. In modern English, all these forms have become simply *you*, which can be singular or plural, subject or object. While the KJV uses *ye* exclusively as a plural pronoun, as in "Blessed be ye poor," meaning "Blessed are all you who are poor" (Luke 6:20), the word eventually came to be used as a highly formal way of addressing one person, still occasionally seen in ecclesiastical and devotional writing, as well as in some spoken prayers, though considered archaic. In modern pseudo–King James English, *ye* is sometimes used to address God, but this usage is incorrect. (See "*thou, thee, thy, thine.*")

The word *ye* as it appears in some pseudo-antiquated names, such as Ye Olde Carde Shoppe, should not be confused with *ye*, the outmoded second-person plural. Early English printers would often use a special character, called a *thorn*, to represent the sound *th*. But since the thorn character looked vaguely like a capital Y, later readers mistook the word *the* for the word *Ye*. Any such use of *ye* as an article should be avoided unless humor is intended.

Yeshua

This Hebrew proper name is sometimes used in English as an alternate name for Jesus (also related to the name *Joshua*). It means "deliverer." In reference to Jesus, *Yeshua* often implies that the user is emphasizing Jesus's Jewish cultural roots. It is also the name for Jesus that is sometimes used among Messianic Jewish Christians.

YHWH, JHWH

Most Bible scholars use *YHWH* rather than *JHWH* for the four letters that stand for the name of God in the Hebrew Bible. (See "*tetragrammaton, tetragram.*") Formerly, those letters were often set in small caps (YHWH and JHWH), but that is less common now, even though the small-cap form is still occasionally seen in the UK. One advantage of the all-cap setting is that it transfers well to online and other digital formats. Unless you have a compelling reason to do otherwise, opt for *YHWH*, in all capitals. (For some Bibles' use of the small-cap *LORD* as a way to translate *YHWH*, see "*LORD, GOD* [CAP-AND-SMALL-CAP FORMS].")

Yiddish

See "*Hebrew, Yiddish.*"

you, You (deity pronoun, second person)

Lowercase the second person of the deity pronoun as you would lowercase the third person. An exception is sometimes made in books of devotion or prayer when the capitalized second-person pronoun is used to address God directly. (For more detail, see "DEITY PRONOUN, THE" as well as "*thou, thee, thy, thine.*")

Yule, Yuletide

Capitalize these terms. In contexts other than Christmas literature or hymns, they carry a hint of sentimentality and are not always understood by readers. Use the more plainspoken *Christmas* or *Christmastime.* Curiously, while *Yule* now refers to the celebration of Christ's nativity, it originated as an Old English word for a pagan midwinter festival.

Z

Zacchaeus, Zaccheus

Of the many biblical names with variant spellings, *Zacchaeus* is one of the most common. It is spelled *Zacchaeus* in most English Bibles (NIV, KJV, NLT, ESV, and others), though *Zaccheus* is occasionally seen (notably NASB, and also the *Webster Bible* [1833] and YLT). Tyndale and Douay-Rheims spell it *Zacheus*. As for Wycliffe, he spelled it *Sache*. For general references, use the common *Zacchaeus*. (See also "*ae.*")

zealot, Zealot

When lowercase, *zealot* means a fanatical believer in a cause (as in *a zealot of campaign-finance reform*). Capitalized, it refers specifically to the first-century religio-political Jewish sect that opposed Rome's occupation of Israel. Jesus's disciple Simon the Zealot (Luke 6:15) was among them, and Barabbas (Mark 15:7) was probably also a Zealot.

Zion

Mount Zion, or simply Zion (which the KJV also occasionally spells *Sion*, as in Rev. 14:1), is a hill in Jerusalem. As a synecdoche, *Zion* can mean the nation of Israel, the Jewish people, or the city of Jerusalem. In the context of some Christian devotional literature, *Zion* is used metaphorically to mean "the people of God," and John Bunyan, in his *Pilgrim's Progress*, uses *Mount Zion* and *the Celestial City* as synonyms for heaven. Since that time, *Zion* and *Mount Zion* have been popularly used in the language of hymns and sermons to mean heaven. If the context is unclear, a careful writer should clarify which meaning is intended: the earthly hill or city of biblical times, the worldwide family of believers, or the heavenly abode of God and the saints.

Zionist, Zionism

Capitalize these terms. A *Zionist* is someone who supported the formation of an independent Jewish state in Palestine or who strongly supports the nation of Israel now. (Some contemporary Christians who support modern Israel as the fulfillment of biblical prophecy are termed "Christian Zionists.") The terms are neutral, but in some political contexts they can imply extremism, so they should be used carefully. Those who oppose a Jewish state are termed *anti-Zionists*—which for some groups implies anti-Semitism.

Notes

1. This list is adapted from items found in William S. Walsh's *Handy Book of Literary Curiosities* (Philadelphia: Lippincott, 1892) and *Brewer's Dictionary of Phrase and Fable* (New York: Harper & Brothers, n.d.).
2. "Prevalence of Visual Impairment," Lighthouse International, lighthouse.org/research/statistics-on-vision-impairment/prevalence-of-vision-impairment/ (accessed October 3, 2013). This information is no longer posted at this site. Lighthouse International is now part of Lighthouse Guild and has changed its website format and information.
3. J. Elaine Kitchel, "APH Guidelines for Print Document Design," *APH.org*, http://www.aph.org/edresearch/lpguide.htm.
4. These guidelines outline Zondervan's own policies and are solely for the information of authors under contract with Zondervan. This information does not constitute legal advice and should not be relied upon by authors for that purpose. Zondervan's right in its sole discretion to decide which materials require permission in a given case is in no way limited by this "Permission Guidelines" outline. Other publishers may have different guidelines, and the information given in this manual should not be referred to in connection with any book that a Zondervan author may be writing for another publisher. Zondervan's authors make certain representations and warranties regarding the content of their books and agree to indemnify Zondervan against certain claims relating to such content. Nothing in this section is intended to modify those obligations of the author or to reduce or restrict the rights and remedies available to Zondervan under its publishing agreements with authors.

Acknowledgments

The editorial staff of Zondervan, a division of HarperCollins Christian Publishing (HCCP), has served as the informal advisory board for *The Christian Writer's Manual of Style, 4th Edition*. Thank you to production editors Chris Beetham, Dirk Buursma, Greg Clouse, Nancy Erickson, Brian Phipps, and Jim Ruark; trade-book acquiring editors Carolyn McCready, Rebecca Philpott, John Sloan, Stephanie Smith, and Sandra Vander Zicht; academic acquiring editors Katya Covrett, Ryan Pazdur, and Madison Trammel; Bible editors Amy Ballor, Shari Vanden Berg, Helen Schmitt, and Mike Vander Klipp; ZonderKidz book editors Jacque Alberta, Mary Hassinger, Barbara Herndon, and Jillian Manning; graphics assets manager Kim Tanner; and publishers Annette Bourland, Paul Engle, Stan Gundry, and David Morris. I cannot imagine a more brilliant and distinguished group of book professionals.

Everything in this book and its previous editions relating to Hebrew, Greek, or Arabic is the work of Verlyn Verbrugge† (1942–2015), Zondervan senior editor-at-large, pastor, author of numerous scholarly works, and a master teacher of biblical languages. It was a privilege to work beside him (literally, in adjacent cubicles) for so many years.

We are indebted to proofreaders Dianne Scent, Charles Taylor, Lauren Schneider, and Tonya Oosterhouse for their hard work in honing the details in this volume.

Over the years, many student interns have contributed their editing and proofreading to portions of this volume: Amy Allen (Calvin), Sarah Kuipers Ball (Calvin), Kasey Cheydleur (Oberlin), Anna Craft (Michigan State), Linsey DeVries (Grand Valley State), Audrey Enters (Calvin), Becky Jen (Calvin), Kelsey Kaemingk (Calvin), Taylor Kemmeter (Hillsdale), Lauren Niswonger (Michigan State), Cassie Shultz (Calvin), Samantha Vandenberg (Calvin), and Peter Vogel (Calvin). Thank you to professors Don Hettinga and Dean Ward of Calvin College for recommending so many top-notch students for the joint Zondervan-Calvin student-internship program. And thank you too to professor Cheryl Forbes (Hobart and Smith), who, as a onetime associate publisher at Zondervan, initiated this program nearly thirty years ago.

Thank you to these individuals who made significant contributions:

Managing editors Kari Moore and Merideth Bliss; editorial coordinators Carly Crookston, Janelle DeBlaay, and Paige Raabe; and editorial assistant Estee Zandee.

Author-care managers Joyce Ondersma and Jackie Aldridge.

Senior directors of production at HCCP, Randy Bishop and Dean Nelson.

Bob Buller, editor of *The SBL Handbook of Style, 2nd Edition.*

Shelley Townsend-Hudson, coeditor of the second edition of this manual, and Abbie Townsend Hudson.

Former Zondervan web content coordinator and information architect Deborah Leiter Nyabuti.

Freelance editor Shauna L. Perez; and Annette Gysen, editor at Reformation Heritage Books.

Judith Markham, formerly of Zondervan, Blue Water Ink, and Discovery House, continues to be a mentor and inspiration to many; her attention to detail and passion for good writing is present on every page of this manual.

Thank you to the hundreds of authors who have worked with Zondervan through the years and who have prompted their editors to track down the answers to the many editorial questions they—and their excellent manuscripts—posed.

An emphatic thank-you to Brian Phipps, a wise and engaging editor, poet, writer, listener, and friend.

Special gratitude to Jim Ruark, who not only wrote the original *Zondervan Manual of Style* but oversaw the editing of this edition as well. He expertly guided this book through the editing, proofreading, and production stages.

Special thanks also to Stan Gundry, who, as academic publisher and vice president of publishing operations, consistently championed this reference.

And finally, thank you to acquiring editor Madison Trammel, who waded through all this material with patience and insight. He is an editor's editor.

References Consulted

Anderson, Laura Killen. *McGraw-Hill's Proofreading Handbook*, 2nd ed. New York: McGraw-Hill, 2006.

Baig, Barbara. *Spellbinding Sentences: A Writer's Guide to Achieving Excellence and Captivating Readers*. Cincinnati: Writer's Digest Books, 2015.

Bernstein, Theodore M. *The Careful Writer: A Modern Guide to English Usage*. New York: Atheneum, 1965.

———. *Dos, Don'ts and Maybes of English Usage*. New York: Times Books, 1977.

———. *Miss Thistlebottom's Hobgoblins: The Careful Writer's Guide to the Taboos, Bugbears and Outmoded Rules of English Usage*. New York: Farrar, Straus & Giroux, 1971.

Brians, Paul. *Common Errors in English Usage*, 3rd ed. Sherwood, Ore.: William, James, 2013.

Bryson, Bill. *Bryson's Dictionary of Troublesome Words: A Writer's Guide to Getting It Right*. New York: Broadway, 2002.

Catholic News Service. *Stylebook on Religion 2000*. Washington, D.C.: Catholic News Service, 2000.

Cook, Bruce, and Harold Martin. *UPI Stylebook and Guide to Newswriting*, 4th ed. Sterling, Va.: Capital Books, 2004.

Crystal, David. *Begat: The King James Bible and the English Language*. Oxford: Oxford University Press, 2010.

———. *Making a Point: The Persnickety Story of English Punctuation*. New York: St. Martin's, 2015.

———. *Spell It Out: The Curious, Enthralling and Extraordinary Story of English Spelling*. New York: St. Martin's, 2013.

———. *The Story of English in 100 Words*. New York: St. Martin's, 2011.

Davidson, Mark. *Right, Wrong, and Risky: A Dictionary of Today's American English Usage*. New York: Norton, 2006.

Dunham, Steve. *The Editor's Companion: An Indispensable Guide to Editing Books, Magazines, Online Publications, and More*. Cincinnati: Writer's Digest Books, 2014.

Evans, Bergen, and Cornella Evans. *A Dictionary of Contemporary American Usage*. New York: Random House, 1957.

Farnsworth, Ward. *Farnsworth's Classical English Rhetoric*. Boston: Godine, 2011.

Fowler, H. W. *A Dictionary of Modern English Usage*. Oxford: Clarendon Press, 1926.

———, and F. G. Fowler. *The King's English*, 3rd ed. Oxford: Oxford University Press, 1931.

Freeman, Jan. *Ambrose Bierce's "Write It Right": The Celebrated Cynic's Language Peeves Deciphered, Appraised, and Annotated for 21st-Century Readers*. New York: Walker, 2009.

Garfield, Simon. *Just My Type: A Book about Fonts*. New York: Gotham Books, 2011.

Garner, Bryan A. *Garner's Modern American Usage*, 3rd ed. Oxford and New York: Oxford University Press, 2009.

———. *The Oxford Dictionary of American Usage and Style*. Oxford: Oxford University Press, 2000.

Goldstein, Norm, ed. *Associated Press Stylebook*. New York: Basic Books, 2007.

Goss, Leonard G., and Carolyn Stanford Goss. *The Little Style Guide to Great Christian Writing and Publishing*. Nashville: Broadman & Holman, 2004.

Hale, Constance. *Sin and Syntax: How to Craft Wickedly Effective Prose*. New York: Broadway Books, 1999.

———. *Vex, Hex, Smash, Smooch: Let Verbs Power Your Writing*. New York: Norton, 2012.

Hale, Constance, and Jessie Scanlon. *Wired Style: Principles of English Usage in the Digital Age*. New York: Broadway Books, 1999.

Hall, Max. *An Embarrassment of Misprints*. Golden, Colo.: Fulcrum, 1995.

Hitchings, Henry. *Language Wars: A History of Proper English*. New York: Farrar, Straus and Giroux, 2011.

Houston, Keith. *Shady Characters: The Secret Life of Punctuation, Symbols and Other Typographical Marks*. New York: Norton, 2013.

Jacobs, Alan. *The Book of Common Prayer: A Biography*. Princeton, N.J.: Princeton University Press, 2013.

Kilian, Crawford. *Writing for the Web*, 4th ed. Bellingham, Wash.: Self-Counsel Press, 2009.

Klinkenborg, Verlyn. *Several Short Sentences about Writing*. New York: Vintage, 2012.

Lerner, Betsy. *The Forest for the Trees: An Editor's Advice to Writers*. New York: Riverhead Books, 2000.

McArthur, Tom, ed. *The Oxford Companion to the English Language*. Oxford: Oxford University Press, 1992.

Mennonite Publishing Network, Inc., Supplement to The Chicago Manual of Style. Scottdale, Pa.: Herald Press, 2006. http://www.heraldpress.com/pdf/0410_mpn_manual_of_style.pdf.

Merton, Thomas. *Echoing Silence: Thomas Merton on the Vocation of Writing*. Ed. Robert Inchausti. Boston: New Seeds, 2007.

Morris, William, and Mary Morris. *Harper Dictionary of Contemporary Usage*, 2nd ed. New York: Harper & Row, 1985.

Nunberg, Geoffrey. *Going Nucular: Language, Politics, and Culture in Confrontational Times*. New York: Public Affairs, 2004.

———. *The Way We Talk Now*. Boston: Houghton Mifflin, 2001.

———. *The Years of Talking Dangerously*. New York: Public Affairs, 2009.

O'Conner, Patricia, and Stewart Kellerman. *Origin of the Specious: Myths and Misconceptions of the English Language*. New York: Random House, 2009.

Plotnik, Arthur. *Spunk and Bite: A Writer's Guide to Punchier, More Engaging Language and Style*. New York: Random House, 2005.

Rabiner, Susan, and Alfred Fortunato. *Thinking like Your Editor: How to Write Great Serious Nonfiction—and Get It Published*. New York: Norton, 2002.

Ritter, R. M. *The Oxford Style Manual*. Oxford: Oxford University Press, 2003.

Rosendorf, Theo. *The Typographic Desk Reference*. New Castle, Del.: Oak Knoll, 2016.

Saller, Carol Fisher. *The Subversive Copy Editor*. Chicago: University of Chicago Press, 2009.

The SBL Handbook of Style: for Biblical Studies and Related Disciplines, 2nd ed. Atlanta: SBL Press, 2014.

Schur, Norman W. *British English A to Zed: A Definitive Guide to the Queen's English*. New York: Skyhorse Publishing, 2013.

Siegal, Allan M., and William G. Connolly. *The New York Times Manual of Style and Usage*, 5th ed. New York: Three Rivers Press, 2015.

Strong, William S. *The Copyright Book: A Practical Guide*, 6th ed. Cambridge, Mass.: MIT Press, 2014.

Stuart, Sally E. *The Writing World Defined A to Z*. Friendswood, Tex.: Bold Vision Books, 2014.

Trask, R. L. *Mind the Gaffe! A Troubleshooter's Guide to English Style and Usage*. New York: HarperCollins, 2006.

U. S. Government Printing Office Style Manual. Washington, D.C.: U.S. Government Printing Office, 2008.

Walsh, Bill. *The Elephants of Style: A Trunkload of Tips on the Big Issues and Gray Areas of Contemporary American English*. New York: McGraw-Hill, 2004.

———. *Yes, I Could Care Less: How to Be a Language Snob without Being a Jerk*. New York: St. Martin's Griffin, 2013.

Zaid, Gabriel. *So Many Books*. Trans. Natasha Wimmer. London: Sort of Books, 2004.

Index

A

a, an, 400
abbot, abbess, abbé, 400
abbreviations
  academic degrees, 18, 32–33
  acronyms, 18
  agencies, 18, 20
  Bible, 331
  Bible books, 18, 21–24, 350–51
  Bible translations, 53–66
  Bible versions, 53–66
  biblical scholarship terms, 19
  book titles, 19
  civil titles, 20
  computer-related words, 18
  corporations, 18, 20
  famous people, 18, 20
  French forms of address, 18
  historical eras, 18
  initialisms, 18, 35–37
  internet-related words, 18
  Latin abbreviations, 307, 351
  measurements, 19
  mid-Atlantic style, 238
  military titles, 20
  notes, 252
  organizations, 18, 20
  periodical titles, 19
  periods, 18–19, 263
  personal initials, 18, 19, 20
  plurals, 19, 295
  provinces, 359–60
  punctuation, 18–19
  religious terms, 25–31
  reverend, 20
  Roman Catholic orders, 343–44
  scholarly abbreviations, 350
  scholarly terms, 31–32
  specific abbreviations, 21
  states, 359–60
  in text, 19
  titles, 20, 25–31
  UK style, 19, 381
  verse/verses, 332
  web style, 19
ABC's, ABCs, 401
abiblical, 401, 524–25
above, below, 401
Abrahamic, Abramic, 401
AC (ante Christum), 413
academic degrees, 18, 32–33
a cappella, 401
accent marks, 150–52, 184–85
accident, 401
acknowledgments, 34–35, 50, 186
acronyms, 18, 35–37
AD (anno Domini), 25, 178, 350, 369, 401, 416–18
Adam's apple, 401
ad card, 48–49, 186
addresses
  publisher addresses, 39, 385–86
  street addresses, 37–38, 256
  web addresses, 38–39
adherent, 402
adjectives
  adjectival phrases, 40, 325
  adverb-adjective combination, 40
  capitalization, 94–97
  comma, 133
  compound adjectives, 40, 201–2
  multiple adjectives, 40
  from personal names, 283–85
  quotation marks, 325
Advent, advent, 402
adverbs
  adverb-adjective combination, 40
  adverbial doubles, 41
  adverbial phrases, 132–33
  capitalization, 89
  headings, 89
  transitional adverbs, 352–53
ae, 402
Afghan, afghan, afghani, 402–3
African American, 403, 423
afterword, 41–42, 49–50
agnostic, atheist, 403
AH (anno Hegirae), 25, 211–12, 370
air force, 403, 412
alleluia, hallelujah, 207, 403, 480–81
All Hallows' Eve, Halloween, Hallowe'en, 481
all right, alright, 403–4
"all rights reserved" notice, 42
All Saints' Day, 404
All Souls' Day, 404
Almighty, almighty, 404
alms, 404
alphabet
phonetic alphabets, 242, 288–89

spelling out letters, 231
alphabetization
articles, 43
letter-for-letter, 42
personal names, 43
pronouns, 43
word-for-word, 42–43
alpha bravo communications code, 242, 288–89
al-Qaeda, 404
altar, 405
although, though, 405
although, while, 590
a.m., 18, 21, 405–6
amen, 207, 406–7
amendments, 407
amid, amidst, 407
Amish style, 292
amoral, immoral, 407, 496
ampersand, 44–45
Anabaptist, Anabaptism, 407–8
anachronisms, 45–47
ancient Palestine, 533
and/or, 408
angel, 408
Anglican Bible, 72
Anglican Church, 408, 436
Anglo-Catholic, 408
Annunciation, annunciation, 408
Antichrist, antichrist, 409
anti-Christian, 409
anticommunist, 409
anti-Semite, anti-Semitic, anti-Semitism, 409
anymore, any more, 409
A-OK, 409
Apocrypha, apocryphal, 71, 410
apostate, 410
Apostle, apostle, 410
apostle, disciple, 453
apostles, twelve, 410–11
Apostles' Creed, 410
Apostolic Fathers, apostolic fathers, 411
apostrophe, 46, 297
appendix, 46, 50
appositives, 131
arabic numeral, 411
archaisms, 46–47
archbishop, 96, 411–12
archdeacon, 412
Arche, L', 412
areligious, 498
arm's length, 412
army, 412
articles, 43
artwork, 235
AS (anno Salutis), 413
as, like, 508–9
ascension, 413
ascetic, ascetical, 413
Asia, Asian, 413
asterisk, 47
asterisms, 47, 154, 367
atheist, agnostic, 403
audio books, 48, 305–14
aureole, 413
author biography, 48, 50
author card, 48–49, 186
author guidelines, 235–36. *See also* manuscripts
author index, 50, 149, 204. *See also* indexes
author inscription, 49
author note, 49, 50
author signature, 49
auxiliary bishop, 414
a while, awhile, 414
aye, 415

B

Baal, Ba'al, 415
baby boomer, 415
baby Jesus, 415
back matter, 41, 48–50, 135
back slash, 357, 378, 392
bacteria, bacterium, 415
bah, humbug, 415
banns of marriage, 415–16
baptism, 419
baptismal name, 416
barista, 416
bated breath, 416
BC (before Christ), 26, 350, 369, 416–17
BCE (before Common Era), 26, 350, 369–70, 417–18
Beast, 418
Beatitudes, beatitude, 419
because, since, 561
Beelzebul, Beelzebub, 419
believer, 419
believers baptism, 419–20
beloved, belovèd, 419–20
below, above, 401
benediction, Benedictus, 420
Benjamite, Benjaminite, 420
bestseller, bestselling, 420
Bethlehem, star of, 564
bi-, semi-, 423
Bible. *See also* Bible versions
abbreviations, 18, 21–24, 53–66, 331
"a"/"b"/"c" system, 332
Anglican Bible, 72
Apocrypha, 71, 410
block quotations, 332
Book of Mormon, 72
books of, 18, 21–24, 97, 331, 350–51
capitalization, 97–98, 421
Catholic Bible, 71
citations, 330–36
copyright page, 330
defining, 69–73
dialogue, 331
Eastern Orthodox Bible, 72
epithets, 96
familiar phrases, 333–34
Greek Old Testament, 70–71
Hebrew Bible, 70
Holy Bible, 488
Jehovah's Witness Bible, 73
Jewish Bible, 70
ligatures, 232, 336
Muslim Bible, 72
names for, 50–51

New Testament, 72, 528–29
Old Testament, 70–71, 528–29
online versions, 52–53
paper quality, 51
paragraphing, 335
paraphrases, 331
parts of, 97–98
permissions, 267–83
poetry, 336
portions of, 51
preferences, 69
pronunciation marks, 335
proper names, 335–36
Protestant Bible, 71–72
quoting, 236, 330–36
Qur'an, 72, 548
red-letter editions, 55, 123, 341–42
referencing, 330–36, 353, 421
Scripture and, 421
semicolon, 353
Septuagint, 70–71
Torah, 72
translations, 53–66, 331
verse numbers, 335
Vulgate, 71, 587
Bible Belt, 420
Bible study, 122, 421
Bible-thumper, Bible-thumping, 421
Bible translations, 53–66
Bible verses, citing, 127, 236, 330–36
Bible versions
abbreviations, 53–66
capitalization, 97
English, 55–64
italicized titles, 216
notorious versions, 66–68
online versions, 52–53
other languages, 64–66
permissions, 267–81
preferences, 69
quoting, 330–31
spellings, 225–26
types of, 52–69, 225–26, 242–43
verb endings, 226–27
biblical, 421
biblical eras, 98
biblical events, 98
biblical hours, 195–96
biblical objects, 98
biblical scholarship terms, 19
biblical studies, Bible study, 421–22
biblical terms, 95–114
Biblicism, Biblicist, 422
bibliography
alphabetizing, 73
citations, 73–74, 245–46
compiling, 73
design, 76
"For Further Reading" lists, 76
multi-author works, 73
periodical citations, 74
placement, 50
proper names, 73
publisher names, 74
software citations, 75
web access dates, 75
webpage citations, 75
bibliolatry, bibliolater, 422
bibliomancy, 422
bio, 48, 50
bishop, 96, 423
black (racial designation), 403, 423
Black Death, 424
Blessed, blessed, blessèd, 424
Blessed Sacrament, 424
blogs
copyright, 78
editing, 76
emoji, 78
emoticon, 78
emphasis, 77–78
fair use, 78
permissions, 78
posts, 424
punctuation, 78
references, 78
repetition, 77
strike throughs, 78
structure, 77
style, 76–79
tone, 77
transitions, 77
web shorthand, 78
blond, 425
blurbs, 166. *See also* endorsements
Body and Blood, 425
body coverings, 193–94
body matter, 79
boldface type, 80
Book, the, 425, 488
book citations, 73–74
book of . . ., 425
Book of Common Prayer, 425
book of hours, 122
Book of Mormon, 72
books. *See also* books, elements of
acknowledgments, 34–35, 50, 186
audio books, 48, 305–14
of Bible, 18, 21–24, 97, 331, 350–51
bibliography, 50, 73–76
blogs into, 76–79
cataloging-in-publication, 115–16
chapters, 116–17
children's books, 118–20
Christian books, 122–23
CIP data, 115–16, 210
coauthored books, 116, 144
concordances, 135–36
contents page, 186, 366
copyright page, 39, 42, 138–41
cover copy, 142
disclaimers, 156–57
endsheets, 168
epigraph, 168, 186
epilogue, 169

flyleaf, 177
folios, 117, 177, 341
footers, 177, 347–48
frontispiece, 185
ISBN, 116, 140, 210
large-print, 228–30
lists, 186
mid-Atlantic style, 237–39
notes, 245–52
omnibus edition, 258
out of print titles, 49
parts of, 94–95, 255
presentation page, 301
promotional page, 305
recto pages, 341
reprints, 116, 210
running heads, 117, 347–48
series, 210
style, 237–39
table of contents, 186, 366
title pages, 186, 193
titles, 142, 253, 347
trim sizes, 375
types of, 118–23, 147–48
verso pages, 341
books, elements of
acknowledgments, 34–35, 50, 186
afterword, 41–42, 49–50
back matter, 41, 48–50, 135
body matter, 79
conclusion, 50, 135
cover copy, 142
dedication page, 120, 144, 186
epilogue, 50, 169
foreword, 184, 186
front matter, 185–86
glossary, 50
introduction, 186, 211
preface, 186, 299–300
prologue, 186, 305
books of Bible, 18, 21–24, 97, 331, 350–51
born again, born-again, 425–26
both ... and, 426
boy, 426
braces, 80
brackets, 80–81, 334
brand names
capitalization, 81–82, 94
common brands, 82–84
generic equivalents, 82–84
nouns, 82
spelling, 85–86
verbs, 82
brethren, 426
Briticism, Britishism, 426
British Isles, 426, 583–84
Brother, brother, 426–27
brunet, 425, 427
bulrush, 427
buttons (keys), 87
by and by, by-and-by, 427
bye, 427, 475
byline, 33, 168

C

cabala, Kabbalah, 503
cadence, 238
calendars, 123–25, 211–13
call, calling, 428
callous, callus, 428
Cambridge, University of, 532
cancer stages, 564
Canon, canon, 428, 429
canoness, 429
Canonical, canonical, 429
canonical hours, 196–97
Canticles, 429
capitalization
adjectives, 94–97
adverbs, 89
biblical eras, 98
biblical events, 98
biblical objects, 98
biblical terms, 95–114
book parts, 94–95
books of Bible, 97
brand names, 81–82, 94
colloquial terms, 89
colons, 89–90, 128
deities, 95, 144–47, 450
denominations, 99
devotionals, 149
drop cap, 117
epithets, 96
eras, 92–93, 98–99, 241
ethnic designations, 90
family relationships, 94
governmental bodies, 92
guidelines, 88–95
headings, 88–89
heaven, 100–101
hell, 100–101
historical eras, 98–99, 241
historic documents, 99
hyphenated compounds, 89
midcaps, 239
organizations, 91–92
particles with names, 90–91
personal titles, 91, 128
personification, 93
place names, 93–94, 99–100
places of worship, 99–100
political organizations, 92
proper names, 90–91, 94–96
racial designations, 90
religious groups, 100
religious movements, 100
religious observances, 99
religious terms, 95–114
religious titles, 96
rites, 99
sacraments, 99
sacred objects, 98
Satan, 96
small caps, 355
Southernisms, 89
standing cap, 117
terms of endearment, 94, 367
thought systems, 93

titles, 88–89, 96
trinity names, 95
vocabulary, 88
captions, 114–15, 263
carat, karat, caret, 429
cardinal, 429–30
cardinal virtues, 470
carol, 200, 430
catalog, catalogue, 430
cataloging-in-publication (CIP)
accuracy, 115
changes, 115
coauthored books, 116
contact information, 116
ISBN, 210
placement, 115
reprints, 116
catechism, 430
Catholic, catholic, 430
Catholic Bible, 71
CAT scan, 431
CBA (Association for Christian Retail), 431
CE (Common Era), 15, 26, 212, 350, 369–70, 417–18
celebrant, 431
Celestial City, 431
celibate, chaste, chastity, 431–32
cell phone, 432
cell phone numbers, 256, 287–88
cenobite, hermit, 486
censer, censor, censure, 432
century, 432
Chanukah, Hanukkah, Hanukah, 481
chaplain, chaplaincy, 432
chapters
epigraph, 168
folios, 117
numbers, 117
openers, 116–17
quotations, 117
running heads, 117, 347–48
text, 117
titles, 117
charismatic, 432
chaste, chastity, celibate, 431–32
cherub, cherubs, 433
cherubim, cherubims, 433
children's books. *See also* books
age ranges, 119–20
cadet edition, 120
copyright page, 120
dedication page, 120
format, 118
justification, 118
lengths, 119–20
letter spacing, 118
margins, 119
page ranges, 119–20
paragraphing, 118–19
style, 118
type face, 118
type size, 118
types of, 119–20
word breaks, 118
word count, 119–20
word spacing, 118
Chinese transliteration, 120–22
chrish, 433
chrismation, 433
Christ, Jesus, 433, 435
Christ, name of, 522
Christendom, Christianity, 433–34
Christ follower, 434
Christian books. *See also* books
Bible studies, 122, 421
book of hours, 122
clerical novel, 122
commentary, 122
concordances, 122, 135–36
devotionals, 122–23, 147–48
end-times novel, 123
genre fiction, 122, 191
hagiography, 123
illuminated manuscripts, 123
lectionary, 123
martyrology, 123
novels, 122–23
red-letter Bible, 55, 123, 341–42
saints' lives, 123
spiritual thriller, 123
types of, 122–23, 147–48
Christian feasts, 123–26
Christian holidays, 123–26
Christianism, Christianist, 434
Christianity, Christendom, 433–34
Christianize, Christianization, 434
Christian name, 434
Christlike, Christlikeness, 435
Christmas, 124, 594
Christmas carol, 200, 430
Christo-, christo-, 435
chronological tables, 50
Church, church, 435–36
church fathers, 436, 467
churchgoer, churchgoing, 436
churchianity, 436
Church of England, 408, 436
Church of Jesus Christ of Latter-day Saints (LDS Church), 506
circa, 436–37
citations. *See also* notes
Bible verses, 127, 236, 330–36
bibliography, 73–74, 245–46
book citations, 73–74
"For Further Reading" lists, 76
periodical citations, 74
software citations, 75
source notes, 245–46, 266
web access dates, 75

webpage citations, 75
city names, 127
civil titles, 20
clauses, 130–32
cleave, 437
clergy, 437
clerical novel, 122
clerical positions, 128, 438
clerical titles, 20, 128, 438, 540–41, 551–52
coauthored books, 116, 144
coauthors, cowriters, 438, 444
coheirs, co-heirs, 438
coliseum, Colosseum, 438
collect, 438
colloquial terms, 89
colon. *See also* semicolon
capitalization after, 89–90, 129
direct quotations, 129
lists, 129
quotations, 128, 129
Scripture references, 129, 332–33
titles/subtitles, 129
volume/page numbers, 129
colophon, 130
Colosseum, 438
come-to-Jesus meeting, 439
comma
adjectives, 133
adverbial phrases, 132–33
ampersand with, 44
appositives, 131
clauses, 131, 132
coordinating conjunctions, 130–31
dependent clauses, 132
disruptions, 133
drama comma, 135
expressions, 132
with "Jr.," 134
numerals, 133, 134, 257
with "oh," 133
Oxford comma, 132, 380
quotations, 133
restrictive clauses, 131
sayings, 133
serial comma, 44, 132, 135, 380
with "Sr.," 134
with "too," 133
verbs, 135
commandments, 439
commentary, 122
Common Era, 439
common sense, common-sense, 439
commonwealths, 565
Communion, 439, 489
Communism, communism, 439
Communist, communist, 439
completed Jew, 439
compose, comprise, 440
compound adjectives, 40, 201–2
compound sentences, 130, 352
compound words, 192, 300, 314
comprise, compose, consist of, 440
computer-related words, 18
conclusion, 50, 135
concordances, 122, 135–36
confession, 440
Congo, 441
congregant, 441
Congress, congressional, 441
conjunctions, 130–31, 260
conservative, 441–42
Constitution, constitutional, 442
contents page, 186, 366
continual, continuous, 442
contractions, 46, 136–37
contributors list, 50
convert, conversion, 442
convict, to, 442
copastor, 442
copyedit, copyeditor, 39, 160, 442
copyright dates, 78, 138, 139
copyright holder, 138, 265
copyright notice, 138–40
Copyright Office, 116
copyright page
"all rights reserved" notice, 42
Bible, 330
children's books, 120
copyright dates, 138, 139
copyright holder, 138, 265
copyright notice, 138–40
country-of-printing notice, 120, 140, 141–42
ISBN, 140
legal notice, 138–39, 140
placement, 139, 141, 186
publication date, 397–98
publisher addresses, 39
corporal, corporeal, 443
corporations, 18, 20
Counter-Reformation, 443
country-of-printing notice, 120, 140, 141–42
couple, 443
court, Supreme Court, 444
covenant, old or new, 444
cover copy, 142
coverings, 193–94
cowriters, coauthors, 438, 444
creation, 444
Creator, creator, 444
crèche, 444
credit line, 266
crosier, 444
cross, stations of, 565
cross, the, 444
cross, way of, 565
cross-references, 80, 205
crossroad, crossroads, 445
crucifix, 445
crucifixion, resurrection, 445, 551
crusade, crusades, 445–46
cult, 446
cultural equivalents, 44
curate, 446
cursed, cursèd, 446
cyber, 447

D

D-Day, 449
Daesh, 448
Dalai Lama, 448
damn, damned, 448
Dark Ages, 448–49
dashes, 143, 162–66, 238, 333, 365, 380
dates
  elided ranges, 252–53
  eras, 369
  inclusive ranges, 252–53
  mid-Atlantic style, 238
  solidus in, 357
  spelling, 238
  systems, 370–71
  in text, 370
  time of day, 368
  UK style, 238, 382
  year dates, 252, 350, 369
David, Star of, 564
days of week, 369
deacon, 449
dead copy, 143
deadly sins, 560
Dead Sea scroll, Dead Sea Scrolls, 449
dean, 449
death dagger, 143
debts, 579–80
Decalogue, 450
decimate, 450
dedication
  coauthored books, 144
  placement, 120, 144, 186
  style, 144
dee-jay, 454
definitions in text, 144
defrock, 450
Dei gratia, Deo gratias, 451
deism, deist, 450, 573
deities
  capitalization, 95, 144–47, 450
  mixed styles, 146
  pronouns, 144–47
  quotations, 147
  style, 144–47
Democrat, democrat, democratic, 451
demonyms, 360–61
denominations, 99
Deo gratias, Dei gratia, 451
dependent clauses, 132
desert, dessert, 451
Deus, deus, 451
deuterocanonical books, 452
Devil, devil, 452
devotional books
  design, 149
  elements of, 122–23, 147–48
  format, 149
  indexes, 149
  types of, 148
devotional caps, 149
devotional contexts, 150
devout, 452
devout Catholic, 452
diacritical marks, 150–52, 184–85
dialogue
  Bible, 331
  disembodied voices, 157–58
  fiction, 152–53
  interrupted dialogue, 153
  numbers, 255
  paragraphing, 260–61
  saying words slowly, 153
  slang dialogue, 153–54
  spelling, 452
Diaspora, diaspora, 453
different, 453
different from, different than, 453
dimensions, 237
dingbat, 154
dis, 453
disability designations, 155–56
disc, disk, 453
disciple, apostle, 453
disclaimers, 156–57, 189
discreet, discrete, 454
diseases, 365
disorders, 365
ditto mark, 158
dive, dived, 454
Dives, 454
divine, divinity, 454
Divine Office, 122, 196, 527
DJ, 454
doctor of the church, 454–55
dogma, 455
Dome of the Rock, 455
dos and don'ts, 455
dot-com, 158
dots, 158
double-check, double check, 455
double-click, double click, 455
double space, 357
double standards, 188
Down syndrome, 455
Doxology, doxology, 456
drama comma, 135
dream sequences, 218
drop cap, 117
drop folio, 117, 177
dummy copy, 158

E

each other's, 457
Earth, earth, 457
Easter, Easter Sunday, 457
Eastern Orthodox, Orthodox, 457
Eastern Orthodox Bible, 72
Eastern Rites, Western Rites, 458
ebook, 458
Ecclesial Latin, 306
Ecclesiastes, Ecclesiasticus, 458
ecclesiastical, ecclesiastic, ecclesial, 458
e-church, 458–59
E. coli, 459
e-compounds, 159
ecumenical, 459
editing tips, 38–39, 159–61

e.g., i.e., 459, 496
either … or, neither … nor, 460
eke, eek, 460
Elder, elder, 460
electronic devices, 87
elegy, eulogy, 460
Eleven, the, 460
eleven disciples, 460
elided numbers, 252–53
ellipses, 161–62, 334, 364, 381
email, 460–61
em dash, 143, 162–64, 238, 365, 380
emergency phone numbers, 288
emergent church, emerging church, 461
Emmanuel, Immanuel, Emanuel, 461, 496
emoji, 78, 165
emoticon, 78, 165
empathic, empathetic, 461
emphasis
blogs, 77–78
italicized words, 217
quotation marks, 324
Empire, empire, 462
en dash, 143, 165–66, 238, 333, 380
endnotes, 245–51. *See also* notes
endorsements, 166–68
endpapers, 168
endsheets, 168
end stop, 173, 263, 321
end times, 462
end-times novel, 123
England, 462, 583–84
English Bible, 55–64
ensure, insure, 462
epigraph, 168–69, 186
epilogue, 50, 169
Episcopal, episcopal, 462
Episcopalian, 462
Episcopalianism, episcopalism, 462
Epistle, epistle, 463
epithets
capitalization, 96
lowercases, 243–44
vulgar epithets, 303
eras
capitalization, 92–93, 98–99, 241
dates, 369
historical eras, 18, 98–99, 241, 252, 350
periods, 536
errata, 170, 186
etc., 463
ethics, 463
ethnic designations, 90, 170–72
ethnic self-identification, 170–71
Eucharist, eucharistic, 463
eulogy, elegy, 460
euphemisms, 240, 303
evangel, evangelical, evangelicalism, 463–64
Evangelist, evangelist, 464
evangelistic, evangelical, 464
evangelize, 464
evildoer, evildoing, evil-minded, 464
ex- (prefix), 464–65
examine, examen, 465
exclamation point, 173
Exodus, exodus, 465
expatriate, 465
explicit, 173
expressions, 132, 207–9
extrabiblical, 465, 524–25
extracts, 327
extreme unction, 465
ezine, 465

F

fair use, 78, 174–75
faith, 466
fall, the, 466
family relationships, 94, 175–76
famous people, 18, 20
fanning, 224
farther, further, 466
Father, father, 466
fathers of the church, 436, 467
feasts, 123–26, 221, 298
fellowship, to, 467
Festschrift, 468
fiancé, fiancée, 468
fiction
brand names, 82
dialogue, 152–53
dream sequences, 218
flashbacks, 218
genre fiction, 122, 191
narrative devices, 218
novels, 122–23
film rights, 137, 364
First Estate, 470
first husband, first gentleman, 468
first lady, First Lady, 468, 540
first person, 176–77
flak, 468
flannelgraph, 468
flashbacks, 218
Flesch-Kincaid reading formula, 340
flood, the, 468
FLOTUS (first lady of the United States), 540
flounder, founder, 469, 470
flyleaf, 177
folios, 117, 177, 341
font, typeface, 118, 337–38, 581
foolhardy, 469
footers, 177, 347–48
footnotes, 178, 239, 245–52, 382. *See also* notes
footwashing, 469
forego, forgo, 469
foreign quotation marks, 325
foreign words/phrases, 178–84, 217
forever, for ever, 469
forevermore, for ever and ever, 469

foreword, 184, 186
"For Further Reading" lists, 76
Fortune 500, 469
forward slash, 356–57, 378
fouls, 143
founder, flounder, 469, 470
Founding Fathers, founding fathers, 470
four cardinal virtues, 470
Fourth Estate, 470
frack, fracked, fracking, 470–71
fractions, 237
free speech, 407
freewill, free will, 471
free world, 471
French forms of address, 18
French style, 184–85
frontispiece, 185
front matter, 185–86
fundamentalism, fundamentalist, 471–72

G

galleys, 143
garden, 473
gay, 508
gehenna, 473
gender-accurate language, 187–90, 579
gender bias, 236
gender self-identification, 190–91
general market, 473
general secretary, 558
generational categories, 191
generic names, 82–84
genre fiction, 122, 191. *See also* fiction
gentile, 473
geographic location, 360–61
gerunds, 298
ghost words, 306
gibe, jibe, jive, 501–2
girl, 473
glossary, 50
Gnostic, gnostic, 474
God
- capitalization, 334–35, 376, 474, 510–11
- compounds, 192
- name of, 522
- pronouns, 144–46
- usage, 474
- word of, 474, 593

Godhead, godhead, 474
God's Word, God's word, 474, 593
golden age, 474
Golden Rule, 474–75
Good Book, 475
goodbye, good-bye, goodby, good-by, 427, 475
good ol' boy, good old boy, 475
Good Samaritan, Good Sam, 475
goodwill, 475
Goody Two-Shoes, 476
Google, google, 476
Gospel, gospel, 97–98, 476
gospeler, 477
gospel side, 476
Gothic, gothic, 477
governmental bodies, 92
grades, 230
grawlix, 192
gray, grey, 477
great (family relationships), 477
Great Britain, 477, 583–84
Great Commission, 477
great Scott, 477
Greek Old Testament, 70–71
green card, 477
greetings/partings, 207, 210
guilt, 478
Gunning "FOG" readability test, 340
Gypsy, gypsy, 478

H

Hades, hades, 479, 483
Hagiographa, hagiography, 479
hagiography, 123
Hail Mary, 479–80
half (family relationships), 480
half-mast, half-staff, 480
half-title page, 193, 206, 352
hallelujah, alleluia, 207, 403, 480–81
hallowed, hallowèd, 481
Halloween, Hallowe'en, All Hallows' Eve, 481
halo, 481
hanged, hung, 481
Hanukkah, Chanukah, Hanukah, 481
hard copy, 193
hate speech, 303
havoc, to wreak, 481
He, he, 481
head coverings, 193–94
headings
- adverbs, 89
- boldface type, 80
- capitalization, 88–89
- endnotes, 247
- hyphenated compounds, 89
- levels, 194–95
- spacing, 195
- subheadings, 194–95

healthcare, 482
hear, hear, 482
Heaven, heaven, 100–101, 482
heavenlies, 482
heavenly host, 482–83
Hebrew, Yiddish, 483
Hebrew Bible, 70
Hebrews, Jews, 483
Hebrew Scriptures, 70
hell, 100–101, 479, 483
helpmate, helpmeet, 484
her, she, 484, 561
heresy, schism, 484–86
hermit, cenobite, 486
hidden endnotes, 247–48
High Church, high church, 486
High Holy Days, 487

High Mass, 514–15
Him, him, 481
Hispanic, 487
historic, historical, 487
historical eras, 18, 98–99, 241, 252, 350
historic documents, 99
HIV/AIDS, 487
holidays, 123–26, 221
holier-than-thou, 487
Holocaust, holocaust, 488
Holy Bible, 488. *See also* Bible
Holy Book, 425, 488
Holy City, 488–89
Holy Communion, 439, 489
holy day of obligation, 489
Holy Days, 487
holy exchange of gifts, 489
holy family, 489
Holy Father, 489
Holy Ghost, 376, 489–92
Holy Grail, 490
Holy Joe, 490
Holy Land, 490
holy of holies, 491
holy orders, 491
Holy Roller, 491
Holy Saturday, 491
holy seasons, 123–26
Holy Spirit, 376, 489–92
Holy Thursday, 492
Holy Trinity, 492
holy war, 492
holy water, 492
Holy Week, 492
Holy Word, holy word, 492–93
Holy Writ, 493
homeschool, homeschooler, 493
horde, hoard, 493
hosanna, hosannah, 207, 493
Host, host, 494
hours, biblical, 195–96
hours, book of, 122
hours, canonical, 196–97
House of Representatives, the House, 494
however, 494
humankind, 494
Humvee, 494
hymnbook, hymnal, 494
hymns
  centering, 328–29
  diacritical marks, 152
  indenting, 328
  meters, 197–99
  texts, 200
  titles, 200
hyphens
  compound adjectives, 201–2
  dashes, 143
  headings, 89
  hyphenated compounds, 89
  noun pairs, 201–2
  prefixes, 201, 300–301, 381
  suffixes, 201
  word divisions, 200–201

I

I Am, 495
ibid., 251, 495
ichthus, ichthys, 495
ID, 495
i.e., e.g., 459, 496
illuminated manuscripts, 123. *See also* manuscripts
immaculate conception, virgin birth, 496, 587
Immanuel, Emmanuel, Emanuel, 461, 496
immoral, amoral, 407, 496
imposition, 354
imprimatur, 203
inclusive language, 187–90
inclusive numbers, 252–53
indexes
  author index, 50, 149, 204
  cross-references, 205
  devotional books, 149
  placement, 50
  preparing, 203–4
  proper-name index, 50, 149, 204
  Scripture index, 50, 149, 205–6
  style, 204–5
  subentries, 204–5
  subject index, 50, 149, 204
in fact, 496
infant Jesus, 415
infinitives, 358
infinity, infinitude, 497
initialisms, 18, 35–37
initials, periods, 263
initials, personal, 18, 19, 20
Inklings, 497, 532
inner city, inner-city, 497
in order to, 497
inscription, author, 49
insensitive language, 236, 303–4
insure, ensure, 462
intensifiers, 206–7
interfaith, interdenominational, 497–98
interjections, 207–10, 233, 303
International Standard Book Number (ISBN), 116, 140, 210
internet, 498
internet-related words, 18
InterVarsity, Inter-Varsity, 498
introduction, 186, 211
irony, 324
irreligious, 498
ISIS, ISIL, 498–99
Islam, Islamic, Islamist, 499
Islamic terms, 211–13
Israeli, Israelite, 499
italic type, 213–16, 335, 499

J

jargon, religious, 219–20
Jehoshaphat, 500
Jehovah's Witness Bible, 73
Jehu, jehu, 500

jeremiad, 500
Jesus
capitalization, 376
events in life of, 172–73
pronouns, 144–46
usage, 433, 435
Jesus Christ, Christ Jesus, 433, 435
Jesus's, Jesus', 500–501
Jew, completed, 439
Jew, Jewish, 501
Jewish, Jew, 501
Jewish Bible, 70
Jewish feasts, 221
Jewish holidays, 221
Jewish rabbi, 501
Jewish terms, 222–24
Jews, Hebrews, 483
JHWH, YHWH, 596
jibe, jive, gibe, 501–2
jogging, 224
journals, 256
Jr., 134, 502
Judaism, 502
Judeo-Christian, 502
judgment, judgement, 502

K

Kabbalah, cabala, 503
karat, carat, caret, 429
Kilns, 503
kingdom, 503
King James Version (KJV). *See also* Bible versions
definition, 503
italicized words, 335
pronunciation marks, 335
spellings, 225–26
King of Kings, 503–4
Koran, Qur'an, 548
koranic, qur'anic, 548

L

L'Arche, 412
large-print books, 228–30
last days, 505
last judgment, 505
last rites, 505
Last Supper, 505
late (deceased person), 505
Latin abbreviations, 307, 351
Latin characters, 351
Latin plurals, 294
Latin pronunciations, 306–7
Latter-day Saints (LDS), 506
Law, law, 506
layity, 506
layperson, 506
lay position, 438, 506
leaped, leapt, 507
lectionary, 123
Lectionary, lectionary, 507
legal deposit, 234
legends, 263
Lent, Lenten, 507
leper, leprosy, 507
lesbian, 508
letter grades, 230
letters
of alphabet, 231
as letters, 230
as shapes, 231
spacing, 118
spelling out, 231
as words, 231
Levant, 507
LGBT, 508
liberal, 508
Libertarian, libertarian, 508
Library of Congress, 140
Library of Congress Control Number (LCCN), 231–32
ligatures, 232, 336
-like (suffix), 508
like, as, 508–9
limited edition, certificate of, 232
limit notice, 232
line spacing, 338, 339
lions' den, 509
lists
book lists, 186
colon with, 129
outlines, 258–59
period with, 263
source lists, 50, 73
Litany, litany, 509
literally, 509
liturgical interjections, 207, 233
liturgical year, 123–26
Liturgy, liturgy, liturgical, 510
live copy, 143
logo style, 233
long-suffering, 510
Lord, 334–35, 510–11
Lord giveth, the, 510
Lord of Lords, 503–4
Lord's Day, 512
lordship of Christ, 512
Lord's Prayer, 512
Lord's Supper, 512
Lord's Table, 512
"lorem ipsum" copy, 158
Low Church, low church, 486
Low Mass, 514–15

M

MacDonald, George, 513
Magdalen, Magdalene, 513
magi, 513
Major Prophets, major prophets, 544
Maker, the, 514
Mammon, mammon, 514
mandatory deposit, 234
mankind, 494
manuscripts
artwork, 235
author guidelines, 235
Bible quotations, 236
charts, 235
font, 235
format, 235
gender bias, 236
illuminated manuscripts, 123
insensitive language, 236
margins, 235
preparing, 235–36
quotation sources, 236
style, 235–36

submitting, 235
tables, 235
text breaks, 367
writing tips, 394–96
marines, 412
Mariology, Mariolatry, 514
marriage, banns of, 415–16
martyrology, 123
-mas (suffix), 514
Mass, mass, 514–15
matins, mattins, 515
May Day, Mayday, 515
measurements
abbreviations, 19
dimensions, 237
fractions, 237
numerals, 236–37, 255
Mecca, mecca, 515
media, medium, 515
medieval era, 448–49, 515
megachurch, 516
Mennonite style, 292
Messiah, messiah, 516
messiahship, 516
messianic, 516
metropolitan, 516
mic, mike, 516
mid- (prefix), 517
mid-Atlantic style, 237–39
midcaps, 239
middle age, middle-aged, 517
Middle Ages, 448–49, 517
midnight, 405–6
military titles, 20, 240
millennium, 517
minced oaths, 240–41, 303
mind-set, 517
minister, 518
Minor Prophets, minor prophets, 544
minus sign, 518
Miranda rights, to Mirandize, 518
mischievous, 518
misnaming, intentional, 241
mission, missions, 518–19
miter, 519
monsignor, monseigneur, 519
Mormon, 506
Mormon Church, 506
Mother Earth, Mother Nature, 519
Mother Superior, 400
Mount, 520
Mount Zion, 597
Muhammad, Mohammed, 520
multifaith, 520
Muslim, 520
Muslim Bible, 72
must-read, 520
myriad, 521
Mystical Supper, 521

N

Name, name of Christ, name of God, 522
names, 18–20, 283–87. *See also* personal names; proper names
namesake, 522
narrative devices, 218. *See also* fiction
narrative notes, 245. *See also* notes
national designations, 170–72
Native American, native American, 522
nativity, 522–23
NATO phonetic alphabet, 242, 288–89
navy, 412
neither … nor, either … or, 460
never-never land, Neverland, Neverlands, 523
New American Standard Bible (NASB), 335
New Atheism, New Atheists, 523
New International Version (NIV), 242–43
New Testament, 72, 528–29
New Year's Day, New Year's Eve, 523
nicknames, 325
Nine-Eleven, 9/11, 9-1-1, 523
Ninety-Five Theses, the, 523
Noah's ark, 412
Noel, 524
no less, no more, 524
nominal Christian, 524
non- (prefix), 524
nonbeliever, unbeliever, 403, 582
nonbiblical, unbiblical, 524–25
noncanonical, 525
non-Christian, unchristian, 582
nonclerical, 525
nonreligious, 498
noon, 405–6
note from author, 49, 50
notes
abbreviations, 252
author references, 249
bibliographic notes, 245–46
book references, 249
citations, 245–49, 252
citing in text, 247
endnotes, 245–51
footnotes, 178, 239, 382
headings, 247
hidden endnotes, 247–48
"ibid." usage, 251
narrative notes, 245
numbering, 247
page citations, 246, 248–49, 252
parenthetical notes, 246–47
periodical references, 250
placement, 50
publisher references, 249
scholarly style, 351
short-form references, 252
source notes, 245–46, 266
substantive notes, 245
superscript numbers, 247

symbol reference marks, 248
UK style, 382
website references, 250–51
nothing less, nothing more, 524
not only … but, 525–26
nouns, 82, 297, 299
novels, 122–23
number of, 526
numbers. *See also* numerals
age ranges, 256
cell phone numbers, 256, 287–88
dialogue, 255
elided numbers, 252–53
emergency number, 288
fictional phone numbers, 288
groups, 253
idiomatic expressions, 254–55
inclusive numbers, 252–53
journal style, 256
ordinal numbers, 253, 370
percentages, 254
periods, 263
phone numbers, 256, 287–88
route numbers, 256
sentences, 255
spelling out, 253–56
street addresses, 37–38, 256
UK style, 382–83
usage, 253–56
verse numbers, 335
webpage style, 256
numerals. *See also* numbers
commas, 133, 134, 257
groups, 253
measurements, 236–37, 255
money references, 255
ordinal numbers, 253, 370
percentages, 254
prefixes, 257
Roman numerals, 344–47, 553
solidus with, 357
spelling out, 253–56, 368
usage, 253–56

O

oaths, minced, 240–41, 303
Occupy movement, 527
offices, 527
Oh, O, 134, 385, 527–28
okay, OK, 528
ol', 528
Old City, 528
old-fashioned, 528
Old Testament, 70–71, 528–29
old times' sake, 529
Old World, New World, 529
-ology (suffix), 529–30
omnibus edition, 258
on accident, by accident, 530
One, the, 530
one another's, 457
online Bible, 52–53
online sources, quoting, 329–30
only begotten Son, 531
on the other hand, 531
oral, verbal, 586
ordinal numbers, 253, 370. *See also* numbers; numerals
organizations, 18, 20, 91–92
Oriental, 413
original sin, 531
orphans, typographic, 343, 387–88
Orthodox, Eastern Orthodox, 457
Our Father, 531
Our Lady, our Lady, 532
outlines, 258–59
out of print titles, 49
Oxford, University of, 532
Oxford comma, 132, 380

P

pages
citing, 246, 248–49, 252
counting, 260, 289
photo sections, 289
signatures, 354–55
palate, palette, pallet, pallette, 533
Palestine, Palestinian State, 533
papacy, 96
Parable, parable, 534
parachurch, 534
Paradise, paradise, 534
paragraphing, 260–61, 335
paraphrasing, 291, 331
parentheses, 261–62
parenthetical notes, 246–47. *See also* notes
Paschal, paschal, 534
passion (of Jesus), the, 534
Pastor, pastor, 535
past tenses, 262, 295–96
Patriarch, the, 535
patriarchs, the, 535
Paul, Saul, 535
pearly gates, 536
Pentecostal, Pentecostalism, 536
people, persons, 536
percent, 536
percentages, 254
performance symbol, 262–63
period, era, 536
periodical citations, 74
periodicals, 19, 249
periods
abbreviations, 18–19, 263
blogs, 78
captions, 263
initials, 263
legends, 263
lists, 263
numbers, 263
sentences, 263
usage, 263–64
permissions

Bible guidelines, 267–81
blogs, 78
to copy, 282–83, 386
general guidelines, 264–67
guidelines, 264–81
notices, 282–83, 386
reader reviews quotes, 282
permission-to-copy notice, 282–83, 386
personal initials, 18, 19, 20
personality types, 581
personal names
adjectives from, 283–85
alphabetization, 43
famous people, 18, 20
initials, 18, 19, 20
misspellings, 285–87
possessives, 297–98
sibilant endings, 297–98
personal titles, 20, 91, 128, 240
personification, 93
persons, people, 536
Pharaoh, pharaoh, 537
Pharisee, Pharisaic, Pharisaical, 537
Philistine, philistine, 537
phonetic alphabets, 242, 288–89
photo sections, 289
Photoshop, photoshop, 537
piety, 537–38
Pilgrims, Pilgrim Fathers, pilgrim, 538, 547
p-in-the-circle symbol, 262–63
pious, piousness, 537–38
pj's, 538
place names, 93–94, 99–100, 127
places of worship, 99–100
plagiarism, 289–91
Plain, plain (Amish), 538–39
Plain style, 292
playdate, 539
plays, 152
pluperfect, 295–96
plurals
abbreviations, 19, 295
apostrophe, 46
irregular plurals, 293–94
Latin plurals, 294
nouns, 82
proper names, 295
regular plurals, 292–93
singulars and, 294–95
p.m., 21, 405–6
podcast, 539
poetry
Bible poetry, 336
centering, 328–29
diacritical marks, 152
indenting, 328
quoting, 296–97
solidus in, 357
titles, 296
political correctness, 297
political organizations, 92
Pontiff, pontiff, 539
Pope, pope, 539–40
pore over, 540
possessives
apostrophe, 46, 297
collective possessives, 299
gerunds, 298
joint possessives, 298–99
nouns, 297, 299
personal names, 297–98
phrases, 299
sibilant endings, 297–98
postal service, 37–38
post-Christian, 541
postconversion, 540, 541
POTUS (president of the United States), 540
Powers-Sumner-Kearl reading formula, 340
prayer books, 123, 540
prayers in text, 299
Preacher, 540–41
preachify, 541
pre-Christian, 541
preconversion, 541
preface, 186, 299–300
prefixes, 201, 257, 300–301, 381
prepositions, 301
presentation page, 301
present writer, 541
President, president, presidential, 541–42
presiding bishop, 542
priest, 542
primate, 542
printer's ornament, 154
printing notice, 141–42
print runs, 232
prior to, previous to, 542–43
prodigal, 543
pro-family, 543
profanity, 192, 240–41, 301–5
profanitype, 192
pro-life, pro-choice, 543
prologue, 186, 305
Promised Land, promised land, 543
promotional page, 305
pronouns
alphabetization, 43
for deities, 144–47, 234
for God, 144–46, 234
male pronouns, 234
neutral pronouns, 189–90
pronunciation guide, 305–14
pronunciation marks, 335
proofreading marks, 316–18
proofreading tips, 314–16
prooftext, 543
proper names
capitalization, 90–91, 94–96
indexes, 50, 149, 204
particles with, 90–91
personal names, 18–20, 283–87
plurals, 295
spelling, 335–36
prophecy, prophesy, 544

Prophets, prophets, 544
proscribe, prescribe, 544
proselytize, 464, 544
Protestant, 544–45
Protestant Bible, 71–72
proved, proven, 545
Proverbs, proverb, 545
Providence, providence, 545
province abbreviations, 359–60
provincial resident names, 360–61
Psalm, psalm, 545–46
psalmist, 546
Psalms, grouping, 319–20
Psalms, numbering, 318–19
Psalter, psalter, 546
Pseudepigrapha, 546
publication date, 397–98
public domain, 265
publisher addresses, 39, 385–86
publisher references, 249
punctuation
  blogs, 78
  colon, 89–90, 128–29, 332–33
  comma, 44, 130–35, 380
  exclamation point, 173
  periods, 18–19, 263–64
  question marks, 173, 321–22
  semicolon, 333, 352–53
  UK publications, 43–44
Purgatory, purgatory, 547
Puritan, Puritanism, Pilgrim, 547

Q

Q&A, Q & A, Q and A, 548
QR codes, 321
Quaker, 548
Quaker style, 321
queries, 91, 315
question marks, 173, 321–22
questions, asking, 349
questions, internal, 322–23
quick-response codes, 321
quotation marks
  "a"/"b"/"c" system, 332
  accuracy, 326
  adjectival phrases, 325
  block quotations, 327–28, 332
  direct discourse, 323
  emphasis, 324
  endorsements, 167
  foreign quotation marks, 325
  indirect discourse, 323
  mid-Atlantic style, 238
  nicknames, 325
  pitfalls, 326
  punctuation, 238, 324, 381
  quotes within quotes, 323
  run-in quotations, 327–28, 332
  sentences, 238, 323–29
  single quotations, 381
  slang, 324
  thoughts, 324, 367–68
  titles, 324–25
  UK style, 381
  usage, 238, 323–29, 381
quotations
  Bible quotations, 236, 330–36
  chapter quotations, 117, 168
  colon, 129
  comma, 133–34
  deities, 147
  direct quotations, 129
  permissions, 266
  poetry quotations, 296–97
  sources, 236, 329–30
quoting Bible, 236, 330–36
quoting online sources, 329–30
Qur'an, Koran, 72, 548
qur'anic, koranic, 548

R

Ra, Re, 549
Rabbi, rabbi, 549
racial designations, 90, 170–72
racial self-identification, 170–71
rack my brain, 549
rapture, the, 549
readability, 337–38
reader response card, 39, 339
reading-level calculation, 339–40
Realtor, realtor, 549
recto (right-hand) pages, 341
rector, 550
recycled-paper statement, 341
red-letter Bible, 55, 123, 341–42
redundancy, 368
references, 50, 78
regalia, 550
religionist, 550
religiose, 550
religious, 550
religious groups, 100
religious movements, 100
religious observances, 99
religious right, religious left, 550
Religious Society of Friends, 548
religious style manuals, 361–62
religious terms, 25–31, 95–114
Renaissance, renaissance, 551
"reprinted by permission" note, 266
reprints, 116, 210, 266, 342, 364
Republican, republican, 551
restrictive clauses, 131
resurrection, crucifixion, 445, 551
Revelation, 551
Reverend, reverend, 20, 551–52
revisions, 210, 342
rights, subsidiary, 137, 364
right-to-life, 552

Rite, rite, 99, 552–53
Ritual Decalogue, 569
rivers, typographic, 343
Roma, Romani, 553
Roman Catholic orders, 343–44
Roman numerals, 344–47, 553
roman type, 499, 553
Rosary, rosary, 553
rubrication, 341
Rule of Benedict, 553
Rule of Five, 291
running footers, 177, 347–48
running heads, 117, 347–48

S

Sabbatarian, 554
Sabbath, sabbath, sabbatical, 554
sacraments, 99, 555
sacred objects, 98
sacred texts, 70–73, 373–75
sacrilegious, 555
Sadducee, 555
said references, 349
Saint, saint, 30, 43, 556
Saints' days, 350
saints' lives, 123
sanctimonious, 556
sanction, 557
sarcophagus, 557
Satan, satanic, satanism, 96, 244, 557
Saul, Paul, 535
Savior, Saviour, 557
sayings, 133–34
scatology, 303
schism, heresy, 484–86
scholarly appearances, 350–51
scholarly terms, 31–32, 217
SCOTUS (Supreme Court of the United States), 540
scribal Latin abbreviations, 351
scribal Latin characters, 351
scribe, 557
scriptural, 558
Scripture, Bible, 421
Scripture, scripture, 558
Scripture index, 50, 149, 205–6. *See also* indexes
Scripture references, 129, 332–33
scripturist, scripturism, 558
second half-title page, 352
secretary-general, 558
secular market, 473
selah, 559
self-identification, 170–71, 190–91
self-plagiarism, 291–92
semi-, bi-, 423
semicolon, 333, 352–53. *See also* colon
Semite, Semitic, Semitism, 559
Senate, 559
sentences
  comma, 44, 130–35, 380
  compound sentences, 130–31, 352
  exclamation point, 173
  fragments, 354
  periods, 263–64
  prepositions ending, 301
  question marks, 173, 321–22
  quotation marks, 238, 323–29
September 11, 2001, 559
Septuagint, 70–71
sepulcher, sepulchre, 559–60
seraph, seraphs, seraphim, seraphims, 560
serial comma, 44, 132, 135, 380. *See also* comma
serial rights, 137, 364
Serpent, serpent, 560
seven deadly sins, 560
seven sacraments, 555
Seven Storey Mountain, 560
Seventh-day Adventist Church, 560
sexist language, 189
shalom, sholom, 561
sharia law, 561
she, her, 484, 561
sic, 561
signature, author, 49
signature breaks, 354–55
sin, original, 531
since, because, 561
single quotation marks, 381
singulars, 294–95
sins, seven deadly, 560
sins, trespasses, 579–80
Sister, sister, 562
sistren, 426
-size, -sized (suffix), 562
skeptic, 562
slang, 153–54, 324. *See also* dialogue
slash mark, 197, 336, 356–57, 378
small caps, 355
smartphone, 562
sneak, sneaked, snuck, 562
so-called, 563
Social Gospel, social gospel, 563
Socialist, socialist, socialism, 563
social media page, 356
Sodomite, sodomite, 563
software citations, 75
solidus, 197, 336, 356–57
Song of Songs, 429
songs, 200, 328–29, 429–30. *See also* hymns
SOTUS (State of the Union Speech), 540
source lists, 50, 73
source notes, 245–46, 266. *See also* notes
South, south, 563
Southernisms, 89
spacing
  double spaces, 357
  headings, 195
  letter spacing, 118
  line spacing, 338, 339, 357

word spacing, 118, 338
speech
dialogue, 152–53
disembodied voices, 157–58
free speech, 407
hate speech, 303
slang, 153–54
taboo speech, 301–4
spelling
brand names, 85–86
King James Version, 225–26
letters, 231
mid-Atlantic style, 238
numerals, 253–56, 368
UK publications, 43–44
UK style, 379–80
words in text, 357–58
Spirit, spirit, 564
spiritual thriller, 123
split infinitives, 358
Sr., 134, 502
stacks, typographic, 358
stained glass, 564
standing cap, 117
Star of Bethlehem, star of Bethlehem, 564
Star of David, 564
Stars and Stripes, Stars and Bars, 564
state abbreviations, 359–60
State of Palestine, 533
state resident names, 360–61
states and commonwealths, 565
stations of the cross, 565
step (family relationships), 565
Stephen Ministries, Stephen Ministry, 565
stereotyping, 171, 187, 236, 297
stigmas, stigmata, 565
still, small voice, 566
storytelling, storyteller, 566
straight and narrow, 566
straitlaced, 566
street addresses, 37–38, 256
study questions, 50
style manuals, religious, 361–62
style sheets, 362–63
subheadings, 194–95
subject index, 50, 149, 204. *See also* indexes
subjunctive, 363–64
subsidiary rights, 137, 364
substantive notes, 245. *See also* notes
subtitles, 129
suffixes, 201, 364
suffragan bishop, 566
Sunday, Sabbath, 554
Sunday school, 566
super Christian, 566
super PAC, 567
superscript numbers, 247
superspiritual, 567
supplicant, 567
Supreme Court, court, 567
suspension point, 364–65, 381
sweet by-and-by, 427
syllogistic words/phrases, 365
symbols
notes reference marks, 248
performance symbol, 262–63
proofreading symbols, 316–18
synagogue, temple, 567
syndromes, 365, 567
Synoptic, synoptic, 567
syntax, 238

T

table of contents, 186, 366
Taizé Community, 568
Taser, taser, 568
Tea Party, 568
Teavangelical, 568
teenage, teenaged, 569
telephone numbers, 256, 287–88
televangelist, televangelism, 569
Temple, temple, 567, 569
temptation, 569
Ten Commandments, 439, 569–70
tenet, tenant, 570
tenses
past tenses, 262, 295–96
pluperfect, 295–96
verbs, 329
Teresa, Thérèse (Saints), 570
terms, defining, 144
terms of endearment, 94, 367
Testament, testament, 570
tetragram, tetragrammaton, 570–71
text breaks, 47, 154, 367
thank you, thank-you, 571
that, which, 571–72
The, the, 572
thee, thou, 574–76
their, theirs, 573
theism, deism, 573
then, 573
theologian, 573
therefore, 573
they, them, 573
Third World, 574
thou, thee, 574–76
though, although, 405
thoughts
quotation marks, 324, 367–68
trailing off, 364–65
unspoken discourse, 367–68
thought systems, 93
thy, thine, 574–76
till, 'til, 576–77
Time magazine, TIME magazine, 577
time of day, 195, 368, 382, 405–6
tironian sign, 44
tithe, 577

title pages, 186, 193, 352, 372
titles
  abbreviations, 20, 25–31
  adverbs, 89
  books, 142, 253, 347
  capitalization, 88–89, 96
  changing, 372
  clerical titles, 20, 128, 438, 540–41, 551–52
  colon, 129
  common texts, 373
  hyphenated compounds, 89
  italicized titles, 215–16
  military titles, 20, 240
  personal titles, 20, 91, 128, 240
  poetry, 296
  prepositions in, 301
  quotation marks, 324–25
  religious titles, 96
  sacred texts, 70–73, 373
to be, 577
too, 577–78
Torah, 72
touchscreen, 578
toward, towards, 578
trademarks, 81–82
transcript, transcription, 578–79
transfiguration, 579
transgender, transsexual, 579
transliteration, 120–22
trespasses, 579–80
trim sizes, 375
Trinity, 95, 375–77, 492, 580
try to, try and, 580
T-shirt, tee, 580
TV, 580
Twelve, the, 581
twelve apostles, 410–11
twelve disciples, 581
Twelve Steps, 581
Twitter, tweet, 581
type A, type B personalities, 581
typeface, font, 118, 337–38, 581
type size, 118, 338
typographic orphans, 343, 387–88
typographic river, 343
typographic symbols, 377–78
typographic widows, 387–88
typos, 315

U

uber- (prefix), 582
UK publications
  Americanizing, 43–44
  cultural equivalents, 44
  punctuation, 43–44
  spelling, 43–44
  vocabulary, 44
Ukraine, 582
UK style
  abbreviations, 19, 381
  dates, 382
  footnotes, 382
  numbering, 382–83
  spelling, 379–80
  time expressions, 382
  vocabulary, 383–84
unbeliever, nonbeliever, 403, 582
unbiblical, nonbiblical, 524–25
unchristian, non-Christian, 582
unchurched, 582–83
unforgivenness, 583
ungodly, 583
United Kingdom, 583–84
United States, 359–61, 565
unreligious, 498
unspoken discourse, 367–68. *See also* thoughts
unspoken prayers, 299
until, till, 'til, 576–77
URLs, 38–39
USA Today, USA TODAY, 584
usher, 584

V

vacation Bible school, 585
Valentine, valentine, 585
venerate, worship, 585
venery, 303
venial, venal, 585–86
verbal, oral, 586
verbs
  abbreviations, 19
  brands, 82
  comma, 135
  tenses, 329
verger, 586
verse, 332
verse numbers, 335
verso (left-hand) pages, 341
versus, 585
very, 586
vespers, 586
Veterans Day, 586
vicar, 587
victuals, vittles, 587
Vietnam, Vietnamese, 587
Virgin, virgin, virgin birth, 496, 587
vocabulary
  capitalization, 88
  italicized words, 214
  meanings, 237–38
  UK publications, 44, 237–38
  UK style, 383–84
vocational terms, 188
vocative O, 134, 385, 527–28
voice
  dialogue, 152–53
  disembodied voices, 157–58
  first person, 176–77
  phrasing, 238
voice mail, 587
VPOTUS (vice president of the United States), 540
v., vs., versus, 585
vulgar epithets, 303
Vulgate, vulgate, 71, 587

W

wages, 588
Wailing Wall, 590
Walmart, 588
warning notice, 385
watches of the night, 588–89
way of the cross, 565
web access dates, 75
web addresses, 38–39
web design, 80
webpage, 256
webpage citations, 75
website, 589
website names, 386
website references, 250–51
web style
- abbreviations, 19
- blogs, 76–79
- emoji, 78
- emoticon, 78
- guidelines, 386–87
- web shorthand, 78

Weltanschauung, 589
West, Western, west, western, 589
Western Rites, Eastern Rites, 458
Western Wall, 590
whatever, what ever, 590
which, that, 571–72
while, although, 590
white (racial designation), 590
Whit Sunday, Whitsunday, 590–91
who, whom, whose, 147, 591
whodunit, 592
whoever, whomever, 591
widows, typographic, 387–88
Wi-Fi, 592
Wisdom Literature, 592
wise men, 592
womankind, 494
Woman's Christian Temperance Union (WCTU), 592
Word, the, 592
wordiness, 365, 392–94
Word of God, word of God, 474, 593
words
- compound words, 192, 300, 314
- defining, 144
- ghost words, 306
- spacing, 118, 338
- taboo words, 301–4
- word choices, 388–89
- word divisions, 389–92

words as words, 392
world's fair, 593
worldview, 593
World War I, World War II, 593
worship, places of, 99–100
worship, venerate, 585
worshiper, worshiping, worshiped, 593
wreak, wreck, 593
writer tips, 394–96

X

Xerox, xerox, 594
Xmas, 594
X-ray, x-ray, 594
Xtian, xtian, 594

Y

ye, 595
yea, yay, yeah, 595
year dates, 252, 350, 369
year of publication, 397–98
Yeshua, 596
YHWH, JHWH, 596
Yiddish, 483
You, you, 596
Yule, Yuletide, 596

Z

Zacchaeus, Zaccheus, 597
Zealot, zealot, 597
Zion, Zionist, Zionism, 597

Personal Style Sheet

All editors have a mental list of words they repeatedly have to look up, personal bugaboos, as it were (for instance, is it *flipflops* or *flip-flops*?). Write them here for quick reference and also use the inside of the front and back covers.

Colophon

This book is printed on 40-pound cream-white offset paper.

It was printed at R. R. Donnelley in Harrisonburg, Virginia.

The text typeface is 10-point Sabon LT Std,

designed by Jan Tschichold in 1967.

The display font is Didot LT Std.

Compositor/interior designer: Kait Lamphere, Beth Shagene

Design manager: Tammy Johnson

Cover designer: William Chiaravalle

Production manager: Fred Jensen

Marketing team: Josh Kessler, Sarah Gombis

Managing editor: Kari Moore

Editorial coordinator: Janelle DeBlaay

Editors: Madison Trammel, Jim Ruark

Proofreaders: Dianne Scent, Charles Taylor,
Lauren Schneider, Tonya Osterhouse